American Indian
Languages

American Indian Languages

CULTURAL AND SOCIAL CONTEXTS

SHIRLEY SILVER
AND
WICK R. MILLER

The University of Arizona Press   Tucson

The University of Arizona Press
© 1997 The Arizona Board of Regents

♾ This book is printed on acid-free, archival-quality paper.
Manufactured in the United States of America

02 01 00 99 98 97   6 5 4 3 2 1

Library of Congress Cataloging-in-Publication Data
Silver, Shirley.
American Indian languages : cultural and social contexts / Shirley Silver and
Wick R. Miller.
     p.   cm.
Includes bibliographical references and index.
ISBN 0-8165-1802-5 (cloth)
1. Indians—Languages—Social aspects.   2. Indians—Languages—Grammar,
Comparative.   3. Anthropological linguistics—America.   4. Indians—Social life
and customs.
I. Miller, Wick R.   II. Title.
PM209.S55   1997
306.44'08997—dc21   97-4817
CIP

British Library Cataloguing-in-Publication Data
A catalogue record for this book is available from the British Library.

In memory of our teacher Mary R. Haas

CONTENTS

ILLUSTRATIONS

TABLES

PREFACE

The purpose of this volume is to introduce the general reader to the mosaic of American Indian languages and cultures as they exist both in time and space. The technical linguistic orientation that we also provide, although limited in scope, encourages and supports further exploration of the interrelations of languages, other aspects of cultures, and ways of knowing.

Some knowledge of phonetics (see appendix 1) comes in handy when considering languages for which there are no established, conventional writing systems. At least an elementary knowledge of phonology (i.e., the sound system of a language) is needed to appreciate how Havasupai words are modified in song (see section 5.4), how the Cherokee syllabary adapts to the Cherokee sound system (see section 8.5), or why Spanish words are modified the way they are when borrowed into the languages of northwest Mexico (see section 13.4). A basic understanding of sentence and word formation helps in gaining insight into the roles of evidentials in Andean and other languages (see section 2.6) or in truly appreciating the relationship between Aztec everyday speech and reverential speech (see section 6.1), the creation of new words as a response to contact with European cultures (see section 11.3), or the modifications in Pomoan languages of the Russian word *butílka* 'bottle' (see section 13.5). Moreover, an understanding of the interconnections between linguistic and nonlinguistic behavior is deepened through exposure to the integration of systematically diverse features of language structure, including semantic aspects (see chapter 3).

We have organized the volume's chapters into six parts: Part I is an overview of languages and their status, Part II languages and structures, Part III languages and cultural domains, Part IV languages and social domains, Part V languages in contact, and Part VI languages in time and space. At the end of each chapter we provide the sources for that chapter and also suggest further readings. For citations that reflect theoretical and other perspectives not included in our discussions, readers with specialist interests should consult the suggested readings. For nonspecialist and specialist alike, the sources and suggested readings cite references that may be of further interest.

There is a great deal of data we could have used but did not. Obviously, one reason has to do with space limitations. Another has to do with our choice of topic: We needed language or other data sources detailed enough to allow treatment of a topic in some depth. There are also particular data sets that it is mandatory to include in a book of this kind: for instance, the Cherokee syllabary when discussing American Indian writing systems (see sections 8.5 and 8.6) or, a classic study of the northern origin of the Navajo (see section 13.1) when discussing linguistic prehistory in North America. In addition, in order to underscore the linguistic diversity of the Americas, we have used a variety of data that have rarely (or never) received attention in the nontechnical anthropological or linguistic literature; and, although we have drawn heavily from our own research areas (the western United States and Mexico), we have included as many other areas of the Americas as we could, given limitations on availability of appropriate data, our access to sources, space, and so on.

This volume has been in preparation for a long time. Over the years both of us have taught courses on American Indian languages to undergraduates. Although we had corresponded about a book such as this one and had exchanged materials used in our respective courses, we did not start putting our ideas together until the spring of 1988 at the University of Utah when we team-taught a course.

Since then, we have profited from students' comments on and reactions to various draft versions. Also helpful have been the comments of colleagues, some of whom have used one version or another in their courses, and have passed on to us student reactions: Pamela Bunte, California State University, Long Beach; Robert Franklin, California State University, Dominguez Hills; Victor Golla, Humboldt State University; Jane Hill, University of Arizona; Leanne Hinton, University of California, Berkeley; William H. Jacobsen, Jr., University of Nevada, Reno; Terrence Kaufman, University of Pittsburgh; Paul V. Kroskrity, University of California at Los Angeles; William Shipley, University of California at Santa Cruz. In addition, we have benefited greatly from the critiques of the persons who reviewed the 1991 draft version for the University of Arizona Press. With the caveat that we are solely responsible for whatever flaws the reader may encounter, we are beholden to all those we mentioned.

I also extend our thanks to others who helped us both in myriad ways, including persons I know Wick would have wanted to mention by name and now cannot. On May 9, 1994, he died tragically as the result of a bicycle accident in Hermosillo, Mexico. I am most grateful to his wife, Joanne, and his son, Cliff, for undertaking the emotionally draining task of tracking down materials he intended to include in the final version. In addition, I must express appreciation to my dear friends, Julia Elliott and Barbara and Ralph Karler, for their supportiveness and encouragement as I continued work on the final version. I am forever indebted to Barbara Karler for magnanimously affording me her superb editorial and computer skills. If not for her generous investment of time and energy and her unstinting help, I would not have finished what Wick and I worked so long and hard over. It saddens me that Wick did not live to see that work brought to fruition. I hope he would have been pleased with the result.

Shirley Silver
Graton, California

Thus they have come to tell it,
thus they have come to record it in their narrations,
and for us they have painted the codices,
the ancient men, the ancient women.
They were our grandfathers, our grandmothers,
our great-grandfathers, our great-grandmothers,
our great-great-grandfathers, our ancestors.
Their account was repeated,
they left it to us;
they bequeathed it forever
to us who live now,
to us who come down from them.
Never will it be lost, never will it be forgotten,
that which they came to do,
that which they came to record in their paintings;
their renown, their history, their memory.
Thus in the future
never will it perish, never will it be forgotten,
always we will treasure it,
we, their children, their grandchildren,
brothers, great-grandchildren,
great-great-grandchildren, descendants,
we who carry their blood and their color,
we will tell it, we will pass it on
to those who do not yet live, who are to be born,
the children of the Mexicans, the children of the Tenochcans.

Aztec historical account from the *Crónica Mexicáyotl*, cited by Miguel León-Portilla in *Pre-Columbian Literatures of Mexico* (Norman: University of Oklahoma Press, 1969), 117; and in "Pre-Hispanic Literature," in *Archaeology of Northern Mesoamerica*, volume 10, part 1, *Handbook of Middle American Indians*, ed. Gordon F. Ekholm and Ignacio Bernal (Austin: University of Texas Press, 1971), 456.

PART I

overview

CHAPTER I

LANGUAGES AND THEIR STATUS

Ever since the inception of the Age of Discovery in the late fifteenth century, the indigenous populations of the Americas have been a source of fascination in the Western world for the average person as well as the scholar, but it is clear that many of the popular notions formed over the years about American Indians are wrong. Although most readers recognize blatantly incorrect notions that characterize American Indians as "noble savages" living a brutish existence in primitive societies with rudimentary cultures and languages, popular misconceptions, many of them subtle, still abound.

The goal of this book is to introduce the general reading public to the indigenous languages of the Americas, an absorbing topic little known outside academic circles. Because we are committed to presenting accurate information, we first need to clear up certain misunderstandings about American Indians in general and about the status of their languages in particular.

I.I POPULAR MISCONCEPTIONS

Most of the misguided views about American Indian languages that have persisted over the years have arisen because of popular notions concerning the degree of diversity in American Indian languages and cultures, "primitiveness," and the relationship between speech and writing.

Diversity

Since the average person knows little about Indian peoples and their cultures, some people tend to think in terms of just one ethnic group, "the Indians," all of whom are supposed to speak a single "Indian dialect." The collective designation "Indian" is a European concept. (There is an American Indian humorous comment to this effect: "It is a good thing Columbus was not looking for the country of Turkey or else we would be called Turkeys instead of Indians.") That "Indian" is not an American Indian concept is neatly illustrated by the fact that at the time of European contact there was no word in any American Indian language that translated the English cover term "Indian." Even though today Indian languages generally have such a word, it is often borrowed from a European language; for example, in Acoma, spoken in New Mexico, ʔíntyu is borrowed from Spanish *indio*. In other cases, the word for "human being" or "person" has come to have two meanings: "human being; Indian." The need for such extensions of meaning arose from the need to differentiate Indians from Europeans (and more generally from non-Indians). In Shasta, a language once spoken in northern California, ʔis 'human being; Indian' contrasts with terms for "Whiteman": pa·stin (a word borrowed from Chinook Jargon [section 10.2] and ultimately from English 'Boston'), or k'an·e·ná·ki, literally 'that which floated to shore', that is, flotsam.

Other English names for Indian groups often do not derive from or coincide with the Indian names for themselves. Two familiar names entered English by way of French. "Iroquois," a term of unknown origin and meaning, refers to a confederacy of six tribes in the Northeast: Mohawk, Oneida, Onondaga, Cayuga, Seneca, and Tuscarora. "Sioux," originally a French shortening of a Chippewa word meaning "adder; enemy," is applied to tribes of the Great Plains who are known in their own languages as "Lakota," "Nakota," and "Dakota."

Labels such as "American Indian," "Iroquois," or "Sioux," however useful they may be for certain purposes, obscure the fact that before European contact, the Americas were peopled by a host of groups manifesting a remarkable diversity of cultures and languages, which are maintained up to this day by many of the descendants of those precontact groups. We hope this book contributes to an appreciation and understanding of this diversity.

"Primitive" Languages

In 1832, after his first contact with the Indians of Tierra del Fuego, Charles Darwin made the following diary entry: "The language of these people barely merits classification as an articulated language." This comment reflects a misconception about American Indian languages that has persisted over time; namely, that Indian languages are "primitive."

When compared with the large urbanizing or urbanized societies found today and in Darwin's time, small-scale foraging and horticultural societies are often considered simpler, with less-elaborated technologies, social organization, ideologies, and the like. Thinking of these societies as "primitive" has led to the common assumption that "primitive" peoples have "primitive" languages. When compared to European languages (e.g., English or Spanish), "primitive" languages are thought to have limited vocabularies, and to lack the grammar as well as the vocabulary necessary to express subtle differences in meaning. Indeed, it is sometimes thought that such languages are so deficient that their speakers, in order to communicate, must depend upon gestures to complete utterances.

Although technologies in small-scale societies may be simple, it is questionable that this is the case with other aspects of culture such as ideology. Moreover, the terms "simple" or "primitive" definitely cannot be applied to the languages of the societies indigenous to the Americas. Every natural language has a highly perfected sound system, an equally well-developed grammar (chapter 2), all the vocabulary required by the culture of its speakers (chapter 3), and the capacity for expressing intellectual and aesthetic ideas and feelings (chapters 5 and 6). In addition, all natural languages are capable of adaptive growth; for example, in the vocabularies of some American Indian languages, there are changes triggered by five centuries of contact with very different European cultures (chapter 11, especially 11.3).

Speech, Writing, and Nonliterate Societies

The notion of "primitiveness" has been fueled by the absence of writing in most of the pre-Columbian societies of the Americas. It is popularly but erroneously believed that a language lacking a writing system is somehow debased, slovenly, or imprecise. In American society today, where it is expected that everyone will learn to read and write early in life, we often confuse language with writing. We frequently speak of writing as though it were a special kind of language, "written," which is thought to be more authentic and precise than "spoken." A more accurate view is that language is represented by two channels: spoken and written, with the written channel secondary inasmuch as it is based on the spoken one. (A third channel, gestured or signed language, is not considered here; but see section 7.3.)

In literate speech communities there are two major cultural techniques related to language. The first is the art of speaking, which literate peoples learn first and share with all humans. The second, the art of writing (representing spoken forms graphically), is acquired later than speaking and distinguishes literate from preliterate peoples.

Learning to read and write a language is a much more deliberate, conscious activity than learning to speak it. Starting around age two, we learn to speak, and by age six we have acquired the major part of the language (except for elaboration in vocabulary). It is not, therefore, until the most significant aspects of language are acquired through the spoken channel that individuals in literate societies are taught to read and write. The fact that reading and writing are deliberate and conscious activities helps breed the idea that writing is somehow the "real" language. This erroneous notion leads to the misconception that languages of nonliterate societies are not as perfectly formed or as precise as those of literate societies.

In reality, however, nonliterate speech communities have their own kinds of linguistic richness (chapter 5), which Western cultures have been slow to recognize and appreciate. Absence of a writing system does not necessarily mean absence of literature. Many nonliterate speech communities in the Americas, as elsewhere, have faithfully preserved their oral traditions. We know little about this vast and wonderfully varied unwritten literature because until recently there had not been much study of American Indian verbal art, and the studies that existed were often based on translations into European languages.

Besides maintaining oral traditions, many modern American Indian groups practice and respect subtle and sophisticated uses of their languages, which for millennia have been spoken no less precisely than languages of literate societies (chapter 6). In the northeastern United States and Canada, for example, speakers of Iroquoian languages cultivate skillful use of language in informal narrative and conversation, as well as in formal oratory; in British Columbia, Bella Coola speakers value the maintenance of a flow of witty and insulting remarks as part of ordinary social interaction; in Chile, the Araucanians consider skill in speaking a sign of masculine intelligence and leadership, with the ideal man expected to speak well and often; and in Bolivia, "politeness," the recognition of a person's humanity, is an obligatory and pervasive aspect of Aymara language use.

Members of all societies make evaluations about language. In 1927 a student of the Menomini (Wisconsin) language noted that even though it was not written, Menomini speakers commented on whether someone spoke well or badly and took note of forms of speech that were incorrect and sounded bad or that were archaic or like the speech of a shaman, and speakers viewed some persons as better models of conduct and speech than others.

In chapters 4, 5, and 6 we show that there are differences in how small-scale nonliterate societies use and evaluate language; however, these differences do not match popular stereotypes of "primitive" languages and "primitive" societies. Assertions, overt or covert, about a language's primitiveness, its lack of variety, or its unsuitability as a means of communication for its users cannot be taken as descriptive of any American Indian language; instead, such assertions reflect a misunderstanding about the nature of human language and an inadequate knowledge of the nature of speech communities, literate and nonliterate.

1.2 POPULATION AND LANGUAGE DIVERSITY

If Europeans were slow to grasp the linguistic diversity of the indigenous American peoples with whom they came in contact, there is evidence from myths and traditions that the Indians themselves have long been aware of it. The Quileute of Washington's Olympic Peninsula believed that originally each person had a separate language and that the culture hero subsequently created the community of languages. The Pit River (Achumawi) of northeastern California have a myth character, Meadowlark, who "knows all the languages"; and, according to the Nomlaki, another northern California people, "everything in the world talks, the trees, rocks, everything. But we can't understand them, just as the white people do not understand Indians."

It is impossible to give accurate figures for either the number of languages or the population of the Americas before European contact. In appendix 2, the list of languages for precontact North America (excluding the West Indies) represents our best estimate: about 250 in Canada and the United States, and well over 100 for Mexico and the rest of Central America. For reasons discussed in chapter 14, the number of distinct languages at the time of European contact clearly must have been much greater, with the total for North America probably closer to 750. The precontact population for North America has been estimated at between one and two million north of Mexico, and from five to twenty-five million in Middle America. The population estimates for South America at the time of contact vary from ten to more than thirty million, and the number of languages is estimated to have been more than five hundred. In 1590, one European observer remarked that "they speak so many languages, so different from each other. . . . In many provinces one doesn't go a league without coming across another language, as remote and distinct from the first as Castilian Spanish from Basque, or from English, or from African languages. . . . In . . . parts of the Indies [Latin America], this reaches such an extreme that in one single village they speak two or three different languages." Although a few of the languages in the Americas were spoken by large numbers of people, most languages seldom had more than a few thousand speakers.Despite the differences in population estimates, at the time of European contact the Americas, even though sparsely populated in many areas, contained possibly one third of all of the world's languages.

Today, the number of speakers of various American Indian languages ranges from millions to a mere handful. Mesoamerica and the Andes were relatively densely populated in precontact times, so it is not surprising that today these are the areas that have indigenous languages with the largest numbers of speakers. Aztec (Nahuatl) in Mexico has at least a half million speakers, perhaps more, and a similar number speak Yucatec Mayan (Yucatán Peninsula), and Quiché (southern Mexico and Guatemala). There are over ten million speakers of Quechua, spoken in Peru and neighboring countries, and as many as three million speakers of Aymara in Bolivia, southern Peru, and northern Chile. In Lowland South America, there are over three million speakers of Guaraní in Paraguay, Brazil, and Argentina.

The most common language north of Mexico is Navajo, spoken by over one hundred thousand speakers in Arizona and adjoining states. Other indigenous languages with fairly large numbers of speakers include Cree, spoken by some eighty thousand people over a wide area in Canada (section 12.1), and Inuit-Inupiaq, an Eskimo language with almost seventy thousand speakers in Greenland and on the northern coasts of Canada and Alaska. Some languages spoken by small numbers are also thriving; for example, Seminole Creek, the language of a few small villages in Florida whose children, in the 1980s, still arrived in school as monolingual Creek speakers.

There is an erroneous idea that the languages of eastern Canada and the United States are all but extinct. Although the western languages have generally fared better than the eastern, there are notable exceptions: Choctaw-Chickasaw (twelve thousand speakers in Mississippi and Oklahoma), Micmac (roughly eight thousand speakers in the maritime provinces of Canada), and Creek (ten thousand speakers in Alabama, Florida, and Oklahoma).

National policy in various countries has brought about forced relocation of some indigenous populations. In the United States, for example, the federal government attempted to remove most of the Indian population to the Indian Territory (what is now Oklahoma). As a result, most of the languages now found in Oklahoma were formerly spoken elsewhere. Some languages, such as Blackfoot (northern Plains), Cherokee (North Carolina), Choctaw-Chickasaw (Mississippi), and Creek (Alabama) are spoken both in their aboriginal homes and in Oklahoma. Cayuga, another language found in Oklahoma, is an example of a language no longer spoken in its original territory, New York State. Due to a set of unfortunate circumstances, Cayuga speakers now live in Ontario, Canada, where the language is still very much alive, and in Oklahoma, where the number of speakers is getting smaller and smaller and there are fewer and fewer occasions for using the language.

Although some languages are spoken by large populations and a few of these are thriving, most languages in the Americas face an uncertain future. As of the 1960s, the best count for languages still spoken north of Mexico came to 175. Of these 175 languages, 136 each had less than 2,000 speakers, 34 of them with 10 speakers each at the most. Many speakers of these 136 languages would have been elderly at the time of the count; additionally, the children in many cases had been growing up monolingual in English; there is, therefore, little likelihood, as of the 1990s, that the 34 languages with ten speakers or less have survived or will survive much longer.

Current figures for Latin America are less accurate than for North America north of Mexico, but it is clear that the process of language extinction is similar. For example, in lowland South America, the least known area of the world linguistically, language extinction is proceeding at an alarming rate. In the past century, more than fifteen out of thirty-five languages have been lost in Venezuela's Río Branco-

Río Orinoco region. In the same period lowland Peru has lost twenty-two of its eighty-five indigenous languages. In lowland Ecuador since the sixteenth century, thirteen out of thirty languages have disappeared. In Brazil, 36 of the approximately 170 Indian languages extant have fewer than 100 speakers each.

Since the beginning of European contact, language extinction has occurred at a rapid rate in the Americas. During the last century it has accelerated on a scale probably never seen before in the world. Only one language, Guaraní of Paraguay (section 9.4), has clearly made the transition into the modern world. Over 90 percent of the Paraguayan population speak Guaraní, which is a significant means of communication for both Indians and non-Indians in contemporary Paraguayan society. Although there are other indigenous languages, such as Greenlandic Eskimo, that have a chance to make analogous transitions, the long-range outlook for the future of the vast majority of American Indian languages, even those with large numbers of speakers, is not optimistic. (See chapter 14 for more information on language distribution and population.)

1.3 LANGUAGE VITALITY

Various factors affect the vitality of a language. Ranging from flourishing to obsolete, the degree of vitality is a reflection of historical factors and the social and cultural position of the language. Quichua, the variety of Quechua spoken in highland Ecuador, provides an example. Its fate will be determined in good part by its positive or negative identification with "Indianness." There have been at least three different responses to Quichua's position in the larger society. First, there are speakers who are maintaining both their native language and culture. Some of these people live in remote areas and have little contact with the national language and culture. Others, who live in less isolated areas, are consciously determined to maintain their traditional language and culture. They do so either for religious reasons or as one way of identifying their ethnicity with certain economic activities defined as "Indian," for example, the manufacture of textiles. Second, there are Quichua speakers who, even though maintaining a strong ethnic identity, are losing their native language. This loss is the apparent result of a new economic base that Quichua speakers themselves do not identify as traditional or "Indian." Last, there are those Indians who are giving up their ancestral ethnic identification and replacing their language and culture with the national language and culture.

When vitality is threatened, speakers often take steps, either consciously or unconsciously, to maintain a language. Among Navajo, Pueblo, and other Indian communities in the United States, concern with language maintenance is sometimes expressed within the religious and ceremonial life of the contemporary community. In communities where the native religion is gaining increased acceptance, extensive language learning or relearning has become important. Where ceremonial knowledge is retained in the ancestral language, traditional institutions provide both invaluable resources for language maintenance and contexts for an approach to language learning consistent with the community's traditional style of teaching and learning. In communities where the tribal council or community-wide meetings are conducted in the local language, young people who participate in these affairs are expected to become fluent in the language of these activities because traditionally based terminologies are required, as well as specialized vocabulary in English. Attendance at these meetings, reinforced by opportunities for language practice in less formal contexts, produces an immediately noticeable growth in the skills necessary for the vitality and maintenance of a language.

1.4 LANGUAGE AND GOVERNMENT POLICY

Political pressure on an Indian community has an impact on language vitality and maintenance. El Salvador provides an example. In the 1930s political repression and agitation for the extermination of the Indian people led many to stop speaking their native languages to avoid being identified as Indians. As a result, Lenca and Cacaopera were completely abandoned, and the use of Pipil came to be so restricted that few of those born after 1932 learned their ancestral speech. While the El Salvadoran example is extreme, it reflects a prevailing assumption on the part of mainstream, European-derived societies in the Americas that the use of indigenous (and other minority) languages threatens a nation's social and political goals. In consequence, national policies in both North and South America implicitly or explicitly encourage ultimate language loss.

In Bolivia, for instance, there are almost thirty minority languages, with two of them, Quechua and Aymara, making up 60 percent of the total national population. It has been tacitly assumed in the educational system that the indigenous languages and cultures must be replaced in order to bring about proficiency in Spanish, the language of wider communication. In the elementary grades, Spanish has been the only language used for teaching children. Moreover, until recently the Bolivian code of education required that native languages were to be used in adult literacy programs only to facilitate the learning of Spanish. An approach to education that stigmatizes the native languages encourages the decline in their use, and languages will be lost unless there is a change in attitudes and educational policy. Fortunately, there are indications of such change in Bolivia.

It is axiomatic that attitudes of the larger society drive governmental policy, which in turn influences vitality and maintenance of Indian (and other minority) languages. A brief examination of the history of official policy in the United States illustrates the point. During the seventeenth and eighteenth centuries, many Indian children in missionary-founded schools were instructed in their native tongue and in English. Those tribes fortunate enough to have this bilingual approach valued it because it provided support for language maintenance. In the late nineteenth century, the federal government created the Bureau of Indian Affairs, which, among other undertakings, was to provide an environment that would turn Indian children away from their tribal customs and tribal languages. The Choctaw, Cherokee, and some other tribes that had taken responsibility for their own education continued to use their native languages in schools until the Bureau of Indian Affairs closed down all mission and tribally run schools and established boarding schools. These boarding schools, usually located far from the home communities of Indian children, served to remove the students from the influences of their ancestral cultures. In the school dormitories, the policy of grouping together persons from different tribes helped guarantee that English was the only language the students had in common. Use of native languages was forbidden, and students were punished, often cruelly, if they were caught speaking Indian languages in the dormitories or on the playground.

As a result of a general investigation of conditions of Indian life, Federal policy began to soften in the 1930s. Bilingual materials were provided to the Sioux and the Navajo, and for a number of Pueblo languages; a program was provided for training teachers in techniques of bilingual instruction. This approach was suspended during World War II and was not reinstituted after the war. By that time, however, the earlier restrictive language policy had already had an effect on many of the languages. As a result, a number of languages are now moribund because parents who had grown up under the earlier system, determined that their children would never suffer the humiliation and hardships that they suffered, often refused to speak their ancestral languages to their children.

Focus has shifted back to the native languages with the enactment of the 1968 Bilingual Education Act because sections and subsequent amendments of the act specifically address Indian language issues. As a result of this legislation and tribal interest in language maintenance, by 1986 there were eighty-nine projects covering fifty-five Indian languages with a total enrollment of 14,384 Indian students. Various Indian communities, however, view these programs differently (views which, in turn, may be different from that intended by federal policy). In some communities (e.g., Tlingit in Alaska and Canada, and some Tewa pueblos in New Mexico and Arizona) children no longer speak the ancestral language. Consequently, the only meaningful goal is language revival, with the traditional language taught as a second language. In communities where children still speak the native language, the aim may be to add English (e.g., Northern Cheyenne [Montana], Choctaw [Missis-sippi], and Zuni [New Mexico]), while in other cases the community's emphasis may be on native language maintenance (e.g., Crow [Montana], Navajo, and Cree).

In 1990 the Native American Languages Act was passed into law, which, in the words of one Senate supporter, declares "a national policy of respect for Native American languages and encouragement of their continued vitality." The bill says that "the right of Native Americans to express themselves through the use of Native American languages shall not be restricted in any public proceeding, including pub-licly supported education programs." The bill further states that it is federal policy to "preserve, protect, and promote the rights and freedom of Native Americans to use, practice and develop Native American languages" and to "encourage and sup-port the use of Native American languages as a medium of instruction in order to encourage and support . . . Native American language survival."

Clearly, federal policy in the United States has been variable; however, one con-sistent theme, reflecting the public attitude in general, has been ever present: Indian languages are to be replaced by English. Time will tell whether or not the Native American Languages Act of 1990 reflects a meaningful change in public attitude—a change that would truly recognize the value of American Indian languages and the significant contributions to the American ethos that American Indians have made, are now making, and will continue to make.

1.5 LITERACY AND LANGUAGE MAINTENANCE

The use of literacy is the one thing that almost all of today's language maintenance approaches have in common. This emphasis reflects the fact that contemporary Indian communities are part of a larger society in which widespread literacy is a ne-cessity. Again, situations are variable across communities, and the uses of literacy in language planning differ; for example, in many Cherokee communities the language is flourishing and there is a long-standing tradition of literacy (section 8.6); among the Navajo the language is also flourishing, but the literacy tradition is new and still restricted to a minority of the community. The approach to maintenance, then, is different in these two cases. In communities in which the languages are obso-lescing, as among the Tanaina of southern Alaska, literacy materials are still being developed and the approach must be different again. Other communities, however, have not developed writing systems and must utilize other, more traditional, strate-gies for maintaining their languages (strategies also available to communities with writing systems). Literacy activities in language planning vary, then, from preliterate stages to the first stages of developing a writing system to the range of adult literacy training needed to provide teachers to the advanced problems of language standardization and modernization.

Depending on the location of the community, English, French, Danish, Spanish, or Portugese (sections 11.4, 11.6) — the languages of dominant societies — have taken on significant roles in the daily life of many American Indian communities; therefore, maintenance of the ancestral languages has assumed great importance. For one thing, if much of the daily activity must be carried out in the dominant language, fluency in the ancestral language is a reminder that no one language has a monopoly over truth, logic, or precision of expression. For another thing, as recognized by the Native American Languages Act, an American Indian language is "an integral part" of an Indian group's culture and identity and forms the basic medium for the transmission, and thus survival of "the society's culture, literature, history, religion, political institutions, and values."

> Agnes Vanderburg sits . . . outside her summer home — a small trailer in the middle of a meadow seven miles up a gravel road on the Flat-head Indian Reservation in northwestern Montana. Marking the way to her meadow are painted wooden signs at every branch in the road: "Agnes' Culture Camp". . . . "Snee-nyeh." She stretches out each syllable as she speaks; it's a stopped sound at the finish. Two girls sitting at her feet listen intently to Agnes repeating the word "owl" in the Salish tongue; they form the sound on their lips, mimicking her. Agnes is an elder of the Salish tribe, . . . one of a number of Salish elders who are passing along . . . a heritage preserved in large measure by language.

SOURCES

In section 1.1 the American Indian comment about "Indian" is from Shutiva 1994; other comments are from the authors' field experiences; discussion of the origin of "Iroquois" and "Sioux" comes from Goddard 1978c and Hodge 1959 [1907], respectively; the Darwin quote is from Clairis 1985:753; treatment of the nature of language and the nature of speech communities draws from Hymes 1964:385–90, 1974a, 1974b, and 1981; mention of Aymara "politeness" is from Briggs 1981; the comment about Menomini speakers is based on Bloomfield 1927. In section 1.2 the Quileute example is from Hymes 1974b:47, the Pit River example from Silver's fieldnotes, and the Nomlaki quote from Goldschmidt 1978. Estimates on number of languages, number of speakers, and the pre-Columbian population are a synthesis of sources: Chafe 1962,

1965, Derbyshire and Pullum 1986, Driver 1961, Grimes 1988, Hodge 1959, Kaufman 1990, Klein and Stark 1985a, McQuown 1955, Olson 1991, Spencer and Jennings 1965, Steward and Faron 1959, and Suárez 1983 (additional sources are listed in chapter 14). The quote regarding the number and diversity of languages in South America is from Mannheim 1991:36. In sections 1.3 through 1.5 the comments on vitality, government policy, literacy, and language maintenance are based on Briggs 1983, Campbell and Muntzel 1989, K. Kroeber et al. 1981, Leap 1981a, 1981b, Spolsky 1978, St. Clair and Leap 1982, Szasz and Rya 1988, and the Native American Languages Act 1990 (Congressional Record, S15024–15030, October 11, 1990). The discussion of language policy draws heavily from Szasz and Rya 1988. The reference to Agnes Vanderburg is from Shaffer 1990.

SUGGESTED READINGS

Using data from Cherokee, Hill 1952 argues against the notion of primitive languages. Bloomfield 1927 may be the first significant analysis of the attitudes of a preliterate community (Menomini) concerning speech standards. Sherzer 1992 presents an excellent overview of the diversity of American Indian languages and literary forms. Spolsky 1978, Zepeda 1991, Hale 1992, and Leap 1993 focus on issues of language vitality and language and government policy. McLaughlin 1992 discusses the role of literacy in Navajo communities. Champagne 1993, using many native voices, presents diverse points of view on culture, language, literature, and so on.

The Society for the Study of the Indigenous Languages of the Americas (SSILA) publishes *Newsletter,* in which a column ("Learning Aids") provides information about published and semi-published teaching materials and tapes for American Indian languages. To acquire a comprehensive listing of these materials, contact the SSILA Newsletter editor, Victor Golla, Department of Ethnic Studies, Humboldt State University, Arcata, CA 95521.

PART II

languages and structures

CHAPTER 2

LANGUAGES AND STRUCTURES

A language is a rule-governed structure consisting of a large but finite set of elements and principles that enables the language user to produce, understand and evaluate utterances. Normally mastered in the early years of childhood, these highly organized systems are, for the most part, below the level of conscious awareness.

Because of the very large number of languages found in the Americas and the considerable variety of language structures, it is impossible to characterize a "typical" American Indian language. Still, there are two things that can be said about these languages: (1) certain structural traits, although not universal, are widespread; and (2) often there are shared features (also found in languages elsewhere in the world) that European languages lack and that seem exotic to speakers of languages such as English and Spanish. One such feature is **polysynthesis,** a process of word formation in which a single word contains grammatical and semantic information that would be expressed in a sentence in Western European languages. Yahi Yana, a language formerly spoken in northern California, provides a good example: *ya·banaumawilǯigummahaʔnigi!* 'Let us, each one, move indeed to the west across (the creek)!' The words in polysynthetic languages have an intricate internal structure and embody many notions that in other languages are indicated by the grouping of independent words in a sentence. Although polysynthesis does not occur in all American Indian languages, it is characteristic of much of the data presented in this chapter. The Yahi Yana form just given provides an illustration of how to read these data. In displaying the internal structure of a word, we place a hyphen between each of the meaningful elements, or **morphemes.** The hyphenated word (freely translated in the Yahi Yana example) is followed by a literal translation of each of the morphemes: *ya·-banauma-wil-ǯi-gumma-ha-ʔnigi!* 'Let us, each one [of us], move indeed to the west across [the creek]!' (several people move-everybody-across-west-indeed-hortatory-we). In some later examples hyphens are not used to separate morphemes if the discussion makes it clear where the divisions occur or if the division is not important for the particular point under discussion. Most of the examples in this chapter, including the Yahi Yana example, are in phonetic script. The values of the phonetic symbols used here and elsewhere in this volume are detailed in appendix I.

SOUND SYSTEMS

The sound system component of language structure, otherwise known as **phonology,** includes an inventory of speech sounds along with the patterns in which these sounds are put together to form syllables and longer sound units. Languages vary as to the nature and size of their sound inventories; for example, as far as consonantal sounds are concerned, Plains Cree (section 12.1) has only ten consonants and semivowels, while Acoma (section 2.1) has thirty-nine, and some Athapaskan and Salish languages have almost fifty. There is no set of speech sounds particularly typical of American Indian languages, other than those typical of the majority of the world's languages such as stops (e.g., [p, t, k]), nasals (e.g., [m, n]), or commonly found vowels such as [i, a, u]. We can, however, mention certain tendencies. Glottalized consonants, for example, are rare in European languages, but occur in a goodly number of American Indian languages (section 12.6). A glottalized consonant is formed when a speaker, in producing a consonant, momentarily closes off the glottis, the opening at the upper part of the larynx between the vocal cords; the result is a consonant with a distinctive popping sound. Another noteworthy tendency is the absence of a contrast between voiceless and voiced consonants (e.g., English [p, t, k] vs. [b, d, g]), which is relatively infrequent in the languages of the Americas, but is a frequent feature of European languages. Moreover, in those languages that do not have the contrast, it is the voiceless rather than the voiced set that almost always occurs.

Although all sound systems contain consonants and vowels, there may be other significant phonological features as well. One such feature is tone, the relative musical pitch of the voice. Like Thai (Southeast Asia) and Yoruba (West Africa) among other languages in the world, some American Indian languages use differences in relative pitch to distinguish meanings; for example, Navajo *nílį* 'you are' and *nilį* 'he is' have the same sequence of consonants and vowels, and are differentiated only by a difference in tone: *nílį* has high tone (marked by [´] over the vowel) on both syllables, while *nilį* has low tone on the first, high tone on the second. Tone is found in a number of other American Indian languages, such as Zapotec (Mexico) and Cherokee.

These three-sound inventory characteristics are found in the now-extinct Shasta language of northern California. Shasta has a contrast between high and low pitch to distinguish meanings, for example, *kipxá·* 'you put your shoes on!' versus *kipxa·* 'you roast it!,' and it has voiceless stops ([p, t, c, č, k, ?]) and glottalized stops ([p', t', c', č', k']), but it does not have voiced stops.

As well as differing in the size and makeup of sound inventories, languages also differ in the patterns that speech sounds form within words. Some languages place severe restrictions on the sequences of sounds that are allowed: In Ute (Utah and Colorado), there are only two syllable types, CV and CVC (C = consonant, V = vowel); CVC only occurs at the ends of words, and consonant clusters (CC) are not allowed. There are, however, other languages that allow sequences of consonants that to the speaker of a European language would seem to defy pronunciation. Among these languages are Coeur d'Alene (Idaho) with word-initial consonant clusters of up to five members, and Bella Coola (British Columbia) in which a word can consist of a sequence of six consonants with no vowels at all: *qpsttx̣* 'take it!' (*qpst-* 'take'; -*t*-, transitive; -*x̣*, imperative). For an expanded discussion of speech sounds see appendix ı.

GRAMMATICAL SYSTEMS

The grammatical component of language includes two subsystems: morphological and syntactic. The **morphology** of a language has to do with word structure and formation; the **syntax** involves sentence structure and formation. Languages vary as to the relative load borne by these two systems; for example, in Acoma (New Mexico), the grammatical notions of subject and object are part of the morphology and are marked by affixation to the verb; in Shoshoni (Nevada and Utah) these notions are part of the syntax and marked by independent words; Aztec, on the other hand, uses both affixation and independent words.

Affixation is a major process in the internal formation of words. A prefix is an affix that precedes the element to which it is added and a suffix follows the element. The Yahi Yana example we discussed earlier has no prefixes; instead, it consists of a root followed by six suffixes:

> *ya·-* 'several people move'   (root)
> > *-banauma-* 'everybody'   (suffix)
> > *-wil-* 'across'   (suffix)
> > *-ǧi-* 'to the west'   (suffix)
> > *-gumma-* 'indeed'   (suffix)
> > *-ha-*, hortatory, i.e., 'let us'   (suffix)
> > *-ʔnigi* 'we'   (suffix)

Affixes are added to stems. A stem might consist of a single root, or a root plus affixes, or it might be derived through compounding by placing two or more roots together, as in this example from Nez Perce (Idaho): *ʔalatálo* 'yellowjacket,' derived from the roots *ʔá·la* 'fire' and *tá·lo* 'testes'. Like affixation, compounding is a significant word-formation technique. Languages do not combine roots, stems, and affixes in just any fashion; there are complex rules for how they are ordered: which can occur together; which classes of affixes are obligatory; which are optional.

Inasmuch as it is beyond the scope of this book to give a full accounting of the linguistic characteristics of the languages of the Americas, what follows is a representative sample of selected aspects. In each case, we give first an example from a particular language, followed by a general discussion for the languages of North America.

2.1 POSSESSION: EXAMPLE FROM ACOMA

Possession as a grammatical notion of necessity precedes any analysis of Acoma, a language spoken at Acoma Pueblo in New Mexico. To start with, a noun may take a possessive pronoun, as in English "**my** house," "**her** pen," "**our** grandmother," "**their** feet." It may also be possessed by another noun, which is typically, but not necessarily, a person or animal: "**the old man's** house," "**Lucinda's** pen," "**the children's** grandmother," "the foot **of the mountain**." Closely allied to noun possession is the possessive sentence, which in English is usually marked by the verb "have": "I **have** a house"; "Lucinda **had** a pen"; "the children **have** two grandmothers"; "they **have** dirty feet."

In Acoma, possessive person reference notions are not marked by separate words, but by prefixation to the noun: *dʸûuni* 'pottery,' *s'a-dʸûuni* 'my pottery,' *k'a-dʸáat'itáan'i* 'her pen,' *dʸaʔáu* 'grandmother,' *k'a-dʸaʔáu* 'her grandmother', *k'a-dʸûuniši* 'their pottery'.

While English possessive pronouns distinguish three **persons**—first person (e.g., "my"), second person (e.g., "your"), and third person (e.g., "hers")—and distinguish three **genders** in the third person—feminine ("hers"), masculine ("his"), and neuter ("its")—Acoma has the same three persons found in English, as well as an additional person, for indefinite; and because Acoma does not distinguish gender, *k'a-dʸàiy'aani* can be translated either as 'his piñon nuts' or 'her piñon nuts'; for example, *s'a-k'úuyá* 'my father's clansman' (first person); *kiça-k'úuyá* 'your father's clansman' (second person); *k'a-k'úuyá* 'his, her father's clansman' (third person); *sk'a-k'úuyá* 'someone's father's clansman' (indefinite person).

English possessive pronouns distinguish two **numbers, singular** (for just one), and **plural** (more than one) but these differences in number are shown by the use of completely different forms: for example, "my" first-person singular versus "our" first-person plural, and "his, hers, its" third-person singular versus "their" third-person plural. In Acoma there are three numbers: singular (for one), dual (for just two), and plural (more than two); however, a change in number is not shown by a change in possessive prefix. Instead, Acoma uses a possessive prefix (sometimes with slight modification) along with a dual prefix or a plural suffix to indicate possession by more than one. (When the dual- and plural-number prefixes are used, there are some changes in the vowel which are too complex to explain here.)

> *k'a-d'ñuuni* 'her (or his) pottery' (third-person singular)
> *k'a-ʔa-d'ñuuni* 'their pottery' (the two of them, third-person dual; *–ʔa–,* dual prefix)
> *k'a-d'ñuuni-ši* (or) *gá-ad'ñuuni-ši* 'their (pl.) pottery' (third-person pl.; *-ši,* pl. suffix)
> *s'a-k'ûiça* 'my sister' (first-person singular)
> *ṣa-ʔa-k'ûiça* 'our (two of us) sister' (first-person dual)
> *ṣa-k'ûiça-ši,* our (more than two of us) sister (first-person pl.)

In the possessive, then, there are two differences between English and Acoma in the expression of number: First, English has two numbers (singular and plural), Acoma, three (singular, dual, and plural); second, the notions of person and number are expressed together in a single element in English, in Acoma, by one set for person and by a different set for number.

When a noun rather than a pronoun indicates the possessor, English marks it with the possessive suffix "-'s" ("the girl**'s** mother") or with "of" ("the mother **of** the redheaded girl"); Acoma employs a different strategy: The possessor noun comes first, followed by the possessed noun prefixed with the appropriate pronominal form(s); for example, *màagíže'eši k'á-nâaya* 'the girl's mother,' literally 'girl her-mother'.

In Acoma there are two patterns of possession, **alienable** and **inalienable.** "Alienable" normally refers to a circumstance in which speakers consider the possessed to be in a temporary or nonessential relationship with a possessor; in other words, the item and its possessor stand in a separable, or alienable, relationship to each other; for example, English "the girl's jeans." "Inalienable" refers to a circumstance in which a possessed item is thought to be in a permanent or necessary relationship to its possessor; that is, the item and its possessor stand in an inseparable, or inalienable, relationship to each other; for example, English "the girl's legs." The alienably possessed Acoma noun class includes terms for objects such as pottery, a pen, piñon nuts, and the like. Like most languages that make a distinction between alienable and inalienable possession, the Acoma inalienably possessed noun category typically includes two kinds of nouns: body parts and kin; that is, a foot must belong to someone, and a father has to be somebody's father.

Nouns in the alienably possessed class differ from those of the inalienably possessed class in two ways: (1) they can occur as unpossessed stems, for example, *d'ñûuni* 'pottery,' and (2) a prefix –(')a– is added to these stems before the possessive prefix is added. In our previous discussion we did not separate these two prefixes. Here, we can give a more accurate writing and show this class marker as a separate element in, for example, the paradigm for "pottery":

> s-'a-d'ñuuni 'my pottery'
> k-'a-d'ñuuni 'her or his pottery'
> kįc-a-d'ñuuni 'your pottery'
> sk-'a-d'ñuuni 'someone's pottery'

We can more clearly see –(')a– as a separate element when we look at paradigms of inalienably possessed nouns. (There are changes in pronoun shapes that depend in part on the nature of the following vowel, but these are beyond the level of discussion that we can provide here):

> s-édí 'my foot'
> ṣ-asdí 'your foot'
> k-asdí 'his or her foot'
> sk-asdí 'someone's foot'

> s-énáska 'my head'
> ṣ-ánáska 'your head'
> g-ánáska 'his or her head'
> sg-ánáska 'someone's head'

> s'í-wáw' 'my face'
> ṣ-'úwáw'i 'your face'
> k-'úwáw'i 'his or her face'
> sk-'uwáw'i 'someone's face'

To someone who does not share in the Acoma worldview it may seem that there are inconsistencies in assigning nouns to the two classes; for example, although almost all body parts are inalienably possessed, a few body-part terms (e.g., pán'aci 'lungs') belong to the alienably possessed class. The kinship terms are about evenly divided between the two classes; for example, s'a-k'ûiça 'my sister (of a man)' is inalienably possessed, while n'âaya 'mother' is alienably possessed. In addition, there are five nouns in the inalienably possessed category that are neither body part terms nor kin terms: s'áuk'îni 'my friend,' s'adyá 'my pet, my domesticated animal,' s'áw'aṣu 'my scar,' s'àiṣa 'my garden,' s'àapaa 'my bag'. We do not have to reach too far to find a rationale for the inclusion of the first four items: Just as a father must be somebody's father, so a friend must be somebody's friend; a pet or domesticated animal must belong to someone, since that is what distinguishes it from a wild animal; a scar, like a body part, belongs to someone; and a garden, in contrast to an uncultivated plot of land, is tended by and belongs to someone. It is unclear, however, why the term for "bag" is on this list, but to provide a proper explanation might take a more extensive description and understanding of Acoma life ways and worldview than we would be able to present here.

Even though inalienably possessed nouns always imply a possessor, there are times when the particular possessor is not important. Acoma provides two solutions to this problem: One is to use the indefinite form, for example, sk'ak'úuyá 'someone's father's clansman,' sk-asdí 'someone's foot'. The other solution is to use the "absolutive," a noun formation restricted to body-part terms and created by adding a prefix h- and a suffix –ni to a body-part term; for example, compare ž̧–ača 'his horn,' with the absolutive form h–áča-ni. Absolutive nouns, then, can be alienably possessed: Notice the contrast between wáakaši ž̧-áča 'the cow's horn' (lit. 'cow her-horn') and s-'a-háčani 'my horn' (e.g., one that I now have that I found in the field).

The possession of animals is expressed in an interesting way in Acoma grammar. The possessive prefixes are not used with animal names; rather, the "pet" word is used: kawâayu s'ad'á 'my horse' (lit. 'horse my-pet'), díya k'ad'á 'his dog' (lit. 'dog his-pet'). (We return to this topic in section 12.6.)

We noted earlier that the possessive sentence is closely allied to noun possession. In Acoma, possessive sentences are identical in form to possessed nouns; for example, the possessed noun s-'a-d'ñuuni 'my pottery,' or the noun phrase k'am'askuk'úuya k-'a-mɨti 'Spider Woman's son' (lit. 'Spider Woman her-son') can function in sentences as subject, object, or any other position that can be filled by a noun or noun phrase. They can also stand as complete sentences with the meaning 'I have pottery' and 'Spider Woman has a son'.

The two features of Acoma possession that we have discussed frequently occur in other languages of North America. One is the use of person references in prefix form, rather than as independent words. This characteristic is shared by languages as different from each other as Navajo, Hopi (northeastern Arizona), and Karuk (northwestern California); but there are also languages, such as Shoshoni (section 2.4), in which person references are expressed as independent words and not as prefixes. The second commonly occurring feature, the distinction between alienable and inalienable possession, is a characteristic of languages as different as Aztec, Yneseño (California), and Cree. While body-part and kin terms are the nouns most typically inalienably possessed, particulars vary from language to language, as do the means for marking the distinction between the two types of possession.

2.2   GENDER: EXAMPLE FROM PLAINS CREE

In section 2.1 we mentioned gender distinctions carried by the English third-person singular possessive pronouns. Very often, in English, words like "her," "his," and "its" (and also "she," "he," "him," and "it") refer to the sex of real-world entities; for example, "his" and "her" can refer to "uncle's" and "aunt's," while "its" refers to the inanimacy of such items as "book's." In contrast to this "**natural**" gender, **grammatical** gender has nothing necessarily to do with such real-world phenomena as sex or animacy; its function in a language is to signal grammatical relationships among sentence elements; for example, in Spanish, nouns are divided into two classes, masculine and feminine; masculine nouns are typically marked by the suffix –*o* as in *libro* 'book,' and feminine nouns by –*a* as in *mesa* 'table'. Modifiers, such as articles and adjectives, must agree in gender with the nouns they modify: *el libro antiguo* 'the old (antique) book,' *la mesa antigua* 'the old (antique) table' (with *el* 'the' and *antiguo* 'old' marking masculine; *la* and *antigua,* feminine). This agreement with the nouns is maintained in the plural forms as well: *los libros antiguos* 'the old books' and *las mesas antiguas* 'the old tables'.

Along with a large number of the world's languages, including many American Indian languages, Acoma gets along very well without making grammatical gender distinctions; thus, the prefix in the Acoma form *k'a-n'âaya,* translated in English as 'his mother' or 'her mother', designates person and possession, but not gender. Some Indian languages, however, have gender systems analogous to those commonly found in European languages, while other languages use gender criteria unfamiliar to speakers of European languages; examples are Wishram (Oregon, Washington), Tunica (Mississippi), now extinct, and the family of Algonquian languages (areas north of Mexico and east of the Rockies). Wishram has a three-gender system: masculine, feminine, and neuter; and Tunica distinguishes two genders, masculine and feminine for both second person ("you") and third person ("he" and "she"). The Algonquian system, however, is based on animacy. There are two genders, **animate** and **inanimate**. Plains Cree (see also section 12.1), an Algonquian language spoken in central Canada, typifies this distinction.

In Cree, although there are some nouns referring to lifeless objects that are considered animate, the reverse is never the case: all nouns referring to humans, animals, spirits, or trees are animate; for example, *na·pe·w* 'man'; *iskwe·sis* 'girl'; *ayahčiyiniw* 'enemy'; *si·si·p* 'duck'; *mo·swa* 'moose'; *atim* 'dog'; *a·tayo·hkan* 'kind of spirit'; *kise·-manito·w* 'God'; *mistik* 'tree'; *sihta* 'spruce'.

Some but not all nouns in each of the following semantic categories are classified as animate: plants and their products, natural objects, body parts, most animal hides and clothing made from them, tobacco and things related to tobacco, and some household objects and items of manufacture. Examples are *ayo·skan* 'raspberry' (but not *ote·himin* 'strawberry'); *paka·n* 'nut'; *mahta·min* 'grain' or 'ear of corn'; *pi·sim* 'sun'; *moonko·na* 'snow'; *nisakitikim* 'my braid'; *nitasiskita·n* 'my calf' (of the leg); *nitihtikow* 'my kidney'; *wa·poswaya·n* 'rabbit skin'; *mostoswaya·n* 'buffalo robe'; *čiste·ma·w* 'tobacco'; *ospwa·kan* 'pipe'; *askihk* 'kettle'; *napwe·nis* 'little frying pan' (borrowed from French la poêle); *asa·m* 'snow shoe'; *so·niya·w* 'gold, money'. In addition, some nouns can be either animate or inanimate, but with an accompanying change of meaning. Some examples: *mistik* 'tree' (animate), 'stick' (inanimate); *asiniy* 'stone' (animate), 'bullet' (inanimate) *nita·s* 'my trousers' (animate), 'my gaiter' (inanimate).

Although there are nouns designating lifeless objects that are animate in gender, the reverse is never true. At first blush, there seems to be a certain logic behind the exceptions; for example, we might claim that it is logical to view the sun as an animate entity, since it is important in Cree cosmology, or that tobacco is viewed as being alive because it is so culturally important. This is, however, after-the-fact circular logic: Is "sun" an animate noun because it is viewed as being alive, or is it viewed as being alive because it is an animate noun in Cree?

The two genders, animate and inanimate, are grammatically marked in the plural, on noun modifiers, and on verbs. The plural has two forms: *–ak* for animate, *–a* for inanimate:

Animate	Inanimate
na·pew-ak 'men'	*astotin-a* 'caps'
si·si·p-ak 'ducks'	*mo·hkoma·n-a* 'knives'
ospwa·kan-ak 'pipes'	*mi·nis-a* 'berries'

Cree nouns are unmarked in the singular, so there is no way to know, simply by its form, whether a singular noun is animate or inanimate. Some Algonquian languages, such as Fox (Michigan), mark the gender in both the singular and plural. A Fox noun must occur with one of these four suffixes: *–a* (anim. sg.); *–aki* (anim. pl.); *–i* (inan. sg.); *–ani* (inan. pl.). Examples are *ineniw-a* 'man'; *ineniw-aki* 'men'; *mi·ša·m-i* 'sacred bundle'; *mi·ša·m-ani* 'sacred bundles'.

Cree noun modifiers usually have two forms, depending on whether they modify animate or inanimate nouns. The forms for 'this' and 'these' provide an example: *awa* (anim. sg.); *o·ki* (anim. pl.); *o·ma* (inan. sg.); *o·hi* (inan. pl.): thus, *awa atim* 'this dog' (anim. sg.); *o·ki atimw-ak* 'these dogs' (anim. pl.); *o·ma mo·hkoma·n* 'this knife' (inan. sg.); *o·hi mo·hkoma·n-a* 'these knives' (inan. pl.).

Finally, animacy is marked in the verb. Intransitive verbs (i.e., verbs with a subject but no object) have two forms, one for animate subject, another for inanimate subject, illustrated in this example with *mihče·tiw* 'to be numerous': *Ospwa·kan-ak mihče·tiw-ak* 'There were many pipes (anim.)'. *Mo·hkoma·n-a mihče·tiw-a* 'There were many knives (inan.)'. Notice how the verb suffixes matching the animate and inanimate subjects are the same as the plural noun suffixes. Transitive verbs (those with both a subject and object) also have two forms, but the gender distinction is based on the animacy of the object, not the subject; examples with *wa·pam-* (anim.); *wa·paht-* (inan.) 'to see'; and *we·pin-* 'to throw away': *ni-wa·pam-a·w ospwa·kan* 'I see the pipe' (anim.); *ni-wa·paht-e·n mo·hkoma·n* 'I see the knife' (inan.); *ni-we·pin-a·w ospwa·kan* 'I threw away the pipe' (anim.); *ni-we·pin-e·n mo·hkoma·n* 'I threw away the knife' (inan.). Since the subject of a transitive verb such as "see" or "throw" is typically animate, whereas the object can easily vary in animacy, it is not surprising that Cree marks animacy for object rather than subject. Typically, animate nouns that are subjects of transitive verbs are doers or agents, and thus normally are human or animal. In certain contexts inanimate entities do occur as actors; for instance, there is a Cree folktale in which a grammatically inanimate form, *mistikwa·n* '(one's) head,' is the protagonist, a rolling head that speaks and does other things more typically associated with animate beings. The fact that it is possible to personify a lifeless object probably accounts for why, in Cree, some lifeless objects are grammatically animate, but no living being or animal is ever treated as inanimate.

As we have seen, the degree of correspondence between grammatical gender and the real-world classification according to "natural" gender varies considerably from language to language. The Spanish words for "hand" and "moon" are feminine, whereas the terms for "foot" and "sun" are masculine; the German word for "girl" is neuter; the Russian words for young living things ("calves," "children," "kittens," "puppies") are masculine in the singular and neuter in the plural. Although most languages with grammatical gender display some correspondence with real-world categories, the Cree example demonstrates that this real-world basis is not always sex.

Sex and animacy are not the only properties playing roles in defining grammatical gender systems; for example, the gender systems of Cree or Acoma or English or Spanish do not provide speakers of those languages with choices that are available to speakers of Oneida (New York), one of the Iroquoian languages. The Iroquoian languages, located in the Great Lakes region, have a grammatical gender system marked in verbs by third-person prefixes that refer to both subjects and objects. In Oneida and some of the other languages, there is one masculine gender and two feminine. The two feminine gender prefixes, labeled FI and FZ in grammatical descriptions, can be used in reference to nonfemales as well as females. The choice of prefix depends on the weighting of several semantic components: (1) animacy, (2) age, (3) indefiniteness (is the specific gender of the referent known or unknown, relevant or irrelevant?), (4) humanness (is an animate being human or animal?), (5) size and gracefulness (is the referent small or graceful, or large, awkward, or aggressive?), and (6) special relationship (is the speaker indifferent, detached in attitude toward the referent, or is there a special feeling of respect?). These components in the verb prefixes interact with similar semantic features in the verb stems to which the prefixes are attached; for example, when the verb stem contains the meaning "young," the two feminines, FI and FZ, can suggest a contrast in size. In other words, whichever prefix occurs on the stem, the verb means "she's young"; however, FZ implies a larger size than FI does. When the verb stem contains the meaning "old," FI and FZ are likely to suggest a contrast in the relationship between the speaker and the referent, with FI implying a closer relationship.

This brief discussion of Oneida feminine gender markers gives only a hint of how a skillful Oneida speaker can manipulate the use of the language's gender system for subtle effects. In the case of these feminine prefixes, a speaker's choice, for any particular utterance, is dependent upon the verbal context and the social relationships that condition the weight given to each of six semantic factors.

2.3 NUMBER: EXAMPLE FROM SHASTA

Some American Indian languages, such as Cree and Aztec, make a distinction between singular and plural nouns in a manner similar to that of languages like Spanish and English: the singular is marked by the absence of any suffix, while the plural is marked by the addition of a suffix: Cree *si·si·p* '(a) duck,' *si·si·p-ak* 'ducks'; Spanish *(un) gato* '(a) cat,' *(los) gato-s* '(the) cats'. Other languages, like Shoshoni, make a three-way distinction between singular (only one), dual (two), and plural (three or more).

Several American Indian languages make no distinction between singular and plural for the noun, or they make distinctions based on quite different criteria. In Shasta (northern California), there is no difference between singular and plural nouns, so that a noun can be translated into English as either singular or plural, depending on context: *suk·ax* 'boy' or 'boys,' *kiyaxá?* 'girl' or 'girls'. Shasta does have, however, a suffix, *–yá·war*, a **collective**, that denotes a group of entities: *suk·ax-**yá·war** '*(a group of) boys' (lit. boy-coll.), *kiyaxá-**yá·war** '*(a group of) girls' (lit. girl-coll.).

The collective suffix *–yá·war* can be added to any noun. Unlike other Shasta nouns, however, the words for 'boy' and 'girl' also have a **paucal** form that can be best translated as 'a few . . .': *?e·warár* '(a few) boys', *yač·apxa·* '(a few) girls'. Each pair of forms, *suk·ax* and *?e·warár*, and *kiyaxá?* and *yač·apxa·* is in a **suppletive** relationship; that is, the forms in each pair, although they have no phonological similarity, are used to indicate a specific grammatical relationship; in this case, the relationship is between singular (e.g., 'one boy'), and paucal (e.g., 'a few boys').

An English example analogous to these particular Shasta examples might be person and people: "person" (singular) and "people" (collective) are in an apparent suppletive relationship, with "person-s" as a plural form. The present and past tense forms "go" and "went," or the comparative forms "good" and "bett-er" are also examples of suppletion in English.

As with nouns, Shasta verbs can be marked for collectivity and, in addition, for **distributive,** that is, an action performed by each person individually: *k'-umpehé·wi-ma* 'he or she swam downstream' (*k'-*, third person; *–umpehé·wi-*, verb stem; *–ma* 'thither'); *k'-umpehé·w-e·ki·-ma* 'they swam downstream' (collectively) (*–e·ki·*, collective suffix); *k'-umpehé·wi-ru-ma* 'they swam downstream' (distributively, i.e., one after another) (*–ru,* distributive suffix). Notice that the prefix *k'-* marks third person, but not gender or number; therefore, the English translations into singular ("he, she, it") and plural ("they") reflect the absence and presence of a collective or distributive marker in the verb.

In Shasta, only in the first person are there distinct forms for singular and plural: *k-* first person singular past ('I'), and *y-* first person plural past ('we'). This provides the opportunity to indicate a paucal form when the first person plural prefix is used. If the verb form is marked for first person and is not marked for collective or distributive, then its meaning includes 'a few': *y-umpihé·wi·-ma* 'a few of us swam down stream'; *y-umpihé·w-e·ki-ma;* 'a group of us swam down stream'; *y-umpihé·wi-ru-ma* 'we (more than a few) swam down stream, one after another'. Many verbs can have collective and distributive forms. In addition, some verbs have suppletive forms for singular versus nonsingular: *k'w-i·?·aka?* 'he looked'; *k'w-ip·aka?* 'they looked'. The use of suppletion to mark singular and plural verbs is quite common. Of the languages examined in this chapter, it is found in Acoma, Aztec, Shoshoni, and the Apachean languages.

2.4 PERSON REFERENCE:
EXAMPLES FROM AZTEC AND SHOSHONI

An examination of personal pronouns entails consideration of, first, what forms the reference takes and, second, the semantic categories involved. In considering form, we are concerned with such matters as whether the person-reference elements are independent words or whether they are affixed. In English, we are used to seeing them as personal pronouns ("I," "you," etc.). In a language such as Spanish, they are fused with tense suffixes. In *habl-o* 'I am speaking,' *habl-as* 'you are speaking,' the suffixes *–o* and *-as* indicate "I" and "you" in the present tense; in *habl-é* 'I spoke' and *habl-aste* 'you spoke,' the suffixes indicate "I" and "you" in the past tense.

Although some American Indian languages employ only independent personal pronouns, quite a few use both independent pronouns and affixes, especially prefixes. Classical Aztec illustrates this point well; it has both prefixes and independent personal pronouns. The independent pronouns are:

neʔhua 'I'	*teʔhuan* 'we'
teʔhua 'you' (sg.)	*ameʔhuan* 'you' (pl.)
yeʔhua 'he, she, it'	*yeʔhuan* 'they'

These forms are used as the subject or object of a verb, or a possessor of a noun. Depending upon how one of these forms is used in a sentence, its English translation will vary accordingly; for example, *neʔhua* is translated as "I," "me," or "my"; *yeʔhuan* as "they," "them," or "their." Use of these independent forms is always optional, and when so used, it is only for emphasis. The prefixes, however, are obligatory, even when the independent forms are used. The subject prefixes are illustrated in this paradigm:

ni-*cochi* 'I sleep'	**ti**-*cochi-ʔ* 'we sleep'
ti-*cochi* 'you (sg.) sleep'	**an**-*cochi-ʔ* 'you (pl.)sleep'
cochi 'he or she sleeps'	*cochi-ʔ* 'they sleep'

Number (singular and plural) is marked not only by the subject pronoun prefix, but also by the use of a suffix (-ʔ) in the plural; additionally, the absence of a prefix marks the third person ("he," "she," "it," "they"), and the presence or absence of the plural suffix (-ʔ) indicates the difference between singular ("he," "she," "it") and plural ("they"). The object prefix follows the subject marker: *ti-**nech**-notza* 'you (sg.) call **me**'; *an-**nech**-notza-ʔ* 'you (pl.) call **me**'; *ni-**mitz**-notza* 'I call **you** (sg.)'; *ti-**k**-notza* 'you (sg.) call **him** or **her**'; *an-**tech**-notza-ʔ* 'you (pl.) call **us**'; *ti-**mech**-notza-ʔ* 'we call **you** (pl.)'; *ti-**kin**-notza* 'you (sg.) call **them**'. When there is an indirect object, three prefixes are present: *ti-**nech-im**-maca in chichimeʔ* 'you gave the dogs to me' (lit. **'you-me-them**-gave the dogs'). The subject is *ti-* (you, sg.), the indirect object is *nech-* (to me), and the direct object is *im-* (the phrase in *chichimeʔ* means "the dogs"). When the object is the same as the subject, there is a special reflexive prefix that marks the object: *ni-**no**-tema* 'I bathe **myself**'; *ti-**mo**-tema* 'you bathe **yourself**'; *ti-**to**-tema-ʔ* 'we bathe **ourselves**'. Prefixes are also used with nouns to show possession:

no-nan 'my mother'	*to-nan* 'our mother'
mo-nan 'your (sg.) mother'	*amo-nan* 'your (pl.) mother'
i-nan 'his or her mother'	*in-nan* 'their mother'
te-nan 'someone's mother' (indefinite)	

We noted in section 2.1 that Acoma uses prefixes to signal possession of nouns. Prefixes are also used with verbs to indicate subject and object. In contrast to Aztec,

Acoma uses a single prefix to indicate both subject and object, for example, *s'-îit'a* 'I stepped on him or her,' where the prefix *s'–* means that the subject is "I," and the object is "him" or "her." A partial paradigm shows how this system works:

> *s'-îit'a* 'I stepped on him': *s'–* = I (sub.), him or her (obj.)
> *ṣ'â-it'a* 'I stepped on you': *ṣ'a–* = I (sub.), you (obj.)
> *tʸ'ûit'a* 'you stepped on me': *tʸ'u–* = you (sub.), me (obj.)
> *sk'û-it'a* 'he stepped on me': *sk'u–* = he or she (sub.), me (obj.)

Acoma is unusual among the languages of the world in that it lacks independent personal pronouns and only uses pronominal prefixes.

The examples from Aztec and Acoma, in which subject and object notions occur as prefixes in the verb form, are demonstrations of polysynthesis as a word-formation process. Such verb words are sometimes known as **sentential verbs;** that is, they contain the grammatical and semantic elements that are essential in the formation of a sentence. Other examples of verb words have been illustrated for Yahi Yana, Cree (section 2.2), and Shasta (section 2.3).

Next we look at Shoshoni personal pronouns, taking our examples from a story about a hunter and his encounter with Mountain Dwarf. A literal word-for-word translation is provided in parenthesis after the free translation:

1. *ɨnnɨn u pekkahkʷcihi, innɨn nookkʷan-tui ɨn kahni-kattun.* 'You will kill it, (and) you will carry (it) to your house'. (you it kill-when, you carry-will your house-to)

2. *Tammɨn wica tɨan u wekkihkʷa.* 'We should look for him'. (we should also him look)

3. *Isɨn tahan haincɨh.* 'He is our friend'. (this our friend)

4. *ɨnnɨn wica ikka nian huueti masunkaa.* 'You should feel my bow'. (you should this my bow feel)

5. *Pɨnnan kahni-kattun koimia.* 'He returned to his house'. (his house-to returned)

6. *Ke un kahni taʔutta.* 'He couldn't find his house'. (not his house find)

7. *Nɨmmɨn ke kaa hɨatɨn.* 'We don't trap rats'. (we not rats trap)

8. *Nɨ ɨkkʷa ke nɨɨwii-tuihantɨn, nuun nia pekka-nuhi.* 'I'm not going to live, so let him kill me'. (I so not live-will, just me kill-let)

9. *Pɨnnan kahni-kattun nukki.* 'She ran to her house'. (her house-to ran)

These pronouns (the numbers refer to the above sentences) occur: (1) *ɨnnɨn* 'you' (subject); *u* 'it,' *ɨn* 'your'; (2) *tammɨn* 'we,' *u* 'him'; (3) *tahan* 'our'; (4) *ɨnnɨn* 'you,' *nian* 'my'; (5) *pinnan* 'his'; (6) *un* 'his'; (7) *nimmin* 'we'; (8) *ni* 'I,' *nia* 'me'; (9) *pinnan* 'her'. At first glance, the Shoshoni system does not seem too different from an English point of view. Person references in Shoshoni, as in English, but not in Acoma and Aztec, are only independent forms, never prefixes. English and Shoshoni are also alike in that they both have distinct forms for subject, object, and possessive; for example, *ni* 'I', *nia* 'me', *nian* 'my'. But as we look further, some differences emerge.

First, several sentences (5, 6, 9) are rendered in English with a subject pronoun "he" or "she," but there is no corresponding pronoun in the Shoshoni sentences. This is because Shoshoni does not have third-person subject pronouns. The absence of a subject pronoun in a Shoshoni sentence signals that the sentence is to be interpreted as having a third-person subject. If a speaker wishes to emphasize, however, that the subject really is a third person, demonstrative pronouns ("this one, that one") are used, as in sentence 3.

A second difference from English is the absence of a gender distinction in the third-person singular pronouns. Context provides the proper translation into English; thus in sentence 1, the object *u* refers to a deer, and is translated as "it"; in 2, *u* refers to a lost man, and is rendered in English as "him"; in 5, the hunter returns to his house; and in 9, Mountain Dwarf's wife returns to her house.

If there are some English distinctions that do not have exact Shoshoni equivalents, there are likewise distinctions in the Shoshoni sentences that do not come out in the English translations. Sentences 5 and 6 both contain 'his house' in the translations, but there are two different pronouns in Shoshoni: in 5, the hunter is returning to his own house, hence *pinnan*, but in 6, the hunter could not find the Mountain Dwarf's house, that is, somebody else's house, hence *un*. We find another use of two different pronouns in 2 and 7, with *tammin* and *nimmin*, which are both rendered by "we." This is because Shoshoni makes a distinction between **inclusive** and **exclusive** in the first person plural that is not reflected by the English pronoun. Inclusive plural *tammin* means "you all and I," while exclusive plural *nimmin* means "I and others, not including you." In 2, the hunter is telling his friends "we (you all and I) should look for him," but in 7 he is telling a newcomer "we (those of us who live here, but excluding you) don't trap rats." Shoshoni also makes a distinction in number that English pronouns do not mark, namely, dual, for just two; the form *tahan* 'our' in sentence 3 is a dual possessive form. (Can you guess whether *tahan* is inclusive or exclusive?) If we use sentence 7 as a model, we can illustrate the three numbers (singular, dual, plural), and the distinction between inclusive and exclusive, for first person subject as follows: *nike kaa hiatin* 'I don't trap rats'; *niwih ke kaa hiatin;* 'we (dl., excl.) don't trap rats'; *tawih ke kaa hiatin* 'we (dl., incl.) don't trap rats'; *nimmin ke kaa hiatin* 'we (pl., excl.) don't trap rats'; *tammin ke kaa hiatin;* 'we (pl., incl.) don't trap rats'.

We also saw the use of dual number in Acoma (section 2.1). While the dual is not

as common as some other grammatical features, it is certainly not uncommon in
North America Indian languages. The same can be said for the distinction between
inclusive and exclusive "we," the use of demonstratives for third person subjects,
and the distinction between "his/her (own)" versus "his/her (someone else's)."

2.5 CLASSIFYING VERBS: EXAMPLES
FROM THE APACHEAN LANGUAGES

The Apachean languages consist of seven closely related languages spoken in New
Mexico and Arizona, including Navajo Apache (usually referred to as simply Navajo),
Chiricahua Apache, Mescalero Apache, and others. These languages belong to the
Athapaskan language family, which contains, in addition to the Apachean languages of the southwestern United States, a number of languages in Alaska, western Canada, and the Pacific coast (see chapter 12 for discussion of "language family,"
and section 14.2 for the classification of this family). Athapaskan languages have a
characteristic set of about a dozen verb stems that classify objects by shape. Two
examples from Chiricahua Apache illustrate the system (the accent marks indicate
tone; for example, hà- has low tone, -ʔą́ has high tone; a hook under a vowel indicates nasalization). In the first instance, hà- is used as follows: hàyó·ʔą́ 'he took it
(a stone ax) out (of a container),' from hà-yi-hó·ʔą́ (hà- 'out of an enclosed space',
yi- third-person object, ho·- tense-like prefix indicating the action is completed,
-ʔą́ verb stem); in the second, -ʔą́ is used as nâiñ·tą́, 'he picked it (a gun) up,' from
ná-yi-di-ni-tą́ (na- . . . -di- 'up', yi-, third-person object, ni- a tense prefix, -tą́ verb
stem). The verb in Athapaskan languages consists of a stem with one or more prefixes. The prefixes indicate such grammatical notions as person (subject and object,
such as yi-, third person, in the examples); adverbial notions that show direction
of the action (such as ha- 'out of an enclosed space', na- . . . -di- 'up'); tense and
mode (such as ho·-, and ni-). When prefixes and stem are joined to make the complete verb, the sounds often change and coalesce; in these examples, the sequence
hà-yi-hó·-ʔą́ becomes hàyó·ʔą́, and ná-yi-di-ni-tą́ becomes nâiñ·tą́.

The stems in the two Chiricahua Apache verbs can most accurately be translated as something like "to handle (a certain kind of) an object." The meaning of a
complete verb, that is, a verb stem with its prefixes, depends on the nature of the
prefixes; thus, in the first example, when the prefix hà- 'out of an enclosed space'
is combined with the stem the resultant meaning can be translated as 'to take out
from'. In the second example, the two-prefix combination na- . . . -di- means 'up';
therefore, this combination plus the stem yields the translation 'to pick up'.

The verb stem in the first example is 'ą́, because the object (a stone ax) is classified as a round object. In the second example, the verb stem is *tą*, because the object (a gun) is a long object. Such verb forms are called **classifying stems,** because use of a particular stem depends on the nature of an object and how it is classified. In the Athapaskan languages shape is the most important classificatory characteristic. The classifying stems in Navajo are:

–'ą́	to handle a roundish object, such as ball, box, hat, knife, book, boot
–tą́	to handle a slender or long stiff object, such as pencil, gun, cigarette, bracelet
–tį́	to handle an animate object, such as a person, bug, mouse, moose, as well as images of living beings, such as a doll, and the carcass of a butchered animal, provided that the backbone, ribs, and neck are still intact
–nil	to handle a set of objects, or plural objects that can be individually distinguished, such as a half dozen eggs, people, coats, sacks of wool, a small number of books, rocks
–jaa'	to handle a mass, or plural objects that cannot be easily distinguished individually, such as a handful of beads, salt, a large number of objects such as books, matches, rocks
–lá	to handle a slender, flexible or ropelike object, such as a rope, belt, snake; also objects that come in pairs such as gloves, shoes, socks
–ką́	to handle an object in an open container, such as a dish of food, a bucket of water, an open bottle of beer, a baby in a cradleboard, an injured person on a stretcher
–tsooz	to handle a flat flexible object, such as a sheet, shirt, handkerchief, as well as a small sackful of objects, such as a small sack of coffee or groceries
–yį́	to handle a large bulky object, in a sack or a load, such as a large sack of wool or potatoes, a truckload of firewood, a saddle
–jool	to handle noncompact or wool-like material, such as loose hay, wool, gaseous matter such as fog, smoke, dust
–tłéé'	to handle mushy objects, such as oatmeal, mud, butter

Every object must be placed into one of these categories when used with a classifying verb of handling. But a speaker does have some leeway. For example, there are two stems for plural objects, depending on whether the items are thought of as a mass or as a set of individual items: In designating a person, one would normally use the stem referring to an animate object; but one can use the stem for mushy objects to refer to a drunk found in a position that resembles an amorphous mass.

This system of classificatory verbs is a hallmark of the Athapaskan languages. Similar systems are found in a number of other languages, such as Keres (the Pueblo Southwest), the Muskogean languages (originally located in the southeastern United States), and the Jaqi languages (Andean area).

2.6 EVIDENTIALS: EXAMPLES FROM THE ANDES

Evidentials have to do with two aspects of reality, namely, the reliability and source of the knowledge embodied in speech: How certain is a speaker that a given statement is true, and what is the source of the information? For example, the first of the following pair of sentences indicates greater reliability or certainty than the second: (1) It rained last night; (2) I think it rained last night. The next sentences differ in sources or types of experience: (1) I saw it raining last night; (2) the ground is wet; it must have rained last night; (3) Amos told me that it rained last night. There is a relationship between degree of certainty and source. Knowledge gained by direct experience through the senses (seeing, hearing, feeling, tasting, smelling) is normally regarded as more reliable than other sources, but the correlation is not perfect and there is cross-cultural variation; for example, some would regard divine revelation as more trustworthy than personal experience, and knowledge gained through dreams, a kind of direct experience, is regarded differently by different cultures.

We examine the evidential system from two Andean languages of the Jaqi language family, Aymara and Jaqaru. Aymara is spoken in Bolivia, Peru, and Chile by well over a million people, whereas Jaqaru is spoken in Peru by only a few thousand. There are differences in detail, but the semantic categories and mechanisms used to mark evidentiality are similar in the two languages. Because these systems are very complex we touch only on the essentials.

Evidentials in these languages are concerned only with the source of the knowledge, not its validity; however, accuracy is a crucial element in a speaker's public reputation. There are three broad categories: (1) personal, knowledge acquired directly through the senses; (2) nonpersonal, knowledge of all situations in which witnesses cannot be expected; and (3) knowledge-through-language, all knowledge gained through the medium of language, written or oral. Although these categories are marked grammatically in various ways, the basic grammatical mechanism involves tense suffixes in verbs and sentence suffixes.

The Aymara personal knowledge suffix is a sentence suffix: *-wa, -w.* It can be added to a single word to form a complete sentence, that is, a sentence that contains no verb: *uta-***wa** 'it is a house' (house-**wa**). This suffix can also be used in sentences with a verb, provided that the tense of the verb does not also incorporate evidentiality as part of its meaning: *jupa-***w** *ut uñji* 'she sees' or 'saw the house' (she-**w** house see/saw); *jupa-***w** *ut uñjani* 'she will see the house' (she-**w** house will-see). By adding the personal knowledge suffix to different words within sentences, different emphases result, as seen in these contrasting Aymara sentences: *Na-***w** *linkwistä^{y}a* 'I (not somebody else) am a linguist'; *Nax linkwistät-***wa** 'I am a linguist (not a biologist or an anthropologist)'.

Some of the tense suffixes indicate only the tense of the verb. Others combine the meaning of tense and evidentiality, as in these Jaqaru examples: *palu-wi* '(he, she) ate' (*-wi*, recent past, personal knowledge); *palk-na* '(he, she) ate' (*-na,* remote past, personal knowledge); *pal-kata* '(he, she) ate' (*-kata*, recent past, nonpersonal knowledge); *pal-wata* '(he, she) ate' (*-wata*, remote past, nonpersonal knowledge). Nonpersonal knowledge frequently involves the remote past and is particularly appropriate for myths, legends, history, and tales of spirit encounters. It is also used for surprises, such as when a speaker suddenly encounters a situation already established, as in this Jaqaru example in which the *-wata*, remote past, nonpersonal knowledge suffix, is used: *Shumayaq mansan palwata* 'Shumaya ate an apple!' Knowledge-through-language (i.e., information gained from reading, hearsay, speeches, and conversation) is marked in Jaqaru by the sentence suffix *-mna: Shumayaq t'ant^{h}q palwimna* 'they say Shumaya ate bread'.

The Jaqi languages provide mechanisms for ambiguous and transitional situations not included in the three broad evidential categories. They are used instead of, or in addition to, the primary categories, when a strong emotion is involved, a personal interaction is the primary motive or focus, there is a reluctance to commit oneself, or there is a desire to obscure the facts without actually lying. The Aymara sentence suffix *-xa*, used when one is not sure of personal knowledge, is an example of a transitional marker: *Iskuyla jutta-xa* 'you are the one who came to school'. The speaker was a school child who added *-xa* to the verb because she was not sure that she recognized the person she was talking to.

The use of evidentials pervades all discourse and narration, including written materials. In fact, it is difficult to produce any sentence without indicating the source of one's information. Moreover, speakers are expected to be skillful and accurate in indicating their source of information. From an English or Spanish speaker's perspective, Jaqi speakers take the matter of knowledge acquired by personal experience very literally, and some types of knowledge that English or Spanish speakers consider general or received knowledge are excluded from the Jaqi personal knowledge category. Therefore, bodily states are personal knowledge in the first person only, whereas knowledge-through-language markers must be used in referring to another person's hunger, thirst, or pain.

There are some exceptions to such literalness. Men may use the personal knowledge system in referring to children as their own, even though they can be certain of this knowledge only through language, that is, from their wives. (Note, however, this saying of a Jaqaru grandmother: *Wallmchinhn qayllpʰq allchinhwa. Lluqllnhan qayllpʰq qachinilli.* 'Child of my daughter is my grandchild. Child of my son, who knows'?) Other exceptions include some types of general information that may be conveyed as personal knowledge, as in this Jaqaru example: *Utʸutʸullquq aqʰin-w utki.* 'Elves live in caves'. The occurrence of the personal knowledge suffix *-w* on *aqʰin* 'cave' indicates an assertion only about where elves live, not about their actual existence.

It is difficult for speakers of the Jaqi languages to believe that there might be a language for which the marking of the source of knowledge is not obligatory; and, since it is language that is most characteristic of human beings, misuse of evidentials can also be considered insulting to a listener. For instance, inasmuch as internal states are only knowable through direct sensation, it is considered rude if a speaker does not carefully adhere to the rules of evidential use when ascribing such a state to another person. There are proverbs used in teaching children the importance of accurate use of evidentials; for example, the following sayings, also used in disputes to impugn the statements of an adversary, encapsulate cultural values concerning the proper use of evidentials. *Uñjasaw (uñjt) sañax, jan uñjasax jani (uñjt) sañakiti* 'Seeing, one can say "I have seen"; without seeing one must not say "I have seen" ' (Aymara); *Illush arma, ish illshuq jan artatxi* 'Seeing, speak; without seeing, do not speak' (Jaqaru).

The belief on the part of Jaqi language speakers that obligatory marking of sources of knowledge is a language universal is reinforced by the fact that local Andean Spanish has been influenced by the local languages and does, in fact, make the same distinctions (section II.6). Outsiders who speak a nonlocal variety of Spanish or who acquire Aymara without learning its evidential system are apt to speak of things that can only be known through language in a way that is interpreted as personal knowledge by the local people. A missionary's statement as personal knowledge that Adam ate the apple is interpreted as a claim of having been present in the Garden of Eden. If a Peace Corps volunteer, reading from a book, states as personal knowledge that certain seeds yield good crops, the perception, again, is of someone trying to deceive. Misunderstandings can also flow in the other direction. If an outsider says, "I am from California," and a Jaqi speaker replies in Andean Spanish or Jaqi, "You say you are from California," the outsider may feel he or she has been accused of lying. From the Jaqi perspective, however, the issue is a matter of accuracy, not morality.

In addition to the Jaqi language family, there are a number of American Indian languages that have well-delineated evidential systems; to name just a few: Makah (Washington), Kwakiutl (British Columbia), Wintu (northern California), Kashaya Pomo (north-central California coast), Maricopa (Arizona), Cayuga (New York), and Quechua (Peru).

All speakers, whatever language they use, must be concerned with the reliability and source of knowledge. In English and most European languages, there is no single grammatical system devoted exclusively to this function; instead, various subsystems within the grammar are pressed into service. English, for example, makes use of modal verbs (could, might, would, etc.), adverbs (maybe, certainly, about), main verbs followed by a subordinate clause (e.g., we think that, they say that, I heard that) and so on. Furthermore, the devices English uses have other, nonevidential functions, such as "think," as in "I think I'll take a walk," or "Julia thinks Joanne is nice."

Although we cannot characterize the evidential systems in the languages of the Americas in any simple or single fashion, we can say that they are much more developed than in the languages of Europe, that they often form a separate and well-delineated system within the grammar, and that obligatory systems are common. In American Indian languages, there is much variation in evidential systems. Some are like English in utilizing a number of techniques. The Iroquoian languages use main verbs (e.g., "say, think"), particles (e.g., "right, possibly"), and verb prefixes and suffixes that have additional, nonevidential functions (e.g., future, contrary to fact, diminutive, etc.). The Jaqi languages stress the source of information, while Quechua languages of Peru are more concerned with the validity of the information, that is, whether a speaker's statement is based on conjecture or on certainty of the facts. The Hopi of northeastern Arizona are also concerned with validity, as these examples show: *wari* 'he ran, runs, is running' (a reported event); *wari-kŋ*ᵂ*e* 'he runs,' for example, on the track team (a statement of general truth); *wari-kni* 'he will run' (anticipated event).

Other languages are like Kashaya Pomo (northern California), which has a set of obligatory verb suffixes that function to indicate that the speaker's source of information is visual, auditory, inferential, hearsay, and the like. The suffix *–ʔdo* 'quotative' indicates that the speaker learned the reported event by hearsay only; *–an* 'aural' indicates that the speaker heard the sounds of an event (but did not see the event); and *–qʰ* 'circumstantial' indicates that the speaker deduced what happened from circumstantial evidence: *sinam-ʔdo* 'they say he drowned'; *sinam-an* 'I heard him drown'; *sinam-qʰ* 'he must have drowned' (i.e., the speaker deduced the drowning from seeing the body on the beach, or floating in the water, or from seeing the capsized boat which the person had been in). Unlike Kashaya Pomo or Hopi, evidential marking in Shasta is just one feature of a set of verb prefixes that simultaneously mark declarative mode (used for making statements), person, tenses, and evidentials:

r–	third-person subject, nonpast, direct evidential; used when the speaker knows of what he speaks from immediate, direct (usually aural or visual) evidence
kw-	third-person subject, nonpast inferential evidential; used when the speaker infers something, on the basis of having perceived the event either directly or indirectly
k'w-	third-person subject, near past, inferential evidential
p'–	third-person subject, distant past inferential evidential
t–	third-person subject, near past, quotative; used when the speaker is reporting something of which he has no personal knowledge
t'w–	third-person subject, distant past quotative

If there is a single obligatory evidential in a language, it is almost always the quotative, which discriminates hearsay from eye-witness reports and is a very common feature of American Indian languages. The quotative can be indicated in a variety of ways: In some languages it is by a sentence suffix that can be added to any word in the sentence, in others by an independent adverb; but, it is more often marked in the verb by a special verb suffix or by a separate set of tense suffixes. It can also be marked by verb prefixes, as in the Shasta example given earlier. Rules of usage vary; in a traditional Wintu tale, only the first sentence is marked with the quotative, while in Shoshoni every sentence in the story must be so marked.

2.7 SOUND SYMBOLISM IN CALIFORNIA LANGUAGES

The term **sound symbolism** refers to the association of certain sounds of a language with particular physical qualities or activities. Thus the English vowel [i] is sometimes associated with **diminutive** (i.e., smallness in size): compare "teeny" ("ee" = [i]) with "tiny" ("i" = [ay]), which is small, but not as small as "teeny." In English, as in most languages, sound symbolism is relegated to some of the more remote corners of the language, where it plays only a minor role. In many California Indian languages, however, such sound symbolism plays a larger structural role. In these languages it is most often associated with size, intensity, or both.

Some languages indicate two degrees of size, a neutral size and a diminutive.

In Hupa (northwestern California), the palatal [ǯ] marks neutral size and its dental counterpart [ẓ] marks diminutive: *ǯəme·l* 'lizard,' *ẓəme·l* 'a cute little lizard' or a species smaller in size than *ǯəme·l*. In other languages, three degrees of size can be marked: neutral, diminutive, and **augmentative** (i.e., 'largeness in size'). In Wiyot (northern California coast) the dental stop [t], which signals neutral size, alternates with the dental affricate [c] to mark diminutive, and with the palatal affricate [č] to indicate augmentative: *dítatk* 'two roundish objects'; *dícack* 'two small roundish objects'; *díčačk* 'two large roundish objects'.

It is not uncommon for diminutive and augmentative marking to become involved with expressions of speaker attitude: the diminutive is used to express affectionate notions, and the augmentative for pejorative comments. This association exists in Spanish where diminutive and augmentative are indicated by suffixes, and not by sound symbolic alternations: *Ros-a* (personal name): *Ros-ita* (dim.), *Ros-ota* (aug.); *manzan-a*, 'apple': *manzan-ita* (dim.), *manzan-ota* (aug.); *carr-o*, 'car': *carr-ito, carr-ote; hij-a, hij-o*, 'daughter, son': *hij-ita, hij-ito* (dim.), *hij-ota, hij-ote* (aug.); *borrach-o*, 'drunk': *borrachón* (aug.). *Hijita*, the diminutive of *hija*, is more apt to be used for 'precious little daughter' rather than simply 'small daughter,' and a form such as *borrachón*, the augmentative of *borracho*, is more apt to be used for 'an ugly drunk' rather than 'a big drunk'.

In Hupa, the diminutive is often associated with endearment, as in the example *ẓəme·l* 'cute little lizard'. In contrast, the Wiyot diminutive usually marks smallness and seldom indicates affection. The Wiyot augmentative, however, frequently has a pejorative sense, especially when referring to people, personified animals and household utensils: *ró?l* 'plate basket,' *ró?račk* 'used' or 'old plate basket'.

Sound symbolic patterns can also be associated with degrees of intensity. In the Ipai dialect of Diegueño (southern California) there are pairs in which retroflex sound [ṣ] is replaced by the dental [s], such as: *xapṣiw* 'to be blue, green,' *xapsiw* 'to be kind of green, dark'. Cocopa (Arizona), a related language, has this set, in which dental [s] alternates with palatal [š], retroflex [ṣ], and lateral [l]: *xpsiw* 'to be blue, green,' *xpšiw* 'to be of turquoise color,' *xpṣiw* 'to be deeply tanned' (color of Indians), *xpliw* 'to be darkish'. The notions of size and intensity seem to be semantically connected; in fact, it has been proposed that the concept of size may stem from that of intensity.

Sound symbolic alternations are used along with special affixes in some languages. For example, in Karuk the diminutive is marked by both the diminutive suffix –*ič*, or –*ač*, and by the change of [θ] to [č], and [r] to [n]: *iθári·p* 'fir tree,' *ičáni·p-**ič*** 'small fir,' *súruvara* 'hole,' *súna**v**an-**ač*** 'little hole'. In Wiyot, symbolic alternations can occur without a diminutive or augmentative suffix, as in the example given earlier, or with –*oc*, –*ic* "diminutive" or –*ačk* "augmentative": **t**awipáhlił 'rope,' **c**awipáhroł-**oc** 'twine' (i.e., small rope), **č**awiphrół-**ačk** 'cable' (i.e., large rope).

In some of the Northwest Coast languages such as Nootka, sound symbolic alternations are also used to mark certain physical or mental characteristics in speaking of or to a person, to refer to particular mythological characters, and to distinguish between ceremonial and everyday speech. This phenomenon is discussed in section 6.5. We also return to sound symbolism in sections 3.5 and 12.6.

2.8 FUNDAMENTALS OF LANGUAGE EXPRESSION

A language in which most grammatical relations are expressed morphologically (by affixation or compounding) is **synthetic** in structure. If it does so to an extreme extent, the language is said to be **polysynthetic,** as discussed in the opening of this chapter. A language that expresses most grammatical relations syntactically (through processes of phrase and sentence formation) is **analytic** in structure. These categories, synthetic and analytic, are not clear cut: few languages are purely one or the other. English, Spanish, and Shoshoni (section 2.4), for example, tend to be analytic, whereas the Apachean languages (section 2.5) and Aztec (section 2.4) tend to be synthetic. Although American Indian languages range in structural type from analytic to synthetic, analytic languages are found much less frequently than synthetic languages.

We have noted that polysynthesis is a widespread structural trait in the Americas. It is a form of grammatical synthesis that creates extremely intricate word structures. Speakers of polysynthetic languages can make use of alternatives in word and sentence formation that are not as readily accessible to speakers of analytic languages; for example, in polysynthetic languages verb forms contain obligatory person-reference affixes that refer to the subjects and objects of sentences and serve to keep straight who did what to whom. If pronouns are also used, they appear only when needed for emphasis or contrast. In languages like English, the order of nouns or pronouns in a sentence identifies the roles of participants in an event and, if that order is changed, the meaning of the sentence changes: contrast "Rover bit Amos" with "Amos bit Rover." In languages that have obligatory person-reference affixes in verb forms, subjects and objects of sentences are automatically identified. Word order, therefore, is not needed to express the function of referents (i.e., which is subject and which is object); instead, word order can be used to indicate the importance to the overall message of each piece of information in the sentence. Typically, new and the most important information appears near the beginning of a sentence, with known (old) and less important information appearing later in the sentence.

The interplay between person-reference affixes and word order is just one of the grammatical resources available to speakers of polysynthetic languages for manipulating the flow of information; for instance, skilled Karuk speakers use separate words to communicate new, salient detail, or to underscore known detail; and they use affixes for background details so that a listener's attention is not diverted. In addition, the morphological systems of polysynthetic languages afford speakers a useful set of mechanisms for creating new, morphologically complex words, and for expanding a language's vocabulary by putting together new combinations.

Common Grammatical Features

In sections 2.1 through 2.7 we have presented in some detail various structural features found in the languages of the Americas: subject and object marking in the verb (section 2.4), noun possession and alienable/inalienable possession (section 2.1), evidential systems (section 2.6), and so on. What follows here are brief mentions of some other grammatical features that are relatively more frequent in American Indian languages than in the languages of the world as a whole.

TENSE AND ASPECT MARKING. As is often the case in many languages of the world, tense and aspect are often marked by suffixes. **Tense** has to do with the location of an event in time, for example, past versus present. **Aspect** has to do with the manner in which a verbal action is experienced or regarded; for example, whether the action is completed ("I've read your book") or in progress ("I've been reading your book"). Examples of tense suffixes from Karuk are: nimmáh-**at** 'I saw him or her' (past tense), nimmáh-**e·š** 'I will see him or her' (future tense). Tunica (Mississippi) provides some examples of aspect suffixes: pa'ta-**wi** 'he or she fell' (semelfactive aspect, i.e, the event took place only once); pa'ta-**ku** 'he or she falls' (habitual aspect). Against this general tendency, however, some languages, such as Chipewyan (northern Canada), use prefixes: **he**-tsaɣ 'he' or 'she is crying' (imperfective aspect: the action is ongoing); **yī**-tsaɣ 'he' or 'she cried' (perfective aspect: the action has been done); **ya**-tsaɣ 'he' or 'she will cry' (future aspect: the action will take place).

CASE MARKING. Nouns in a number of languages take suffixes with the meaning of "location," as illustrated in Karuk: ʔáas-**ak** '**in** the water', impaa-**k** '**on** the road,' ʔáfiva-**ak** '**at** the bottom'. While functioning semantically in ways analogous to the prepositions that occur in such languages as English, French, and Spanish, these suffixes differ from prepositions in that (1) they are not independent words and (2) they are postposed, not preposed. Formations like ʔáas-ak are also reminiscent of case systems, found in languages like Finnish, German, Latin, and Russian.

Case is a grammatical category occurring with nouns that identifies a particular set of syntactic relationships that nouns participate in; Latin, for example, has these forms for *lup–* 'wolf':

> *lup-**us**,*   nominative case (used as subject, as in "the wolf howled")
>> *lup-**e**,*   vocative case (used in address, as in "Wolf!," as it might occur in a myth)
>> *lup-**um**,*   accusative case (used as object, as in "he killed the wolf"
>> *lup-**ī**,*   genitive case (used in possession, as in "the wolf's howl")
>> *lup-**ō***   dative case (used as indirect object, as in "they threw the baby to the wolf")
>> *lup-**ō***   ablative case (used in a variety of functions, including marking the noun as the instrument with which something is done)

Analogous systems occur in some American Indian languages, as in Luiseño, a language of southern California:

> *kíi-**ča***   'house' (nominative case)
>> *kíi-**š***   'house' (accusative case)
>> *kíi-**k***   'to the house' (dative case)
>> *kíi-**ŋay***   'from the house' (ablative postposition)
>> *kíi-**ŋa***   'in the house' (locative postposition)
>> *kíi-**tal***   'by means of the house' (instrumental postposition)

Other Grammatical Features

There are also other grammatical features, some of which have already been illustrated, that occur frequently enough to deserve comment.

INCLUSIVE-EXCLUSIVE DISTINCTION. In Shoshoni (section 2.4), we saw a differentiation between inclusive and exclusive person, a distinction found in the Algonquian languages, the Jaqi languages, Washo (California-Nevada border), and others.

NUMBER. Whereas many languages do not make a distinction in number, others do in a variety of ways. Some languages are like English, making a distinction only between singular and plural, while others, such as Acoma (section 2.1), Shoshoni (section 2.4), Lake Miwok (central California), Navajo, and more, make a three-way distinction among singular, dual, and plural. In addition, there is Shasta (section 2.3) with its focus on collective and distributive.

REDUPLICATION. The morphological process of **reduplication** is a noteworthy characteristic of various Indian languages. This grammatical process is one in which all or part of a root is repeated. With verbs, it is often used to indicate distributed or repeated action, as in Karuk: *ʔimyah* 'breathe,' *ʔimyah-yah* 'pant' (i.e., take many breaths). In Puget Sound Salish (Northwest) we find such forms as *oqʼalb* 'it's raining,' *oqʼal-qalb* 'it's raining continuously'; *x̣ódx̣ód* 'to talk,' *ox̣ódod-x̣ódcot čed* 'I just talked to myself' (*čed* is first person singular). Reduplication of nouns is sometimes used to form the plural, as in Oʼodham (Arizona): *gogs* 'dog', *go-gogs* 'dogs'.

SUPPLETION. As illustrated in Shasta (section 2.3), **suppletion** is a term for a specific grammatical relationship among forms that have no phonological similarity. In one Shasta example, suppletion marked a change in number in verb roots. Analogous patterns are found in other languages, such as Navajo or (as in the following example) Karuk: *ʔikpuh* 'one swims,' *ʔiθpuh* 'two swim,' *ʔihtak* 'several swim'. We also cited an example from Shasta in which suppletion marked the relationship between singular and paucal in a restricted set of nouns. Other languages also use suppletion for indicating number for nouns, as in Shoshoni: *tuinɨ* 'boy' (sg.), *piianɨwɨh* '(two) boys' (dual), *piianɨɨ* 'boys' (pl.).

LOCATION-DIRECTION AFFIXATION. Through the use of prefixes or suffixes, verb forms frequently specify the location or direction of an action, as in Karuk: *paaθroov* 'throw upriver,' *paaθraa* 'throw uphill,' *paaθripaa* 'throw across-stream'. There are thirty-eight such forms in Karuk. (See section 3.2 for a similar system with nouns in Guarijío [Mexico].)

INSTRUMENTAL PREFIXES. Some languages specify the instrument of action. The following examples from Kashaya Pomo show the prefix *ba–* 'with the mouth or nose': *ba-hcʰaw* 'to knock over with the snout' (e.g., a pig rooting around), *ba-deedu* 'to push along with the snout', 'to carry in the beak' (of birds), 'to give vocal directions on how to go somewhere' (for action by a human being). There are twenty such prefixes in Kashaya Pomo. They designate many types of things that may be involved in the action or state denoted by the verb root, and are organized semantically into (1) natural forces, such as fire, gravity, wind; (2) body parts, such as eye, mouth, tongue, hand, foot; (3) instruments, such as long object, nonlong object, object with a handle; (4) movements, such as lengthwise, sidewise, through the air. A number of other languages also have instrumental prefix systems; among them are the Maidun languages (northeastern California), Shoshoni, and the Siouan languages.

NOUN-OBJECT INCORPORATION. Aztec, the Iroquoian languages, and Tewa (New Mexico) are just a few of the languages which incorporate the noun object directly into the verb. The following example is from Oneida: *la-yʌ́tho-s* 'he' or 'she plants' (*la-* 'he', *-yʌ-* 'to plant', *-s* present tense); *lanʌstayʌ́sthos* 'he' or 'she plants **corn**' (*-nʌst-*, incorporated form of *o·nʌ́ste?* 'corn').

By way of summary, it is important to note that most of the grammatical and semantic distinctions we have discussed in this chapter are obligatory rather than optional. In English, for instance, number marking for nouns is obligatory: an English speaker must either say dog (sg.), or dogs (pl.). As an obligatory distinction, number in nouns is absent in many American Indian languages; however, there are always optional mechanisms available. Similarly, evidential marking is obligatory in many American Indian languages but optional in English.

An early student of American Indian language structures once pointed out that languages differ not so much in what they **can** say, but in what they **must** say; in other words, obligatory grammatical categories vary across languages.

SOURCES

The Yahi Yana example is from Sapir 1929a. Examples in the sound system discussion are from Silver 1966 (Shasta) and a personal communication from Dale Kinkade (Bella Coola). In the grammatical system discussion, the Nez Perce example is from Aoki 1970. Section 2.1 is based on Miller 1965; 2.2. on Bloomfield 1946, Wolfart 1973b, Wolfart and Carroll 1981 (Cree), and Abbott 1984 (Oneida); 2.3. on Silver 1966; 2.4 on Sullivan 1988 (Aztec), and Miller n.d.a. (Shoshoni); 2.5. on Hoijer 1945, and Young and Morgan 1980. Section 2.6 draws from Chafe and Nichols 1986, Hardman 1986 (Jaqi), Oswalt 1961 (Kashaya Pomo), Silver 1966 (Shasta), and Whorf 1940 (Hopi); 2.7 from Bright 1957 (Karuk), Haas 1970, 1973a, Langdon 1971, Nichols 1971, Teeter 1959 (Wiyot); 2.8 from Bright 1957 (Karok), Haas 1946 (Tunica), Kroeber and Grace 1960 (Luiseño), Li 1946 (Chipewyan), Miller n.d.a. (Shoshoni), Mithun 1983, Oswalt 1961 (Kashaya Pomo), Saxton and Saxton 1969 (O'odham), Silver 1966 (Shasta), and Snyder 1968 (Salish). The comment that languages differ in what they must say is from Boas 1911.

SUGGESTED READINGS

There are a number of excellent sources concerned with structural and other aspects of the languages of the Americas; for example, scholarly journals such as *Anthropological Linguistics, International Journal of American Linguistics* and the *Journal of Linguistic Anthropology* are of particular importance. Unfortunately for the interested lay person, many articles in these journals, as well as other substantive writings, are technical and demand a background in linguistics. Two important early studies that do not presuppose much background are Boas 1911 and Sapir and Swadesh 1946. The general reader might also want to consult Hoijer 1954, the inspiration for section 2.8. A source of interest to the nonspecialist and specialist is Hinton 1994, which focuses on the indigenous languages of California.

The following set of references is mostly technical and concerns aspects of structural features we do not treat in our discussions. This set also includes relevant topics we were unable to consider because of space limitations. The asterisked items do not require extensive background in linguistics, although they may present some difficulties to the uninitiated. On alienable/inalienable possession: see Nichols 1988, and Velásquez-Castillo 1993; on aspect see Hardy and Montler 1988 (aspect and morphological processes in Alabama); on diminutivization see Munro 1988 (diminutive syntax in Lakota, Chickasaw, and Maricopa); on ergativity see Abbott 1991 and Chapman and Derbyshire 1991 (grammatical sketches of the Amazonian languages Macushi and Paumarí); on gender see Jacobsen 1979d* (Washo); see also Darnell and Vanek 1976*, Black-Rogers 1982*, Craik 1982*, Strauss and Brightman 1982* (semantic basis for gender in Algonquian languages). On grammaticalization see Craig 1986 (Jacaltec)and Wichmann 1993 (review of grammaticalization phenomena attested in Mixe-Zoquean languages); on inclusive/exclusive see Jacobsen 1980*; on morphosyntax see Gerdts and Michelson 1989 (Dogrib, Ojibwa, Eskimo, Halkomelem) and Payne 1990 (lowland Amazonian languages); on noun incorporation see Sapir 1911 (seminal article)*, Bonvillain 1989 (noun incorporation and the formation of semantic units in Akwesasne Mohawk)and Norcross 1993 (application of various grammatical theories in determining whether Shawnee noun incorporation is a lexical or a syntactic process); on number and number suppletion see Langdon 1988* (Yuman languages) and Mithun 1988* (Central Pomo); on obviative see Wolfart 1978 (Cree); on possession see Jelinek and Escalante 1988 (Yaqui); on polysynthesis see Mithun 1983* and Denny 1989 (Algonquian and Eskimo); on reduplication see Kimball 1988* (Koasati); on sound symbolism see Oswalt 1971a* (Pomoan languages), Ultan 1971* (Konkow), Watahomigie et al. 1982*, and Gensler 1993 (Walapai); on switch reference see Jacobsen 1967 (seminal article on a device for pronominal reference), Haiman and Munro 1993, and Farrell et al. 1991.

PART III

languages and cultural domains

CHAPTER 3

LANGUAGES AND CULTURAL DOMAINS

What is the extent of the relationship between a language and the needs and culture of the people who speak it? What areas of language structure are involved in this relationship? In exploring these questions, an early student of American Indian languages noted that languages differ according to how groups of ideas are classified and how they may be expressed (morphemes, words, phrases, etc.). In making his point, he cites two examples, one from English and one from Eskimo.

> [In English,] we find that the idea of WATER is expressed in a great variety of forms: one term serves to express water as a LIQUID; another one, water in the form of a large expanse (LAKE); others, water as running in a large body or in a small body (RIVER and BROOK); still other terms express water in the form of RAIN, DEW, WAVE and FOAM. It is perfectly conceivable that this variety of ideas, each of which is expressed by a single independent term in English, might be expressed in other languages by derivations from the same term.
>
> Another example of the same kind, the words for SNOW in Eskimo, may be given. Here we find one word, *aput*, expressing SNOW ON THE GROUND; another one, *qana*, FALLING SNOW; a third one, *piqsirpoq*, DRIFTING SNOW, and a fourth one, *qimuqsuq*, A SNOWDRIFT.

We note two things about these examples: They involve a relationship with the physical environment and they involve vocabulary. What about other areas of English-speaking and Eskimo-speaking lives—more abstract aspects, such as ideology? And what about areas of language other than vocabulary, such as grammatical patterns? As we move from more concrete to more abstract aspects of a people's life, and as we move from vocabulary to grammar, we find that the relationship between language and the lives of the speakers becomes much more difficult to specify; indeed, we will discover that in certain areas there is some question of any relationship at all.

Culture is a fundamental element of human existence and human nature. It entails knowledge and learned behavior and it is transmitted by the social group. It includes, among other things, knowledge about plants and animals and how people use them; knowledge of the physical environment, how the environment is used, and how people locate themselves in the environment; the rules for appropriate intersocial behavior; counting systems; and many other things like jokes, supernatural beliefs, and how to fix a flat tire. Language, as a part of culture, is also an expression of culture. Some aspects of culture, such as how to carry objects (e.g., in the hand, on the head), are infrequent topics of discussion; but other aspects, particularly those that are more abstract and those belonging to ideology and belief systems, are often topics of intense discussion that are manifested primarily through language.

3.1 CULTURAL DOMAIN AND PLANT
TAXONOMY: KASHAYA POMO

It is useful to think of the vocabulary of a language as a dictionary that contains all the words of that language, with each entry consisting of information about meaning, part of speech, and pronunciation. In some sense, speakers carry such a dictionary in their heads and, if they speak more than one language, they have more than one dictionary. But how is such a dictionary organized? The easiest physical representation might be alphabetical, from A to Z. However useful for easy reference, this is not how a dictionary is represented in people's heads. We can never really know how vocabulary is mentally organized, but there are ways of studying the organization of words that shed light on their semantic and cultural connections; if done properly, such studies should provide insights into the underlying organizing principles used by speakers.

The past several decades have seen advances in the study of vocabulary and semantic domains. American Indian languages have played a significant role in these studies and have helped delineate the relationship between language and other aspects of culture. The analysis of folk taxonomies, classifications that group things into increasingly more inclusive categories, is one of several ways for studying the organization of a semantic domain. We must emphasize here that we are interested in **folk taxonomies**, not scientific ones. In a scientific taxonomy, "beaver" would be considered a kind of "rodent," which in turn is a kind of "mammal" and ultimately a kind of "animal." But most English speakers would consider a "beaver" simply as a kind of "animal," at least in their folk taxonomy.

The units of folk taxonomic analysis are **generics,** which are defined as "a kind of—." In English, generics include such terms as "owl," "maple," "spider" and "beaver," which can be defined as "a kind of bird," "a kind of tree," "a kind of bug," and "a kind of animal," respectively. The resulting analysis yields a taxonomic **tree** (see figure 3.1), a diagram in which lines branch out from a **node,** a central point. In a

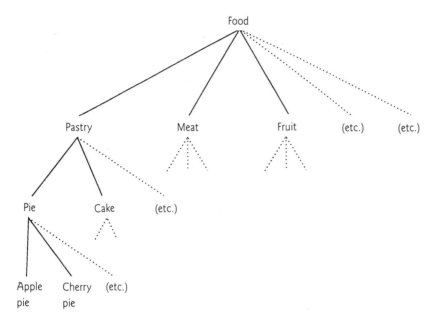

Figure 3.1.—A partial taxonomic tree, showing the place of "apple pie" in the English domain of "food."

taxonomic tree, there is at least one node that has several **branches.** For instance, in an English taxonomic tree, the node "animal" includes among its branches "beaver," "bear," "deer" and others (but not "maple"). Some generics may include lower **levels;** for example, for some English speakers "black bear" and "grizzly bear" are kinds of "bears."

Two cultural domains, plants and animals, are well suited for folk-taxonomic analysis and such analyses have been especially insightful cross-culturally. The folk taxonomies of these domains have a limited depth (i.e., a limited number of possible levels or nodes that a taxonomic tree can have), and there is a certain degree of agreement across cultures as to what levels can be found within a taxonomy.

Our discussion of the plant taxonomy of the Kashaya Pomo, whose territory is located in a coastal area of northern California, is based on a thorough study that, with eighty-six Kashaya plant names, is probably close to being exhaustive (see figure 3.2). In the Kashaya language, the term *qʰale* 'plant' includes what in English would be called "tree, bush, grass, fern," and the like, but excludes "seaweed" and "mushroom." Kashaya speakers divide *qʰale* into three groups; two groups are named (*qʰale* 'trees', *hahse* 'bushes'), while the third, which includes all

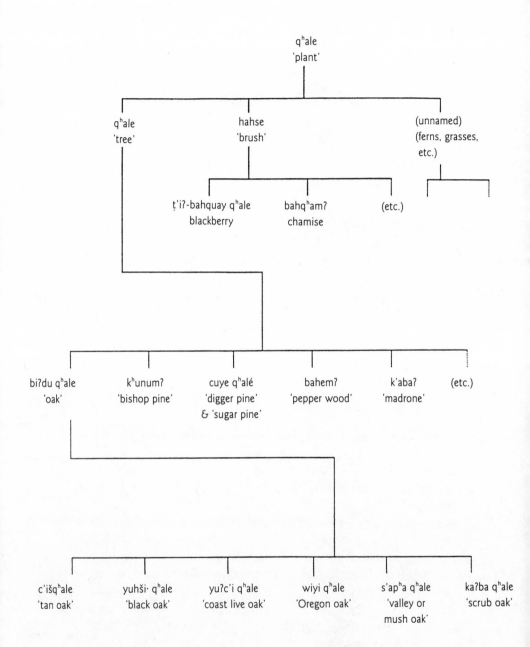

Figure 3.2.—A partial taxonomy of the Kashaya Pomo "plant" domain.

other plants, is unnamed. Notice the ambiguity: q^hale stands for either "plant" or "tree," depending on which taxonomic level the speaker is concerned with. Ambiguities of this sort are common in taxonomic systems and seldom cause speakers problems. Some English speakers may use *coke* to mean "Coca-cola" and any other kind of cola drink. Speakers who use *coke* in this fashion can ask, "What kind of coke do you want?" and can expect an answer something like "Pepsi."

Under q^hale 'tree' we find such terms as: $k^hunum?$ 'bishop pine' (*Pinus muricata*), *cuye q^halé* 'digger pine' (*Pinus sabiniana*), 'sugar pine' (*Pinus lambertiana*), literally 'pinenut tree', *bahem?* 'pepperwood', 'California bay' (*Umbellularia californica*), *k'aba?* 'madrone' (*Arbutus menziessii*). Examples of *hahse* 'bush' are *t'i?-bahqhay q^hale* 'blackberry' (*Rubus ursinus* or *R. vitifolius*), literally 'thorn-manzanita berry plant'; *bahq^ham?* 'chamise' (*Adenostoma fasciculatum*). Among the third, unnamed, group of plants are ferns, grasses, and the like.

Under q^hale 'tree', there are six oak trees: *c'išq^hale* 'tan oak' (*Lithocarpus densiflora*); *yuhši·q^hale* 'black oak' (*Quercus Kelloggii*); *yu?c'i q^hale* 'coast live oak' (*Quercus agrifolia*); *wiyi q^hale* 'Oregon oak' (*Quercus Garryana*); *s'ap^ha q^hale* 'valley' or 'mush oak' (*Quercus lobata*); *ka?ba q^hale* 'scrub oak' (Quercus *dumosa*). All of the oak trees except for the tan oak are, literally, 'acorn tree', with the word for 'acorn' referring specifically to the species of oak that it comes from, so that *yuhši·* is 'acorn of the black oak', *yu?c'i* is 'acorn of the coast live oak', and so on. There is also a general word for acorn, *bi?du*, which can be applied instead of the more specific terms; thus acorn for each oak tree is *bi?du* 'tan oak acorn'; *yuhši·* or *bi?du* 'black oak acorn'; *yu?c'i* or *bi?du* 'coast live oak acorn'; *wiyi* or *bi?du* 'Oregon oak acorn'; *s'ap^ha* or *bi?du* 'acorn of the valley or mush oak'; *ka?ba* or *bi?du* 'scrub oak acorn.' The six oak trees are grouped together under the name *bi?du q^hale*, literally 'acorn tree', the only trees in Kashaya that allow such a grouping.

The reason for the elaboration of 'oak' and 'acorn' in the Kashaya plant taxonomy is not hard to find: among the Kashaya Pomo (along with most California Indian groups), the oak and its fruit, the acorn, figure in important ways in many aspects of the culture. As the economically most important oak, *c'iš-q^hale* 'tan oak' (*c'iš-* 'beautiful', hence lit. 'beautiful-tree') is accorded a special position, as are its acorns. The term *bi?du* is ambiguous, depending on taxonomic level: 'acorn of the tan oak' or 'acorn (of any oak)'.

Although Kashaya Pomo territory comprises only three hundred square miles, it is ecologically varied; that is, modern biology recognizes eight plant communities. The Kashaya have also recognized these communities, since each one has provided its own unique contribution to the native economy: mixed evergreen forest, *kulu·*; oak woodland, *kulu·*; redwood forest, *šiyo*; Douglas fir forest, *kulu·* or *šiyo*; chaparral, *hahse*; coastal scrub, *hahse*; grassland, *qahqo*; coastal strand, no linguistic label. The *kulu·* communities have been the most important economically. The Douglas fir forest has undergone some changes in the past century, which may explain the use of two labels. In earlier times, the stands of fir were much reduced and occurred in a more open forest, with tan oak, madrone, and other trees typical of the *kulu·* communities. Modern logging practice has encouraged the development of dense single-species stands of fir, which more closely resemble the impenetrable *šiyo* redwood forest. Thus *kulu·* is applied to the older Douglas fir forests that more closely resemble the more open mixed evergreen and oak woodland communities, whereas *šiyo* is used for the denser stands. The term *hahse* for chaparral and coastal scrub communities is the same term we saw earlier for 'bush', which contrasts taxonomically with *qʰale* 'tree', since the typical plants in these two communities are *hahse*.

Generics are the basic unit in biological folk taxonomies. These are the units that get classified; frequently they correspond to what the biologist recognizes as a species. Kashaya *kʼabaʔ* 'madrone' (*Arbutus menziessii*), and *bahqʰamʔ* 'chamise' (*Adenostoma fasciculatum*) are examples. Sometimes more than one species are grouped together under a single generic name, especially if the species are not very important culturally; thus the Kashaya use *cuye qʰalé* for two species, 'digger pine' (*Pinus sabiniana*), 'sugar pine' (*Pinus lambertiana*). When a generic term includes more than one species, it does not mean that speakers cannot tell the difference between them, but rather that they have chosen not to give them distinctive labels. A knowledgeable person frequently will say something like "there are two Xs," and then proceed to describe the differences.

Folk taxonomies will frequently, but not universally, group generic terms into higher level units and give them names, as with the Kashaya *qʰale* 'tree', and *hahse* 'bush'; comparable terms are often found for fauna, for example, English "bird." Less common are intermediate terms such as Kashaya *biʔdu qʰale*, a term that groups together the six oak trees.

In contrast to modern urban societies, small-scale societies tend to have fewer words that group biological generic terms together into higher order categories. In fact, the highest order terms, "plant" and "animal," are frequently missing in small-scale societies. There is further evidence that among such societies nonagricultural peoples do less grouping than agriculturalists. It would be a mistake to view less development of higher level terms as a sign of "primitiveness." Plants and animals are of particular importance in foraging groups, so that names for generics are especially important, whereas higher order labels are less useful. Higher order labels sometimes are a convenient way of grouping objects whose individual identification is not of much cultural use. An outstanding English example is *weed*. Most people do not know the names of the species that go by this label, unless they are particularly noxious, like *nettle* or *poison oak*. We will return to the question of the place of taxonomies in culture in section 3.6 when we consider numeral classifiers in northern California.

3.2 CULTURAL DOMAIN AND GEOGRAPHIC ORIENTATION

Guarijío Directionals

Every cultural group must have a way of talking about directions and a way of locating itself within its physical environment. The nature of the environment helps to shape the directional system but, as we shall see, it does not determine it.

Our example is the directional system of the Guarijío, a horticultural group of northwest Mexico who live in rugged country with deep canyons, steep hillsides, and restricted areas of flat land. The language has a directional system tied to a larger postpositional system. **Postpositions** are like prepositions, except that they come after the noun (are postposed) and not before it (preposed). In Guarijío, they are suffixed forms, not free and independent words. The directional suffixes occur with great frequency in most conversations, particularly when discussing coming and going to the corn fields, to the store, or visiting friends and relatives in neighboring hamlets. Here is an example in which the speaker is telling of an unusual amount of water coming down the river: *waʔágia aštóna paʔwí werú* 'lots of water came on down from there' (lit. 'there-down-from came water much'). The first word, *waʔágia*, is composed of a locative *waʔá* 'there', plus the directional suffix *-gia* 'down.' The directionals can be added directly to a locative, as in the last example, or to placenames, which are a special type of locative: *Simiré Sehčiéboreru* 'He went down to Arechuyvo' (lit. 'went Arechuyvo-down-to'; *Sehčiébo* = 'Arechuyvo', *-reru* = 'down to'). These special directional postpositions, however, cannot be added directly to a noun, but instead must be added to a noun that has another (nondirectional) postposition: *Tetúmi simpáira lančóci wohkotéreru* 'They went below down through the pines to the ranch' (lit. 'below went ranch-to pines-among-down-to'; *wohkó* = 'pine tree', *-tére* = 'among, through', *-ru* = 'down to').

Three postpositions have been illustrated in these sentences, *-gia*, *-reru*, and *-ru*, and they all translate 'down'; but the three are not identical in meaning. A directional in Guarijío always includes four components of meaning: (1) relative height: up or down; (2) distance: near or far; (3) direction: hither or thither (coming or going, from or to); and (4) degree of slope: steep or not steep; thus *-gia* is 'down, near, hither, not steep', *-reru*, 'down, near, thither, not steep', and *-ru*, 'down, near, thither, steep.' Each directional can be seen as belonging to four pairs, or binary sets, with the other member of the set showing the opposite component; for example, the four that stand in opposition to *-ru* (down, near, thither, steep) are: *-re*, opposite in height (**up,** near, thither, steep); *-rebo*, opposite in distance (down, **far,** thither, steep); *-reba*, opposite in direction (down, near, **hither,** steep); and *-reru*, opposite in degree of slope (down, near, thither, **not steep**). With four components in pairs or binary sets, there are sixteen suffixes ($2 \times 2 \times 2 \times 2 = 16$). Four additional directional suffixes bring the total to twenty, suffixes that include only the components for distance and direction, and which are used when the direction is on the level, as in *Wahkipára ye?nisíga wa?ábo pa?wí* 'He went there to measure the water (in the river)' (lit. 'went to-measure there-thither water'; *wa?á* = 'there', *-bo* = 'near, thither').

Some of the directional suffixes appear to be made up of smaller elements; thus in our examples we see *-re*, *-ru*, and *-bo* recurring with other elements. But if these are treated as compound suffixes, it turns out to be impossible to assign these smaller parts a consistent meaning. Doubtless at an earlier period in the history of the language they were meaningful elements that combined into compound suffixes, but today they must be considered single semantic units.

There are a number of locative adverbs that form a part of the total directional system, adverbs to which the directionals can be added. The most important and, next to *wa?á* 'there', the most frequent in conversation is *paó* 'the other side of a water course'; for example: **Paó** *ohóna mulá wa?ábo* 'The mules are walking on the other side of the arroyo' (lit. 'other-side walk mule[s] there-thither'). *Paó* occurs with a slightly different subset of directional suffixes, which form a special subsystem within the larger directional system.

With this very complex system of directionals, Guarijío gets along very well without the cardinal directions for north, east, south, and west. Those directionals used for "far" and "not steep" can, however, be used for "east" and "west," as *-reribona* 'from the west' (up, far, thither, not steep). This usage reflects the location of the Guarijío on the western side of the Sierra Madre Mountains, in which the mountains slope gradually to the western coastal plain. This can lead to ambiguity, however, because it is possible in some places to be gradually coming up from afar, but from the east rather than the west.

It is interesting to compare this system with that used by the local Spanish-speaking population. The two cultures are very different in most aspects, but in one way they are very similar: They make similar cultural use of the environment, probably because the Spanish learned the techniques for farming this very difficult terrain from the Guarijío and their traveling patterns are similar. All of the semantic components found in the Guarijío systems are expressed in the local Spanish, except that each component is expressed separately; thus 'steep' is *barranca*, 'hither' is *pa' allá*, 'other side of a water course' is *otra banda*, and so on. It is not merely that these concepts can be translated into local Spanish (these last few paragraphs illustrate that they can be translated into English as well), but rather that these terms are part of the local Spanish directional system, and they are in very frequent use. There are two formal differences between the Guarijío and local Spanish system: First, in Guarijío the terms are integrated into the larger postpositional system; and second, in Guaríjio, the various semantic components are combined into a single suffix, while in Spanish they are expressed separately. These differences are a reflection of two facts: first, Spanish lacks a postpositional system (using prepositions, instead), and second, the tighter integration in Guaríjio reflects greater antiquity of the system.

Other Directional Systems

There are at least two other types of directional systems common in North America. One uses the coast and rivers as points of reference, the other uses the cardinal directions. The first type is utilized by most of the peoples from northern California to southern Alaska, an area that shows a certain uniformity of culture, but a variety of very different languages. The directions are "out to sea," "towards the coast," "up the coast," and "down the coast," or, with rivers, "up river," "down river," "to the left bank," "to the right bank." As in the Guaríjio case, the systems within the various languages are normally very tightly integrated into the grammar.

The Pueblo groups of New Mexico and Arizona, like the groups in the Northwest Coast area, display a fairly uniform culture, but several different languages and language families are represented. There we find a cardinal direction system, but one that incorporates "the zenith" (up) and "the nadir" (down), giving six, rather than four, cardinal directions. The directional system is a direct reflection of an elaborate ceremonial system in which the six cardinal directions play an important part. In some of the languages, direction of movement is always given in terms of north, east, south, and west (with ways of being able to give intermediate points on the compass), and if up or down is not included with the direction, it is understood that the movement is on the level. Again, we find the directionals are well integrated into the adverbial system of the languages. This integration illustrates especially well the relationship between linguistic structure and a particular cultural orientation.

3.3   CULTURAL DOMAIN AND GEOGRAPHIC ORIENTATION

Chumash Placenames

Just as there are cultural and linguistic differences in how people orient themselves in the physical environment, so, too, are there differences in how they apply names to the landscape. We saw that cultural uses and linguistic resources are important for gaining an understanding of locational systems; exactly the same is true in understanding how placenames are composed and bestowed.

The Chumashan languages were spoken along the coast of southern California and on the Santa Barbara Channel Islands. There were perhaps six languages: Ventureño, Barbareño, Yneseño, Purisimeño, Island Chumash, and Obispeño. At the turn of the century most of the languages still had fluent speakers with extensive knowledge of the placenames; and before the last Chumash language became extinct in 1960, a considerable amount of linguistic and cultural data was recorded. Although the six Chumashan languages are distinct from one another, it is clear that the placename patterns were uniform across the languages.

Examples are given here with a translation of the placename, followed, in parentheses, by the name of the language that the term comes from (e.g., Yneseño, Ventureño), and whether the term is the name of a village, hill, and so on (absence of information indicates unavailability). Not infrequently the English placename is derived from the Chumash, in which case it is listed with ">," to be read as "becomes"; thus, ʔawahay' 'moon' (Ventureño; > Ojai). English placenames that are of Chumash origin have come by way of Spanish, so they have a hispanicized spelling; thus the "j" in Ojai is pronounced as English "h," and the "qu" in Lisque Creek is pronounced "k."

First we consider the linguistic mechanisms, then the semantic aspects of placename formation. Most placenames are formed from noun or verb roots, using a limited number of linguistic mechanisms. Sometimes a bare noun is used: stuk 'wooden bowl' (Yneseño; name of a village); muwu 'beach' (Ventureño; name of a village; > Mugu). The noun root is also used in formation with certain affixes, such as the third-person prefix with inalienably possessed nouns (section 2.1): s-ʔaxpil'il 'its root' (Barbareño; name of a village); s-ʔeqp'e 'its kneecap' (Ventureño; > Sespe). Other nouns have a definite article prefix "the," which has different forms in the various languages: ma-šul-šulu 'the shale bed' (Yneseño ma- = 'the'; name of a white bluff by a river); he-l-ʔoʔ 'the water' (Barbareño he-l- = 'the'; name of a village on Goleta Slough); sa-ʔ-aqti-k'oy, 'a thing sheltered from the wind' (Ventureño sa- = 'the'; > Saticoy). Other placename-forming techniques using noun roots include the use of the locative prefixes mi- and ʔal-, the use of reduplication to indicate a collective, and the use of polysynthetic forms in which the verbal prefix ka- 'it is . . .' occurs: mi-čʰumaš 'place of the islanders' (name for Santa Cruz Island; čʰumaš is the name for the inhabitants of the Channel Islands, and comes into English as "Chumash"); ʔas'aka 'in its bed' (Purisimeño; > Zaca Station) [ʔas'aka is derived, by regular phonetic rule, from ʔal-s-ʔakay]; ʔal-iswey 'at the tarweed' (Purisimeño; > Lisque Creek); woq-woqo 'much tar' (Barbareño); ka-mulus 'it is the juniper' (> Camulos); ka-s-tiq 'it is its eye, face' (> Castaic).

Verb roots in placenames usually occur with one or more affixes: the third person subject prefix s- ("he, she, it"), the agentive prefix ʔal- ("one who, one that . . ."), the locative prefix mi- ("where" or "place of"), or the locative suffix –muʔ: s-yux-tun 'it splits in two' (Barbareño; name of a village); ka-s-tixwanuč 'it is scratched' (Barbareño; name of a hill); ʔal-wat'alam 'one that is congested' (Barbareño; name of a weedy lake) **mi**-s-waskɨn 'where it spreads open' (Yneseño; name of a place along a river); *wenem'u* 'sleeping place' (Ventureño; > Hueneme) [*wenem'u* is derived from *wen'-muʔ*]; *kašin'ašmu* 'where much is stored' (Ventureño; name of a village) [*kašin'ašmu* is derived from *ka-sin'ay-š-mu*].

Turning now to the semantic characteristics, we find it is common to name a place after plants, animals, or material characteristics of that place. Examples in addition to those already given are: *ʔal-iswey* 'in the tarweed' (Purisimeño; name of a village; > Rancho Suey, Suey Crossing); *xonxoni ataʔ* 'tall oak' (Purisimeño; name of a village); *mikiw* 'place of the mussel' (name of a village); *si-haw-haw* 'the foxes' (a spot near Ojai); *šɨš u-č'iʔ* 'den of the woodrat' (Barbareño; name of a village; in Yneseño *u-č'iʔ* lit. 'the-rat', is replaced in this placename with *a-č'iʔ*, to correspond with the differences in the definite article in these two languages); *pismuʔ* 'tar, black stuff' (Obispeño; > English Pismo Beach); *huya* 'soapstone' (name for Santa Catalina Island, because soapstone, an important raw material for fashioning artifacts, is found there).

There are also descriptive terms based on body parts: *s-is'a* 'the eyelash' (Ventureño; the name of a horizontally striated mountain, and of a nearby village); *šnoxš* 'nose' (Barbareño; name of a bluff in the hills behind Santa Barbara); *kas'elew* 'tongue' (name of a village near a sharply protruding rock). Some places are named for characteristic uses or activities of the area. One of the best examples was given earlier, *wenem'u* 'sleeping place', so called because it was the closest place on the mainland to the Channel Islands for islanders to spend the night before returning home. Names based on legendary or mythological incidents are also found, such as *masʔap haqsi* 'the house of the sun'.

Some of the names are only partly analyzable into meaningful elements; others are totally without etymologies, such as *takuy'* (which survives in the English names Tecuya Creek and Tecuya Mountain), and *teqepš* 'Tequepis Canyon'. (The historical significance of names without etymologies is explored in section 13.3.)

General qualifiers that are so common in English placenames, such as "creek," "point," or "mountain" (e.g., "Lisque Creek," "Point Mugu," "Little Water Peak," or "The Smoky Mountains") are not used in the Chumashan languages. Nor are places named after people (cf. "Finland," or "England," originally "Land of the Angles"); instead, we find the reverse: People are named by where they lived, as in *ʔalap-kalawašaq'* 'people of kalawašaq' (Yneseño), *ʔanap-qasil* 'people of quasil' (Barbareño), *ʔat'ap-muwu* 'people of Mugu.'

Other Placenames

The Kwakiutl, a coastal people of British Columbia, and the Eskimo share an interest in the sea and seacoast, yet their naming of coast features is very different.

The Kwakiutl placenames are a good example of the intersecting role of linguistic form and cultural focus in naming. Kwakiutl has a large number of locative suffixes, so that placenames that translate something like "island at the point, island in the middle, island in front," and the like, were popular. Inasmuch as Eskimo does not have such suffixes, names of this sort in Eskimo would be just as awkward as the English translations are. Some languages, like Tewa (New Mexico), make compounds readily, and use them in placenames. Polysynthetic languages like Dakota favor nominalizations that encapsulate in words ideas that in English are expressed in a phrase or sentence: "buffaloes that return running"; "hill wearing blue robe"; "smoke arises from the ground (hot springs)."

Turning to cultural considerations, the Dakota interest in history is reflected both in placenames and in personal names, with placenames like "Four-Bears camp"; "abandoned site of the Pawnee"; "they caused the enemies to swim"; and personal names like "he finds a woman." Those features that get named also reflect other cultural interests. Until quite recently, the Guarijío seldom traveled more than twenty-five or fifty miles within their mountain home, so that large geographic features, such as rivers, creeks, canyons, and mountain ranges were of little interest to them, and received no names. Instead, the river pools, bends in the river, creek, or canyon, and individual mountains received names.

3.4 LANGUAGES AND SOCIAL SPACE: SHOSHONI DEIXIS

All languages have a set of deictic words, words that point, and hence, their meaning is variable, depending on the relative position of the speaker and hearer. The most common deictic words are demonstratives (e.g. English "this"), and we will use demonstratives as a point of departure in discussing deixis. English recognizes two degrees (and, for the demonstratives, two numbers): "this," "these" (near the speaker), and "that," "those" (far from the speaker). Shoshoni recognizes four degrees: *sitin* 'this' (near the speaker); *setin* 'this' or 'that' (usually near the hearer); *satin* 'that' (farther away, but in sight); and *sutin* 'that' (out of sight). There are four more terms, without the initial *s-*, which are less definite that those with the *s-*: *itin*, *etin*, *atin*, and *utin*. There is a ninth form, *matin* 'this, that', which is used when the speaker does not wish to commit him- or herself on relative position. (Three numbers are recognized in the demonstratives: singular, dual, and plural, bringing the total number of demonstrative forms to twenty-seven.) Some dialects of Shoshoni use *sotin* in place of *sutin*, or as an additional out-of-sight demonstrative, but which is closer than *sutin*.

The recurring element in these forms is –tïn. Accordingly, it is the initial syllable, consisting of a single vowel or consonant plus vowel, that carries the deictic semantic load: i-, si- 'close' (near the speaker); e-, se- 'far' (or near the hearer); a-, sa- 'still farther'; o-, so- (out of sight, closer than u-, su-); u-, su- 'out of sight' (usually farther than a-, sa-); ma- 'indefinite location'.

To understand the significance of the vowel that marks the deixis, we need a short technical discussion of the Shoshoni vowel system. The two most important phonetic features for describing vowels (and the only two we need to be concerned with for the question at hand) are relative tongue height and relative tongue position. For tongue height, we can distinguish high, mid, and low vowels. The tongue is close to the roof of the mouth for a high vowel, as in English "reed" and "rude" (phonetically [rid] and [rud]); the tongue drops down and is distant from the roof of the mouth for a low vowel, as in English "rod" (phonetically [rad]); and a mid vowel is mid-way between a high and low vowel, as in English "raid" and "road" (phonetically [red] and [rod]). Concerning relative tongue position, a front vowel has the tongue forward in the mouth, as English "reed" and "raid" ([rid] and [red]), well back in for back vowels, as in English "rude" and "road" ([rud] and [rod]), and in between for central vowels, as in English "rod" [rad].

Shoshoni has six vowels, the same five that English has, which we have discussed above, plus a sixth not found in English, [ɨ], a high central vowel. They can be charted as follows:

	Front	Central	Back
High	i	ɨ	u
Mid	e		o
Low		a	

If we chart only those vowels that are used in the deixis system, we get:

	Front	Central	Back
High	i		u
Mid	e		(o)
Low		a	

(The mid back vowel [o] is placed in parentheses because it is part of the system in only some dialects.) We can trace the relative distance on the vowel chart, starting with the high front [i] for "near, in sight," down through [e] and [a], and ending up at the high back [u], "far, out of sight." This is another example of **sound symbolism,** which we discussed in section 2.7. In this case, however, the semantic dimension of relative size (small vs. large) is extended to relative distance (near vs. far). High front vowels (along with palatal consonants, which are articulated in the same position) are often associated with smallness and nearness, while back vowels are often associated with largeness and distance; note, for example, the Spanish diminutive suffix *-ita, -ito (casita* 'little house'), and the augmentative *-on (borrachón* 'drunkard, big drinker'); or English *these* [ðiz] as opposed to *those* [ðoz].

One of the outstanding characteristics of language is its **arbitrariness,** which is to say there is an arbitrary association between the sounds in a word and the meaning of the word. Nevertheless there are a few exceptions to the arbitrariness of language, and sound symbolism is one of the outstanding examples. Human beings, speaking whatever language, find the association of certain sounds to certain meanings frequent enough that it can be no accident, and arbitrariness cannot be evoked.

The Shoshoni deictic system has a much broader application than its English counterpart. Here is a listing of just some of the stems they are found with (illustrating with *i-* and *u-*): *ikkih, ukkuh* (here, there); *ipe, upe* (then, here, about this time; then, there, about that time); *ipaka, upaka* (this big, that big); *innih, unnih* (thus, like this; thus, like that); *sihoi, suhoi* (around here, around this; around there, around that).

The underlying relative position of deixis is spatial, but through metaphorical extension, deictic terms can be used to refer to time. Contrast "I don't need a car at *this time*" (i.e., now), with "we didn't have a car at *that time*" (i.e., then). They can also extend to psychological distance; for example: "I like *this coat* better than *that old ugly coat.*" Such extensions are also common in Shoshoni (and probably all languages); thus if the diminutive suffix *-cci* is used, a suffix that also indicates endearment, it is natural to use the noun with an *i-* deictic element: *sitïn piacci* 'this (dear) mother'. The combination *sutïn piacci* sounds strange to the Shoshoni ear, since it would imply 'that (out of sight, and by implication out of mind) dear mother'; but without the diminutive suffix, *sutïn pia* 'that (out of sight, hence depreciated) mother', the phrase is acceptable. In these cases, then, *sitïn* and *sutïn* do not refer to real location, but rather to psychological location. Shoshoni uses demonstratives where English would use third-person pronouns and definite articles, since Shoshoni does not have these elements; as a result, Shoshoni uses the deictic elements more than English does, and the extension of these elements into psychological space is much more frequent. Inasmuch as there are four (in some dialects five) degrees of distance, subtle shades of meaning are often indicated.

3.5 LANGUAGE AND COUNTING SYSTEMS

The Aztec Vigesimal System

The decimal counting system, based on tens, is probably the most common type in the languages of the world. English provides an example: There are unique numbers from one through ten, with most higher numbers based on these lower numbers ("eleven" and "twelve" are exceptional; historically they are derived from lower numbers, but they are probably unitary names for the average English speaker), and unique names for some of the higher multiples, such as "hundred" and "thousand." Both multiplicative and additive functions are used; thus "twenty" and "sixty" are "two × ten" and "six × ten," and "twenty-four" (or "four and twenty") are "two × ten + four" (or "four + two × ten"). Seldom is the counting system absolutely a pure expression of the particular type, and this is the case for our decimal system, which has a few extra wrinkles in the teens.

Whereas the decimal counting system is well represented in the Americas, other types are found, such as the vigesimal system (based on twenty), of the Aztec. Using the traditional Hispanicized writing system, as described in appendix I, the numbers one to twenty are:

ce	1	ma?tlactli once	11
ome	2	ma?tlactli omome	12
eyi	3	ma?tlactli omeyi	13
nahui	4	ma?tlactli onnahui	14
macuilli	5	caxtolli	15
chicuace	6	caxtolli once	16
chicome	7	caxtolli omome	17
chicueyi	8	caxtolli omeyi	18
chiconahui	9	caxtolli onnahui	19
ma?tlactli	10	cempohualli	20

The numbers one through four are the basic ones. Five, ten, and fifteen are nouns, a fact reflected by the noun suffix –tli (which is changed to –li after the consonant [l]). Macuil-li 'five' is derived from the verb macui 'to grasp in the hand'. The numbers six through nine are derived from a stem chicua– plus the numbers one through four; thus chicua– 'five' plus ce 'one' = chicuace 'six'. Ma?tlac-tli 'ten' is probably from mai– 'hand' and tlac-tli 'torso, upper body' (e.g., the ten digits on the hands, but excluding the ten digits on the feet). The word for fifteen (caxtol-li) does not seem to be related to any other word. The numbers eleven through fourteen and sixteen through nineteen are derived from ten and fifteen, respectively, plus om-, on– 'two' (i.e., "again" or "plus"), plus the numbers one through four.

The count is based on the human body with twenty digits, and further divided into four groups of five, reflecting the four limbs each with five digits; thus underlying this vigesimal system is a quinary system, based on five.

The word for 'twenty' is literally 'one count': cem– 'one', pohua 'to count', and the nouns suffix –tli. The numbers from twenty-one to thirty-nine are formed by adding the numbers one through nineteen to twenty; for example, cempohualli *ommacuilli* 'twenty-five' (literally 'twenty + five'). The count changes to *ompohualli* at forty, which is literally 'two counts'. The numbers continue in this fashion up to 380; for example,

ompohualli	40	('2 counts')
eyipohualli	60	('3 counts')

And so forth, up to:

caxtolli onnauhpohualli	360	('18 counts')

After this the counting continues as follows:

centzontli	400	('1 head of hair')
ontzontli	800	('2 heads of hair')
etzontli	1,200	('3 heads of hair')
nauhtzontli	1,600	('4 heads of hair')

And so on, up to:

caxtolli onnauhtzontli	7,600	('19 heads of hair')

The next change takes place at 8,000:

cenxiquipilli	8,000	(lit. 'one bag')
onxiquipilli	16,000	(2 × 8,000)
macuilxiquipilli	40,000	(5 × 8,000)
maʔtlacxiquipilli	80,000	(10 × 8,000)
caxtolli omome xiquipilli	136,000	(17 × 8,000)
cempohualxiquipilli	160,000	(20 × 8,000)
centzonxiquipilli	3,200,00	(400 × 8,000)
cempohualtzonxiquipilli	64,000,000	(20 × 400× 8,000)

Other Counting Systems

The simplest counting systems have only three unique numbers: "one," "two," and "three" (in certain contexts these may mean "one," "few" and "many"). They are found in only a few small-scale societies, including some lowland South American groups such as the Siriona, Yanoma, and Bacairi. Higher numbers are expressed additively, never by multiplication. An example from Bacairi:

1 *tokale*
2 *ahage*
3 *ahewao*

4 *ahage ahage* (two + two)

5 *ahage ahage tokale* (two + two + one)

It is sometimes claimed that peoples with such systems cannot count beyond three, but this is clearly false. Higher numbers are not easily expressed, so that even a number like twenty-four becomes awkward, for example, "three (and) three (and) three (and) three (and) three (and) three (and) three (and) three." Again, there is a relationship to cultural complexity: simple counting systems of this sort are only found in those societies where there is little need for counting. But the relationship is not straightforward, since more complex systems that are multiplicative as well as additive (though not as complex as those found in Mesoamerica) are also found in some of the small-scale societies where the need for counting is minimal.

California Counting Systems

Vigesimal, decimal, and simple additive systems with only three numbers are not the only types of systems found in the Americas. Because of the variety of types, a brief examination of those in California is instructive. All of the systems can easily handle one hundred, and a few can easily reach the thousands. Unlike Mesoamerica, in precontact California there was no calendar for keeping track of the days and the years over long periods of time, but counting of strings of shell beads was important, especially in the north, where wealth was a central cultural motif.

A number of languages use a decimal system, and vigesimal systems are found in a few places. But most common are quinary systems (based on five), in which the numbers between six and nine are related to the numbers between one and four; thus in Cahto, an Athapaskan language of northern California, six is *yiban ɫaxaʔ*, with *yiban* meaning 'on the other side' (i.e., the other hand), and *ɫaxaʔ* meaning 'one.' As in other parts of the Americas, the word for five, less often ten, is related to the word for hand: Lake Miwok five is *kedékku* 'one hand', ten is *ʔukúukoci* 'two hands'; Cahto five is *laʔsane*, ten was *laʔɫbaʔan*, with both words related to *la* 'hand'.

Some California languages use a quaternary system (based on four). An example is Ventureño Chumash (southern California):

1 *pakeet*	9 *etspá*
2 *eshkóm*	10 *kashkóm*
3 *maség*	11 *telú*
4 *skumú*	12 *maség skumú* ('3 [×] 4')
5 *itipakés* ('1 more')	13 *maség skumú kampakeet* ('3 [×] 4 + 1')
6 *yetishkóm* ('2 more')	14 *eshkóm laliét* ('2 less [than 16]')
7 *itimaség* ('3 more')	15 *pakeet sihué* ('1 less [than 16]')
8 *malahua*	16 *chigípsh*

The anatomical basis (five digits and four limbs) is still there, as is seen from Yuki of northern California, which also has a quaternary system. The Yuki count not by their fingers, but by the spaces between the fingers. Numbers are visualized by placing twigs between the digits.

Counting Systems in the Americas

The Aztec system is rare in that it can be classified as purely vigesimal. Most systems have certain irregularities (compare the teen sequence in the English decimal system). Some systems (not illustrated in this discussion) are mixed, using one type for lower numbers, another for higher, or in some cases offering a choice of types for certain of the numbers. All systems use additive functions; most also use multiplicative functions; and a few make occasional use of other functions. Nine, for example, is sometimes expressed as "one less than ten," "one lacking" or "not ten." There appears to be little relation between the type of system (quaternary, quinary, decimal, or vigesimal) and the nature of the culture, with the type that is found probably being a historical accident. But the degree of elaboration and ease of expressing higher numbers does seem to be a function, at least in part, of the degree of elaboration of the culture, with small-scale societies that do not use higher numbers on a daily basis often having less elaborated systems. We should make clear that degree of elaboration and ease of expression are not necessarily related to degree of mathematical sophistication. Often it is possible to form higher numbers in a small-scale society very clearly, using a consistent and logical system, but using a rather long phrase, as Ventureño Chumash thirty, *eshkóm sihué eshkóm chigípsh* 'two less than two × sixteen'.

3.6 CLASSIFICATORY SYSTEMS AND WORLDVIEW: NUMERAL CLASSIFIERS IN NORTHWEST CALIFORNIA LANGUAGES

Classification is inherent in nouns. English words like "stone," "tree," or "uncle" will include certain objects or people and will exclude others. We can see by examples such as the Kashaya Pomo names in the plant world that different peoples and different languages have a variety of ways of ordering and classifying what is about and around them. In some languages, we find the classification of whole sets of words by means of **classifiers.** These are words used in certain grammatical contexts in which each classifier is used with a certain set of words with some common semantic characteristic. English has a hint of classifiers in phrases such as, "three **head** of cattle," "four **bottles** of milk" or "six **sacks** of potatoes." The system is not complete; we can say either "two beers" or "two **cans** of beer," and we say "eight dogs" and "two potatoes," but not "eight **head** of dogs" or "two **??** of potatoes." In addition, the classification hugs the semantic ground of the real world rather closely: we could say "three **sacks** of moose" if we could envision sacks large enough to put moose into.

In languages with true classifiers, however, certain classifiers are used with certain sets of nouns, and their use is obligatory in certain well-defined grammatical situations. Languages vary as to which grammatical setting requires a classifier, but a common one is in counting. Mandarin Chinese is an example of a language with such a numeral classifier system. When one speaks of "three umbrellas," or "three cats," one must use the appropriate classifier, which, for umbrellas, is the classifier used with objects with a handle and, for cats, the classifier used with animals. An elaborated set of numeral classifiers is a well-developed characteristic of all Chinese languages, as well as of most of the languages contiguous to Chinese in Southeast Asia, such as Thai, Vietnamese, and Burmese.

Although less common than in Asia, classifier systems are found in a number of languages in the Americas; for example, in Wiyot of northwestern California, Kwakiutl and some of the Salish languages in the Northwest Coast and most of the Mayan languages of Mesoamerica. In some cases it is a numeral classificatory system (e.g., Tzeltal, a Mayan language of southern Mexico), while in other cases it is based on criteria other than enumeration (e.g., Jacaltec, a Mayan language of Guatemala.) (The use of a classifier in the possession of pets is discussed in section 12.3.)

One of the most complex numeral classifier systems in North America is found in Yurok, a language of northwestern California. Here the classifier is a suffix added to a number when an item is counted: *koht-e?r tepo·* 'one tree' (lit. 'one-**classifier** tree'); *ni?-ił pegək* 'two men' (lit. 'two-**classifier** man'); *nahks-oh ha?a·g* 'three rocks' (lit. 'three-**classifier** rock'). The classifier *–e?r* is used with straight objects, *–ił* with human beings, and *–oh* with round objects.

Some of the numeral classifiers are *–ił, –eł, –eył* 'human beings'; *–aa?y, –ə?əył,* all animals except snakes; *–ek'wo?n* 'bushlike objects' (e.g., plants, bushes, hips, songs); *–e?r* 'straight objects' (e.g., trees, ferns, sticks, bridges, legs); *–oh* 'round objects' (e.g., rocks, silver dollars, drums, hats, flowers, berries, nuts, heads, hearts, eyes); *–ek'* 'rope-like objects' (e.g., ropes, strings, snakes, necks, tongues); *–ok's* 'flat objects' (e.g., boards); *–əpi?* 'pointed objects or tools' (e.g., obsidian blades, knives, men's spoons); *–e?n* 'amorphous objects' (e.g., body parts that are not bushlike, straight, round or rope-like; utensils; streams). Additional categories include houses; boats and boat-shaped objects; dentalium shells; strings of dentalia; woodpecker scalps; white deer skins; and still others. Some of these are seemingly rather specialized, such as dentalium shells and woodpecker scalps, but they make sense once we realize that these objects are of cultural or ceremonial significance for the Yurok.

We may observe that there is a basic dichotomy between animate objects (the first two classifiers) and nonanimate objects. Snakes, which are placed in the non-animate category (specifically rope-like objects), represent the only exception to the dichotomy. The animates are divided in two, human and nonhuman. The nonanimates are classified mainly by shape, although some culturally significant objects have their own classifier. Although the assignment to the various categories is normally regular, there are a few arbitrary placements, such as snakes into rope-like objects and songs into bushlike objects. In some cases, there is a choice, in which case there is a corresponding change in meaning; thus ci·sep' means 'flower bush' when used with the bushlike classifier, but 'flower' when used with the round classifier.

It should be noted that numeral classifiers divide the Yurok plant world into a limited number of shape categories: bushlike, straight, and round objects. But plants can also be classified into taxonomic groupings similar to those discussed earlier in this chapter for the Kashaya Pomo plants. This method yields a different set of categories: tree, bush, grass, flower, and berry; and it is also noteworthy that the criteria for classification are entirely different in the two cases.

In a comparison of the taxonomic systems for plants and animals for Yurok, Karuk, and Californian Athapaskan, it is interesting that, although these three northwestern California groups share a similar culture and the taxonomic systems for plants and animals are remarkably similar across languages, the languages belong to different families. If, however, different criteria are used, namely, nontaxonomic criteria, some similarities are still to be found, but they are not nearly so striking. Hupa, which belongs to the Californian Athapaskan group, has a system of classificatory verbs similar to the system we described for Apachean languages in section 2.5. The categories are round object; long or stick-like object; living being, human or animal; container with contents; fabric-like object; several objects or rope-like object; granular mass; dough-like or mud-like object; piled-up fabric (blanket). Some of these categories are similar to those in Yurok, but others are strikingly different. Notice that one of the Hupa categories is for living beings, but unlike the Yurok categories, there is no distinction between human and nonhuman. There is, however, a weakly developed classifier (perhaps a numeral classifier?) system that does distinguish humans from all other objects. Although the data base has not allowed a full comparative analysis of classification in the three languages, there are enough examples to be suggestive and to raise interesting questions about their historical origins and about the psychological reality of the categories for the speakers.

3.7 WORLDVIEW AND THE HOPI

Since the time of Aristotle at least, the question of the relation between language and culture (or more generally, between linguistic and nonlinguistic behavior) has bemused scholars as well as the proverbial man in the street. Sometimes a relationship has been assumed based on little or no evidence, with the hypothesis stated simplistically: German is a logical language better suited for science and mathematics; Italian is better suited for music; and so on. Such relationships are unproved and unprovable. We cannot, however, dismiss all hypotheses in this easy fashion. Sometimes the grander the scheme, the more difficult it is to substantiate and evaluate, but a claim cannot be shouldered aside simply because it is difficult to evaluate. There have been scholars in such diverse fields as anthropology, linguistics, literature, philosophy, and psychology who have made sweeping claims about the interconnections of language, culture, and thought. In the period from the late 1920s to the early 1940s, within the context of American Indian languages, a controversy was sparked in the linguistic scholarly community by the contention that, since language plays such an important role in an individual's understanding of reality, the particular language the individual speaks is important in shaping that reality. There is nothing very controversial about the idea that language plays an important role in culture and human thought. At issue, however, are (1) the question of linguistic relativity—is the relationship of language, thought, and culture the same for all languages, or do particular languages have particular relationships, and (2) the question of linguistic determinism—to what extent does language shape and control, or just reflect, a view of the world?

Using Hopi, the Uto-Aztecan language spoken in several Pueblos in northeastern Arizona, as the immediate arena for the controversy, it was claimed that English, German and French reflect a very similar reality, and that the differences between them seem minimal when contrasted to the very different reality reflected in Hopi; that is, Western scientific concepts of time, space, and matter are based on a reality embedded in the Western European languages, whereas in Hopi concepts of time, space, and matter are treated very differently—so much so that, had the Hopi developed a science of physics, it would have been very different from physics as we know it. Moreover, Hopi was described as superior to the Western European languages in the reporting and validating of experience; and, with some hyperbole, English was compared to Hopi as a bludgeon is to a rapier where thinking and rational analysis are concerned.

In using Hopi to demonstrate how all aspects of language are related in some fashion to thought and culture, focus was placed on vocabulary differences among languages and how they reflect the fact that experience is classified differently by different languages; for instance, since Hopi has one noun that covers every thing or being (except birds) that flies, this single Hopi word is used when in English three words would be used, "insect, airplane, aviator"; English, however, has one word, "water," to match two words in Hopi that distinguish between water in a container and water found freely occurring in nature.

In support of the notion that language shapes and controls a view of the world, evidence from Shawnee and Nootka, as well as from Hopi and English, was marshalled to demonstrate the different ways in which the formation of morphologically complex words reflects different views of reality. Another aspect of the relationship between linguistic and nonlinguistic behavior that came up for discussion was the role of overt and covert grammatical categories. An overt category is formally marked in every sentence containing a member of that category; for example, in English, the plural of a noun is an overt category usually marked by the suffix –s ("table, tables"). A covert category is marked only in certain types of sentences and not in every sentence in which a word belonging to that category occurs. In English, gender is a covert category because, for example, its marking only occurs when there is need to refer to a noun by a singular personal pronoun ("the table . . . it").

In Hopi there are two noun classes: animate and inanimate, which are covert because the nouns are not overtly marked for animacy or inanimacy. Each class of noun, animate and inanimate, has a distinctive way of forming the plural; for instance, a language learner knows that the Hopi word for "cloud" is animate because in its plural form it is treated as animate. Examples such as "cloud," taken together with the importance of cloud-gods in Hopi ceremonial life, suggest that the covert nature of the animate and inanimate grammatical categories in Hopi is significant as a subtle indicator of aspects of Hopi thought; that is, covert linguistic categories reveal more than overt about how a cultural group experiences reality. Although one may choose to disagree over the significance of overt and covert grammatical categories in relation to nonlinguistic behavior, there is no doubt they are important linguistic concepts, and these early discussions foreshadowed their treatment in modern linguistic theory by many years.

With reference to the Hopi verb, again contrasting it with English, there appear to be ways in which obligatory categories in Hopi differ from those in English, and it was claimed that these differences indicate that the two languages encapsulate very different views of time, space, and matter. Consider the notion "flash." To express this in English, the language's sentence patterns require a subject noun or pronoun, as in "a light flashed" or "it flashed." Flashing and light are, however, the same notion; there is no doer (i.e., "it" or "light") and no performing of an action; in this case, the Hopi form is just *rehpi*, a verb without a subject. It has been suggested that because Hopi can use verbs without subjects it has greater power as a logical tool for understanding various cosmological concepts.

Finally, the early discussion about "fashions of speaking" was based on the assumption that, within one language, systematically diverse features of linguistic structure (lexicon, morphology, syntax, etc.) were integrated in a variety of ways that functioned to express and shape cognitive orientation. This discussion anticipated today's sociolinguistic concept of "ways of speaking," which assumes that a particular fashion of speaking may have quite different cognitive results when one considers how it was acquired and its place in the linguistic repertoire of an individual and a community.

3.8 WORLDVIEW, CLASSIFICATORY SYSTEMS, AND NAVAJO

In consequence of the ideas about language, thought, and culture prevalent in the previous decade, a number of language and culture studies, with American Indian languages as their focus, appeared in the 1940s and 1950s. One example was a study of the Wintu (northern California) in which the connections between Wintu language and thought seemed to infer patterning in Wintu culture from aspects of the structure of the Wintu language. Another study, this time focusing on Navajo, also traced connections between structural patterning in the language and aspects of the culture.

Although a cause-and-effect relationship was never fully claimed by those who favored a close linkage, critics of the approaches taken in the aforementioned language and culture studies have said that correlations between linguistic and nonlinguistic behavior, such as those claimed for Hopi, Navajo, and Wintu, could always be found because they were after-the-fact correlations: in other words, after an investigator comes across some linguistic subsystem that he or she finds intriguing, the investigator rummages around in the culture to find a match.

It has turned out to be extraordinarily difficult to devise experiments that adequately test aspects of the "language shapes world view" hypothesis; for example, how does one test the claim that Hopi would have provided a better medium than Western European languages for the development of modern physics? In spite of the obvious difficulties, a number of studies emerged in the 1950s, one of which focused on the classificatory system of the Navajo verb. We noted earlier (section 2.5) that Navajo classifies objects into a variety of categories, depending on such characteristics as shape and rigidity, for example, round object, long rigid object, long flexible object, flat flexible object, large bulky object, and so on. Therefore, the category to which an object belongs determines which verb stem is used in talking about it: for instance, depending upon shape and rigidity of object, the verb for "pick up" will be different in sentences such as "I pick up a cigarette," "I pick up a blanket," and "I pick up a rope." This study was limited to just three categories, long rigid (e.g., a cigarette), flat flexible (e.g., a blanket), and long flexible (e.g., a rope), and it was predicted that a Navajo speaker's nonlinguistic categorization of such objects would conform to the linguistic categorizations. Navajo- and non-Navajo-speaking subjects were presented with sets of four objects, which could be variously placed into two logical groups by form (following the Navajo verb categories), by color, by material, or by function; thus one set consisted of a blue ruler, a green tape, a green candle, and a blue electric cord. Another set consisted of a metal bolt, a flexible metal wire, a cigar, and a string of artificial pearls; still another, of a red ruler, a gold-colored chain, a wooden paint brush, and a length of rope. The subjects were asked to divide each set of four into logical groups with two members each. It was expected, of course, that the Navajo- and non-Navajo-speaking subjects would categorize differently, and that Navajos would use the form category more than the others. But there was no significant difference in the way the two groups of subjects categorized. Such results are typical of most experiments based on an assumption that patterns of linguistic traits channel cultural behavior. Although these results do not support such hypotheses, they do not necessarily disprove them. If there is a causal relationship between linguistic and nonlinguistic behavior, it is not obvious, and certainly not as strong as the casual observer might think. As has been pointed out, languages are "sets of verbal tools . . . and they, like other tools, condition what they produce, without wholly determining it."

3.9 THE CULTURAL USES OF TAXONOMIES: THE SLAVE CLASSIFICATION OF ICE

Among the Slave Indians of the Northwest Territories a taxonomy of ice is used in assessing travel conditions. There are thirteen ice categories grouped into three unnamed or covert groupings: solid ice, melting ice, and cracking ice. The thirteen terms are not totally distinct words, but rather are formed from the single root tę 'ice'. A few examples: tędeizile 'brittle ice' (a kind of solid ice); tęgá 'white ice' (a kind of melting ice); tętseiyindlá 'seamed ice' (a kind of cracking ice).

Winter travel is by foot, snowshoe, or dogsled. Some types of ice are suitable for travel by all three means, some are not suitable for any kind of travel, and some are suitable for some but not all three means of travel. With thirteen categories of ice and three means of travel, there are thirty-nine situations and for each there are three possible approaches: (1) cross the ice, (2) make a detour, or (3) proceed cautiously and examine the ice.

Fathers play a question-and-answer game with their sons to teach them safe travel. The adult presents the boy with a category of ice (e.g., *tẹdeiẑile* 'brittle ice') and a given situation (e.g., *at'ák'ènatséde* 'traveling from place to place by snow-shoe'). The boy's task is to decide which of the three approaches is the appropriate one. If he gives the correct answer, the father presents him with another category of ice and travel situation. If the answer is incorrect, the boy is expected to ask why, so that an explanation can be given.

3.10 LANGUAGE, COGNITION, AND CULTURE

It is insightful to know how a particular set of words or semantic domain, such as ice, is divided up. But we can learn more once we know the organizing principle behind the vocabulary in a particular domain. One way to get at organizing principles is to group the words into grammatical categories, as Hopi nouns were separated into covert animate and inanimate classes. The noun classes involved in the Yurok numeral classifier system are also covert classes, classes that reflect in part culturally significant categories. Another way is to study botanical and zoological folk taxonomies, as was done with the Kashaya Pomo plant terminology. There is also the application of a componential analysis, that is, the division into binary semantic components, as in the case of the Guarijío directional system. Although the occurrence of binary features in a directional system is rare, and perhaps unique to the Guarijío, componential analysis has been applied with great success to other semantic domains. Although there are yet other ways in which culturally important vocabulary can be organized, we have given examples of the most useful and most commonly used methods.

Scholars have had greater success in dealing with more concrete aspects of culture, less success with the more abstract. This probably tells us that more concrete things are easier to deal with, not that the relationship between language and culture is stronger in this area. There has also been greater success in dealing with lexical material than with grammatical. The areas of grammar that have yielded most readily are those enmeshed with the lexicon, as in the case of the Guarijío directionals and the Yurok numeral classifiers. There has been very little success in dealing with large abstract grammatical systems, such as that represented by the Hopi verb (section 3.7). Is this because such systems are less susceptible to cultural connections, or is it because they are more difficult to study? Considering the number of attempts that have been made to find such linkages between language and culture, we would be inclined to think there is little or at best only a tenuous connection in these cases, but this is far from being an established fact.

In the 1940s and 1950s there was a rather extreme emphasis on linguistic relativity; since that time there has been an increasing interest in linguistic universals. It seems there is a limited set of possible obligatory linguistic categories. Furthermore, the category that is obligatory in one language is often found in other languages as a covert category, turning up sometimes in subtle and less obvious corners of the language; for example, the division of nouns into animate and inanimate is an obligatory (and overt) category in the Algonquian languages, is the basic division for the use of numeral classifiers in Yurok, but is a covert distinction (based on plural formation) for Hopi nouns. Animacy is not an important grammatical category for English, but we do find it as a covert category made evident in questions where we must choose between "who" and "what." It may be that the presence of an overt category has little effect on our thinking or on nonlinguistic behavior, and probably there is little or no causal relationship in these cases. But that does not necessarily mean that such overt categories have no cultural significance. At the very least, we need to raise the question: Why is a linguistic category obligatory and overt in one language and not another? For example, why do Navajo verbs divide nouns into different classes based on their form? And why does English not use this division? The answer to this and related questions is simple: We do not know.

SOURCES

The chapter opens with a quote from Boas 1911:25f. In section 3.1, the Kashaya Pomo data are from Goodrich, Lawson, and Lawson 1980. The Guarijío data in section 3.2 are from Miller 1988; other discussion draws from Boas 1934, Harrington 1916, and Miller 1965. In section 3.3 Chumash data is from Applegate 1974; other discussion draws from Boas 1934 and Miller n.d.a. Section 3.4 is from Miller n.d.a. Section 3.5 is based on Beeler 1964, 1986, Campbell, Kaufman, and Smith-Stark 1986, Closs 1986a,1986b, Payne and Closs 1986, Hinton 1989a, Kroeber 1925–26:877–79, and Sullivan 1988. The Yurok data in section 3.6 comes from Kroeber 1911, Robins 1958, and Haas 1967; Hupa data are from Victor Golla (cited in Haas 1967); additional discussion draws from Berlin and Romney 1964, Bright and Bright 1965,and Craig 1979. Discussion in section 3.7 is based on Whorf 1938, 1940, 1941a, 1941b, 1945, 1956 and Hymes 1974a, 1974b. Wintu discussion in section 3.8 is based on Lee 1938 and 1944b; Navajo, on Hoijer 1951 and Maclay 1958; other discussion is drawn from Hymes 1966 and 1983 with quote from Hymes 1983:174. Section 3.9 is based on Basso 1972.

SUGGESTED READINGS

Over the years, reference to Franz Boas (1911) and his citation of the Eskimo terms for snow has become a favorite example for those interested in how a people's way of life influences vocabulary. Martin 1986, however, discusses how "embroidering" and sloppiness in using secondary sources has led to a count ranging from three to two hundred or more "Eskimo words for snow." For a discussion of the problems raised by a question such as, "How many Eskimo words for snow are there?" see Pullum 1991:168–71.

With reference to section 3.1, studies that have contributed to an understanding of folk taxonomies include Trager 1939 (tree terms in the Pueblo languages), Metzger and Williams 1966 (Tzeltal firewood taxonomy), Perchonock and Werner 1968 (Navajo food terms), Frisch 1968 (Maricopa food terms), Berlin et al. 1974 (Tzeltal plant taxonomy), Hage and Miller 1976 (Shoshoni bird taxonomy), and Berlin 1976 (Aguarana folk botany); general studies include Berlin 1972, Berlin, Breedlove, and Raven 1973, and Wierzbicka 1984. For section 3.2, Brown 1983 discusses origins of cardinal direction terms; Brugman 1983 discusses body-part terms as locatives (Chalcatongo Mixtec); and Payne 1982 reports on directionals as time referentials (Asheninca). For section 3.3 refer to two papers by Basso (1984 and 1988) that analyze the role placenames play in Western Apache culture. For section 3.4 Hanks 1990 presents a study of Maya deixis. With regard to section 3.5 refer to Closs 1986b, who includes chapters by various authorities on number systems in North and South America; Payne and Closs 1986 discuss the Aztec system in detail, including the use of numbers in prehispanic Aztec culture. Bunte and Franklin 1988 examine the San Juan Southern Paiute numeral system and its present-day uses. For section 3.7 Malotki 1983 provides an in-depth study of Hopi time expressions with a reevaluation of the claim that Hopi is a "timeless" language. On sections 3.8 and 3.10 for aspects of Wintu language and world view, see Lee 1943, 1944a, 1944b, and 1946. For discussions of language and world view that postdates the 1950s see McCormack and Wurm 1977 and Gardner 1985; for a relatively recent treatment of Navajo world view, see Witherspoon 1977 and 1980.

PART IV

languages and social domains

CHAPTER 4

LANGUAGES AND SOCIAL ORGANIZATION

The uses to which languages are put vary within communities and across cultures, and a language reflects in many ways—some small, some not so small—how the members of a particular society and culture use it. The nature of language use is affected by such things as the size of the community; the community's social organization, including the role kinship plays; whether the community is mobile or settled; visiting patterns within and across communities; the nature of the boundaries between the community and other communities; whether neighboring communities speak the same language, similar languages, or entirely different languages; the presence or absence of multilingualism; the nature of language variation; how areas of cultural focus relate to language and language use; and patterns of language learning.

A particular society's social structure and cultural orientation also affect attitudes that its members may have toward language (how language is valued or not valued); attitudes toward speakers (who are considered the good speakers, what is considered "good speech" and why); and the presence and characteristics of fashions of speaking (e.g., baby talk, respect speech, styles used in speechmaking, storytelling, and the like).

In this chapter, we examine the place of language in four sets of communities: the Great Basin, the Pueblos of New Mexico and Arizona, the Creek Confederacy, and the preconquest Aztec empire. In addition, we explore some general questions about the relationship between language use and the community.

4.1 LANGUAGE COMMUNITIES IN THE GREAT BASIN

Since ancestral times, the Indian peoples of the Great Basin have been identified with an area now divided into Utah, Nevada, and portions of neighboring states. The area is characterized by low rainfall, extremes of temperature, and variation in the topography. The valleys range from about three thousand to six thousand feet in altitude and are separated by north-to-south running mountains that range between eight thousand and twelve thousand feet in elevation. In earlier times, the available plant and animal resources were scanty and unevenly distributed, but extremely diverse because of the variation in topography.

Two linguistic groups have inhabited the Great Basin, the Washo and the Numic. The Washo, numbering perhaps a thousand at the time of contact, lived and still live in a relatively restricted area in the vicinity of Lake Tahoe in western Nevada and eastern California. The Washo language appears to be distantly related to languages to the west in California. The Numic-speaking communities covered the rest of the Great Basin and even spilled into southern California and to the east on to the Great Plains. There are several Numic languages, all closely related. Within the basin are Mono (western Nevada), Northern Paiute (western Nevada, southeast Oregon), Bannock (a dialect of Northern Paiute but spoken in southern Idaho in primarily Shoshoni-speaking territory), Panamint (Death Valley region of Nevada and California), Shoshoni (eastern Nevada, northern Utah, Southern Idaho), Southern Paiute (southern Nevada and southern Utah), and Ute (southern Utah, western Colorado). Those languages that have covered large geographical areas, namely Northern Paiute, Shoshoni, and Southern Paiute, also display considerable dialect diversity. On the other hand, the early Numic-speaking populations numbered about twenty thousand, a rather small number considering the large area involved. Like the topographical conditions of the Great Basin, the distribution of people was variable, but population density was usually quite low, sometimes much less than one person per square mile.

Even though the languages are very different, in ancestral times the Numic-speaking peoples and the Washo were culturally similar and shared a similar ecological adaptation. Most of the Great Basin peoples were foragers, depending on hunting and gathering with fishing important in some areas; and they were, of necessity, seasonally nomadic. The subsistence activities of the Western Shoshoni of eastern Nevada will serve as a general model. The winter was spent in villages of about five households in or near the pine-nut groves located in the foothills of the mountains. Pine nuts served as the staple winter food and were stored in large quantities in the hope that there would be enough to last the winter. When spring arrived, the village broke up into individual family units and headed for the lowest valleys where the spring food plants were ready earliest. As summer approached, the families moved into the higher valleys and mountains, following the ripening of the food plants. Autumn, when people could gather in larger numbers for a limited period, was the time of the rabbit hunt, a cooperative venture carried out by driving the animals into nets and clubbing them to death. It was also the time for another cooperative venture—the antelope hunt when the animals were driven into corral-like surrounds. While the local resources allowed, sometimes as long as three weeks, as many as a hundred people could be gathered in one place. It was a gala time of all-night dancing, the hand game (a type of gambling game), socializing, telling stories, and swapping gossip and news. With the coming of winter, the seasonal round began again. In spring there might be smaller gatherings for shorter periods, for example, when the Bear Dance was performed. Families apparently preferred to return to the same places each year, since they would be familiar with both the area and the people in it. They might, however, have to spend the winter in a different location with different people if, for example, there had been a pine-nut failure in their favorite locale. Clearly, then, the specifics of this yearly Great Basin migratory round were highly variable.

Social Groupings

A typical household in the Great Basin, consisting of perhaps five or six people, often included individuals other than the nuclear family (husband, wife and their children): perhaps an unmarried younger brother, an aged grandfather, a widowed aunt. If there were a great many children, one or more might live with a grandparent or with a childless aunt and uncle. In most places in the Great Basin the nuclear family was the largest permanent social unit, probably as a result of the way of life and necessary adjustments to the environment. In certain areas (particularly in the south and west), however, there was a certain permanency in larger social groupings. Residence patterns after marriage were discretionary: while it seemed that a man should move in with his wife's family until children were born, local conditions and personal preferences often led to the new couple residing with the husband's family or his brother or to the establishment of a new household or a variety of other arrangements.

Local groups, composed of several families, had names. In the north, they called themselves after a distinctive food source (though not necessarily the main food resource), such as "the salmon eaters," "the rye grass eaters," or "the mountain sheep eaters." In the south, the names tended to be geographical, so they would be "people of such and such a mountain." In some cases, groups formed a loose political unit; in other cases the local group served to distinguish "us" versus "others," with no clear-cut dividing line between.

The economic division of labor was primarily sex-dictated: Men hunted large animals, older men past their prime trapped small animals, and the women and children gathered wild plant foods. The division, however, was not as strict as it might seem, for both men and women took part in the rabbit drives, the antelope drives, and (in areas where fishing was important) the fish drives. By the same token, men often gathered plant foods when it was a group activity, as in the gathering of the pine nuts.

Given the nature of the social groupings and subsistence activities, it is not surprising that leadership roles were limited. There were individuals whose title has been translated into English as "chief," but such persons did not wield anything close to absolute authority. The headmen or band leaders wielded power through persuasion rather than coercion, for they were good speakers who had good sense and advice worth listening to. Among the Shoshoni these leaders are called *tekʷahni*, a term derived from a verb meaning 'talk'. (Among the Northern Paiute they are called *poinapi*, also based on a verb for 'talk'; in Southern Paiute the term is *niavi*, based on the word for 'name' or 'renown'.) Leadership posts varied, so that the person in charge of the rabbit hunt (usually the owner of a rabbit net) might or might not be the head man at the winter village. The leader of the autumn round dance or the spring bear dance was normally the person who knew the most songs and had the most pleasing voice; he might or might not play a leadership role in other activities. The leader of the antelope hunt had to be an antelope shaman (i.e., a shaman who had a helping spirit from the antelope) so that the animals would be charmed and willingly enter the antelope surround.

A shaman (also called "Indian doctor") played an important leadership role, for he or she possessed the power to cure: a power that came from the spirits of such entities as deer, antelope, bear, lightning, and the mythological Water Baby. The spirits of specific beings were often associated with particular powers, and a very powerful shaman could claim power from more than one source. At curing ceremonies some shamans worked with a "speaker" who taught the audience the shaman's song (given to a shaman by her or his power source) so that they might help in the curing process. This "speaker" also explained to the audience what the shaman was doing at various steps during the ceremony. Although shamans tended to be intellectual and, as such, were respected, they were also feared because their power to cure and do good could be turned to do harm.

Good storytellers were also respected. They did not form a special group; they were merely men and women known for their storytelling ability and often were versatile individuals who were capable of filling leadership roles.

The picture that emerges then of ancestral societies in the Great Basin is one of impermanent communities with no restrictive boundaries. There were no well-delineated political or social groups larger than the family; instead, there were interlocking networks of kin-related groups spread throughout the area, each man the center of his own concentric circles.

While there were linguistic differences throughout the Great Basin, there were few sharp linguistic boundaries separating the languages, perhaps a reflection of the absence of fixed social and political boundaries. Between the Northern Paiute speakers in western Nevada and the Shoshoni speakers in eastern Nevada, there was a zone of about a hundred miles wide peopled by speakers of both languages who intermarried and were for the most part bilingual. The fact that Shoshoni and

Northern Paiute are closely related languages no doubt facilitated this situation, but it can hardly explain it, since a similar situation along the Washo and Northern Paiute border involved fundamentally different and unrelated languages. Notice that it was not the languages that were mixed, but rather the speakers that were inter-mingled—a circumstance that, along with the concomitant bilingualism, makes it impossible to draw sharp geographic boundaries between the languages. Moreover, a change in language did not always entail a change in society or culture; from group to group in the Great Basin, cultural changes might be slight for neighbor-ing groups but could be considerable between groups at some distance from each other. Similarly, linguistic changes (either dialectal within the same language or to other languages) could be slight or considerable. Although the linguistic and cul-tural changes did not correlate very closely with one another, the apparent absence of sharp boundaries quite probably led to the spread of regional linguistic features, a topic discussed in chapter 12.

Linguistic Enculturation

Studies of various cultural groups have shown that the varieties of speech a child learns are influenced by the group around him or her. A Washo- or Numic-speaking child, for instance, grew up in an environment that included a rather small group of persons who were linguistically diverse. His or her most frequent contact was with immediate family members who, among the Shoshoni, for example, might include a Ute mother who spoke Shoshoni with a Ute accent, or a mother and father who spoke slightly different dialects of Shoshoni, possibly a grandmother or uncle from a different area, and so on. A child with no siblings very likely would have no contact with a peer group because there would be no opportunity to interact with other children except during the winter camp or the autumn gatherings. During these gatherings, however, a child was exposed to great linguistic diversity, for there might be in attendance twenty-five, seventy-five, or even as many as a hundred or more persons (the largest, which seldom lasted more than a week or so). Moreover, it was not uncommon for a family to loan out a child for a season, or even a few years, to grandparents, to an aunt and uncle (especially if the family had too many mouths to feed and the aunt and uncle were childless), or to other relatives who might live in a different linguistic area. Unfortunately, we do not know just what effect a linguistically diverse environment and such factors as linguistic identification and prestige had on language learning in the Great Basin; nor do we know how individu-als learned the fashions of speaking that reflected the various areas of cultural focus.

Fashions of Speaking and Cultural Focus

In every community there are appropriate ways of behaving; frequently what is culturally appropriate behavior for one activity is not appropriate for other activities.
Appropriate cultural activity includes ways or fashions of speaking. A particular
fashion of speaking is called a speech style and particular styles are associated with
particular activities. For example, one style is appropriate for speechmaking, another
for storytelling, and yet another for speaking to small children. The use of the same
style for more than one cultural activity indicates that a speech community views
those activities as similar in some way. Some styles, such as the one used in oratory, carry prestige; others, such as baby talk or swearing, do not and may even be
undervalued (see chapter 6 for a detailed discussion of style). Differences in fashions
of speaking reflect what is important for a community; for instance, in all communities, speechmaking is of some importance and is marked off, linguistically, from
everyday or casual speech; if it is especially important, we can expect the speechmaking style to be especially well marked and differentiated from everyday speech.

Areas of cultural focus in the Great Basin include mythology, song, and the curing
ceremonies performed by the shaman. Coyote, who is trickster, culture hero, and
buffoon, all wrapped into one, is the central figure in the basin's rich mythology; for
instance, in Shoshoni, Coyote's speech is marked by a special suffix -pai that may
be added to any word in direct quotes of his speech, which then sounds ludicrous
and hilarious to a Shoshoni audience. In these cases, Coyote is speaking in a halting
manner and the more pai suffixes in a sentence, the more ludicrous and hilarious he
sounds. In a similar way, Blue Jay adds the suffix -cai to his speech; however, this
simply marks Blue Jay's way of speaking and does not make his speech sound ludicrous or hilarious. There are also other standardized markers, and in telling Coyote
stories, each practiced storyteller has his or her own variations.

Songs form an important genre among the Great Basin people and, at least among
the Numic speakers, special features differentiate songs from casual speech. First
of all, songs are an integral part of some myths and play a role in the Bear Dance,
the round dance, shamanistic curing ceremonies, and hand games. Although techniques overlap, there are also linguistic and thematic differences that separate the
various categories of songs. The songs of the Shoshoni offer some examples.

Unlike all other categories of songs, the hand-game songs contain passages,
either in part or in whole, with nonsense or meaningless words, sometimes with
sounds, such as the [l] sound, that are not otherwise found in Shoshoni. Shoshoni
dance and shaman songs utilize a phonetic marking involving geminated stops (e.g.,
pp, kk, etc.) and prenasalized stops (e.g., mg, ŋg, etc.). In songs, noninitial voiceless geminated stops (e.g., [wekkumbičč̣ł] 'buzzard', [huuppi] 'wood', and [tosattsi]
'little White One') are usually (but not always) changed to prenasalized voiced

stops (e.g., [weŋgumbinjɨ], [huumbɨ], and [tosandzɨ]). Because geminated stops occur frequently, the phonetic effect is very striking. The prenasalization sometimes leads to ambiguity, which is purposely manipulated for poetic effect. Thematic differences mark different song styles; that is, Bear-dance songs will have references to Bear and her characteristics (often in an oblique fashion), doctoring songs have oblique references to the shaman's power, and round-dance songs often refer to aspects of nature. Bear-dance songs are part of the ceremony. Doctoring songs come to the shaman in a dream, when the power first comes to him or her, and they are the doctor's personal property. Round-dance songs, available for anyone to use, are freely composed, and frequently the composer of the song is known. One well-known Shoshoni, who is remembered from the nineteenth century and respected because of the many songs he composed, has the name Pia Hupia, literally "Big Song." (It is interesting to note that Shoshoni round-dance songs were used in the Ghost Dance, a cultural revival movement that played a prominent role in the massacre at Wounded Knee.)

Tammɨn Yampa Satɨɨcci 'Our Pet Carrot Dog' is an example of a round-dance song:

Tammɨn Yampa Satɨɨcci,	Our Pet Carrot Dog,
Okʷaimanti puikɨnɨkkina.	He stands gazing toward the river.
Yampa tai,	Friend of the carrot,
Yampa tai,	Friend of the carrot,
Yampa tai.	Friend of the carrot.

Yampa is "wild carrot," or *Perideridia Gairdneri,* an important edible root harvested in late spring and early summer. The opening phrase is literally "our carrot dog," a phrase difficult to translate into English in such a way that it still carries the connotation it has for the Shoshoni listener. The reference is to some unidentified animal, which perhaps showed up on one occasion while a group was gathering carrots; a composer then memorialized the event with a song.

Shoshoni round-dance and doctoring songs differ thematically, and round-dance songs are public property, while doctoring songs are owned by the shaman. Even so, today, doctoring songs that certain round-dance singers find particularly pleasing are sometimes used in round dances. Whether this present-day practice was carried on in ancestral times is not known.

In earlier times, it appears that the speech style used by a Shoshoni shaman in a doctoring ceremony was well marked off from casual speech, but we have no records to indicate exactly how it may have been different. We do know, however, that a shaman's helper, or *tekʷawoppi* 'talker', who spoke for the shaman, would deliver a prayer in highly poetic language. Indeed, prayers, sometimes as part of a doctoring ceremony, or given on other occasions, are still heard at funerals. They constitute a distinct style, often with special words, for example, Northern Paiute *puusaattɨ* in place of the usual *taba* 'sun'.

The Great Basin oratorical style has been described by a Tubatulabal (a member of a neighboring California group) as being "just like a peanut vendor." A leader, or other respected person (man or woman), may give a speech at a public gathering; the style, which seems similar to that found generally in western America, is marked by content (the audience is admonished to lead the good life, be virtuous, industrious and the like), by a particular tone of voice, and by repetition.

Slang, a fashion of speaking characteristically associated with the young and peer groups, was apparently missing in the linguistic repertoires of most early Great Basin societies—most likely because the way of life did not lend itself to the development of peer groups, since children came together in groups for only a limited period of time.

Fashions of Speaking and Social Category

In all cultures, people of different social categories are addressed differently. The way one talks to a young child or baby is not the same way one addresses respected elders, close kin, or strangers; however, the fashions of speaking reflecting these social categories appear to have been only weakly developed in the Great Basin. Baby talk has been reported among the Ute, it is missing among the Western Shoshoni, and elsewhere the record is silent. No specially marked differences between men's and women's speech have been reported, nor any specially marked respected speech. Among the Ute, however, there was a special way for older people to talk, a fashion of speaking used only in certain contexts; and it was marked by certain phonological changes.

Multilingualism and Multidialectalism

At the time of European contact, a great deal of bilingualism existed in the Great Basin in those areas where two languages bordered each other. Bilingualism was facilitated by the close relationship of the Numic languages, a fact that has been noted by the Numic speakers themselves. We have already mentioned the strip of territory, up to a hundred miles wide, between the Shoshoni and Northern Paiute, in which the whole population was bilingual. Many Shoshonis and Southern Paiutes of southern Nevada spoke each other's languages. There was also a fair degree of bilingualism between the Washo and Northern Paiute, and in the border area there were groups called "half Paiute." In these cases, since they did not signal cultural differences, language differences were not used as symbols for cultural identity.

Shoshoni-Northern Paiute bilingualism persists today because there are a number of present-day communities that include speakers of both languages. Trilingual individuals, those who speak Shoshoni, Northern Paiute and English, are not uncommon. "Passive bilingualism," the ability to understand but not speak a second language, frequently occurs in groups of speakers of closely related languages. It is common today in the Numic area and was probably common in ancestral times as well.

Because of accidents of personal history, some speakers of a Numic language are bidialectal. They may have grown up in more than one locality, their spouse might be from a different dialect area, they might have moved as adults (often moving to the spouse's community), or they might have engaged in extensive travel. Extensive exposure does not guarantee bidialectalism, however, since a number of people thus exposed remain monodialectal. Among the Numic-speaking peoples in the Great Basin, the ability to control more than one dialect is admired, but the inability to do so is not stigmatized. In general terms, learning another dialect can lead to three possible results: some individuals change dialects, losing their native dialect; others learn an additional dialect, keeping the two distinct; and still others end up with a mixture. All three, and with various gradations, are found in the Great Basin.

Bilingualism and bidialectalism are slightly more common among men than women, which is probably a reflection of the fact that men are more apt to be travelers. There is, however, no expectation that these abilities belong only or primarily to men. Numbers of speakers also play a part; for example, most Panamint speakers, who are relatively few in number, have learned to speak or understand the very closely related Shoshoni, but only a few Shoshonis understand Panamint. Today, English serves as the language of wider communication, but there is no evidence that any one language served this function in precontact times.

Linguistic Awareness and Attitudes

The Southern Paiutes and Utes (Southern Numic) use dialect differences as a marker of ethnic difference, with this exception: language and dialect differences are not used as symbols of cultural identity and no one dialect or language carries greater prestige than another. Great Basin peoples are well aware of linguistic differences, although they attach little social significance to them: People from different areas speak different dialects or languages, but these dialects and languages are neither better nor worse; they are simply different. If a person from a different dialect area is able to use the host dialect, that is fine; however, there is no expectation that he or she must do so. People are often able to identify particular words as being typical of the speech of certain localities, but there are no standard shibboleths generally cited to characterize speakers of a certain area. We must, however, take note of the very close linguistic similarities between the Numic languages. As one Shoshoni speaker said, "Ute has a lot of the same words [as Shoshoni], but sometimes they mean different things." Washo, however, which is unrelated to the Numic languages, is sometimes characterized as "like Chinese."

In many parts of North America there is a phenomenon called **word taboo,** a term that refers to the avoidance of certain words, or their replacement by synonyms or phrases. Although not as predominant a feature as in some parts of North America, it is found in the Great Basin among some groups. 'Bear' is sometimes referred to as 'aunt', particularly during the pine-nut harvest, and the word for 'rattlesnake' in Northern Paiute, *tokokkʷa*, was replaced with *waʔyaciciʔi* 'dear little waving one'. Name taboo, in which the name of a dead person is avoided, seems to have been practiced only among the Southern Paiute.

In summary, good storytellers, good singers and song composers, and good speech makers are admired, but in all other respects, the approach among the Numic-speaking peoples of the Great Basin toward language reflects a casual attitude. There is a relative absence of elaboration of styles relating to social category (styles for showing respect, for men's and women's speech, for baby talk, and the like), there is a laissez-faire attitude toward multilingualism and dialect shifting, and neither language nor dialect is generally used as a symbol for cultural identity.

4.2 LANGUAGE COMMUNITIES IN THE PUEBLOS

The Pueblo peoples of the southwestern part of the United States live in some twenty villages and speak six languages: Hopi, Zuni, Keres, and three Tanoan languages, Tiwa, Tewa, and Towa. The Hopi live in several pueblos or villages on three mesas in northeastern Arizona. Zuni speakers live in a single pueblo in northwestern New Mexico. Keres is spoken at seven pueblos in and near the northern Rio Grande Valley in New Mexico. Speakers of the Tanoan languages reside in pueblos also located in the Rio Grande Valley and there is one outlier group, the Arizona Tewa, found among the Hopi. Zuni and Towa (spoken at Jemez) are spoken at single pueblos and display no dialect variation. The other languages are spoken at from two to seven pueblos, with a slightly different dialect at each pueblo. Hopi, a Uto-Aztecan language, has linguistic relatives over a wide area in western North America and Tanoan may also be related to Uto-Aztecan. In contrast, Zuni and Keres have no known or proven linguistic relatives. Although there is cultural variation among the pueblos, it does not match the degree of linguistic variation.

The Pueblo peoples have lived a similar way of life in settled farming villages for some fifteen hundred years, and have a rich and highly developed ceremonial life. Each pueblo, consisting of a single village, or one central village with satellite villages, is a socially, politically, and ceremonially autonomous unit. Populations range from a few hundred to a few thousand.

The Pueblo groups have been able to maintain their social and cultural identity, in spite of almost four hundred years of contact with European culture. Even so, there have been social and cultural changes, occasioned by the late sixteenth-century arrival of the Spanish who especially affected the eastern Pueblos, and by the presence for over a hundred years of Anglo-Americans whose influence has been more intense than that of the Spanish. Until well into the twentieth century, the native languages of the Pueblos were the first languages learned. It has only been in recent years that English has become quite common as a first language.

Social Groupings

Although there is variation across villages, there is enough commonality in social groups to allow a general sketch. In most cases, clans are matrilineal and exogamous. There are a dozen or so clans, and an individual is born into the clan of his or her mother and cannot marry an individual from this clan. Among all the pueblos, the residential unit is the extended family, consisting of married couples and their married children; in the pueblos with matrilineal clans, wives are from the same clan and husbands from different clans. Crosscutting the clan system are a number of religious societies, which play important roles in both ceremonial and political affairs.

In the past, government was largely a theocracy, in which leadership roles were closely tied to the religious societies. Nowadays, some leadership positions are filled by election because patterns of political organization are changing in response to the larger Euro-American society of which the Pueblo world is now a part. One fact remains unchanged, however: There are certain leadership positions that have specific duties and responsibilities attached to them. These positions are filled by formal mechanisms, whether by affiliation in religious societies or by election, and they show a certain commonality across pueblos. For example, in most villages one person is responsible for contact and communication with outsiders (usually called the "governor"), another for mobilizing the community for communal work (e.g., repairing the irrigation ditches each spring), another for the organization of the various religious ceremonies, and so on.

The most important contrast between the Pueblo and Great Basin speech communities is that each pueblo is an independent suprafamilial political and social unit. Also, in contrast to the communities considered later in this chapter, it appears that, at least in pre-Columbian times, political links between pueblos were few. There was, and is today, however, a network of social relationships. Considerable interpueblo trade of nonfood items and considerable contact between ceremonial leaders have been ongoing since ancestral times. These interpueblo contacts

have not had a dampening effect on the strong sense of identity of each pueblo—
a sense of identity fostered by the fact that individuals normally have genealogical
and fictive ties with the majority of the individuals in the village. Some observers
see this identity with the pueblo as an expression of ethnocentrism: Members of a
given pueblo take note of variations in language, ceremonialism, and other aspects
of culture, and assume that those in their own pueblo are right and superior to
those found among their neighbors.

Linguistic Enculturation

The pueblo that the child grows up in has well-delineated boundaries. In the past
the child was probably not much influenced by either Indians or non-Indians outside the pueblo, but today outside events and institutions, like school, are of considerable importance.

A Pueblo household includes more than the nuclear family, so that there are
many adults to provide a linguistic model for a child. Older sisters typically spend a
substantial part of their time as baby tenders and introduce the child early to well-
developed play and peer groups.

Learning of the various styles of speech comes in late childhood or early adulthood. Slang is picked up informally from peer group members, but more formal
varieties of speech come with more deliberate training. In an early journal account
an observer noted that a Hopi chief "will take his nephew out herding with him not
only as a shepherd or donkey boy but to teach him prayer-songs."

Fashions of Speaking and Cultural Focus

Speech styles are well defined in relation to the richly developed ceremonial life and
political systems that form the foundation of Pueblo culture. The most important
style is ceremonial speech, present in all the pueblos, and best described for Zuni and
Keres. It is used in the kiva (the sacred ceremonial chamber) and on all ceremonial
or ritualistic occasions. Certain words are replaced by special "ceremonial words,"
words that are often felt to be archaic. At other times metaphor is used, for example, Zuni *takka* 'frog', and its ceremonial equivalent *woliye tinan k?ayapa*, literally
'several-are-in-a-shallow-container they-sitting they-are-in-liquid'. Not all words
have a ceremonial equivalent, and words considered coarse, undignified, or ritually
impure are omitted in ceremonial speech, as are Spanish and English loan words.

A well-developed oratorical style is used at most public functions. The Tewa
have a term for speechmaking, *tumahe*, which has been described as formulas that
"are learned by heart, either by listening to more experienced speakers or by taking
actual lessons from elder relatives and friends. . . . The conventional style approved

was smooth, low-voiced, unemphatic: originality of form was to be avoided, and the object was to clothe originality of matter in traditional form, so as to be able to say of any proposal 'all this I heard from your fathers and uncles'." It has been suggested that the style reflected "reluctance to be assertive and conspicuous," which is typical of general Pueblo behavior.

Closely allied to speeches are chants, used by so-called chanters, criers, or announcers. This highly and rigidly structured style is found mainly in the western Pueblos and is especially well developed among the Hopi, where it is clearly differentiated from both singing and speaking by a special term. There is an official crier or "speech chief" who makes the official public and religious announcements. Even though anyone can make a secular announcement from the house top on personal matters, such as lost or stolen property, a speech chief is usually asked to do this. There is special training for the crier chief, the one who performs the religious (as opposed to the secular) chants.

Storytelling is important for proper moral training, since past events are important guides for present and future behavior. Stories are typically told in the home on winter nights. Storytellers do not undergo any formal training, but simply learn by listening. The genre is well marked by special linguistic markings (chapter 5) and is labeled in the native cultures by special names, for example, in Arizona Tewa pę́·yuʔu and Zuni *telapnaawe*.

The language used in song differs from ordinary speech, at least in some cases, but there is no systematic discussion of this topic in the ethnographic literature. Sacred songs at Cochiti seem to use ceremonial speech. Songs are often borrowed and Keres seems to be a popular source.

Fashions of Speaking and Social Category

Social categories are important in determining fashions of speaking in the Pueblo communities. A specialized baby-talk vocabulary has been reported for Keres and for Hopi, and it is likely a pan-Pueblo development. In Acoma (Keres) there are some thirty baby-talk words that replace their adult equivalents, words like 'mommy', 'bite', 'sleep', and 'kitty-cat'. Adults claim the main reason for their use is their easier pronunciation, though an objective examination of the two sets of words does not always bear this out, for example, as in the use of glottalized consonants: m'éum'éu (baby talk), múusa (adult speech) 'cat'; ʔák'ɨʔák'ɨ (baby talk) ʔɨsk'a (adult speech) 'drink'. The vocabulary of men's and women's speech is differentiated for a few items in Hopi, Keres, and Tewa. The number of words that are differentiated is small, but the words are of frequent occurrence so that the effect is very noticeable. An article published in 1955 reports that slang, used by teenagers and young adults, was a fashion of speaking in Zuni that older people viewed as a worthless but harmless form of speech that the young outgrew. Younger speakers are expected to address their elders in a respectful manner. Among the Arizona Tewa, this normally entails using appropriate kin terms and greeting forms.

Spanish and English function as additional styles for those who speak them. Although English has been replacing it, Spanish still retains a place in the communicative network, particularly in the eastern Pueblos. In the 1950s, at Cochiti, a pueblo with Spanish Americans living right in the pueblo, teenagers learned each other's languages and Spanish was normally the appropriate language in dealing with Spanish Americans. English, in addition to being a lingua franca (i.e., a language of wider communication), was, for example, the appropriate language for baseball. At a few of the more highly acculturated pueblos, and among families that live away from the pueblo, English is used widely in a variety of contexts, especially by the young.

Multilingualism and Multidialectalism

In the modern pueblos almost everyone is bilingual in English, largely because of its use in schools. Although English has replaced Spanish as the lingua franca, Spanish is still used, especially by older people and by the Rio Grande Pueblos, which are located in an area containing large numbers of native Spanish speakers.

The six hundred or so Arizona Tewa represent the most notable example of native bilingualism. The Arizona Tewa are descendants of those who took refuge among the Hopi after fleeing the oppression of the Spanish in the Rio Grande. They share First Mesa with the Hopi and speak their language. Other examples of native bilingualism are sporadic, with a frequency about as low as any place of comparable linguistic diversity in North America. Although learning another native language was not undervalued, neither was it highly valued. The one exception seemed to be ceremonial leaders, who would sometimes be in contact with their counterparts in other villages and would then learn each others' languages to facilitate these contacts. There was also some bilingualism as a result of trading practices, with Navajo, a nonpueblo language, perhaps the most important language in this regard. Other reasons for bilingualism were intertribal marriages (rare) and the moving of a group to another pueblo, usually in times of distress, such as famine. Evidence indicating that native bilingualism has declined since the wider currency of Spanish and English may support the notion that such bilingualism is not highly valued. It also does not appear that any Indian language ever served as a lingua franca in the Southwest.

Some pueblos have an interpreter, which may be a reflection of the low level of Indian language bilingualism. It cannot be determined whether or not this is a recent practice. It has been reported that a Zuni interpreter must know Zuni, English, and Spanish, and that the Hopis of First Mesa select Arizona Tewas as interpreters, because of their ability to speak several languages.

Linguistic Awareness and Attitudes

Words for speech acts, genres, and other fashions of speaking indicate an acute awareness of speech. Examples from Arizona Tewa are –cíkáy 'to inquire', -yon 'to command', -túkyɛnu 'to put a curse on someone', –pę́·yuʔu 'stories', wo·waci '(life) histories', khaw 'songs', teʔe hi·li 'kiva talk' (i.e., ceremonial speech), t'owabí hi·li 'mundane talk'.

The proper use of speech is highly regarded and the ability to use the more elevated styles, especially the ceremonial language, is admired. As reported in the 1950s, the sacred vocabulary had overtones of dignity and prestige for a native speaker of Zuni. Although younger Zuni speakers admitted that they could not explain all religious terms, both young and old had no trouble identifying certain words and phrases as belonging to the sacred rather than the everyday vocabulary.

As we have indicated, the relatively self-contained nature of each pueblo fosters a high degree of identity with that pueblo on the part of the individual, and each pueblo feels superior to its neighbors. When similarities of custom are noted, it is assumed that the neighboring pueblo did the borrowing. These ethnocentric notions extend to language; for example, in 1935 an observer noted that the Santo Domingo Indians laughed at the way other Keresan Pueblos "talked" Keres. No single language or dialect is granted greater prestige; thus, the conditions are met for language to serve as a symbol for self-identity and also for identifying other groups.

It is consistent with pueblo ethnocentrism that bilingualism, although not undervalued, is neither highly valued nor widely practiced. The Arizona Tewa are again the exception, because they take great pride in being completely bilingual in Hopi. According to a well-known historical account, knowledge of Hopi is supposed to be open to the Tewa, but knowledge of Tewa closed to the Hopi. Some Hopis do, in fact, know Tewa, particularly those married to Tewas, but such knowledge is usually concealed.

4.3 LANGUAGE COMMUNITIES
OF THE CREEK CONFEDERACY

In ancestral times, the Indians living in what is now the southeastern United States had a fairly uniform culture. Most groups lived in settled towns. Horticulture, based primarily on corn, beans, and squash, provided the economic base, although hunting and gathering were not unimportant. The southeastern peoples had evolved the most highly developed social and political systems of any peoples north of Mexico, in particular, those of the Natchez and their neighbors in the lower Mississippi area. Among these groups, a class or caste system apparently was well developed, and the power of the chief came closer to being absolute than it was in any other groups north of Mexico.

Accounts of the ancestral communities are sometimes scanty, largely because of the removal of southeastern Indians to Indian Territory (now eastern Oklahoma) in the last century. We must depend primarily on the accounts of early travelers and missionaries and accounts of older Indians told to ethnographers during the late nineteenth and early twentieth centuries. Unfortunately, although the Oklahoma communities retained many of their preremoval characteristics, most ethnographers focused on earlier aspects of Indian life.

Information on the Indians of the Creek Confederacy is fuller than for some other groups in the Southeast. The Confederacy was a loose one, comprised of about fifty towns, located in Georgia and adjacent areas. After the early contact with European powers, the inhabitants of these towns moved to Alabama and remained there until the United States government "removed" them to Oklahoma in 1832. Once resettled in Oklahoma, they maintained much of their original social and political organization for a number of years.

Each town governed its own affairs. Town leadership was vested in a chief along with other governmental and religious officials. Normally, the chief and many of the other officials were chosen from certain clans; the specific clans, however, might vary from town to town. Associated with each town was a plaza with its public buildings. The government of the Confederacy was a larger version of the government of the town. Delegates from the member towns normally met once a year. Confederacy business pertained only to external affairs: conducting war, maintaining peace among members, and dealing with outsiders, both European and Indian.

The most important unit from a linguistic point of view was the town. A child's linguistic enculturation probably took place in the town, with outside influence being minimal, at least during early childhood. Town sizes seemed to range from a hundred to over a thousand. Most towns spoke one or another Muskogean language: Creek, Alabama, Koasati, Hitchiti, Mikasuki, and Apalachee; but non-Muskogean languages were represented as well: Natchez, Yuchi, and Shawnee. Creek, the politically and numerically dominant language, was divided into a number of dialects.

Bilingualism

Bilingualism is known to have been a significant means of communication among the various groups of the Confederacy. (A sign language also existed—one that differed from the well-known Plains variety; but, since little is known about it, we can do no more than mention it in passing.) Because of the multiplicity of languages spoken in the affiliated towns of the Confederacy, it is very likely that skill in communicating in more than one language was a hallmark of political leadership. Among the speakers of the various languages there was a high degree of bilingualism that persisted into modern times. One observer has reported that during the removal to Oklahoma, although everybody spoke different languages, nearly all the young people understood and spoke Creek. The same observer also commented that the Yuchis had maintained their distinctive identity more than other groups; for example, not many spoke Creek and they rarely intermarried with the Creeks. Most Yuchis, however, were bilingual in Creek by 1940, even though Shawnee, their primary second language in the seventeenth century, was still used by a few into the twentieth century.

Native speakers of minority languages were much more apt to speak Creek than the reverse and, during the 1930s and 1940s, the fathers of many men or the men themselves could speak Creek plus another Indian language. A scholar writing in the 1920s seemed to think that there was more bilingualism among men than women, probably because of the importance of Creek in political life, but this view was not borne out in the 1930s and 1940s when it was possible to come across as many women as men who were bi- and multilingual.

Bilingualism was sometimes the first step in language shift and language replacement (i.e., the giving up of one language and replacing it with another; see section 9.4). In eastern Oklahoma, there was a postremoval shift in the Old Creek Nation from non-Creek languages to Creek. Although preremoval shifts to Creek had been common, there were a few cases in which a shift was to another language. The shifting was probably an ongoing process in various stages of development in various towns. For example, the Yuchi did not seem to be as far along the road to cultural and linguistic assimilation as were, for example, the Hitchiti. The foreign origin of the Yuchi, probably relative newcomers to the Confederacy, was better reflected in their town culture than like origins were for other towns that had (or were reputed to have had) a foreign origin.

We do not know the social or cultural context of precontact bilingualism in the Confederacy. In postcontact times among the descendants of the groups participating in the Confederacy, bilingualism has sometimes been the result of interlingual marriages, with the children learning the language of both parents. At other times, it has been through exposure to other languages, either as a child or later in life, with some individuals exhibiting a passion for piling up languages as they got older. Some families have been bi- and multilingual for generations, indicating that bilingualism does not always lead to language shift. An early trader reported the presence of passive bilingualism in the Confederacy, and it has been common well into the latter part of the twentieth century.

Fashions of Speaking

Descriptions of speech styles tend to be sketchy, but it is clear that respected varieties were well developed. Speaking at the annual spring meeting of the Confederacy was a highly regarded skill; and, next to success in war, it was the major means of social advancement. It had religious associations, and before a public speech the Creek speaker used to spit four times with deliberation and repeat a formula. Speeches began with a formulaic opening sentence and were delivered in a high-pitched, monotonous tone interrupted from time to time by a rather abrupt rise followed by a drop in tone. The oratorical language was full of metaphorical allusions, with irony and satire preferred to denunciation. Speeches were appropriate at all public gatherings: the Busk or Green Corn Ceremonies, ball games, funerals, or before embarking on a raiding trip. Although not as common as in the past, speechmaking was heard as recently as 1973 by a visitor to a Creek-speaking community in Oklahoma.

Heralds or criers have been reported for both the Yuchi and the Creek. A chief never made a public address; instead, he had a speaker do it for him.

Storytelling was circumscribed by well-defined conventions. Natchez stories could only be told at night after the first frost. They began with a formula such as *akiNca seNci··· wa··· ma·ka···* 'the-tale is-sitting (particle) saying'. The ending was *akiNca kecikti··· wa···* 'the-tale is-broken (particle)'. Sometimes there were special words that substituted for ordinary ones that were called "cannibal's talk." Among the Creek, there were a number of myth names for Rabbit, who was the major mythological character in the southeast, and some also for Wolf, which were used to show special respect; thus *cofí*, the ordinary word for 'rabbit', could be replaced by *pa·sokó·la*, or *tama·timí·kko (mí·kko* 'chief, king'). Among the Yuchi, good narrators of stories were also generally respected and, like the Natchez stories, Yuchi narratives began with stereotyped phrases.

Medicine songs and formulas had to be memorized because exact recitation was necessary. One description claims that the songs contained everyday words, sometimes with nonsense syllables, but with no special vocabulary or special phonetic changes. A conflicting description claims that the song texts were often not clearly understood because they evidently contained the vocabulary used by the shaman, and there were also grammatical and phonological changes. Ceremonial and mythological texts (in contrast to stories) were like medicine songs and formulas, in that memorization and exact repetition were important. Such texts started with no introduction, were given with a slow, monotonous delivery, and contained a minimum of repetition.

It has been noted that public speeches "contained certain 'peculiar' words," without any indication as to what "peculiar" meant. In addition, an early French explorer reported that the language used by the shaman or "knower" (it is not clear which) had nothing in common with the people's language. These facts, along with the comments about the difficult-to-understand medicine songs and formulas, may point to an earlier ceremonial "language" or vocabulary, like that noted for the Pueblos.

There was, at an earlier time, a well-defined difference between men's and women's speech in the Eastern Muskogean language of Koasati. The men's form was made from the women's form by adding –s or replacing the last element with –s:

Women's	Men's	
ka·	ka·s	'he is saying'
molhil	molhís	'we are peeling it'
í·p	í·ps	'he is eating it'

In the 1930s, when this system was studied, only older Koasatis maintained the distinctions, and the women's forms were being replaced by the men's forms. The appropriate sex forms were used in telling a story when quoting a person of the opposite sex; and parents of both sexes would correct young children if they used the wrong form. One male speaker thought women's speech sounded better than men's: it was "easy, slow, and soft. It sounds pretty. Men's speech has too much sss." Was he reacting to women's speech as such or to the fact that, being replaced by men's speech, it was becoming "archaic"?

Fragmentary evidence indicates that the Creek and Hitchiti distinctions were similar to those in Koasati. An early observer found an example of women's speech in a Hitchiti hunting song, hunting being an activity normally associated with men.

Linguistic Awareness and Attitudes

Information on language attitudes is sketchy, but a few points stand out. We know that ability in public speaking was highly regarded. Creek was the language of wider communication and in 1971 was reported as the language still used by the Florida Mikasukis with outsiders; therefore, we might expect it to carry greater prestige. But we have no information on this matter. Creek speakers seemed to relegate Yuchi to a lower position, judging from some comments made by Creeks. One Creek is quoted as follows: "When the Creator made the ancestors of the Indians he gave them different languages until he had none left. He found that there were still some Indians whom he had not provided for. These were the Yuchi. Having no language for them, he kicked them in the buttocks saying 'Ba!' which explains why the Yuchi have such an unintelligible speech." Another Creek claimed that "It [Yuchi] sounds more like a fellow sick and gruntin' like." At least part of this attitude may stem from the fact that Yuchi has a much richer consonantal system than any other language in the Confederacy, including a full set of glottalized consonants. The last point we can make here about language attitudes has to do with English: In the 1930s, although bilingualism seemed to be accepted as a matter of course, at least between Indian languages, more conservative Indians still had an aversion to or dislike of English.

4.4 LANGUAGE COMMUNITIES OF THE AZTEC EMPIRE

Well-developed, stratified civilizations existed in the pre-Columbian Americas in two places, Mesoamerica and the Andes. Mesoamerican civilization began more than three thousand years ago, encompassing an area from the central Mexican highland through the Yucatán Peninsula, Guatemala, and neighboring areas.

The subsistence base depended primarily on the cultivation of corn, which was most commonly made into tortillas and tamales. Other plants such as beans played a subsidiary but important role. Wild plants and hunting declined in importance as the population increased. Efficient and intensive farming methods led to increased population and urbanization, along with a complex network for the distribution of food that was managed and controlled by the central governments. Surplus food allowed for the development of full-time specialists in nonfood-producing occupations and to a social stratification with nobles, commoners, and other classes. The political unit was the city-state and was governed by a ruler or king, along with other bureaucratic officials. Sometimes, a city-state would extend its dominion over other cities to form empires that were often multiethnic and multilingual. These empires were of varying sizes and existed for varying periods of time. The archeological record shows that once-powerful empires sometimes disintegrated, only to be replaced by others.

There was an elaborate pantheon, a richly developed ceremonialism, and a type of warfare that was almost ceremonial. Considerable human capital was spent in the construction of public buildings, including those very impressive temples where most of the public ceremonies took place. A principal object of warfare was to capture sacrificial victims, who would have their hearts ripped out so that the blood could feed the sun; without this immolation, the sun would cease its daily trip across the sky, so a staggering number of captives were sacrificed to this end each year. The warrior who made a capture gained prestige and the victim was assured of an honorable afterlife.

A solar calendar of 365 days and a ritual calendar of 260 days were used. The latter was used in tracking a complex set of ceremonies and was also consulted in a system of divination. No activity was undertaken without consulting a soothsayer and his Book of Days, in order to determine which days were lucky or unlucky for the particular activity. As we will see in chapter 8, the calendar played an important role in the development of Mesoamerican writing.

The city-states formed speech communities quite different from the last three types that we have considered. Most cities had between fifteen and thirty thousand inhabitants, although a few were considerably larger. The rural area that supplied the city with food extended out about ten kilometers. The city was sometimes independent, sometimes in a loose confederation with another city or cities, sometimes a tribute-paying vassal to a conquering city.

Our interest is in a group of Nahuatl-speaking people called the Mexica (pronounced *meshē'kə*), who at the beginning of the fourteenth century lived in a series of small cities in the Valley of Mexico. Three of these cities, Tenochtitlán, Tlatelolco, and Texcoco, rose to prominence and formed the Triple Alliance that, by the time of the Spanish Conquest, controlled most of central Mexico. Allegiance was demanded and tribute collected from most of the other Nahuatl cities, as well as from a variety of foreign ethnic groups who spoke different languages. This empire stretched from the Gulf Coast to the Pacific through Oaxaca and to the border of the tropical lowlands (see map 4.1).

Nahuatl speakers occupied most of the central highlands of Mexico in the northwestern part of Mesoamerica; and their language belongs to the Aztecan branch, the most southern of the Uto-Aztecan language family (section 12.4). Tradition claimed that the Nahuatl speakers were a nomadic people whose homeland was to the northwest on an island called Aztlan (hence the name "Aztec"). When the Spanish arrived in the early sixteenth century, there were several million Indians who spoke a variety of Nahuatl dialects.

Mesoamerica was also home to almost one hundred other languages (section 14.3). Some, like Nahuatl, were spoken by large populations, while others were (by Mesoamerican standards) more modest in size. Some, like Tarascan, were linguistic isolates, while others fit into diversified language families. There was considerable contact between these ethnically and linguistically diverse people — contact through diplomatic channels, through long-distance trade in luxury items and raw materials unique to certain areas, through war, and, at least in the case of the Mexica, through the administration of vassal states and the collection of tax and tribute.

The Aztec Empire was the largest but not the first in Mesoamerica. The city of

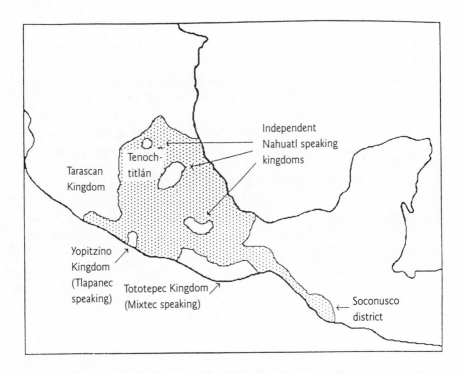

Map 4.1.—The Aztec Empire at the time of conquest, 1519 (based on maps and other data in Berdan 1982, Davies 1987, Suárez 1983, and Voorhies 1989).

Teotihuacán, in the northeastern part of the Valley of Mexico, was the region's capital from the second century B.C. until the eighth century A.D., during which time it exercised cultural and probably political control over a large area. Between A.D. 900 and 1150, the Toltecs held sway from their capital of Tula to the north. The Mexica considered themselves to be the spiritual descendants of both Teotihuacán and the Toltecs.

Tenochtitlán was the political center of the Triple Alliance, Tlatelolco, with its great market, was the commercial center, and Texcoco was the intellectual and cultural center. It has been estimated that the population of Tenochtitlán was two hundred thousand; the Valley of Mexico, about one million; and the total empire, more than five million.

The Spanish Conquest of 1519–1521 brought an end to the Aztec empire and to the Mexica social order. The conquest was short and brutal, and in its aftermath European diseases decimated the native populations. Temples were destroyed, books were burned, and few traces of the indigenous religion were allowed to remain. Mexico City was built on the site of Tenochtitlán and the stones from the principal temple (i.e., the Templo Mayor) were used to build the Catedral de la Asunción. With the destruction of the old social order, Mexico City came to be inhabited primarily by mestizos, offsprings of the Spanish conquistadores and Indians; their language was Spanish, but their culture was a synthesis of European and indigenous elements.

In the rural areas outside Mexico City, a new social order emerged, with the Indians becoming a dependent peasant population. Although the culture changed, particularly in the area of religion with the imposition of Christianity, a remarkable amount of Nahuatl language and culture still persists.

We know a great deal about the Mexica language and culture, ironically because of the Franciscan missionaries, the very ones who attempted to snuff out the native cultures. Most of them learned Nahuatl in order to be in a better position to proselytize and, in order to better understand their charges, some missionaries recorded native beliefs and customs. The most important was Fray Bernardino de Sahagún, who arrived in New Spain in 1529, very soon after the conquest. For over fifty years he put together an extraordinarily detailed account of preconquest society and culture and of the conquest itself as seen through native eyes. Under his watchful eye, this account was dictated in Nahuatl by former nobles, merchants, and artisans, and was written down by younger literate Indians. It also includes a Spanish paraphrase. The perspective is selective, because the topics were circumscribed by what the missionaries asked about (Sahagún tended to talk only to specialists), and what the Mexica were interested in talking about. At the same time, however, many aspects of the sacred and profane life are covered in detail and, because they were described by preconquest experts, they represent an insider's view.

The language of Tenochtitlán which the missionary linguists recorded in the sixteenth century has come to be called Classical Nahuatl, or Classical Aztec, or sometimes simply Aztec, although this can be confused with the Nahuatl that is spoken today. The varieties of Nahuatl that continue to be spoken in the areas outside Mexico City are noticeably different from Classical Nahuatl, a reflection of the earlier situation, in which there was (and still is) considerable dialect diversity, which is hardly surprising for a language that once counted its speakers in the millions.

Social Groupings

Mexica society was sharply divided into a number of social classes. Highest in status were the nobility. They were called *pillōtl*, and nobleman or noblewoman *pilli*, both words being derived from –*pil* 'offspring' (either son or daughter). They were the ruling class and were those from whom the ruler or king (*tlaʔtoāni*, from *tlaʔtoā* 'to speak') was chosen. From this class were also drawn the *tētēuctin* 'lords' (singular *tēuctli*), who served the state in a variety of bureaucratic positions. (In this chapter, we write Aztec in the traditional Hispanicized writing system, as described in appendix I.)

Next in status were the long-distance merchants, the *pōchtēcaʔ* (sg. *pōchtēcatl*), who traveled to the frontiers of the empire and beyond, trafficking in luxury goods. The artisans who produced luxury items for the nobility were called *Tōltēcaʔ* (sg. *Tōltēcatl*) 'Toltecs', because in theory it was the Toltecs, the inhabitants of Tula, who developed the art of goldsmithing, silversmithing, feather working, and working with gem stones. In status they ranked right after the *pōchtēcaʔ*.

Finally there were the commoners, or *mācēhualtin* (sg. *mācēhualli*), who made up the bulk of the population, but did not form a unified group in either rank or occupation. There were local merchants (not to be confused with the *pōchtēcaʔ* or long-distance merchants) who sold goods in the markets that were to be found in each city. The cities were also served by carpenters, haulers of water, and a host of other workers. Unlike the artisans who produced luxury items, those who made utilitarian objects, such as pottery or mats, were usually part-time craftsmen. In the countryside, most of the commoners were farmers.

Rank, occupation, and ethnic affiliation were marked by differences in dress and personal ornamentation; for example, only nobles wore cotton clothing, while commoners wore clothing of maguey fiber. Although there is no mention of speech differences based on rank or occupation, we do know that there were differences of address based on the rank of the speaker and addressee. Birth was the most important factor in establishing rank, but merit and ability also played a role. An individual's position within the nobility was validated by that person's deeds and a commoner could move to the noble ranks. The priesthood cut across the system of rank; noble and commoner parents alike could dedicate a son or a daughter to the temple, where they would be trained to conduct the various religious rites. Each occupational group had its patron god and various religious rites associated with it. The *pōchtēcaʔ* and luxury artisans had their own gods, temples, priests and priestesses, and associated religious rites.

The basic social unit beyond the family was the *calpōlli* (from *cal–* 'house', plus a passive form of *pōhua* 'count'), a land-holding unit composed of a group of related families. Those in the city were often quite large, numbering several thousand people. Each *calpōlli* had its own temple and school. The artisans of luxury goods (who were often imported from foreign lands) and the long-distance merchants formed their own *calpōlli*. The *calpōllec*, the elected leader, dealt directly with the state; he kept track of the boundaries of the communal land and allocated fields to the individual families; he was in charge of organizing the communal labor for the state and raising the army units in time of war and was responsible for the collection of taxes.

Education and the Verbal Arts

Parents were responsible for instructing a child in morals and in practical knowledge, such as farming, weaving, cooking and the like; the elders (over fifty) were responsible for passing on more esoteric knowledge. A child's education began at birth. The midwife spoke to the baby, telling it what kind of world it was born into, and what kind of life to expect; for example, "Thou hast come to reach the earth, where thy relatives, thy kinsmen suffer exhaustion, where they suffer fatigue. It becometh hot, it becometh cold, the wind bloweth. It is a place of thirst, a place of hunger, a place of no gladness, a place of no joy, a place of exhaustion, of fatigue, of torment." This pessimistic view of life is one that the Mexica child could expect to hear for the rest of its life.

Nothing is known of the informal linguistic enculturation that took place during the child's first few years, but we have a fairly complete picture of later years because the well-developed institutions of formal education have been fully discussed in the early records. There were two institutions, one religious, the *calmecac*, the other secular or military, the *tēlpōchcalli*. Each temple, dedicated to a particular god, had its associated *calmecac* (*cal–* 'house', *meca–* 'rope', but in this context, 'lineage'). In charge were the *tlamatinime?* (*tlamatini*, sg., from *tla–mati* 'to know something, be knowledgeable'), 'wise men, sages'. In theory, the *calmecac* was only open to the children of nobility, but those from the merchant class, as well as an occasional commoner, attended as well. If children were dedicated by their parents to a temple, they would, after completing the *calmecac*, enter the priesthood; this possibility was open to both the nobility and commoners and to both sexes. A *calmecac* education was also a prerequisite for entering the higher occupations reserved for the nobility, such as kings, governors, public administrators, lawyers, judges, and the like. Some authorities said instruction began at age six or seven and lasted to age twenty; others said it started at age fifteen. We may guess that those of higher rank and those who dedicated their children to the temple may have started earlier and thus received a fuller education. The young scholar learned, among other things, the art of rhetoric, the various religious rites, which included learning the sacred verses by heart, and the art of writing (or better, near writing; see later discussion).

Each *calpōlli* had its own *tēlpōchcalli* (*tēlpōch–* 'young man', *cal–* 'house'), which was open to boys of all classes and, indeed, was mandatory for those who did not enter the *calmecac*. The training was intellectually and physically less rigorous and was of shorter duration. It began at about age twelve and finished at about age fifteen. The emphasis was on the martial arts and community service.

Far more important for intellectual and language instruction than the *tēlpōchcalli*, however, was the *cuīcalli* or *cuīcacalli*, 'song house'. There boys and girls between the ages of about twelve and fifteen were gathered before sunset and instructed in music, dance, rhetoric, and morals. Each *calpōlli*, whether of nobles or commoners, had a *cuīcalli*, and elders of both sexes in the *calpōlli* were the instructors.

These formal institutions were the means for introducing the young to the rich set of Mexica verbal arts that formed such an important part of Mexica intellectual life. Although military achievement was important for a man's advancement in Mexica political life, it needed to be coupled with a knowledge of public speaking. The king, the highest public official, was called *tlaʔtoāni*, literally 'speaker'. He did not simply inherit his position by birth; rather, he was chosen from a leading family, with his ability as an orator given particular consideration. Verbal knowledge, ability, and expression were also the foundation for advancement in more purely intellectual pursuits such as the priesthood.

Fashions of Speaking and the Verbal Arts

We know very little about the everyday fashions of speaking, but a great deal about the well-developed aspects of verbal art, including oratory, poetry, the verbal aspects of religious rites, and sacred and profane knowledge codified in memorized treatises on a variety of subjects ranging from history to the sciences. Much of this knowledge was memorized by the scholar-priests. We also know what parents told their children about various aspects of exemplary behavior, including proper speaking. Moderation was stressed in all aspects of behavior, be it dress, manner of walking, eating and, in particular, speech. Thus a noble father told his son:

> Thou art to speak very slowly, very deliberately; thou art not to speak
> hurriedly, not to pant, nor to squeak, lest it be said of thee that thou
> art a groaner, a growler, a squeaker. Also thou art not to cry out, lest
> thou be known as an imbecile, a shameless one, a rustic, very much
> a rustic. Moderately, middlingly art thou to carry, to emit thy spirit,
> thy words. And thou art to improve, to soften thy words, thy voice.

These were words from "our forefathers as they departed, in order that thou mayest dwell with others on earth, in order that thou mayest be prudent in all things." Inasmuch as they were words from the ancients, they represented, by implication, the wisdom of the ages. It was expected that a great warrior might speak boastfully and in an immoderate fashion but, according to Sahagún, such people were unadapted for the tasks of government. Keep in mind that many of Sahagún's sources were Mexica scholars, so we cannot be sure the warriors would have subscribed to this view.

The Mexica produced a vast and varied quantity of literature and, even though a considerable amount of it exists today, it appears to be only a fraction of the original. Although some of it seems to be traditional, a good deal was composed by individuals who are identified by name. Almost all was in verse, to facilitate memorization. Because there was a leisure class that had the time to devote itself to cultivation of the arts, the Mexica were able to do so on a wider scale than the simpler speech communities that we have considered earlier in this chapter. Among the *tlamatini*, there were some who specialized in literature and among the nobility there were some noted authors. Texcoco was the acknowledged cultural center of the empire and parents from the nobility who wished their children to have a cultured education would send their children to a *calmecac* in that city.

Since the topic of Nahuatl verbal art is too extensive to cover here, we will look at only three types: oratory and moral instruction, poetry, and historical chronicles.

Oratory and Moral Instruction

It is not clear that the Nahuatl scholar recognized these two types of speech as a single genre. We will, nonetheless, consider them together, because their structure and intent are similar. It is clear, however, that moral instructions, moral admonitions on proper deportment, constituted a Nahuatl genre, since it had a name: *huehuetla?tōlli*, literally 'words of the ancient ones' or 'discourse of the elders'. The *huehuetla?tōlli* were important in Mexica society, which put such a heavy stress on ethical behavior, moderation, and a very strong work ethic.

Some of the best examples of oratory and *huehuetla?tōlli* followed a similar structure or plan. First in a speech was a greeting to the person or persons being addressed; for example, this speech by an elderly dignitary after the newly installed ruler had spoken to the citizens of the city: "O master, O ruler, O our lord, thy vassals here take, here grasp, here rejoice in, here take pleasure in the little, the small bit of thy spirit, thy word, which cometh forth, which sparketh forth; that which our lord gave thee, which he placed within thee: the precious, the wonderful, the incomparable, which lieth inert, lieth folded in thy lap, within thy breast." After the introduction, the orator usually showed his modesty by depreciating himself, as in this example in which the king replied to the priests who had just installed him as the new ruler of the city: "Perhaps thou hast mistaken me for another, I who am a commoner; I who am a laborer. In excrement, in filth hath my lifetime been—I who am unreliable; I who am of filth, of vice. And I am an imbecile. Why? For what reason? It is perhaps my desert, my merit that thou takest me from the excrement, from the filth, that thou placest me on the reed mat, on the reed seat?" Depreciation of the speaker is not found in the *huehuetlaʔtōlli*, probably because, unlike oratory, these words are not those of the speaker but rather words that represent the wisdom of the ancient ones.

The body of most speeches and *huehuetlaʔtōlli* included admonitions on how to behave and how not to behave. We gave an example earlier from a moral discourse, in which a noble father told his son how to speak. A typical ending is seen in the following discourse from an older merchant to a young merchant going out on his first trip: "Perhaps once more thy mothers, thy fathers, and thy kinsmen will look thee in the face. Verily, what thou shalt eat and drink will be the advice we here give thee. For with all this we gird, fortify, and bind thee. We thy mothers and fathers implore thee: pay good attention; look well; take care, O my son. Go in peace, leaving thy aunts and uncles."

Poetry

Poetry was called *in xōchitl in cuīcatl* (literally 'the flower, the song'), indicating that it was recognized as a distinct genre and, within that poetry, several different kinds of both sacred and profane types were recognized. Poetry was sung to the accompaniment of a drum and sometimes a flute. Topics were varied and included themes dealing with nature, especially flowers, one's place in nature, and religion. An example dealing with nature follows, composed by a foreign diplomat, who viewed the Valley of Mexico from the mountains, as he was coming into the capital, Tenochtitlán:

I climb; I reach the height.
The huge blue-green lake
Now quiet, now angry,
Foams and sings among the rocks . . .
Flowery water, green-stone water,
Where the splendid swan
With its rippling feathers
Calling swims to and fro.

In addition to poetry by known authors, there were poems or songs that were an integral part of religious ceremonies.

Historical Chronicles

The Mexica were interested in history in order to validate their cultural roots, as well as to trace and validate royal genealogies. The following example describes the arrival of the Mexica's legendary ancestors at the Toltec capital of Tula:

Year 2-House:
here for the first time was made the "binding of years" [cycle of 52 years]
On the hill of Coatepetl the fire was lighted, in the year 2-Reed.
In the year 3-Flint:
the Mexicans arrived at Tula.
In the year 9-Reed:
the Mexicans had been twenty years in Tula.
Year 10-Flint:
they arrived at Atlitlalaquian.
There they remained eleven years.
In the year 8-Reed they came to Tlemaco.
In Tlemaco they remained five years.
In the year 13-Flint:
they arrived at Atotonilco.
Four years the Mexicans remained in Atotonilco. . . .

Mexica scholars did not make a clear separation between what we might term myth or legend versus history; this seems curious only if we view this genre from our cultural point of view rather than from theirs. From the Mexica perspective, it was not important if the account was totally "correct," or partly legend or purely legendary; what was important was that it was believed to be a true account of their origins. Many of the chronicles, especially those that came closer to the historical period (in the European sense), were rooted in a chronology through use of the Aztec calendar with references to the years: 2-House, 3-Flint, and so on, as just illustrated.

Doublets and Metaphors

In Nahuatl pictorial writing, speech was indicated by a scroll coming from the speaker's mouth; if it was song or poetry, flowers were added to the scrolls. From the samples we have cited, we can see that the Mexica greatly valued flowery language; but the samples of highly regarded speech from the fifteenth and sixteenth centuries are for the most part the product of scholars and educated gentlemen and ladies, so we do not know to what extent these kinds of speech touched the common people.

A number of devices were used to produce flowery speech. One is the use of a set of grammatical devices called the reverential, which is discussed in section 6.1. Another device uses doublets, the pairing of words or phrases in which the meaning of the two parts is the same. The Nahuatl verbal artist enjoyed saying the same thing a second time, using different words. This device was used in *machiyōtla?tōlli* ('words of example') or metaphors. For example:

> 'poetry'   *in xōchitl in cuīcatl* (the flower, the
>   song)

'war'	*in ātl in tlachinolli* (the water, the conflagration)
'governmental authority'	*in petlatl in icpalli* (the mat, the chair)
'city'	*in ātl in tepētl* (the water, the mountain)
'his speech'	*itlaʔtōl iʔyo* (his word, his breath)

Doublets are also used to good effect in oratory and other prose. An example from a *huehuetlaʔtōlli* in which the father is admonishing his daughter:

> *Huel xiccaqui nochpochtze, nopiltze. Ayeccan in tlalticpac, amo pacoaya, amo huellamachohuaya. Zan mitoa ciauhcapacohuaya, chichinacapacohuaya tlalticpac.*

> Listen well, my child, my little girl. There is no place of well-being on the earth, there is no happiness, no pleasure. They say that the earth is a place of painful pleasure, of grievous happiness.

The pairs are:

nochpochtze, nopiltze	'oh my daughter, oh my child'
amo pacoaya, amo huellamachohuaya	'there is no happiness, there is no pleasure'
ciauhcapacohuaya, chichinacapacohuaya	'it is weary happiness, it is painful happiness'

(The other words in the passage are: *huel* 'well'; *xiccaqui* 'listen!'; *ayeccan* 'not a good or just place'; *in tlalticpac* 'on earth'; *zan* 'just, only'; *mitoa* 'it is said'.) The doublets also have parallel linguistic structure; for example, the first pair uses the prefix *no–* 'my', and the honorific vocative suffix *–tze*, the negative *amo* is used with both verbs in the second; and the verbs in both the second and third doublet are in the imperfect (suffix *–ya*).

The Place of Writing

The students in the *calmecac* were under the watchful eye of the scholar-priests and were carefully taught what were called the "gods' songs," which were inscribed in books (i.e., codices). Students were also all taught "the reckoning of the days, the book of dreams and the book of years." Their accomplishments are celebrated in poetry; for example,

I sing the pictures of the book
and see them spread out;
I am an elegant bird
for I make the codices speak
within the house of pictures.

The so-called writing of the ancient Aztecs was a notational system that was more than simply pictographic, yet less than full writing, a system that has been termed a mixed or transitional system of writing. The Nahuatl called the system *tlaʔcuilōlli* 'writing, painting' (derived from *tlaʔcuiloā, iʔcuiloā* 'to write, paint'), because the symbols were most commonly painted on paper (*āmatl* 'paper, book'). Modern scholars have come to call the symbols glyphs, and the manner of notation hieroglyphic. The books are referred to as codices (sg. codex). The scribe was called *tlaʔcuiloʔ* 'writer, painter'. He used a variety of colors, since most glyphs had their own characteristic color; for this reason the books in bright and varied colors were metaphorically called *in tlīlli in tlapalli* 'the black, the red', a term that could be extended to refer to the wisdom of the ancient ones. With some exceptions (e.g., numbers and dates), the notations were not "read" in the usual sense; instead, a scholar memorized the text and used the writing to jog the memory. The verb used for 'to read' is *pōhua*, the basic meaning of which is 'to count, to relate'. We specifically focus here on the place of "the black and the red" in Aztec society; for discussion of the writing system, see section 8.3.

The most frequent uses of the notational system were tied, directly or indirectly, to the calendar. The codices include *xiuhāmatl* 'the book of years' (*xiuh–* 'year', *āma–* 'book'), *tōnalāmatl* 'the book of days' (*tōnal–* 'sun, day'), *tēmicāmatl* 'the book of dreams' (*tēmic–* 'dream'), *tōnalpōhualli* 'the reckoning of days' (*pōhualli* 'the count'). These works were indispensable for the priest in conducting the yearly round of ceremonies, for the astrologer and diviner (*tonālpōuhqui*, with *–pōuhqui* from *pōhua* 'to count'), and for others who needed to refer to the calendar to know which days were propitious for undertaking a certain activity, for selecting the day for naming the newborn infant, and the like.

History, also rooted in a chronology, was another important subject for the codices. Although dates and numbers were very accurately written, the narrative parts were indicated by mnemonic devices; for example, the migration of the ancestral Nahuatl people is shown by a picture of the priests carrying their patron god, with footprints showing the direction of travel. The notational system was also used for more mundane purposes. Judges, for example "calmly and prudently . . . heard the plaints of the vassals; in the picture writing which recorded the case, they studied the complaints." In addition, the system was used to keep track of taxes and tribute, accounts in the royal storehouses and, on a more local level, it was used by officials within the *calpōlli* who needed to keep records for such things as the allocation of the communal lands and a roster of men available for public service work and the military.

The books did not replace memorization. On the contrary, they nurtured it. Much of the student's academic study at the *calmecac* was devoted to memorizing traditional lore and other verbal material that was written in cryptic fashion in the codices. This practice is reminiscent of the preliterate society of ancient India, which had a very strong academic tradition, from which an incredible amount of scholarly material was put to memory, a practice that continued long after Sanskrit became a written language.

We do not know what proportion of the population was able to interpret the glyphs. We do know that writing was primarily an activity of the nobility, but was not restricted to them. Some merchants knew the system, as well as an occasional commoner, especially those who had official duties within the *calpōlli*, for example, persons responsible for tabulating the taxes, keeping track of men available for military service, keeping track of the communal lands and so on. We also know that scribes enjoyed considerable prestige.

The Place of Nahuatl in Mesoamerica

Almost half a millennium after the fall of the Aztec Empire, modern Nahuatl is spoken with considerable dialect variation by perhaps half a million speakers. Does this modern diversity of dialects reflect the linguistic picture of the time of the empire when there were several million speakers? Although we do not have much specific information regarding precontact dialect diversity, early Spanish observers, as well as the Mexica themselves, noted that there were differences between the Nahuatl spoken in the Mexica heartland and some of the more distant communities. In the modern communities, there is a marked tendency for the speech of those areas that were not a part of the Aztec empire to show the greatest divergence, even though there are still some striking differences between the communities that were within the empire. It seems safe to extrapolate (in a general fashion, at least) this situation back to the time of Classical Nahuatl.

As we have said before, the Mexica considered themselves the spiritual and cultural descendants of the Toltec, a civilization whose capital of Tula was about a hundred kilometers north of Tenochtitlán. The prestige of the Toltec rubbed off on the language they spoke: According to Sahagún's account, "These Tolteca, as is said, were Nahua; they did not speak a barbarous tongue. However, their language they called Nonoalca. They said as they conversed: 'my noble lord: my lord younger brother; my lord elder brother'." This passage suggests that the Toltecs were admired for their appropriate use of speech etiquette (i.e., a fashion of speaking). There are, however, suggestions in Sahagún and elsewhere that the speech of Tula may have been dialectally slightly different. In another passage from Sahagún, we are also told that "All the Nahua, those who speak clearly, not the speakers of a barbarous tongue, are the descendants of the Tolteca." The Mexica believed that the people of Tula moved to the southern end of the Valley of Mexico and that a woman from one of these communities brought the language to Texcoco during the reign of Techotlalatzin. Again, the truth of this statement is not important (in fact, from what we know of the nature of language transmission, it is unlikely), but the statement tells us what the Mexica thought about the speech of the Toltecs. As the acknowledged cultural leaders within the Triple Alliance, the nobles of Texcoco were thought to preserve the best and purest form of the language.

We do not know if the Nahuatl spoken by the Mexica enjoyed greater status in other Nahuatl-speaking cities of the empire; however, contemporary dialect studies show that linguistic innovations that originated in the Valley of Mexico (perhaps from Tenochtitlán, perhaps from Texcoco, or perhaps in an even earlier time from Tula) had spread to other Nahuatl-speaking communities; presumably this expansion is not recent, but goes back to the time of the empire. If linguistic innovations were spreading from the Valley of Mexico to the hinterland, it is likely that the variety of Nahuatl spoken by the Mexica was considered more prestigious.

Whereas the majority of the cities that were incorporated into the empire spoke Nahuatl, there were many ethnic groups that spoke other languages. Some of the major groups included: Otomí, found mainly to the north and west of the Mexica, but with scattered enclaves in other places; the Mayan language of Huastec, spoken in the north on the Gulf Coast; the Totonac languages, on the Gulf Coast to the northeast; the Zapotecan, Popolocan, and Mazatecan languages to the southeast; Cuitlatec, Tlapanec, and Mixtec to the south; and Matlazinca to the west. Many of these languages were also spoken in areas outside the empire. The most distant part of the empire was the Soconusco district in what is now Chiapas, where Pipil (an Aztecan language), Zoque, and Mangue were spoken, and perhaps also some Mayan languages. In addition, the Mexica knew most of those people outside the empire who were part of the civilized Mesoamerican world, mostly because of trade relations. They knew all too well the Tarascans on their western frontier, whom they fought against in a bitter war, but failed to bring into the empire. They also knew and traded with cities in the Mayan area where there were (and still are) some thirty quite different languages; however, the Mexica were perhaps less familiar with their languages than those closer to home because the Mayan languages, with the exception of the Huastec found to the north on the Gulf Coast, were located in the far southern and eastern parts of Mesoamerica and were the most distant from the Mexica.

As a result of conquest and warfare, there were dislocations in the distribution of populations, and depopulated areas were resettled by governmental design.

Although some of the dislocations concerned only Nahuatl-speaking populations, perhaps peoples of diverse Nahuatl dialects were also reshuffled. In other cases, enclaves of Nahuatl or other languages were located outside their home area and consequently surrounded by peoples speaking different languages.

Valuable insights into the native view of foreign languages are found in Sahagún; for example, he writes that the Matlatzinca "spoke a barbarous tongue, but there were those who spoke Nahuatl. The way they pronounced their language made it somewhat unintelligible; in their language was the letter 'r' "; or concerning the Totonac: "Their language was a barbarous tongue, although some spoke Otomí, some spoke Nahuatl, some spoke also the Huaxteca [Huastec] language." The translation, "their language was a barbarous tongue," is in Totonac: *In intlatol popoloca*; the word *intlatol* means 'their language', while *popoloca* means 'to speak a language badly, to speak a foreign language, to speak unintelligibly'. Today several languages have the unflattering name *Popoloca*, which, as one might guess, is not the name the speakers gave to their own language.

On the northern frontier were tribes who lived a nomadic way of life, hunting and gathering. Collectively known under the name Chichimec, they are discussed at length in Sahagún. Concerning language: "There were also the Nahuachichimeca, those who understood, who also therefore spoke, the Nahuatl language and a barbarous tongue. Also there were the so-called Otonchichimeca. These were called Otonchichimeca because they spoke a barbarous tongue and Otomí. Also there were the Cuextecachichimeca, who were called Cuextecachichimeca because they spoke a barbarous tongue and Cuexteca." The attitude toward the so-called Chichimec was ambivalent: on the one hand, the Mexica looked down on them for their unsettled way of life and rustic ways; on the other hand, they were admired for their simple virtues and physical stamina. The Mexica were proud of a mythology that claimed a recent Chichimec past. In chapter 13, we will see that there is some basis for positing a northern origin for the Mexica (and other Nahuatl-speaking peoples); however, what is again important here is not what the true situation might be, but rather the fact that the Mexica believed in the Chichimec connection and that it colored their attitude toward the Chichimec tribes and their languages.

Markets, Traders, and Artisans

The market, along with the traders and artisans—the two groups most responsible for its development—had a profound effect on the speech communities. Long-distance trade in luxury goods goes back to 1200 B.C. and it is likely that the marketplace, along with traders and artisans, played an equally ancient role in Mesoamerican society.

Every city had its *tiānquiztli* or 'market' (from *tiāmiqui* 'to buy and sell'). In smaller towns, market day came once a week (which was five days long in the Aztec calendar); the larger cities would have a daily market, but with a larger one every fifth day, on that city's market day. The market was a standard feature not just of the Nahuatl area, but throughout Mesoamerica. The largest one was in Tlatelolco, the commercial center for the Triple Alliance; the early Spanish arrivals estimated that there were between twenty- and twenty-five thousand people in the market each day and forty to fifty thousand on market day. The language of the market was, of course, Nahuatl, but it was not always the first language of the traders; it was not uncommon to see Otomí or other foreign traders who had come to market to sell their goods.

As we have seen, the trader, or *pōchtēca?*, formed a special class in the Mexica social order. Tlatelolco was the commercial center in the Triple Alliance and had the most important and influential merchant guild, but there were also guilds in Tenochtitlán, Texcoco, and several other Nahuatl-speaking cities in the Valley of Mexico. The traders often learned the languages of the foreign lands they visited; but this was not always necessary, because Nahuatl was widely used as a trade language, not only within the empire, but also beyond. There is evidence that its use as a trade language predates the rise of the Aztec Empire and that the dialect used was a little different from that used in the cities of the Triple Alliance.

There was a special group of merchants called "disguised traders" who undertook journeys to foreign lands. Their mode of dress and their haircuts were, for example, like the dress and haircuts of Tzinacantla, Cimatlan, or Otomí natives and, according to Sahagún, "they learned their tongue to enter in disguise. And no one at all could tell whether they were perchance Mexicans when they were anointed with ochre." Their purpose was not only trade, but also the searching out of intelligence for the army's next conquest. They were highly motivated to speak the language like a native with no trace of Nahuatl accent, for detection would mean an end not only to their trading expedition, but their lives as well.

Because the artisans of luxury goods from certain conquered nations had a reputation of being highly skilled, they were brought to the capital, sometimes from other Nahuatl-speaking cities, but other times from faraway places, and these foreign artisans formed ethnic enclaves of Mixtec-speaking peoples from Oaxaca and people from the Gulf Coast. There is archaeological evidence that this was a long-standing practice in Mesoamerica, to be found in such ancient prehistoric cities as Teotihuacán before the rise of the Aztec Empire.

4.5   SPEECH COMMUNITY, THE
SOCIAL GROUP, AND CULTURE

The nature of the speech community reflects both the nature of the society and the
nature of the culture. For this reason, it is necessary to understand the differences
among societal types (or what some anthropologists would call societal levels).
We distinguish these types: (1) nomadic foraging societies, (2) village societies,
(3) stratified states. These societal types are defined primarily in terms of economic
and political organization. Our paramount interest, however, is how the nature of
the societal type affects settlement patterns and, in turn, linguistic interaction.

Examples of the first type include the societies in the Great Basin, the Eskimo and
the Northern Athapaskan, and most northern Algonquian tribes of the subarctic.
Political units larger than the family did not usually play a large role. Suprafamilial
groupings and leadership were limited and often temporary. Individuals belonged to
interlocking networks of kinfolk.

For settled village societies, farming often provides the economic base, as among
the southwestern Pueblos, the villages of the Creek Confederacy and other groups
in the Southeast, the Iroquois and eastern Algonquians of the northeastern woodlands, and some of the tribes of the eastern Plains. Village life, however, is not limited to farming communities; a favorable environment can lead to settled life, as in
California and the Northwest Coast, where there are well-developed suprafamilial
organizations and leadership is more permanent. The buffalo-hunting groups of the
High Plains also belong in this category. Even though they were nomadic and split
into small groups during part of the year, they did constitute a political unit and
their leadership was typical of that found in village groups. There are no classes
in these village societies; thus, in the Northwest Coast all men were fishermen,
whereas in the Pueblos and villages of the Creek Confederacy, all men were farmers.
In some cases, as in the Northwest Coast and in the Creek Confederacy, rank is important, with individuals being born to families or kin groups (such as clans) that
had greater or lesser wealth or prestige. Rank, however, is missing in other village
groups, such as the Pueblos.

An example of a stratified state is seen in the society of the Natchez who lived
along the lower Mississippi, but such societies were more typical farther south, in
Mesoamerica and in the Andes of South America. The Aztec had a well-developed
class system in which a person was born into the class of nobles (the ruling class),
traders, artisans, or commoners (although, as we saw, there was some chance for
mobility). In some cases, the political unit was a local group or city; in other cases,
it was a larger group or empire that incorporated a number of different ethnic and
linguistic groups.

The Society, Language Boundaries, and Linguistic Diversity

Nomadic foragers typically lack sharp boundaries, since there are no permanent residential units larger than the family. Instead, one finds a network of relationships over a wide area. When two very different cultural types adjoin, there may be a sharp boundary (e.g., Northern Athapaskan and Eskimo, or Cree and Eskimo), but they can be blurred with extended contact (e.g., Washo and Northern Paiute). The latter case shows that language difference does not mean that there will necessarily be a difference in culture. There need not even be a sharp language boundary (e.g., Northern Paiute and Shoshoni; Cree and Ojibwa).

We saw from the example of Great Basin societies that there can be internal diversity in unstratified communities; however, because such speech communities are small face-to-face groups, they offer less potential for diversity than more complex groups. In a stratified society, such as the Aztec, there is opportunity for internal differences, both between classes and between different ethnic groups, for stratified societies can be multiethnic.

Language shift through replacive bilingualism (the giving up of one language for another, as discussed in section 9.4) can take place in unstratified societies, as we saw in the Creek example, but it is not as common or sweeping as in stratified societies. There is always a tendency (sometimes slight, sometimes great) for homogenization of the linguistic diversity within a stratified society. We saw this tendency in Aztec, in which linguistic innovations spread out from the Valley of Mexico to Nahuatl-speaking communities in the hinterlands of the empire.

Stratified and village societies with sharper societal boundaries offer a greater potential for linguistic diversity than foraging societies. Stratified states, especially empires, while displaying greater internal diversity, often exhibit homogenizing tendencies, so that village societies actually offer the greatest potential for overall diversity (i.e., measuring the number of languages and/or distinct dialects, say, per one hundred thousand people); thus, the Pueblos and Creek Confederacy village societies displayed greater per capita diversity than the Great Basin on the one hand, and the Aztec Empire on the other.

While villages offer the greatest potential for linguistic diversity, such diversity is not guaranteed. Other factors must be considered: History plays a part, but is largely unrecoverable for nonliterate societies; the density, distribution, and stability of the population are important, and these depend partly on societal type, partly on the distribution and availability of the natural resources. Precontact California exhibited greater diversification of resources in a smaller area than any other place in North America; a considerable variety of biotic resources were often available in a range of just a few square miles; thus, small groups could be self-sufficient in small areas, in permanently settled villages. These conditions, along with the fact that most California societies are well-bounded tribal societies, contributed to a diversity of languages that is probably unsurpassed elsewhere in the world, except in New Guinea.

With sharper societal boundaries, dialects are often easier to delineate among village dwellers than nomadic foragers; thus, Keres is spoken in seven isolatable dialects in seven pueblos, among which intermarriage is at a minimum. The dialect situation among the Yokuts of California seems to have been similar. Shoshoni, on the other hand, displays as much dialect diversity, but the transitions are gradual.

The question of numbers is important also. In the whole of the Great Basin, there were about twenty thousand people, the same number reported to be present at the market on an ordinary (nonmarket) day in Tlatelolco. In the Great Basin, contact with just a handful of families or even a single family speaking a foreign dialect or language could have an effect on the communicative network of the local speech community. In Mesoamerica, contact with a single family speaking a foreign language would be a drop in the bucket; we must in this case be concerned instead with groups of people instead of a handful of families or a single family. Although it is the interaction between individuals that is important for understanding all speech communities, with larger numbers there is a different chemistry, which in turn affects the results of the language contact. In the Great Basin, people knew, from personal experience, the language repertoire of almost everybody with whom they came in contact. In a large stratified society, one is often in contact with strangers (as in the market place, for example). The Aztec solved this problem by using dress and personal adornment as a means of marking class and ethnic identity (a very common solution in stratified societies), so that one would know how to address a stranger and what language to use.

Language and dialects are always available as symbols of identity; however, they can be used as a symbol for group solidarity ("us" vs. "them") only if there are clear boundaries; therefore, there is less potential in foraging groups than in the other two types. Language is more apt to be used as a symbol of identity in areas of linguistic diversity, in cases in which the languages are unique (e.g., Zuni, spoken at one Pueblo, as contrasted with Tewa, spoken at several), and in cases in which the linguistic differences are greater (e.g., Hopi and Arizona Tewa as contrasted with the Keres dialects). (It should, however, be noted that a strong sense of group identity or solidarity can also develop without language as the symbol to express it.)

Linguistic enculturation in foraging societies is influenced by the absence of sharp boundaries and by the fact that the child is in contact with a small but linguistically variable group of people. Such societies do not seem to allow for the development of a peer group, probably a necessary ingredient for the development of slang, which was apparently absent in the basin, but present at Zuni.

Culture, Belief Systems, and Language

There is considerable cross-cultural variation in the beliefs about language, but, for the most part, the variation corresponds to other aspects of cultural variation and not to societal type; for example, many peoples believe their own language or dialect to be superior to others. This belief is present in the Pueblos and is related to Pueblo ethnocentrism, while it is absent in the Great Basin. That this is not simply a difference between foraging and village societies is apparent from Australian foraging societies, which have very strong beliefs in the superiority of their own forms of speech. Somewhat different, however, is the notion that a particular language or dialect, not necessarily one's own, should be granted favored status because it is the best. Such a belief is common in stratified societies and is found sporadically in the more complex societies of North America: for example, the favored position of Creek in the Creek Confederacy, of Mohawk in the Iroquois League, and of Hupa in northwestern California. This attitude was more sharply defined in Aztec society, where it was felt that the language spoken at Texcoco was superior to that spoken in other Nahuatl-speaking cities. Prestige and belief in language superiority lead to the development of standard languages, a characteristic of modern industrialized society.

Involuted societies provide the potential for a greater range of fashions of speaking; for example, the Pueblo communities have a well-developed ceremonial style, a well-developed chanting style for making public announcements (for the western Pueblos only), and a well-developed style for public speaking; these styles are not as developed in the Great Basin. Cultural attitudes about language, however, are more important than societal type: A society that greatly values language is more apt to elaborate fashions of speaking (e.g., Australian societies, where language is highly valued, and styles are highly elaborated).

Limiting Factors

Certain features are limited to or only fully elaborated in stratified societies, namely, social dialects, honorifics, writing, trade languages, and lingua francas. Dialects arise from isolation. If the isolation is geographic, regional dialects result, if social, social dialects result. Social isolation is most often associated with social-class boundaries, hence social dialects are usually limited to stratified societies. (A familiar example in the United States is African-American English, which is used by many members of the African-American communities located in most large cities in the United States.) We saw hints of social dialects among the Nahuatl speakers, with the cultured speech of the nobility at Texcoco being highly esteemed. Unfortunately information from the historical record is not full enough for us to know the details of the situation.

All speech communities recognize that a change of speech is called for in addressing people of higher status and sometimes, also, when talking about such a person or when talking about an exalted topic. Some languages have institutionalized this difference by having well-marked differences in vocabulary, or special respect or honorific forms that are embedded in the core of the grammatical or phonological system. Although respect forms exist in North American languages, complex elaboration is found more commonly in the languages of stratified societies, as for example the Aztec (see chapter 6 for fuller discussion).

As discussed in chapter 8, writing is seldom found unless there is a need for the storing and transfer of information on a scale that cannot be handled by oral means, a condition never met in unstratified societies. The presence of writing can cause oral traditions to become less elaborated and less important, particularly for those involved in the cultural transmission of information from one generation to the next. This did not happen in the Aztec case, however, because the near-writing system served as a mnemonic for memorization, which then served to greatly stimulate the oral tradition. Writing was introduced or its invention was stimulated after European contact (e.g., the Cree and the Cherokee, see chapter 8) in groups that in precontact times were unstratified; in these cases, the groups in question had become part of a larger, composite, European-derived society.

Trade languages, for example, Nahuatl in Mesoamerican trade, are limited to societies that have large-scale, institutionalized trade. The marketplace and other such institutions that are a product of stratified societies are often important. Chinook Jargon, a lingua franca (discussed in section 10.2), seems to have been a pre-Columbian development, but it was not widely used until the development of the fur trade, a post-European contact development. Although lingua francas are found in unstratified societies, they are given greater scope in stratified societies.

American Indian Speech Communities Today

We have seen how language use and function played out in aboriginal times in four quite different communities in the Americas. These communities have undergone considerable change since European contact. Two facts stand out: first, they are now part of larger societies and, second, the language of the dominant society plays an increasingly important role. Although most of the Great Basin groups today live in permanent settlements ranging from a few families to over a thousand, there is still much coming and going between the communities, which reflects the ancestral migratory habits. Very little of the original political structure remains, but many other cultural and social patterns persist. The Pueblo communities remain intact, with modified but still ancestral patterns of political and social interaction. The communities that made up the Creek Confederacy have changed after more than three centuries of contact, after moving first from Georgia to Alabama and then being moved to Oklahoma; however, most members still maintain their ethnic and community identity. The Aztecs have undergone the greatest change: The political and intellectual accomplishments, the elaborate social structure and the rich religious traditions are now a thing of the past. Many of the descendants of the Aztec Empire have been absorbed into the Mexican mestizo society; those that have not been absorbed retain their language and certain aspects of their original culture, though in modified form, and belong to peasant communities that are marginal to the larger society. Many aspects of Nahuatl language etiquette persisted well into the colonial period and still persist today in the rural Nahuatl-speaking areas.

English and Spanish, the languages of the dominant societies, play an increasingly greater role, and the indigenous languages in these societies and those in almost all other indigenous communities of the Americas are endangered. But even in communities that are undergoing or have undergone a language shift, many patterns of ancestral language function and use still remain. (See chapter II for a discussion of linguistic acculturation and language shift.)

SOURCES

In section 4.1 discussion on ecological setting and social structure is from Steward 1938, 1965, and 1970; on culture and social structure from d'Azevedo 1963, 1986a, Downs 1966, C. Fowler 1982a, Fowler and Liljeblad 1986, D. Fowler 1966, Hopkins 1883, Kelly and Fowler 1986, Murphy and Murphy 1986, and Thomas et al. 1986; on language from Jacobsen 1966, Liljeblad 1986, and Miller 1966, 1970, 1986, n.d.b. In addition, discussion on language communities is from Leland 1986 (Numic-speaking populations); on linguistic acculturation from Hill 1978 and Owen 1965; on fashions of speaking and cultural focus from Sapir 1910 (Southern Paiute song) and Crum 1980 (Shoshoni song); on fashions of speaking and social category from Stewart 1960 (Ute baby talk), Goss ms. (elder speech), and Downs 1966 ("half-Paiute"). In section 4.2, the general discussion of society and culture is from Dozier 1970, Eggan 1950, 1979, and Ortiz 1979 passim; on linguistic acculturation from Dennis 1940 (Hopi), Newman 1955 (Zuni), and Stephen 1936 (Hopi). Fashions of speaking and cultural focus discussions include ceremonial speech, from Newman 1955 and 1955:347 (Zuni) and White 1944 (Keres); loanwords, from Newman 1955 and Trager 1944; tumahe formulas, from Dozier 1954:272 (Tewa); oratorical style, from Fox 1959:558–59 (Cochiti); chants, from Dozier 1954:272 (Hopi), Black 1967 (Hopi), and Voegelin and Euler 1957 (Hopi); speech chief, from Stephen 1936:941 (Hopi); storytelling, from Kroskrity 1985 (Zuni and Arizona Tewa); language used in song, from Fox 1959:559 (Cochiti); borrowed songs, from Stevenson 1904:183, 225, 424, and Stephen 1936:137, 406 (Keres as source). Fashions of speaking and social category include baby talk, discussed by Miller 1965, 1965:112, Parsons 1923:168 (Keres), Dennis 1940:35, Titiev 1946, and Voegelin and Voegelin 1957:50 (Hopi); men's and women's speech, found in Titiev 1946 (Hopi), Sims and Valiquette 1990 (Keres), and Kroskrity 1983 (Tewa); slang, from Newman 1955 (Zuni); address forms, in Kroskrity p.c. (Arizona Tewa); uses of Spanish and English, from Lange 1959:19, Fox 1959 (Cochiti), Voegelin, Voegelin, and Schutz 1967, Brandt 1970, and Leap: 1973, 1974; multilingualism and multidialectalism, from Dozier 1954:291-92 (Hopi, Arizona Tewa), Kroskrity 1981, Leap 1973:277, Dozier 1954:297, 399, Stephen 1936:xxvii, White 1935:80, and Smith and Roberts 1954:27. Linguistic awareness and attitudes include terms for speech usages, discussed in Kroskrity 1993b (Arizona Tewa); sacred and everyday vocabulary, from Newman 1955: 346, 352 (Zuni); ethnocentrism, in Dozier 1970:209 and White 1935:28-29 (Keres); bilingualism, discussed in Dozier 1954:292 and Stephen 1936:556-57 (Hopi, Tewa). Discussion in section 4.3 on Southeast culture is from Swanton 1928a, 1946; on the Creek Confederacy, Swanton 1922, 1928c, and Opler 1952; on town size, Gatschet 1884:120; on Creek dialects, Haas 1945:69, 1973b:1211-16; on bilingualism, Haas 1945: 69-70, Foreman 1930:120, 121, Haas 1974 p.c. (Yuchi, Creek), Thwaites 1896-1901:114-15, and Speck 1909 (Shawnee, Yuchi); on men and women, Swanton 1922:314 and Haas 1974 p.c.; on language shift: Haas 1945:69-70 (postremoval), Swanton 1922: 12-31, 215 (preremoval), Speck 1909 (Yuchi), Haas 1974 p.c. (bi- and multilingual families), Swanton 1922:314, Haas p.c. (passive bilingualism), and Swanton 1928c:446 (sign language). Fashions of speaking include oratorical styles, discussed in Swanton 1928c:313, Haas 1974 p.c., Swanton 1928b:610, Williams 1930:12, 66 (settings), and Haas 1974 p.c. (recent past); heralds or criers in Speck 1909:82 (Yuchi) and Swanton 1928b:610-11; storytelling in Haas 1974 p.c. (Natchez, Creek), Speck 1909:101 (Yuchi); medicine songs and formulas in Swanton 1928b:639 and Speck 1911:215; ceremonial and myth texts in Wolff 1951; "peculiar words" in Swanton 1928b:611, 616; men's and women's speech in Haas 1944 (Koasati)and Gatschet 1884:79 (Hichiti). Linguistic awareness and attitudes of Creek are discussed in Sturtevant 1971:112 (Florida Mikasukis), Speck 1909:12, and Haas 1974 p.c. (Yuchi); and of English in Haas 1974 p.c. Discussions in section 4.4 are from Berdan 1982; Carrasco 1971, Davies 1987, Fagan 1984, Soustelle 1962, and Sanders 1971:15-16 (city-states); on Mexica language and culture from Nicolau d'Olwer 1987, and León-Portilla 1969:14-18 (Sahagún). Passages from Sahagún are taken from the Dibble and Anderson translation, but written in an orthography that has come to be standard for citing Classical Nahuatl (Sullivan 1988). Unless otherwise indicated, English translations of Sahagún are by Dibble and Anderson. Suárez 1983 is the standard source for the Mesoamerican languages. Discussion on education and the verbal arts is from Sahagún 6:168 (quoted passage); fashions of speaking and the verbal arts is from Sahagún 6:122 (quoted passage),

Soustelle 1962 (Sahagún quote) 2:22 (warrior speech), Cornyn 1938:233 (verse and memorization); oratory and moral instruction is from Sahagún 6:83 (quoted passage—greeting), Sahagún 6:41 (quoted passage—depreciation of speaker), Sahagún 4:63 (quoted passage—admonition); poetry is from León-Portilla 1969:78, Soustelle 1962: 236–43 (musical accompaniment), Soustelle 1962:242 (quoted passage); on historical chronicles see León-Portilla 1969:126 (quoted passage); on doublets and metaphors see Bright 1990, Sahagún 6:93, León-Portilla 1971b:455 (quoted passage—admonition); on the place of writing see Sahagún 365, León-Portilla 1969:11 (quoted passage—poem), Dibble 1971:330 (mixed system of writing), León-Portilla 1969:12, 14–15, Fagan 1984:55 (mnemonic devices), Sahagún 8:42 (quote—judges and notational system), Berdan 1982:37 (taxes and tribute); the place of Nahuatl in the wider world of Mesoamerica: Lastra 1986:189–233, Canger 1978, 1980, Sahagún 10:170 (quote—Toltec prestige), Sahagún 10:170 (quote—Nahua), Soustelle 1962:219 (Tula woman), 232 (nobility of Texcoco); Canger 1978, 1980, Lastra 1986:211 (spread of linguistic innovations), Sahagún Book 10, Suárez 1983:148, Voorhies 1989:9–11 (Mayan languages), Calnek 1976:189–91, Carrasco 1971:374, 366 (population dislocations), Sahagún 10:182 (quote—Matlatzinca), Sahagún 10:184 (quote—Totonac), Karttunen 1983 (popoloca), Sahagún 10:175 (quote—Chichimec languages); information on markets, traders, and artisans is from Fagan 1984:204, Davies 1987:138, Berdan 1982: 32, Soustelle 1962:60, Dakin 1981, Sahagún 9:21 (quote—disguised traders), Sahagún 9:80 (Nahuatl speakers), Fagan, 1984:147–48, Berdan 1982:57, Noguera 1971, Carrasco 1971:366, Calnek 1976:289 (Mixtec-speaking peoples). In section 4.5, information on the society, language boundaries and linguistic diversity is from Wolfart 1973a (Cree, Ojibwa), Kroeber 1906:657–58, 1925–26:474 (Yokuts dialects), Newman 1955 (Zuni); culture, belief systems, and language: Strehlow 1947 (Australian foraging societies), Speck 1945:28 (Mohawk), Powers 1877:72–73 (Hupa), Garvin and Mathiot 1960, Haugen 1966:1–26 (standard languages), Karttunen and Lockhart 1991, Hill and Hill 1978 (Nahuatl language etiquette), and Philips 1970, 1983 (contemporary language use).

SUGGESTED READINGS

On section 4.1 see Crum 1980 for a discussion of Shoshoni poetry songs. In section 4.4, in-depth studies of Nahuatl literature include Cornyn 1938, Garibay K. 1954–1955, 1964 and León-Portilla 1969, 1971a, 1971b. For section 4.5, there are several very good works available on the role language plays in contemporary communities: Hill and Hill 1978, 1986, for a Nahuatl-speaking rural community in Mexico; Philips 1970, 1983, for a community in Oregon; and Kroskrity 1993b, for the trilingual Hopi-Tewa community of Arizona.

CHAPTER 5

PERFORMERS AND PERFORMANCES

The notion of **performance** is important in the study of folklore, and a grow-ing number of scholars have applied it to the study of Native American oral tra-ditions, including kinds of speech behavior other than storytelling. We examined some examples in the previous chapter: in the Great Basin songs, shamanistic or curing ceremonies, and oratory, as well as storytelling; among the Pueblos ora-tory (including the Tewa *tumahe*), chants (found only in the Western Pueblos) and songs; in the Creek Confederacy oratory, medicine songs and formulas, as well as stories; among the Aztecs oratory, moral instruction (*huehuetlaʔtōlli*), poetry, and historical chronicles. (It is possible to think of a number of examples from current Euro-American speech communities, e.g., nominating speeches, commencement addresses, prayers, sermons, jokes, jump rope songs, children's bedtime stories, and so on.)

In this chapter, we first present an overview of California Indian storytelling, and then follow it with an excerpt from an interview with a person who tells us of his understanding of the importance of this performance type. We next look at spe-cific kinds of performance in four cultures: a Chinook narrative, a Havasupai song, a Navajo prayer, and three Kuna performance types.

5.1 CALIFORNIA STORYTELLERS AND STORYTELLING

Reading traditional American Indian literature in translation or even reading a printed version in the original language often obscures certain essential character-istics of the story's telling. To persons used to English narrative styles, a story in translation may plod along with little sense of action and with a lot of seemingly unnecessary repetition. In a printed version of a myth or story, the reader's at-tention is most likely focused on the content of one storyteller's single narration. Moreover, printed versions seldom incorporate contextual information relevant to storyteller behavior, narrative style, audience participation, and settings. As a re-sult, crucial aesthetic dimensions of American Indian literary art are unavailable to readers: a sense of the storyteller, the audience, and the place and time of the telling is missing. In other words, each telling of an American Indian myth or story is a performance, and no two performances are the same.

From statements made today by Indians who remember "the old ways" (either through personal participation as children or because of information passed on to them by their "old people"), along with nineteenth- and early twentieth-century observers who described the life ways and languages of various Indian peoples, it is possible to develop a general picture of the art of storytelling as it was practiced in what is now California.

A skilled storyteller did not simply repeat a story he or she had heard or learned, but would recreate a story by arranging the incidents and plots into unique forms pleasing to the listeners. For instance, an Owens Valley Paiute narrator sometimes used only the central theme of a narrative and embellished it with new episodes and characters, and Karuk tellers of Coyote stories, besides elaborating small details, transposed, reshuffled, and omitted episodes. However, even though a storyteller would improvise and originate, she or he could not be too inventive. The audience, very much aware that there was a conventional way of treating a particular myth or tale, would disapprove of tellings that departed too much from the time-honored standard version.

In addition to being inventive, a storyteller needed other talents to win audience approval. A gift for speaking in public was essential. Additionally, the teller had to be able to use a style that contained a variety of set phrases and differed from the ordinary speech of conversation. Practically all Mohave myths were told in ritualized style. Pomoan storytelling has been compared to Bible-reading, and Achumawi storytelling to novel-reading or theater-going. A narrator also had to be an actor, able to impersonate characters by changing his or her voice to fit that of a character, to mimic facial expressions, and to illustrate the actions of various characters with appropriate hand and body movements. A storyteller identified with the characters in the story, mimicking voices and singing songs associated with particular characters. For instance, a Yokuts narrator often imitated the characteristic sounds of the birds and animals that played a part in the sequence of events. Lastly, a gifted teller of stories needed a prodigious memory. Persons who excelled as tellers of stories had so much literary material stored in their memories that they could perform for hours at a time and night after night without repeating themselves. A Nomlaki is quoted as saying that "the old people would sit in the sweathouse and tell stories for a week without repeating one."

Storytelling in California was not a specialized occupation; nevertheless, gifted storytellers were greatly admired and their services were much in demand. Exceptionally talented Miwokan narrators with well-stocked repertoires traveled from village to village to entertain listeners. They were rewarded with gifts of food, baskets, and furs, as were narrators among other groups, the Modoc and Maidu, for example.

Much storytelling knowledge was absorbed informally, almost unconsciously. From their earliest years, children heard the traditional stories recited countless times until they knew the basic substance and many of the important details by heart. Because of individual interest, special aptitude, or family tradition, some absorbed more than others.

In northern California, especially to make certain that the body of myths was properly preserved and perpetuated, an older relative often took a hand in instructing a child who showed interest and aptitude. Karuk and Shasta elders subjected children to a stringent learning process: After dark in the sweathouse, the sleeping quarters for males, a Karuk elder recited myths to boys who repeated them after him, a passage at a time. Girls received instruction in the same manner from female relatives. Shasta children experienced similar training, and it was believed that they would grow up humpbacked if they did not learn the stories. Yuki instruction took a more institutionalized form: There was a "boys' high school," and the time put in was long and arduous. This ritualistic period of instruction was supervised by an old man, and a good part of it was devoted to the teaching of mythology surrounding Taikomol, the supreme being.

In contrast to these northern groups, the Mohave and Yuma in the south felt that no training in myth-telling was necessary, since they believed that individuals dreamed the stories they told. They did, however, have a mechanism for standardizing the various accounts and their manner of presentation: a myth would be recited in the presence of older men who freely criticized a narrator's version and his delivery.

There were "rules" associated with storytelling performances. In some groups, when narrating a tale, the storyteller remained seated; in others, he or she stood facing the audience. A Kamia storyteller not only stood but swayed from side to side as the narration progressed. Certain other rules also had to be carefully observed; for example, once having started a story, a Karuk narrator had to finish it. To fail to do so would cause his back to become crooked. Among the Owens Valley Paiute, tribal traditions had to be recited with deep seriousness because improper or frivolous telling insulted the animals and natural phenomena mentioned, which in turn avenged themselves.

There were also rules for audience behavior. The Yuki had a rule that men, allowed to smoke while listening to a nonsacred story, had to put their pipes away when a myth began. Many groups had a rule that listeners must lie down; otherwise, according to Sierra Miwok and Pomoan beliefs, they would become hunchbacked. Whatever the rules, listeners actively participated. They expressed amazement at marvelous happenings, laughed at Coyote's shenanigans, and shuddered and indicated loathing at the evil deeds of cannibals and other fearsome characters. On occasion, they would exhibit, through demonstrations or statements, approval or disapproval of a character's behavior. There were also times when the audience was required to be thoughtfully silent: for instance, when a Yuki storyteller introduced a narrative with, "this is a story they told long ago," the audience knew that a myth was to follow and that its telling called for silence; listeners would interrupt from time to time only to make such comments as, "That's been done," or "It happened like that."

A traditional form, often with set phrases, was used for myth-telling. Literary devices included phrases such as, "it is said," quotatives (see section 2.6) and repetition. The frequency of reiteration depended upon the number held sacred by the group. If the sacred number was four, for example, the repetitions occurred in sets of four. The stories often had set openings and closings. In Shasta, *t'we·we?e* 'they were living (there)' would open a narration and the closing would be *mi·paw ké* 'that's all' or *mi·ké tuti·k* 'that's the way it was'. A Pomoan ritual closing, "from the east and the west may the Mallard girls hurry and bring the morning," was used to make daylight come quickly.

Stories set in the prehuman, mythical era had to be told only in the proper season and at the proper time: in the winter and at night. According to many northern California groups (e.g., Modoc, Shasta, Atsugewi, Achumawi, Wintu, Northeastern Maidu), myth-telling in the summer attracted rattlesnakes, and the Shasta believed that Rattlesnake took offense at summertime storytelling in the same way a person resented mention of the name of a deceased relative. The Wintu and Northeastern Maidu also felt that telling myths in the wrong season hastened the arrival of winter. Miwokan storytellers began myth recitations after the first rains fell; and the Achumawi season began with the first December moon and ended the middle of March. Pomoan groups and the Yuki believed that a narrator who described happenings of the mythic past during daylight hours would become hunchbacked.

Activities surrounding the performance did not end when the telling of a myth was over; for example, at the end of a story told to a group of Shasta children, the elderly woman narrator would take each child in turn and, starting at the top of the spinal column, press on successive vertebrae, while reciting the various animal characteristics the listener should have: "This is Grizzly Bear and you must be strong and brave like the grizzly bear" and so on. The Shasta believed in the direct magical effect of storytelling, so, mentioning a prehuman character in this fashion, brought about the desired results. In many groups, listeners had to bathe early the following morning to make themselves "healthy." Among the Tubatulabal, the previous night's auditors were roused by the old people when the morning star appeared and ordered outside to jump in an icy pool—to make them "strong," to "keep them healthy." Persons who wished to avoid this early morning dip gave the storyteller some pine nuts, acorns, or other seeds. During a night's session, in order to escape incurring any obligation at all, a man might cover his head with a blanket so that he could sleep and not hear the narration.

The restrictions that pertained to myth-telling did not apply to ordinary stories. Among the Shasta, for instance, adults used story fragments to illustrate points in conversation, and the Cahuilla used quotes from the oral literature to assess the value or appropriateness of taking action in crisis situations. In northeastern California, people recounted anecdotes based on the actual experiences of living persons whenever possible. In addition, parents, or more often, grandparents, told children ordinary stories any time the children wanted to hear them.

5.2   A CONVERSATION WITH
A CALIFORNIA STORYTELLER

Some of the points discussed in section 5.1 come up in the following conversation about "old time" storytellers and storytelling. This edited segment is from a larger interview, in English, that was recorded in 1977 with Ike Leaf, a member of the Hammawi band of Pit River (Achumawi). IL indicates Ike Leaf, SS indicates the interviewer.

IL: My uncle [father's brother] used to tell me *a lot of* stories. He was forty-five or fifty years old—quite a bit older than my father. I believe I was nearly seven or eight.

SS: Did he ever tell you how *he* heard the stories?

IL: Well—, he heard stories in various places from different people —older people. A few of the older people remembered stories. Only a few families would know some of the stories, and those families would be good storytellers.

SS: Did anybody ever tell you how in the *real old* times they used to tell the stories?

IL: Well—yes. People used to tell me that when a story was going to be told, maybe two families would get in the winter house and listen, or they'd place people all round inside the house there. Then this one guy would tell the story. And he'd tell the story to these people again. Then if these same people want to hear the story again sometime later—if they missed something—well, he tells it again. And that way they—, the story was well heard and well remembered. And the storytellers were pretty particular when they were telling stories. One would say, "You'll sit there, and you'll sit there, you'll sit there." Or, to

some kids sitting there: "You kids, I don't want you to make
noise or go to sleep. That way you won't have a crooked back.
You'll be straight. Don't sleep when someone is telling a story."
That's what he'd tell them.

SS: So, that was kind of a rule—

IL: It is a *rule*. It's good in that way and keeps the kids awake.

SS: Were there any rules for the storyteller? Were there any rules
about whether the storyteller was supposed to sit or lie down
or—

IL: No, he was sitting on something.

SS: There weren't any rules about how he was supposed to sit—
like he had to sit straight up all the time?

IL: No, but they generally sat up straight, in the early days. They
doubled their legs in front and sat like that. Just like you're sitting on a chair, only legs'd be crossed. That's how Indians sat in
the early days. But, the main rule they had was that the young
ones were not to go to sleep while he was talking . . . the people
there would wake up the kids if they felt sleepy. So, it's good
in two ways: the kids can remember the story, they can hear
it all; and, next thing, is they put a little scare in them. They'd
say, "If you go to sleep, when the story's telling, you'll have a
crooked back; you're going to bend over, and then you're going
to sleep in that shape." So, for that reason, it was a good rule.

SS: Right, it was a good rule. Did you ever hear people talk about
how the kids, once they heard the story, did they ever practice
it among themselves? Would the kids tell stories to themselves
to learn how to be a storyteller?

IL: Yeah. Someone would tell just what he remembered, maybe
something important to him—, he'd tell that part, something
that's *strict*. Another'd talk about how he'd want to go to sleep
when they tell the story. And another kid, doing *this* story,
would remember some important thing to him. Well, then the
next time a kid suggests having the same kind of storytelling,
well, that kid'll just add some more to it.

SS: I see. This'd be kids among themselves, kids telling stories to
themselves to learn how to tell the stories right. Did anybody
ever talk about what the special features were that a good storyteller had? What made a person a good storyteller?

IL: Well, a good storyteller will describe things, it's not mixed up,
it's on one line, whatever it is. If it is a deer hunting, or fishing,

he just makes it sound like you're there. And if some kid was
interested, well, he'd sure *pick it up*. Well, maybe in another
twenty or thirty years, he'll be a storyteller too. Maybe there'd
be *two* out of five or six kids, or maybe one. But that's how the
story never got old, or nothing got added. If anything was added
to it, then other people would say "No, he didn't say that."

ss: He didn't tell it right, huh?

IL: He didn't tell it, yeah. So, he'd correct himself by going back
and listening again. But they don't jump up and ask him, "Well,
I heard it *this* way." No, you got to take that to the storyteller,
because he's the main guy that understands all the ways to
make it sound like you're right there.

5.3   BUNGLING HOST, BENEVOLENT HOST:
A CHINOOK NARRATIVE

Chinook territory is located along the Columbia River from the mouth to the
Deschutes River, in what are now Oregon and Washington. There are two, possibly
three, closely related Chinook languages: Wishram Chinook, Wasco, and Lower
Chinook. Although the Chinook distinguish between myth and tale (their words
for them are different) both can be divided into acts, scenes, stanzas, verses, and
lines. Changes in acts and scenes correspond to changes in location and actor(s),
respectively. The other units (stanzas, verses and lines) are discussed in the treatment of a Wishram Chinook Coyote story that follows.

In American Indian oral literature there are sets of stories about prehuman inhabitants of the earth, prehumans that are identified with animals, yet had human
virtues and failings. When humans were created or arrived on earth, these prehuman creatures became the present-day animals. Although the stories are often
similar from area to area, the animal characters change with the environment; for
example, in North America, fish and sea mammals are emphasized in the Northwest; fox, deer, and rabbit in the Eastern Woodlands; and coyote and buffalo in
the Plains, Plateau, and Prairies. The central figure of many stories is a trickster;
and, although Raven (parts of the Northwest Coast), Rabbit (parts of the Southeast), and other animal characters fill this role, it is Coyote who is the preeminent
trickster figure. Coyote both aids and hinders. On the one hand, he is wise and responsible for most of the good things that humans enjoy, such as the use of fire.
On the other hand, he is foolish, outrageous, and double-dealing, a buffoon who

cannot do things right and constantly makes a fool of himself. Pointing up human weaknesses is one of the many purposes the telling of Coyote stories serves.

The sample Chinook story is one of those in which Coyote cannot do things right. He visits Deer, who provides him with food he makes from his own flesh and blood. Coyote visits Deer again and the incident is repeated. Coyote invites Deer to visit him and tries to emulate Deer's deeds. But instead of cutting himself to provide the food, he tries to cut his own wife. Both Deer and Coyote's wife are horrified, and they make Coyote stop. Coyote's wife scolds him for acting so badly, and Deer again provides food. We give here the opening scene:

A	(a)	*Ǧayuyá: (I)sk'úlya.*	Coyote went on and on;	1
	(b)	*Ná:wit gayúyam Ič'ánkb(a) idiáqł.*	Straightway he arrived at Deer's house.	2
	(c)	*Aga kwápt štâ··xt.*	Now then the two sit and sit.	3
	(d)	*Aga kwápt galikim Isk'úlya: "Ag(a) anxk'wáya."*	Now then Coyote said: "Now I'll go home."	4 / 5
	(e)	*"A-u,"*	"All right,"	6
		gacĭux Ič'ánk.	Deer responded to him.	7
B	(f)	*Aga kwápt gačagálg(a) aq'éwiqe;*	Now then he took a knife,	8
		a-iłq'oá··b gacĭux igéwaq iáłqba.	he just sliced meat from his body	9
	(g)	*Aga kwápt gaqǐlud(a) Isk'úlya.*	Now then it was given Coyote	10
	(h)	*Kwádau išiágačb(a) ik'ámunaq galixəlúqłkwačk.*	And he pushed wood up his nose	11
	(i)	*Aga kwápt galigálb(a) iłiágawəlqt;*	Now then his blood flowed out;	12
		pá··ł at'íwat.	filling a bucket	13
	(j)	*Aga kwápt Isk'úlya gaqǐlut.*	Now then Coyote was given it.	14
C	(k)	*Aga kwápt itqułiámt galixk'wá.*	Now then he went home to the house.	15

This section of the narrative divides into three stanzas (A, B, C), eleven verses (a–e, f–j, and k), and fifteen lines. In Chinook, adverbial elements that occur in sentence initial position (i.e., initial particles) are important in marking verses. The one occurring most frequently in this selection is *aga kwápt* 'now then' (lines 3, 4, 8, 10, 12, and 15). Stanzas are marked by a variety of techniques, including the patterning and interplay of linguistic markers (form), and content (the meaning and internal logic of the narrative). The lines, verses and stanzas are arranged in a hierarchy of units based on three and five, the culturally significant numbers in the Northwest Coast.

Further analysis of Chinook narratives reveals more structure, or "architecture"; for example, in the patterning of the pronouns and nouns within the stanzas, and in the way the thematic content is unfolded. The interlocking of the various devices provides the narrator with a structure that entails both constraints on and opportunities for artistic expression. Retellings of the same narratives by the same speaker vary: each telling or performance is a new re-creation. There is also variation from narrator to narrator, which partly reflects the fact that some narrators are more skillful than others, but also reflects differences in individual style.

Investigators have found that the use of verse in American Indian narratives is not at all rare. Indeed, it may not be too sweeping to say that most oral traditions (at least among preliterate peoples) are told in verse, but the structural features that identify the verses vary across language communities.

5.4 AN OLD LADY'S LAMENT:
A HAVASUPAI SONG

The five hundred or so Havasupai who live in northern Arizona speak a Yuman language, a language they share with their neighbors, the Walapai and Yavapai. As a performance type, Havasupai song is well developed. The song that is the object of our attention occurs within a story. A woman lives alone with her two sons. When the woman has grown old, her sons, now young men, set out for a canyon, a dangerous place called Rocks Clap Together (identified with Havasupai Canyon), which is owned by Owl, who causes the canyon walls to clap together so as to kill all intruders. The young men kill Owl 'and make the canyon safe by so placing a log that the walls can no longer clap together. This is only a fragment of the story, but enough to provide a context for the song. The mother sings the song to the boys in a futile attempt to dissuade them from setting out on their dangerous journey. There are nine verses, with most of them consisting of four lines:

1a	ʔaáawéʔe gəmóleʔe,	My only baby,
1b	ʔaáawéʔe gəmóleʔe,	my only baby,
1c	ʔaáawéʔe gəmóleʔe,	my only baby,
1d	gəmóleʔṁ,	my only one,
2a	ʔabáʔa hánigaʔa,	a healthy man,
2b	ʔabáʔa hánigaʔa,	a healthy man,
2c	gavóʔo ñiyúgaʔa,	how will you be that,
2d	ñiyúgaʔṁ?	will you be?

3a	ñiwáʔa niyíjigaʔa,	The ones who want that,
3b	ñiyáʔa ñiyójəgaʔm,	the ones who are like that,
3c	ʔagʷé e jijámugaʔa,	(if) they make mistakes,
4a	ñivoʔo niyúhawaʔa,	if someone is like that (makes mistakes),
4b	ñiwáʔa tiʔóbəmeʔe	he isn't that way (is not healthy),
4c	ʔəáawéʔe gəmóleʔe,	my only baby,
4d	gəmóleʔm̀.	my only one.
5a	ʔabáʔa ʔiyúhiʔje,	Owl Man,
5b	ʔawéʔe gəgábaʔa,	Rocks Clap Together (placename),
5c	gayáŋa vəʔíjimeʔe,	this is what they say,
5d	vəíjimeʔe.	what they say.
6a	gaááʔal ñiwágaʔm,	He lives in there,
6b	ʔabáʔa haʔi waʔa,	the man I told you about,
6c	ñevóʔo ñiwégaʔa,	he owns that place,
6d	gaáá ñiwa.	he lives there.
7a	ʔawáʔa ʔiʔí maʔm,	I'm telling (you),
7b	metéʔe tigáyvega,	you are making a mistake,
7c	gaááʔa miyámagaʔa	if you go there
7d	miyújəhaʔa.	if you ever do.
8a	ayúʔu geʔiteʔe	Don't let it be thus
8b	ʔəáawéʔe gəmóleʔe,	my only baby,
8c	gayáʔa məʔévogaʔa	listen to (my words)
8d	miyújəhaʔa.	always.
9a	ayúʔu geímaʔa.	That is how it is.

What is there about these several sentences that make it an aesthetic experience for the Havasupai singer and hearer, and that qualify it as a performance? The next few paragraphs provide some of the technical information necessary for answering this question. (Unfortunately, space limitations do not allow us to present the accompanying melody and rhythm, indispensable for understanding the total aesthetic experience.)

Havasupai, like other Yuman languages, has a complex set of phonological rules that change vowels and consonants when stems and affixes are joined together. How these sounds are changed depends on their resulting position in the word and the nature of the other vowels and consonants that are adjacent. The rules that apply to song, however, are not identical to those that apply to speech; some are special to song; in other cases, rules that apply to speech are suspended in song.

An important phonological difference of song, as contrasted to speech, is that "open" sounds [e], [a], and [o], are favored over "closed" sounds, [i] and [u]. One

of the several rules that brings this about is a change from /u/ to [o] in songs; for
example, /vu/ 'that', is a demonstrative usually used when speaking of a person or
object recently but not currently present. While not common in speech, it is quite
common in song. In this song text, it occurs three times (2c, 4a, 6c), and in each
case, the vowel is changed to [o]: [-vó(ʔo)]. However, this [u] to [o] rule is optional,
as illustrated by the form /yu/ 'be'. In 3b, it is changed to [yo], but elsewhere the
vowel is unaltered: 2d, 4a, 7d, 8a, 8d, and 9a.

Not only does the operation of the phonological rules bring about a greater frequency of open sounds, but also the choice of elements plays a part; thus elements
that contain nasals (e.g., /ñ/, more open) are more apt to be chosen than those that
contain stops (e.g., /b, t/, more closed). An example is the deictic element /ñ-/, the
function of which is usually to add emphasis. It is used much more in songs than
in speech, so much so that its deictic meaning tends to be bleached out in songs.
Its high frequency of use, then, contributes to the higher frequency of nasals: 2c,
2d, 3a, 3b (twice), 4a, 4b, 6a, and 6c (twice).

Nonsense syllables are added in most songs, syllables that tend to fill out the
rhythmic pattern of the line. The choice of the phonetic elements, particularly the
vowels, can be partly predicted by rules. We will not give the rules (they are complex), but their operation contributes to more open sounds. Some examples:

[gəmóleʔe], from /g–mol/ prefix + 'only' (1a)
[hánigaʔa], from /han–g/ 'good' + 'same subject' suffix (2a)
[niyúhawaʔa], from /ñ–yu-h/ 'deictic' + 'be' + 'irrealis' suffix (4a)

The use of more open sounds in songs is certainly not unique to Havasupai,
and in fact may be universal. Notice that nonsense syllables in English songs, even
though they are introduced by very different rules, result in more open sounds, for
example, "Deck the halls with boughs of holly, fa la la la la la la la la," with [a] being
a very open vowel, and [l] a rather open consonant sound.

Havasupai songs differ grammatically from speech in a number of ways. Here
we examine only two: the use of nominal sentences and the use of the possessive prefix /g-/. As in most languages, the Havasupai sentence typically contains a
verb. A formal characteristic that can help in identifying a verb (for a finite or non-
subordinated verb) is the fact that the verb will normally take one of two suffixes,
/-g/, which we can gloss as 'same subject', or /-m/, 'different subject'. (We omit
the syntactic criteria that differentiate 'same subject' and 'different subject', since
they are rather complex.) In the following examples from the song test, 'ss' is 'same
subject', 'ds' is 'different subject'):

[ñevóʔo ñiwégaʔa], from /ñ-vu ñ-wii-g/ (deictic-demonstrative
deictic- possess-ss), 'he owns that place', 6c

[ʔabáʔa hánigaʔa], from /ʔbaa han-g/ (man good-ss), 'a healthy
man', 2a

[ñiwáʔa tiʔóbəmeʔe], from /ñ-wa t-ob-m/ (deictic-demonstrative
negative-negative-ds), 'he isn't that way', 4b

[gaááʔal ñiwágaʔm], from /ga+áa-l ñ-wag-m/ (indefinite +
demonstrative-inessive deictic-live-ds), 'he lives in there', 6a

As these examples show, verbs, with their characteristic suffixes /-g/ and /-m/, do
occur in Havasupai song texts, but one of the defining features of song is a higher
frequency of sentences lacking those suffixes: that is, sentences that are more noun-
like than verb-like are much more common in songs than in speech. Among the
examples are: 'My only baby' (1a), 'Owl Man' (5a), 'This is what they say' (5c), 'If
you ever do' (7d).

In speaking, first and second person inalienable possession (see section 2.1) is
indicated by prefixes, along with an independent pronoun: /ña ʔ-áot-v/ (me my-arm-
demonstrative) 'my arm'; /ma m-áot-ñ/ (you your-arm-demonstrative) 'your arm'. In
singing, the prefix is often /g-/, found only in songs: /áaw-e g-mol/ (baby-vocative g-
only) 'My only baby' (perhaps more literally 'Baby! my only one'), 1a. These are just
some of the phonological and grammatical characteristics that set songs apart from
speech. They are the kinds of things that are sometimes referred to as poetic license.

The Havasupai story song varies slightly from performance to performance. A
song consists of a number of lines, with a given performance drawing on most or
all of the lines. Although the singer has a certain freedom in putting them together,
there are certain constraints as well, the most obvious one being that there has to be
rough adherence to the story line. Repetition of lines is common, particularly at the
beginning; thus the first line of "An Old Lady's Lament" is: "My only baby / my only
baby / my only baby / my only one." (It should be noted, however, that the first verse
in a performance does not invariably include repetition.) It is also common to repeat
lines that occur near the beginning later on in the song. Thus 'My only baby', 1a, is
also found in 4c and 8b, and 'my only one', 1d, is found in 4d. What we might call
shortened repetitions also occur: 'My only baby / my only one' (1c, 1d); 'This is what
they say / what they say' (5c, 5d); 'He lives in there / . . . / he lives there' (6a, 6d).

Although Havasupai narratives are always in the third person, the story songs
inserted into the story are in the first person and are a way of introducing a direct
quote. The story songs belong to a larger category of songs that we can call fully
worded (though they do contain some nonsense syllables).

Almost all fully worded songs are in the first person, and most types are sung
by one person—necessarily so, since the songs vary somewhat from performance
to performance. Besides the story song, the fully worded song type includes shaman (or doctoring) songs and love songs. Unlike the other kinds of songs, shaman

songs are the personal property of the doctor (a very common practice in western North America) and are dreamed, or at least the right to use them is dreamed. Love songs (also called "women's songs" by the Havasupai, even though a few are also really men's songs) are composed to express the author's feelings about a sweetheart, a person the author would like to have as a sweetheart, or a spouse. (A song about a spouse often expresses disappointment about married life.) If a love song is artfully composed, then others learn and sing it, and the content of the song becomes memorialized within Havasupai tradition.

In addition to the fully worded type, there are partially worded songs and songs without words (which contain only nonsense syllables). Round-dance songs (section 4.1) are an example of partially worded songs, while sweathouse and funeral songs are examples of songs without words. Group activities are the occasions for these songs, which are sung by more than one person. It is easier for them to be sung by a group because, unlike the fully worded songs, the texts are set (i.e., they do not vary from one performance to the next). One such cluster of songs, "horse songs," is used in the training of horses and has been borrowed from Navajo. Inasmuch as these songs are not intelligible from the Havasupai point of view, they must also be considered songs without words. (Theoretically they are interpretable in Navajo, although they have been changed in their transmission into Havasupai, so that Navajos, when hearing recordings of these songs, find them only partially interpretable.)

Fully worded songs can be used as a very powerful form of social control. Although most of them are in the first person, they represent quotes of another (except in those rare cases in which the singer is also the composer); consequently, they can be used as an indirect way of expressing opinions or feelings. For instance, there is a rather long and very well-known song about a fight that split the whole community, a fight triggered by a trivial incident that was misinterpreted. When a heated argument broke out at a PTA meeting, a member of the group started singing this song. She needed only to sing the first verse to get the message across.

In comparing Havasupai song traditions to those found among other groups, we find similarities. In regard to phonological changes that set songs apart from speech we have noted the same phenomenon in the Great Basin (section 4.1), and it is widespread in North America. The variable performances of the worded songs are also not unique to Havasupai; however, set renditions are not uncommon either, particularly for sacred songs in which an exact repetition of the words is necessary. The use of song for directly quoting in narratives, in what has been called "song recitatives," is also common in western America. In addition, there has been the rather frequent occurrence of borrowing songs from foreign groups, with words that were unintelligible to the borrowers—a phenomenon we also noted for the Pueblo communities (section 4.2). Furthermore, the distinction between fully worded songs, partially worded songs, and songs without words is widespread, though their use in the various types is varied. In the Great Basin, for instance, round-dance and doctoring songs are fully worded, story songs are sometimes fully, sometimes partially worded; and hand-game songs use nonsense syllables. Singers often say that the songs used in sacred contexts represent archaic forms of the language. Although this explanation accounts for some of the partially worded songs in some languages, it cannot explain all cases; moreover, an appeal to an archaic language may, at least in some cases, simply be a rationalization for why the speakers cannot understand everything in the song.

The use of song as a means of social control has been reported for other groups, for example, the Eskimo. In some societies, most notably in Africa, proverbs are widely used for social control, for they allow one to appeal to an outside authority, without directly involving the speaker. Since proverbs are only weakly developed in American Indian societies, it may be that songs replace proverbs in this function.

5.5 MALE SHOOTING CHANT EVIL-CHASING: A NAVAJO PRAYER

Navajo religious practice includes simple prayers that may be uttered by anyone whenever circumstances warrant it. Athough such prayers have a clear-cut structure, they are variable, not memorized pieces. In addition, there are a large number of memorized prayers, often referred to as chants, that are the property of specialists known as chanters. The function of a chant is to cure the sick. The chanter, the patient, and an audience consisting of relatives and friends of the patient make up the participants in a performance. Efficacy depends on exact repetition. Prayers are passed on from an experienced chanter to a novice, who must learn each chant as a whole, and not piecemeal. Because each one runs several hundred lines, a considerable amount of intellectual capital must be spent to learn them. A single mistake not only renders the prayer ineffectual, but can also place the participants in danger; thus a chanter who contracts to perform a prayer undertakes a considerable responsibility for the patient as well as others present at the performance. Not everyone has the intellectual ability, the will, and the level of social responsibility necessary to become a chanter.

Navajo ideology includes a belief that is common throughout the world, though not universal: a belief in the power of the word. If a prayer is properly presented to a god or other supernatural power, the prayer must be answered. The Christian god may grant or deny a request, according to his will, and according to the worthiness of the petitioner. But Navajo gods are powerless to express their volition before a properly presented prayer. It is no wonder, then, that exact repetition of the prayer is so important.

For our illustrative example, we draw upon a study appropriately titled "Prayer: The Compulsive Word," in which there is an analysis of the first night's prayer from the Male Shooting Chant Evil-chasing. We present only excerpts of the 399-line chant. Note that a full understanding and appreciation of the prayer depends on an understanding of Navajo theology and symbolism, which we do not provide, since our discussion is limited to the structure of the prayer.

A prayer can consist of a single unit or of multiple units. A multiple-unit prayer usually has four (four being the Navajo ritual number), with each unit displaying parallel structure; it can also consist of five units, with the last unit used to close out the prayer. The Male Shooting Chant Evil-chasing prayer is of this last type, with unit A being lines 1–76; B, lines 77–161; C, lines 162–245; D, lines 246–325; and E, lines 326–399.

A unit most commonly consists of three divisions: an invocation, a petition and a benediction. Units A–D in our example are so constructed, while unit E consists solely of a benediction. The four invocations identify the place and the supernatural being at that place that is being petitioned:

1	*dził yildiliigi,*	at Rumbling Mountain,
2	*ʔatseebeist'áan bił xaxookǫsíi dinéé diyiní,*	Holy Man who with the eagle tail-feathered arrow glides out,
77	*dził yildiliigi,*	At Rumbling Mountain,
78	*gish yist'áan bił xaxookǫsíi ch'ikéé̜ diyiní,*	Holy Woman who with the feathered wand glides out,
162	*dził yildiliigi,*	At Rumbling Mountain,
163	*tseek'ishdiitsoi bił xaxoo kǫsí kiyéé diyiní,*	Holy Boy with the yellow tail-feathered arrow glides out,
246	*dził yildiliigi,*	At Rumbling Mountain,
247	*t'áłchíi k'aaʔ bił xaxookǫsí ʔat'ééd diyiní,*	Holy Girl with the red-feathered arrow glides out,

The only differences in each of the invocations are the beings that are addressed (*dinéé, ch'ikéé̜, kiyéé, ʔat'ééd*), along with the sacred objects associated with each one (*ʔatseebeist'áan, gish yist'áan, tseek'ishdiitsoi, t'áłchíi k'aaʔ*). The invocation in other prayers is sometimes longer, but the petition usually makes up the bulk of the prayer. The benediction in this prayer, which follows, is of variable length, being between seven and fourteen in units A–D, while the whole of unit E is a benediction.

A petition normally contains one or more series of comparison couplets, in which a quality of the supernatural is listed in the first line of the couplet, which is then compared with and petitioned for in the second line. An example of a series of such couplets from Unit A:

48   Just as you are the one from whom weakness passes,
49   So may weakness pass away from me.
50   Just as you are the one whom weakness merely grazes,
51   So may weakness merely graze me.
52   Just as you are the one who transforms evil,
53   So may I transform evil.
54   Just as you are the one dreaded by evil because of these things,
55   So may I be dreaded by evil because of these things.
56   Just as you are the one who has become evil (i.e., in control of evil)
        because of these things,
57   So may I become evil because of them.

(The last couplet, lines 56 and 57, summarizes all of the characteristics listed in the preceding couplets.) Couplets of comparison are composed with exactly the same structure in both lines, which we can illustrate by looking at the Navajo of one:

48   *t'aa bee nts'a xoníyêeii,*
49   *t'áa ʔái bee sits'á xoníyée? doo.*

Each line begins with *t'aa* 'just (as)', followed by *bee* 'by means of'. Each line of the couplet ends with the same verb, except that in the first line the verb is relativized or nominalized by the suffix *–ii* 'the one who', while the verb on the comparison line lacks this suffix: *xoníyêeii* 'the one from whom weakness passes', and *xoníyée? doo* 'weakness passes'. The verb in the second line is always followed by *doo* or *dooleeł* 'it will be, it will become'. The first line contains a second person that is changed to the first person in the comparison line. This change is indicated by a prefix either with the verb, or with a postposition; in this couplet, the prefix is on a postposition: *nts'á* 'from you', *sits'á* 'from me'.

    The prayer contains sets of lines that vary by only a single word. For example, in these five lines near the beginning of unit A, the lines vary only in the first word, a possessed body part: *nikeeʔ* 'your feet', *nijáad* 'your legs', and so on.

5   *nikeeʔ niɣéeʔii díi bee shich'ą́a ńdidíidáał*   With your strong feet
                                                      rise up to protect me,
6   *nijáad niɣéeʔii díi bee shich'ą́a ńdidíidáał*   With your strong legs
                                                      rise up to protect me,
7   *nits'íis niɣéeʔii díi bee shich'ą́a ńdidíidáał* With your strong body
                                                      rise up to protect me,
8   *nínii niɣéeʔii díi bee shich'ą́a ńdidíidáał*   With your strong mind
                                                      rise up to protect me,

9   *niinéeʔ niɣéeʔii díi bee shich'ą́a ńdidíidáał*   With your strong sound
                                                            rise up to protect me,

Blocks of lines of this sort are repeated in later units, sometimes with additional lines added, and sometimes with the blocks placed in a slightly different order. This variation is not haphazard; it is done in a skillful fashion so that the number of lines in each of these blocks produces a unified structure.

As these few examples have illustrated, a Navajo prayer, composed in formulaic fashion, is constructed with very skillful use of formula. In order to give some feeling for the beauty of the prayer, we give in translation only the first twenty-three lines of unit A, and the benediction of unit D:

1   At Rumbling Mountain,
2   Holy Man who with the eagle tail-feathered arrow glides out,
3   This day I have come to be trustful,
4   This day I look to you (for help),
5   With your strong feet rise up to protect me,
6   With your strong legs rise up to protect me,
7   With your strong body rise up to protect me,
8   With your strong mind rise up to protect me,
9   With your strong sound rise up to protect me,
10 Carrying the dark bow and the eagle tail-feathered arrow with which you
                    transformed evil,
11   By these means you will protect me,
12 These you will hold me,
13 So that I being at a place behind you, evils will pass me,
14 Evil ghost power of all kinds will go past me,
15   This day from the tips of my toes it will move out,
16   From the tips of my body it will move out,
17   From the tips of my fingers it will move out,
18   From the tip of my speech it will move out,
19 No weapon of evil sorcery can harm me as I go about,
20   This day I shall recover
21   Safely may I go about,
22   Your child I have become
23   Your grandchild I have become.

317 Surely this day happily I go about, I say.
318   May it be beautiful before me,
319   May it be beautiful behind me,
320   May it be beautiful under me,
321   May it be beautiful above me,
322   May it be beautiful around me,

323   May my speech be controlled,
324   Restoration-to-youth According-to-beauty I have become, I say
325   May all these things be so.

5.6 THE LANGUAGE OF THREE KUNA
PERFORMANCE TYPES

On the border between Panama and Colombia, approximately twenty-five thousand
Kunas live in villages on islands and the mainland along the Caribbean coast. Culturally the Kuna are affiliated with the South American lowland area. The extensive
documentation of their very rich verbal life consists of the best and most complete
description and analysis of an indigenous American speech community currently
available.

The Kuna distinguish *tule kaya*, literally 'person speech', that is, "everyday Kuna"
from three special varieties of speech: *sakla kaya* 'chief language', *suar nuču kaya*
'stick doll language', and *kantule kaya* 'puberty rite language' (*kan-tule* lit. 'flute person', the official who performs the puberty rite, and so called because the flute is
an indispensable piece of equipment for the ceremony). Although the three special
styles differ, there are similarities in the techniques that utilize changes in vocabulary, phonology, morphology, syntax, structure, and such nonlinguistic features as
tone of voice. In referring to these varieties, we use English translations of the
Kuna terms, "chief language," "stick doll language," and "puberty language"; keep
in mind, however, that these labels represent different varieties of speech in Kuna,
rather than different languages.

These three varieties of speech correspond to the three areas of greatest cultural
elaboration among the Kuna, and each variety has an appropriate context for its
use. "Chief language" is used by "chiefs," respected elders who occupy positions of
respect and limited political authority. In the center of each village there is a gathering house. One of the local chiefs or sometimes a visiting chief delivers a speech in
the evening. It can be on a variety of topics—history, local events, politics, and so
on—and the speeches in the gathering house are a nightly event. "Stick doll language" is used by curing specialists and is so named because stick dolls are part of
the necessary paraphernalia for a curing performance. "Puberty language" is used by
the official who conducts the girl's puberty ritual. Of the three events, the puberty
ritual is the least frequent. It is performed two or three times a year in each village
and is occasioned by a girl's first menses. Although a speech in the "chief language"
follows very strict guidelines, it is a free composition and shows the least amount
of deviation from everyday speech. As for "stick doll language" and "puberty lan-

guage," the rituals are from memorized texts that allow no variation. The longest and most elaborate is the puberty ritual, which takes several days to perform.

Even though everyone knows everyday Kuna, every Kuna speaker does not have equal access to being able to understand or use the three special varieties. In these varieties, special words replace certain everyday words, for example:

Everyday language	Stick doll language	Puberty language
ome 'woman'	walepunkʷa	yai
tii 'water'	wiasali	nukku kia

There are also a number of prefixes, for example, olo-, uu-, ulu-, ilukka-, ipepo-, esa-, po– (and others); and suffixes, for example, –pilli, –kači, –lele (and others), which are used to derive new words:

kana 'bench'	olo-kana (chief language)
kači 'hammock'	po-kači (chief language)
	ipepo-kači-pilli (stick doll language)
puti 'blowgun'	olo-puti (stick doll language)
mola 'blouse, shirt'	uu-mola (stick doll language)
	ilukka-mola (puberty language)
wini 'beads'	esa-wini-kači (puberty language)
toke 'to enter'	ulu-toke (puberty language)

These affixes have no meaning in and of themselves other than to derive new words for these special styles. They are affixed not only to everyday words (as in the above examples), but also to words not found except in this combination, for example, olo–welip–lele 'white-lipped peccary' (yannu is the everyday word). In some cases, there is more than one term in a special style, such as:

Everyday language	Chief language	Stick doll language
sikli 'curassow'	olo-kupyakki-lele	sitoni
	olo-miikinya-liler	mii
moli 'tapir'	olo-alikinyali-lele	ekʷilamakkatola
	olo-halikiny-appi	ekʷirmakka
	olo-swikinya-liler	

As it does in all languages, metaphor plays an important part in everyday Kuna, but it plays a still more important role in the special varieties; for example,

ome 'woman'	tuttu (lit. 'flower'; chief language)
mala 'thunder'	pap kinki sakla (lit. 'God's rifle'; chief language)
poni 'evil spirit'	urwetule (lit. 'angry person'; stick doll language)
kʷallulke 'to be born'	akteke (lit. 'to land'; stick doll language)

> *kallis* 'pieces of meat'   *ipya suli* (lit. 'no eyes'; puberty language)
> *kope* 'to drink'   *pulku sae* (lit. 'to do like a drinking gourd';
>   puberty language)

The lexical replacements are not limited to nouns, but, as the examples show, this lexical class is the one most commonly affected.

The final vowel (in some cases the entire final syllable) of a suffix, stem, or prefix may be lost. Under certain phonological conditions, this loss is obligatory, but in most cases, it is optional. Because Kuna phonology does not allow a sequence of more than two consonants, a sequence must be simplified to two consonants, if vowel loss brings more than two consonants together; for example, *tuppu* (island) + *takke* (see) > *tup-takke* 'he sees the island'. In addition, a number of other consonant changes take place after vowel loss; for instance, the change of /l/ to /r/ when it is in final position or before another consonant, the change of /k/ to /y/ when it is before another consonant, the change of /ss/ to /č/, and still others.

Because the dropping of vowels is sometimes optional, there is a range between the longest possible form, in which only obligatory loss takes place, and the shortest possible form, in which all possible shortenings have taken place. For example, the sequence *takke-sa-suli-moka* 'he did not see either' (lit. 'see-past-negative-either') becomes:

> *takk(e)-sa-suli-moka* > *taysasulimoka* (longest form)
> *takk(e)-s(a)-sul(i)-mo(ka)* > *tačurmo* (shortest form)

(The elements that are lost are placed in parentheses.) The shortest forms are characteristic of the most casual, rapid, everyday speech. The more formal, less casual, or more careful the speech, the longer the forms, with the fullest forms being found in the "stick doll" and "puberty languages."

Notice that vocabulary replacement is categorical: either a special word replaces an everyday word, or it does not. But the shortening is on a continuous scale: a word can be in its longest possible form, shortest possible form, or various points in between. The effect is similar to contractions in English, which can also show various degrees: *Did you see him? Did ya see 'im? Didja see 'im? 'Dja see 'im?*

Except for the particular affixes used in the special styles to form new vocabulary, there are no grammatical differences between everyday Kuna and special styles: the same set of affixes and the same set of syntactic rules are used in all the speech varieties. Some grammatical features occur so frequently, however, that their use is characteristic of these three "languages." A case in point is the suffix *–ye*, which ordinarily adds an optative meaning to verbs, and a vocative meaning to nouns. It is used so often, almost bleached of its everyday meanings, that it functions instead as an embellishment, a poetic line marker, or filler.

Tone of voice and other paralinguistic features are also important markers of
the three "languages." Each has a particular kind of "chant," with a characteristic
melodic contour and characteristic rhythm; in addition, the "puberty language" is
normally shouted.

Manner of organization and restrictions in thematic content mark the special
styles as different from everyday speech. Repetition and parallelism are common.
Lines are often marked at their beginnings and ends by certain characteristic words
or affixes; for example, a chief often uses words with meanings like 'see', 'hear',
'say', and 'in truth' to end a line; and in a speech given by two chiefs, the main or
chanting chief gives a verse, normally of two lines, which the responding chief then
punctuates with *teki* 'indeed'.

The following examples from each special variety illustrate all of the marking
techniques, except the paralinguistic features, for which we would need a notation
indicating rhythm and pitch. First a segment of *sakla kaya* 'chief language', from a
speech in which the chanting chief describes the plants and animals provided by
God (cc is chanting chief, RC responding chief):

CC:	*We yalase papal anparmialimarye sokel ittole.*	God sent us to this mountain world.
	Eka masmul akkʷekarye oparwe.	In order to care for banana roots for him.
RC:	*Teki.*	Indeed.
CC:	*Ekal inso tarkʷamul akkʷekarye sokel ittolete.*	In order thus to care for taro roots for him.
	Sunna ipiti oparwe.	In truth, utter.
RC:	*Teki.*	Indeed.
CC:	*Al inso ekal wakup tulal akkwekar sokel ittole.*	Thus in order to care for living yams for him.
	Al ipiti oparwe.	Utter.
RC:	*Teki.*	Indeed.
CC:	*Al insol eka moe tulal akkʷekar sokel ittole.*	Thus in order to care for living squash for him.
	Al ipiti oparwe.	Utter.
RC:	*Teki.*	Indeed.

The boldface vowels are normally omitted in everyday speech, their loss often producing sequences of consonants that would undergo further changes. Words that
close a line (and are omitted from the translation) include *soke-l* 'say', *ittole* 'hear',
and *opar-we* 'utter', which also illustrate the use of suffixes, *-l* and *-we*. These
suffixes, while not unique to the "chief language," occur much more frequently in
it. The final vowel of each verse is lengthened; that is, the responding chief's reply
teki begins before the lengthening in the chanting chief's verse is completed; and,

likewise, the chanting chief's next verse begins before the responding chief finishes lengthening the final vowel of *teki*. The parallelism and repetition typical of the special styles are evident in this particular segment, which is particularly characteristic of "chief language" because its vocabulary items all occur in everyday speech.

The next sample, of the *suar nuču kaya* 'stick doll language', is addressed to spirits, asking them to effect the cure:

Kurkin ipekantinaye.	Owners of kurkin.
*Olopillise pupawal**a**kan akkue**k**ʷiči̇ye.*	To the level of gold your roots reach.
Kurkin ipekantinaye.	Owners of kurkin.
*Olopillise pe maliwaskakan upo**e**kʷiči̇ye.*	Into the level of gold your small roots are placed.
Kurkin ipekantinaye.	Owners of kurkin.
*Olopillisepe maliwaskakan**a** pioklek**e**kʷiči̇ye.*	Into the level of gold your small roots are nailed.
Kurkin ipekantinaye.	Owners of kurkin.
*Olopillipiye ap**i**kae**k**ʷiči̇ye kurkin ipekantinaye.*	Within the very level of gold you are resisting, owners of kurkin.

Vowels normally omitted in everyday speech are boldfaced. Every line ends with the optative suffix –*ye*, and the first line of each couplet ends with the sequence of suffixes, –*ti-na-ye*; these suffixes are found in everyday speech, but not with the same frequency as in this variety of speech. The first word of the second line of each couplet has *olo*-, a prefix used only to derive words in the special styles. The first line of each couplet includes two special vocabulary items: *kurkin* 'brainpower' (a metaphorical extension of 'hat' in everyday language), and *ipe*– 'owners'; another special word is found on line two: *pupawala*– 'to reach'. The repetition and parallelism that we saw in the "chief language" segment is even more striking in the "stick doll language," probably in part because a speech by a chief is a new composition, while the texts of the "stick doll language" are set, memorized pieces.

Our last sample is of "puberty language." Because the girl and the general public are separated during a puberty rite, the *kantule*, who officiates in the ceremony, gives a running description of what is happening:

Yaikana uuparpa imakte.	The women's underwear makes noise.
Yaikana uuparpa pukki nite.	The women's underwear can be heard far away.
Yaikana kala tere imakte.	The women's coin necklaces make noise.
Yaikana kala tere pukki nite.	The women's coin necklaces can be heard far away.
Yaikana kala purwa imakte.	The women's bead necklaces make noise.
Yaikana kala purwa pukki nite.	The women's bead necklaces can be heard far away.

This short passage illustrates the very tight structure of these texts: each of the six lines begins with the same noun, *yaikana* 'women' (*yai* 'woman' in "puberty language," –*kana* plural suffix). The noun that follows *yaikana* in each line of a couplet is the same: *uuparpa* 'underwear' in the first couplet, *kala tere* 'coin necklaces' in the second, and *kala purwa* 'bead necklaces' in the third. The first line of each couplet ends with the same verb, *imakte*, and the second line with the verb, *pukki nite*; both verbs end with the same tense-aspect and line final marker *te* 'then'. In this sample, only the verb *imak-* 'to make noise', is not a special word. Of the three varieties of speech, the "puberty language" displays the greatest lexical substitution; consequently, for the nonspecialist, this style is more difficult to understand than are the other two styles.

5.7   PERFORMANCES AND CROSS-CULTURAL COMPARISON

To what extent are various types of performances valid from a cross-cultural perspective? Since a performance in a particular language is always rooted in a cultural tradition, we could take an extreme position by saying that performance types can only be discussed within a particular cultural tradition. Strictly speaking this is true, as illustrated by the Kuna example. But such a statement precludes any attempts at generalization. We do not know enough about Indian language communities in particular, or language communities in general, to make definitive statements concerning similarities across cultures or universal features of performance. We do know enough, however, to be certain that such similarities and universals exist. We can even make some general statements, however tentative; for instance, the fact that the terms for certain kinds of performances translate more easily than others suggests that some performance types are better candidates for valid cross-cultural comparison than others. Consider a performance like song. We feel comfortable using the English word "song" in translating the terms in most languages for this performance type. However, the use of English translations such as "prayer," "sermon," and "speech" is more problematical. How do we translate the Aztec *huehuetlaʔtōlli* 'moral admonition' (literally 'speech of the old ones') into our cultural experience? "Sermon" might be our closest cultural equivalent, but not everything we call a "sermon" would be an Aztec *huehuetlaʔtōlli*, or vice versa.

Cross-cultural comparison is also made difficult by the fact that some peoples have two or more categories where others have only one; for example, what English speakers might call "stories" may represent more than one type in another culture. (Technical discussions use terms such as "myth," "legend," "narrative," "fairy tale," and the like, but it is doubtful that these terms represent clearcut categories in contemporary twentieth-century cultures.) Furthermore, the existence of a named category does not guarantee internal consistency. Great Basin communities have a kind of story often labeled in the anthropological literature as "Coyote stories," even though there are some "Coyote stories" from which Coyote is absent. These stories are accounts of events that took place during an era "when animals were people" (similar to the genre found among the Chinook and many Californian groups). The stories range from those that are extremely important for understanding religious thought and ethics to those that serve primarily to entertain. At the theologically less important end of the scale, there are a few stories in which Coyote (interpret as "Indian") finds some way to trick Cowboy (interpret as "Whiteman"); whatever the purpose(s) of such stories, it is doubtful that many Great Basin Indians regard them as historically true.

Performances have one characteristic that sets them apart from other varieties of verbal behavior: they have a very tight structure, both in terms of the organization of thematic content and in the linguistic devices that are used for the formal expression of the content. Although some of the structure is apparent in a good translation, many of the more important structural features are displayed only through a careful study of the linguistic details of the performance. The structure is especially rigid, with repetition and parallelism well developed, when the texts demand exact repetition, as in the case of the Navajo prayers and the Kuna "stick doll language" and "puberty language." Although exact repetition is more common for sacred texts, it is sometimes found for nonsacred songs and poems, as well. The performance's structural requirements often offer a speaker great latitude. The speakers most skilled at manipulating and taking advantage of the structural requirements are those recognized as the best performers (e.g., the best orators, the best storytellers, the best singers, etc.). Greater latitude is normally allowed in oratory and speechmaking (as with the Kuna speeches) than for stories or songs: in the former, new material is often introduced; in the latter, the storyteller or singer must at least adhere to the story line.

There are certain performance types available to all, as, for example, Havasupai story songs. Other types may be limited to use by particular subgroups; for example, just men, just women, just children (e.g., jump-rope songs in Euro-American culture), or just elders (e.g., the Aztec *huehuetlaʔtōlli*). Even more limited in use are such types as Havasupai curing songs (owned by the doctors), Navajo chants, learned by specialists, or the Kuna "puberty rite language." The more restricted in use a particular performance type is, the greater possibility there is for a specialized variety of speech that is different enough from ordinary speech to be partially or wholly unintelligible to the uninitiated. This is most likely if the addressee in the performance is a nonhuman (a god or spirit), rather than an ordinary member of the general population.

Performances, be they stories, songs, oratory, or rituals, are found in both nonliterate and literate societies, but they function differently in nonliterate societies and in societies in which literacy plays a limited role (see section 8.9 for discussion of how literacy changes society). The place of oral traditions and language in non-literate societies is nicely characterized in this statement by N. Scott Momaday, the well-known Kiowa writer:

> I have studied the oral traditions of the Native American for many years and I have come to know that we have lost a certain ability to understand the belief in language that was shared by people long ago, not only Native American people, but others as well. . . . One of the things we know is that a person who does without writing must speak with greater care . . . and he must remember more carefully. Oral tradition represents a much greater realization of the power of language. Writing can be great: we know that, we have great litera-ture, but writing is not the same use of language. Before Beowulf was written down, when it was still recited by itinerant storytellers, I think it had greater power.

5.8   PROSE, POETRY, AND PLAYWRITING

It is tempting to think of American Indian tales and myth as relics of the past; yet narrative creativity did not end with the arrival of outsiders. There are stories that predict the arrival of the Whites, that join Jesus and the tricksters, that send Coy-ote out over the ocean in an airplane. As ancestral communities became part of the larger contemporary society, some types of performances were lost, others changed and adapted over time to the new circumstances. In addition, oral traditions and performances often continue in English as well as in Indian languages.

Today, American Indians also display their verbal creativity in writing. In North America there are such examples as a body of poetry written in Navajo, a collection of poems written in O'odham, and an edition of Tlingit narratives, written in Tlingit with English translations by speakers who are literate in their language. In Meso-america writings of various kinds in Nahuatl are flourishing, and there has been a resurgence of indigenous literature among the Yucatecan Maya of Mexico. "Chuyma Manghit Yurir Arunaka: Suxtalla," an Aymara poem by Juana Vásquez, published with Spanish translation, is but one example of the output from Latin American communities.

In 1829, William Apes (Pequot) published *A Son of the Forest*, thought to be the first full-length autobiography written in English and published by an American

Indian author. In 1912, Mourning Dove [Christine Quintasket] (Okanagan) completed the first draft of *Cogewea, the Half-Blood*, a novel published in 1927. Mourning Dove was the first American Indian writer to incorporate into a novel an Indian people's oral traditions and aspects of their daily life and religion.

In 1847, George Copway (Ojibway) published his autobiography, generally considered to be the first book in English by a Canadian Native. In 1886, there appeared *Poésies religieuses et politiques*, by Louis Riel (Métis), a famous Native writer of the time. One of Canada's best-known Native writers, E. Pauline Johnson (Mohawk), writing around the turn of the last century, produced poetry and prose that focused on Native peoples and her own heritage.

Published Native contemporary poetry in book form includes, for example: *The Wishing Bone Cycle*, a collection of Swampy Cree narrative poems; *Indians Don't Cry*, a collection of the poetry and short prose of George Kenny (Ojibway); and *Song of Eskasoni*, a volume of poetry by Rita Joe (Micmac). Poets published in various journals include Anneharte (Saulteaux), Shirley Bruised Head (Blood), J.B. Joe (Nootka), and Joane Cardinal Schubert (Peigan).

The appearance in 1970 of *Harpoon of the Hunter*, a novel by Markoosie, an Inuit, is thought to have signaled the beginning of contemporary Native fiction. More recent novels include, among many others, *Raven Steals the Light*, by Bill Reid (Haida) and *Slash*, by Jeanette Armstrong (Okanagan). Tomson Highway (Cree), author of *The Rez Sisters*, a critically acclaimed play, is one of a growing number of Canadian Native playwrights. Since the 1960s the proliferation of Native writers in Canada has been rapid. Contributing to the vigor of contemporary Native drama, prose and poetry are theater companies that hold workshops and produce Native plays, journals, magazines, and newspapers that specialize in Native materials, and Native-managed publishing companies and small presses interested in Native materials. In Ontario, the Native Theatre School trains Native people in acting, playwriting, and stagecraft. In British Columbia, the En'Owkin Centre for Native Writers, the first Native-managed school of its kind in North America, operates on the premise that young Native writers learn best from other Native writers who understand their concerns. The writing is directed in two ways: (1) toward the Native communities themselves in order to breathe life into traditions that have been lost or put aside due to the impact of colonialization, and (2) toward the world at large, and white audiences in particular.

In the United States, the works of American Indian writers who publish in English, with American Indian themes and in a voice that often echoes ancestral oral traditions, take various literary forms: autobiography, mysteries, novels, nonfiction, plays, poetry, and short stories. We unfortunately can offer here only a very brief listing of this large and ever-increasing body of literature.

Autobiography: *The Names*, N. Scott Momaday (Kiowa); *Life among the Piutes: Their Wrongs and Claims*, Sarah Winnemucca Hopkins (Paiute).

Mystery: *Stallion Gate*, Martin Cruz Smith (Seneca-Yaqui).

Novel: *Waterlily*, Ella Deloria (Dakota); *A Yellow Raft on Blue Water*, Michael Dorris (Modoc); *Jailing of Cecelia Capture*, Janet Campbell Hale (Coeur d'Alene-Kutenai); *Wind from an Enemy Sky*, D'Arcy McNickle (Métis-Flathead); *Almanac of the Dead. A Novel*, Leslie Silko (Laguna); *The Heirs of Columbus*, Gerald Vizenor (Ojibwa); *Indian Lawyer*, James Welch (Blackfeet-Gros Ventre).

Non-fiction: *We Talk, You Listen*, Vine Deloria, Jr. (Sioux); *Fus Fixico Letters*, Alexander Posey (Chickasaw-Creek); *Keeping Slug Woman Alive*, Greg Sarris (Kashaya Pomo-Coast Miwok).

Plays: *New Native American Drama*, Hanay Geiogamah (Kiowa-Delaware); *Green Grow the Lilacs* [basis for Rodgers and Hammersteins's "Oklahoma!"], Lynn Riggs (Cherokee).

Poetry: *In Mad Love and War*, Joy Harjo (Creek); *In Summer This Bear*, Maurice Kenny (Seneca-Mohawk); *Mud Woman: Poems from the Clay*, Nora Naranjo-Morse (Santa Clara); *Songs for the Harvester of Dreams*, Duane Niatum (Klallam); *Woven Stone*, Simon Ortiz (Acoma); *Round Valley Songs*, William Oandasan (Yuki); *An Eagle Nation*, Carter Revard (Osage); *What Happened When the Hopi Hit New York*, Wendy Rose (Hopi-Miwok); *A Breeze Swept Through*, Luci Tapahonso (Navajo); *Star Quilt*, Roberta Hill Whiteman (Oneida).

Short Stories: *Grandmothers of the Light*, Paula Gunn Allen (Laguna-Sioux); *Earth Power Coming: Short Fiction in Native American Literature*, Simon Ortiz, ed.

Various other examples and discussion of contemporary Native American writing can be found in anthologies and collections of short stories.

SOURCES

Information in section 5.1 is from Wallace 1978 and Silver fieldnotes; in addition, see Olmsted and Stewart 1978:234 (Achumawi storytelling). For section 5.2, see Silver fieldnotes and tape. Section 5.3 is from Hymes 1981 (structure of Chinook myths and tales) and 1984 (sample Chinook story); in addition, see Levitas et al. 1974 (central animal characters). For section 5.4, see Hinton 1984; see also Sapir 1910, Miller ms., and Chamberlain 1910 (Western America, the Great Basin and the Eskimo). For section 5.5, see Reichard 1944. Section 5.6 is from Sherzer 1983, 1986, and 1990. On section 5.8, see Hymes 1990 (Coyote in an airplane), Rex 1989 (poetry in Navajo), Zepeda 1982 (poems in O'odham), Dauenhauer and Dauenhauer 1987 (Tlingit), León-Portilla 1993 (Nahuatl), Vasquez 1992 (Aymara poem), Peyer 1994 (William Apes), Brown 1994 (Mourning Dove), Ruoff 1994 (Copway), King 1994 (Riel and Johnson), Atwood 1990 (The En'Owkin Centre for Native Writers), Norman 1976 (*The Wishing Bone Cycle*), Kenny 1977, Joe 1988, King 1994 (Canadian Native writing), Markoosie 1970, Reid 1984, Armstrong 1985, Highway 1988, Momaday 1976, Winnemucca Hopkins 1883, Smith 1986, Deloria 1988, Dorris 1988, Hale 1985, McNickle 1978, Silko 1991, Vizenor 1991, Welch 1990, Deloria, Jr. 1970, Posey 1993, Sarris 1993, Geiogamah 1980, Riggs 1936, Harjo 1990, Kenny 1985, Naranjo-Morse 1992, Niatum 1981, Ortiz 1992, Oandasan 1984, Revard 1993, Rose 1982, Tapahonso 1987, Whiteman 1984, Allen 1991, and Ortiz 1983.

SUGGESTED READINGS

See Basso 1984 on the role of stories in Western Apache culture and Hymes 1981, must reading for those interested in performance. For section 5.1, see Howard 1987 on the Cree Trickster who "brought words over" from animals to people; Kroskrity 1993a on formal devices used by Tewa storytellers to create an "authoritative" storytelling voice; Lang 1994 on a collection of traditional Karuk [or Karok] texts; Rice 1987 on Meadowlark, the bird that spoke Lakota; and Shipley 1991 on Maidu myths and stories. For section 5.3, Hymes 1984 provides a fuller (and more convincing) analysis of the Deer and Coyote narrative than we have had space to present; Koller et al. 1982 offers a variety of perspectives on Coyote; and Babcock and Cox 1994 consider the trickster in both oral and written American Indian literature. See Bright 1990 for an account of Nahuatl couplets, along with a short and very readable general discussion of ethnopoetics; other good descriptions include Foster 1974a and 1974b on Iroquois oratory; Bright 1984:98 on Karuk verse); and Sherzer and Woodbury 1987 for examples from Tonkawa, Sahaptin, Kuna, Quiché Maya, and Eskimo. For section 5.4, see Evers and Molina 1987 on Yaqui Deer Songs; Hill 1993 on transformations of everyday discourse in ritual singing; and Vander 1988 on Wind River Shoshoni songs. For section 5.6 see Sherzer and Urban 1986 on ritual speech and Chafe 1981 on colloquial and ritual Seneca. In section 5.7, for regional coverage of verbal art, see Hymes 1990 on Northwest Coast cultures and Liljeblad 1986 on the Great Basin. For regional coverage of oral literature, see Wiget 1994. Hinton and Watahomigie

1984 is a bilingual edition of the verbal art of eight Yuman communities (Hualapai, Havasupai, Yavapai, Paipai, Diegueño, Maricopa, Mohave, and Quechan). For section 5.8 see Coltelli 1990 in which eleven American Indian writers discuss, among other things, links between past and present in the creative process; Lerner 1990, anthology of contemporary northwest American Indian writing; Peyer 1990, early short stories by North American Indians; Purdy 1989 on the novels of D'Arcy McNickle; Sarris 1993 on oral traditions continued in English; Tapahonso 1993, a collection of Navajo poems and stories; and Wiget 1994, a history of emergence of Native American writing and consideration of Native American writing from 1967 to the present.

CHAPTER 6

FASHIONS OF SPEAKING

The Yurok (northwestern California) make a distinction between ordinary and *wo·gey* speech. *Wo·gey* speech is considered educated speech, used in discussing esoteric subjects, in reciting myths, and on those occasions when ordinary language would be considered too coarse. It is purposely taught and consciously learned after ordinary language is mastered. Control of *wo·gey* speech is a sign of education and good breeding, and it is said that only those born into high ranking or high status families learn it. *Wo·gey* speech is not a separate language distinct from ordinary Yurok; rather, it differs from ordinary speech only in its lexicon, that is, its vocabulary, and not all words in the lexicon are different. In some cases, the two styles of speaking use the same word with different meanings; thus *pegerk* is 'man (adult male human)' in ordinary talk, but 'real man, rich man, independent person (male or female)' in *wo·gey*. Lexical changes also involve use of special words in *wo·gey* not found in ordinary speech.

Form and function are two facets of speech **styles** (i.e., fashions of speaking). Under form, we ask, how is the style marked? Under function, the question is, under what conditions is it used and what does it signify? In this chapter our emphasis is on form—linguistic techniques used in marking fashions of speaking. The changes in form that differentiate Yurok everyday speech from *wo·gey* speech are similar (or analogous) to changes associated with the speech styles used in the performances considered in chapter 5, **marked** off from other speaking styles by special aspects of language structure (e.g., pronunciations, grammatical constructions, lexicon).

If a speech community gives names to speech varieties (e.g., English "preaching"; "gossiping," etc.), it is likely that the names indicate significant sociocultural functions for those varieties; see, for example, Shoshoni *hupia* 'song', and *natikʷinappɨh* '(traditional) story', and Tewa *tuhame* 'speechmaking' (sections 4.1 and 4.2.). If a fashion of speaking is not named, this may indicate that it is of less cultural significance than one with a name. It is, however, important not to jump to conclusions; sometimes a culturally significant speech style is unnamed. Seneca (New York, Ontario) speakers, for instance, commonly use three distinct styles of speaking for which there are no Seneca terms: a conversational style used in everyday social interaction; a preaching style used in a four-day ritual involving recitations of the message of Handsome Lake, the Seneca prophet; and a chanting style used in thanksgiving rituals. Inasmuch as each style relates to a different aspect of Seneca daily life, it is highly likely that speakers immediately recognize inappropriateness of use.

Changes from one form of speech to another may not be well marked; for instance, formal conversational speech styles in English are set off from informal (or **casual**) styles by more frequent use of several structural features, among which are pronunciations such as -ing ("Martha is leaving tomorrow") versus -in' ("Martha's leavin' tomorrow"), uncontracted forms, "Martha is . ." versus contracted forms "Martha's . . . ," and the use of which ("the speech which Martha is giving . . .") versus that ("the speech that Martha's givin' . . ."). Depending upon the nature of the social interaction, however, features that mark informal conversational styles may also occur in formal styles ("the speech that Martha's giving. . ."), and vice versa.

Differences between fashions of speaking can also be well marked; for example, in American English, the speech used in marriage rituals, when praying, when advertising used cars, and so on. Moreover, the members of a speech community often have definite attitudes about what constitutes the best (i.e., "good") speaking styles. Songs among the Shoshoni, chanting among the Hopi, the ceremonial language of the Pueblo, oratory among the Creek, or huehuetlaʔtōlli among the Aztec are examples of highly valued styles, as are all the styles illustrated in chapter 5. Typically, the best styles are considered special, important, sometimes sacred. Sometimes certain features of highly valued fashions of speaking are considered archaic; for example, English -eth, as in "He mak**eth** me to lie down in green pastures"; other times, uninterpretable features arise through borrowings from foreign dialects or languages (see the songs borrowed from Navajo into Havasupai, section 5.4).

We can also distinguish between everyday conversational styles (i.e., casual styles) and **expressive** fashions of speaking, which include baby talk, slang, swearing, word taboo, speech play, and related phenomena. These expressive styles sometimes carry prestige but, more often, in many social contexts their features mark them as inappropriate; for example, it has been reported for Yokuts (California) that there is a kind of morphological construction used by children that adults have felt too "silly" to be used in serious discussion. We also noted in chapter 4 that the Zuni have viewed slang as worthless, but harmless. Some expressive speech styles (e.g., profanity) may even be thought of as harmful.

As we have said, each fashion of speaking is marked by characteristic linguistic features. A particular style may be marked by any combination of features: (1) phonetic, (2) grammatical (either morphological or syntactic), (3) lexical (use of special vocabulary), (4) paralinguistic (i.e., by such features as "tone of voice," careful articulation, etc.), or (5) rhetorical and thematic.

It is probably impossible to specify the number of fashions of speaking that a cultural group recognizes, partly because some styles are unnamed and not (consciously) recognized, partly because differences in styles may become less well marked, and partly because new social circumstances may give rise to appropriate new styles. It is, of course, the well-differentiated styles and those considered best (or, for that matter, "not good") that are most apt to be easily (and consciously) recognized. Because an exhaustive classification of style types would be very difficult, if not impossible, especially cross-culturally, we settle here for a representative sample of style types in American Indian communities, using the following three-way framework: (1) styles that are examples of a performance, such as narrative, song, prayer (already discussed in the last chapter); (2) styles that indicate social relationships between speaker and hearer, such as respect speech and men's and women's speech (sections 6.1 and 6.2); and (3) expressive styles, including speech play, word taboo, and swearing (section 6.4). This three-way framework is not exclusive: for instance, baby talk (section 6.3) is an expressive style that also indicates social relationships between speaker and hearer, and the well-developed varieties of expressive speech in the Northwest Coast (section 6.5) often indicate social relationships and are often used in performances. Finally, our three-way framework ignores the fact that the use of ritual speech is not limited to performances.

6.1 SPEECH AND SOCIAL CATEGORY: RESPECT SPEECH AMONG THE AZTEC AND GUARIJÍO

In this section and the next two (6.2 and 6.3) we consider variation in speech that is a consequence of the particular participants; but such variation is seldom entirely independent of other variables, such as setting, topic, and attitude. Speakers in every speech community show deference when speaking to individuals who command respect, and often, also, when talking about other people or even objects that are felt to be special. A well-marked special speech style is sometimes used in such situations. We illustrate with two examples: one from Classical Aztec called the reverential, and the other from Guarijío called "speaking for two."

Aztec Reverential

The Aztec use a special form of speech called reverential speech when the speaker wants to show special respect to the hearer or to the subject of discourse. It was used in Classical Aztec in pre-Columbian times and continues to be used in the modern versions of the language. Because the linguistic and social rules of usage are slightly different between Classical and modern times, we will describe the rules as they applied to Classical Aztec, using the traditional orthography described in appendix I for writing Aztec.

The reverential form of the noun and pronoun is formed by adding the diminutive suffix *–tzin*:

taʔ-tli	'father'	*taʔ–tzin-tli*	'honored father'
ilama	'old woman'	*ilama-tzin*	'revered old woman'
coco-tli	'turtle dove'	*cocoʔ-tzin-tli*	'beloved turtle dove'
a-tl	'water'	*a-tzin-tli*	'holy water'
teʔhua	'you'	*teʔhua-tzin*	'honored you'

(The absolute suffix *–tli, –tl,* which is added to most nouns has a grammatical rather than a semantic function, and thus is untranslatable.)

The formation of the reverential form of the verb is a two-step process. First, the verb is made reflexive; the reflexive is illustrated with the verb *itta* 'to see'. In its non-reflexive form, the order of elements is SUBJECT PREFIX + OBJECT PREFIX + VERB STEM: *ni-mitz-itta* 'I see you' (lit. 'I-you-see'); *ti-nech-itta* 'you see me' (lit. 'you-me-see'). The order of elements for the reflexive is the same, but the object pronoun is replaced by a special reflexive form: *ni-no-itta* 'I see myself' (lit. 'I-myself-see'); *ti-mo-itta* 'you see yourself' (lit. 'you-yourself-see'). Next, a suffix is added, with the choice of suffix depending on the type of verb. Intransitive verbs add the causative suffix *–tia,* which we illustrate with the verb *cochi* 'to sleep'; in the example, we give the intransitive, the causative, and the reverential: *ni-cochi* 'I sleep' (intr.); *ti-cochi* 'you sleep' (intr.); *ni-mitz-cochi-tia* 'I make you sleep' (caus., lit. 'I-you-sleep-cause'); *ti-nech-cochi-tia* 'you make me sleep' (caus, lit. 'you-me-sleep-cause'); *ti-mo-cochi-tia* 'you sleep' (rev., lit. 'you-yourself-sleep-cause'). If the verb is transitive, the applicative suffix *–lia* is added. In its nonreverential function, the applicative is used when something is done for somebody else's benefit: *ni-tequiti* 'I work'; *ni-mitz-tequiti-lia* 'I work for you' (appl., lit. 'I-you-work-benefit'); *ni-mitz-caqui* 'I hear you'; *ni-mitz-tla-caqui-lia* 'I hear something for you' (appl., lit. 'I-you-something-hear-benefit'); *ni-mitz-no-caqui-lia* 'I hear you' (rev., lit. 'I-you-myself-hear-benefit', that is, 'I hear you for myself'). If the verb is already reflexive, then the special reverential suffix *–tzinoa* is added: *ti-mo-tataca* 'you scratch yourself'; *ti-mo-tataca-tzinoa* 'you scratch yourself (rev.)'. The reverential form of the verb is ambiguous; it shows reverence to either the subject or the object of the verb, unless one of them is the first person ("I," "we," "me," or "us"), since the first person cannot be honored. There are other changes, involving demonstrative prefixes on the verb and postpositions added to the noun, which we omit from this discussion.

Guarijío Speaking for Two

The Guarijío of northwest Mexico have a special respect style called *eméwame*, which is marked by three grammatical changes: (1) the first person plural pronouns *remé* 'we', *tamó* 'us, our' replace the first and second person singular *neé* 'I', *noó* 'me, my', and *muú* 'you', *amó* 'you (obj.), your'; (2) a passive tense suffix replaces an active tense suffix on the verb if the subject of *remé* 'we' really refers to second person 'you', but the active tense suffix remains if the subject is really 'I'; and (3) the plural replaces singular forms of nouns, verbs, and adjectives. An example of the replacement of 'we' for 'I': *mukére neé kuʔírabi* 'I carried it on my shoulders for a little while' (ordinary speech); *mukére remé kuʔírabi* (same meaning, *eméwame* speech). An example of the replacement of 'we' for 'you', with the verb made passive is *Mukére muú kuʔírabi?* 'Did you carry it on your shoulders for a little while?' (ordinary speech); *Mukéru remé kuʔírabi?* (same meaning, *eméwame* speech). In the last sentence, the verb *muké* 'to carry it on one's shoulders' has the past passive suffix *–ru* in place of the past active suffix *–re*, that is: *mukéru* 'it was carried', passive, versus *mukére* 'carried it', active.

The use of the plural is not as important in marking this special style as it might seem, since only a few nouns (and only nouns referring to people), verbs, and adjectives have special plural forms, such as *teʔmarí* 'boy'; *tehtémari* 'boys'; *kahtí* 'seated' (sg. subj.); *močiwá* 'seated' (pl. subj.); *tehpekúma* 'long' (sg.); *tetepéruma* 'long' (pl.); *tohsáname* 'white' (sg.); *toʔtósame* 'white' (pl.).

The Guarijío respect speech is limited to certain situations and to certain categories of in-laws, with whom it is used reciprocally. It is used when the speaker wishes to include the in-law (comparable to the way a nurse might say to a patient in our speech community, "How are we today?" but would not be likely to say, "We are running a fever," meaning "You are running a fever"). The in-laws with whom respect speech is used are: *moʔné* 'son-in-law', 'younger sister's husband'; *moʔóri* 'daughter-in-law', 'younger brother's wife'; *siʔá* 'father-in-law', 'wife or husband's older brother'; *wasí* 'mother-in-law', 'wife or husband's older sister'. Notice that the terms for parents-in-law and children-in-law are extended to certain categories of brother- and sister-in-law. Some speakers use terms derived from Spanish for the sibling-in-laws: *kompári* (< *compadre*) 'younger sister's husband', 'wife or husband's older brother'; *komári* (< *comadre*) 'younger brother's wife', 'wife or husband's older sister'. However, the respect speech remains unchanged. Respect speech is not used with the other siblings-in-law (older sister's husband, older brother's wife, spouse's younger brother or sister), relatives that have a different set of kinship terms. Bilingual Guarijío speakers translate *eméwame* into Spanish either as *"hablando por dos"* ("speaking for two"), which characterizes the linguistic markings, or as *"habla de los compadres"* (*"compadre* speech"), which characterizes the people between whom it is used.

Respect Speech

Grammatical markers used in respect speech systems usually succeed in distancing (metaphorically and psychologically) the person or object being respected. Using the plural is one common technique to accomplish this. We saw its use in the Guarijío respect system. The plurals are also used in much of northern California for addressing strangers and in-laws, and by certain Athapaskan-speaking peoples in addressing a mother-in-law. Greater psychological distance is also gained by adding an extra direct or indirect object through the use of certain morphological elements or by distancing the subject through the use of the passive, as in the Aztec and Guarijío systems.

Another common technique for showing respect is the use of the diminutive (as in Aztec), a semantic category often associated with endearment. In this case, psychological distance is decreased rather than increased, because respect is marked by showing that an endearing relationship exists between the speaker and addressee. Although the use of grammatical markers is especially common in respect speech, lexical marking is also frequently used. The Natchez of the lower Mississippi used this technique.

There is a relationship between respect speech usage (or social meaning) and the nature of the society. We find respect usage in many contemporary European systems in the use of polite (respect style) and familiar (casual style), and in certain Asian systems, such as Japanese and Korean. In these highly stratified societies, we find two usages: one is reciprocal, the other, nonreciprocal. The reciprocal usage is between equals in which the polite pronoun (e.g., Spanish *usted* 'you' polite) is used between people who are more distant (strangers, casual acquaintances), while the familiar (e.g., Spanish *tu* 'you' familiar) is used between people who are less distant (close friends, family members). The nonreciprocal usage is used between people of unequal status, with the person of higher status using the familiar form and the person of lower status answering with the polite form. The Classical Aztec usage seems to have paralleled modern European and Asian systems in being used both reciprocally and nonreciprocally; but reciprocal usage is common, while nonreciprocal usage is rare in such small-scale societies as the Guarijío. Moreover, the people who use it are almost always defined in terms of kinship categories, with in-laws, cross-sex ties, and senior versus junior (i.e., older/younger, ascending/descending generations) being the most common kinship parameters.

6.2 SPEECH AND SOCIAL CATEGORY:
MEN'S AND WOMEN'S SPEECH IN YANA

The Yana of northern California made a distinction between the speech of men and women. Most of the differences can be described by means of two rules, the application of which results in forms in women's speech being shorter than those in men's. The first rule applies to all noun forms that are two syllables or more in length, and to many verb forms that end in short /a/, /i/, and /u/. The form in women's speech is made by devoicing the final vowel and, if the consonant before the vowel is a plain unaspirated stop, it is changed to the corresponding aspirated stop:

men's	women's	
sika·ka	*sika·kʰA*	'quail'
mic'i	*mic'I*	'coyote'
šu·šu	*šu·šU*	'dog, horse'
hi·si	*hi·sI*	'man'
môhi	*môhI*	'to eat'
pʰača	*pʰačʰA*	'snow'

The second rule applies to nouns of one syllable, to nouns that do not end with a short /a/, /i/, or /u/, to demonstratives, and to certain verbs. In this case the men's speech form ends with –na, while the women's speech form ends with –h:

men's	women's	
ʔina	*ʔih*	'tree, stick'
yuna	*yuh*	'shelled acorn'
ya·na	*ya·h*	'person'
yu·čʰaina	*yu·čʰaih*	'acorn mush'
hič'inna	*hič'inh*	'wildcat'

Men's speech was used by men when talking to men. In all other cases, women's speech was used, that is, in men talking to women, and women talking to either men or women. Women, however, would use the men's speech if giving a direct quote, for example, in a tale quoting a male character talking to another male character.

We saw earlier (section 4.3) that the Koasati also made a distinction between men's and women's speech. In both Koasati and Yana, the style changes are marked phonetically. The systems differ in two regards, however. The Yana system is sensitive to both the speaker and the hearer, with the men's style used by men only when talking to men, and the women's style used in all other cases. The Koasati system is sensitive only to the sex of the speaker. In addition, in Koasati the forms in men's speech are derived by applying the rules to the forms that make women's speech, while in Yana the women's speech contains shortened forms of the men's.

Another example of phonetically marked sex-based style is found among the Gros Ventre, a Plains Indian community; also, a study done early in the century reported that among some Eskimo-speaking groups the final stops /p, t, k, q/ in men's speech are replaced by corresponding nasals /m, n, ŋ, ·ŋ/ in women's speech. Lexical and grammatical means are also used as markers of sex differences in speech. In the languages of some Pueblo groups, the differences are marked lexically (section 4.2); and in the Biloxi and Lakota languages the distinction is grammatically marked by differences in form for certain enclitics.

There have been numerous studies in recent years of sex-based gender differences in language, particularly in American English. These studies have made clear that, through investigating language use, we can learn a great deal about male-female social interactional behavior, both same-sex and different-sex. In addition, exploration of language use yields insights into attitudes speakers have about their own and the other sex. But it is tempting and all-too-easy to draw false conclusions from limited information; for instance, consider the Yana and Koasati sex-based gender styles. Do the linguistic rules that account for these special speech styles have social meaning? No, because the rules are categorical. Social meaning can be attached only when the speaker has a choice of whether or not to apply the given rule. About the only safe conclusion to reach concerning categorical use of sex-based gender rules in a speech style is that it signals the society's recognition of a difference between the two sexes, a fact that hardly needs linguistic evidence to support it.

Do societies with languages that have special sex-based gender styles (as opposed to the noncategorical, subtle style changes found in American English) recognize greater social differences between the sexes? Empirical examination of the two types does not lend support to this notion. It could be just as easy to conclude that the reverse is the case: Those societies that subtly indicate sex-based speech differences through noncategorical styles are in a better position to exercise "thought control" through language than societies for which sex-based gender differences are obvious and categorical. But there is no empirical support for this conclusion either. Or, what about the notion that women were better placed in Koasati society than they were in Yana society because Koasati linguistic rules derive men's speech forms from women's forms, while the Yana rules do the opposite? Once again, empirical support is not there: The setting up of "basic" forms (Koasati women's; Yana men's) is simply a linguist's descriptive device for the stating of linguistic rules, rules that tell us nothing about social relations between the sexes.

What of differences based on the sex of the hearer? As we have seen in Yana, a man used one style in speaking to other men, another when speaking to women. But in Koasati, the choice of gender style depends solely on the sex of the speaker, not the addressee. In other words, in the Koasati system, choice of gender style is totally fixed by the sex of the speaker, while in the Yana system the choice varies as the addressee varies. What might be the particular social significance of these differences? Too little is known about Yana society, and hypotheses based on such differences cannot be tested since sufficient cross-cultural and cross-linguistic data are lacking.

6.3 BABY TALK IN COCOPA

Cocopa, a Yuman language spoken along the lower Colorado River in Arizona and Mexico, employs a rather complex system for converting words and phrases of adult speech into baby talk, that is, speech used by adults in talking to small children. Some examples:

	Adult Speech	Baby Talk	
1	aṣú· ikm	anvú· ikm	'later'
2	umic wa·yá·c	unvít anyá·t	'she goes around crying'
3	lu·p mu·kʷi· kmyu	lu·p unvi·s yu	'what will you buy?'
4	xucáq	xunvák	'she's bad'
5	kʷanʸuk	kanvúk	'baby'
6	ṣuʔúl	sunvúl	'she washes'
7	xasány	ván	'little girl'
8	nʸi·šá·ɫy	ninvá·ɫ	'her hand'
9	mapúc msunáy inʸá·m	mapút nay na·m	'you are telling a big lie'
10	rapm	inlápm	'if it hurts'
11	mapúc mi·yá·y pi·t yum	putʸ vetʸ yo·m	'you're crazy'
12	cmwi·m ma·k myuxɫʸ	anví·m va·k yus	'go wherever you want!'

An examination of some of the baby-talk words, such as anvú· for adult aṣú· (1), anyá·t for adult wa·yá·c (2), or unvi·s for mu·kʷi (3) might lead to the conclusion that the baby words and the adult words are entirely different, in the same way that the English baby word "choo-choo" is different from "train." In most cases, however, the Cocopa baby words are not substitutes for adult words; instead, they are phonetically modified versions of adult forms, analogous, for example, to the English baby words "tumtum" and "wabbit," phonetically modified forms of "stomach" and "rabbit."

We give some of the rules for phonetic modification. Examples of each rule are taken from the list above and referred to it by the number in that list. Since the rules are complex, and often more than one rule applies to a given form, the reader will have to pay close attention to detail and may have to read through the rules more than once to understand how they operate in the examples given. If an example shows no change, the operation of the rules is optional. The reader should look carefully at the two charts of Cocopa consonants, one for consonants found in adult words, the other for those found in baby words:

Cocopa Consonants (Adult Words)

p	t	ṭ	c	k	kʷ	q	qʷ	ʔ
	s	ṣ	š	x	xʷ			
		ł	łʸ					
		l,r	lʸ					
m		n	nʸ					
w			y					

(Positions of articulation: labial, dental, alveolar, palatal, velar, labiovelar, post velar, post labiovelar, and glottal; see appendix 1.)

Cocopa Consonants (Baby Words)

p		ṭ		k
	s			x
v				
		ł		
		l		
m		n		
w		y		

The changes from adult to baby words are summarized in the series of rules given next. These rules change consonants or vowels (Rules 1, 3, 6), introduce consonants (Rules 2 and 5), drop consonants (Rule 4), or add the diminutive prefix (-)n- (Rule 7). Their application results in a reduction in the number of consonants used in baby words, and also the addition of a consonant, /v/ (Rule 2), not found in adult words.

RULE 1. Certain groups of consonants are replaced by a single consonant. The replacements are:

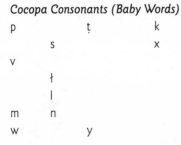

t, ṭ, c	> t
k, kʷ, q, qʷ	> k
s, ṣ, š	> s
x, xʷ	> x
ł, łʸ	> ł
l, lʸ, r	> l
n, nʸ	> n

Some examples, with the consonant under consideration in bold type:

Adult form		Baby form
wa·yác	>	*anyá·t* (2)
xucáq	>	**x**unvák (4)
kʷanʸuk	>	**k**anvúk (5)
ṣuʔúl	>	**s**unvúl (6)
nʸi·šá·tʸ	>	**n**invá·t (8)

RULE 2, CONSONANT REPLACEMENT. The consonant before the root syllable (which is the stressed syllable) is replaced by /v/, a consonant that is not otherwise found in Cocopa:

xu**c**áq	>	xun**v**ák (4)
kʷ**a**nʸuk	>	kan**v**úk (5)

Sometimes Rule 1 is applied in contexts where Rule 2 would be expected:

rapm	>	in**ł**ápm (10)
i**nʸ**á·m	>	**n**a·m (9)

Sometimes neither rule is applied, as in:

mapúc	>	mapút (9)
msunáy	>	nay (9)

RULE 3, PALATALIZATION. This rule is not used very often, but when it is, it is in place of Rule 1. In this case, dental, alveolar, and palatal consonants are replaced as follows:

t, ṭ, c	> tʸ
s, ṣ, š	> š
ł, łʸ	> łʸ
l, lʸ	> lʸ
n, nʸ	> nʸ

The consonant /tʸ/ does not otherwise occur in Cocopa as an independent consonant:

ma**p**úc	>	pu**t**ʸ (11)
pi**ṭ**	>	ve**t**ʸ (11)

RULE 4, CONSONANT DROPPING. Consonants that are not part of the root (i.e., are part of prefixes or suffixes) may be dropped. If a vowel that is part of a prefix follows a dropped consonant, that vowel usually drops as well:

kmyu	>	yu (3)
msunáy	>	nay (9)
mapúc	>	put^y (11)

RULE 5, –S SUFFIXATION. The consonant /-s/ may be added to the vowel of the root. In some cases, the adult form contains no suffix, while in other cases, the –s suffix takes the place of one that was dropped because of Rule 4:

| mu·k^{w}i· | > | unvi·**s** (3) |
| myuxɬ^y | > | yu**s** (12) |

RULE 6, VOWEL CHANGES. Long vowels in prefixes (but not in roots), if they have not been lost by Rule 4, are usually shortened, and the vowels /i, u/ are sometimes changed to /e, o/, respectively:

n^y**i**·šá·ɬ^y	>	n**i**nvá·ɬ (9)
p**i**·t	>	v**e**t^y (11)
yu**m**	>	yo·m (11)

The reader may have also noticed other places where there is a vowel found in one form, but missing in the corresponding adult or baby word. This is because Cocopa has a complex rule for vowel insertion, a rule that is part of adult grammar, rather than just for forming baby words. Because of various other changes brought on by the operation of the baby-word rules, it is sometimes the case that vowel insertion takes place in one form, but not the other.

RULE 7, PREFIX OF DIMINUTIVE N–. This is not a phonetic rule, but a grammatical one, in which the diminutive prefix n– is usually (but not necessarily always) added to the baby word. It is not prefixed to the very beginning of the word, but rather to the consonant of the root:

wa·yác	>	a**n**yá·t (2)
xucáq	>	xu**n**vák (4)
k^{w}an^{y}uk	>	ka**n**vúk (5)
ṣuʔúl	>	su**n**vúl (6)
n^{y}išá·ɬ^y	>	ni**n**vá·ɬ (8)

There are additional rules, but these seven account for the most common and most pervasive changes found in baby talk. Often several rules apply to a given word so that the similarity of the baby word to the adult word is opaque. For example, to the adult word mu·k^{w}i· (3), apply Rules 2, 4, 5, 6, and 7, and the result is unvi·s. Or to xasán^y (7), apply Rules 1, 2, 4 to yield van. With so many rules to apply to just a single word, it is hardly surprising that the rules are not applied 100 percent of the time; it is just possible that the speaker simply "forgets" and drops a rule. It is also noteworthy that there are options, so that Rule 3 (palatalization) is an option for Rule 1 (consonant fronting). There is also variation across speakers, so that, for example, some Cocopa speakers use a consonant other than /v/ in Rule 2 (consonant replacement).

Among the Cocopa, men use the diminutive prefix *n–* in baby talk, but the use of consonant changes is limited to women; baby talk is used with boys and girls up to about the age of five or six; and young girls will use it in answering their mothers. A mother will sometimes use it with older children in a teasing situation, and often it will be used between a mother and her youngest adolescent daughter to show affection. But baby talk is never used after the daughter marries.

Although baby talk is very common, it is not always a special style, as it is among the Cocopa, where it can be described by a set of formal rules. Baby talk is not to be confused with child language, a simplified version that children use before they have mastered the full language. Where found, baby talk is typically a formalized, institutionalized type of speech that is normally used by adults in talking to young children, and that young children often use (and must learn to use) in return.

A limited number of techniques are used for marking baby talk. The technique favored by the Cocopa, namely, phonetic substitutions, is found in other systems, but seldom are the rules as pervasive and complex as in this case. It is likely that rules for phonetic substitution have their origin in adults mimicking what they perceive as young children's mistakes. The Cocopa and other such systems are more than just the "mistakes" of infants, however, because they utilize a *particular* set of phonetic substitutions. The systems among young children, on the other hand, while showing certain trends, such as the simplification of consonants, dropping certain consonants (especially in final position), and so on, are idiosyncratic when compared across children. Thus a Cocopa infant's early phonological system may display certain features found in the baby-talk system, but it will not be identical to it; in fact, the child will have to learn that system as well as the regular adult system as well.

Lexical marking, the use of special baby-talk vocabulary, is a technique more common than phonetic substitution for distinguishing this special style. We noted the use of lexical marking in Keres (section 4.2) and there is a similar system among the Comanche. Lexical marking usually involves a few dozen special baby words for objects and activities common in the child's world.

Baby-talk styles may also make use of grammatical marking. In the Comanche system there are two grammatical techniques, reduplication (cf. English "choo-choo") and use of the diminutive suffix (cf. English "bunny," "kitty," "horsie"), both of which occur frequently across languages. We noted that Cocopa also makes extensive use of the diminutive. In addition, Cocopa uses reduplication, which we did not illustrate because it is less commonly found in baby-talk styles. Except for the diminutive and reduplication, the use of special morphological or grammatical devices is not very widespread. One can, however, find a few examples, for instance, the use of a particular morphological derivation in Yokuts that is found only in baby talk.

Finally, the marking devices may involve paralinguistic features; for example, Quiché, a Guatemalan language, uses whispering; and a very common feature of baby-talk systems combines the use of palatal consonants (again, see Cocopa) with heavy palatalization and special voice characteristics in which the voice is placed at a higher pitch, often almost squeaking.

When speakers are asked why they use baby talk, they frequently suggest that it is easier and simpler for the child to learn to speak and understand. The Kuna use of full, uncontracted forms when talking to children (and to foreigners), very likely does make it easier for the child; however, complex sets of rules in systems such as Cocopa make suspect the validity of the notion of "easier and simpler." A notion more apt to be valid is that baby talk shows endearment, another explanation speakers sometimes offer.

Even when baby talk is absent as a special style or formalized institution, it is usually present in a more informal fashion in the use of such devices as palatalization, nonstandardized phonetic substitutions, greater use of diminutive forms, and the like. Although baby talk has been reported to be absent among a few American Indian groups—the Hidatsa, Gros Ventre, Shoshoni, Havasupai, and Kaska— we strongly suspect that more intensive investigation would show it present as an informal system in the speech of at least some of these groups.

6.4 EXPRESSIVE SPEECH: SWEARING, SPEECH PLAY, AND WORD TABOO

Language use in most cultures includes speech varieties that can be labeled swearing, verbal abuse, cursing, profanity, or vulgarity, and speakers will agree that such varieties are bad or harmful, but it is important to keep in mind that what is profane or vulgar varies from culture to culture; for instance, swearing is sometimes reported absent in American Indian communities, but such reports may hinge on the culturally defined notions of investigators. Among the Delaware, elements of scatological and sexual reference are incorporated into nouns and verbs: *húnti hú kpanš·e·t·iyéhala!* 'pretty soon you'll fall the hell off!', with *–š·e·t·iye(·)–* 'anus' inserted between the initial and final elements of *kpaníhala* 'you fall'; *mpas·alák·ay* 'the damned bus', from *mpás* 'bus' plus an element meaning 'penis'. The use of elements of scatological or sexual reference is also encountered in the speech of various other American Indian groups, and similar topics are used in swearing in Apache.

Death, especially of a relative, is an even more frequent theme for verbal abuse. In Blackfoot (northern Plains) it is delivered in the third person: *máipaxkóxsinisikápoko-mipúminàs* 'his (meaning: your) lice have a very bad-death-dirty taste'.

In Crow (Montana) a curse can be "you are a ghost," meaning you are practically invisible, crazy, and alone in the world; "you have no one to talk to," meaning, all your relatives are gone, there is no one to support you, and hence you cannot be of any account; "no one at all owns you," meaning you completely lack emotional ties, no one cares for you or feels for you; or a person can be likened to a lower animal.

If profanity and verbal abuse represent the dark side of expressive speech, speech play represents the light side. It includes puns, tongue-twisters, word games, and we might include slang. Although these genres are found in American Indian communities, they are not well developed and have not been extensively reported. Pig Latin-like word-play games, common through Eurasia, have not been reported for North America. They are, however, extensively developed among the Kuna of Panama, who have several types. In one type, *sorsik summakke* or *arepečunmakke* 'talking backwards', the first syllable of the word is moved to the end of the word: *osi > sio* 'pineapple'; *ope > peo* 'to bathe'; *takke > ketak* 'to see'; *take > keta* 'to come'; *ipya > yaip* 'eye'; *uwaya > wayau* 'ear'. In a type the Kuna call *ottukkuar sunmakke* 'concealed talking', the sequence /ppV/ is inserted after the first consonant and vowel of each syllable (/V/ indicates that the vowel after /pp/ is identical to the vowel of the preceding syllable): *merki > mepperkippi* 'North American'; *pia > ppippiappa* 'where'; *ua > uppuappa* 'fish'.

Word taboo is a manifestation of the belief in the power of the word. Death taboo has been reported for the Plains and is especially common in the Northwest Coast and California. Among the Coast Salish of the Northwest Coast, a person's name becomes taboo immediately after death. At a following feast a word phonetically similar to the name is made taboo and replaced by a descriptive phrase; the taboo is lifted when the name is later given to a member of the deceased person's lineage. In the nineteenth century, for example, when *xát^was* and *č'atádad* died, *x̣átx̣at* 'mallard duck' was replaced by *hɔ́hɔbšəd* 'red foot', and *sč'atá* 'rock' was replaced by *k^{'w}îlʔílas* 'round object for cooking'. The word for mallard duck was permanently replaced by 'red foot', and in the 1940s only a few older people remembered the old word. The word for 'rock', however, came back into use after the taboo was lifted.

Death is not the only context for the operation of word taboo. Animal names in particular seem to evoke this phenomenon; for example, among the Kuna the names of a number of plants and animals are not uttered at night, being replaced instead by euphemisms:

Ordinary (day) names	*Night names*
marya 'guava'	*kaya piri* (lit. 'curved mouth')
salu 'snail'	*tios uwaya* (lit. 'God's ears')
nalup 'peach palm'	*ikko turpa* (lit. spine fruit)

In many parts of North America, the bear is believed to be powerful and supernaturally dangerous, and its name is avoided on certain occasions. The Shoshoni avoid its name during pine-nut picking time, replacing it with a number of special words and phrases such as *paha* 'aunt' (the kinship position Bear usually has in Shoshoni mythology). The names for owl are also avoided in wide areas of North America, because the owl's call is closely associated with death.

6.5 DIMINUTIVE, AUGMENTATIVE, AND
EXPRESSIVE SPEECH IN THE NORTHWEST COAST

We saw in section 2.7 that many languages have a special diminutive form to refer to something small; it is most commonly marked by a suffix or by sound symbolism. Some languages also have an augmentative to refer to something large. It is very common for diminutive and augmentative systems to become involved in defining different styles, as we have seen with the diminutive frequently being used in baby talk, and the diminutive noun suffix being used in Classical Aztec in the reverential.

The languages along the coast of Washington and British Columbia have developed a complex diminutive and augmentative system, using both suffixes and sound symbolism. These systems have been incorporated into a number of special styles used to talk to and about a wide variety of different kinds of people. They have been described for the Nootka of Vancouver Island, and the Quileute of Washington State, and have been reported for a number of other groups in the area. We give a sample of the categories in the system used by the Nootka of Vancouver Island.

In speaking to or about children, the diminutive suffix –*ʔis* is used to show affection or love to a child: *waɬ-šiƛ-aH* 'I am going home' (*waƛ* 'to return', –*šiƛ* inceptive action, –*aHƛ* 'I'); *waɬ-šiƛ-ʔis-aH* 'I am going home, little one' in lullabies. It can also be used to belittle an adult. The augmentative suffix –*aq* is used in talking to or about fat or large people: *haʔ-ǫkʷ-it-Ha-k* 'Did you eat?' (*haʔ* 'eat', –*ǫkʷ* intransitive suffix, –*it* 'past time', –*Ha* question marker, –*k* 'you'); *haʔ-ǫkʷ-áq-it-Ha-k* 'Did you eat, fatty?' In talking about unusually small people and also about small birds, the diminutive suffix is used, along with a consonant change, in which [s] and [š] are changed to [ś], [c] and [č] to [ć], and [c'] and [č'] to [ć']. Notice that the diminutive suffix –*ʔis* is, by this rule, changed to –*ʔiś*: *hín-t-šiƛ-weʔini* 'he comes, they say'; *hín-t-śiƛ-ʔiś-weʔini* 'he, little man, comes, they say'. When talking to or about persons with eye defects, the diminutive suffix is used, along with another change pattern, in which the same six consonants are changed to the laterals [ɬ], [ƛ], and [ƛ']. Again the diminutive suffix changes, this time to [-ʔiɬ]: qʷís-mah 'he does so'; qʷíɬ-ʔiɬ-mah 'he does so, weak eyes'; semi 'Sammy' (the English name given to a cross-eyed Nootka man); ɬemi-ʔiɬ 'little cross-eyed Sammy'. This manner of speaking, called ƛ'aƛ'áčk'ini 'to talk in a sore-eyed fashion', is also used to refer to the mythological characters Deer and Mink, whose style of talking contains the changes to lateral consonants unaccompanied by use of the diminutive. When speaking of lame people, the diminutive suffix is used, along with the element –ƛš– or –ƛši–, which is stuck inside the word at any point: hin-ínɪ-ʔaƛ-ma 'he comes now' (hin– 'be, do'; –inɪ 'come'; –ʔaƛ 'now'; –ma tense suffix); hin-ínɪ-**ƛ̌ší-ʔic'**-aƛ-ma 'the lame chap is coming'. (The diminutive suffix combined with –ƛš becomes –ʔic'). For talking to or about left-handed people, the element –čHᵃ– is inserted after the first syllable, along with the diminutive suffix: yáaɬ-ʔaƛ-ma 'there now he is' (yáaɬ 'be there'; –ʔaƛ 'now'; –ma tense suffix); yáaɬ-**čHᵃ-ʔic'**-aƛ-ma 'there now the left handed person is'. It is also usual, particularly when joking, to use this method of marking speech when referring to bears, which are thought to be left-handed. It is appropriate to use the diminutive marking in speaking to or about children, but the other marking patterns are only used with reference to a person, unless an insult is intended. There are also special forms for hunchbacks, circumcised males, greedy people, and cowards.

The Quileute of Washington have a similar system, along with a form used by men in speaking directly to women, but used by women when speaking about women. An early study reports that the Haida of Queen Charlotte Islands used a suffix –ʔl in talking to a slave, in a kindly manner to an equal, or in belittling oneself, out of courtesy.

Although full-blown systems of the Nootka type seem to be limited to the Northwest Coast, simpler versions have been reported in other parts of western North America in the special speech of animals in stories. In Nez Perce (Idaho) stories, Bear changes consonants to ɬ; Skunk, besides nasalizing in a highpitched voice and changing certain consonants, changes a to e·; and Coyote changes n to l and s to š. In the stories of various California groups, Coyote talk is also marked by changes from ordinary speech; for example, in Chemehuevi (southeastern California) Coyote uses the suffix -aykʸʔ; and in Yahi (northern California) he substitutes n for the ordinary Yahi l. In stories told in other parts of the West there are still other variations: Bear, in Takelma (Oregon) stories, sometimes prefixes ɬ– to words; and in Cocopa Coyote sometimes inserts the segments –lʸ– or –l– when he speaks, and Mountain Lion's speech may contain extra –r– segments. Story animals are not the only ones who use these sorts of special speech: Cocopas, for example, use special sounds in talking to cats and other domesticated animals, and in depicting how they talk.

Animal speech of the kind we have mentioned is not limited to American Indian languages: In depictions of animal talk in movie cartoons, for instance, Tweety Bird substitutes *t* for a number of ordinary American English speech sounds; and Sylvester the Cat changes various sounds to *t^y*, a non-English speech sound that sounds "slurpy" to English speakers. The varieties of consonantal play used to portray animal speech or, as in Nootka, to express judgments about particular group characteristics, reflect attitudinal patterns of a culture rather than the feelings or mood of an individual. It is not unusual at all in languages for this kind of expressive use to be associated with cultural notions about respect, sex-differences and humor, as well as smallness, largeness, affection, and contempt (section 2.7).

6.6   FORM AND FUNCTION

Phonetic markings are a common means of defining speech styles. We have seen it as a marker for defining baby talk (e.g., Cocopa), men's and women's speech (e.g., Koasati), and expressive speech in the Northwest Coast and Kuna ("talking backwards"). We found no examples in our sample of phonetically marked respect speech; however, not enough is known about respect speech in languages to draw a conclusion that phonetic marking is seldom used for this genre. Phonetic marking is very commonly used in song (e.g., Havasupai, Shoshoni), and while it is not rare with other performance types (e.g., Kuna), neither is it common.

Grammatical markings are commonly used to mark respect speech (e.g., Classical Aztec, Guarijío). This type of device is also found in baby talk (e.g., the common occurrence of reduplication and the diminutive), less commonly in differentiating men's and women's speech. Sometimes special grammatical markers are used in performance types (e.g., the special prefixes and suffixes used in Kuna), but more common is the preferential use of certain morphological and syntactic constructions, for example, the more frequent use of nominal sentences in Havasupai songs or the more frequent use of the optative suffix –*ye* in Kuna performances.

Lexical marking (the use of special vocabulary items, as well as the use of metaphor) is such a common device for all style types that we hardly need to list specific examples. We find it for all varieties of performance (oratory, song, prayer, and others), respect speech, men's and women's speech, baby talk, and (even though we gave no examples) slang and profanity.

Paralinguistic marking is found for almost all types of styles, but it is particularly diagnostic with certain types. Palatalization, often along with a high pitched voice, is a very common marker of baby talk. A tone of voice that many members of the

American English speech community would recognize by the term "preacher talk" is quite common in oratory. Manner of organization and thematic content are also important marking devices in performance types.

We have discussed the relation between form and function in those cases where it is possible to gain some insight into the origins of these marking techniques: the use of grammatical devices to increase or decrease psychological distance in respect speech; the reduction of consonant sequences and other similar simplifications in baby talk, simplifications that mimic the infant's learning of the language; the use of more "open" sounds in song, and so on. A number of questions remain, however, particularly for phonetic and lexical markings. Why, in certain Eskimo communities, for example, did men use voiceless stops, while women used the corresponding nasals? The replacement of geminated voiceless stops by corresponding nasals plus voiced stops in Shoshoni songs is congruent with the fact that more open sound occurs in songs; but why this *particular* substitution? The use of metaphor in lexical replacement is not hard to understand, but the simple substitution of one lexical item for another is not: for example, *ome* 'woman' is replaced by *yai* in the Kuna "puberty language"; where did *yai* come from?

In some cases, it can be shown that phonetic rules and lexical replacements are borrowings from neighboring dialects or languages; for example, Siberian Yupik Eskimo has borrowed a pattern from Sirenikski, another Eskimo language, and uses it in stories in the speech of small children or of adults in addressing small children. In Sirenikski, most noninitial vowels have become [ə]. In folktales, Siberian Yupik Eskimo uses the diminutive suffix –*kəłə*, and makes vowel changes similar to those that occurred in Sirenikski, for speech to small children in folktales; thus a giant addresses a small girl: *Panəkəłəmaaŋ saməŋ* piiqsin? 'Little daughter dear, what are you saying?' *Panə-kəłə-maaŋ* (lit. 'daughter-diminutive-vocative') would be *pani-kəłə-maaŋ* in normal speech.

Examples of lexical borrowing are found in the Keres-speaking Pueblos of New Mexico, in which some of the words that are ceremonial words in one Pueblo Keres dialect are everyday words in another Keres dialect. Although in most cases we do not know, nor are we apt to know, the history of a particular phonetic or lexical marking, it is probable that some cases are the result of borrowing; but it is very unlikely that all such phonetic and lexical markings have arisen in this fashion. Unfortunately, then, the origin of the nasals inserted before a stop in Shoshoni songs, and of *yai* 'woman' in Kuna "puberty language" will probably always remain a mystery.

SOURCES

The introduction draws from Buckley 1984 (Yurok speech styles), Chafe 1993:73 (Seneca), and Gayton and Newman 1940 (Yokuts example). Section 6.1 is based on Andrews 1974, Sullivan 1976, 1988 (Aztec reverential speech), Miller 1980 (Guarijío respect speech); the general respect speech comments draw from Miller n.d.b. In section 6.2, men's and women's speech discussion is based on Sapir 1951 (Yana), and Haas 1944 (Koasati); other examples are from Flannery 1953, Taylor 1982 (Gros Ventre), Boas 1911:79 and Kalmár 1979 (Eskimo), and Haas 1944 and Alan Taylor p.c. (Biloxi and Lakota). In section 6.3, the baby-talk treatment is based on Crawford 1970 and 1978a, with mention of Comanche drawn from Casagrande 1948, and Yokuts example from Gayton and Newman 1940; references to Quiché and Kuna from Pye 1986, Sherzer 1983:39; speculation about presence or absence of baby talk in Hidatsa, Gros Ventre, Shoshoni, Havasupai, and Kaska is from Miller n.d.a. In section 6.4, the verbal-abuse discussion draws from Laski 1958:149 and Ransom 1946: 54 (reported absence of, in American Indian communities), with examples from Ives Goddard p.c. (Delaware), Opler 1941:457, Devereux 1951 (Apache), Alan Taylor p.c. (Blackfoot), and Lowie 1959:105 (Crow); Kuna speech-play discussion draws from Sherzer 1970, 1976; word-taboo references about the Northwest Coast, California and the Plains are from Elmendorf 1951, Kroeber 1925–26:181, 360, 469, 499, 749, and Lowie 1935:68; the Coast Salish example is from Elmendorf 1951. Examples of Kuna word taboos are from Sherzer 1983:29–30. In section 6.5, the discussion of the Nootka diminutive-augmentative system is based on Sapir 1915, and the Haida example is from Swanton 1911:254. Examples concerning special speech of animals and depictions by speakers of how animals talk are drawn from Aoki 1970 (Nez Perce), Langdon 1978 and Hinton 1989b (Chemehuevi, Yahi, Takelma, Cocopa, and American English). In regard to section 6.6, see de Reuse 1989 for an example of Siberian Yupik Eskimo borrowing of a phonetic pattern and White 1944 for comment on lexical borrowing between Keres dialects.

SUGGESTED READINGS

Regarding the introduction, see Voegelin 1960 for discussion of casual and non-casual speech styles; Basso 1990:114–17 for a typology of style categories in Western Apache speech and a discussion of stylistic and functional differences in Western Apache narratives; and Sherzer 1983:18–20 for a discussion of problems of considering style variation in a cross-cultural perspective. See Schlicter 1981 for description of a Wintu speech style—shamanistic jargon. On section 6.1 see Hill and Hill 1978 for a study of respect forms in modern Nahuatl. On section 6.2 see Briggs 1992 for a study of Warao women's use of language in ritual wailing; Halpern 1980 for discussion of sex differences in Quechan narration; Kroskrity 1983 for consideration of male and female speech in Pueblos; and Kimball 1987 and Saville-Troike 1988 for discussions of a reappraisal of Haas' 1944 study of Koasati men's and women's speech. On section 6.3, Kess and Kess 1986 present a study of Nootka baby talk. On section 6.4, Bright 1979 considers how dead kin are named in northwestern California; Carranza 1983 discusses Quechua insults. 6.5: Egesdal 1992 is a study of Thompson Salish speech stylization.

CHAPTER 7

NONVERBAL COMMUNICATION

Language is so closely associated with humanness that we tend to overlook the fact that it is just one of many channels of socially organized communication. Among these channels are highly patterned nonverbal communication systems such as kinesics (the social uses of posture, facial expressions, and eye movements), proxemics (the social uses of space, including how close or far people position themselves from one another while interacting), and paralanguage (the social uses of nonlinguistic vocal behavior: how voices sound ["throaty," "hoarse," etc.]; how speakers use voice pitch, careful articulation, length [e.g., "drawled" or "clipped" speech], etc.; and how they use sounds that function like words [e.g., "shhh," "psst," "tsk-tsk," etc.]). In previous chapters we have mentioned in passing aspects of paralanguage, and, in effect, we cannot do much more. Information about nonverbal communication systems and how they integrate with spoken language to form culture-specific modes of communication is at best sketchy for all speech communities, not just American Indian communities.

In this chapter, our discussion of American Indian forms of nonverbal communication centers on uses of silence, speech surrogates, and direct signaling systems. Silence, the absence of talk, connects with speech in ways that speakers are unaware of for the most part. A speech surrogate is based on language, and the components of the surrogate represent features of a particular language. The most highly developed of these is writing, which we consider in chapter 8. In writing, a symbol such as a letter or logographic sign (= word character, see section 8.2) is a direct substitute for a sound or a word in the language. In speech surrogates based on musical pitch, certain aspects of language (tones, certain classes of vowels and consonants) are represented by changes in pitch and character of the musical notes. Surrogates based on whistling or whistle-like systems have sprung up in widely scattered places in the world, and two of them, the Kickapoo and Mazatec systems, are considered in this chapter. Surrogates based on musical pitch are never as "full" as writing. In alphabetic writing, an attempt is made, though never completely successful, to represent all the sounds of the language. In whistle surrogates, for example, only classes of sounds are represented.

So-called sign "languages" have also sprung up in a variety of places in the world. They are difficult to classify, since sometimes they have characteristics that are based in part on the spoken language; and, other times, a sign-language system displays language-like characteristics, but is not based on any specific language. This seems to be the case with Plains Sign Language, which is considered in this chapter. Despite similarities to spoken language, sign languages are seldom speech surrogates. Exceptions are the so-called spelling systems sometimes used in modern nonhearing communities. These are true surrogates, but because they are based on writing (e.g., signed English), which is in turn based on a spoken language, they are a surrogate of a surrogate.

In contrast to speech surrogates, direct signaling systems and mnemonics have no connection with language; the message can be understood without translation into the language of the signaler. The signals have conventional meanings, sometimes the result of prearranged agreements ("one if by land, two if by sea"), and other times by tacit agreement.

7.1 SILENCE: THE WESTERN APACHE

Silence, which all cultures use in certain settings to convey meaning, is often misinterpreted across cultures; for instance, cross-cultural misinterpretation can arise because the pauses between alternating utterances in a conversation are longer in many American Indian communities than they are in Euro-American communities. Silence often makes us feel uncomfortable. In certain contexts, it can be interpreted as hostile behavior. Strangers seated next to one another on a journey may feel they must make chitchat, even if they really have nothing to say. The old saw, "Children should be seen and not heard," indicates that there are also settings in which silence is appropriate. In a mainstream American classroom, for instance, silence communicates attention and receptivity. Just as there are cross-cultural differences concerning what is appropriate verbal behavior in various settings and situations, including what to say, there are also differing views of what not to say and when to say nothing. In order to behave in culturally acceptable ways it is as important to know a community's conventions about when not to speak as it is to know what to say.

Even though American Indian communities do not all use silence in the same ways, they share certain similarities, at least when contrasted with Euro-American communities. The discussion that follows is drawn from a study of the uses of silence among the Western Apache of Arizona.

The Western Apache use silence in three situations: (1) to show respect to another, usually a person of authority, (2) in certain ritual settings, by a specialist during certain periods of preparation, and (3) when the relationship between the participants in an interaction is seen as potentially ambiguous or unpredictable. It is this last situation that non-Apaches find most difficult to understand. The most obvious case of an unpredictable relationship is when two strangers meet. In our society, we feel free to talk after introductions, which can even be self-introductions. In Western Apache society, introductions between strangers would be out of place; by the time two people know each other well enough to talk together, an introduction is not needed. In one situation a work party included two individuals who were strangers. During the first four days, the two said nothing to each other; then on the fourth day, one of them said: "Well, I know there is a stranger to me here, but I've been watching him and I know he is all right." After that, the two felt free to talk to each other.

Courtship and a child's return home from boarding school are other unpredictable circumstances that call for silence for a period of time. In a courtship situation, a couple are together for some time before they feel comfortable in speaking freely to each other. When children return home from boarding school, parents and children do not speak to each other for a while. Because the children have been away in an alien environment and perhaps have changed, the situation is unpredictable. It is up to the children to speak first since it is their behavior, not the parents', that is potentially unpredictable. Unpredictable behavior is also characteristic of persons who get angry and speak angrily to others, or are drunk, or are sick with grief because of the death of a relative. Western Apaches do not talk to such persons until they are back in their right minds. Speaking to persons in such states might just make it more difficult for them to return to normal. It is easy to see how this silence behavior could lead to intercultural miscommunication between Western Apaches and Euro-Americans. If a Euro-American gets mad at someone who turns out to be blameless, that person is expected "to stick up for him- or herself," rather than remain silent, since silence might be interpreted as an admission of guilt.

7.2 KICKAPOO AND MAZATEC WHISTLE SPEECH

Kickapoo Whistle Speech

Original Kickapoo territory was in the Great Lakes region. Forced out of their homeland, most Kickapoos reside today on reservations in Kansas and Oklahoma; however, in the middle of the nineteenth century, some left the United States to settle on lands provided by the Mexican government in the state of Coahuila. Of the various Kickapoo groups, only the Mexican Kickapoo use *onowéčikepi* 'whistling', a form of nonverbal communication that is an adaptation of a love flute that was widely used in precontact times in the area from which the Kickapoo emigrated.

"Whistle speech" is a misnomer because this mode of communication is analogous to fluting in both production and sound. The indigenous flute, obsolete in Mexico since the early twentieth century, has been replaced by hand fluting. Notes are produced by cupping the hands together to form a chamber into which air is blown by placing the lips against the knuckles of the thumbs. Pitch is regulated by lifting the fingers of the outside hand, which forms the back of the chamber. Fluted notes represent features of spoken Kickapoo: pitch and length of vowels, vowel clusters, and intonational contours. Vowel qualities and most consonants are not represented. In Kickapoo, accented vowels have high pitch and unaccented vowels have low pitch, and there are regular rules for the assignment of these pitches to sentences of several types. Consequently, fluted speech has a complex set of possible sentence melodies. In addition, the frequent deletion of intervocalic semivowels produces triple-length vowels. It is the interaction of sentence melodies with vowels of from one to three units of length that permits accurate identification of fluted messages. In fluted speech, notes within a word are separated by a brief silence with glottal closure, words are separated by a longer silence, and a sentence consists of a sequence of notes of various lengths and pitches. In spoken Kickapoo an emphatic meaning is added to a sentence by replacing the low pitch on the last vowel in the sentence with a falling or level pitch, and the vowel is often drawled. In fluted speech this device can be used to end a sentence.

Kickapoo whistle speech is restricted almost completely to courtship and is principally the property of adolescents and young adults. Most post-adolescent Mexican Kickapoos understand it, even though they may no longer practice it. Young people of both sexes "whistle," although ordinarily girls do not initiate conversations, but will reply when addressed. The fluting is generally done in the evening between dusk and midnight when the young men congregate at popular gathering places near the village. They are often accompanied by younger brothers who use these occasions for learning the system. The young men send fluted messages to their girlfriends. Sounds and fluting styles of the whistlers differ, so each girl (and often everyone else in the village) can identify the originator of her message. Since everyone in the community understands the whistle speech, a young man must be careful of what he says to his girlfriend. Sometimes a couple will get together to work out their whistling messages, which tend to be stereotyped phrases, such as "Come on!" "Wait a minute!" "What's keeping you?" "I'm thinking of you." Not all messages appear to be stereotyped, however, and it may be that a full conversation can be carried on through this sort of fluting.

Mazatec Whistle Speech

The principle of substituting musical notes for language features is a simple one, and comparable systems have evolved independently in several parts of the world. Another example from the Americas is the whistled and hummed speech of the Mazatec, an Indian group located in the Mexican state of Oaxaca. As described by an observer in 1948, Mazatec whistle speech is a male activity in constant use until males reach middle age. Boys learn it at about the same time they learn to speak Mazatec; old men, however, seldom use it. Although women do not use it, they understand it. Unlike the Mexican Kickapoo usage of fluted speech, Mazatec men and boys ordinarily whistle only to other men and boys, although there are some situations of cross-sex communication; for example, a boy will whistle a message to a girl (e.g., to tease her) and she will give a spoken reply, or young boys will whistle a reply in response to their mothers' spoken summons.

Whistle speech is most often used when spoken words do not carry well over distances. Men scattered over a wide area while working plots of ground will often talk to one another with whistles; similarly, travelers on trails will keep in touch with each other by whistling. Whistle speech is also used to call or get the attention of someone (even though that person may be within easy speaking distance), to converse without interfering with the spoken conversation of others, to make secret comments in the presence of a non-Mazatec and to warn that strangers are coming.

Whistled conversations lasting as long as three minutes have been reported, and there appears to be no reason why a conversation could not continue indefinitely. Because most Mazatec whistled conversations begin with one of a rather limited number of topics, an easily identifiable cultural context is quickly established. What begins as a whistled conversation at a distance may conclude as a spoken one when the conversation partners near each other. In such cases the usual formal greetings that serve as preludes to spoken conversations can, optionally, be ignored in going from whistling to speaking.

The Mazatec system does not simply consist of signals with limited meanings about which there is common agreement and, unlike the whistles used as signals to animals, signals that have no spoken language equivalents, the system is based on spoken Mazatec; that is, it is a speech surrogate. When a Mazatec is asked what a person "said" in whistle speech, he responds with a very specific, literal rendering in the spoken language.

The fact that Mazatec is a tone language has facilitated the development of a speech surrogate based on whistled notes. The spoken language has four tones that are, with only one minor exception, transferred to the whistle speech. In both speech and whistling, the main word stress falls on the last syllable of the stem, and in both channels of communication, intensity of stress and spread between pitch registers vary according to whether the communication takes place over a short or long distance: the greater the distance, the greater the intensity and the spread. In addition, the distance involved causes key changes: while the key is raised when whistling or shouting over long distances, it is lowered over short distances or if the communication is carried on in a secretive manner. The key is established by the first speaker. Failure to stay in pitch causes difficulty for the other party to the conversation who may misunderstand an utterance that is correct as to pitch contour but off-key.

Any word or sentence that can be spoken in Mazatec can be whistled. In the spoken language many words and phrases have identical tonal patterns and consonants or vowels usually distinguish tonally identical words and phrases. Because there are no consonants and vowels in whistled speech, ambiguity is possible when a context permits two or more interpretations. The whistling of proper names is one of the most frequent causes of ambiguity because the Mazatec use Spanish names and the assimilation of Spanish words and names to the Mazatec tonal system follows restricted patterns; thus, names such as *Modesto, Gustavo,* and *Ricardo* all take an identical tone pattern and there is no way, aside from context, to differentiate the names. In spite of potential ambiguities, the actual instances where confusion occurs are few because the contexts in which whistle speech takes place are more limited than the ones in which speech is used, and the topics of conversation are usually obvious.

7.3 PLAINS SIGN LANGUAGE

The sign language of the Plains Indians has captured the imagination of all who have come in contact with it, be they amateurs or professional scholars. The first Europeans to enter the Plains reported its use, and it continues to be used in the twentieth century, albeit in a changed cultural context. We consider first the nature of the system, then its origin, use, and function.

The System

In most sign-language systems, including Plains Sign, many of the signs are **iconic**, that is, there is a direct relation between the sign and its referent. In contrast, spoken language symbols are almost always **arbitrary**; that is, there is no necessary natural relationship between the symbol and its referent. What is called *dog* in English is *perro* in Spanish, *chien* in French, *pó·ko* in Hopi, *ɬíí* in Navajo, and so on. This arbitrariness is one of the outstanding characteristics of human language; however, there are marginal exceptions in languages, for example, sound symbolism (sections 2.7, 3.4, and 12.5), which approaches iconicity.

Iconicity may be illustrated by the Plains Sign for "eat." The tips of the five fingers of the right hand are compressed, in a line, slightly curled, and placed in front of the mouth; with wrist action, the fingers are moved downward, in front of the mouth. Both hands are used to indicate rapid eating, eating a lot or many people eating.

The fact that a sign is iconic does not mean that its meaning is immediately obvious; for example, the sign for "dog" is formed by holding the first and second fingers of the right hand in a forked position, with the thumb and other fingers closed; the forked fingers point to the left, and the hand is moved to the right. This sign is an icon for a travois, a Plains device pulled by dogs that consisted of two sets of tipi poles lashed to the side of the dog, with the tent laced in between the poles and dragged behind. It is doubtful that even a Plains Indian familiar with the travois would automatically interpret the sign without tutoring. "Bad" presents another example: the hand is held up, in a clenched position, then brought down, opened with a partial snap and with the fingers flung out and separated, as though throwing something away. There are, however, some signs that are arbitrary or appear to render an iconic interpretation difficult. "Question" is indicated by holding the right hand up, about shoulder high, fingers pointing up and loosely separated; the hand is moved two or three times, either to the left and right, or slightly rotated.

We noted in chapter 2 that spoken language has a grammatical system consisting of an inventory of sounds that recur in a variety of patterned sequences to produce words; that is, the sequences of sounds that make up words are meaningful but, taken individually, sounds are meaningless. Does a sign language have an analogous system? Signs are comparable to words of spoken language; they are the meaningful elements. Obviously, they are not composed of sounds, but that does not preclude the possibility that they are composed of a constellation of smaller elements, which taken individually are without meaning. In fact, it seems that in all sign languages that have been studied adequately, including Plains Sign Language, all, or at least most, of the signs are susceptible to a decompositional analysis of this sort. Three basic types of units are posited for Plains Sign: the configuration of the hand, the type of movement (or lack of movement for some signs) and the position of the hand in relation to the body. There are, for example, eighteen basic hand configurations (e.g., open hand, clenched hand, one or more fingers extended with the other closed, etc.) and forty body positions. These are used to make up eighty gestural units and a typical sign consists of three or four of these gestural units. Even the obviously iconic signs are susceptible to this analysis.

Spoken languages also have a grammatical component and they all contain elements (sometimes words, sometimes prefixes or suffixes), more grammatical than conceptual in nature, that mark grammatical relationships; for example, the English sentence, "Butch wants to chew the bone." The suffix –s (on "wants") shows the verb is present tense and that the subject is singular, while to marks the grammatical relationship between the two verbs ("want" and "chew"). How does Plains Sign mark grammatical relationships? What is its grammar like? In most sign languages, many or all of the signs are conceptual in nature, and Plains Sign is no different. Among its few grammatical markers are the "question" sign placed at the beginning of the sentence, and "no," placed after the word it negates. Certain conceptual signs do double duty and also perform grammatical functions; for example, instead of tense markers, adverbial signs like "now" and "long ago" indicate time; and the sign for "push," when added to the main sign in a sentence, loses its conceptual meaning and becomes an imperative marker, indicating a command.

Some signed words are compounds consisting of two or more signs: The first sign is normally the head of the compound, while the following sign or signs modify and delimit the initial sign; for example:

Whiteman + soldier + walk = "infantry"
man + marry + no = "bachelor"
brother + possess + wife = "sister-in-law"

Some of the compounds include a rather large number of elements. The longest recorded compound is for "skunk," which consists of these elements: (1) small animal, (2) plumed tail, (3) striped back, (4) stink, (5) bad, (6) egg, (7) smash. Because longer compounds usually display some redundancy, it is possible to leave out certain elements; for example, it is possible to indicate "skunk" by these abbreviated sequences:

1 + 3	(small animal + striped back)
1 + 4 + 5	(small animal + stink + bad)
1 + 6 + 7	(small animal + egg + smash)
2 + 4 + 5	(plumed tail + stink + bad)
2 + 4	(plumed tail + stink)
2 + 6 + 7	(plumed tail + egg + smash)
3 + 4	(striped back + stink)
3	(striped back)
3 + 4 + 5	(striped back + stink + bad)
3 + 6 + 7	(striped back + egg + smash)
4 + 5 + 6 + 7	(stink + bad + egg + smash)

Notice that "egg + smash" (6 + 7) occurs as a unit, that is, one never occurs without the other.

Sign words are strung together to make sentences. The order is fairly flexible, but not entirely free. To give some notion of the nature of the Plains Sign syntax and of the language's communicative potential, here is a representation of a short passage recorded in the last century; each English word in the passage is a gloss, that is, rough translation, of the individual sign:

> I + arrive + here + today + make + treaty. My + hundred + lodge + camp + beyond + Hills + Black + near + river + called + Elk. You + chief + great + pity + me. I + poor. My + five + child + sick + food + all-gone. Snow + deep + cold + strong. Perhaps + chief + great + above + see + me. I + go. Moon + die + I + arrive + there + my + camp.

A free translation:

> I arrived here today to make a treaty. My one hundred lodges are camped beyond the Black Hills, near the Yellowstone River. You are a great chief, pity me. I am poor. My five children are sick and have nothing to eat. The snow is deep and the weather intensely cold. Perhaps God sees me. I am going. In one month I shall reach my camp.

It is difficult to estimate the size of Plains Sign vocabulary. Clearly some signers have a larger vocabulary than others. The largest vocabulary recorded for a single individual is thirty-five hundred signs; however, there are signers who function quite well with five hundred to a thousand. The semantic range of the vocabulary is quite broad, so that almost any topic can be discussed. There are, however, some limitations; for example, there are not many signs for the different species of plants. This is understandable when we realize that an important function of the language was for intertribal communication. In intratribal contexts, where plants were used for food, medicine, and so on, plant names would be important, but in intertribal settings there would be little call for identifying plants. Evaluative and emotive terms are few and cause-and-effect statements are difficult to express; however, spatial relationships, physical activities, enumeration, specification, and comparison are easily expressed, as are animal names, descriptions of animal characteristics and movements, personal names, and placenames. Moreover, just as spoken languages do, Plains Sign coins new terms when the need arises; for example, there are signs for twentieth-century technological items such as "car" and "airplane."

Plains Sign Language is not a speech surrogate because it is not based on or derived from any of the spoken languages of the Plains. Nevertheless, to classify it as a direct signaling system does not do it justice, because it has many language-like characteristics: It has a structure and grammar very much like spoken language; new signs can be formed by compounding; and the signs are susceptible to analysis into smaller gestural components, much as words are susceptible to analysis into phonetic elements. In addition, its communicative ability approaches or is equal to that of vocal language.

Origin, Use, and Function

It is not known exactly where the Plains Sign Language originated or who invented it, but the weight of the evidence suggests that it came from the south and then spread north. Its age is unknown, but it was probably pre-European, since it was reported by the earliest European travelers in the Plains.

Why did it arise? There have been a number of hypotheses, one of which is that it was an adaptation of long-distance signaling for hunting or raiding parties, but none of them have been proven and, given the skimpiness of any support-ing evidence, they are probably not subject to verification. One of the most likely suggestions is that the system sprang up among the tribes along the Gulf Coast between Louisiana and northern Mexico as a response to the considerable linguis-tic diversity in that area. On the other hand, it is not at all clear why, in an area of linguistic diversity, a sign language would develop rather than multilingualism or a lingua franca (chapter 10) based on a spoken language.

Plains Sign spread from south to north in the Plains during a period of great change. Groups from the east were being pushed onto the Plains by European settle-ment along the Atlantic coast and the adjacent interior; the horse was introduced by the Spanish from the south and made buffalo hunting as a way of life much more attractive, so that those groups who previously had made marginal use of the Plains moved much more centrally into the area in pursuit of the buffalo. Con-sequently, groups that had had only sporadic or no contact with each other were now in frequent contact. Linguistically, the Plains Indians are a mixed bag and sign language offered a ready means for intertribal contact. It became the area's lingua franca, particularly for trade, but whether trade was the impetus for its develop-ment is not known. It continued to be used as the language of intertribal contact until this century when the near-universal knowledge of English replaced it as the language of intertribal contact.

In the nineteenth century, Plains Sign was used by tribes speaking over three dozen languages belonging to about a dozen linguistic groups. The tribes, arranged by linguistic families, were as follows:

> **(Athapaskan):** Sarsi, Jicarilla Apache, Mescalero Apache, Kiowa
> Apache, Lipan Apache
> **(Algonquian):** Plains Ojibway, Plains Cree, Blackfoot (including
> Blood, Piegan), Cheyenne, Arapaho (including Gros Ventre)
> **(Salish):** Coeur d'Alene, Kalispel, Flathead, Spokan

(Sahaptin): Nez Perce, Yakima, Umatilla

(Siouan): Dakota (including Stoney, Yankton, Assiniboine, Santee,
Teton), Hidatsa, Mandan, Crow, Kansas, Osage, Omaha, Ponca

(Uto-Aztecan): Wind River Shoshoni, Comanche, Southern
Paiute, Ute

(Caddoan): Arikara, Pawnee, Wichita, Caddo

(Kiowa-Tanoan): Kiowa, Taos

(Linguistic Isolates): Cayuse, Kutenai, Tonkawa, Karankawa

These tribal groups occupied the Plains and adjacent areas and their locations in the Plains were roughly as follows: the Sarsi in the north with the remaining Atha-paskan tribes (the Apachean branch) in the south and (outside the Plains, proper) in the Southwest; the Algonquian-speaking tribes in the north; the Salish and Sahap-tin groups (outside the Plains) in the Plateau region to the northwest; the Siouan-speaking groups in the north and east; the Uto-Aztecan-speaking groups on the western fringe and adjoining Great Basin; the Caddoan-speaking tribes scattered along the eastern edge; the Kiowa in the southern Plains; and Taos, the northern-most Pueblo village in New Mexico. The speakers of linguistic isolates (i.e., lan-guages not belonging to any clearly related linguistic grouping) were the Cayuse and Kutenai in the Plateau, and Tonkawa and Karankawa in southern Texas. In addition, some displaced eastern tribes entered the area and learned the Sign: the Delaware, Kickapoo and Shawnee (Algonquian), and Wyandot and Cherokee (Iroquoian).

When Europeans first came in contact with Plains Sign in the sixteenth and seventeenth centuries, it was still in the process of spreading north and did not reach the northern Plains and the adjoining Plateau region to the west until quite late, with some tribes not using it until the nineteenth century and, in a few cases, the twentieth. Because the area involved was a thousand miles from east to west and even farther from north to south, it is not surprising that there were dialect differences, including differences in some of the signs, differences in style of execu-tion, and differences in stance.

The heyday of Plains Sign was the nineteenth century, at least in the central and northern Plains. Not everyone in the tribe learned it and not all tribes were equally proficient or fluent in its use. In general, men were more proficient and more fre-quent signers than women, but there were some women who were known to be very good signers. In the north the Crow, known as the most proficient users, were followed closely by the Northern Cheyennes and the Blackfoot. In the southern Plains the Kiowa were considered the best signers.

Originally, as we have noted, the main use of Plains Sign was as a means of communication between linguistically diverse tribes and, at least at first, especially for trading. By the nineteenth century it was also often used between members of the same tribe, serving simply as an alternative to speech. It would be used, for example, with those hard of hearing or as a way to converse with some members of a group without interrupting others when a spoken conversation was underway. It could also be used as a means for long-distance communication. Additional important functions included entertainment, oratory, and storytelling and, in fact, these are its main uses today now that English has taken over the function of intertribal communication. Storytelling is its primary function today in the far northern Plains and nearby Plateau area. It is also used by many, especially younger, Indians today for its symbolic value as an expression of Indianness.

Plains Sign Language has captured the imagination of the larger society, where it is also a symbol of Indianness. It has even been enshrined in general American culture: generations of Boy Scouts have learned some of it, including the three-fingered salute, derived from the sign meaning "wolf" or "scout," and have earned thousands of sign-language merit badges.

7.4   DIRECT-SIGNALING SYSTEMS
AND THEIR COMMUNICATIVE PURPOSES

Long-Distance Systems

In addition to Plains Sign, a number of direct-signaling systems were used in North America. In the Plains (as well as in some other areas), there were long-distance systems used in war and hunting. Distance signaling conveyed limited kinds of information; some signals were conventional, announcing presence of game, enemies, or friends. In other cases, systems consisted of prearranged sets of signals specific to particular situations.

Signals were both visual and audible. In the Plains, whistling or imitations of animal and bird cries were used in warpath communication, and smoke signaling was used both in warfare and for indicating camp movements and conditions. The Karankawas of south Texas had more than twenty different types of smoke signal, including columns, spirals, zig-zags, and diverging lines. Other visual systems included full-body signaling and signaling by hand-held mirrors. Body signals were made up of gestures and postures combined with various kinds and directions of movement on foot. If there was a particular need to communicate from a distance, anyone might use body signaling; however, it was mostly used by scouts and lookouts. A mirror-signaling system transmitted information according to number and kinds of flashes and the movement of the light beam during a flash. Mirror signals were used in various ways: for example, scouts and hunters used them to communicate information about numbers and locations of enemies or game; suitors used them in communications with sweethearts. It is also reported that they were used within a camp to inform unexpected guests that food was being prepared and that they could expect to be served a meal. Terrain and degree of visibility determined the type of long-distance visual signaling to be used; that is, smoke signaling was used more or less all over North America, but body signaling and mirror signaling, which needed wide visibility, were limited to the Plains and the Southwest.

Picture "Writing"

Pictography, or picture "writing," was practiced in some parts of North America. Various materials were used as surfaces: rock, dirt, bark, hides, and so on. The method used for inscription depended on how hard, soft, or porous a surface was, on the availability of materials and tools, and on the preferences of the "writer." Although never language specific, picture writing is definitely tied to particular cultural contexts; for example, the "rock art" of the Chumash (California), which is some of the most spectacular pictography in North America; however, someone who can figure out, in general, the topic of a pictograph or a series of pictographs, is not really able to "get the message" unless he or she has access to explicit and implicit cultural detail, including detail about the pictographer and the actual events depicted. The following description of a Plains pictographic message drawn in the dirt is an excellent illustration of the relation of picture writing to specific cultural contexts:

> I saw . . . a little stick standing in the bank, and attached to the top of it a piece of birch bark. On examination, I found the mark of a rattlesnake with a knife, the handle touching the snake, and the point sticking into a bear, the head of the latter being down. Near the rattlesnake was the mark of a beaver, one of its dugs, it being a female, touching the snake. This was left for my information, and I learned from it that Wa-me-gon-a-biew, whose totem was She-she-gwah, the rattlesnake, had killed a man whose totem was Muk-kwa, the bear. The murderer could be no other than Wa-me-gon-a-biew, as it was specified that he was the son of a woman whose totem was the beaver, and this I knew could be no other than Net-no-kwa. As there were but few of the bear totem in our band, I was confident the man killed was a young man call Ke-zha-zhoons. That he was dead, and not wounded merely, was indicated by the drooping down of the head of the bear.

Pictography was used in two ways: to convey new information and to aid in recalling information. As illustrated in the foregoing Plains example, conveying new information could involve various kinds of communications such as invitation, warnings, or notices of conditions at another community, for example, illness or famine. In precontact times, a "writer" would leave a pictographic message where the intended "reader" would find it or the message might be carried to its recipient by a third party. In the Plains, in the late nineteenth century, such messages might even be sent by "U.S. mail."

As an aid to recall, pictography was used in the Plains for the maintenance of historical information. Tribal historical records, or "winter counts" (from their Dakota name), were kept on hides with each year represented by one or two depictions of memorable happenings in that year; for example, painted on a robe, there is a Crow winter count of an encounter in which thirty Dakotas were killed. Pictography was also used as a mnemonic device for maintaining religious information: The correct version of a chant, for example, might be in an archaic or esoteric form of language, so, to aid in recall of the chant's proper order and content, a single picture, otherwise meaningless, would represent each phrase. This sort of mnemonic pictography is in some ways like the mnemonic devices described for the Aztec in sections 4.4 and 8.3.

Inasmuch as direct-signaling systems are independent of spoken language, it is not surprising that certain American Indian systems came to be used to some extent by non-Indians. We have already commented on the Boy Scouts' use of sign language; in addition, in the large cattle drives on the Plains in the third quarter of the nineteenth century, certain body signals were used by White cowboys on horseback. Mirror signaling was officially used by the United States Army for a time after the Civil War, and pictography, in reinterpreted form, can be found in the sun on New Mexico's state flag and, at one time, on New Mexico's automobile license plates.

Wampum

Wampum were tubular beads made from clam shells. They were used before European contact, but were not in common use until afterwards. Although it is popularly, but incorrectly, believed that wampum served primarily as money, their primary function was, in fact, political: among certain Iroquoian and Algonquian tribes in the Northeast, wampum acted as badges of accreditation for ambassadors, and they were used as sacred symbols in the sealing of treaty agreements. They also functioned as mnemonic devices whose designs recorded events, conveyed messages, or set out the correct recitation of a ritual.

Totem Carvings

The totem carvings of the Northwest Coast peoples are part of a sophisticated art tradition that reflects a strongly evolved aesthetic sense. Totem carving, however, is more than just an art form: Among the Tlingit, Haida, and Tsimshian, for example, it was closely tied to a social system characterized by a high degree of stratification. This system gave rise to a ceremonial display of carved crests that are symbols of rank and descent, similar in some ways to European coats-of-arms. Owned by particular lineages and functioning as a historical record, crests and combinations of crests act as mnemonic devices in recapitulating a lineage's history, memorializing its legendary supernatural contacts, and illustrating lineage myths.

Quipus

The use of knotted cords as mnemonic devices was widespread in the Americas; their use was reported also for the Eastern Algonquian groups, various Plains tribes, several tribes in the American Southwest, the Huichol of Mexico, and others. The primary function of these knotted devices was to record dates and numbers and to aid in the recall of stories, songs, genealogies, traditions, and religious laws.

One of the most complex systems was the Quechua *quipu* 'knot'. Composed of colored and knotted cords attached to a base cord, it was used by Quechua-speaking administrators of the Inca Empire to record the results of computations. The numerical system used was decimal: there was a separate cord for each position (tens, hundreds, thousands, etc.), and the number of a particular position was indicated by the number of knots. The uses and functions of the quipus are not well understood because so little information about them survived the Spanish destruction of the Inca Empire, although it appears that quipus functioned as registers of all the activities of the Incan realm: Statistical quipus kept detailed records of the empire's material resources and other quipus helped fix in memories facts about laws, rites, treaties, speeches, and history.

SOURCES

The introduction to chapter 7 draws in part from Leeds-Hurwitz 1989 (chapter 5). Section 7.1 is based on Basso 1970. In section 7.2 the Kickapoo whistle-speech discussion is drawn from Ritzenthaler and Peterson 1954, Taylor 1975, and Voorhis 1971; the Mazatec whistle speech discussion comes from Cowan 1948. Section 7.3 is based primarily on Taylor 1975, 1978, and 1981; other important sources (Clark

1885, Mallery 1880, 1881, Tomkins 1929, [especially] West 1960) we did not directly consult, but they are well summarized in Taylor's material. Section 7.4 draws in general from Taylor 1975 (distance signaling, pictography), Tooker 1978 (wampum), Holm 1990 (totem carvings), Ascher 1986, and Day 1967 (quipus). The description in section 7.4 of a pictographic message is cited in Taylor 1975; the references for Chumash rock art are Clewlow 1978 and Hudson and Lee 1981.

SUGGESTED READINGS

For discussion of silence as communicative behavior, see Saville-Troike 1985 and Scollon 1985. See Taylor 1975, 1978, and 1981 for treatments of nonverbal communication in North America and Plains Sign Language in particular. See Umiker-Sebeok and Sebeok 1978 for a general discussion of indigenous sign languages and Ascher and Ascher 1981 for a detailed discussion of how to make a quipu, the cultural context of quipus, and the position of quipu makers in Incan society.

CHAPTER 8

THE WRITTEN WORD

There are three types of writing systems: **logographic, syllabic,** and **alphabetic**. In a logographic system (8.2), the basic symbols stand for a word (or, more accurately, a morpheme, see Chapter 2); in a syllabic writing system (8.5, 8.7), the basic symbols stand for a syllable; in an alphabetic system (8.8), the basic symbols stand for a sound (consonant or vowel). In the Americas before European contact, only a few writing systems existed, all in Mesoamerica and all logographic. Since that time, both syllabic and alphabetic systems have been developed in a number of indigenous languages in the Americas.

8.1 MESOAMERICAN WRITING

Writing in Mesoamerica is more than two thousand years old. It first evolved in what is today southern Mexico, Belize, and Guatemala, where inscriptions (a few isolated words) have been found that can be dated to the fifth century B.C. Full writing (words forming sentences) dates from the first or second century B.C. The earliest written inscriptions relate to calendar dates, names, and places, and the oldest (a post-Olmec carving recently found near Vera Cruz carrying the dates A.D. 143 and 156) is written in Zoquean, "an early ancestor of four languages spoken today in Vera Cruz, Tabasco, Oaxaca, and Chiapas," according to one of the decipherers. All of the other early inscriptions are written in Yucatec and Chol, two of about thirty Mayan languages. Thanks to the great strides that have been made in recent years in deciphering Mesoamerican writing, we know now that both the "Epi-Olmec" and Mayan systems were fully developed. Although the Aztec were in the process of evolving a form of writing at the time of European contact, it was not yet a complete system. Because the early missionaries to the Aztec, unlike those to the other Mesoamerican peoples, made a very complete record of almost every aspect of Aztec life (section 4.4), the modus operandi of Aztec scribes is well documented. The writing systems for other Mesoamerican languages are not well understood, but they were probably, like the Aztec, incomplete systems or "near writing."

Because dates and numbers play such an important part in most Mesoamerican texts, a thorough appreciation of the writing is possible only with a concomitant understanding of the calendar and vigesimal number system, two important features of the Mesoamerican ethos prevalent throughout the area and not just where writing was present. Whereas the systems for any one cultural group might vary in the details, they were all similar in the generalities. Since we discussed the Aztec and Tequistlatec vigesimal number systems in section 3.5, here we will consider only the calendar, using the Mayan as an example.

Mesoamericans had both a ritual and a solar calendar. The ritual calendar consisted of 260 days. We can show how it worked with the twenty Yucatec Mayan day names:

(1) *Imix*	(5) *Chicchan*	(9) *Muluc*	(13) *Ben*	(17) *Caban*
(2) *Ik*	(6) *Cimi*	(10) *Oc*	(14) *Ix*	(18) *Eznab*
(3) *Akbal*	(7) *Manik*	(11) *Chuen*	(15) *Men*	(19) *Cauac*
(4) *Kan*	(8) *Lamat*	(12) *Eb*	(16) *Cib*	(20) *Ahau*

Each day name occurred with a number from one to thirteen; thus if the starting point were *One Imix*, next would come *Two Ik, Three Akbal, Four Kan*, and so on. When *Thirteen Ben* was reached, the next day would be *One Ix* followed by *Two Men*, and so on. After reaching the twentieth day, *Seven Ahau*, the count would return to *Imix* again: *Eight Imix, Nine Ik*, and so on. The days went on in an endless repetition, with a given number and day name being repeated once in every 260 days (that is, twenty day names times thirteen).

The solar calendar consisted of eighteen divisions, each lasting twenty days, plus a nineteenth division of five days, or $18 \times 20 + 5 = 365$. After 18,980 days, which is exactly fifty-two solar years and seventy-three ritual years, the two calendars return to the same day. Although the Mesoamerican astronomers knew that the solar year actually consisted of 365 days plus a fraction, they did not correct for the additional quarter day, as we do with leap year, because it would have disrupted the perfect repetition of the twenty-day and the fifty-two-year cycles.

Texts dealing with ritual and ceremony, histories, genealogies, astronomical calculations, and treatises concerning the moon and planets—all these important intellectual writings clearly required a calendar and Mesoamericans were adequately served by the two, ritual and solar. In addition, people were given day names, so that the various lords and ladies who figure in histories and genealogies have names like *One Ahau* or *Seven Imix*.

Writing was most commonly found in codices, carved in stone, or painted on pottery. A codex was a manuscript using paper or paper-like material, such as bark, skin, or the like. Whatever the medium, writing was used less often than in the modern world for mundane, utilitarian, or practical purposes. Writing was an art, and the scribes, a highly respected class, were as mindful of the aesthetics of their work as of the content, particularly for the monumental inscriptions. Very frequently a text includes a scene depicting pictorially the same event recorded in the text, a practice that has facilitated the deciphering of the writing.

The indigenous writing systems died out soon after the Spanish Conquest, partly because writing was closely associated with the native religion, which the missionaries undertook to repress as a preliminary to Christianizing the Indians. Although the missionaries to the Aztecs preserved a number of codices, elsewhere, for instance, in the Mayan area, the destruction of codices was zealously pursued. Another factor contributing to the demise of the indigenous writing systems was the introduction of a Hispanicized version of the Roman alphabet, so that the Mesoamerican languages continued to be written for some time, now in the Roman alphabet, with the result that writing probably became more widespread.

8.2 THE MAYAN HIEROGLYPHIC SYSTEM

In 1549 a contingent of Spanish missionaries disembarked at Mérida on the Yucatán Peninsula. Among them was a young Franciscan, Fray Diego de Landa, who, ambitious and doctrinaire, rose quickly to a high position where he could effect the destruction of most of the Mayan codices because they had nothing in them, he said, but superstition and lies of the devil. Before long, however, Landa's overzealousness brought about his recall to Spain where (ca. 1566) he wrote his justly famous *Relación de las Cosas de Yucatán*, a work of self-justification that paradoxically conveyed a sense of wonder and appreciation of the Mayan ethos. Within this apologia there was also a description of the Mayan hieroglyphic system and an explication of how numbers, day names, and month names were written, as well as an "alphabet." Landa was subsequently exonerated and dispatched back to the Yucatán now as Bishop Landa, while his report along with the three—possibly four—surviving codices were soon consigned to a dusty church archive until the rediscovery and publication of *Relación* in 1864.

In the nineteenth century an archaeological and antiquarian enthusiasm turned an avid eye to the civilizations of the Americas and there, in the jungles among the romantically splendid ruins, found a new set of hieroglyphics.

Hieroglyphic (*hiero* 'sacred', *glyph* 'carving') is a term that was first applied to Egyptian pictographs; subsequently it has been used to describe other forms of logographic writing, particularly Mesoamerican inscriptions in which each symbol is referred to as a "glyph."

With typical nineteenth-century optimism, scholars and amateurs alike plunged into the work of demystifying the exotic remains of the Mesoamerican civilizations.

When Bishop Landa's "alphabet" was unearthed, it was hailed as a new Rosetta Stone; however, the would-be archaeologists and epigraphers were swiftly disabused, for the Mayan glyphs refused to yield their secrets and all attempts to apply the "alphabet" brought forth only gibberish. Other parts of the *Relación*, however, along with the three newly rediscovered codices went a long way toward the elucidation of the Mayan calendar and number system. Nevertheless, the glyphic writing remained a mystery. At best, Landa's observations offered a toehold, but did not allow a full reading. Even so, there were three factors that helped the frustrated decipherers: First, many of the inscriptions included a pictorial representation along with the written text; second, many of the texts were placed in a very rigid format, almost formulaically, with the same type of information appearing in predictable places; and third, the languages were well known and, indeed, are still spoken today.

A Mayan hieroglyphic is basically logographic; that is, a glyph represents a word, rather than a sound in the language. The glyphs are usually placed in vertical pairs. The topmost pair is read from left to right, then the pair placed below, and so on. The left-most double column is read first, and then the double column to the right. The glyphs are placed in glyph blocks, and it appears that the artistic rendition of the glyphs was at least as important as the functional aspects of the writing, for the individual glyph blocks are uniformly balanced; as a result, a glyph block may contain a single glyph, or more. If more than one is included, the glyphs are arranged in an artistic manner, which is sometimes left to right, sometimes top to bottom, sometimes with one inserted ("infixed") within the other, and sometimes merged ("conflated") into a single glyph in such a way as to be aesthetically satisfying. As one might imagine, these diverse arrangements create difficulties for the modern reader, who must engage in a process of unscrambling.

The Mayan writing system contains about eight hundred different glyphs, which can be grouped into three types: word glyphs, phonetic complements, and rebus signs. A word glyph is a symbol that represents a word. Many Mayan glyphs are iconic, that is, they represent the object in picture form. Although not all word glyphs are iconic, Mayan numerals are a good example of the iconic word glyph. Like most other Mesoamerican writing systems, the Mayan uses bar and dot numerals, which take advantage of the vigesimal number system. The numbers from one to four are expressed by dots, which are most commonly placed in a column to the left, or in a horizontal row at the bottom of the glyph. Five is indicated by a bar, which is vertical (if to the left), or horizontal (if at the bottom). The numbers from six to nineteen are expressed by combinations of bars and dots; thus six is shown by a bar and a dot, nineteen by three bars and four dots, and so on. If the number is to the left, then the dots are to the left of the bars; if the number is at the bottom, then the dots are placed over the bars. The numbers found in the codices are usually written in a straightforward manner, but those inscribed in monuments are frequently adorned in various ways. Those numbers that include one or more bars, along with one or two dots (six, seven, eleven, twelve, sixteen, and seventeen) are ornamented in such a way as to fill up the empty space that would otherwise result; it appears that vacant space was habitually eschewed by the Mayan artist.

The Maya developed a symbol for zero, which made the execution of higher numbers very easy. A dot ($= 1$) with a zero renders twenty (i.e., 1×20); a dot with two zeros, four hundred ($1 \times 20 \times 20$); a dot with three zeros, eight thousand ($1 \times 20 \times 20 \times 20$); and so on.

There was also a second iconic way to write numerals. Each number had a god associated with it, so that a clearly identifiable picture of the appropriate god (either as a head or full body glyph) indicates a number.

The nearly serendipitous discovery of phonetic complements in the Mayan system led first to the realization that the inscriptions are not in just one language but two, Yucatec and Chol; and, second, Bishop Landa's "alphabet" finally became clear. In their exasperation, some of the early epigraphers had claimed that it was a hoax on the part of Bishop Landa, or the scribe, or that there had been a misunderstanding between the two. We now know (since the 1960s) that no hoax was involved, but that there was indeed a misunderstanding, for the Mayans did not use an alphabet, but rather a **syllabary**, in which the symbol represents a consonant plus a following vowel. Landa must have thought that the symbols stood for letters, individual consonants and vowels, as in the Roman alphabet used in Spanish. He obviously went through the Spanish alphabet, which is sounded (in Spanish) *a, be, se, de, e, efe, ge, ache*, and so on, asking the scribe for each "letter." The Mayan scribe recognized these as syllables, not letters, and gave the syllabic symbol for each. Because all this information was filtered through the Spanish alphabet, there are many syllabic characters that Landa did not record; that is, from the letter "b" Landa recorded the syllable BE, but not BA, BI, and so on. Likewise, there are a number of consonants that have no counterpart in the Spanish alphabet, and so were unrecorded by Landa. One of the mysteries of the Landa alphabet—that is, some of the "letters" seem to include more than one syllable—is easily solved by the recognition that some Spanish letters are pronounced as two syllables; for example, *h* and *l* are pronounced "a-che" and "e-le," so that the scribe wrote these as two syllables, A-CHE and E-LE. The phonetic complement in the Mayan system thus consists of a consonant plus vowel. Some are derived from word glyphs, for example, the complement for KA, which is identical with the word glyph for *kay* 'fish'. Many complements, however, cannot be shown to be derived from word glyphs.

Although the phonetic complements have the shape, consonant + vowel, or CV, always ending with a vowel, not all Mayan words end with a vowel, and in fact, the most common phonetic shape of root words is CVC, and a final consonant is spelled as if it ended with the vowel identical to the vowel just before it. Thus *cutz* 'turkey' is spelled with two phonetic complements, CU-TZU; *witz* 'hill' also with two, WI-TZI; *pakal* 'shield' with three, PA-KA-LA; and so on. (A Hispanicized orthography is used here in writing Yucatec, so that *cutz, witz,* and *pakal* are phonetically [kuc], [wic], and [pak'al]; see appendix I for the phonetic values of these symbols. It has become customary in Mayan hieroglyphic studies to represent the complements by capital letters separated by a hyphen, so that, for example, the writing PA-KA-LA represents three Mayan complements.)

About one hundred phonetic complements have been identified, but since some syllables can be written in more than one way (e.g., four versions are known for NA), they represent only about fifty-five distinct syllables. There are still many gaps; thus NA, NI, and NU are known, but there should also be glyphs for the complements NE and NO.

The third type of glyph in Mayan writing, the **rebus sign**, is a kind of word glyph that takes advantage of homonyms or near homonyms. The word glyph, for example, for *na?* 'mother' is also used for *nah* 'first'; the glyphs for 'four', 'sky', and 'snake', words that are nearly homophonous in Mayan, are sometimes used interchangeably, and Mayan artists indulged in such pictorial punning as painting snakes above a scene in place of the sky.

8.3 AZTEC WRITING

At the time of the Spanish Conquest, the Aztec were in the process of developing a writing system, which can best be termed "near writing," since it has characteristics that place it between a pictographic system and full writing. **Pictographs** are a form of graphic communication system in which the ideas expressed are not dependent on a particular language (section 7.4). Although most of the symbols are pictorial representations, some may be conventionalized and abstract. The key to determining if a system is pictographic or "full writing" is not how conventional or abstract the symbols are, but rather whether the symbols represent ideas that could be expressed in any language, or whether they represent words of a particular language. The Mayan hieroglyphic writing shows us that symbols in a full writing system can be pictorial to a large degree; but there are two characteristics that distinguish the Mayan system from a pictographic system: The pictures stand for words in the language, not ideas, and full sentences can be represented, not just individual words. The greater use of pictorial forms in the Aztec system is not what keeps it from being a full writing system, but rather this characteristic is a reflection of the fact that it was not a full writing system.

Many of the Aztec glyphs are simply pictures of the object: a picture of a rabbit for 'rabbit', a picture of an arm for 'arm', a tree with water at its base for 'willow', the lower half of a human body, the undevoured part, protruding from the mouth of a jaguar for 'place where people are devoured' (a placename), and the like. Some of the pictures are highly stylized and conventional, so that someone not familiar with the tradition might not recognize glyphs for such objects as 'water', 'smoke', 'joy', and others.

Some glyphs are more complex and are expressed as metaphors; for example, 'speech' is represented by a scroll coming from the mouth, or 'song' or 'poetry' if it is a flowered scroll; 'conquest' by a burning temple; 'war' by the metaphor 'water and conflagration' (in atl, in tlachinolli); 'authority, rulership, government' by 'mat and chair' (in petlatl, in icpalli). Color was also important, so that, for example, the glyph for 'war' had a black background.

The rebus sign was used in some cases, especially for placenames and personal names, and in these cases the glyphs were not pictographs, since they were clearly tied to specific words composed of specific sounds in the Aztec language. For example, Coyocac 'place of the Coyoca people' was represented by a picture of a coyote (coyō-tl), and sandals (cac-tli) (the noun suffixes –tl, –tli, –li were ignored in the rebus writing); Mapachtepec literally 'Raccoon Mountain', by a picture of an arm (mai-tl), Spanish moss (pach-tli), and a mountain (tepe-tl); Tlalchich-tli, a personal name, by pictures of a screech owl, a rectangle for a field, and teeth: the screech owl (chich-tli) indicates the syllable chich, the rectangle either tlal-li 'land' or mil-li 'corn field', and the picture of teeth (tlan-tli) shows that the reading for the rectangle is for tlal-li rather than mil-li. Placenames frequently ended with the suffix –pan 'on' and –tlan 'near'; these endings were often indicated by a flag (pan-tli) and teeth (tlan-tli).

It is clear that Aztec writing is more than just pictographs, that is, images detached from the particular language: The artists were trying to write certain words, not just to communicate ideas. There were conventions for writing some of these words; and there were attempts to indicate the sounds of some of the words. The conventions were, however, rather loose. A name could be written more than one way, often within the same document; sometimes the rebus principle was used, sometimes not, and sometimes a different rebus sign was used for the same name. The glyphs often stood for words, and there were some standardized conventions, but the artist or scribe was given some latitude in just how to indicate the words. It is doubtful, however, if whole sentences of the Aztec language were ever written. We are told, for example, that young priests, who had to memorize verbatim certain prayers and songs, used ritual codices as mnemonic devices. The codices could not be interpreted by one who had not learned the rituals, but only by someone who had already memorized the "script."

8.4 THE USE OF WRITING IN MESOAMERICA

Most of the uses of Aztec "near writing" centered around the Mesoamerican calendrical system in one way or another (section 4.4); that is, genealogies (especially for tracing and validating royal lines), history, divination involving the book of years, and astronomy. This notational system was also used where no dates were involved, for example, by accountants in the royal storehouses and by judges hearing a case; these uses, however, were less common. Among the Maya, inscriptions on stone and associated with pyramids and other monuments deal principally with political history and genealogies; the codices (only three—possibly four—have been preserved) deal with astronomy and related calendrical and ritualistic topics; ceramic writings, most often found on pottery in tombs, are related to death and the underworld. Finally, the Zapotec of Oaxaca used their notational system almost exclusively to record political history.

8.5 THE INVENTION OF THE CHEROKEE SYLLABARY

In 1819 a remarkable intellectual achievement came to fruition in the Americas. That was the year of the completion of the Cherokee syllabary, a writing system invented by Sequoyah, a Cherokee who knew no English and did not know how to read or write in any language. He did know that English speakers used "talking leaves"; that is, they were able to represent their language with marks on paper. If English speakers could do that, he asked himself, why could he not do it for his language. What is fairly amazing is that since Sequoyah had no knowledge of the nature of the English writing system, he had no way of knowing if the symbols (i.e., "letters") stood for ideas, words, or sounds. He began by developing a logographic system, in which each symbol stood for an individual word; but, having invested several years in the task, he came to realize that such a system would be very clumsy, and that it would tax the human memory to its utmost. He then hit upon the idea of having the symbols stand for sounds rather than words, so that a much reduced number of symbols could be used to represent the language.

Those of us who have been literate in an alphabetic system since childhood tend to think it natural that we can represent the sounds of our language with written symbols; it is easy, therefore, for us to miss the full significance of Sequoyah's discovery. But if we look at the history of writing it becomes apparent that the idea is anything but obvious. Although Sequoyah did not dream up the idea of writing by himself; that is, he got the idea from the "talking leaves" that literate English speakers used, everything else appears to be his own invention: the development of the writing system, and perhaps also the recognition that a limited number of symbols could be used to stand for sounds, rather than the much larger number of symbols that would be needed if they stood for words.

New writing systems have been invented a number of times at a number of places throughout the world; but in most cases the idea of writing was borrowed from a neighboring group, and this is certainly the case for Sequoyah. It is not clear how many times writing has been invented from scratch (i.e., the idea of writing as distinct from the particular systems), but there are two clear examples: one in Mesoamerica, the other in the ancient Middle East. In these cases the systems were logographic (except for the Mayan use of phonetic complements) and used a large number of symbols to represent the words of the language rather than a small number of symbols for the sounds. The Sumerian and Egyptian systems were invented about 3,000 B.C.; it took another fifteen hundred years before the Phoenicians discovered that language could be represented by written symbols that stand for sounds instead of whole words. In the space of a few years Sequoyah implemented what it took our intellectual ancestors fifteen hundred years to discover.

What Sequoyah invented was not an alphabet, but a close cousin to it: a syllabary. There are eighty-five "letters" (it will become clear that they are not "letters" in the usual sense, but this is the term that has come to be used for the symbols). Six of them are used for vowels, one for the consonant "s," and the remaining seventy-eight are used for combinations of a consonant and following vowel (originally there were eighty-six letters, but one has dropped out of use).

Where did the letters come from? Some appear to be letters from the Roman alphabet, both capital and small letters, sometimes standing in their usual orientation, at other times inverted or on their sides; some seem to be modifications of Roman letters; others appear to be wholly new inventions. Sequoyah may have borrowed some letters from the Roman alphabet, but it is clear that he did not borrow the phonetic values; thus "A" is used for the Cherokee sequence [go], "B" for [yɨ], "b" for [si], "C" for [tli], "D" for [a], and "E" for [gɨ].

The syllabary does not do a perfect job of representing all the Cherokee sounds. The language has six vowels and nineteen consonants. Each of the six vowels is represented in the syllabary, but the syllable combinations of consonant plus vowel are underrepresented. For a perfect representation, there should be 114 (6 vowels times 19 consonants), in place of the 78. What Sequoyah did was to write certain pairs of syllable with the same letter, so that, for example, [go] and [ko] are written "A," [la] and [ła] are written "W," [dlɨ] and [tlɨ] are written "P," and so on. Sequoyah grouped the pairs in a very systematic fashion: in every pair, the vowels are the same, and a voiced consonant (e.g., [g], [l], [dl]) is paired with its voiceless counterpart (e.g., [k], [ɬ], [tl]). Only those of low frequency were paired; that is, the pairing is somewhat comparable to the English use of "th" for both [θ] and [ð], as in 'thigh' and 'thy'.

Words consisting of sequences of vowels and consonants, such as *amageʔe* 'hominy' present no problem for the syllabary; this word is spelled with four letters, and analyzed (for purposes of the syllabary) as *a-ma-ge-öe*. Consonant clusters of [s] plus a consonant are no problem, either, inasmuch as there is a separate letter for the single consonant [s]; thus *kodesdi* 'spade' is spelled with four letters, and is treated as *ko-de-s-di*. But sequences of other consonants are spelled as if there were a vowel between them: *dineɬdi* 'dolls' is spelled as if it were pronounced *di-ne-ɬo-di*, and *taʔlsogo* 'twenty' as if it were *ta-li-so-ko*.

Two features of the Cherokee sound system are ignored in the syllabary, that is, vowel length and tones. The six vowels occur both long and short, and this difference is important for distinguishing meaning, as in *ama* (with the first vowel short) 'salt', and *a·ma* (with the first vowel long) 'water'. These two words, though pronounced differently, are written the same in the syllabary; in English, comparably, two readings are given *to lead* (one reading meaning 'to follow', the other meaning 'a kind of metal'), or *to read* (e.g., "he wants to read" vs. "he has read"). Cherokee also uses tones to differentiate words; that is, it is a tone language, like Navajo or Chinese; however, these tones go unmarked in the syllabary.

It may seem that there are a number of imperfections in the syllabary, since it is not able to represent all of the distinctive sounds and sound sequences in the language. While it is probably the case that it would not be a good writing system to use for someone learning Cherokee as a second language, it seems to create few problems for a Cherokee speaker learning to read. In fact, it seems to be a better fit for the language than the writing system used for English. It is said, in fact, that a Cherokee invests less time in becoming literate in the syllabary than does an English speaker becoming literate in the Roman alphabet.

8.6 THE USE OF THE CHEROKEE SYLLABARY

Sequoyah's twelve-year effort in developing the syllabary aroused little interest or enthusiasm among his tribesmen. When the syllabary was perfected, only two people were privy to its completion: Sequoyah and his daughter. In 1819, a demonstration was arranged: a message was spoken to Sequoyah, who wrote it down in Cherokee. It was then sent to his daughter, who in turn read it back before a group of tribal leaders. According to all reports, the importance of this writing demonstration was recognized immediately, and it electrified the Cherokee nation.

Within a year, thousands of Cherokees had learned to read and write their native tongue; letter-writing became common; the Bible was translated and written in the syllabary; Indian doctors wrote down songs and formulas that until that time had been passed on only orally from one generation to the next; and in 1828, a printing press was set up in New Echota, the capital of the Cherokee nation. The printing press published a weekly newspaper, the *Cherokee Phoenix*, which appeared in both Cherokee and English. It also published portions of the Bible, a hymn book, temperance tracts, and laws passed by the National Council. There was a brief halt in the use of the printing press when, in 1839, the Cherokee nation was moved along the infamous Trail of Tears from northeast Georgia and contiguous parts of neighboring states to the Indian Territory (now Oklahoma). The printing press was set up in the new capital of Tahlequah and undertook even more publishing activity than before, including a bimonthly religious magazine, the constitution of the Cherokee nation, spelling books, arithmetic books and other primers, and the complete New Testament. There is a great deal of manuscript material (church records, curing formulas, Christian songs, and letters) from the second half of the nineteenth century still preserved by the Smithsonian Institution and the American Philosophical Society.

Estimates on literacy rates among the Cherokee in the early nineteenth century vary widely, from 25 percent to 90 percent. Even if we accept the lower rate, it is clear that writing played an important part in Cherokee life and it is interesting to note that literacy was highest in the traditional, "full blood" communities.

The year 1906 marked the end of printing in the syllabary. The United States government created the state of Oklahoma, dissolved the Indian Territory and the Cherokee Nation, replaced the Cherokee-run school system with one run by the Bureau of Indian Affairs, and confiscated the printing press. But Cherokee literacy had become too much a part of Cherokee life to be stamped out that easily. Indeed, in current Cherokee culture, literacy is associated with knowledge and is still a prerequisite for certain activities. Cherokee literacy, however, has declined and is common today in only two cultural activities, the church and native doctoring. To be a full participant in a Cherokee congregation, one has to be able to read aloud from the Bible; that is, the reader must give a public demonstration that he or she is able to read the syllabary. The use of writing in native medicine, however, is different, because the doctor uses writing to preserve medicinal knowledge, and hence must be able to write, as well as read. At present, only those over thirty read, which is not necessarily a reflection that literacy is on the decline, but rather that literacy is associated with knowledge, and hence is an adult activity. Today adult literacy in the Cherokee syllabary ranges between about 35 percent and 65 percent (depending on the community). While a formal classroom setting is occasionally used, most learning, as in Sequoyah's days, involves one person teaching another.

If we ask why literacy became such an important part of Cherokee culture in the nineteenth century, we will be confronted with a number of possible answers, none of them definitive: a writing system became available—that is important, but it does not explain why it caught on. It is, however, a sine qua non that skills come about because there is a need for them and writing is one of those skills that nonurban societies have little use for. Surely the Cherokee had no need for literacy in pre-Columbian times; but in the United States of the nineteenth century there were different conditions, probably many of them engendered by the pressure of proximity to the dominant Euro-American society. For one thing, there was a new sense of ethnic identity and nationhood, and then there was the development of new institutions (e.g., tribal government, tribal judicial system, a formal education system). All these probably came together to create the proper climate for literacy to be welcomed as a necessary adjunct to the changing Cherokee society.

8.7 THE CREE SYLLABARY

In 1823, James Evans, a young missionary from England, was assigned to the Ojibwa tribe. It is said that he learned to speak the language fluently, but he felt that the Roman alphabet was unsuited for writing it because the sounds in Ojibwa were quite different from English. He therefore devised a syllabary, which he presented to his superiors in Toronto in 1836, and asked permission to use it for writing scriptures and other religious material. To his disappointment, permission was denied, probably because there was already a system created by earlier missionaries with existing written material in the Roman alphabet.

In 1840, Evans moved to Norway House, a Cree mission on Lake Winnipeg, where he once again trotted out his syllabary because Cree and Ojibwa, both Algonquian languages, are very closely related (section 12.1). After teaching the syllabary to a number of young Cree speakers, Evans devised a crude printing press, and reported: "My type answers well. The hymn beginning with 'Jesus my all to heaven is gone' is in press." He later ran off copies of other hymns and then had better luck in persuading the mission board to allow the use of the syllabary, perhaps because the mission had not previously tried to write Cree so there was no competing orthographic tradition, and perhaps because the mission authorities simply accepted the fact that it was an accomplished deed: The Cree themselves had in fact taken up the syllabary, and it had spread among them very rapidly. Although devised by an outsider, the system seemed to be their own, possibly because the forms of the letters were different from the alphabet used for writing English and French.

Cree and most other Algonquian languages are well suited for a syllabary, in fact, better suited than Cherokee. The language has a small number of consonants, and only four vowels. The syllable has the shape CV, which is optionally followed by a "final" (i.e., final consonant). Evans worked out an ingenious method for indicating the final consonant and following vowel: each consonant has its distinctive shape, which is then rotated in one of four ways (up, down, left, right) to show which vowel follows.

As with the Cherokee syllabary, it spread rapidly from Indian to Indian, and in fact, it spread beyond the Cree to other Algonquian languages in Canada. By 1880, it was even adapted for use in some Eskimo communities and in some Canadian Athapaskan languages.

During its use in the nineteenth century, most printed material was produced by the missions and was restricted to religious material: the Bible, hymns, the Book of Common Prayer, catechism, and the Ten Commandments. It was used not only by the Church of England missions (from which the syllabary sprang), but by Catholic and other missions as well. Such nonreligious materials as newspapers came to be printed in the syllabary with increasing frequency in the latter part of the twentieth century. The Cree and other linguistic groups who adopted the syllabary have used it and continue to use it in other homelier contexts as well, such as for writing letters, messages, grocery lists, and the like.

8.8 OTHER POST-COLUMBIAN WRITING TRADITIONS

A number of other languages have developed literacy traditions, but (with some exceptions) these traditions are not very strong. In the United States and Canada, some of the writing systems were developed by native speakers, but the majority were devised by outsiders, particularly English- or French-speaking missionaries. With Cherokee and Cree as the outstanding exceptions, the orthographies are usually based on the Roman alphabet, sometimes with spelling conventions of English or French; in Alaska, the Cyrillic alphabet was introduced into some Aleut and Eskimo communities by Russian missionaries. The different orthographies that have come into use vary considerably in how well they are adapted to the language in question. Even when poorly adapted and used by few speakers, the orthographies have come to be freighted with sentiment and are not easily replaced with better, more scientifically accurate orthographies. Often the bulk of printed material is of a religious nature, which also helps to confer prestige on the spelling system.

In Mexico, pre-Columbian hieroglyphics were replaced by the Roman alphabet, most frequently with the conventions of Spanish spelling, for example, the use of "que" for [ke], "qui" for [ki], "x" for [š], and so on. Although Nahuatl and Yucatec

Mayan were widely used in Colonial times in both religious instruction and political administration, the use of written Spanish came to replace the use of written Nahuatl, Yucatec, and other local languages as bilingualism became more widespread.

Orthographies for many languages have been created by the Summer Institute of Linguistics (SIL), a group whose primary goal is to translate the Bible into indigenous languages. They have done some work in English-speaking North America, but much more in Latin America where, as a general rule, the indigenous languages are more viable. Using modern linguistic practices, they have not only devised these orthographies, but have promoted native literacy through the publication of literacy materials, adult-education materials, bilingual dictionaries, and reference grammars.

In an increasing number of American Indian communities in the United States and Canada, the indigenous languages are giving way to English or French. Tribal elders, concerned that language loss will also lead to a loss of native culture and ethnic identity, have sometimes instituted language classes for the children of the community. Although these classes have usually been of questionable utility in stemming the loss of language, they are often useful for instilling ethnic consciousness and pride. Whatever the impact of these classes on the Indian ethos, the fact that the classes are usually conducted in a formal classroom setting, with the preparation of language lessons, means that the material must be presented in written form: Therefore, if the language was not previously written, an orthography must be constructed.

8.9 WRITING AND ITS USES

Writing comes about as a response to a society's needs, and it appears that the written word is not a necessity until that society has reached a certain level of development—be it a critical mass of people, the fact of urbanization, or the emergence of social stratification. Hunter-gatherers, pastoral folk, village dwellers—these small communities have little use for writing. The important everyday information, that is, names, numbers of livestock, distances from one place to another, can be carried around in the head or notched on a stick; the other, weightier information, like the history of the tribe or the ingredients for a poultice to use on an arrow wound, can be left to the storyteller and the shaman-healer, respectively. Such was the nature of the majority of the pre-Columbian indigenous communities north of Mesoamerica.

In Mesoamerica the situation was vastly different, but not unlike the Mesopotamian society that developed the earliest form of writing. Probably because of the highly successful intense cultivation of maize, Mesoamerican populations exploded from time to time and from place to place, and archaeologists can tell us of veritable cities: probably 18 thousand inhabitants around La Venta (ca. 900–400 B.C.), 125 to 250 thousand at Teotihuacan before A.D. 600, upwards of 20 thousand at Monte Albán before A.D. 700; at Tikal estimates range from 20 to 125 thousand people, and in Tenochtitlan at the time of the Conquest there were no fewer than 100 thousand souls. Agglomerations of these sizes needed something more than a family memory, a counter of sheep, and a wise woman. Some way had to be found to record who lived where, who worked which land, whose family still owed labor and goods to the state and why. Moreover, religion, ever more intricate, demanded a record of the gods and their earthly counterparts, the kings, their histories, their rituals and what they required of their devotees. No mere storyteller could handle this assignment; what was needed was a regiment of priests and, alongside them, an army of scribes.

Writing, however, can also come about through mere proximity. There is no doubt that writing spread from place to place throughout the Yucatán Peninsula, just as in the Old World it had spread from Mesopotamia to Egypt, to Crete and probably to India and China. Similarly, the Cherokee Sequoyah was inspired to devise his syllabary because he had heard of the Whites' "talking leaves." Sequoyah, however, had probably understood that, without the "talking leaves," his people would be left behind. In other words, he felt the pressures of trying to keep up and compete with the dominant Euro-American society that had proliferated at the expense of the indigenous peoples of the Americas.

Possibly the quickest way of spreading the written word is to impose it, whether by military conquest or religious proselytization. We have seen it from the Aztecs to the Cree syllabary.

Writing in its earliest stages takes the form of pictures. As it develops, the pictographs tend to become logograms; that is, symbols that stand for words (morphemes). As we saw (section 8.3) in pre-Columbian America, Aztec "near writing" was largely pictographic, while Mayan (section 8.2) was fully logographic or hieroglyphic and word glyphs were combined with phonetic complements. Both forms of writing, however, had answered the requirements of large urban populations, fully stratified and possessed of large quantities of information that needed to be manipulated: stored, transferred, communicated, disseminated, and so on. This information related to public administration, history, trade, legal processes, education, science, and so forth. Although it is possible for a "state" to function and handle large quantities of information without writing (the Incan Empire with its elaborate quipu system comes to mind), it is manifestly easier when a written system of recording and notation has evolved.

In chapter 6 a distinction was made between "casual" and "noncasual" forms of speech; the same sort of distinction can be made in writing. In the simplest terms, noncasual writing was found carved in stone; casual writing was relegated to more impermanent materials, such as books, scrolls, codices. The stone inscriptions recorded the histories of the gods and the lives and genealogies of their descendants, the kings. These noncasual texts were often read at public ceremonies where, doubtless, the audiences were duly awed by the reminders of their heritage and destiny and their place in the scheme of things—perhaps we might consider this a form of "mind control." On the more mundane, civic level of control, the casual form of writing played an enormous role in the everyday lives of the people, in the inventory of royal storehouses, in the verification of land-holders, in the transcription of legal disputes, and so forth. Somewhere between the casual and noncasual there lay an area that encompassed the intellectual, the scholarly, the scientific; for example, the Mayan codices that listed the synodic periods of Venus tabulated and codified information that, difficult to manipulate in an exclusively oral society, had the value of adding to the society's accumulation of knowledge through the development of a scholarly tradition and a class of erudites. In post-Columbian Indian societies the uses of writing, often now in a foreign alphabet, still continued the work of public administration and government (a prime example is the Cherokee Nation's use of the syllabary) and was still the handmaiden of religion, albeit a different one.

SOURCES

Section 8.1 is a synthesis based on Dibble 1971, Coe 1976, Houston 1989, Marcus 1976, 1980, Schele 1982, 1984, Soustelle 1962, Stuart and Houston 1989, and Thompson 1972; for quote (from John Justeson) about oldest inscription, written in Zoquean, see Stuart 1993:110, with Coe 1976, Capitaine 1988 and Justeson et al. 1985 as related references; for history of scholarship see Kelley 1976:1–8, Houston 1989:8–19; see Morley 1975 for Yucatec day names. Section 8.2 is a synthesis based on Hanks 1989, Martha Macri p.c., Schele 1982, 1984, Stuart and Houston 1989, and Thompson 1972. The discussion of phonetic complements draws from Kelley 1976:178–79 and Houston 1989:38–42. Section 8.3 is based on Dibble 1963, 1971, and 1972; the discussion of glyphs as metaphors draws from Soustelle 1962:233. For section 8.4 see Coe 1973 (Maya inscriptions); Marcus 1980 (Zapotec notational system). Sections 8.5. and 8.6 are based on Monteith 1984, Walker 1969, 1975, 1981, n.d., and White 1962; see Monteith 1984:64 for comment about literacy in the traditional communities. Section 8.7 is based on Burwash 1911, Walker 1981, n.d., and Rhodes and Todd 1981. Section 8.8 makes extensive use of Walker 1969, 1981, n.d. On section 8.9 see Goody 1977 (influence of writing on communication).

SUGGESTED READINGS

For section 8.1 see Marcus 1992 for a comparison of the writing systems of the Aztec, Mixtec, Zapotec, and Maya states. For section 8.2 see Houston 1989 for a lively account of the Mayan writing system and its decipherment. For section 8.3 see Dibble 1963, 1971, and 1972 for discussion of Aztec near writing. For section 8.4 see Marcus 1976, 1980 for accounts of Zapotec near writing and its use. For sections 8.5 through 8.8 see Walker 1969, 1975, 1981, n.d., for discussions of the Cherokee syllabary and modern literacy and writing systems in North America, and Walker and Sarbaugh 1993 for an early history of the Cherokee syllabary. In section 8.9, for accounts of the place of literacy and writing systems in American Indian societies, see Goddard and Bragdon 1988 (Introduction) for Massachusetts, one of the first indigenous American languages to develop a literary tradition as a result of European contact; McLaughlin 1992 for the role of literacy in Navajo society; Karttunen 1983 for use of a standardized written Nahuatl in Mexico's Spanish colonial administration.

PART V

languages in contact

CHAPTER 9

MULTILINGUALISM

When speakers of different languages interact, language-in-contact situations arise in which the communities and speakers involved accommodate to each others' language behavior by becoming bilingual or multilingual. If groups speaking different languages are more or less in permanent contact, the most straightforward solution for effective communication is for some or all of the groups' members to learn each others' languages. If intergroup contact is limited, a few individuals are enough to provide the necessary communication links (see discussion in sections 4.1 and 4.2 of the Great Basin and Pueblo communities). In the past, to deal with intergroup communication problems, many American Indian groups used as mediators persons whose bilingualism often resulted from factors like intermarriage or length of an individual's residence with an alien group. However, continuing and widespread intercommunity contact frequently leads to a large-scale multilingualism that encompasses most or even all of one or more of the communities in contact. In the case of some Indian groups, multilingualism has been deliberately cultivated through the maintenance of intimate political and social contacts across tribes for many generations.

As the terms imply, bilingualism involves the alternative use of two languages and multilingualism the alternative use of three or more languages. Bilingual and multilingual speakers may differ widely in their actual linguistic skills, so it is possible to distinguish different degrees of proficiency: for example, **incipient bilingualism, ambilingualism,** and **functional bilingualism**. The term "incipient bilingual," which first occurred in a description of pre-bilingualism among the Huave of southern Mexico, designates an individual who may know a large number of words, mostly nouns, in a second language, but does not know how to form sentences with them.

At the opposite end of the scale from incipient bilingualism is ambilingualism, the ability to use, in every sphere of activity and equally well, more than one language without any traces of one language in the uses of the other. Complete ambilingualism most likely does not exist. Since the functions of language mesh so tightly with the variety of circumstances occurring throughout an individual's lifetime, there is little chance that a bilingual can make equal use of both languages in all activities and experiences. Domains exist in which bilinguals use both their languages equally well; however, when using a language other than the one in which they would normally talk about a particular activity, they may not be able spontaneously to come up with the necessary exact terms or structures. Given specific domains of activity, even professional interpreters who presumably have native speaker proficiency in more than one language will work more easily from one language into another. (There are, however, many individuals whose proficiency in two languages closely approaches ambilingualism; they are "fluent" bilinguals.) Proficiency intermediate between ambilingualism and incipient bilingualism is referred to as functional bilingualism. Functional bilinguals can use both languages to satisfactorily carry out all activities, even though their speech may show significant signs of transfer in pronunciation, grammar, and vocabulary from one language to the other. As long as these transfer features do not hinder communication between speaker and listener, they do not stand in the way of functional bilingualism.

Distinguishing degrees of bi- (or multi-) lingual proficiency is just one of a number of ways to consider individual bilingualism. Whatever the perspective, there are important factors to keep in mind. First, abilities in the languages involved may or may not be equal. Second, the way the languages are used plays a highly significant role. Last, the basic principles affecting language usage are the same whether a speaker is bilingual or multilingual.

In multilingual settings, a number of individual bilinguals usually serve as linguistic mediators between the different language groups involved. These mediators represent the link between individual and societal bilingualism or multilingualism. Studies of societal bilingualism and multilingualism are concerned with how a speech community's language varieties interrelate, and with the links between language and various sociocultural factors.

In sections 9.1 and 9.2 we present two case studies which emphasize significant sociocultural factors that support individual multilingualism in two geographic areas: the Vaupés region of lowland South America and precontact California. In section 9.3 we consider a brief example of societal multilingualism that involves three languages in the pre-Columbian Inca empire. The fourth study (section 9.4) focuses on the societal bilingualism arising out of Spanish-Guaraní contact in Paraguay; and in section 9.5 we consider the role of Navajo-English bilingual "code talkers" in World War II as an example of a specific use of individual bilingualism.

9.1 THE VAUPÉS

The Vaupés River Basin, half in Colombia and half in Brazil, is part of the Amazon river drainage. In an area a little larger than New England, about ten thousand Indians and perhaps as many as fifteen hundred non-Indians live in settlements

along major rivers. This culturally homogeneous region is considerably diverse linguistically. There are some twenty-five or more languages, most of which belong to
Eastern Tukanoan, the oldest indigenous language family in the area; the rest of the
languages belong to either the Arawakan or the Carib families. The cultural norm is
societal multilingualism, with almost every individual speaking three, four or more
languages well.

Two kinds of multilingualism occur in the region. One, discussed in section 10.4,
entails the use of four lingua francas: a local language and three others brought in
from outside the area. The other, which we consider here, has its roots in settlement patterns and social structure. Vaupés Indians are semisedentary farmers who
travel by canoe on the rivers that lace the area. Their settlements, "longhouses,"
are located along these rivers two hours' to a day's travel away from each other.
The longhouse is a multilingual community. The basic ceremonial and political unit,
it consists of four to eight families, with a total population between twenty and
forty. According to marriage rules, a man must marry a woman from outside his
longhouse community. Appropriate outside groups are defined by language; that is,
a wife must come from a longhouse belonging to a language group different from
that of her husband. A person's descent is traced through his or her father's side,
and when a man marries he and his family reside in his father's longhouse community. An individual's formal language affiliation, therefore, is determined by his or
her "father language," and not by the language that identifies his or her mother's
language group (i.e., "mother language").

Although men must choose their wives from a longhouse with a different father
language, the marriage rules are not so simple. A language group is represented by
a series of longhouses and is part of yet a larger social unit that includes other language groups. In the Vaupés, this social unit, a phratry, claims common descent
from a mythological ancestor, and intermarriage within a phratry is not allowed. A
Bará speaker says, for example, "My brothers are those who speak my own language.
I call Tukanos 'brothers' because we used to speak the same language." In other
words, men and women with Bará and Tukano as father languages cannot marry
each other because these languages are included in the same phratric grouping. The
Vaupés phratries do not correspond to a scientific classification of the languages of
the area into linguistic families and subfamilies. Instead, as a useful means for regu-
lating marriages, the phratry groupings reflect a belief system that unites language
and kinship, with persons speaking the same language seen as brothers and sisters;
for instance, Tukano, a father language, is also a lingua franca, learned in addition
to other languages by most of the inhabitants of the Vaupés. When one man was
asked why everyone did not simply use Tukano, he replied, "If we all were Tukano
speakers, where would we get our women?"

All the residents know the various languages spoken in the longhouse. Among husbands and wives, each speaks to the other in the husband's language, while in other areas each speaks his or her own language to the other; however, in some areas the wife speaks the husband's language to him. The local father language is used among men and to men, and a woman uses it when talking with her children. In addition, it is used when women from different language groups or phratries interact. In a longhouse of any size, there are usually several women, each with her own original father language. In frequent same-group interactions, women converse in their own languages, and men, if within hearing, understand them. Even though ordinarily speaking the longhouse father language when talking to both parents and others, a child is usually fluent in languages of both parents. Knowing his mother's language can be very important for a young man because of the cultural preference for marrying someone from his mother's language group. In addition, children are in contact with the languages spoken by married women from various language groups, and they also have contact with languages spoken by visitors to the longhouse.

Each longhouse has its distinctive repertoire, consisting of a father language and one or more mother languages; for instance, there are longhouses along the Inambú River, near the confluence with the Papuri River, that have Tuyuka as their father language. In most of them, three mother languages are spoken: Desano, Tukano, and Bará. Even though the same four languages remain in all the longhouse repertoires, the proportions of speakers of these languages change from longhouse to longhouse: The farther away a longhouse is from the Desano-speaking area and the closer it is to the Bará-speaking area, the number of Desano-speaking wives drops and there is a corresponding rise in the number in Bará-speaking wives.

Besides the multilingualism characteristic of the longhouses, there are personal language repertoires that each individual, over time, develops. For an adult, a personal repertoire can be considerably larger than the longhouse repertoire. While it is the norm for children to be fluent in from three to five languages, there are adults who use as many as seven to ten languages with varying degrees of proficiency. Languages other than the longhouse languages are encountered through travel. Visits to other settlements are frequent for courtship, trade, and ceremonies; and trips, lasting from a few days to several months, afford opportunities for learning additional languages. An unmarried youth, for example, may spend considerable time traveling, checking out prospective mates, and learning new languages, particularly if his bride-to-be speaks a father language not in his repertoire (i.e., if it is not one of the mother languages of his longhouse). Even after courtship and marriage, additional languages are often learned throughout adulthood and into old age.

Language is a symbol of social identity among Vaupés Indians. The one thing known about a person before anything else is his or her language group membership. During a visit, for example, participants begin a conversation in their father languages. In the opening phase of the conversation, new information is seldom presented since the interaction serves to signal both identity with a father language and also distinctiveness from others; after this first phase, the conversation shifts into whatever language is most convenient. The particular set of languages used in any specific encounter depends on various factors like the father languages of the participants, the language of the longhouse, the language of the senior male participants, a lingua franca, or perhaps yet another language.

Language mixing is not approved of and a person does not like to speak a language until he or she knows it well, particularly if the new language is quite similar to one already known. Consequently, a learner will spend some time listening before trying to speak. In addition, there are conversational customs that probably aid in learning: for example, it is proper etiquette for listeners to repeat the last word of the speaker's sentence in order to indicate that they are listening and taking part in the conversation. Because sentences end in verbs in the Tukanoan languages and verbs frequently include inflectional affixes that encapsulate the semantic and syntactic relationships of the entire sentence, this conversational custom would appear to be an effective language-learning strategy.

In the Vaupés, people would be puzzled by such a question as, "How many languages do you know?" Because multilingualism is the norm, it is not thought of as being particularly remarkable; however, if Vaupés Indians are asked language by language, they can provide clear evaluations of their knowledge of each: "none," "only understand," "a few words," "half-way" or "some but not well" (usually meaning some failings in pronunciation), "just a little lacks," or "all." Such ratings are underestimates. According to one student of Vaupés languages, "when an Indian says he speaks such-and-such a language 'some,' we would be more prone in English-speaking culture to say he speaks it 'quite well.'"

The multilingualism that exists among the Tukanoan language groups differs from many other multilingual situations. First of all, if we consider such factors as numbers of languages and verbal repertoires, the degree of multilingualism is unusually widespread. With a population of approximately ten thousand, a dispersed settlement pattern, and low population density, the Vaupés situation supports a view that the formation of multilingual speech communities does not necessarily depend on high population density or a large number of speakers per language. Second, language is the most important marker of group identification in the region. In other cases of multilingualism, several markers, such as physical characteristics, differences in technology, dress, and so on, are equally as important as language. Last of all, in many other multilingual environments, factors like setting, activity, role or participant, topic, and so on, may determine the use of one language or dialect in encounters, regardless of the various languages or dialects participants may have in common. In Vaupés encounters, situational and other constraints always operate together with the particular father-language identities of participants.

Vaupés multilingualism represents one of the world's most complex sociolinguistic situations. The Tukanoan peoples of the Vaupés think highly of multilingualism, of large language repertoires and of the ability to speak languages well without mixing them. In addition, language survival is so closely related to the maintenance of group and individual identity that many of the groups have made extraordinary efforts to preserve their languages. These facts together with the fact that the region displays considerable cultural uniformity, call into question the often-held assumption that linguistic diversity necessarily leads to barriers in communication and, therefore, to cultural diversity. In-depth study of Vaupés multilingualism (which we have not attempted here) might shed some light on just how cultural patterns and values, language attitudes, and language survival are interrelated.

9.2 CALIFORNIA

Linguistically diverse, with a multilingualism rooted in cultural patterns of marriage, ceremonialism, and trade, the precontact geographic area now called California might seem similar to the Vaupés region of today. Before Euro-American contact, however, the California area was not only much more populous but was also culturally and ethnically much more diverse than the Vaupés region. In addition, it exhibited greater linguistic diversity, which was still evident in 1871 and 1872 when a visitor among Indian groups in the northern two-thirds of California reported traveling in some regions where "a new language has to be looked to every ten miles."

Before Euro-Americans appeared on the scene, the approximately three hundred thousand inhabitants of the area spoke somewhere between sixty and eighty languages. These languages, many of which had large numbers of dialects, have been grouped into twenty-two language families, some of which are remotely related, or are likely to be remotely related. The extent of this linguistic diversity and the fact that languages and populations were not equally distributed throughout the region are factors contributing to the particular overall character of multilingualism in precontact California. Chimariko, for instance, was spoken by a few hundred people along a twenty-mile stretch of the Trinity River in northern California; Esselen, by a similar number on the central coast; and Cupeño, in southern California by five hundred people living in two villages. In contrast, the seven Pomoan languages, located in north-central California between the coast and the Sacramento Valley, were spoken in over thirty villages by a total of eight thousand speakers; and

Yokuts, in the San Joaquin Valley, had eighteen thousand speakers located in about fifty or sixty villages, with each village speaking a slightly different dialect.

Even though there is no systematic, direct evidence of specific multilingual situations that may have been present in the area for millennia before Euro-American contact, comments buried here and there in various reports and studies indicate that "bilingualism and multilingualism were common among California Indians, [and were] undoubtedly accompanied over the centuries by a steady process of acculturation and exchange of linguistic material in all directions." In the northwest part of the area, people living in settlements near language-group boundaries habitually spoke both their own languages and those of adjacent groups. One report comments that the Yurok and their neighbors were very similar as far as culture went, but spoke totally different languages, and "two of them will sit and . . . gossip for hours, each speaking in his own tongue." According to another source, the Yurok elite enjoyed being able to speak a language other than Yurok. A remark of this kind indicates that there were circumstances in which it may have been considered prestigious to speak a second language. In the northeast, Atsugewis were bilingual in Atsugewi and Achumawi, the language of a neighboring group; but even though Atsugewis often learned the Achumawi language, Achumawis did not learn Atsugewi. It appears that there were also contexts that drew upon multilingual skills: "If the [Atsugewi] shaman were unsuccessful in a cure, a shaman from another village or tribe might be called in. . . . A pain . . . entered his body . . . and spoke through him using Achumawi, Atsugewi or the Maidu language."

In the north-central area, some Cahtos spoke Northern Pomo in addition to their own language and, on the Wailaki-Northern Pomo border, nearly everyone understood the languages of both groups. The Coast Pomo and the Central Pomo were in intimate contact to the north with the Coast Yuki, Huchnom, Valley Yuki, and Cahto; to the east with the Eastern Pomo, Southeastern Pomo, Patwin, Lake Miwok, and Wappo; and to the south with the Coast Miwok. Altogether, this contact involved twelve languages, some of them very different from each other. Most Pomoan peoples knew more than one Pomoan language, with boys often sent to learn the languages of neighboring villages. As for the Wappo, one report, in stating that Wappos "display great readiness in learning their neighbors' tongues," comments that an old Wappo man was reputed to have known fourteen languages. For the south-central area, there is mention of Yokuts-Mono bilingualism on the western slopes of the Sierra Nevada. For the south, a report that Ipais were in contact with Luiseños, Cupeños, and Cahuillas indicates the possibility of either bilingualism or multilingualism or both.

The foregoing patchwork of passing remarks about some of the language-in-contact situations in various areas of precontact California gives hints of widespread and intricately patterned multilingual networks of communication that were severely disrupted after contact. Societal and cultural complexities contributed mightily to the intricacies of this multilingual patterning. Even though much of the ethnically diverse population spread throughout the area shared certain cultural traits that unify the region into a distinct "culture area," there were also subareas with their own particular characteristic features, which were evidence of cultural ties with areas beyond the boundaries of the present-day state. For instance, the central California subarea was culturally the most distinctively "Californian"; northwestern California had features that aligned it with the north Pacific coast culture area; the northeastern subarea had affiliations with the Great Basin and Plateau areas; and southern California reflected Southwest or Pueblo influences. (In addition, desert populations along the eastern edge of present-day California were not part of the California culture area at all. Their cultural orientations were Great Basin in type.)

Throughout California the village society, or "tribelet," was the basic self-governing and independent social unit. These communities were made up of types of family and household group that varied according to subarea. In southern and south-central California, tribelets were organized into clearly defined, complex sociopolitical groups that traced descent through the male line. Often several lineages were linked into clans, or in some cases there would be several unrelated lineages. In northern California loosely organized tribelets were generally made up of settlements consisting of extended family groups. After marriage, a couple could choose to reside with either the man's or the woman's kin group; however, in some areas there was a tendency to favor residence with the man's kin group.

The tribelet was an autonomous, land-holding political unit united under the leadership of a local headman. Sometimes a cluster of closely linked settlements, or a group of scattered settlements (as in the north), were under the authority of a single headman; for instance, the fifty or sixty Yokuts settlements were united into thirty-seven village communities and the approximately thirty-five Pomoan settlements were united into about twenty-five tribelets. Although commonality of language did not help define sociopolitical units larger than the village community, sometimes two or more tribelets speaking the same language were federated under a single political authority. Political confederations of this kind were characteristic of some of the Shasta, Miwokan, Chumashan, Gabrielino, and Salinan groups.

Tribelets were strongly connected with each other by both formal and informal interlocking links, and stable trade and military alliances often involved communities that were members of various language groups. Alliance structures occurred throughout the precontact California area from west to east and from north to south. In addition, there were communities that served as cross-tribelet interface centers, sometimes involving several hundred to several thousand people in intense sociopolitical and economic interaction. Three linkage patterns in particular fostered multilingualism: marriage alliances, ceremonial cooperation, and economic exchange.

Marriage

All through precontact California marriage practices tended to create environments in which children often grew up as functional bilinguals or multilinguals. In addition to an area-wide rule that an individual married someone from outside his or her kin-based group (family, extended family, lineage, and so on), there was also a rule against marriage to any relative within three to five generations, with the number varying in different parts of California. These rules fostered the development of multilingualism, by encouraging marriages involving persons from different language groups; for example, in southern California, because of the lineage system and the generation rule, the average tribelet of only a few hundred members would be virtually without potential spouses for its members. As a case in point, a single Gabrielino tribelet in southern California had intermarriages with thirteen other tribelets, three of which belonged to foreign-language groups.

Cross-language marriage alliances were especially common among the elite. Throughout California, there were social class distinctions based on wealth and rank, and as a rule tied to family traditions. The elite class consisted of headmen and their immediate families, as well as bureaucrats, religious specialists, and crafts specialists, all of whom were often members of the headman's extended family. Since the elite, a minority within the population-at-large, preferred to marry within their own class, this sort of preferential marriage practice, in addition to the "marrying out" and generational rules, further restricted spouse selection. As a result, among the elite there tended to be an emphasis on intermarriage between members of distinct language groups. In addition, it was generally considered proper for a headman to have more than one wife at the same time. As economic administrators who managed the distribution and exchange of goods for the benefit of the group, headmen needed ties with other political units. One way to establish such ties was through marriage, and frequently a headman married several women, all of whom, often speaking different languages, would be daughters of influential families in different tribelets. By the same token, among religious specialists, a shaman (in groups where men were shamans) often had more than one wife, as this was an indication of the wealth he possessed and of a willingness of families to ally with him.

Ritual Alliances

Four ritual complexes, the World Renewal, the Kuksu, the Toloache, and the Mourning Anniversaries, forged networks of ceremonial cooperation throughout large regions of precontact California and were intimately involved, through ritual events, in the social and economic aspects of California societies.

In northwestern California, the Karuk, Yurok, Hupa, Tolowa, and some of their neighbors held annual cycles of World-Renewal rites in order to maintain world order and the health of individuals, to insure the productivity and availability of food and other resources, to avoid natural disasters, and to gain assistance from the supernaturals. A large number of ritual specialists conducted the rites, which were accompanied by dance cycles lasting up to sixteen days. These specialists, who had to be well versed in a large body of esoteric and sacred lore, represented a number of different language groups, as did the thousands of participants, who were organized into large "ritual congregations."

In north-central California, practitioners of the Kuksu religion participated in cycles of rites and ceremonies during which gods, spirits, or ghosts were impersonated in order to recreate sacred time and restore people to the untainted state prevailing at the time of creation. The god most widely impersonated is called *kúksu* in Eastern Pomo and there are similar terms in other languages. To the west in portions of the coast ranges, the practitioners were the Cahto, speakers of the various Pomoan and Yukian languages, and the Coast and Lake Miwok. To the east in portions of the Sacramento Valley the main practitioners were speakers of various Maiduan languages, as well as the Patwin, the Northeastern Pomo, and the Plains Miwok. The Kuksu system consisted of a number of secret societies composed of learned men (and sometimes women) who administered and led the cycles of public rites and ceremonies. The tendency for membership in the Kuksu societies to run in families indicates the likelihood that they were used to strengthen marriage ties, thereby operating as intertribelet alliances. Although specific ritual features varied considerably from region to region, all the Kuksu societies were characterized by complexity and a formalized organization that incorporated a number of tribelets. As was the case with the northwestern World-Renewal rites, performances were large undertakings that lasted for several days and drew performers and audiences from a wide, multilingual area.

The Toloache religious complex, with its stress on ritual death and rebirth, reflected an overriding concern with personal and cosmic death and renewal. The Toloache religions spread throughout the southern and south-central California culture areas, from the Yuman peoples of the south, north through the Yokuts, and up as far as the Central Sierra Miwok. Religious practices were based on the ritual use of *Datura stramonium*, a hallucinogenic plant commonly known as jimsonweed or toloache (from Nahuatl *toloatzin* via Spanish). In southern California, datura drinking was the esoteric part of the rites associated with the initiation at puberty of young males. Such ceremonies were core traits of the Toloache religion of the Luiseño-Juaneño, Cahuilla, Ipai, Tipai, Cupeño, and Gabrielino. In the south-central

coastal area, among the Chumash, datura use centered around an elite socioreli-
gious guild made up of ritual officers whose primary responsibility was the performance of dances and other rituals at large public ceremonies. From time to time
many of these ritual specialists participated in ceremonies held in widely scattered
locations throughout the area where different Chumashan languages were spoken.

Accompanying the Toloache complex was the "Mourning Anniversary." Carried
out by most of the southern California groups, this practice extended outside the
south-central and southern culture areas to northern California, where the Nisenan, and possibly the Konkow, performed the ceremony in conjunction with Kuksu
rites. Mourning Anniversaries were large public gatherings in which those assembled
mourned their dead; for example, when the Wickchamni Yokuts held their annual
ceremony, guests came by the hundreds to participate in six days of special rites.
The occasions often served other purposes as well, including expressions of reci-
procity between kin groups.

Although each of the four major religious systems we have briefly sketched was
distinctive, and there was a great deal of local variation within a single system,
they (and many less prominent ritual activities) performed significant nonreligious
functions, which included acting as social and economic regulatory mechanisms
and creating networks of political organization. In doing so, they helped promote
multilingualism in a variety of ways. First, they required the participation of religious leaders from several neighboring groups, many of whom did not speak the
same first languages. Second, their public ceremonies drew together large numbers
of people from different language groups widely spread over the surrounding areas.
Last, through the development of major religious centers, they created centers of
economic, social, and political interaction. In northern California, World-Renewal
rites were celebrated at thirteen ritual centers and in the south, at least among the
Gabrielino and Chumash, there were similar centers for the Toloache rites. In those
parts of California that lacked fixed or permanent centers, each community served
as a ritual center when a ceremony was hosted by local leaders. The end result was
the integration of thousands of people, often from scores of tribelets, into many
intersecting networks with a radius of fifty to seventy-five miles. Presumably, this
integration supported the proliferation of complex patterns of multilingualism.

Trade

Trade was a very important and active undertaking in precontact California. The
considerable social and political interaction associated with religious gatherings
provided an arena for important trading activities. But trade occurred in other contexts as well, one of the most important of which was a trade feast. A community
hosting a trade feast served as a center for intense sociopolitical and economic inter-

action that could involve a dozen or more tribelets speaking two or more languages and coming from differing ecological spheres. The entire Pomoan area, for example, was part of a much larger interrelated economic system that included most groups in northern California and made possible the exchange of goods, services, ceremonies, and marriage partners over a wide area. Pomoan groups held trade feasts between neighboring settlements; and it was among the duties of Eastern Pomo and Southeastern Pomo headmen, for instance, to open trade feasts with appropriate speeches.

Inasmuch as trade was important in strengthening cross-tribelet ties, formalized trading-partner relationships, sometimes reinforced by intermarriage, existed throughout the California area. Trading partnerships were one way to extend to foreign groups the advantages of the reciprocal economic relationships generally found within lineages or extended families. In the northeast prominent Atsugewi men had special trading partners, often relatives, in each neighboring group. Trading partnerships also occurred in the northwest among the Yurok, and in southern California they regularized reciprocal exchanges with groups from the Southwest culture area.

Trade routes were along trails that connected settlements and tribelets, and trails from one settlement to another might extend into the territory of neighboring groups and from there on to adjoining groups. Although traders usually traveled only short distances along trade trails, objects of trade would often end up hundreds of miles from their source, since routes extended for hundreds of miles, north and south, east and west. These trade routes crossed many linguistic boundaries, with trails combining to form continuous lines of communication: north-south, from the Mexican border to the Oregon line; east-west, from the Pacific coastal areas to the Great Basin.

In summary, marriage practices, ritual complexes, and trading patterns in pre-contact California were major factors in the weaving together of over five hundred autonomous village communities, representing at least sixty languages, into intricately constructed networks of communication that promoted a great deal of societal as well as individual multilingualism.

9.3 THE INCA EMPIRE

Societal multilingualism is common in stratified societies. There are a number of examples from pre-Columbian Mesoamerica where each language had its own functions. In Chapter 4, for example, we examined the Aztec Empire, in which the Aztec language was used for diplomacy, politics, and trade. In South America, in the Andes, three languages were involved in the establishment of the Inca Empire:

Puquina, Quechua, and Aymara. Puquina was the language of the Inca royal family and conquering group, whose initial conquest was of a Quechua-speaking state in the Cuzco area; however, when the Puquina-speaking conquerors took over, they left the Quechua-speaking administration in place; in addition, as the Incas extended their empire, they used Quechua and not Puquina as the imperial language. The two most common languages of the multilingual area they controlled were Quechua and Aymara, each with several million speakers.

In addition to these three languages, there were many local languages spoken in limited areas. The empire was a cultural and linguistic mosaic brought about in part by imperial resettlement policies. The pattern of language intermingling was analogous to the pattern in the Vaupés region (section 9.1). Because of its use in administration, Quechua was learned as a second language by local leaders and sometimes by the whole community; and in some communities it replaced the local language. Although a number of local languages were involved, the replaced language was often Aymara. Nevertheless, Aymara persisted as a local language to a significant degree; therefore, in the Inca Empire there was a large population bilingual in Quechua and Aymara. The original conquering group and the royal family continued to use Puquina, their native language, along with Quechua for administrative purposes. In addition, many members of this social stratum also spoke Aymara as their third language. When the Spanish conquered the Inca Empire in the sixteenth century, the capital, Cuzco, was a trilingual city. After the Spanish Conquest, colonial and church policy brought about an even greater spread of Quechua at the expense of Aymara.

9.4 PARAGUAY

Modern-day Paraguay presents us with an example of societal bilingualism and a languages-in-contact situation much different from those of the Vaupés and precontact California. Paraguay is a nation of approximately three million people, 92 percent of whom speak Guaraní, an indigenous language, and 60 percent Spanish: 8 percent are monolingual in Spanish; 52 percent are bilingual in Spanish and Guaraní; and 40 percent are monolingual Guaraní speakers. Although Guaraní is more prevalent in rural areas than in urban ones, three quarters of the population in the capital, Asunción, speak the language. Contrast these figures with those of the capital cities of two other Latin American nations that also have large American Indian populations: fewer than 15 percent of the inhabitants of the capital city of Peru speak an Indian language, and in the capital city of Mexico, fewer than 10 percent.

In most parts of the Americas, to speak an indigenous language is to be an

Indian, since non-Indians rarely use or have knowledge of an American Indian language. This is not so in Paraguay, where most people of non-Indian descent learn Guaraní; in fact, every president of Paraguay has been able to speak the language, and speaking Guaraní reinforces a person's identity as a Paraguayan, whatever his or her class, ethnicity, or geographical background. Accordingly, the status of Guaraní in Paraguay is unique in the Americas: it is not only an Indian language, but also a symbol of national identity. Both Guaraní and Spanish are recognized as national languages and bilingualism is officially sanctioned.

To understand how Guaraní came to occupy its distinctive position, we need to trace the historical process that contributed to Paraguay's particular pattern of bilingualism. During the beginning phase of Spanish colonization early in the sixteenth century, mutual cooperation between the Guaraní people and the Spanish was reinforced by familial alliances that the men from the Spanish expeditions entered into when they married or had extramarital relationships with Guaraní women. These alliances ultimately yielded a high percentage of households of mixed Spanish-Guaraní ancestry, in which Guaraní was the primary language spoken. The primacy of Guaraní was also reinforced by Jesuit educators who, early in the seventeenth century, were promoting literacy and pride in Guaraní.

In the early colonial period, the pattern of interaction between the Spanish and the Guaraní in Paraguay was similar in some ways to what occurred in other parts of Latin America with large indigenous populations; for instance, it was not uncommon for those of Spanish descent in colonial Mexico to speak Nahuatl, or in the Andean colonies to speak Quechua or Aymara. Two things, however, happened in Mexico and the Andean areas that did not happen in Paraguay during the period following contact: first, a Spanish-speaking elite developed that was insulated from the masses and, second, there was a considerable flow of Spanish-speaking immigrants attracted by exploitable natural resources. The use of Spanish did not overtake that of Guaraní because Paraguay did not develop a sharply defined class system with an elite set apart by language, education, and economic status. Moreover, since Paraguay had no readily exploitable natural resources, there was no large influx of Spaniards to add to the Spanish-speaking element of the population.

Paraguay became independent from Spain in 1811. From 1814 to 1840 its borders were closed to trade and immigration, and cultural contact with the outside world came to a standstill until they reopened in 1840. In 1864 Guaraní became a national unifying symbol when Paraguay entered into a disastrous war against Brazil, Argentina and Uruguay. By the end of this war, however, with over half of its population destroyed, Paraguay was under the control of Argentina and Brazil, and a disdain of Guaraní developed that lasted some sixty or so years. During those years, the Spanish language was emphasized and in many homes in the metropolitan area children were forbidden to learn Guaraní. But the association between Paraguayan nationalism and Guaraní was reinforced when the Indian language was used to rally the troops during the Chaco war of 1932–1935 against Argentina. After the Chaco War, because of an increase in Paraguayan contact with other nations, there was an emphasis on Spanish, the language of wider communication; but in the 1950s, sponsored by the government, interest in Guaraní increased and, in 1967, this Indian language's position was enshrined in Paraguay's constitution, which designates both Guaraní and Spanish as national languages.

Paraguayans praise Guaraní as "the heart of the nation" and "the symbol of the true soul of the people." Those who speak Guaraní are fellow Paraguayans; those who speak only Spanish, even though living in Paraguay, are "gringos." Paraguayans also consider the language well suited for discussing such topics as botany, agriculture, and medicine, as well as being appropriate for poetry, for making declarations of love, and for telling jokes. Since Spanish, however, is the official language of government and education and schooling is only in Spanish, Guaraní is often denigrated. Lack of Spanish indicates lack of education, and monolinguals in Guaraní are seen as less intelligent than those who are bilingual.

An understanding of the different domains and functions of the two languages in Paraguayan society helps shed light on the ambivalent attitudes toward Guaraní. In rural areas, Guaraní is the language used in most contexts. The major exception is in school, where Spanish is the language of instruction. In urban contexts, however, several factors come into play in the choice of language. Depending upon such variables as where a conversation takes place, what the particular circumstances are, and what the topic is, people will alternate between the two languages when conversing. Spanish is expected in formal settings, while in informal settings the language is more apt to be Guaraní. Intimacy is also a factor: close friends use Guaraní, while newly introduced people will probably use Spanish; and courtship normally begins in Spanish, then shifts to Guaraní as the relationship becomes closer. In recent years, the use of Spanish has been spreading from the urban to the rural areas, but it has not been replacing Guaraní; rather, there are places for the use of both languages because it is patterns of usage, the extralinguistic rules that govern the choices between the two languages, that have been spreading.

In most parts of the Americas, bilingualism involving a national and an indigenous language is normally transitory, the first step in language replacement. In modern nation-states, the communicative functions of the Indian language (or languages) become more and more restricted to the traditional local society or societies (section 11.4). In this respect, Guaraní is exceptional since it shares dominance with Spanish and has certain functions and roles distinct from those of Spanish that are part of modern Paraguayan culture and society.

9.5 NAVAJO CODE TALKERS

Since early in the European occupation of the Americas, powers in conflicts among themselves have used American Indian languages for one purpose or another. Paraguay used Guaraní in its conflicts with Brazil, Argentina and Uruguay. In World War I the United States Army employed speakers of Choctaw and Comanche, and "Michigan and Wisconsin" Indians (perhaps Chippewas) in sending secret messages. The fullest and most systematic military use of an indigenous language occurred during World War II, when the United States Marine Corps recruited over four hundred Navajos for use in the Pacific theater to send radio messages in a code secure from enemy interception. "Navajo code," as it was called, played a crucial role in many battles, including the battle at Iwo Jima, where it was used for the entire military operation. In this code, the letter values come from the English translations of the Navajo terms: a message was encoded by using Navaho words, say, the three words for "ant," "bear" and "cat"; the message was then decoded by translating the Navaho words into English and using the initials of the English words to render, perhaps, the name of an operation called "ABC." Thus, the Japanese name Suribachi was spelled "sheep," "uncle," "ram," "ice," "bear," "ant," "cat," "horse," "ice." Past efforts to use Indian languages in military contexts had encountered difficulties because of a lack of fixed conventions for military terms. In Navajo code, this problem was solved through the invention of 413 "code words"; for example, the Navajo word for "chicken hawk" was used for "dive bomber"; "hummingbird" for "fighter plane"; "iron fish" for "submarine."

The Navajo language was a logical choice as a "code language": first of all, it was an unwritten language and "exotic" from the Japanese point of view; second, since it has the largest number of native speakers of any Indian language in the United States, it was easier to find recruits who could act as "code talkers."

To recapitulate at this point, the Navajo code talkers are an example of a group of individual bilinguals whose proficiency in two languages (Navajo and English) was utilized by a nation in time of war. In the other language-in-contact situations we have discussed, both individual speakers and communities are involved; and there are several factors influencing the extent of multilingualism. One factor, of course, is the degree of linguistic diversity, although diversity alone does not guarantee multilingualism. As our Vaupés and precontact California discussion has shown, the roles played by social institutions are also important. For individual multilingualism in unstratified societies, such as those in the Vaupés region, probably the single most important factor is the marriage link; that is, the language of spouses and their families or (from the point of view of the children) of parents and their families. In precontact California, individual multilingualism was influenced by a complex of cultural patterns. Attitudes (Is language learning considered easy? Is multilingualism valued?) also play a role in shaping the nature and degree of multilingualism, and are probably shaped by the relationship of the languages to social institutions, as in the Vaupés region where multilingualism is highly valued and intimately connected with social structure.

The Incan and Paraguayan examples illustrate how, in societal bilingualism and multilingualism, function is especially important in determining the choice of language. The Paraguayan situation also provides an example of something else that is usual in bilingual and stratified societies of the modern, urbanizing world: one language is often linked with a set of sociopolitical institutions and used in formal settings, while the other language is associated with informal institutions and settings. In Paraguay, Spanish is the language of government and education, and of legal and business affairs; but Guaraní, the language of intimacy, also plays an important role in establishing the identities of groups and individuals as Paraguayan when they are outside their country.

SOURCES

The introductory section draws from Baetens Beardsmore 1986, Diebold 1960, Gumperz 1962, Halliday, McIntosh and Strevens 1965, and Weinreich 1953. Section 9.1 is based on Sorensen 1967, 1985, Jackson 1974, 1983, and Grimes 1985; for quotes: see Jackson 1983:92, 170 from a Bará speaker and for the use of Tukano; Sorensen 1967 for ratings of fluency. Section 9.2 is based on Bean 1976, 1978, Bean and Smith 1978, Bean and Theodoratus 1978, Bean and Vane 1978, Blackburn 1976, Buckley 1989, Garth 1978, Gayton 1976, Heizer 1978, Kroeber 1925, 1962, 1971, Luomala 1978, McLendon and Lowy 1978, Miller 1978, Myers 1978, Pilling 1978, Shipley 1978, and Spier 1978; for quotes see Powers 1877:347, 144, 198 on language diversity, the Yurok and their neighbors, the Wappo; Olmsted and Stewart 1978:231 on shamans' use of languages; Shipley 1978:81 for quote on bi- and multilingualism. Section 9.3 is based on Hardman 1985a, 1985b, Heath and Laprade 1982, Mannheim 1991. Section 9.4 is based on Rubin 1968, 1985, Service 1954, Sorensen 1973, and Stark 1983. Section 9.5 is based on Walker 1980 and 1983.

SUGGESTED READINGS

On sections 9.1, 9.3, and 9.4 see Urban 1991 for a discussion of State-Indian linguistic relationships in Peru, Paraguay, and Brazil.

CHAPTER 10

LINGUA FRANCAS

In chapter 9 we saw that bilingualism and multilingualism are natural and common responses in contact situations in which the participants speak different languages. A special kind of bilingualism involves the use of a **lingua franca**, a language used by non-native speakers when interacting with speakers of different languages; in other words, the lingua franca makes it possible for persons from diverse ethnic and linguistic groups to communicate with each other. English and French are often used in this way in the world today; for instance, in buying a train ticket in Munich, a traveler, whether from Salt Lake City or Tokyo, is likely to use English when speaking with the ticket agent. The use of a lingua franca is usually limited to a certain kind of interaction, with trade the most common one; however, lingua francas are also used in political, diplomatic, religious, and exploitative labor settings.

In the Americas, after European contact, the various European languages—English, Danish, French, Portuguese, Russian, Spanish—have been used as lingua francas at various times and in different places. We have already noted the place of Spanish and later English in the Pueblo Southwest (section 4.2). Danish is the language of education and public administration in Greenland, while Greenlandic Eskimo is the language of the home. In (pre)colonial times, French served as a lingua franca between French speakers and Indians and sometimes between different Indian groups in the French colonies in Canada and Louisiana; today its use is limited to some Indian groups in Quebec. Russian was used in certain parts of Alaska, and Spanish and Portuguese have been widely used in many parts of Latin America. Indigenous lingua francas had greatest scope in the Aztec and Inca Empires: Nahuatl was used in government, diplomacy, and trade in the Aztec Empire and beyond (section 4.4), and Quechua was the imperial language of the Inca Empire (section 9.3).

We noted earlier that no lingua franca was present in the nomadic foraging societies of the Great Basin (section 4.1). Lingua francas are sometimes missing in village societies, as in the Pueblos (section 4.2), and sometimes present as, for example, the use of Creek as the medium for conducting politics in the Confederacy (section 4.3). Other examples in village societies include the use of Hupa among the surrounding groups in northwestern California and the use of Mohawk in the Iroquois League. The position of Tuscarora among surrounding tribes in the Southeast was noted by an early traveler, who stated, "the most powerful Nation of these Savages scorns to treat or trade with any others . . . in any other Tongue but their own, which serves for the lingua of the Country, with which we travel and deal." It is in stratified societies like the Aztec and Inca empires, however, that a lingua franca has the greatest scope.

A lingua franca does not have to be a verbal language; for instance, Plains Sign Language was used as the language for intertribal contact in the Plains (section 7.3). Moreover, there are language varieties known as pidgins and creoles that are also used as lingua francas.

10.1 PIDGINS AND CREOLES

The terms "pidgin" and "creole" are used here in their technical, scholarly meanings rather than the way they are used in a popular sense. In popular usage, "pidgin" sometimes refers derisively to varieties of English that have low social standing. "Creole" often refers to descendants of the French settlers of Louisiana who speak a regional dialect of French, or it refers to African-Americans who speak what is, in technical usage, a French-based creole.

Pidgins arise in contact situations among speakers of different languages, and a pidgin is a form of natural language that has a limited vocabulary and simplified phonological and grammatical structures. The vocabulary of a pidgin consists of those words necessary for carrying on conversations restricted to particular contexts, for example, trade or work. Sometimes the vocabulary is based primarily on words from a single language, a **base language,** which is supplemented with some words from other languages. In other cases, the vocabulary is from such a mix of languages that it makes little sense to identify any one language as the base language. The sound system of a pidgin, usually a simplified version of the base language, often shows phonetic influence from the other languages in the contact situation. In comparison with the grammatical system of a "full" language, a pidgin's grammatical structure is streamlined. Some pidgins have grammatical structures that are greatly simplified versions of the grammars of the base languages; other pidgins have the same grammatical categories that occur in the full languages of the contact setting, but the forms in which the categories are expressed may be entirely different. Moreover, a pidgin often develops new grammatical categories not found in any of the languages in contact. It is important to keep in mind that, although the structures of pidgins may be streamlined when compared to those of full languages, pidgins are rule-governed structures, and sentences are constructed accordingly.

A pidgin arises then out of contact situations and has restricted communicative functions; but unlike a full language used as a lingua franca, a pidgin has no native speakers and is a second (or third or fourth, etc.) language for all of its speakers.

Pidgins seem to spring up as a natural response in multilingual contact settings where there is a need for a language to serve as a medium of communication, but the contact is not intimate enough for full bilingualism to develop.

Sometimes a pidgin is short-lived; it is a way station before full bilingualism develops. Under the right sociocultural conditions, however, it can persist for a long period of time. If that happens, two things take place: first, the extreme variation of usage among speakers characteristic of pidgins in their early stages becomes stabilized and the language crystallizes into a definite form; second, the grammatical structure becomes more complex, usually developing from its own resources rather than borrowing from the grammar of the full languages in the contact situation. Once this happens, the pidgin may (if the sociocultural conditions are conducive) become creolized and then can be learned as a first language by children.

A creole develops from a pidgin used as a native language. The emergent creole is now no longer restricted in its communicative settings because, as a first language, it must be used in all settings and fulfill all the communicative functions of a speech community. It is now a full language, with a full vocabulary, phonology, and grammar; however, its linguistic structure will often have features inherited from its pidginized past that mark its historical origin.

Some of the developments of pidginized varieties of American Indian languages can be seen as a response to European contact and expansion. There are, however, two American Indian pidgins (Chinook Jargon and Mobilian Jargon, discussed next) that are possibly internal, precontact developments, but even in these cases European contact led to their geographic expansion.

10.2 CHINOOK JARGON

The best known example of an American Indian pidgin is called a "jargon," namely, Chinook Jargon. Chinook Jargon was a pidgin widely spoken in the Pacific Northwest in the nineteenth century. It is not to be confused with Chinook, two full languages (Lower Chinook and Upper Chinook), which were formerly spoken along the Columbia River. First contact between Northwest Coast Indians and Europeans took place at the end of the eighteenth century and the first recordings of Chinook Jargon were made in the early nineteenth century. Although the data are not conclusive, evidence strongly suggests that this pidgin was in existence before European contact. It is clear, however, that European contact, particularly the expansion of the fur trade to the Pacific Northwest, greatly stimulated the development and expansion of Chinook Jargon. In the early part of the nineteenth century its use was limited to the lower Columbia River and surrounding area. By the end of the century it had spread to include a much-expanded geographic area: the coastal area from southern Alaska to Oregon and inland as far as Montana.

Most of the vocabulary of Chinook Jargon comes from four sources: Lower Chinook, Nootka, French, and English. The following examples are from Lower Chinook, with Chinook Jargon (CJ) in the left column, and the source, Lower Chinook (LC), in the right. The prefixes *t-* and *i-* are number-gender prefixes in Lower Chinook, which are sometimes dropped, sometimes incorporated into the stem when brought over into Chinook Jargon.

tílixəm	'people'	< LC *t-élxəm*	
kaním	'canoe'	< LC *i-kaniím*	
ísik	'ash (the wood)'	< LC *i-sik*	'paddle'
t'álapas	'coyote'	< LC *i-t'aálaps*	
tq'ix	'to like'	< LC *tq'eex*	
úlu	'hungry'	< LC *oó-lo*	'hunger'
náika	'I, me, mine'	< LC *náika*	'I' (emphatic)

Following are examples of Chinook Jargon terms from Nootka (Nt), spoken on Vancouver Island:

tənás	'child'	< Nt *t'an'a*	
pátač	'give'	< Nt *p'a-čiƛ–*	'to potlatch'
wínapi	'by and by'	< Nt *wiinapi*	'stopping'
wik	'not'	< Nt *wik*	

Some examples from French (Fr) are:

kocó	'pig'	< Fr *cochon*	
labáb	'beard'	< Fr *la barbe*	'the beard'
likák	'rooster'	< Fr *le coq*	'the rooster'

Examples from English (Eng):

ápəls	'apple'	< Eng apple
bástən	'American'	< Eng Boston
dret	'straight, true, correct'	< Eng straight
úlman	'husband'	< Eng old man

Besides a number of words of unknown origin, there are also terms from other Indian languages, in particular Chehalis, a Salish language of British Columbia, and Cree, spoken in eastern Canada and introduced by wives of the French fur trappers.

Chinook Jargon vocabulary varied considerably from place to place, not surprising considering that it was used as a trade language over an immense area. As the language spread, some words of Indian language origin were replaced by French words,

and some of these were, in turn, later replaced by English words. Because the language was used in an ever-widening set of contexts, new words were also added as
new concepts were needed. As is typical of pidgins, the vocabulary was restricted:
estimates of its size range between five hundred and one thousand words. As a result (and again typical of pidgins), a given word often had a rather broad semantic
range, which could be further specified and narrowed through compounding; thus
mamuk or *maŋk* 'to make, do' entered into a variety of compounds to yield, among
others, terms translated in English as "bring, boil, begin, think, correct, twist, finish." The inventory of Chinook Jargon consonants and vowels is presented below
in chart form (see appendix I for the interpretation of the symbols):

p	t		c	č	k	kʷ	q	qʷ	ʔ
p'	t'	λ'	c'		k'	k'ʷ	q'	q'ʷ	
b	d				g				
		ł	s	č	x	xʷ	x̣	x̣ʷ	
m	n								
	r	l							
w			y						

The vowels are:

i		u
e	ə	o
	a	

The consonant pattern is very typical of the Indian languages of the region; however,
many of the consonants are exotic from the point of view of French and English,
especially the lateral affricate and fricative [λ', ł], the glottalized consonants [p', t',
λ', c', k', q', k'ʷ, q'ʷ], and the contrast between front velars [k, kʷ, k', k'ʷ, x, xʷ]
and back velars [q, qʷ, q', q'ʷ, x̣, x̣ʷ]. Native speakers of French and English often
substituted more familiar sounds when speaking Chinook Jargon, for example, they
replaced the glottalized consonants [p', t'], and so on, with [p, t], and so on, and
[λ'] (i.e., a glottalized "tl" sound) in initial position with [kl]. Words in Chinook
Jargon taken from Lower Chinook usually retained these "exotic" sounds; however,
the fact that the pronunciation of words from Nootka was usually changed is one
of the clues that words taken from Nootka entered the vocabulary via speakers of
European languages, not directly from Nootka speakers.

    Just as other pidgins do, Chinook Jargon has a greatly simplified grammatical
structure, which is in stark contrast to the very complicated structures of Lower
Chinook and other languages of the region. There are, however, specific grammatical features that are similar to patterns in Lower Chinook and other Northwest
Coast languages, that is, the patterns involved in the formation of negative sen-

tences, yes-no questions, imperatives, and the use of double marking of subjects with pronoun and noun. In negative sentences, a negative word, either *wik* or *xilu*, is usually placed at the beginning of the sentence, rather than before the verb, as in English (a literal word-for-word translation follows the free translation):

Wik ałqi msáyka náyka.	'You won't have to wait for me.' (not future you-plural wait me)
Xilu mayka saman?	'Don't you have salmon?' (not you salmon)
Xilu mayka kʼʷas.	'Don't be afraid.' (not you afraid)

There are two ways to mark yes-no questions. One way is to place the question particle *na* after the first word, while the other is to mark the sentence as a question by simply ending with a rising intonation or tone of voice. An example of each type: *Mika **na** klap mika kiuatan?* 'Did you find your horse? (you **Q** find you horse)'; *Mika mamook kow mika kiuatan?* 'Have you tied your horse? (you make tie you horse)'. The use of a question particle (in noninitial position, not necessarily in only second position) is typical for most Northwest Coast languages.

The imperative is marked by *łuš* 'good', or *łuš spus* 'good if' (*spus* from English 'suppose'). In addition to being prevalent in many languages of the area, this pattern is also a very common way to make a polite request in many other languages, including English, for example, "It would be good if. . . ." An example: *łuš (spus) mayka łatwa!* 'Go! (or) You should go!' (good if you go). The last example to consider here is again one that is common to Lower Chinook and most other languages of the region, that is, the use of a pronoun along with a noun subject. This pattern occurs in nonstandard, but not standard, English discourse, for example, "And then the dog he started barking." Some Chinook Jargon examples are: *t'alap'as pi lilu **łaska** małayt ixt-ixt łaska xaws* 'a coyote and a wolf lived with their houses side by side' (coyote and wolf **they** live one-one they house); *Ixt man yáka kúli kúpa lamotáy* 'one man went to the mountains' (one man he go to mountain)'; *Jesus yaka kumtuks kanawey tilikums* 'Jesus knows all nations' (Jesus he know all people). There is some variation in Chinook Jargon grammatical structure, which reflects the fact that the speakers came from a variety of language backgrounds. Even so, the grammatical variation is not as great as that found in the vocabulary and phonology.

Chinook Jargon functioned in a way typical for that of pidgins. It was used as a lingua franca among Indians speaking different native languages; and, in their interactions with Indians, European missionaries and traders—especially fur traders—also used it. The contact among Europeans and Indians facilitated the pidgin's geographic spread, which was more often an indirect rather than direct result of contact, with one Indian group learning from another within the context of the fur trade.

During the last quarter of the nineteenth century, the heyday of its use, Chinook

Jargon was spoken by perhaps a hundred thousand people, from the Alaskan pan-handle to northern California, and from the coast into the interior of British Colum-bia, Washington, Oregon, Idaho, and western Montana. During the early days of European contact at Fort Vancouver, and perhaps at other places as well, some of the children of European fathers and Indian mothers spoke Chinook Jargon as their first language, so that for these speakers, it was a creole rather than a pidgin. This development was very short lived, however, inasmuch as French or English came to replace Chinook Jargon as the language of the offspring of Indian and European parents.

Those most expert in the use of the pidgin were the speakers of the two Chinook languages, the southern Coast Salish languages, the two Sahaptin languages, the linguistic isolates Kalapuya and Molale, and speakers of other languages located in and near the Columbia River, the area from which Chinook Jargon dispersed.

Europeans, who spoke English or French as their native languages, were not only responsible for the introduction of English and French words, but probably were also responsible for the introduction of words from Nootka, a language of Vancouver Island. Nootka speakers were some of the earliest contacts with American Indians in the Northwest Coast that Europeans had; they most likely learned some Nootka words and then used them in subsequent contact with other Indian groups, as-suming these words were in "the Indian language" and, therefore, understandable by any Indian. This scenario best accounts for the fact that words of Nootka origin do not retain "exotic" consonants in Chinook Jargon, while those originating from Lower Chinook and other Indian languages do.

As it spread eastward, Chinook Jargon met the Plains Sign Language, another lingua franca, which was spreading north and west out of the Plains. At the same time, English was becoming common as the lingua franca between Indians, and between Indians and Euro-Americans. The use of Chinook Jargon soon began to decline and now, in the late twentieth century, few Indians can speak it.

Historical records make clear that the arrival of Europeans, and particularly French-speaking fur traders, was the catalyst for the spread of Chinook Jargon, but the historical picture is murky in regard to its origin. Did Chinook Jargon originate before or after contact with speakers of French and English? Both the ethnohistoric record and the linguistic record favor but do not provide proof of a precontact origin.

The situation in the Northwest Coast was one of multilingualism and linguis-tic diversity similar to the picture we painted for California (section 9.2; see also section 12.6). As in California, patterns of intermarriage, ceremonialism and trade contributed to multilingualism; however, although the linguistic diversity was con-siderable, it was not as great as it was in California. The existence of extensive multilingualism would be an argument against the precontact use of a pidgin lan-guage; that is, if multilingualism was so prevalent, why would there be any need for a lingua franca? The answer to this question lies in the fact that Northwest Coast life and California life differed in two important ways: (1) how trading was carried on, and (2) the widespread practice of slavery in the Northwest Coast, but not in California. Both of these factors contributed to a context that could have nurtured the use of a lingua franca.

In California, most travel was by foot. In the Northwest Coast, for moving over long distances, travelers used ocean-going canoes on the ocean and major rivers. The Chinook were important middlemen for the trade route that entered the mouth of the Columbia River, a major highway to the interior; and, within Chinook territory, an important trading center developed near The Dalles on the Columbia River Gorge. Because of rapids there, it was an especially favorable place to fish during the annual salmon run. Once a year, Indians from hundreds of miles around congregated to trade salmon, slaves, and other commodities. Multilingualism in the Northwest Coast, as in California, involved the languages of immediate neighbors; however, it was of little use in communicative settings in which those people coming from long distances to trade were brought into contact. This trading center near The Dalles provided a setting conducive to the development of a pidginized version of Chinook as a lingua franca.

The Chinook, as well as many other groups in the Northwest Coast, held large numbers of slaves. Sometimes working alongside their masters, sometimes not, slaves were used by wealthy families for doing domestic work. Acquired by long-distance raiding, they then were often sold or traded. We have no documented evidence concerning the language or languages used between slave and master, or between slaves from different groups; however, the fact that slaves in any given village were taken from a variety of distant locations, not from immediate neighbors, would encourage the development of a pidgin, just as long-distance trade did.

The linguistic evidence is also suggestive for a precontact origin. First, the consonantal system of Chinook Jargon is very much like that of a number of Northwest Coast languages, and not at all like French or English. Second, there are several grammatical features characteristic of languages of the area that do not occur in French or English. In addition, the fact that Chinook Jargon had already crystallized into a definite form by the time Europeans arrived at the mouth of the Columbia River in the early eighteenth century argues in favor of its having been in existence for some time.

10.3 OTHER AMERICAN INDIAN PIDGINS

Mobilian

Mobilian, also known as Chickasaw Trade Jargon, is a pidgin widely used in the Southeast as a lingua franca. Data on it are skimpier than those for Chinook Jargon. French domination of the lower Mississippi started at the beginning of the eighteenth century. The area was one of considerable indigenous linguistic diversity and multilingualism; however, we do not know if, at the beginning of the century, any particular language served as a lingua franca. By the end of the first quarter of the century, Mobilian was used as a lingua franca as far north as the Ohio River, westward into Texas, and eastward to what are now the borders between Alabama, Georgia, and western Florida. By the 1970s, there were still a few elderly speakers.

It is not certain that Mobilian existed before French exploration. It is clear, however, that Frenchmen, in dealings with Indians, used it widely and contributed to its spread. Its grammar is based on a simplification of two Muskogean languages, Alabama and Choctaw (or possibly Chickasaw, which is closely related to Choctaw). Most of its vocabulary also comes from these languages.

Other Pidgins

Other American Indian pidgins have developed for limited periods. A pidginized form of Delaware, an Algonquian language, was used in the seventeenth century in parts of what are now New Jersey, Delaware, New York, and Pennsylvania. Developed in the context of trade between Europeans and the Delaware, its vocabulary was largely from Delaware along with some words from related Algonquian languages, as well as Dutch, English, and Spanish. The grammatical structure of Delaware was largely eliminated and words were strung together in English word order.

A recent pidgin and one still in use is Trader Navajo, a pidginized form of Navajo used as a means of communication between White traders and Navajos on the Navajo reservation. Some White traders do not make the distinction between full Navajo and Trader Navajo, believing that they are speaking Navajo when in fact they are speaking the pidgin.

Failure to distinguish between a pidgin and the full language is quite common. In 1633 the French missionary Paul Le Jeune wrote the following about a pidginized variety of Montagnais, an Algonquian language of eastern Canada: "When the French use it, they think they are speaking the Savage Tongue, and the Savages, in using it, think they are speaking good French."

10.4 THE VAUPÉS: LINGUA FRANCAS

In section 9.1, we discussed the linguistic situation in the Vaupés region as one of individual multilingualism involving the local languages, plus the acquisition of a father language and a mother language, as well as additional languages. There are some indications that outside Euro-American pressures have helped shape this particular pattern; nevertheless, evidence indicates that the general pattern of multilingualism predates direct European contact.

Four languages have been used as lingua francas in the Vaupés region: Nheengatú (an Indian language), Portuguese, Spanish, and Tukano. With the possible exception of Tukano, the use of these languages as lingua francas is the result of European contact and penetration into the area; however, this pattern of societal multilingualism, even though postcontact, easily became part of an already existing cultural configuration in which learning additional languages was accepted very easily.

Until the middle of the nineteenth century, outsiders did not significantly begin to make contact with and penetrate the Vaupés region, which is divided by a border between Colombia and Brazil. The first Jesuit mission was established in 1852 and as of 1970 there were seven missions operated by Portuguese or Spanish speakers, depending on which side of the border a mission was located. A rubber boom from 1875 to 1920 brought in rubber gatherers, most of whom were speakers of Nheengatú and Portuguese; and there are a few non-Indian settlements on the outskirts of the Vaupés region. The largest of these, Mitú, located just to the north, has a population of one thousand.

Although areas adjacent to the Vaupés region have been much more influenced by outside pressures, they continue to retain their indigenous multilingual character. Just to the west is the former rubber-gathering region, now occupied by former inhabitants of the central Vaupés area. These people, having given up the original father language–mother language pattern, all speak Tukano, and almost all speak Spanish as well. To the north live people who are locally called *Cabucos* (from Portuguese *cabocos* or *caboclos* 'backwoodsmen'). They are descendants of rubber gatherers who remained after the rubber boom, marrying Indian women who speak Cubeo, a language belonging to the Eastern Tukanoan language family. Cubeo speakers, like those of the Vaupés region, are multilingual, but they do not take part in the exogamous marriage system that produces the pattern of father language and mother language. All the Cabucos speak Spanish, all at least understand and most speak Cubeo. To the south and east, in the vicinity of lower Vaupés and middle Río Negro, is the area of longest contact with outsiders. There, Tukano, one of the most widespread father languages, has now almost completely replaced other father languages, at least among younger speakers. Nheengatú and Portuguese are also spoken by almost everyone, with Nheengatú functioning as a home language on equal footing with Tukano.

Nheengatú, also known as Lingua Geral, is a member of the Tupí-Guaraní language family. A lingua franca spoken over a wide area of Amazonia, it was introduced by colonists and others involved in a variety of extractive industries in Brazil, and it has become the first language of a good-sized population. Introduced into the Vaupés region by Jesuit missionaries and rubber gatherers, Nheengatú served as a lingua franca for the indigenous populations on both sides of the Brazilian-Colombian border into the first two or three decades of the twentieth century. Tukano has now replaced it as a lingua franca, and today Nheengatú is known by only a few people in the area.

Tukano, as both a father language and a mother language (section 9.1), is involved in a web of individual multilingualism; as one of the largest of the father languages, it also serves as a lingua franca. In fact, it is the most commonly used lingua franca in the Vaupés region and is spoken by about 90 percent of the population. Although its use as a lingua franca is clearly an indigenous development, it is not clear that this development is independent of the contact pressures of the past 150 years. Because the region is divided by the border between Brazil and Colombia, a Brazilian Indian who knows Portuguese but not Spanish finds that Portuguese is not understood if he goes any distance into Colombia; the reverse situation results when a Spanish-speaking Colombian Indian travels any distance into Brazil. Tukano fills the position once occupied by Nheengatú by being the only lingua franca used throughout the whole area.

In most places in the Americas, widespread bilingualism involving a European language is frequently a replacive bilingualism leading to the loss of the native language. This has not happened, at least up to this time, among the speakers of indigenous languages in the Vaupés and surrounding areas. The monolingual Portuguese and Spanish speakers in the region find this surprising, since they view their "civilized" languages as superior and do not understand why the Indians do not acknowledge this superiority by giving up the indigenous languages. The native speakers of Indian languages of the region, however, have a different perspective: Multilingualism is the ordinary state of affairs; therefore, it is only natural that Portuguese and Spanish are to be added to their existing linguistic repertoires.

Unlike the situation in the Vaupés region, where Portuguese and Spanish are not necessarily used as lingua francas, in many circumstances involving American Indian communities, a colonial language initially used as a lingua franca has now become the first language of a community or an area. In such a situation, we can no longer speak of a lingua franca; instead, such a change in use is an example of language replacement. This topic is considered in the next chapter.

SOURCES

In the introduction, see Halliday et al. 1965 for general comments about lingua francas and Crawford 1978b:5 for the comment about the position of Tuscarora. In section 10.2 the discussion of Chinook Jargon is based on Hajda et al. 1988, Hymes 1980, Kaufman 1971, Thomason 1983, and Thomason and Kaufman 1988:256-63. In section 10.3 the Mobilian segment is based on Crawford 1978b and Haas 1975; see Taylor 1981 for the comments on other pidgins and Taylor 1981:183 for quote concerning a pidginized variety of Montagnais. Section 10.4 draws from Jackson 1983, Rodrigues 1985, and Sorensen 1967, 1985.

SUGGESTED READINGS

In regard to sections 10.1 and 10.2, for in-depth consideration of aspects of creole studies, see Valdman and Highfield 1980 and Bickerton 1981; see Bakker 1991 for an overview of Newfoundland and Labrador trade languages, including Micmac-Montagnais Pidgin and Micmac Pidgin English. On section 10.3 see Moore et al. 1994 for an overview of the history of Nheengatú.

CHAPTER II

LANGUAGE CONTACT

Contact between groups speaking different languages is often a catalyst for language change. Change in vocabulary is the change most often brought about through contact. Borrowing words from another language is a frequent way of introducing new vocabulary items (sections 11.1 and 11.2); however, there are other vocabulary-building techniques as well (section 11.3). If contact is extensive, language contact can bring about structural changes in the phonology (section 11.2) and in the grammar (section 11.5). In some situations contact results in language loss; that is, a community shifts from one language to another (section 11.4). In sections 11.1. and 11.2 we consider cases in which the contact is between American Indian languages; in sections 11.3 through 11.5, cases in which American Indian languages change because of contact with European colonial languages, and in section 11.6 situations in which European colonial languages change because of contact with American Indian languages.

II.I LOANWORDS IN HUASTECA NAHUATL

The majority of the Nahuatl-speaking population is found in the Mexican highlands. There are, however, Nahuatl-speaking islands, separated from the main body of speakers and surrounded by speakers of other languages. One such island is Huasteca Nahuatl, located on the Gulf Coast to the north of the central highlands. Although it is a distinct dialect, the differences between it and other varieties of Nahuatl are not great.

   Totonac, to the south, separates Huasteca Nahuatl from the main body of Nahuatl speakers. Huastec, a Mayan language to the north of Huasteca Nahuatl, is also a linguistic island as most of the Mayan languages are spoken on the Yucatán Peninsula, in Guatemala, and in nearby regions. Huastec is a language, not a dialect, whereas Huasteca Nahuatl is only dialectally different from Nahuatl. The fact that both are linguistic islands, separated from their respective linguistic cousins, is evidence that Huastec speakers and Huasteca Nahuatl speakers are, relatively speaking, newcomers to the Gulf Coast. The time of movement for the Huastec is measured in millennia, for the Huasteca Nahuatl, in centuries.

When the speakers of Huasteca Nahuatl came to the tropical coast, they entered a new environment and encountered a number of new plants and animals for which they had no names. One strategy for acquiring new vocabulary, utilized frequently by the world's languages, is to take words from a neighboring language. This process is called **(lexical) borrowing** and the resulting forms are called **loanwords**. In Huasteca Nahuatl (HN) there are over a dozen botanical terms that are loans from Huastec (H); here are some examples (read "<" as "is borrowed from"): HN *apač-λiʔ* < H *apac'* 'palm leaf' (*Sabal mexicana*); HN *wale:yaʔ* < H *bale:ya* 'watermelon' (*Citrullus* lanatus); HN *čičih-λiʔ* < H *čičiθ* 'quebracho tree' (*Diphysa robinoides*); and HN *koyolih* < H *k'oyol* 'coyol palm' (*Yucca* c.f. *treculeana*). Loanwords for birds and animals include names such as: HN *kokoh-cih* < H *kukuʔ* 'turtle dove' (*–cih* is the diminutive suffix); HN *osowih-λiʔ* < H *oθo:w* 'iguana'. (The Nahuatl noun suffix *–λiʔ, –λ*, is added to many of the noun borrowings.) Among the few loans that are not for either plants or animals: HN *taka:-niʔ* 'to touch' < H *taka:l* 'to strike metal'; HN *šipa:l-oaʔ* < H *θipa:l* 'to braid someone's hair'; HN *caka:-niaʔ* 'to peck' < H *c'ik'kàa:l* 'to sting; bite'; HN *ciciliaʔ* 'to make noise' < H *c'iliy* 'noise'.

When language contact is intense, the borrowing language will frequently borrow both phonological and morphological patterns from the donor language; but, if it is not intense, as in this case, the borrowing language will remake the word to fit the native phonological and morphological patterns. The data given earlier display examples of phonological adaptation; for instance, Huastec, along with other Mayan languages, distinguishes between plain and glottalized stops (e.g., [k] vs. [k']), a distinction that Nahuatl lacks. Consequently, both types of stops are borrowed into Huasteca Nahuatl as plain stops: *kukuʔ* > *kokoh-cih* and *k'oyol*. Huastec has two back vowels, [u] and [o], while Huasteca Nahuatl has only one, [o], so that both vowels appear as [o]: *tuyu:m* > *toyoʔ* and *oθo:w* > *osowih-λiʔ*. Huastec has the voiced stop [b], replaced in Huasteca Nahuatl by [w]: *bale:ya* > *wale:ya* and *mabak* > *mawakih-λiʔ*. Lastly, the fricative [θ], which Huastec has and Nahuatl lacks, is replaced in Huasteca Nahuatl by a variety of other consonants: [h] (*čičih-λiʔ*), [s] (*osowih-λiʔ*), and [š] (*šipa:l-oaʔ*).

Other directions of borrowing existed among the languages of this area. There are a small number of words in Huasteca Nahuatl that are borrowed from Totonac and also a slightly larger number of words from Huasteca Nahuatl into Totonac. When the same words appear in both languages, it is possible to determine the direction of borrowing by looking at the language families involved. The forms borrowed from Huasteca Nahuatl into Totonac are also found in other varieties of Nahuatl, while those borrowed from Totonac into Huasteca Nahuatl are not found elsewhere in the Nahuatl-speaking world. A handful of words in Huasteca Nahuatl, mostly plant and bird names, could be borrowings from either Huastec or Totonac. Inasmuch as the Huastec are also newcomers to the area, although not as recent as the Huasteca Nahuatl, Totonac may well be the ultimate source for these; however, this guess, which is based on nonlinguistic evidence, does not tell us whether the loans in Huasteca Nahuatl came directly from Totonac, or by way of Huastec. It is clear that these considerations are of historical interest, a topic explored at greater length in chapter 13.

11.2 LAKE MIWOK: A CASE OF BORROWING AND STRUCTURAL CHANGE

Structural borrowing, or the borrowing of phonological or grammatical material, sometimes accompanies intense lexical borrowing, particularly if there is a large bilingual population. Such is the case for Lake Miwok in California. The Miwokan family of languages consists of two main branches, Eastern and Western. In precontact times, the five Eastern languages formed a continuous block from the eastern edge of San Francisco Bay to the foothills of the Sierra Nevada Range. The two Western languages, geographically isolated from each other as well as from the Eastern languages, are Coast Miwok, found north of San Francisco in and near what is now Marin County, and Lake Miwok, located about eighty miles north of San Francisco on the southern shore of Clear Lake. Although the Miwokan languages are closely related, they clearly constitute seven distinct languages, not dialects.

Even though geographically separated, speakers of the two Western languages were in frequent contact with each other. Lake Miwok speakers were, however, in even closer and more frequent contact with their more immediate neighbors, Hill Patwins, to the east; speakers of some of the Pomoan languages (Southeastern Pomo, Eastern Pomo, Central Pomo, Southern Pomo) to the north and west; and Wappo speakers, with the main body found to the south and a small enclave to the northwest. The Lake Miwoks were also in contact with speakers of other Pomoan languages who were not their next-door neighbors. The Pomoan family of languages, like the Miwokan, consists of several closely related, yet distinct, languages. Likewise there were several Patwin languages, Patwin (proper), River Patwin, and Nomlaki.

Lake Miwok has a much larger inventory of consonants than the other Miwokan languages. Take, for instance, the stops and affricates, which in all the Miwokan languages, save Lake Miwok, configurate as

   p   t   ṭ   k
        c

(Points of articulation for stops are [from left to right] labial, dental, retroflex, velar; the affricate /c/ is dental [ts] in some languages, alveolar [č] in others; see appendix 1 for more phonetic details on the use of these symbols.) This configuration consists of a single series of stops, voiceless and unaspirated, and a single voiceless unaspirated affricate. Lake Miwok has, in addition, voiceless aspirated, glottalized, and voiced stops, along with a larger set of affricates:

p	t	ṭ		k
pʰ	tʰ	ṭʰ		kʰ
p'	t'	ṭ'		k'
b	d			
	c	č		
	c'	č'	λ'	

There are three possible explanations for this situation. One is that there have been internal changes within Lake Miwok to produce the extra consonants. The second is that Lake Miwok reflects a pattern found at an earlier time in all the Miwokan languages and that all the other languages except Lake Miwok simplified the consonant system. One can find parallels for both types of changes in the languages of the world; however, if either of these types of changes had occurred, we would expect that the words showing the extra consonants in Lake Miwok would also turn up in other Miwokan languages; that is, in the other languages, words similar in form and meaning would have voiceless unaspirated consonants in places where Lake Miwok has the aspirated, glottalized or voiced stops. With some marginal exceptions, however, such forms do not occur in other Miwokan languages. The third possible explanation is that Lake Miwok borrowed words from surrounding languages. An examination of these languages shows that this is, in fact, what happened. If we look at the stop and affricate system of the surrounding languages, we discover that they have the consonants in question in their inventory of stops and affricates. First, Hill Patwin:

p	t	ṭ	k
pʰ	tʰ		kʰ
p'	t'		k'
b	d		
	c		č'
		λ'	

then, Wappo:

p	t	ṭ	c	č	k
p'	t'	ṭ	c'	č'	k'

and, lastly, we give the stops and affricates for Eastern Pomo only; the system is very similar in the other Pomoan languages:

p	t	ṭ	c	č	k	q
pʰ	tʰ	ṭʰ	cʰ	čʰ	kʰ	
p'	t'	ṭ'	c'	č'	k'	q'
b	d					

Of 260 Lake Miwok words that contain the consonants not found in other Miwokan languages, 78 have resemblant forms in one or more of the surrounding languages. Because there has been so much borrowing back and forth between the languages in this part of California, it is not always easy to establish who borrowed first from whom. The task has been complicated by the fact that the appropriate form for comparison was not always available in all of the languages; consequently, the original donor language may not always have been represented in the material available. Some examples (the gloss is given only once if it is the same in all the languages):

Lake Miwok	*Other Languages*
pʰákpʰak 'egg'	Hill Patwin: *pʰakpʰak*
p'ócci, pócci 'woman'	Nomlaki: *p'ota:s*
	Hill Patwin: *p'okita*
búkʰal 'fish trap'	SW Pomo: *buhqʰal* 'burden basket'
	E Pomo: *bu:xál* 'fish trap'
t'éele 'breast'	River Patwin: *t'e:li* 'chest, breast of bird'
t'éele 'to slice meat'	Hill Patwin: *t'ellaʔ* 'to slice'
	Wappo: *t'e, t'el* 'to cut open'
kanáamota, kanáamot'o	Wappo: *kána:mot'a*
'Mount St. Helena'	
dolóomen 'throat'	Patwin: *dol, dolomʔ* 'Adam's apple'
ṭukú-nni 'to spot'	Hill Patwin: *t'ok-u:ro* 'spotting'
ṭúmma 'bowl-like basket'	Patwin: *t'omo:y* 'small burden basket'
kʰába-ṭi 'bump one's head'	SE Pomo: *q'abélla, q'abél-yaq'o* 'skull'
k'éeliṣ 'to peel'	Patwin: *k'er-ta*
k'éni 'storage basket'	Patwin: *k'eniʔ* 'plate basket'
c'ée 'angleworm'	Hill Patwin: *č'ee* 'fish worm'
c'ówka 'small bluebird'	Hill Patwin: *č'owkoč'owko*
	Patwin: *č'oka*

A great deal of intermarriage and daily contact between the different linguistic groups and a concomitant multilingualism created the perfect setting for intense borrowing. Unlike the Huasteca Nahuatl speakers, the Lake Miwok speakers did not replace new sounds with their closest Miwokan counterpart; instead, the new sounds were borrowed along with the words containing them. In the Huasteca Nahuatl situation, most of the borrowings involved names for new plants and animals. In the Lake Miwok case all semantic areas of the lexicon are represented, including rather basic notions (e.g., "egg," "breast"), specific activities (e.g., "to bump the head," "to slice meat") and placenames. Although only seventy-eight resemblant sets have been found, with fuller records of the surrounding languages the number might well be much greater. The fact that some of the pairs look very similar and others not so similar probably means that some words were borrowed recently, others not so recently. These facts are relevant for interpreting linguistic prehistory (sections 12.6 and 13.5).

11.3 LEXICAL ACCULTURATION
IN A COLONIAL SETTING

The term **acculturation** refers to the changes brought about by cultural contact. The concept has most often been invoked when the influencing culture is a complex one (especially European or European-derived) and the influenced or acculturating group is a small-scale society. The term **linguistic acculturation** refers to this process as it applies to language and **lexical acculturation** refers still more narrowly to the lexicon or vocabulary of a language. The previous two sections dealt with lexical acculturation in precontact settings. Now we turn our attention to post-Columbian linguistic acculturation and, specifically, to lexical acculturation.

When the European colonists arrived, the indigenous populations became familiar with a host of new objects and concepts, including items of European material culture (guns, buttons, metal, etc.), new domesticated plants and animals, new foods, and often a new religion—all of which needed names. Names were also needed for new categories of people, such as "soldier," "missionary," and the like, as well as a way for differentiating "Indians" from the newcomers. Several techniques can be used to augment vocabulary in an acculturating setting. We saw in sections 11.1 and 11.2 that borrowing is one such means, but it is not the only one, as our examination of the following three cases reveals.

Mountain Pima

The speakers of this Uto-Aztecan language live in the mountains along the border of the Mexican states of Sonora and Chihuahua. Contact with Spanish speakers began at the beginning of the sixteenth century; however, initial contact was not very close because of the isolated location. In fact, a great deal of the early contact was probably indirect and mediated by such neighbors as the Opata, Eudeve, and Pima

Alta, who, like the Mountain Pima, spoke related Uto-Aztecan languages. Speakers of these other languages, living in less isolated locations, were in greater contact with Spanish speakers during an earlier period. Among these groups, language shift has taken place and, for the most part, there has been a shift in cultural identity as well, a fate that probably also awaits the Mountain Pima. A study conducted in 1965 and 1966 found that even though Mountain Pima was still in everyday use, Spanish was widely spoken as a second language and linguistic acculturation was evident in all aspects of the Mountain Pima language.

Mountain Pima speakers have utilized several techniques in providing for new vocabulary, but borrowing from Spanish has been by far the favorite (in the following sample, read "<" as meaning "from Spanish"):

ʔáahar	'garlic'	< ajo
ʔalgdóon	'cotton'	< algodón
ʔawióon	'airplane'	< avión
buur	'burro'	< burro
domk	'Sunday, week'	< domingo
díršinʸ	'peach' (and fruit in general)	< durazno
dʸooš'	'God'	< Dios
fiéer, fíeer	'iron'	< fierro
gasolíi, gasolíin	'gasoline'	< gasolina
ʔiig, ʔíigiš	'fig'	< higo
ʔistúuf, estúuf	'stove'	< estufa
kaar	'automobile'	< carro
kaw	'horse'	< caballo
kurš	'cross'	< cruz
káawilʸ	'sheep'	< cabra 'goat'
kompanʸíi	'company'	< companía
kóowar	'copper'	< cobre
lašáart-	'pray'	< rezar
lámpar	'lamp'	< lámpara
mantakíiy	'butter'	< mantequilla
meeš	'table'	< mesa
membríiy	'quince'	< membrillo
miéerkoliš	'Wednesday'	< miércoles
máaškar	'mask'	< máscara
naráŋh	'orange'	< naranja
nawáah	'knife'	< navaja
paadéer	'wall'	< pared

paal^y	'priest'	< *padre*

paal^y   'priest'   < *padre*
piaart, fiaart   'borrow'   < *fiar*
pióon, pióon-gar   'employee'   < *peón*
pyéehid^y   'fiesta'   < *fiesta*
ralóoh, šalóon, rilóon, 'clock, watch'   < *reloj*
sanóore, sanóori   'carrot'   < *zanahoria*
šeewóoy   'onion'   < *cebolla*
šoop   'pasta, rice'   < *sopa*
šíiwkil^y   'goat'   < *chiva*
tíl^y*ig, tél*^y*ig*   'wheat'   < *trigo*
tómin^y   'money'   < *tomín* (a coin
                                                 used during
                                                 colonial times)
wahkéehal^y   'cowboy'   < *vaquero*
wandéer   'flag'   < *bandera*
wáalat   'bucket'   < *balde*

This list of loanwords is by no means complete. Most of the items belong to a limited number of semantic areas: religious terms, days of the week, newly introduced domestic animals and plants, new foods, and newly introduced objects of Spanish and Mexican origin. The loanwords in the sample have been borrowed from all historical periods; thus, *tómin*^y 'money' must be early because the Spanish word it is derived from was used only in the early colonial period; while *ʔawióon* 'airplane' must be recent since it refers to a newly introduced object. Likewise *káawil*^y 'sheep' is probably early; although it means 'sheep' in Mountain Pima, it is borrowed from Spanish *cabra* 'goat', a word that has been replaced by *chiva* 'goat' in present-day local Spanish.

The period of borrowing of the various forms is reflected not only in the semantics, but in the phonology as well. Early loans are made to fit the native phonological patterns, with the result that often they are quite different from the original Spanish model; later borrowings are more faithful to Spanish phonology, introducing new features into the language. (Some of the distortions of early borrowings are the result of indirect or intertribal borrowings.) Spanish words, for example, that begin with a sequence of consonants, a pattern foreign to native Mountain Pima phonology, are changed in early borrowings (e.g., *kurš* 'cross' and *tíl*^y*ig* 'wheat'), while the consonant clusters are retained in later borrowings (e.g., *pláatan* 'banana' < *plátano*; *granáad* 'pomegranate' < *granado*). In early borrowings, the non-native sounds [f], [s], [l], and [r] are replaced by [p], [š], [l^y] and [l^y], respectively, but these new sounds are retained in later borrowings. The non-native vowel [e] is kept in later borrowings, while in early ones it is replaced by a native vowel, usually [a] or [i].

Some words that we might expect on semantic grounds to be early have the new sounds. It is likely that they have been touched up more recently by fluent bilinguals and, in fact, the places where we find multiple renditions would seem to reflect this as an ongoing process: *šaríi, seríi, šeríi* 'matches'; *ralóoh, šalóon, rilóon* 'clock'; *ʔistúuf, estúuf* 'stove'. The early period, in which there were few bilinguals, produced a pattern of borrowing comparable to that found in Huasteca Nahuatl, while the later period more closely resembles the Lake Miwok situation.

The loan words have been well integrated into Mountain Pima grammar; for example, the plural is formed by reduplication of the first consonant and vowel, usually with the dropping of the first vowel in the stem; that is, CV- is reduplicated as CVCV-, which then changes to CVC-. Along with this loss of vowel, there are also frequent changes in vowel length.

košnéer, kokšnéenar	'cook, cooks'
kurš, kúukriš	'cross, crosses'
káawilʸ, kákwilʸ	'sheep' (sg. and pl.)
look, lolk	'crazy' (sg. and pl.)
múušik, múumšik	'music' (sg. and pl.)
paal, pápal	'shovel, shovels'
políiš, pópliš	'police, policemen'
riik, rírk	'rich' (sg. and pl.)

The following examples illustrate, in addition, a phonological rule that applies to native words as well, namely, the change of stem initial [w] to [p] in the reduplicated form:

wahkéehalʸ, wapkéhalʸ	'cowboy, cowboys'
wootéey, woppthéhi	'bottle, bottles'
wáati, waptéhi	'washtub, washtubs'

Loan words can also undergo the same morphological derivations used with native words: *kaafée* 'coffee', *kaaféeč-* 'to make coffee'; *mantéek* 'lard', *mantéekmag* 'greasy'; *múušik* 'music', *muušik-giwdam, múumšik-giwdam* 'musician(s)'.

New derivations, or new coinages, and **extensions of meaning** are techniques of vocabulary expansion that utilize the resources of the native language. Although Mountain Pima clearly prefers borrowing, these two methods are well represented. Sometimes a loanword exists beside a new formation, which may indicate that the use of native resources was more popular in earlier days and that such words were sometimes replaced (and continue to be replaced) by Spanish loanwords, once bilingualism became more common. Some examples of new derivations follow (with a literal translation placed in parentheses):

biič-kám	'bathroom' ('place for excrement')
gášikar	'broom' (derived from the verb *gašʉ-* 'to sweep')
haaʔt gagardam	'customer' ('things buyer')
haat-núunkaam	'rich person' ('thing haver', alongside the loanword *riik* < Spanish *rico*)
káawilʸ wópar	'wool' ('sheep hair'; also simply *wópar*; and the loanword *laan* < Spanish *lana*)
šuudag hugidʸám	'beach' ('at the edge of the water')
wákinʸ-díʔɨr	Godmother ('washing [i.e., baptizing] mother')
wáknag tóoʔop tám	'to baptize' ('to wash in the church')
wɨ́iškar móoʔtkar	'magistrate' ('the head of everyone')

Examples of extensions of meaning are:

ʔalšim	'needle','bone awl'
ʔóidʸig	'heaven' (original meaning?)
ʔóoʔoon	'letter','drawing'
gaat	'gun, 'bow'
ʔak	'irrigation ditch','river' (also *kanáal,* irrigation ditch < Spanish *canal*)
mášad	'month', 'moon'
šóoihig	'livestock','pet'
típar	'ax' (evidence from nearby related languages shows that originally it probably was 'stone ax')
tɨraw	'potato' (evidence from nearby related languages shows that originally it referred a kind of native tuber)

This list illustrates something that occurs quite often in an acculturating setting; that is, when the meaning of a word is extended to refer to a newly introduced item, the native item frequently becomes much less common or is even dropped. Often the word for the old item must be modified to differentiate it from the new one; thus 'bow' and 'bone awl' can be referred to as *gaat* and *ʔalšim*, respectively, but because these words more often refer to 'gun' and 'needle', the ambiguity can be resolved by a qualifying term: *ʔuuš-gaat* 'bow' ('wood-gun'); *ʔóoʔor ʔalšim* 'bone awl' ('bone needle'). New compounds and new phrases have been constructed in Mountain Pima using the borrowed lexicon: *gáaš lámpar* 'gas lamp'; *kar motóorgar:* 'car motor' (*–gar* is a possessive suffix); *kompanʸíi pióon-gar* 'employee of the company'; *priisk dúršinʸ* 'prisco' (kind of small peach). These phrases reflect Mountain Pima word order, with the modifying elements first, rather than Spanish word order ("*lámpara de gas*," "*el motor del carro*," etc.).

There are also mixed compounds and phrases, using native and borrowed items in what are called **loan blends**: *fewréer mášad* 'February' ('February + month (or) moon'); *manšáan ʔíibdar* 'apple' ('apple tree + fruit'); *poošt am kíik* 'house post' ('post + of + house'); *toáah gasolíi* 'white gas' ('white + gasoline'). With Spanish loanwords numbering in the hundreds, Mountain Pima is an example of very intense language contact. Although the Mountain Pima pattern is no exception to the general rule that loanwords taken into a language are most commonly nouns, the borrowing of forms in other word classes is not insignificant.

Mountain Pima society is slowly fading into the general Mexican society. This **mestizoizing** is a process that began in Mexico in the fifteenth century with the Aztecs of central Mexico, and continues to occur in other parts of indigenous Mexico. It is reflected in the very large number of loans in the Mountain Pima language, as well as in the loanwords for nonintroduced concepts, for many of which there were perfectly viable native words; for example,

barwakoáa	'to pit barbecue'	< *barbacoa* (also native *gáʔi báhi*, 'roast [in the] ground')
fiéewar	'fever'	< *fiebre* (also native *tónʸim*, from *toonʸ* 'hot')
kaašp	'dandruff'	< *caspa* (also native *wúhiwar*)
krúudag	'hangover'	< *cruda* (also native *dóʔi*)
nʸéet-ag,		
nʸéet-gar,		
niéet	'grandchild'	< *nieto, nieta*
pariént-ag	'relatives'	< *parientes*
pooš	'spring' (water)	< *pozo*
syéet	'seven'	< *siete* (also native *wúšinʸdam hímak*)
šeelóoš	'jealous'	< *celoso*
wašúur	'garbage'	< *basura* (also native *náanak*)
káasi	'almost'	< *casi* (also native *tímp*)
kúmu	'as'	< *como*
nee	'neither'	< *ni*
paakii	'in order to'	< *para que*
peer	'but'	< *pero*
pork	'because'	< *porque*

It seems reasonable to assume that the Mountain Pima had grandchildren, dandruff, and fevers, utilized springs, and expressed jealousy before the Spaniards arrived.

Comanche

When speakers of Comanche first appeared on the historical scene in the early eighteenth century, they were already on horseback. They were hunting buffalo and marauding their Indian neighbors and the Spanish settlements in New Mexico and Texas. Their contact with the Spanish, sometimes friendly, sometimes hostile, was not particularly intense, but was sufficient for the borrowing of a few Spanish words, such as *paanu* 'white bread' (< *pan*); *paapasi* 'potatoes' (< *papas*, plural form); *tohtíya?* 'wheat', 'bread' (< *tortilla*); *toorosi?* 'cattle' (< *toros* 'bulls'); *kucára?* 'small spoon' (< *cuchara*), and a few others. Contact with English speakers began a century later, at the beginning of the nineteenth century. At first, the contact was casual, as it had been with the Spanish speakers; then, after the Comanche were rounded up in 1875 by the United States Army and taken to Fort Sill, Oklahoma, it became more intense.

Although not as numerous as Spanish loanwords in Mountain Pima, English loanwords in Comanche occur frequently. Here are a few examples: *kaat* 'God'; *pooka* 'poker' (card game); *sikvic* 'six bits'; *waikin* 'wagon'. There are also some examples of **loan translations** (or **calques**); that is, the formation of new vocabulary by means of literal translation: *wa?oo-rihkapih* 'catsup' ('cat-food'); *woko-rihkapih* 'pineapple' ('pine –food'); *kuhcu-ataivoo?* 'cowboy' ('cow-boy'); *ta ?ahpi?* 'Our Father', that is, 'God' ('our father'). Like borrowings, and unlike new formations and extensions of meaning, loan translations depend on familiarity with the contact language. The technique, not commonly used in Comanche, is seldom used extensively in other cases of lexical acculturation. (Note, however, the Mountain Pima word for 'hang-over' *dó?i*, which has as its central meaning "raw." Its use to mean "hangover" is a direct translation of the Spanish *cruda*.)

Comanche examples of extension of meaning include *kiika* 'onion', 'wild onion'; *kʷataci* 'sausage', 'big intestine'; *taave* 'clock', 'sun'; *tihiya* 'horse' (formerly 'deer'); *?a-tika* 'horned-food' is now 'deer').

New formations, that is, words coined using native word-building techniques, make up 65 percent of the Comanche acculturated vocabulary; for example, *?oha-vicippih* 'butter' ('yellow milk'); *puhi-vihnaa?* 'watermelon' ('plant sweet'); *pia ?eeti* 'gun' ('big bow'); *tuu-paa* 'coffee' ('black water'); *na-kari-?* 'chair' ('reciprocal pre-fix + sit + noun suffix').

As new words have entered the Comanche lexicon to reflect a new way of life, words reflecting an older way of life have been dropped. Here are a few of the words that were known only to older people in 1940: *?eena* 'jerky meat'; *?itanuci* 'tipi pegs'; *so?me?* 'tanned buffalo hide'; *naninasu?aiti* 'taboo against mentioning the name of a dead person'.

Semantic Extension in Western Apache

Mountain Pima and Comanche provide examples of extension of meaning from native words to cover new concepts, a technique used to a greater or lesser extent in all acculturating settings. Western Apache provides an example of the semantic extension of an entire set of terms, namely, the application of human body part terms to the parts of pickup trucks and cars:

Anatomical terms		Extended meanings
biwos	'shoulder'	front fender
bigan	'hand and arm'	front wheel
biyedaa'	'chin and jaw'	front bumper
bikee'	'foot'	rear wheel
binii'	'face'	from top of windshield to bumper
bita'	'forehead'	windshield
bichįh	'nose'	hood
bigháń	'back'	bed of truck
bik'ai	'hip and buttocks'	rear fender
bizé'	'mouth'	gas pipe opening
bidáá'	'eye'	headlight
bits'ǫǫs	'vein'	electrical wiring
bibiiye'	'innards'	all items under hood
bizig	'liver'	battery
pit	'stomach'	gas tank
bijíí	'heart'	distributor
bijíí'izólé	'lung'	radiator
bich'í'	'intestine(s)'	radiator hose(s)
bi'ik'ah	'fat'	grease

Western Apaches began to buy and drive pickup trucks and cars in the early 1930s, a time when most adults were still monolingual. Since the pickup replaced the horse as the main means of transportation, the set of body-part terms related to the horse could be considered the source of the extensions; however, a better explanation is that the set was extended in its entirety because natbiil 'pickup, car' was placed in the same semantic class as other entities that had body parts; that is, natbiil belongs to the category 'ihi'dahí, a category that includes people, quadrupeds, birds, reptiles, fish, and a few machines such as bulldozers, tractors, and steam shovels. What holds this set together semantically is that all entities in it move by themselves and that they contain similar (body) parts. In Western Apache, one can talk about an "automobile's body" (*naɫbiil bits'í*) in the same way one can talk about a "human being's body."

In considering linguistic acculturation in Western Apache, Comanche, and Mountain Pima contexts, we have reviewed five techniques of word building: borrowing, loan translation, native word building, semantic extension, and loan blends. Because word building and semantic extension do not necessarily depend on knowing the contact language, greater use of native word-building and semantic extension occurs more often in the earliest periods of contact. Borrowing (along with loan translation) often depends on knowledge of the contact language; therefore, there may be greater emphasis on borrowing in the later periods. Beyond this, some languages seem to prefer certain strategies over others; for example, Mountain Pima prefers borrowing, while Comanche prefers to make up its own words, and Eastern Pomo, one of Lake Miwok's neighbors, has responded differently to two colonial languages, borrowing about 150 words from Spanish but only a handful from English. In much closer contact with English than they were with Spanish, Eastern Pomo speakers just use English when their conversations involve semantic domains introduced via acculturation.

Structural considerations, including the structural "fit" or similarity of the languages in contact, probably play a role in lexical acculturation. In the past, scholars observed that the Athapaskan languages (Navajo and the other Apachean languages and languages in the interior of western Canada and Alaska, some in southern Oregon and northern California) seldom used loanwords. Since these languages are widely separated geographically and the cultures of their speakers vary, it was thought that the similarities in linguistic structure led to a similar response to linguistic acculturation, that is, the morphological structure of these languages made borrowing difficult; therefore, native word-building techniques and semantic extensions were preferred. In recent years, however, some of these languages have been exposed to intense contact with English, and the floodgate to English loanwords has been opened. At present, about all we can suggest is that intensity of contact, linguistic structure, and cultural factors (including cultural attitudes) all play a role in shaping the response in lexical acculturation. Just how these three factors interact is yet to be established.

11.4   A SHIFT TO THE COLONIAL LANGUAGES

Linguistic acculturation often represents the first step in language shift, the process by which a first language is replaced by a second language. It is understandable that as a culture comes in contact with new concepts, the vocabulary of its language incorporates new words through borrowing or use of other linguistic techniques. With intense contact, a language may begin to incorporate loanwords into old, native semantic domains. This is not a necessary result of intense contact (it happened with the Mountain Pima but not with the Comanche), but, if it happens, it is usually a sign that a language shift is about to take place. A speaker maintains more than one language if they serve different functions, with each language used for its respective domain. When the line between the sets of functions begins to erode, then one or more of the languages becomes redundant.

The situation with Comanche is typical of a number of Indian communities in which language shift has taken, or is taking, place. In 1940, there was a full range of bilingualism among the twenty-four hundred or so Comanche. Those over sixty spoke little or no English and those under thirty, little or no Comanche. The in-between generation, between thirty and sixty, formed the bilingual generation, but only a small number were equally at home in both languages. The degree of fluency in English manifested by any individual Comanche was a fairly reliable indication of that person's relative acculturation to patterns of American culture and could best be determined by observing the person's choice of language and his or her command of it in a variety of speech situations ranging from intimate ones found in family contexts to casual ones found in religious, economic, or administrative contexts.

The speech habits of the older Comanche were reflected in their use of English, particularly if they had learned it after they had learned Comanche. They spoke English with what would be called, in popular terms, a "Comanche accent," and their use of English grammatical structures was influenced by Comanche structure. The Comanche of younger speakers showed a great deal of simplification, dropping final glottal stops, as well as final vowels (which are normally voiceless in Comanche, making them hard for native English speakers to hear), and using affixes incorrectly or leaving them out entirely. In addition, modern descriptive words were often used in place of forgotten older words and English words and phrases were used more frequently. Today, there are no more than fifty people who remember and can speak Comanche with any fluency. Why this rapid language shift? It is not simply that the speakers were "forced" to abandon the language or because they were numerically overwhelmed, although these factors did play a role. Rather, it has to do with the cultural position of Comanche and English in the Comanche community and the role of the two languages in nonlinguistic aspects of Comanche acculturation to the dominant society. Some of the contexts in which Comanche was the appropriate language, for example, telling traditional stories, holding traditional ceremonies, became less and less frequent, while the settings in which English was appropriate, for example, school, meetings with government officials, became more and more frequent.

The shift from Comanche to English represents a type of language shift impossible in pre-Columbian times. Many indigenous societies have become dependent on the institutions of the societies represented by the colonial languages. Acculturation brings changes that sometimes, but not necessarily, result in total assimilation into the larger society. Whether or not assimilation is total, new institutions develop; for instance, schools and the institutions associated with Christianity. Ordinarily, the colonial language is the appropriate language for these institutions. At the same time, there is a loss of some of the institutions for which the indigenous languages are best suited; for example, the Plains War Societies, the institutions surrounding traditional storytelling, or older indigenous institutions are transformed into ones for which the colonial language is appropriate. Two examples in North America are the intertribal Powwow and the Peyote religion. English is used in both cases. In other words, as an indigenous society changes and evolves, the contexts in which the native language would be appropriate become fewer and less frequent, while the reverse holds true for the newer institutions and the use of the colonial language. The survival of an indigenous language depends on its taking on new, introduced functions. So far, only Guaraní in Paraguay has been successful in doing this.

Although the colonial language occupies an important position in most Indian communities, its position is seldom the same as that found in the larger society. Rules of usage for both the written and spoken language often reflect indigenous practices. Most Indian communities in the United States use a social dialect that has come to be called "Indian English." It seems to have originated in the boarding schools that the Bureau of Indian Affairs (BIA) began operating at the turn of the century. In these schools, English was used as the lingua franca because the students came from various linguistic backgrounds and the resultant variety of English used was apparently transmitted from one generation of students to the next.

Government language policies in the United States, at least until recent years, have not been conducive to the maintenance of Indian languages (section 1.4). Many Indian adults who are products of BIA schools place the blame with the BIA for language loss. Moreover, when adults are asked why they use English in the home and with their children, they often reply that they do not want their children to experience the same problems they encountered when they entered school knowing no English. The language policies of the BIA accurately reflected the attitudes of the members of the dominant society, in which Indian languages were (and still are, to a large extent) viewed as an impediment to "the Indian's advancement."

In a setting in which a language shift is taking place, the terms "flourishing" and "obsolete" represent the two ends of a scale for language vitality, with "obsolescing" used to refer to a midpoint. Because the scale is a sliding one, these terms do not represent fixed positions. A **flourishing** language is one in which the contact or colonial language is used almost entirely as a second language. Children entering school and perhaps some older adults do not speak the contact language or are incipient bilinguals. In the last decade of the twentieth century, few Indian communities in the United States and Canada have languages that fit this category: Navajo, Mississippi Choctaw, some Cree communities, and a few others. The number of flourishing languages is somewhat larger in Latin America; for example, Tarahumara in northern Mexico, Kuna in Panama (section 5.6), languages in the Vaupés (section 9.1), Aymara and Quechua in the Andes (section 9.3), Guaraní in Paraguay (section 9.4), and others.

In **obsolescing** language communities, the native language still serves as a vehicle for social interaction, but the settings in which it is used become more and more restricted. The few children who are bilingual learn the native and contact languages at the same time, so the contact language cannot be regarded as a second language, whereas the youngest speakers who are not proficient in their use of the native language can only be referred to as "semi-speakers." In communities of rapid transition, the in-between generation uses the contact language as its primary language: The speakers are fluent in it and feel more at home using it, even though it was not their first language. Older speakers often comment on how younger people speak the language; for example: "The youngsters speak a funny Arapaho; they don't use all the big words that we do and that our fathers did, and they take many short cuts. We can understand them alright, but it doesn't sound the way we would say it." Examples of this obsolescing phase include Comanche as it existed in 1940 and a Menomini speech community in the 1920s. In the late twentieth century we find, among others, Shoshoni and languages of various Plains communities in progress, with some of the Pueblo languages just entering this phase.

An **obsolete** language is known (better, remembered) by some of the adults in the community. Technically the language is still living, but sociologically it is dead. The comment of a Gros Ventre speaker to a visiting linguist is typical: "That's a tough language you ran into, pardner. . . . That's why we don't speak it ourselves; it's a hard language to learn. You can tell that—when we talk our own language, we have to think before we tell you." The obsolescing Comanche of 1940 has, by the end of the twentieth century, become an obsolete language. Other examples of this phase include many of the languages of California and some in the Northwest Coast. In 1959, while doing a field study of the then obsolete language of Serrano in southern California, Miller, in asking about terms for items of acculturation (e.g., television, lipstick, etc.), was told repeatedly, "we didn't have that (e.g., television) in the old days." Silver, working at the same time and also a few years later, in an analogous situation with a speaker of Shasta would be told, "we didn't do that [or have that] before the white man came." In effect, both Serrano and Shasta had become "old days" languages. Serrano has since become an extinct language and Shasta most likely has as the last speaker may have died in the 1980s. If a language is recently extinct, there may often be persons who remember some words and phrases and sometimes may even have a little bit of the native sound system still intact.

There are certain similarities in the language shift of obsolescing American Indian speech communities and immigrant speech communities. In both cases, three-generation households show the same pattern of language use. Frequently, the grandparents speak to the children in the ancestral language but are answered in English. The parents, the in-between generation, speak to the children in English but to the grandparents in the ancestral language. Although English has been learned as a second language by the in-between generation, it has often become their primary and preferred language even though the form they may speak reflects influences from their first language. In lay parlance, they "speak English with an accent."

There are, however, a number of differences between the two types of speech communities. When an American Indian community no longer speaks its ancestral language, the language is gone forever. When an immigrant community no longer speaks Italian, German, Spanish, Japanese, or the like, the language is still alive in "the old country." It is possible for a third generation member to make an extended visit to relatives in the old country in order to learn or to refresh her or his knowledge of an ancestral language. Such opportunities would not be available in most American Indian contexts. The awareness of the language in "the old country" often leads to what one observer has called "bilingual norms"; that is, the awareness that an acculturated or "Americanized" version of a language (e.g., "Americanized Norwegian") is appropriate in certain contexts, while a "pure" version is appropriate in other contexts.

11.5 MITCHIF: A SPECIAL CASE

Mitchif is a language composed of elements from Plains Cree and French. It is spoken by a group of people known as the Métis. A product of the fur trade, the Métis emerged as an identifiable group at the end of the eighteenth century. They are primarily descendants of French Canadian men and Indian, mostly Cree, women. Later intermarriages were mostly with Cree or other Indian groups rather than with French, so that in today's population, the Indian component is greater than the French. Highly mobile, the Métis live in scattered groups, mostly in western Canada, where they form a link between the Indian and Euro-Canadian populations.

The boundary between the Métis and the Cree is not always clear, in part because they both have low social standing and are often denigrated by both the Indian and the White communities. This makes it difficult to get an accurate population tally, but the number seems to be less than five thousand. Those who still speak Mitchif comprise a still smaller group, perhaps a few hundred. Most of these live at the Turtle Mountain reservation in North Dakota and additional speakers are found in Manitoba, Saskatchewan, and perhaps elsewhere. In addition to Mitchif, they speak French and English. In 1977, there were no speakers under forty; English was in the process of replacing both Mitchif and French.

Mitchif is the language of the home, and it is what gives the speakers a measure of self-identity. French and Cree are used with outsiders. It is not the case that the Métis simply take French and Cree and mix them together. The two are combined in a patterned fashion and at least some speakers have a notion of what is "proper" Mitchif.

The noun system of Mitchif is derived primarily from French, the verb system comes entirely from Cree, and the language of origin is reflected in the lexicon, phonology, and morphology in these two Mitchif systems. Here we focus on the noun system because it reflects the area of interaction between French and Cree; however, we also have to touch upon certain aspects of the verb system, since the verb is important in distinguishing animate nouns from inanimate nouns.

Five nouns ("mother," "father," "grandfather," "grandmother" and "chokecherry") are of Cree origin. All the remaining nouns (excluding a few from English) are from French, as are all the adjectives. Except for the five words of Cree origin, all nouns (including those of English origin) must occur with an indefinite article, a definite article or a possessive pronoun; for example,

ãn mæzɔ̃m	'a house'	(ãn, indef. article)
lɪstor	'the store'	(lɪ, def. article; stor < English)
mi pul	'my chickens'	(mi, first person plural possessive pronoun)
lɪ bɔ̃ ĵä	'God'	('the good God')
lɪ pči ãfã	'the little child'	('the little child')
lɪ vyü bwa šɛš	'the dry old wood'	('the old wood dry')
lɪ pat dɪ twezu	'the bird's leg'	('the leg of bird')

As in French, there are a few adjectives that occur before the noun, while all others follow it.

The articles and possessive pronouns are from French; and, as in French, the articles are marked for gender (masculine, feminine), and the definite article also specifies number:

	Masculine	Feminine	Prevocalic (Masc. or Fem.)
indef.	æ̃	æ̃(n)	æ̃n
def.sg	lɪ	la	l
def.pl	li	li	liz

Gender is governed by the choice of the article that is used with the noun, not by any intrinsic meaning of the nouns. Thus, *garsɔ* 'boy', *zæf* 'egg' and *rum* 'room' are masculine because they occur with *lɪ* and *ãn*, while *fiy* 'girl' and *plüm* 'pen' are feminine because they occur with *la* and *æ̃(n)*.

In section 2.2 we saw that Cree, like other Algonquian languages, has gender classes in its noun system, distinguished not by sex gender (masculine and feminine), but by animacy (animate and inanimate). Cree nouns take four different endings, depending on whether the noun is animate singular, animate plural, inanimate singular, or inanimate plural. Because almost all nouns in Mitchif are from French, they do not take the Cree endings for animacy and number; however, Mitchif nouns can still be divided into two classes based on animacy because, in Cree and Mitchif alike, verbs must agree in animacy with both subject and object; for example:

gi·-wa·pama·w lɪ garsɔ	'I saw the boy'	(*garsɔ*, 'boy', animate; –*wa·pama·w*, 'see', animate object; *gi·-*, "I," past tense)
gi·-wa·pahtæ̃·n lɪ fizi	'I saw the gun'	(*fizi*, 'gun', inanimate; –*wapahtæ̃·n*, 'see', inanimate object)
la pul ki·-šišuw	'the chicken is cooked'	(*pul*, 'chicken', animate; –*šišuw*, 'is cooked', animate subject; *ki·-*, past tense)
la vyæ̃d ki·-šite·w	'the meat is cooked'	(*vyæ̃d*, 'meat', inanimate; –*šite·w*, 'is cooked', inanimate subject)

The animacy and sex genders crosscut, so that a noun will belong to any one of four classes; for example,

animate, masculine:	*lɪ garsɔ*	'the boy'
	lɪ wægɔ	'the wagon'
animate, feminine:	*la fiy*	'the girl'
	la rɔš	'the rock'
inanimate, masculine:	*lɪ mãži*	'the food'
	lɪ fizi	'the gun'
inanimate, feminine:	*la mæzɔ*	'the house'
	la sæs	'the hunt'

The natural classification breaks down at points here, just as it does in most sex gender systems; for example, "boy" and "girl" are animate, "food," "gun," "house," and "hunt" are inanimate, but "wagon" and "rock" are classified as animate.

The demonstratives in Mitchif are from Cree, and they distinguish singular and plural, as well as animate and inanimate. There are three degrees of distance, "this" (near by), "that" (intermediate distance), and "that" (farthest distance). The forms for "this, these" are *awa* 'this' (animate), *u·ma* 'this' (inanimate), *ō·kik* 'these' (animate), *ō·hī* 'these' (inanimate). The demonstratives, which are used with the definite article, must agree in animacy and number with the nouns, for example: *awa la fiy* 'this girl' ('this [anim. sg.] the girl'), *u·ma lɪ zæf* 'this egg' ('this [inanim. sg.] the egg'). Thus, the division of animate versus inanimate in nouns is marked not only by their agreement with the verb, but also by their agreement with the demonstrative.

The five nouns of Cree origin cannot take an article; however, when they take a pronominal possessor, they may be possessed in one of two ways: with an independent pronoun of French origin or with an affix of Cree origin; for example

ma mušu·m	'my grandfather'	(*ma* 'my', of French origin); or
ni-mušu·m	'my grandfather'	(*ni–* 'my', of Cree origin)
su mušu·m	'his grandfather'	(*su* 'his, her', of French origin); or
u-mušu·m	'his grandfather'	(*u–* 'his, her', of Cree origin)

For all other nouns, possession is by means of the independent pronouns, never the affixes: *ma mæ̃* 'my hand' (never **ni-mæ̃*). When nouns of Cree origin are also modified by an adjective, only the independent possessive pronoun is used: *nɔt vyü mušu·m gra* 'our fat old grandfather' ('our old grandfather fat').

One other aspect that reflects the Cree noun system is the use of the obviative (section 12.1), a grammatical category typical of Cree and other Algonquian languages. The obviative suffix is added to a noun to show that it is least important of two third persons (sometimes it is called the "fourth person"); thus, *la fãm mičimine·w lɪ pči-wa* 'the woman is holding the child' ('the woman is—holding the child—obviative'). Unlike Cree, the obviative is optional in Mitchif: either *pčiwa* or *pči* could be used in this sentence. In addition, there are other grammatical contexts in which the obviative is used in Cree, but not in Mitchif.

It is tempting to say that Mitchif is simply a kind of Cree that has borrowed most of its nouns and all of its adjectives from French. If this were all that had happened, then it would resemble Mountain Pima, which has borrowed extensively from Spanish nouns. There is, however, an important difference; for example, Spanish nouns have been integrated into the Mountain Pima grammatical system and do not take the Spanish plural nor do they take the Spanish articles; instead, they are inflected for number by reduplication, just like native Mountain Pima nouns. Furthermore, Mountain Pima shows all the signs of a language in transition, a language that is about to be replaced by Spanish. Mitchif, on the other hand, has crystallized into a distinctive, stabilized form. It does not resemble a language used by a community undergoing a language shift; rather, it is more like a case of arrested language shift.

11.6   CHANGES IN THE AMERICAS'
COLONIAL LANGUAGES

The languages of the major colonial powers to come to the Americas, Danish (in Greenland), Russian, French, English, Spanish, and Portuguese, have left their mark on American Indian languages. In turn, these colonial languages have been influenced by indigenous languages, even though to a far lesser extent. We consider three cases, American English, Mexican Spanish, and Andean Spanish.

American English

A good dictionary of American English will show words that have American Indian origins and will give their etymologies, as in the following (mostly) familiar items:

> abalone < Spanish < Costanoan (a Californian language)
> bayou < Louisiana French < Choctaw *bayuk* 'creek'
> caribou < Canadian French < Algonquian (Micmac?) *khalibu*
>   'pawer, scratcher'
> catalpa < Creek *kutuhlpa* 'head with wings', from shape of the
>   flower
> chinchilla < Spanish, probably < Aymara or Quechua, name of
>   the animal
> chipmunk < Algonquian (Ojibwa) *atchitamo* 'squirrel'
> cougar < French < Portuguese < Tupi *suasuacada* 'like a deer'
> guano < Spanish, probably < Quechua *huanu* 'dung'
> guava < Spanish *guayaba* < Arawakan *goyaba* or Tupi *guaiaba*
> hickory < Virginian Algonquian *pawcohiccoro*
> hominy < Algonquian *rockahominie* 'parched corn'
> igloo < Eskimo *iglu* 'house'
> jaguar < Portuguese or Spanish < Tupi *jaguara*
> moose < Algonquian (Natick) *moosu* 'he trims, shaves', from habit
>   of stripping bark
> opossum < Virginian Algonquian (Powhatan) *apasum* 'white animal'
> pecan < Algonquian (Cree) *pacan*
> persimmon Algonquian (Cree) *pasiminan* 'dried fruit'
> pone < Algonquian (Delaware) *apan* 'baked'
> potato < Spanish < Taino *batata*
> powwow < Algonquian (Massachusetts) *pauwaw* 'he dreams',
>   (Natick) *pauwau* 'conjurer, he uses divination'

raccoon < Algonquian *arakunem* 'hand-scratcher', Virginian
    Algonquian *arahhkumen* 'he scratches with his hands'
skunk < Algonquian *seganku*
squash < Algonquian (Massachusetts) *askoota*
succotash < Algonquian (Narraganset) *misickquatash* 'ear of corn',
    (Narraganset) *msakwatas* 'something broken into pieces'
tepee < Siouan (Dakota) *tipi* < *ti* 'to dwell' + *pi* 'used for'
tobacco < Spanish < Taino or Carib; or Tupi *taboca* 'a reed'
toboggan < Canadian French < Algonquian (Micmac) *tobakun*
tomato < Spanish < Nahuatl *tomatl*
totem < Algonquian (Ojibwa) *ototeman* 'his relations'
woodchuck (by way of folk etymology) < Algonquian (Ojibwa)
    otchig 'fisher', 'marten' or Creek *otchek*

Most dictionaries do a very poor job of representing the American Indian pronunciations and there are often minor, sometimes major, errors in etymology; for example, many dictionaries list "caucus" as perhaps from an Algonquian language form *caucauasu* 'advisor'. More likely, however, is the suggestion in the *Random House Dictionary of the English Language* (second edition, unabridged, 1987) that "caucus" is from Medieval Latin *caucus* 'drinking vessel' ("alleged Virginia Algonquian orig. less probable").

Some words, like "avocado" (< Spanish *aguacate* < Nahuatl *ahuacatl*), "bayou" and "potato" have entered English via another colonial language. Many American Indian terms have found their way into the vocabulary of the major languages of the world and thus are a part of an international vocabulary, rather than being specific to American English. The earliest such words first came into Spanish from Caribbean languages, especially Taíno, during the first period of Spanish occupation in the West Indies. A few such words are (listed with the Spanish form first, followed by the English): *barbacoa* 'barbecue', *hamaca* 'hammock', *huracán* 'hurricane', *iguana* 'iguana', *maíz* 'maize', *papaya* 'papaya'.

Other words of Indian origin in American English are of limited or local usage, such as "pogonip" ('a cold fog, also called 'frost fog' < Paiute), "quahog" ('edible clam' < Narraganset *poquauhock*), or "potlatch" (< Chinook *patshatl* 'gift'). All of the loanwords in American English came into the language as nouns, and it is no accident that many of the terms are from eastern Algonquian languages because the English colonists encountered speakers of these languages first (e.g., Natick, Narraganset, Powhatan, Delaware, et al.). Although there are terms that are difficult to categorize, many loanwords are plant terms, for example, "persimmon," "squash"; others are food terms, for example, "hominy," "succotash"; still others are for animals such as "skunk," "raccoon." In addition, there are terms for material objects associated with Indian culture; for example, "tepee," "moccasin" < Natick *mokkusin* (or) Narraganset *mocuussin* 'shoe'.

Mexican Spanish

Mexican Spanish has also borrowed a number of words from indigenous languages. Some are of only local currency, such as these that are found in northwest Mexico: *yori* 'non-Indian, Mexican person', *huari* 'basket', *mahuechi* 'corn field', Although local borrowings of this sort exist in American English (cf. *pogonip*), such borrowings are much more common in Mexican Spanish (and for that matter, in most languages of Latin America) than in American English.

The largest number of loanwords came from Nahuatl, spoken in the area where the first extended contact took place between the Spanish and an indigenous group. Most of these terms are known all over Mexico and sometimes beyond; but, with a few exceptions, they are not known in Spain. Here is a sample selection:

aguacate	'avocado'	< āhuaca-tl
cacahuate	'peanut'	< cacahua-tl 'cacao, chocolate bean' (Nahuatl 'peanut' is tlā-cacahua-tl, lit. 'earth-[chocolate] bean')
camote	'sweet potato'	< camoʔ-tli
coyote	'coyote'	< coyō-tl
cuate(s)	'twin(s)'	< cōā-tl 'snake','twin'
chamaco	'boy'	(cp. chamāhuac 'child to grow up', from verb meaning 'to swell up')
chia	'chia', 'kind of plant with edible seeds'	< chiyan-tli
chicle	'chewing gum'	< tzic-tli (cp. English 'chiclets')
chichi	'breast' (colloquial)	< chīchī 'to suckle'
chile	'chili'	< chīl-li
chipichipi	'drizzle'	< chipīni 'to drip'
chocolate	'chocolate'	< chocolā-tl

ejote	'green beans'	< exō-tl
elote	'fresh corn, corn on the cob'	< ēlō-tl
escuincle	'brat'	< itzcuīn-tli 'dog'
esquite	'toasted corn kernels' (Mexico's answer to beer nuts)	< īzqui-tl 'pop corn'
guacal	'basket for carrying burdens on the shoulders'	< huacal-li
guacamole	'guacamole sauce'	< āhuaca-mōl-li (lit. 'avocado-sauce')
guajalote	'turkey'	< hue?xōlō-tl
huipil	'kind of blouse'	< huīpīl-li
hule	'rubber'	< ol-li
jícama	'kind of edible root'	< xicama-tl
jiote	'ringworm'	< xiyō-tl 'itch, mange'
jitomate	'tomato'	< xī-toma-tli (lit. 'green-tomato')
jocoyote	'youngest child'	< xōcoyō-tl
mapache	'raccoon'	< māpachin
mecate	'rope'	< meca-tl
mezcal	'mescal', a distilled alcoholic drink, and the name of the kind of maguey plant from which it is made	< mexcal-li
milpa	'cornfield'	< mīl-pan (lit. 'field-in')
mole	'kind of sauce made from chile and chocolate'	< mōl-li
nixtamal	'hominy' (corn boiled with lime and ready to be ground into meal for making tortillas)	< nex-tamal-li (lit. 'ashes-tamale')
nopal	'prickly pear cactus'	< nopal-li
ocelote	'ocelot, jaguar'	< ōcēlō-tl
olote	'corncob'	< olo-tl
otate	'bamboo'	< otla-tl
petate	'sleeping mat'	< petla-tl

peyote	'peyote'	< peyo-tl
pinole	'a watery gruel drink made from ground toasted corn'	< pinol-li
quelite	'greens, such as pigweed or lamb's quarters'	< quili-tl
quexqueme	'kind of poncho worn by women'	< quech-quemi-tl (lit. 'neck-garment')
tamal	'tamale'	< tamal-li
tecolote	'owl'	< tecolō-tl
temascal	'sweat house'	< temāz-cal-li (lit. 'bathe-house')
tianquis	'flea market, swap meet'	< tiānquiztli 'market' (based on tiāmiqui 'to buy and sell')
tlacuache, tacuache	'opossum'	< tlacuātzin
tomate	'tomato'	< toma-tl
tule	'reed'	< tōl-in
yagual	'head-pad, for carrying loads on the head'	< yahual-li
zacate	'grass'	< zaca-tl
zoquete	'mud'	< zoqui-tl

The pattern of borrowing into Mexican Spanish shows some similarities to that found for American English. There are a number of words for new plants, new foods, and new animals. (It is interesting that the most important Aztec contribution to Mexican cuisine, the tortilla, is not a loanword, but is composed of Spanish elements, *torta* 'cake' plus a diminutive suffix.) In the pattern of borrowing, however, the differences between American English and Mexican Spanish outnumber the similarities. Many words do not fit into the three categories the borrowing languages share; for example, *cuates, chipichipi, escuincle, jacal* ('hut' < *xaʔ-cal-li* lit. 'sand-house'), *ocote* ('pine tree, evergreen tree; torch' < *oco-tl* lit. 'pine tree'), *petaca* ('trunk, hamper' < *petlā-cal-li* lit. 'mat-house'), *tocayo* ('person having the same name as another' < *tōcā-yoʔ* from 'name' plus a suffix that forms abstract nouns), and several others. In a number of cases, such as *mecate, tecolote, zacate*, there was already a native Spanish word, which was replaced by the Nahuatl. Although most of the words are nouns, there are also verbs, for example, *pizcar* ('to harvest' < *pixca* 'to harvest').

As in American English, the structure of morphologically complex words was lost in the borrowing process. This is seen most readily in the Nahuatl noun suffix with the variant shapes -*tli*, -*tl*, -*li*, which become most commonly -*te* (e.g., *chicle* < *tzic-tli*); *metate* 'grinding stone' < *metla-tl*) or -*le* (e.g., *pozole* 'hominy stew' < *pozol-li*); in other words, this element must be analyzed as a suffix in Nahuatl but is simply part of the stem in the Spanish word. Just as sounds foreign to English were changed to their closest English counterpart, sounds foreign to Spanish were changed into their closest Spanish counterpart. A good example is the reduction of Nahuatl short and long vowels into a single vowel type in Spanish because Spanish does not distinguish vowel length. Thus, the long [ā] in *comāl-li* and the short [a] in *copal-li* are rendered in an identical fashion in Spanish *comal* 'griddle' and *copal* 'incense'. In one case, however, Spanish has shown partial accommodation: the lateral affricate [ʎ] (written "tl") usually becomes Spanish [t], as in *petla-tl* > *petate*, but in some cases the foreign phonetic pattern is retained, as in *tlacuātzin*, which in Spanish is either *tlacuache* or *tacuache*.

The reason for the differences in the borrowing pattern in American English and Mexican Spanish is not hard to find. The English colonists simply transplanted their culture to the North American shores and, during the early colonial period, the number of native speakers of English bilingual in an Indian language was relatively few and became even fewer in the years that followed. Although many Indian groups may have become bilingual in English, their numbers are few in relation to the surrounding monolingual English-speaking population.

In contrast to American culture (i.e., the culture of the United States), Mexican culture is a synthesis of Spanish and Indian (in particular Nahuatl) elements. During the early colonial period, native speakers of Spanish adopted many aspects of Mexican Indian life and many of them learned Nahuatl. More importantly, a large proportion of the Spanish-speaking population learned Nahuatl as their second language and these people were the catalyst for change.

Andean Spanish

In section 2.6, we looked at a number of Andean languages possessing a rich evidential system; that is, a speaker must indicate if a fact is known to be true from personal experience, from the experience of another, and so on, and we mentioned that the Spanish of the area has come to make some of these same distinctions. The indigenous languages indicate evidentiality grammatically in various ways, which include a set of suffixes. The local Spanish has come to mark evidential distinctions by redefining the meaning and function of certain tenses and of certain adverbs and conjunctions, such as *pues, pero, siempre*; for instance, in the example that follows, the past perfect is marked by the use of a past tense of *haber* (*había* in the example) plus the past participle of the verb *ver* (*visto* in the example): *había visto la casa* 'she saw the house' (nonpersonal or surprise). In the rest of the Spanish-speaking world, this sentence would be the equivalent of the English, "she had seen the house." The future tense provides another example; there are two futures in Spanish: one is an inflected future form in which a future suffix is added to the verb stem; this future form is often translated by English "will . . ." The other future is formed by using a form of *ir* 'to go', followed by an infinitive, and is often translated by "going to . . ." or "gonna . . . ," as in: *vendré* 'I will come'; *voy a venir* 'I'm gonna come'. The English equivalents of these Andean Spanish constructions would be *vendré* 'I will come (maybe, but don't wait for me)' (nonpersonal); *voy a venir* 'I will come (and do wait)' (personal).

The differences between Andean Spanish and the varieties of Spanish spoken elsewhere are subtle and often go unnoticed by nonlocal Spanish speakers; indeed, sometimes there are misunderstandings, usually without the speakers realizing the source of the misunderstandings.

The Andean and Mexican colonial settings had much in common. A large proportion of the population in these settings was bilingual, speaking a local language as their native language and Spanish as their second language. Their Spanish was influenced by their native languages. Their offspring became, in increasing numbers, monolingual in the variety of Spanish spoken by their bilingual forefathers, not that of the Spanish-speaking colonists. In a relatively short time, the features of Spanish that developed because of the contact situations spread as well to the descendants of the colonists, a minority of the population. Although the historical record is not conclusive, it supports this sequence, of which we can be fairly certain because better documented language contact cases show that influence of this sort proceeds in this fashion.

11.7 LANGUAGE CONTACT AND BILINGUALISM

A great deal of what we know about languages in contact has come through studying the results of contact, rather than through observation of contact itself. For rather obvious reasons, this is particularly true of contact between Indian languages, as contrasted with that between Indian and colonial languages: The contact between Indian languages and cultures was largely disrupted soon after Europeans arrived; consequently, the past processes of contact could seldom be directly observed.

Language changes that are the result of language contact are mediated by the bilingual individual; therefore, understanding the nature of the bilingual situation is the key to understanding the nature of language contact. The distinction between individual and societal bilingualism is important (section 9.4); so, too, is the distinction between casual and intense contact, which is closely related to the kinds of bilingualism (incipient, functional, or fluent), discussed in the introduction to chapter 9. Lexical borrowing takes place through either casual or intense contact; however, intense contact, ordinarily associated with a sizable body of fluent bilinguals, is necessary for structural change of the sort we saw with Lake Miwok, Mountain Pima, and Mitchif.

Influence may be in one direction only, as the influence of Spanish has been on Mountain Pima; it may also be mutual, as has been the borrowing among Huasteca Nahuatl, Huastec, and Totonac (although more borrowing has taken place into Huasteca Nahuatl than the reverse). Prestige acts as an important factor: If the societies in question—and, by extension, the languages—are of equal prestige, influence is more apt to be mutual. If there is inequality, the borrowing is more apt to be one way, flowing from the more prestigious language and society to the one(s) with lower prestige. There are other factors at work as well. Consider, for instance, the greater borrowing of Nahuatl into Mexican Spanish as compared to borrowing from Indian languages into American English. Furthermore, the borrowing into Huasteca Nahuatl, although mutual to some extent, was greater in this direction, because, as newcomers, the Huasteca Nahuatl had need for new names in a new environment.

The individual bilingualism typical of small-scale societies is the perfect context for mutual borrowing. California is a case in point, where the degree of borrowing of all types—lexical, phonological, and grammatical—is so heavy and in so many directions that it is sometimes difficult to sort out who borrowed what from whom. Individual bilingualism also provides a good context for lexical borrowing in many cultural areas, including everyday or basic vocabulary. Lexical borrowing that accompanies societal bilingualism, on the other hand, tends to be limited to those cultural areas involved in the bilingual contact, be they political, religious, commercial, or other spheres. Individual bilingualism, however, does not guarantee borrowing. In the Vaupés each language is also a badge for kin-group identity; as a result, speakers consciously try to keep the languages distinct. Although it is difficult to believe that after centuries of multilingualism there has not been some mutual influence, such influence would have been minimal and very different from that in the California case.

Widespread bilingualism can be the harbinger of language shift, but only under certain conditions. Stable bilingualism and multilingualism existed for centuries, perhaps millennia, in California and it still exists in the Vaupés. Replacive bilingualism and language shifts on a grand scale are more often associated with societal bilingualism and most often in such stratified societies as those represented by precontact societies in the Andes and in the Aztec Empire. They are also associated with the shift from an ancestral to a colonial language in postcontact times. Such a shift took place on a modest scale in the Creek Confederacy when Creek replaced the languages of individual villages. In the Northwest Coast and in California, individual bilingualism also led to language shift, but again only on a modest scale. In the Northwest Coast individual bilingualism was the enabling mechanism for the languages of the coastal area, which had greater prestige, to make slow inroads upstream and into the interior. In the village societies of California relative numbers were less important than they are in highly stratified societies. A number of languages with only five hundred or a thousand speakers who lived in only a few villages seemed to be holding their own, an understandable situation when we realize that the unit of interaction, the speech community, was the village rather than the total population of speakers of a particular language. In a highly stratified society the survival of a language with only five hundred or a thousand speakers would be very unlikely, if not inconceivable.

Acculturation of nonlinguistic aspects of culture occur in such a way that a truly mixed culture can result; modern Mexican culture is an example. A mixed language, however, is almost impossible because language works differently from other aspects of culture. It has been said that "language is probably the most self-contained, the most massively resistant of all social phenomena. It is easier to kill it off than to disintegrate its individual form." Dialect mixture is possible and is, in fact, a fairly frequent phenomenon, as is the mixture of fairly closely related languages. But the mixture of fundamentally different languages is difficult. Although it has been reported, in almost every case for which there is sufficient evidence to assess the claim, the claim has been shown to be false. It is understandable, then, that without considerable supporting evidence, there is scholarly reluctance to accept claims of mixed linguistic ancestry. While Mitchif, being neither Cree nor French, is cited as a plausible example, mixed languages are still very rare. Moreover, there are too few examples to even allow speculation as to what must be necessary in a social and linguistic context for a mixed language to arise; but the rarity attests that the circumstances must be very, very special.

Areal features arising in the context of prolonged contact and bilingualism are another product of language contact. Because there is no appropriate historical documentation for the indigenous languages, we have been unable to explore the processes of contact and change that lead to the development of areal feature. We can, however, discuss examples of end results, which we present in sections 12.3 through 12.6.

SOURCES

Section 11.1 is based on Kimball 1989; section 11.2 on Callaghan 1964. In section 11.3 the Mountain Pima discussion is based on De Wolf n.d.; Comanche on Casagrande 1954, 1955; Western Apache on Basso 1967. The mention of Eastern Pomo is drawn from McLendon 1969; discussion of structural "fit" draws from Sapir 1921b: 197. In section 11.4 discussion of Comanche draws from Casagrande 1954, 1955 and of "Indian English" from Spicer 1962:440, Harvey 1974, and Leap 1993; the comments about Arapaho and Gros Ventre are from Salzmann 1951:100, 1969:307; the mention of Menomini draws from Bloomfield 1927; the reference to bilingual norms is from Haugen 1950. In section 11.5 the Mitchif discussion is based on Rhodes 1977, with Métis references from Slobodin 1981. In section 11.6 class notes provide the basis for discussion of loans into American English; Karttunen 1983, Santamaría 1974, and Molina 1977 are the sources for the treatment of loans into Mexican Spanish; discussion of Andean Spanish draws from Hardman 1986. In section 11.7 mention of language shift in the Northwest Coast is based on Jacobs 1937; the quote concerning language is from Sapir 1921b:206; the mixed language discussion draws from Thomason and Kaufman 1988.

SUGGESTED READINGS

For an overview of North American Indian languages contact, see Bright 1973. For section 11.3 there are a number of very good studies concerned with lexical acculturation as the central or one of the principal topics. We have discussed two, Casagrande 1954, 1955 and Basso 1967. Some others are Trager 1944, Bright 1952, Dozier 1956 (see also Dedrick 1977), Bright 1960, Shipley 1962, McLendon 1969, and Kroskrity and Reinhardt (1984). These observers note the value of such studies, since the semantic areas affected by linguistic acculturation are a good index of the nature of acculturation in general. Regarding section 11.4, Philips 1970, 1983 discusses contemporary language use in a multiethnic Indian community; Kroskrity 1993b considers the use of English, Hopi, and Arizona Tewa in a Tewa community; see Darnell 1985 for a discussion of communicative patterns in Cree communities in Alberta; Miller 1972 discusses Shoshoni as an obsolescing language; Sorensen 1985 considers a Latin American example of governmental attitudes regarding American Indian languages. For section 11.5, Thomason and Kaufman 1988 examine a number of cases, both in and outside the Americas, that involve language contact and structural change. For section 11.6 see Cotton and Sharp 1988 regarding patterns of lexical change in Latin America.

PART VI

languages in time and space

CHAPTER 12

LANGUAGES AND SHARED HISTORIES

We can classify languages into groups that display similarities and share certain features. The classifications are of three types: genetic, areal, and typological. These are complementary, not competing classifications. They highlight different kinds of phenomena and give different kinds of information.

Languages that belong to the same language family are **genetically related** (or, simply, related). Such languages derive from a single ancestral language or **proto-language.** If the protolanguage was spoken only a few hundred years ago, its descendants, rather than being distinct languages, are dialects of the same language; for instance, the varieties of English (American, Australian, British, Canadian, etc.) and of Spanish (Colombian, Cuban, Iberian, Mexican, Puerto Rican, etc.) spoken in various areas of the world. If the protolanguage was spoken one or two thousand years ago, its descendants are distinct languages that are closely and obviously related: examples would be the Romance languages (French, Italian, Spanish, etc.), which are descended from Latin, and the various Slavic languages (Russian, Czech, Polish, etc.). If the ancestral language was spoken several thousand years ago, then the languages are more distantly related, and the relationships are not obvious: here we find the Indo-European languages, a group that includes, among others, Albanian, Greek, the languages of northern India, and the Romance, Slavic, and Germanic languages.

Related languages can be grouped into **language families:** for example, Romance, Slavic, and Germanic. Remote relationships, which frequently include groupings of two or more families, can be called language or linguistic **stocks** or **phyla;** for example, the "Indo-European stock," or the "Indo-European phylum." (Some language historians make a distinction between stocks and phyla: a phylum is a more inclusive grouping.) A language or a small group of closely related languages with no clear linguistic relatives is called a **language isolate**; a familiar example from Europe is Basque. "Isolate" is also used to speak of an "orphan" language that is part of a remotely related linguistic stock; for instance, Greek and Albanian are isolates within Indo-European.

Neighboring languages often share certain features that are the result of prolonged contact (usually with extensive multilingualism) rather than genetic relationship. If a number of features are shared, it is sometimes possible to place the languages into an areal grouping; however, similarities among the languages in an areal group may be the result of genetic as well as areal factors, since some of the languages may be related and others unrelated (or so distantly related that the relationship is not a significant factor). If contact between neighboring groups is intense and long lasting (several hundreds or even thousands of years), it becomes difficult or impossible to sort out the similarities that are the result of genetic relationship from those that are areally spread through contact over time.

Typologically similar languages are simply those that share types of structural features, such as tone, or a distinction between alienable and inalienable possession, regardless of the historical origin of the shared features. This sharing of features may be the result of relationship; it may be the result of contact; or it may be the result of chance. We touched on this topic in chapter 2 when we discussed structural features. Typological classifications are a touchstone for learning about the nature of language, because certain features often cluster together; for example, languages that place the direct object after the verb most often have prepositions and most often place adjectives after the noun, while languages that place the object before the verb do the opposite; typically they have postpositions and place the adjective before the noun. Inasmuch as we discussed structural features in chapter 2 and are concerned here with similarities that are the result of shared histories, our discussion in this chapter is limited to genetic relationship and areal phenomena and does not treat typological phenomena further.

12.1   THE CREE DIALECTS

In ordinary usage, **dialect** often refers to a variety of speech varying from the standard or national language; however, we use the term in the technical linguistic sense in which it simply refers to varieties of speech across speakers, but within the same language. According to this usage, the type of speech variety in a language (e.g., English) commonly referred to as "the standard language" (e.g., "standard English") is a social dialect. Dialect variation is both regional and social; in the latter case, the linguistic variation is between speakers of the same speech community who belong to different social groups. Since social dialects are more commonly associated with stratified societies, our use of "dialect," unless otherwise indicated, refers to regional rather than social dialects.

The Cree language is spoken by about eighty thousand persons in the Canadian provinces of Labrador, Quebec, Ontario, Manitoba, Saskatchewan, and Alberta. The language is not uniform, which is hardly surprising, considering the immense area involved. The basic division is between Western Cree and Eastern Cree. Western Cree consists of Plains Cree, Woods Cree, West Swampy Cree, East Swampy and Moose Cree, and Attikamek; Eastern Cree is represented by Mistassini Cree, Naskapi, and Montagnais. While we will refer to these varieties as the dialects of Cree, it will become clear that divisions into discrete dialects should not be taken too seriously.

Characteristic Features

The Plains Cree dialect is our point of departure, not because it has any linguistic primacy but because it is the best studied, since it has the most speakers. The sound inventory of Plains Cree includes eight consonants (/p, t, č, k, s, h, m, n/), two semivowels (/w, y/), four long vowels (/i·, e·, a·, o·/), and three short vowels (/i, a, o/). Any of these three elements (consonant, semivowel, vowel) may begin or end a word: *atim* 'dog', *watay* 'his (her, its) belly', *ni·so* 'two'.

The semivowel /w/ can follow most initial or medial consonants, and the consonants /h/ and /s/ can precede most medial or final consonants: *kwayask* 'properly, straight', *mo·swa* 'moose', *askihk* 'kettle', *te·pakohp* 'seven', *ospwa·kan* 'pipe', *pahkwe·sikan* 'bannock'.

Number and gender were discussed earlier (section 2.2). Another salient grammatical feature that deserves mention is the system for marking person (e.g., "I," "you," "he"). Person is marked for verbs by a rather complicated system of prefixes and suffixes. Some examples with the stem *wa·pam–* 'to see' (animate object):

ni-wa·pam-a·-w	'I see him, her'
ki-wa·pam-a·-w	'you see him, her'
ni-wa·pam-a·-na·n	'we (exclusive) see him, her'
ki-wa·pam-a·-naw	'we (inclusive) see him, her'
ki-wa·pam-a·-wa·w	'you (plural) see him, her'
ki-wa·pam-it-in	'you see me'
ni-wa·pam-ik-(w)	'he, she sees me'
ki-wa·pam-ik-(w)	'he, she sees you'
ki-wa·pam-i-(i)n	'I see you'

(Elements that are dropped in certain phonetic contexts are placed in parentheses.) Notice that it is not the prefix or the suffix alone that marks person, but rather the combination of the two. Thus the complex *ni-* . . . *-w* indicates first person ("I, me") and third person ("he/she, him/her"); the suffix *–a·* after the stem shows that the subject is "I" ("I see him/her"), but with *–ik*, it is "he/she" ("he/she sees me"). The same set of prefixes and suffixes (with slight modifications) are used with nouns, to show possession:

Table 12.1. Illustration of Three Consonants in Western Cree

	I	it is windy	sand	it goes well	one	properly	man	my dog
Plains Cree	niya	yo·tin	ye·kaw	miyopayiw	pe·yak	kwayask	na·pe·w	nite·m
Woods Cree	niða	ðo·tin	ðe·kaw	miðopaðiw	pe·yak	kwayask	na·pe·w	nite·m
West Swampy Cree	nina	no·tin	ne·kaw	minopaniw	pe·yak	kwayask	na·pe·w	nite·m
East Swampy Cree	nina	no·tin	ne·kaw	minopaniw	pe·yak	kwayask	na·pe·w	nite·m
Moose Cree	nila	lo·tin	le·kaw	milopaliw	pe·yak	kwayask	na·pe·w	nite·m
Attikamet	nira	ro·tin	re·kaw	miropariw	pe·yak	kwayas	na·pe·w	nite·m

Note: The first four words contain /y, ð, n, l, r/, depending on dialect. The next two contain /y/ in all dialects. (Based on Wolfart 1981 and Rhodes and Todd 1981.)

ni-moso·m	'my grandfather'
ki-moso·m	'your grandfather'
o-moso·m	'his, her grandfather'
ni-moso·m-ina·n	'our (exclusive) grandfather'
ki-moso·m-inaw	'our (inclusive) grandfather'

One last feature to be mentioned is the category of **obviative.** When there are two actors, the more prominent (called the **proximate**) is unmarked, while the less prominent, or obviative, takes an obviative suffix *–a*. The obviative has a number of grammatical functions, one of which is to indicate which noun (in this case *na·pe·w* 'man', and *atim(w)* 'dog') is subject or object: *Wa·pame·w na·pe·w atimw-a.* 'The man saw the dog'. *Wa·pame·w na·pe·w-a atim.* 'The dog saw the man'. Recall that Cree distinguishes between two genders, animate and inanimate (section 2.2). Only animate nouns, like *atim* 'dog', distinguish the obviative. In Plains Cree, an inanimate noun, like *mo·hkoma·n* 'knife', is unchanged in this context: *Wa·pahtam na·pew mo·hkoma·n.* 'The man saw the knife'. (In this case the verb is *wa·paht-* 'to see [inan. obj.] rather than *wa·pam–* 'to see [anim. obj.]', because the object is 'knife'.) That 'knife' is unmarked is not surprising, since it would take a rather bizarre semantic context for 'the knife saw the man'.

Dialect Differences

While the similarities of the Cree dialects far outnumber their differences, the differences are prominent enough to enable a listener to determine where a speaker is from. One of the more important diagnostic phonetic features in Western Cree entails /y/ in the Plains Cree dialect. There are a number of words in Plains Cree that contain /y/, and in these words the other Western dialects always have /y/ as well; see 'one' and 'properly' (table 12.1). In Plains Cree, however, /y/ corresponds to other consonants in the other Western dialects; see "l," "it is windy," "sand," and "it goes well" in table 12.1.

There are two possible explanations for this sort of situation. One is that originally Cree had /y/ in all six of the example words and that in certain words the /y/ remained in all dialects, while in other words it changed in all dialects except Plains Cree. If this hypothesis were correct, we would expect to find something existing in the phonetic environment in one case and absent in the other; for example, that certain vowels followed or preceded /y/ when it changed or other vowels when it remained the same. We do not find this to be the case. We can, therefore, entertain a second hypothesis, namely, that Cree originally had two consonants. In Plains Cree one of these consonants became /y/ and merged with original /y/ while in the other dialects it developed in different directions. The question is: What was that sound

Table 12.2. Correspondences of the Three Consonants in Western Cree Dialects

Original Cree	*l	*y	*n
Plains Cree	y	y	n
Woods Cree	ð	y	n
West Swampy Cree	n	y	n
East Swampy Cree	n	y	n
Mosse Cree	l	y	n
Attikamek	r	y	n

originally? A likely candidate would be one of the consonants found in the other dialects, namely, /ð/ (as in Woods Cree), /n/ (as in West and East Swampy Cree), /l/ (as in Moose Cree), or /r/ (as in Attikamek). We can eliminate the possibility of /n/, since this consonant is found in all Western Cree dialects in certain words (for example 'man' and 'my dog' in table 12.1). But /ð/, /l/, and /r/ are all possibilities, inasmuch as these consonants are never found outside the pattern being discussed. Evidence from Eastern Cree and related Algonquian languages shows that the consonant was probably /l/; but even without this outside evidence, it is clear that the ancestral language, called Proto-Cree, had a contrast of three distinct consonants. This pattern is maintained in Woods Cree and Attikamek (along with Moose Cree), even though the particular phonetic value of the consonant has changed. Plains Cree and Swampy Cree, on the other hand, have both innovated, but in different ways. In Plains Cree, the original /l/ fell together with /y/. In Swampy Cree, this /l/ fell together with original /n/. This pattern is shown in table 12.2. The original or Proto-Cree consonants are marked with an asterisk to show that they are **reconstructed** forms. Reconstructed forms are always hypothetical forms. Since we are dealing with closely related dialects, the hypothesis for the existence of these three consonants in the protolanguage is a very strong one, especially for *y and *n; but one thing is quite certain: The ancestral language had a pattern of three distinct consonants, even if we cannot be absolutely sure of their phonetic value.

In one other area there is dialect variation in the Western Cree dialects that entails the consonants, namely, a variation between /š/ and /s/. These sounds are kept distinct in East Swampy Cree, Moose Cree, and Attikamek, as seen in *ši·ši·p* 'duck', contrasted with *sa·kahikan* 'lake'. On the other hand /š/ and /s/ fall together in Plains Cree, Woods Cree, and West Swampy Cree, as in *si·si·p* and *sa·kahikan*. We must reconstruct Proto-Cree, then, with the two consonants *s and *š; thus the total consonant inventory for Proto-Cree includes the eight found in Plains Cree, *p, *t, *č, *k, *s, *h, *m, *n, plus two additional ones, *l and *š.

There are two important phonological characteristics that mark the major division between Western and Eastern Cree. One is the change in the eastern dialects of /k/ to /č/ before front vowels: Western Cree ki·we·w, but Eastern Cree čiwew 'he goes home'. The other is the reinterpretation in the eastern dialects of the contrast of vowel quantity (i.e., long and short vowels) to one of vowel quality. Most western Cree dialects preserve the original pattern with /i·, e·, a·, o·/ and /i, a, o/, while the Eastern dialects have /i, e, a, o/ and /ɪ, ə, u/.

The Cree dialects, like dialects of all languages, are not static. There are generational differences and changes that spread from community to community. In some Montagnais communities, for example, a change of [šk] and [šp] to [x] and [ɸ] is taking place, a change that has left older speakers unaffected:

Older Speakers	*Younger Speakers*	
nöškat	nəxat	'my leg'
əšpmöt	ɸmət	'up'

One of the more striking differences between the dialects pertains to the differences between slow and careful versus fast and casual speech. In some dialects, vowels between certain consonants are omitted. An example from Plains Cree, which often omits vowels between /n/ and /s/, and between /s/ and /t/:

Kinisitohtawin či·?	'Do you understand me?' (slow speech)
Kinstohtawin či·?	(same sentence, fast speech)

Another example from Plains Cree:

niki·nipa·n	'I had slept' (slow speech)
nki·npa·n	(faster speech)
ŋgi·mpa·n	(still faster speech)

Thus the /i/ in the sequence /nik/ is dropped, which brings the voiced nasal /n/ into contact with the voiceless velar stop /k/; the nasal changes to velar /ŋ/, the position of articulation for /k/, and the /k/ in turn becomes voiced /g/, now being next to the voiced nasal. In some Cree dialects, the nasal is dropped, so that the first person prefix ("I") is signaled solely by the change of voiceless to voiced of the stem initial stop. There are two important facts involving these changes: first, while most of the dialects have optional changes of this sort for fast speech, the details of the rules change somewhat from dialect to dialect; second, certain rules that are optional in some dialects have become obligatory in others. The end result is that there is greater similarity across dialects in slow speech than in fast speech.

The dialects display not only variation in phonology, but also in vocabulary and grammar; as with phonology, however, the differences are not major. The word for 'canoe' offers an example: In most of the Cree-speaking area the word is *o·ši* (or *o·si*, in those dialects that have lost the contrast between /š/ and /s/), but in some Plains Cree communities it is *ci·ma·n*. For grammar, most of the features we have sketched for Plains Cree are shared by other dialects: the distinction between ani-mate and inanimate nouns, between singular and plural nouns, and between prox-imate and obviate nouns, the same person affixes for verbs and nouns, and so on. There are differences in detail, so that, for example, some Plains Cree dialects treat *so·niya·w* 'gold, money' as an inanimate noun (where, in terms of a natural classi-fication, we would expect to find it), while others treat it as an animate noun. In another case, most dialects do not distinguish the obviative for inanimate nouns, but East Swampy and Mistassini Cree do; thus, the obviative suffix *–iniw* is used with inanimate nouns (like 'knife') in East Swampy Cree, but not in Plains Cree:

Wa·pahtam mo·hkoma·n.	'He saw the knife'. (Plains Cree)
Wa·pahtam mo·hkoma·n-iniw.	(same sentence, East Swampy Cree)

The pattern of dialect variation within the Cree language is well represented in these samples. The deepest and most basic division is in the Western and Eastern dialects. However, we repeat that division into discrete dialects should not be taken too seriously. In the Eastern Cree area, in particular, the dialect changes are gradual and result in a **dialect continuum.** In Western Cree, the dialect divisions are a bit more sharply defined; however, there is variation within the six delineated dia-lects. The dialect boundaries are rather fuzzy, because most of the dialect features do not correspond exactly to proposed dialect divisions; for example, an innova-tion that characterizes Woods Cree from other dialects is a change of /e·/ to /i·/; thus *me·skanaw* 'road' and *pe·yak* 'one', as it is pronounced by most Cree speakers, is pronounced *mi·skanaw* and *pi·yak* in Woods Cree. This innovation, however, is shared by some of the adjacent Plains Cree communities.

Many Cree speakers have been very mobile, in pre-Columbian times as well as today, which has led, over time, to the intermingling of speakers of different dialects, to a high degree of bidialectalism and even multidialectalism, and to the transporting of dialect features to speakers of diverse dialects. Such developments have made the delineation of dialects for the Cree language (and for that matter for most languages) often somewhat arbitrary and, consequently, make difficulties for the mapping of both dialect and language boundaries, a common problem for many American Indian languages.

Dialect development is the result of two factors: linguistic change and isolation. The isolation may be either geographical or social, but in unstratified societies it is almost always geographical. Some of the variation that is natural to all languages becomes ossified with the passing of time and the generations. If the language is spoken in a single community, the result is simply linguistic change; but more commonly the language is spoken in several communities, which may be isolated from each other. In that case, the changes are independent so that the resulting speech in each community is dialectally distinct. Almost never is the isolation complete, however. Speakers are aware of the dialect differences found in neighboring communities, and these differences can then feed into the linguistic flux found in all communities. Neighboring dialects can influence each other, and dialect features can spread. Other things being equal (and of course often they are not), the greater the geographic extent of a language, the greater the isolation, which in turn leads to greater dialect variation.

Dialect variation can be considerable without having a great effect on intelligibility. In fact, intelligibility is the most common means of distinguishing dialects from languages: If two varieties of speech are mutually intelligible, they are dialects of the same language; if not, they are distinct and separate languages. There are, however, two problems. First, what constitutes mutual intelligibility? People speaking divergent dialects may be able to communicate effectively when speaking slowly and carefully and when the topic of conversation is narrowly defined, but they may be utterly lost in the give-and-take of everyday informal rapid conversation. There is a drop, but not an absence, of intelligibility at the borders between some of the Western Cree dialects, for example between Plains and Woods Cree, between Woods and Western Swampy Cree, and between Western and Eastern Swampy Cree. Second, dialect variation may be gradual throughout an area, so that there are few or no clear dialect or language breaks, yet the varieties of speech at two ends of a dialect continuum may be different enough to be mutually unintelligible. It is very likely, for example, that speakers of Cree at the far western end (Plains Cree) and the far eastern end (Montagnais) would find it very difficult or impossible to understand each other. The distinction between dialect and language is, nevertheless, a useful one, which can be ignored in those cases in which the facts or the interpretation of the facts are not clear.

12.2 THE UTO-AZTECAN FAMILY

The Uto-Aztecan language family consists of approximately thirty languages spoken over a wide area in Mesoamerica and the western United States. In our examination of the Cree dialects, we saw that there were slight differences in vocabulary, phonology, and grammar. In the case of the Uto-Aztecan languages, the differences are

Table 12.3. Basic Vocabulary Items in Seven Uto-Aztecan Languages

	Shoshone	Tubatulabal	Luiseño	Hopi	Guarijío	Cora	Nahuatl
nose	mupi	mupi·-t	múvi-l	yaqa	yahk-a	cuʔuri	yaka-ƛ
ear	nenki	naŋha-l	náq-la	naq-vi	nahk-a	našai	naka-·s-ƛi
eye	puih	punzi-l	púš-la	po·si	pusi	hiʔi	i·š-telolo-ƛ
tooth	tama	taman-t	tamá-t	tama	tamé	tamé	ƛan-ƛi
breast	pici	pi·-l	pi·-t	pi·-ht	čiči	ciʔi-mé	čičiwal-li
heart	pihyi	su·na-l	sún-la	inaŋʷt	sulá	sáihnʸuʔuka-ri	yo·l-o-·ƛ
bone	cuhmi	o·-n	kuká·wu·-t	ö·qa	oʔá	karí	omi-ƛ
urinate	si·	ši·tt	ši·ʔa-	sisiuki	siʔa-ní	séʔe	a·síši
excrement	kʷita-ppih	ša·-l	ša·ʔi-š	kʷita	wihtá	čʷitá	kʷiƛa-ƛ
tail	kʷesi	wiši·	-piqʷsiv	siri	wahsí	kʷasí	kʷiƛa-pil-li
dog	sati·	puku-biš-t	awá-l	po·ko	čuhčú-ri	čiʔi	či·č·
moon	mia	mi·ya-bis-t	m-oy-la	mɨ·yawɨ	mečá	máškiraʔi	me·c-ƛi
water	pa·	pa·-l	pa·-la	pa·-ht	paʔwí	háh	a-·ƛ
stone	tim-pi	tɨn-t	to·-ta	owa	tehté	tʼetʼé	te·ƛ
salt	ona-pi	o·na-l	eŋ-la	oŋʷa	oná	unáh	ista-ƛ
road	poʔe	poh-t	pé-t	pö·-ht	poé	huyé	oʔ-ƛi
two	waha-	wo·-	wéh	lö·yö-m	woká	wáʔapwa	o·-me
dry	pasa	wa·g-it	a-wáx-ve	la·qu	wagi-ná	wáči	i·š-wa·k-ki
heavy	pɨtɨ	pɨłiʔ	wima-	pɨtɨ	pehté-ni	tʼi-hetʼe	et-k
stand	wɨnɨ-	ɨ-wɨn-	wɨ·ta	wɨnɨ	weri	áh-če-si	iʔka-·k
give	uttu	maha	óvi-	maqa	kiʔá-ni	-ša	maka
die	tiai	mu·g-it	piʔ-muk	mo·ki	mugu-ná	mɨʔɨ	miki

much greater, because the **time depth** is much greater, that is, the span of time from when the ancestral or protolanguage was spoken to the present. In families of closely related languages, such as Germanic, Romance, or Algonquian, the similarities are obvious, and so is the fact that the languages are genetically related. But the similarities are not immediately obvious between languages in families, such as Indo-European or Uto-Aztecan, in which the languages are more distantly related. In such cases careful analysis is necessary for discovering them.

Cognates and Regular Sound Correspondences

We begin our analysis by examining **basic vocabulary:** everyday words that are learned early in life, such as body parts, natural phenomena, basic activities, terms for closely related kin, and the like. These words are more resistant to replacement and are less apt to be borrowed than others. Some basic vocabulary items are listed in table 12.3. A casual inspection shows similarities in some of the words; for example the word for 'ear' is similar in all seven languages, as is the word for 'stone' in all languages but Hopi. If we can show that these similarities are the result of their derivation from a common source in the protolanguage, we refer to them as **cognates.** While the search for cognates begins by looking for similarities, we shall see that similarity is not the necessary characteristic for establishing the fact that given vocabulary items are cognate.

For a variety of reasons not all the basic vocabulary items in table 12.3 are cognate. Although such words are more resistant to replacement than those less basic, they can be replaced, which is apparently what happened to the word for 'stone' in Hopi, and in a number of other cases in which a given language seems not to have a cognate form. In some cases, the cognate is preserved, but with a change in the meaning. For example, Hopi does preserve the old word for "stone" in words like *tɨmkᵞe* 'edge of a cliff'. Also Shoshoni *pihyɨ* 'heart' is not cognate with any of the other words that are listed in table 12.3, but there is a prefix *sun–* 'with the mind' that goes with these words. Likewise Hopi *ináŋʷɨ* 'heart' is not cognate, but *só:na* 'seed' is. Shoshoni *uttu* 'give' finds no cognate in the chart, but *maka–* 'feed' (i.e., 'give food') does. In some cases, as in the word for 'nose', a given item seems to have two cognate sets: The more northern languages (Shoshoni, Tubatulabal, and Luiseño) seem to share one cognate, while the more southern languages (Hopi, Guarijío, and Aztec) seem to share another. It turns out, however, that some of the more northern languages do in fact preserve the southern cognate, but with the meaning 'point'; for example Tubatulabal *yahaawi-t* 'summit, point'. Proto-Uto-Aztecan, then, had the word **yaka*, but it is not clear if the original meaning was 'nose', or 'point', or both.

We start by looking for phonetically similar items in the basic vocabulary items but, because we know that words can change their meanings, we can also find

Table 12.4. Cognate Sets in Seven Uto-Aztecan Languages

	Shoshone	Tubatulabal	Luiseño	Hopi	Guarijío	Cora	Nahuatl
water	pa·	pa-	pá-	pa-	paʔw	háh	a-
tooth	tama	taman-	tamá	tama	tamé	tamé	λan-
dry		wa·g-	-wáx-	la·q	wagi-	wáči	-wa·k-
nose (1)				yaqa	yakó		yaka-
give		maha		maqa			maka
ear	nenki	naŋha-	náq-	naq-	nahká	našai	naka-
tail	kʷesi	wiší·	—qʷsi-		wahsí	kʷasí	
stone	tïm-	tïn	tó·-		tehté	tʼetʼe	te-
heavy	pitti	pïtï?		pitï	pehté-	-hetʼe	eti-
moon	mïa	mï·ya-	móy-	mï·ya-	mečá		me·c-
stand	wïnï-	ïwïn-		wïnï	weri		
road	poʔe	poh-	pé-	pö·	poé	huyé	oʔ-
bone		o-		o·qa	oʔá		omí-
two		wo·-	wéh	lö·yö	wokó		o-
salt	ona-	o·na-	eŋ-	o·ŋʷa	onó	unáh	
breast (1)	pici	pi-	pí-	pi-			
breast (2)					cičí	ciʔi-	cičiwal-
urinate	si·	si-	si·ʔa-	sisi-	siʔa-		-šiša
excrement	kʷita-	punzi-	púš-	kʷita	wihtá	cʷitá	kʷiλa-
eye	puïh	mupi-	mú·vi-	po·si	pusí	híʔï	ïš-
nose (2)	mupi	su·na-	sún-				
heart					sulá		
die		mu·g-	-muk	mo·ki	mugu-	mïʔï	miki
dog (1)				po·ko			
dog		puku-			cuhčú-ri	či·čí·	ci·čí·

Note: The Tubatulabal word for (tail) is probably cognate, but the first vowel does not match the regular correspondences.

Table 12.5. Uto-Aztecan Vowel Correspondences in Initial Syllables

Shoshone	a, e	ɨ	o	i	u
Tubatulabal	a	ɨ	o	i	u
Luiseño	a	o	e	i	u
Hopi	a	ɨ	ö	i	o
Guarijío	a	e	o	i	u
Cora	a	e	o	i	ɨ
Nahuatl	a	e	o	i	i
Proto-Uto-Aztecan	*a	*ɨ	*o	*i	*u

Notes:

*a supported by: "water," "tooth," "dry," "nose (1)," "give," "ear," "tail";

*ɨ supported by: "stone," "heavy," "moon," "stand";

*o supported by: "road," "bone," "two," "salt";

*i supported by: "breast (1)," "breast (2)," "urinate," "excrement";

*u supported by: "eye," "nose (2)," "heart," "die," "dog (1)," "dog (2)."

cognate items with different but related meanings. What is to prevent us from searching the vocabulary of a given language for words that are phonetically similar to words in another language, whether or not they mean the same thing, and simply declaring them to be cognate? In our discussion of Cree *l, *y, and *n, we noted that *l changed to another sound in some of the dialects, while *y and *n remained unchanged. It is the regularity of sound change, which leads to (**regular**) **sound correspondences**, that provides the necessary safeguard. However, because the relationship of the Uto-Aztecan languages is distant, we can expect that the languages will display a larger number of sound changes, illustrated by a smaller number of cognates, than was the case for Cree. Further, the greater number of sound changes may obscure some of the similarities so that some cognates might not be discovered on the first pass.

By omitting the noncognate material and by stripping away prefixes and affixes so only roots are left (table 12.4), we can more readily observe the sound correspondences. The cognates are also reordered so as to illustrate the vowel correspondences of the initial syllable. These correspondences, along with the reconstructed Proto-Uto-Aztecan vowels, are given in table 12.5.

The data for reconstructing the consonants can be organized in a similar fashion. Table 12.6 is a list of a number of Uto-Aztecan cognate sets, arranged to illustrate initial consonant correspondences, all of which are given in table 12.7. In some cases, there are multiple correspondences, which in each case are explainable in terms of

Table 12.6. Uto-Aztecan Cognate Sets, Illustrating Initial Consonant Correspondences

	Shoshone	Tubatulabal	Luiseño	Hopi	Guarijío	Cora	Nahuatl	Proto-Uto-Aztecan
water	pá·	pa·-	pá-	pa·-	paʔwí	háh	a·-	*p-
stone	tɨm-	tɨn	tó·-		tehté	tʼetʼe	te-	*t-
tooth	tama	taman-	tamá-	tama	tamé	tamé	λan-	*t-
bitter			čí·v		cihpú-	-cíh-viʔi		*c-
hair, head	co-	čomo·-					con-	*c-
suckle, breast		ci·n			čiʔí-	ciʔí-	čiči	*c
sit	katɨ	halti-	qál-	qalti-	kahti	-kaɪ		*k-
house	kahni	hanii·-		qeni	karí		kal-	*k-
husband	kuhma	ku·ŋa	-kú·ŋ	ko·ŋʸa	kuná	-kin		*k-
bite (k)	ki-	kiʔt	kóʔi-	kɨ·(ki)		-čéʔe	keʔ(coma)	*k-
excrement	kʷita-		-qʷsi-	kʷita	wihtá	cʷitá	kʷiλa-	*kʷ
tail	kʷesi	-wiši·			wahsí	kʷasí		*kʷ-
urinate	sɨ·	sɨ-	sɨ·ʔa-	sɨsɨ	siʔa-		-šiša	*s-
cold	sɨ-	sɨ(ʔbɨ)-	su(vó)-	sɨsɨ(ŋ)	seh(ko)-	-se·		*s-
moon	mɨa	mɨ·ya-	móy-	mɨ·ya-	mečá		me·c-	*m-
hand	ma-	ma-	má-	ma-	ma(tála)	mʷá(hkaʔa)	ma·-	*m-
nose	nenki	naŋha-	náq-	naq-	nahká	na(šaɪ)	naka·-	
dry		wa·g-	-wáx-	la·qu	wagi-	wáči	-wa·k-	*w-
stand	wɨni-	ɨ·wɨn-		wɨnɨ	werí			*w-
pine	wonko-	wo·ŋha-	wixéʔ(tu)-	löqö	wohkó		oko-	*w-
nose	ya·	yaha·(wi)-	yá·w-	yaqa	yahká		yaka-	*y-
carry	ya·		yá·w-	ya·w-				*y-
stick, arrow	hu·-	ʔu·-	hú·-	ho·-	uá	iʔí(ri)		*h-
wind	hu·-	ʔa·ka(wa·)-		hɨ·kʼaʳ(ŋʷ)	ega-	éka	eʔe·ka-	*h-

Note: Only roots are listed, with noncognate material placed in parentheses. There are meaning changes in some languages, which are not indicated. The initial consonant of the Proto-Uto-Aztecan word is reconstructed and indicated by an asterisk.

Table 12.7. Uto-Aztecan Consonant Correspondences in Initial Syllables

	*p	*t	*c	*k	*kʷ	*s	*m	*n	*w	*y	*h
Shoshone	p	t	c	k	kʷ	s	m	n	w	y	h
Tubatulabal	p	t	c, č	k, h	w	s, š	m	n	w	y	Ø
Luiseño	p	t	c	k, q	kʷ, qʷ	s, ṣ, s	m	n	w	y	h
Hopi	p	t	c	k, q	kʷ	s	m	n	w, l	y	h
Guarijío	p	t	č	k	w	s	m	n	w	y	Ø
Cora	h	t, tʸ	c	k, č	kʷ, cʷ	s	m, mʷ	n	w	y	Ø
Nahuatl	Ø	t, λ	c, č	k	kʷ	s, š	m	n	w	y	Ø
Proto-Uto-Aztecan	*p	*t	*c	*k	*kʷ	*s	*m	*n	*w	*y	*h

Note: Ø indicates "nothing," that is, the consonant is dropped.

the phonetic environment. For example: in Hopi, Proto-Uto-Aztecan *w > /l/ before the vowels /a/ and /o/, but remains /w/ before other vowels; in Cora, Proto-Uto-Aztecan *k and *kʷ > /č/ and /čʷ/, respectively, before the front vowels /i/ and /e/, but remain /k/ and /kʷ/ before other vowels. The other multiple correspondences (*k > Tubatulabal /k, h/, and Luiseño and Hopi /k, q/; *t > Aztec /t, tl/; etc.) can be explained in a similar fashion.

This discussion does not exhaust the Uto-Aztecan sound changes. There are certain changes of consonants in noninitial position that are different from those in initial position; consonants in final position must be reconstructed; and many of the languages have contrastive vowel length that must be taken into consideration. But, in principle, the procedure is the same as that illustrated for vowels and initial consonants.

It should be clear by now that the search for cognates is not simply a search for similar sounding words, but is a search for words that fit into a matrix of regular sound correspondences. The initial search must involve basic vocabulary and words of identical meaning. Once the sound correspondences have been identified, we can include words of changed meaning; for instance, we can count Shoshoni *sun*– 'with the mind' and Hopi *so:na* 'seed' as cognate with the word for 'heart' in other Uto-Aztecan languages. The establishment of sound-correspondence patterns also allows us to recognize as cognates words that are phonetically very different. What is required is not phonetic similarity, but strict adherence to the sound correspondences. The cognate set for *pu:si 'eye' illustrates this point: Shoshoni *puih* and Aztec *i·š*– share, phonetically, very little; however, they fit the sound correspondences. In Shoshoni, vowel length is lost and medial *s is lost in certain environments; in Aztec, initial *p is lost, *u become [i], *s becomes [š] before *i, and final short vowels are lost. The characterization of these changes is not made on an ad hoc basis, but on the basis of a number of cognate sets that demonstrate the validity of the sound changes (not all of which have been illustrated here); for example, the loss of *p in initial position in Aztec is illustrated not only in 'eye', but also in 'road' and 'water', as well as many others not shown here.

Loanwords

One of the values of searching for systematic correspondences is that it allows us to distinguish vocabulary similarities that have a different historical explanation. An example is provided by Guarijío, a language spoken in two varieties, the River dialect and the Mountain dialect. The word for 'tobacco' is *pipá* in River Guarijío, while it is *wipá* in Mountain Guarijío. Cognates in other Uto-Aztecan languages include Luiseño *pí·va-t*, Hopi *pi·va-t*, and Mayo *bí·ba-m*, and the Proto-Uto-Aztecan root can be reconstructed as *pi·pa. We have already seen that initial Proto-Uto-

Aztecan *p should remain unchanged in Guaríjío (see 'water', 'heavy', 'road', and 'eye'), which then would indicate that the word in River Guaríjío is cognate, while in Mountain Guaríjío it is not. We find, however, that initial Proto-Uto-Aztecan *p has undergone a change to /w/ in the Tepiman languages; further, Mountain Guaríjío borders the Tepiman languages, while River Guaríjío does not. 'Tobacco' is not a basic vocabulary item, but rather belongs to cultural vocabulary (tobacco is of ceremonial significance in most American Indian communities), which means that borrowing is more likely than with basic vocabulary items. (The utility for distinguishing cognates from loanwords for studying culture history in discussed in the next chapter.)

Internal Classification

The Uto-Aztecan languages are found in two geographically separated locations, with a northern group found in the western United States, and a southern group stretching from northwest Mexico southward into Central America (see map 12.1). Do these two geographic units also reflect linguistic units? They probably do, but before we discuss the case at hand, we must discuss some general questions of internal classification.

In our discussion of the Cree dialects, we noted that language change is universal and, further, that if a given language is spoken in more than one community, it will change in different directions in each community. At first, the differences are dialectal, as in the Cree case, but given more time, the dialects will evolve into mutually unintelligible languages. Each of these languages is itself a potential protolanguage, which can develop diverse dialects and, next, distinct languages.

Returning now to the Uto-Aztecan languages, we can rephrase the question as follows: Are each of the geographic units, the northern and southern Uto-Aztecan languages, derived from their own respective intermediate protolanguages? If they are, they would constitute two **branches** within the language family and we would expect languages within a branch to share greater similarity in phonology, vocabulary, and grammar than those outside the branch. Sometimes the question of greater similarity is obvious. In these two cases, it is not, so we resort to a search for **shared innovations.** These are changes common to a group of languages that would place them into a branch and would imply an intermediate protolanguage. There are three clear cases of shared innovations for the southern languages (> = "becomes"): Proto-Uto-Aztecan *ɨ > Southern Uto-Aztecan *e, Proto-Uto-Aztecan medial *n > Southern Uto-Aztecan *l (and in some languages further becomes /r/ in certain environments), and Proto-Uto-Aztecan medial *ŋ > Southern Uto-Aztecan *n. For example Proto-Uto-Aztecan *su·na 'heart' > Guaríjío sulá (cf. Hopi so·na); Proto-Uto-Aztecan *o·ŋa 'salt' > Cora ʔuná (cf. Luiseño éŋ-la); and Proto-Uto-Aztecan

Map 12.1.—The Uto-Aztecan language family.

*pɨtɨ 'heavy' > Guarijío *pehté*, Cora *–hetʸe* (cf. Shoshoni *pɨttɨ*, Tubatulabal *pɨtɨʔ*). (In some of the southern languages, Southern Uto-Aztecan *l has further become /r/ in certain environments; and Proto-Uto-Aztecan medial *ŋ has also become /n/ in Shoshoni; but this is clearly an independent development, since languages very closely related to Shoshoni and belonging to the same subbranch still retain /ŋ/.)

The reader might ask how we know that the direction of change is in fact as we have given it. How do we know that Proto-Uto-Aztecan did not originally have medial *l, medial *n, and *e, which changed to /n/, /ŋ/, and /ɨ/ in the northern languages? In such a case, the northern languages would be the innovators, with the evidence for subgrouping the northern rather than the southern languages into a genetic subgroup. Unfortunately, to demonstrate that the changes were in the direction we have given them would take us too far afield in a technical discussion.

Concerning the northern languages, some Uto-Aztecan scholars claim that there is evidence of shared innovations that would allow for the positing of a Northern Uto-Aztecan branch. The evidence, however, is less clear than for the southern languages, so that this is still an open question. In the classification that follows, a northern branch is not assumed:

1. Numic
    A. Western Numic: Mono, Northern Paiute
    B. Central Numic: Panamint, Shoshoni, Comanche
    C. Southern Numic: Kawaiisu, Ute-Southern Paiute
2. Tubatulabal
3. Takic
    A. Serrano-Gabrielino (extinct): Serrano, Kitanemuk, Gabrielino
    B. Cupan: Cupeño, Cahuilla, Luiseño
4. Hopi
5. Southern Uto-Aztecan
    A. Sonoran
        a. Tepiman: O'odham, Mountain Piman, Northern Tepehuan, Southern Tepehuan
        b. Tarahumaran: Tarahumara, Guarijío
        c. Opatan (extinct): Opata, Eudeve
        d. Cahita (two dialects, Mayo and Yaqui)
        e. Tubar (extinct)
        f. Corachol: Cora, Huichol
    B. Aztecan: General Aztec (many Nahuatl dialects, including Classical Aztec), Pipil, and Pochutec (extinct)

This classification implies sudden splits and a number of intermediate proto-languages, which can be represented in a tree diagram (see figure 12.1). There are problems, however; for example, the Corachol languages (Cora and Huichol) spoken in the mountains of the Mexican state of Nayarit, are the southernmost of the Sonoran languages and are still today in closest geographic proximity to the Aztecan languages. Phonologically, grammatically, and lexically, therefore, they should be grouped with the Sonoran languages rather than with Aztecan. To give one illustration: Proto-Uto-Aztecan *n in medial position became a retroflex (= tongue curled up, as in English [r]) consonant, usually retroflex [ɽ] (as in Cora and Huichol), though

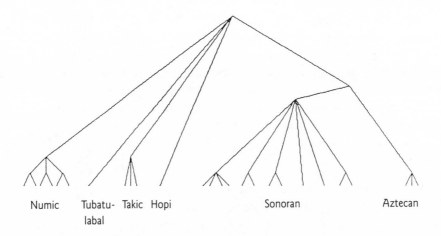

Numic   Tubatu- Takic Hopi   Sonoran   Aztecan
          labal

Figure 12.1.—Uto-Aztecan Family Tree. Major branches rather than individual languages are labeled.

in some Sonoran languages it is a retroflex [ḷ] (see 'house' and 'stand', table 12.6).
In the Aztecan languages, however, this consonant became a dental [l]. Nevertheless, Cora and Huichol do have some features that link them with the Aztecan languages; for example, Proto-Uto-Aztecan initial *p became [h] in Cora and Huichol,
and was dropped in the Aztecan languages; probably the change in Aztec was by
way of [h], that is to say, the change was from *p to an intermediate *h, and then
was dropped. In a similar fashion, Proto-Uto-Aztecan *u, a back rounded vowel,
became a back unrounded vowel, [ɨ], in Cora and Huichol, and then it was fronted
to a front unrounded [i] (and fell together with original *i) in Aztec.

Tubatulabal presents another example. This language shares certain features with
the Numic languages to the east, and still different features with the Takic languages to the south. If the Takic languages did not exist, we might be tempted to
classify the Numic languages as one branch and Tubatulabal as a second branch of
a still larger grouping within Uto-Aztecan. If, on the other hand, the Numic languages did not exist, we would be tempted to group Tubatulabal and Takic into a
larger grouping (see figure 12.2).

What is the cause of these patterns? A family-tree classification presupposes
sudden cleavages, as well as lack of contact and mutual influence after splits have
taken place. Very seldom do either of these two things happen. More commonly,
divergent varieties of speech slowly develop from similar dialects into distinct languages. In section 12.1 we saw that one can seldom draw sharp boundaries between

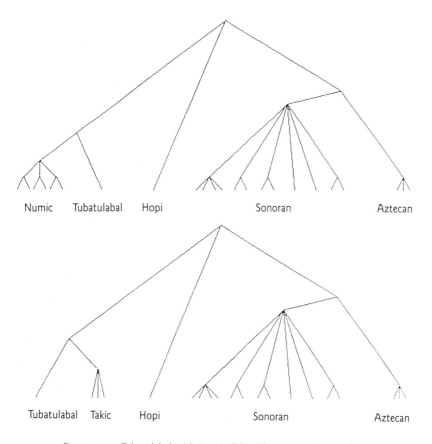

Numic   Tubatulabal   Hopi   Sonoran   Aztecan

Tubatulabal   Takic   Hopi   Sonoran   Aztecan

Figure 12.2.—Tubatulabal with Numic/Takic. The upper diagram shows
the apparent grouping of Tubatulabal with Numic if the Takic branch is
not taken into consideration. The lower diagram shows the apparent
grouping of Tubatulabal with Takic if the Numic branch is not taken into
consideration.

dialects; they intergrade, forming a **dialect chain** or **net.** As time passes and
the differences between the dialects become more pronounced, they develop into
closely related but mutually unintelligible languages. If population movements or
other disturbing factors have not come into play, the old intergraded dialect relationships may still be reflected. It is also common for speakers of these languages
to be in contact with one another, so that changes in the various languages are
not independent; instead, there is mutual influence in the direction of the changes,

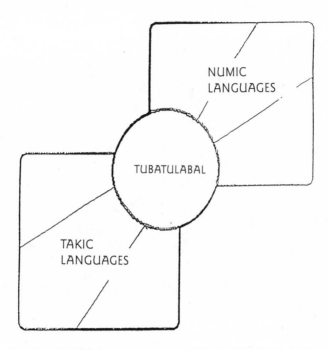

Figure 12.3.—Numic branch, Tubatulabal, and Takic branch of Uto-Aztecan, represented by a net diagram.

which leads to the situation reflected by the Corachol languages and by Tubatulabal. Such patterns can better be shown in the form of a net (see figure 12.3).

Time Depth, Dating, and Glottochronology

The time depth of the various branches in Uto-Aztecan is variable. The Numic languages are very closely related and very similar to each other. The degree of difference between the languages is comparable to that of the Romance languages, which would put Proto-Numic at about two thousand years. The Takic languages are somewhat more diverse than the Germanic languages, which would give them a time depth of three thousand to thirty-five hundred years. The Southern Uto-Aztecan group has a time depth of about four thousand years. Uto-Aztecan as a whole is about as diverse as Indo-European or perhaps slightly more so, so that the time depth is somewhere between five and six thousand years.

This method of dating involves making an educated guess. There is another method, called **glottochronology,** which can be applied in a more objective fashion, but the resulting dates are not necessarily any more accurate. The method calibrates changes in vocabulary and time depth. All aspects of language, phonological, grammatical, and lexical, change in time, but only lexical changes can be counted and quantified in a more or less consistent fashion.

Because it is assumed that basic vocabulary changes more slowly and, more importantly, that basic vocabulary changes at a constant rate, only basic vocabulary is used. The assumption of a constant rate of change is critical for the method and it should be noted that there are critics who do not feel that the assumption has been proven. The method utilizes a standard list of one hundred basic vocabulary terms and compares pairs of languages to determine the percentage of cognate forms in the list; thus for 'heart' Tubatulabal *su·na-l* and Luiseño *sún-la* count as cognate, while Tubatulabal *su·na-l* and Hopi *inaŋʷi* do not. Hopi has a cognate, *só·na* 'seed', but it is not counted in this case, because to be counted as "glottochronologically the same" the cognate must be retained with the same meaning. Based on test cases of languages with a long written history, it has been determined that a language will maintain about 81 percent of its glottochronological basic vocabulary over a thousand-year period. Two languages, then, derived from a protolanguage that was spoken one thousand years ago will retain 81 percent of the protolanguage's glottochronological basic vocabulary; since it is assumed that the changes are independent in the daughter languages, these two languages will share 65 percent between themselves, that is, 81 percent of 81 percent. After the percentages of cognates for each pair of languages are tabulated, the data can be arranged in cognate density charts, which can then be used for calculating the dates, using a formula derived from the test cases, to convert the percentages into years. See Table 12.8.

The method is not without its detractors. If it is to work at all, it must be applied very carefully, with the sound changes identified, so that true cognates can be counted. Note that Shoshoni *puih* and Aztec *i·š-* 'eye' would easily be missed if the sound correspondences had not been worked out. When a glottochronological date does not match the educated guess date, one suspects that the glottochronological date is inaccurate.

The cognate density charts can also be used for classification. In one sense, the use of vocabulary is not as useful for classifying as the data from phonology and grammar, because there is no way to determine shared innovations. But it often reflects old dialect nets and chain phenomena more readily; thus the intermediate position of Tubatulabal is apparent in table 12.8.

This discussion highlights a methodological problem in classification that relates to the influence that neighboring languages (related or not) can exert on one another, a pet topic of ours that is discussed in the next several sections.

Table 12.8.   Cognate Density of Twelve Uto-Aztecan Languages

Sh	Shoshoni (Central Numic)										
Cm	88	Comanche (Central Numic)									
SP	62	59	Southern Paiute (Southern Numic)								
Tb	38	35	39	Tubatulabal							
Sr	24	21	27	35	Serrano (Takic)						
Ca	27	24	31	38	50	Cahuilla (Takic)					
Ls	24	22	27	34	35	50	Luiseño (Takic)				
Hp	23	22	31	38	29	31	26	Hopi			
Oo	25	23	28	35	27	31	25	32	O'odham (Sonoran)		
Gu	23	24	25	36	34	34	28	32	44	Guarijío (Son.)	
Cr	23	21	22	30	21	24	22	26	34	42	Cora (Son.)
Az	16	14	16	24	22	23	19	24	29	32	37	Aztec

Note: Figures represent percentage of cognates, from a 100-item basic vocabulary, between pairs of languages. (From Miller, 1984:14.)

12.3   THE POSSESSION OF "PET": AN AREAL TRAIT IN THE SOUTHWEST

In Keres, one of the Pueblo languages of New Mexico, one cannot directly possess an animal. One cannot say, for example, "I have a chicken," or "my son has a horse." Instead, one must use the inalienably possessed noun –ad'á, which translates, roughly, as 'pet': "I have a (pet) chicken," or "my son has a (pet) horse." An example from the Acoma dialect: *kawâayu k'úučín'i s'a-**d'á** '*I had a palomino horse' (lit. 'horse yellow I-had-pet'). The word –ad'á is a **classifier,** a type of grammatical word that, as discussed in section 3.6, must be used in certain grammatical contexts. In this case, its use is limited to animal names, and it must be used whenever an animal is possessed.

The obligatory use of a pet classifier in the possession of animals is found in a number of languages in the southwestern United States and northwest Mexico. Some examples:

> Diegueño (Southern California, Yuman family): *ʔxaṭ ʔ–nʸ–xaṭ* 'I have a dog' (dog I-prefix-pet; the prefix nʸ– indicates the noun is alienably possessed.)

Seri (northwest Mexico, a language isolate): *sii kanao ʔi–x̣š* 'my cat'
(thing cat my-pet)
Serrano (southern California, Uto-Aztecan family, Takic branch):
pɨɨ–ʔašta–m kavaayuʔia–m 'their horses' (their-pet-plural
horse-plural)
Guarijío (northwest Mexico, Uto-Aztecan family, Sonoran branch):
noʔópuhku–wá cuʔcúri 'my dog' (my pet-possessive dog)
Washo (western Nevada and central California, a language isolate):
di–gúšuʔ síisu 'my bird' (my-pet bird)

In some languages, the use of a pet classifier is optional:

Walapai (Arizona, Yuman family): *waksí ña ʔ–wíi–v–č yu.* 'It's my
cow'. (cow I-have-the-subj. be)
or: *waksí ña ñi–hát–v–č yu.* 'It's my cow'. (cow I
prefix-pet-the-subj. be; the prefix *ñi–* is cognate to
the prefix in Diegueño that indicates the noun is
alienably possessed)
Hopi (Arizona, Uto-Aztecan family): *maana–t moosa–ʔat* 'the girl's
cat' (girl-'s cat-her)
ʔi–kʷáay–vooko 'my (pet) eagle' (my-eagle-pet)

In other languages its use is limited to certain contexts, for example, in Shoshoni
it is not used with animals that are ordinarily possessed, such as horse, mule or
dog, but it must be used with animals that are not ordinarily possessed, such as
chipmunk or robin: *nɨ muuta* 'my mule' (my mule), but *nɨ punku woʔi* 'my (pet)
chipmunk' (my pet chipmunk). When used without an animal term, the pet word
normally refers to the most typical domestic animal: 'dog' (e.g., Diegueño, Hopi,
Washo), 'horse' (e.g., Shoshoni), or 'cattle' (e.g., Guarijío). We translate the noun,
when used as a classifier, as 'pet'; this must be viewed, however, as a convenient
gloss (that is, a short, one-word translation for identification purposes), which does
not do justice to the full range of meanings found in the various languages, where
it is often a culturally charged word. In Luiseño for example, it is used for 'guard-
ian spirit', in O'odham, it is derived from a verb 'to be pitiful', while in some other
languages, it is related to words meaning 'slave', 'orphan', or 'adopted child'.

When a particular linguistic trait is shared by a number of contiguous languages,
one suspects there is a historical explanation. If the contiguous languages are genetically related, then one suspects the shared feature to be a common retention,
which is to say that the feature is a legacy from the ancestral language. If the feature is found in contiguous languages but crosscuts genetic boundaries, then one
suspects it is an **areal feature,** a shared trait that is the result of contact. The "pet"

classifier is an example, since it is found in two language families: Yuman (present in all of the languages except Kiliwa, the most southern Yuman language, spoken in Baja California) and Uto-Aztecan (present in the Numic, Tubatulabal, Takic, and Hopi branches, some of the languages of the Sonoran branch, and missing in the Aztecan branch). It is also found in three language isolates: Keres, Seri, and Washo. It is absent in all languages contiguous to these languages (see map 12.2).

The spread of a linguistic feature can be the result of direct borrowing, but more often the influence is indirect. In the case at hand, the word for "pet" has not been borrowed, as is evident by the fact that the form of the word is quite different from language group to language group. Instead, what has been borrowed is the use of an existing word, usually "dog," as a classifier.

The identification of the "pet" classifier as an areal feature is enhanced by two factors: the number of languages involved and the particularity of the feature. Chance could be an explanation if only two or three languages were involved. But chance is unlikely here, inasmuch as the feature is found in five genetic units that include over twenty-five languages. Chance is a more plausible explanation for linguistic features that are relatively common in the languages of the world, such as a contrast between voiced stops (e.g., [b, d, g]) and voiceless stops (e.g., [p, t, k]). The same is true of features for which there are limited possibilities, such as the relative position of the verb and direct object where there are only two possibilities: either the verb comes after or before the object (with or without intervening material, such as the subject). While the use of classifiers is not particularly rare in the languages of the world, two facts make this a somewhat more particular phenomenon: the classifier is used with "pets" or domesticated animals and it is used when the animal is possessed. It is unlikely that this constellation of traits arose independently more than once.

Genetic considerations often play a role and become intertwined with areal factors in such a way that it is often difficult to separate the effects of the two phenomena. In the Yuman examples, we saw that the "pet" word was ʔxaṭ in Diegueño, and hat in Walapai. There are cognate forms in all the Yuman languages that allow us to reconstruct Proto-Yuman *ʔxat. (The reader will have to take it on faith that the sound correspondences have been worked out in Yuman, in much the same way as illustrated earlier for Uto-Aztecan, so that this reconstruction is valid.) In all of the Yuman languages, the cognate forms mean 'dog'. It is also used as the "pet" classifier in all the Yuman languages except Kiliwa, a language in Baja California that is geographically most removed from the "pet" phenomenon as well as linguistically most distant within the Yuman family. There are two possible interpretations: either the pet classifier postdates Proto-Yuman and the split up of the ancestral language into the daughter languages so that *ʔxat meant only 'dog' in Proto-Yuman, or the word was used as a classifier in Proto-Yuman so that it meant both 'dog' and 'pet', but the classifier usage of 'pet' was lost in Kiliwa. If we con-

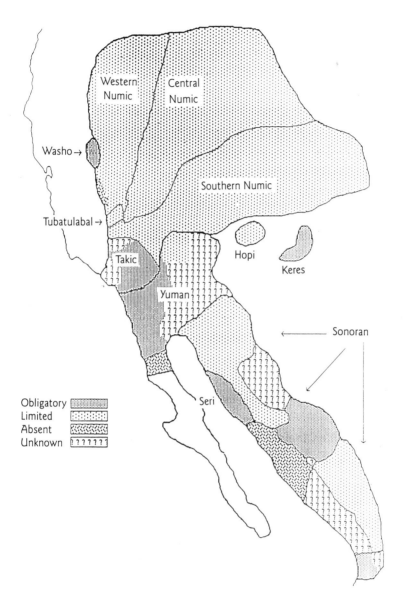

Map 12.2.—Distribution of the "pet" classifier used in possessive phrases.

sider only the Yuman evidence, the two hypotheses are equally attractive; but with
the evidence that we consider next, the first hypothesis is a little more probable.

The evidence within the Uto-Aztecan languages is less equivocal. As in Proto-
Yuman, the reconstructed word, *punku, probably meant 'dog'. Notice, however,
that the Takic languages do not use a word from *punku, but rather a word that in
Proto-Takic was *ʔáči-la; thus it is very unlikely that *punku was used as a classifier in Proto-Uto-Aztecan times, though the Proto-Takic *ʔáči-la might have been
so used.

Concerning the geographic origin for the "pet" classifier, we can postulate that
it arose in either Yuman or Takic languages, since these languages represent the core
area, both in terms of geography and intensity of usage. From there, it spread to the
other Uto-Aztecan languages, as well as to Seri, Keres, and Washo. We emphasize
again that it was the use of "pet" as a classifier that spread, not the word itself.

Proto-Uto-Aztecan has a greater time depth (five thousand or more years) than
Proto-Yuman (about four thousand years), which in turn has a greater time depth
than Proto-Takic (about three thousand years). Inasmuch as the evidence does not
support the use of the classifier as far back as Proto-Uto-Aztecan, it is not likely
that it came into use before Proto-Yuman; the most likely guess would be a point
of time between Proto-Yuman and Proto-Takic.

12.4 A LINGUISTIC AREA: MESOAMERICA

An area that contains a group of languages that share a cluster of features is referred to as a **linguistic area.** This term is used provided that there is convincing
evidence that the traits in question are the result of contact and not other factors
(e.g., chance or genetic inheritance), and provided that the area can be fairly clearly
delineated. We use the term **diffusional area** in those instances in which it is
clear that shared linguistic features are at least partly the result of contact, but it is
difficult to sort out with confidence the effect of genetic relationship and contact,
or to clearly define the geographic limits of areal influence. We discuss and give
an example of a linguistic area in this section and reserve discussion of diffusional
areas for sections 12.5 and 12.6.

Mesoamerica provides an excellent example of a linguistic area (see map 12.3).
The languages in question belong to several different language families:

1.   Otomanguean: a well-diversified language family of over
     twenty languages, belonging to eight branches. One language,
     Chichimeco Jonaz, and some varieties of Pame are outside the
     Mesoamerican area.

Map 12.3.—The Mesoamerican linguistic area (after Campbell, Kaufman, and Smith-Stark, 1986).

2. Aztecan: a branch of Uto-Aztecan that consists of three closely related languages. The other branches of Uto-Aztecan are to the north and outside the Mesoamerican area.

3. Totonacan: a family consisting of two languages.

4. Mixe-Zoquean: a family consisting of two branches, Mixean and Zoquean, with three languages in each branch.

5. Mayan: a family of thirty languages, belonging to five branches.

6. Tarascan: a linguistic isolate consisting of a single language.

7. Cuitlatec: a linguistic isolate consisting of a single language.

8.   Tequistlatecan: a linguistic isolate consisting of two languages.
9.   Huave: a linguistic isolate consisting of a single language.
10. Xinca: a linguistic isolate consisting of four languages.

(See appendix 2 for more details on the location of these languages.)

A rather large number of linguistic features are common to a number of Meso-american languages. Here we are only interested in those features that are diagnos-tic, that is, helpful in defining Mesoamerica as a linguistic area, and those that have these characteristics: (1) they are particular rather than common or near universal in the world's languages; (2) they are found widely throughout the languages in question; and (3) they do not extend beyond or much beyond the borders of the languages in question. We will look at four morphological and syntactic features that meet, or nearly meet, these criteria: They relate to noun possession, the num-ber system, basic word order, and locatives derived from body parts. We will also look at a number of calques, or loan translations, that are widely shared in the area.

The order of elements for noun possession places the possessed noun first, fol-lowed by the possessor, and the third person pronoun is prefixed to the possessed noun. For example:

> Quiché (Mayan): *u-c'i·ʔ le· ačih,* the man's dog (lit. his-dog
>   the man)
> Classical Aztec: *i-huanyolque cihuatl,* the woman's relatives (lit.
>   her-relatives woman)

The most common order is with the possessed noun first, followed by the posses-sor, but sometimes the order is reversed. Since there are only a limited number of ways of showing noun possession, the trait is not as particular as we might want (see section 2.1). But it is very striking that this method and order of elements is very common throughout the Mesoamerican languages, and that the languages bordering Mesoamerica do not use this method.

Almost all the Mesoamerican languages use a vigesimal number system (sec-tion 3.5). Some of the bordering languages (e.g., several of the Uto-Aztecan lan-guages in northwest Mexico) share this trait. It is, nevertheless, a rather particular trait, being one of the less common ways of forming numbers in the languages of the world.

All of the Mesoamerican languages place the object after the verb, sometimes immediately after (e.g., subject + verb + object), other times non-immediately (e.g., verb + subject + object). An example from Classical Aztec: *Auh i·wa·n niman iʔkʷa·k kitlatike in teo·kalli* 'And it was also when they burned the temple' ('and also then when they-burned the temple'). With only two orders possible, the trait is not as useful a characteristic as one might like, but in this case it is particularly striking that all the languages show this order, and that the Mesoamerican languages are surrounded by a sea of verb-final languages, with some marginal exceptions (e.g., some of the bordering Uto-Aztecan languages show both orders).

The last feature, which is morphological, has to do with locatives derived from body parts. Some examples from Mixtec are *čïhi* 'stomach; in(side), under'; *ini* 'heart; in, inside'; *nuu* 'face; to, at, from'; *šinï* 'back; behind'. Examples from Cakchiquel, a Mayan language, are *–pan* 'stomach; in, inside'; *–či* 'mouth; to, in, at'; *–x* 'back; behind'; *–wi* 'head hair; on, on top of'. One can find parallels in other languages, such as English prepositional phrases that are derived from body parts, for example, "at the foot of the mountain," "in the face of the wind," or "at the mouth of the river." What is noteworthy about the Mesoamerican examples, however, is that the feature is extremely pervasive in these languages, and there is usually no formal difference between the locative and its body-part counterpart. On this second point, we can contrast English, in which body-part words are used in locative phrases, but they cannot function independently as prepositions, so that we cannot say, for example, "foot the mountain," "face the wind" (meaning "in the face of the wind"), or "mouth the river."

A calque, or loan translation, is a literal translation from one language to the next: for example, Spanish *rascacielos* (*rasca* 'scrapes', *cielos* 'skies') compared to English skyscraper. One study has identified over fifty calques in the Mesoamerican area, thirteen of which are widely distributed within the area, but not beyond: knee = head of leg; wrist = neck of hand; boa constrictor = deer-snake; lime = ash, or stone ash; egg = stone of bird, or bone of bird; vein = road (of blood); molar = grinding stone; edge = mouth; thumb = mother of hand; finger = child of hand; gold or silver = god-excrement, or sun-excrement; alive = awake; town = water-mountain; porcupine = thorn opossum, or thorn plus some animal.

In most cases, language families that are represented in the Mesoamerican language area are totally within the area. The two exceptions are rather telling. The Otopamean family (which is a member of the larger Otomanguean group) includes one language, Chichimeco Jonaz, which is found just to the north of the Mesoamerican area; this language lacks the features we discussed earlier. The three Aztecan languages (Nahuatl [Aztec], Pochutec, and Pipil), which belong to the most southern branch of Uto-Aztecan, share the Mesoamerican linguistic features, while the other Uto-Aztecan languages (with a few exceptions) do not. Even though the Aztecan-speaking peoples are relative newcomers to Mesoamerica, having arrived within the past one or two thousand years, there still has been ample time for them to develop the characteristic linguistic features of the area.

12.5 SOUND SYMBOLISM: A DIFFUSIONAL
TRAIT OF THE PACIFIC COAST

In section 2.7 we introduced the notion of sound symbolism with examples from several California languages. Phonologically and semantically complex systems of sound symbolism have been reported for a number of languages in this area. We will examine four systems: (1) consonant alternations used in diminutive shifting in northern California, (2) vowel alternations in the Konkow language of north-central California, (3) the interplay of consonants and vowels in inanimate imitatives of the Pomoan languages of central California, and (4) sound symbolic alternation for size and intensity in the Yuman languages of southern California and contiguous Baja California and Arizona. All our examples come from California, but the reader should be aware that similar systems are found in Pacific Coast languages to the north.

Diminutive shifting, a type of consonantal sound symbolism conveying diminutive meaning, crosses a number of genetic boundaries in the Pacific Northwest and California. In northern California, it is found as an active process in Hupa (Athapaskan), Wiyot and Yurok (Algic), and Karuk, Yana, and Achumawi (Hokan). It is documented as occurring vestigially in Southern Sierra Miwok, a central California Utian language. It shows up as an inactive process in Luiseño, a Uto-Aztecan language of southern California, and as an active one in Diegueño and Cocopa, Yuman languages in southernmost California.

In northern California, the consonantal alternations are not identical, but they are similar, often involving alternations of /l ≈ r/, /t, θ ≈ c, č/, and /s ≈ š/. An example from Karuk of /θ ≈ č/ and /r ≈ n/: *θufkírik* 'great horned owl'; *čufkínik-ič* 'little great horned owl' (*-ič*, diminutive suffix). An Achumawi example of /l ≈ r/: *cilléqʰ* 'baby'; *cinnéqʰ-ča* 'teeny baby' (*-ča*, diminutive suffix). In Karuk, Achumawi, and Yana, diminutive shifting occurs with the diminutive suffix. In Hupa and Wiyot, some forms are diminutivized without a diminutive suffix, while in Yurok there is no diminutive suffix, so that diminutive shifting takes place only through consonant alternations: *seʔlet-*, 'to scrape off mud'; *seʔreč-*, 'to whittle wood' (/l ≈ r/ and /t ≈ č/). Besides having similar consonant alternations, some of these languages have diminutive suffixes that are similar in shape: Hupa, *-c*; Wiyot, *-oc ≈ -ic*; Karuk, *-ič ≈ -ač*; Achumawi, *-ča*.

Konkow, a Maiduan language just south of and contiguous with Yana, also has diminutive and augmentative symbolism, but with no affixation. Konkow, however, presents a new aspect of the Pacific Coast sound-symbolism puzzle because in Konkow diminutive shifting involves vocalic, not consonantal, alternations; for example: *c'í-ʔit'in* 'squeak'; *c'ǝ-ʔat'in* 'creak'; *c'á-ʔat'in* 'creak' (lower pitch); *héde* 'now' (proximal); *hódo* 'then, later' (distal). The second example is a metaphorical extension of the vocalic system reminiscent of the use of vowels in marking Shoshoni deixis (section 3.4). Just what connection, if any, the phonology and semantics of the Konkow mode of sound symbolism may have with the diminutive shifting found further north is unknown.

In the western part of north-central California, and not contiguous with any of the languages discussed so far, are three Pomoan languages that have a sound-meaning system that uses both vowels and consonants. As in the case of Konkow, just what this system has, or does not have, in common with the diminutive shifting to the north is an open question. Kashaya Pomo provides a good example of the complexities involved in Pomoan sound symbolism. Kashaya has a set of forms, inanimate imitatives, which, through the use of specific consonant and vowel combinations, copy sounds produced by the action of or manipulation of inanimate objects. These inanimate imitative forms all have the shape CVC, with restrictions as to which consonants may begin the syllable and which may end it. Three vowels, [a, o, i], contrast regularly to designate specific sound qualities: [a] represents flatness of sound, [o] indicates a sound that comes from a three-dimensional object (usually solid) of medium size, and [i] most frequently represents the lowest pitched, loudest, most massive sounds, but it can also represent light, high-pitched sounds:

> ṭam,   reverberating sound from striking something flat, like a door
> or wall; sound of piling lumber; sound of distant gunfire
> when it re-echoes
> ṭom,   clang of a cowbell or of hitting a can; sound of a small drum
> ṭim,   sound of a thunder clap, boom of a large drum
> t'ip',   sound of the snap of breaking a string or thread

Whereas the vowels indicate size and shape symbolism, the consonants are **onomatopoetic,** that is, they mimic the sounds themselves rather than symbolizing the shape or size of the thing from which the sound comes; for example, in syllable final position, [l] indicates that the sound emitted vibrates or resonates for a noticeable length of time (ṭil 'thud with reverberation, rumble') [ṭ] symbolizes that the sound is close, while [k] is used for distant sounds.

The Kashaya inanimate imitatives demonstrate yet another facet of the various ways in which sound symbolism is manifested in Pacific Coast languages. Although the consonantal symbolism introduces a systematic onomatopoetic dimension not found (or at least not readily apparent) in the languages to the north, the vocalic symbolism involving size is reminiscent of Konkow's diminutive-augmentative symbolism.

Kashaya sound symbolism also introduces an emphasis on size and intensity that is reflected in the Yuman languages of southern California, northern Baja California, and Arizona. In the Ipai dialect of Diegueño, there is both consonantal and vocalic symbolism. While the vocalic symbolism is vestigial, the consonant symbolism is significantly present in the language, with two different types recognized: size symbolism and intensity symbolism. Size symbolic alternations include /ł ≈ l/, /ł^y ≈ l^y/, and /ɽ ≈ r/:

cəkułk	'(large) hole through something'
cəkulk	'small hole through something'
ʔəsał^y	'my hand, arm'
ʔəsal^y	'my little hand, arm'
yaɽəyaɽ	'to be (large and) circular'
yarəyar	'to be small and circular'

Intensity symbolism involves a complex set of consonantal alternations affecting sets of two or more forms; for example:

məwas	'to be soft, tender'
məwaṣ	'to be real fine'
məwal	'to be powdery, fine' (like flour)
məwal^y	'to be pliable, mushy'
məwał	'to be limp, paralyzed'
səmiləmilp	'roll like log'
səmil^y	'roll over quickly'
səmiṇəmiṇp	'roll back and forth'

We have provided only a sketch of four very complex systems of sound symbolism from California. Our discussion has been limited, not only because the phenomena are far too complex to present in a few pages, but also because the data base is limited. We have detailed descriptions of the sound symbolic systems for only a few languages.

We sympathize with those who have found it difficult to thread their way through the detailed and complex patterns of sound symbolism. The least we can hope is that the reader can appreciate that these patterns, often shared or partially shared by neighbors who may or may not speak related languages, clamor for a historical explanation. The occurrence of sound symbolism in so many neighboring languages would argue against proposing independent innovation as an explanation for the phenomenon. A historical explanation will have to take into account both genetic relationships and areal diffusion. Unfortunately, we do not have at hand the data that will allow us to give a satisfactory historical explanation, and we may never have it.

12.6 CALIFORNIA: LANGUAGE FAMILIES AND DIFFUSIONAL AREAS

Mesoamerica provided a clear example of a linguistic area, one in which linguistic features crosscut the genetic units. In that particular case, we had a fairly clear idea of what the genetic units were, so that we were usually able to distinguish similarities that were the result of genetic relationship from those that were the result of areal influence.

Precontact California presents a more difficult case. It was one of the most culturally and linguistically diverse areas in the world and, in addition, there was a great deal of intergroup social interaction (section 9.2) which led to the spread of areal features. But distinguishing genetic from areal similarities in California is an exceedingly difficult task. After almost a century of intensive research, we are beginning to get a general picture of the linguistic prehistory of California, both genetic and areal, but there is still much that we do not know, some of which will never be known. We present first what we know (or think we know) about the genetic units, then follow with a discussion of selected areal features.

(The borders of the state of California were, of course, drawn in postcontact times, and bear no relation to where California Indians actually resided. We need not be concerned here with an exact definition, so that when we speak of California, it should be understood as only roughly coinciding with state borders.)

Genetic Units

At the time of first contact, there were approximately 90 languages and an unknowable number of dialects, but with an estimate of over 150. The earliest classification, known as the Powell Classification, was published in 1891 (section 12.7) and grouped the languages into more than twenty genetic units. Subsequent research suggests that several of them may be grouped into two more inclusive genetic units, Hokan and Penutian, which, if correct, reduces the number of genetic units to six. It is instructive to take a look at the history of the scholarship for these two putative stocks, since there is no general agreement among knowledgeable scholars as to the validity or membership of the two constructs. The remaining genetic units (Uto-Aztecan, Algic, Athapaskan, and Yukian) are discussed more briefly, inasmuch as there is clear agreement concerning their validity.

Hokan

The Hokan stock consists of thirteen genetic units, eleven of which are found at least partly within California. Seven are situated north of San Francisco: Karuk; Chimariko (extinct); four Shastan languages (extinct); two Palaihnihan languages, Achumawi and Atsugewi; two Yanan languages (extinct); seven Pomoan languages (one, most likely two, extinct); and Washo, located on the California-Nevada border around Lake Tahoe. The genetic units found in central California are all extinct: Esselen, Salinan, and the six Chumashan languages. The Yuman family is represented by Diegueño (consisting at least of Tipai, Ipai, and Kamia, three quite distinct dialects or possibly three closely related languages), Cocopa, Mohave, and Quechan in southern California and adjacent areas of Mexico and Arizona. The other Yuman languages are found in Baja California and western Arizona. The last two genetic units in the stock are located in Mexico: Seri, a single language on the coast of Sonora, and Tequistlatecan, two languages in Oaxaca. Three of the genetic units are well-diversified families consisting of several languages: Pomoan, Chumashan, and Yuman. The rest are isolates or small families of closely related languages.

The word for "two" begins with *hok*– or something similar in a number of languages (e.g., Atsugewi *húki*, Chimariko *xókhu*, and Shasta *xukʼ·a*), and is the source for the name Hokan. In the first proposal of the Hokan hypothesis, the evidence consisted of only five presumed cognate sets: "eye," "tongue," "water," "stone," and "sleep." Additional lexical evidence was presented later, along with a tentative set of general structural characteristics: absence of plural markers in nouns and suppletion between singular and plural verb stems (2.3); verb suffixes indicating plurality; instrumental prefixes; direction-location verb suffixes; and affixed pronominal elements, usually prefixes (see also section 2.8).

Most language prehistorians concede that Hokan is at least a useful and plausible hypothesis and a few even believe in it; but there is universal agreement that it has not been validated, at least not in same sense that, for example, Uto-Aztecan and Indo-European have been. The position of some branches within the stock is particularly problematical, namely Karuk, Chimariko, Salinan, Washo, and Chumash. The position of Esselen is especially tenuous and will always remain so, since the linguistic records of this extinct language are sparse.

Penutian

The postulation of a Penutian stock originally just consisted of languages in California but now includes languages elsewhere, particularly the Pacific Northwest. There are five centrally located California Penutian language families. The Wintuan and Maiduan families, with three members each, are situated north of San Francisco in the Sacramento Valley and its immediate environs. The Yokutsan family, located south of San Francisco in the San Joaquin Valley and its environs, was composed of an uncertain number of languages; there were two groups, each with six inter-linking dialects or closely related languages. The seven Miwokan languages, three of which are extinct, are located in central California from the coast to the southeast. The eight Costanoan languages, all extinct, were distributed along the California coast from San Francisco south.

The name Penutian is derived from the word for 'two', in the "Pen" languages: Maiduan, Wintuan, and Yokutsan (cf. Proto-Maiduan *pé·ne*), and in the "Uti" languages: Miwok and Costanoan (cf. Proto-Costanoan *ut̲x̲i*). The first effort to link these five families was made on the basis of a number of lexical resemblances. Next came the observation that it was typical in Penutian languages for stem morphemes to have a shape, CVCV(C), in which the vowels were often the same. With that observation came the claim that the California Penutian languages were related to certain languages in the Pacific Northwest.

Clear and convincing evidence for the Utian languages (Miwokan and Costa-noan) has been found, so that the relationship can be considered validated. While it is unquestioned that there are similarities among the "Pen" languages (Maiduan, Wintuan, and Yokutsan), clear and convincing proof that they are related to each other or to the Utian languages is not yet at hand, so many language prehistorians consider Penutian to be a plausible but unverified set of hypotheses. Those who are skeptical about the validity of California Penutian are even more skeptical about the inclusion of the additional languages in the Pacific Northwest.

Other Genetic Units

The Uto-Aztecan languages have been discussed in section 12.2. Tubatulabal and the six Takic languages are in southern California. There are also two languages belonging to the Numic branch: Kawaiisu in southern California and some dialects of Mono farther north and on the east side of the Sierra Nevada. There are additional Numic languages spoken within state boundaries, but they are culturally aligned with the Great Basin, not California (section 4.1).

Algic consists of three genetic units: One, Algonquian, is a family found in eastern North America, while the other two, Wiyot and Yurok, are isolates spoken along the northern coast of California. The linguistic diversity is probably about as great as that found in Uto-Aztecan. Algic is discussed in more detail in section 12.7.

The Athapaskan family contains over thirty closely related languages, spoken in three areas: (1) western Canada and interior Alaska, (2) Arizona and New Mexico, and (3) the Pacific Coast. The five Pacific Coast languages were spoken in two geographic areas: Chasta Costa and Tolowa along the Oregon-California coast; and

Hupa, Mattole, and Wailaki, in northwestern California and separated from the Chasta Costa and Tolowa by the Yurok. Except for Hupa, these languages are either extinct or nearly so. Three of these languages, the Chasta Costa, Mattole, and Wailaki, constitute a dialect chain.

The Yukian family consists of two groups and at least as many languages, Wappo and Yuki, which were separated from each other by the Pomoan languages. Both are extinct or nearly so. Wappo was spoken near Clear Lake. The Yuki speakers were located farther north; it is not clear if they spoke a single language with three distinctive dialects or three closely related languages: Yuki (proper), Coast Yuki, and Huchnom.

Diffusion of Linguistic Traits

In addition to difficulties presented by the differences in time depths involved in the genetic history of the indigenous languages and language families in California, there are also problems involving diffusion of linguistic features among languages, both related and unrelated:

> Even where genetic relationship is clearly indicated, as in the case of the Athapaskan and the Algonkian-Wiyot-Yurok families, the evidence of diffusion of traits from neighboring tribes, related or not, is seen on every hand. This makes the task of determining the validity of the various alleged Hokan languages and the various alleged Penutian languages all the more difficult. . . . It points up the desirability of pursuing diffusional studies along with genetic studies. This is nowhere more necessary than in the case of the Hokan and Penutian languages . . . , particularly in California where they may well have existed side by side for many millennia.

The language prehistorian, then, faces a tremendous challenge in California. At the beginning of this chapter, we noted that similarities requiring a historical explanation are of two types (those resulting from genetic relationship and those resulting from contact) and that these two types are the basis for the two types of classification, genetic and areal. As we have seen, in this and in the last chapter, all aspects of language are subject to diffusion: lexical, phonological, grammatical, and semantic. Even where the genetic situation is clear, separating out features that are the result of areal diffusion from genetic unity is not easy. But the task becomes even more difficult and in some instances may prove impossible in areas such as prehistoric California in which contact between linguistic groups has been intense and has occurred over long periods of time. Serious work on these topics in California has become possible only in recent years, now that the data base is becoming reasonably full and the genetic picture is becoming clarified. We have already discussed two examples from California, namely the diffusion of aspirated, glottalized, and voiced stops into Lake Miwok (section 11.2), and the distribution of sound symbolism (section 12.5). Additional examples follow in which we see how complex an interweaving of genetic and diffusional factors can be.

Front and Back [t], a Diffused Phonetic Trait

The languages that have a contrast between front and back [t] fall into three types:

1. Languages in which there is a two-way contrast between true stops, that is, [t] and [ṭ]: all Pomoan languages (Hokan); Southern Sierra Miwok (Penutian), Yuki, and Wappo; and three Yuman languages, Diegueño, Quechan, and Cocopa (Hokan). Of the languages north of Mexico, this contrast is limited to just these languages, and thus constitutes a specifically Californian trait.

2. Languages in which there is a two-way contrast between a stop and an affricate, that is, [t] and [c̣], or [ṭ] and [c̣]: Tolowa (Athapaskan); Chimariko (Hokan), Costanoan (Penutian), Salinan (Hokan), Yokuts (Penutian), and Kitanemuk and Serrano (Uto-Aztecan). This contrast is well attested outside of California, for example, among the northern Athapaskan languages and the Keres language of New Mexico.

3. Languages in which there is a three-way contrast between [t], [ṭ], and [c̣]: Lake Miwok and Yawelmani Yokuts, both Penutian languages. Like the first type, the trait is limited to California.

This trait, which has three variants, is found in languages that encompass half the state: a large continuous area extending north and south of San Francisco Bay, with a lone northern outlier (Chimariko) and a set of southern outliers (all Yuman). Cutting across genetic linguistic boundaries, the trait appears in Yukian, the family isolate; and some but not all of the Hokan branches: Chimariko, Pomoan, Esselen, Salinan, and Yuman (except for those spoken outside California, which are without the contrast). It also occurs in some Penutian families: Costanoan, Miwokan, and Yokutsan, but again not in all of them.

The trait is absent in Uto-Aztecan languages, with the exception of Kitanemuk and Serrano, languages that abut Yokuts, the presumed donor. It is conspicuously absent in Athapaskan (excepting Tolowa) and Algic. Uto-Aztecan and Athapaskan, at least, are known to have originated in other areas (section 13.4) and are candidates for late arrival in California.

A closer examination of the distribution of this trait raises many questions we cannot explore here. Suffice it to say that the problem cries out for a historical explanation in which diffusion plays a major role, even though we are not in a position to give a detailed historical account that will totally explain its distribution.

Other Diffused Phonetic Traits

There are many other phonetic traits that have an areal distribution. We will list just a few. A number of languages have a three-way contrast between plain, aspirated, and glottalized consonants (e.g., /t, tʰ, t'/): the Athapaskan languages, some neighboring Hokan and Penutian languages, and some Penutian and Hokan languages farther south. The three-way contrast is not specifically a California trait, since it is also found among a number of languages to the south, in Mexico, Central America, and the west coast of South America. This trait is part of a larger diffusional area of glottalized consonants, a feature very common in languages of western North America, but rare in the languages of eastern North America. Glottalized consonants are also found in many languages of Mesoamerica and western South America.

Klamath-Modoc and Wintu (Penutian), and Chimariko and Pomoan (Hokan) have front and back velar consonants (e.g., /k, q/), a feature highly characteristic of the Northwest Coast area; this trait appears to be an old one that is distributed spottily along the Pacific Coasts of North and South America.

In addition to phonetic traits having wide distributions, there are some with a limited distribution. One such trait is a subareal feature: the voiced stops, [b] and [d], rare in northern California but occurring in a narrow east-west strip of languages including Kashaya Pomo (Hokan), and Wintu-Patwin, Lake Miwok, and Maiduan (Penutian).

Number Systems

In discussing number systems (section 3.6), we noted that Californian Indians use a variety of systems. In northern California, these systems are primarily decimal, quinary, senary, or quaternary, with a distribution that suggests areal spread. To cite a few examples:

1. Wiyot and Yurok, two branches of the Algic family, have decimal systems, thus bearing more resemblance to neighboring Athapaskan languages than to the languages of the third Algic branch, Algonquian, most of which have quinary systems.

2. One would expect Cahto to use a decimal system just as its Athapaskan relatives do; however, it has a quinary system that seems to be due to the influence of some of the Hokan languages of the area, even though at the time of contact Cahto was not geographically contiguous with these languages.

3. The Wintun languages, with quinary systems, have a propensity for using multiplication in forming numerals of the second quine, and there are neighboring languages, for example, Eastern Pomo (Hokan) and Maidu (Penutian), which reflect the same method in their quinary systems.

4. The Miwokan languages reflect various features: for example, Saclan, which

has a senary system, resembles some of the Costanoan languages, and Central Sierra Miwok may retain a trace of this system in its word for seven. Lake Miwok, in using multiplication (two times four) in its word for eight, seems to show the influence of its near neighbor Patwin, a Wintun language.

Linguistic diffusion will not obscure close linguistic relationships, though it can introduce problems in reconstructing a detailed protolanguage. Diffusion can, however, present problems for more distant and remote relationships of the sort considered next.

12.7 DISCOVERING REMOTE RELATIONSHIPS

Now that we have examined the nature of linguistic evidence in discovering genetic relationships (sections 12.1 and 12.2) and have seen how diffusional factors can muddy the waters (sections 12.3 through 12.6), we are in a position to examine how to use linguistic evidence in the more difficult cases. Two cases will be examined: Algic and Macro-Siouan.

Algic

A 1913 study proposed a relationship between the Algonquian language family and two languages of northern California, Wiyot and Yurok, a grouping that has since come to be called the Algic linguistic stock. The argument was based on evidence from grammar and vocabulary. The grammatical evidence was derived from striking similarities in a set of pronominal prefixes; the evidence is listed here:

Proto-Algonquian	Wiyot	Yurok	
*ne–	d(u)–	?ne–	first person
*ke–	kh(u)–	k' e–	second person
*we–	w–,u(?)–	?we–, ?u–	third person
*me–	b–	me–	indefinite

The phonetic correspondences are still more striking when we know that Wiyot [d] and [b] (voiced alveolar and bilabial stops, respectively) alternate in certain well-defined contexts with [n] and [m], which are the corresponding alveolar and bilabial nasals. What is especially convincing is not the similarities of the individual prefixes, but rather the total complex. Details concerning the use of these prefixes in the three groups provides still more evidence: they are used both with nouns (for possession) and verbs (for subject); in Algonquian and Wiyot (but not Yurok) the consonant [t] is inserted after the prefix if a following noun begins with a vowel, and still more.

The vocabulary evidence is less striking. In the 1913 study, over a hundred possible cognates were identified. This was done before there had been much work in comparative Algonquian. Today, Algonquian is one of the best-known families in the Americas, which has been a great help in evaluating the potential cognates within Algic. Based on this better evidence, a number of the early suggestions of cognate sets had to be abandoned, so that perhaps not many more than fifty clear and convincing cognate sets remain that are shared by at least two of the three branches. Part of the problem in discovering cognate sets may be in recognizing the sound changes that underlie the phonetic correspondences, but most likely the greatest problem rests on the fact that two of the three branches consist of only single languages, so that much of the cognate material has been lost to the ravages of time. Sound correspondences have been identified but, to date at least, there are not enough cognate sets to allow the reconstruction of the full phonological system of Proto-Algic.

Algic is a classic example for illustrating the importance of grammatical evidence in discovering remote genetic relationships. The evidence from the vocabulary alone would probably be enough for proving the relationship of the three branches. We could, however, prove the case from the grammatical evidence alone, since the grammatical correspondences are quite detailed. The probability that they are the result of chance or borrowing is almost zero.

Algic and Uto-Aztecan are probably of comparable time depth, but validating the genetic unity of Uto-Aztecan is easier simply because there are several branches, many of which contain several languages, while Algic consists of only three branches, with two of them being isolates. Further, the geographic dispersal of Uto-Aztecan is much greater, so that problems caused by diffusion of linguistic traits are minimal and easily detected, whereas Wiyot and Yurok have been living next to each other for who knows how long.

Macro-Siouan

Starting in the middle of the nineteenth century, a number of observers have suggested a distant relationship between three language families: Iroquoian (the Great Lakes region and the Southeast), Caddoan (the eastern Plains) and Siouan (the eastern Plains and Southeast). Evidence to support this hypothesized relationship consists of too few possible cognates to attempt to construct a theory of sound correspondences. The best evidence concerns a rather large number of striking similarities in the verb structure; for example, the Iroquoian and Caddoan verb consists of four major parts, which are, from left to right: (1) a prefix that gives information on tense, subordination, mood, things such as negation, and the like, (2) a pronominal prefix, (3) the verb stem, and (4) a tense or aspect suffix. A number of similarities were noted in the pronominal prefixes, both in their form as well as in the kinds of grammatical categories that are expressed, in the way the dual and plural are marked, and so on. How many similarities of this sort are needed so that one must assume that they result from a remote genetic relationship, rather than from chance or from contact? The similarities do not entail the kind of interlocking detail that we saw for Algic, so that the case for genetic relationship is not as good. Opinion on Macro-Siouan is divided among responsible scholars; most would agree that the similarities listed are extremely suggestive, but that the case has yet to be proven. It should be noted that comparative work in the reconstruction of the families within the hypothesized stock is still in progress; much of the earlier work consisted of comparing individual languages within each group, rather than comparing Proto-Iroquian, Proto-Caddoan, and Proto-Siouan with each other. When the various branches of the family are more closely related, as in the case of the branches within Uto-Aztecan, this is not a major obstacle; but with remote relationships, the comparison of protolanguage forms, rather than of individual languages, facilitates the process.

History of Classification

Attempts to show deep genetic relationships of American Indian languages have a long history. At earlier times, before the beginning of serious study of the languages of the Americas, it was assumed that all of these languages must be related. It was thought to be simply a matter of finding out which languages went together more closely. By the nineteenth century, it was apparent that there was much more linguistic diversity than previously suspected. Recognition of that diversity was expressed in the so-called Powell Classification, published in 1891 and conducted under the aegis of the Bureau of American Ethnology. The classification, the result of the work of several scholars, was not the first classification of American Indian languages, but it was the first to be undertaken in a systematic fashion, with the attempt to gather comparable and uniform data from as many languages as possible. It was restricted to North America north of Mexico, and it was conservative: Only clearly related languages were placed within the same family. The resulting classification recognized fifty-eight families. Some of the families were quite large and often diverse, such as Algonquian in the northeast and northern Plains, Siouan in the Plains and Southeast, Athapaskan in the Western Subarctic and southwestern United States, and Salish in the northwestern United States and Canadian Southeast. Others consisted of isolates, such as Beothuk, the extinct language of Newfoundland; Zuni, in New Mexico; and Yuchi, a language of Georgia, now spoken in Oklahoma. The Powell Classification has served for over a century as the base line for later comparative and classificatory work.

We have noted (section 12.6) that California provided the scene for a great deal of post-Powell classificatory work in attempts to find remote genetic relationships. That California (along with nearby areas, particularly on or near the coast to the north) should provide a major theater for attempts at deep genetic comparisons is hardly surprising, since it is the area of greatest linguistic diversity in the Americas.

Such classificatory work, however, was not limited to California. One of the early ambitious schemes claimed to present evidence to link all the languages in North America (including most in Mesoamerica) into a single language family. The most influential scheme grouped Powell's families, along with a few from Mexico, into six so-called super stocks. It was noted that the scheme was "suggestive but far from demonstrable in all its features at the present time," a cautionary note that many later observers failed to heed. The groupings range from those that had been, or came to be, validated (e.g., Uto-Aztecan, Algic) to those that have been discarded (e.g., Zuni with Uto-Aztecan).

The most ambitious scheme to emerge in recent years proposes three groups: (1) Eskimo-Aleut, (2) Na-dene, which includes Athapaskan, Eyak, Tlingit, and Haida (section 14.2), and (3) Amerind, which includes all the remaining languages in the Americas. The first two groups are proposals from earlier workers. The Eskimo-Aleut family consists of two clearly related branches and is universally accepted. Na-dene, one of the six super stocks, is accepted by some prehistorians, but not all; the relationship between Athapaskan, Eyak, and Tlingit is universally accepted, but that of Haida is problematical. The Amerind family is a new invention. It is divided into eleven large branches, four of which are found principally in North and Central America, and seven principally in South America. Many of the North and Central American groupings follow suggestions made by earlier workers. The evidence for Amerind is based on lexical and grammatical similarities, and the lexical evidence is given in a listing of 281 proposed cognate sets. Each proposed cognate set includes items from at least two of the branches, with some of the sets including entries from most or all of the proposed branches. This lexical evidence cannot be properly evaluated because there is no set of sound correspondences provided, nor is there evidence for the proposed grouping into the eleven branches.

A few scholars find this latest classification convincing, although most are skeptical at best. Trying to prove genetic relationships and to provide an internal classification without a theory of grammatical and sound correspondences will work for closely related languages, and even moderately well for distantly related languages such as Uto-Aztecan, but it becomes very chancy for remote genetic relationships. Even if all, or a significant portion, of Amerind is validated by future work, it is unlikely that the internal classification will remain unchallenged. Likely some parts of the scheme will withstand the test of time, particularly those parts that were proposed by earlier workers, and for which evidence for the relationship had already been gathered. From this discussion, the reader may correctly infer that there is, as yet, no consensus on remote genetic relationships and, by the very nature of the problem, there may never be any.

SOURCES

Section 12.1 is based on Rhodes and Todd 1981, Wolfart 1973b, and Wolfart and Carroll 1981. Section 12.2 stems from Miller 1983 and 1984. Section 12.3 is based on Miller 1987. Section 12.4 is based on Campbell, Kaufman, and Smith-Stark 1986; see Smith-Stark 1982 for specific reference to calques. Section 12.5 is based on Gamble 1975 (Yokuts); Haas 1970, 1973a, 1978a; Langdon 1970, 1971 (Diegueño); Nichols 1971, Oswalt 1971a (Pomo); Teeter 1959 (Wiyot); and Ultan 1970, 1971 (Konkow). Section 12.6 is based on Campbell and Mithun 1979, Jacobsen 1979c, and Shipley 1978. In addition on genetic units, see Powell 1891 (earliest classification of languages in California); on Hokan, see Dixon and Kroeber 1913, 1919, Sapir 1917, 1925 (Hokan hypothesis), Dixon and Kroeber 1913 (cognate sets), Campbell and Mithun 1979:25, Jacobsen 1979c:545 (general structural characteristics), and Shipley 1978:85–86 and Campbell and Mithun 1979:43 (plausibility of hypothesis). Sources on Penutian include Dixon and Kroeber 1913, 1919 (California Penutian proposal), Dixon and Kroeber 1913 (use of lexical resemblances to link "Pen" and "Uti" languages), Sapir 1923 (typical Penutian stem), Shipley 1978:82, and Silverstein 1979:651–53 (relation of California Penutian to Pacific Northwest languages). On diffusion of linguistic traits, see Haas 1978a:368 (quote) and Langdon and Silver 1984 (diffusion of phonetic trait). Section 12.7 is based on Goddard 1975, 1986, Haas 1958, and Sapir 1913. In addition, on Algic, see Sapir 1913 (relationship between Algonquian and Wiyot, Yurok), Goddard 1975, 1978 (grammatical evidence), and Sapir 1913 (identification of possible cognates). Macro-Siouan is discussed in Chafe 1973 (evidence supporting Iroquoian-Caddoan hypothesis); on the history of classificatory work, see Powell 1891 (first systematic classification), Radin 1919 (ambitious classificatory scheme), Sapir 1921a, 1929a (most influential classificatory scheme), Sapir 1951[1929]:172 (quote: cautionary note), Greenberg 1987 (most recent ambitious scheme), and Greenberg 1987:181–270 (lexical evidence).

SUGGESTED READINGS

For discussion and appraisals of the Greenberg classification, see *Current Anthropology* 1986 27(5), 1987 28(1), 28(3), 28(5), Campbell 1988, Rankin 1992. See Darnell and Hymes (1986) for discussion of the Sapir classification.

CHAPTER 13

THE USE OF LANGUAGE
AS A TOOL FOR PREHISTORY

Language can be used as a touchstone for unraveling events of the past. Linguistic evidence can help in determining earlier cultural and social patterns, in tracing movements of people and discovering areas of dispersal, and in establishing prehistoric contact between peoples. The most important tool for the language prehistorian in this endeavor is the comparative method, which allows for the reconstruction of vocabulary in the protolanguage. But as we will see, it is not the only tool. We give a number of case studies.

13.1 NAVAJO ETYMOLOGIES, AND
RECONSTRUCTED VOCABULARY

Navajo belongs to the Apachean branch of the Athapaskan languages, languages found in three geographic zones: the subarctic of interior Alaska and western Canada, the Pacific coast in southern Oregon and California, and the Southwest in Arizona and New Mexico. Navajo, along with the other Apachean languages, is found in the more southern area. How is one to account for this distribution? The most likely hypothesis is that the Athapaskan-speaking peoples originated in one of these three places and migrated to the two other zones.

One of the earliest and still today most elegant studies in American Indian linguistic prehistory examined four Navajo words and showed that they reflected a northern origin. The words were ?adee 'gourd', –sas 'seed lies', naadąą? 'corn', and –keeh, a verb stem used in an idiomatic expression referring to sleeplessness.

The word for 'gourd' is ?adee?, which also means 'gourd dipper, ladle'. It is also used for dipper, ladle, and spoon, in general, with the gourd ladle being the most typical ladle or spoon. Thus an earthen spoon is called "mud ?adee?," and a tablespoon is called "metal ?adee?." The word also means 'someone's horn', and is composed of the indefinite possessive prefix ?a– plus –dee? 'horn' (cf. bi-dee? 'his [animal's] horn'). Unpossessed, the form is dé 'horn'. With the meaning "gourd, dipper, ladle, spoon," and "horn," the element ?a– has lost its force as a possessive prefix, as shown by the fact that this element remains when other possessive prefixes are added: *be-ʔedeeʔ* (assimilated from *bi-ʔadeeʔ*) 'his gourd ladle'.

Comparison with other languages shows that these forms come from Proto-Athapaskan **dé* 'horn' (unpossessed form) and **-dèeʔ* 'horn' (possessed form). Further, one finds that in the northern languages, the cognate forms not only have the meaning 'horn', but also 'spoon made of horn'. We can trace the history of the Navajo meaning as follows: (1) an animal's horn, (2) spoon, ladle made of horn, (3) any spoon or ladle, (4) gourd spoon or ladle, and finally (5) gourd. Stage 1 would be Proto-Athapaskan; stage 2 if not Proto-Athapaskan, then at least a widespread feature of the northern languages, reflecting the use of horns for making spoons; and stages 3, 4, and 5 a Navajo, and at least in part a more general Apachean development. With stage 2 no longer represented in Navajo, the meanings 'one's horn' and 'spoon, ladle, gourd' have become disconnected, so that they are now thought to be two distinct and unrelated words, an idea strengthened by the fact that it is taboo to make spoons from deer horn.

Whereas the verb *–sas* normally means 'seed lies', its meaning is more general: 'the mass of finely divided particles (e.g., grain, sand) lies'. A derived verb form *naasas* means both 'I scatter the seeds' as well as 'I let the mass (of grain, sand) spill; I sprinkle it (e.g., sand, water)'.

There do not appear to be cognates of this verb in other Athapaskan languages, at least no cognates of verbs in this particular form; however, internal linguistic evidence from within Navajo provides the touchstone for related forms in the Athapaskan language family. Navajo phonology is such that all verbs beginning with /y/ must be from an underlying form that includes a prefix of rather general meaning, called a classifier in Athapaskan grammar. The /s/ would be from a classifier –ł– plus either /y/ or /z/; thus the form *–sas* in Navajo must derive from an underlying *yas* or *zas*. As it turns out, there is a word *yas* 'snow', which is the underlying form. The Proto-Athapaskan form is reconstructed as **yáxs*, with cognates in almost all the languages, for example, Chipewyan *yaθ*, Babine *yìs*, Beaver *yas*, and so on. Thus the verb for a new activity, the sowing of seeds, is derived from the root of an old and familiar item, namely snow.

The word *naadąąʔ* 'corn' is composed of two elements. The second element, *–dąąʔ* occurs in a number of compounds, such as: *maʔii-dąąʔ* 'juniper berries', literally 'coyote's corn'; *gahtsoh-dąąʔ* 'winterfat', literally 'jackrabbit's corn'. The form of this element is clearly a possessed form, shown by the fact that this is the form when used with possessive prefixes (e.g., *shi-dąąʔ* 'my corn'), as well as by an analysis of the phonetic form which we will not provide here. Originally the element meant 'food', and later became narrowed to what came to be the most important food, namely, corn; thus a literal translation for *maʔii-dąąʔ* at an earlier time was not 'coyote's corn', but 'coyote's food'. The current word for food is *ch'i-yaan*, based on the root *-yaan* 'to be eatable', the same root that *-ḍąą?* is based on.

The current word for corn, then, can be taken to mean '*nàa-*'s corn' or '*nàa-*'s food'. What, then, is *nàa-*, the first element of 'corn'? It must be an animate being, since the second element of 'corn' is possessed. It is an element, still found today in the Navajo names for neighboring groups, meaning 'aliens' or 'enemy': *nàa-sht'ézhí* 'Zuni Indians' (second element, 'the one's who are blackened'); *nàa-łáŋ* 'Comanche Indians' (second element, 'the many'). The element is found in many other Athapaskan languages and is clearly inherited from Proto-Athapaskan. The original meaning of the Navajo word for 'corn' was 'enemy food' or 'alien food'.

The verb *-kéeh* is limited to an expression for 'sleeplessness', for example *bił sits'anakeeh* 'sleeplessness always bothers me'. In this idiom, the subject is always *bił* 'sleep', and the one who lacks sleep is always indicated by an indirect object pronoun (in this case *-si-* 'me'). The adverbial prefix *-ts'á-* 'away from' is always used with the verb, which gives a sense of motion to the verb, with the feeling that 'sleep slips away, moves away, glides away'.

The closely related Chiricahua Apache has a verb identical in form, but with a different meaning, 'several to run, trot'. The difference in meaning leaves one wondering if the two verbs are cognate. When the northern languages are examined, however, the relationship becomes clear; for example, Chipewayan *-kaih*, Beaver *-kɛ*, and others, all meaning 'to travel by canoe', always with plural subject, and in some languages also '(plural objects) to float or move in water'. The desert dwelling speakers of Apachean languages lost the central meaning of moving by canoe, but retained the word with a shift in meaning or in an idiomatic expression.

These etymologies in Navajo give us glimpses of earlier cultural practices, when animal horns rather than gourds were used for making spoons and ladles, and when the canoe was a common means of travel. They also present us a picture of a people who have, in relatively recent times, been introduced to agriculture, and who, at an earlier time, lived in a different environment, with their northern neighbors. We can thus conclude that the Navajo (and others in the Southwest who speak languages belonging to the Apachean branch of Athapaskan) left their northern relatives and moved south, rather than the reverse.

The reconstruction of vocabulary items that refer to specific cultural traditions can be a powerful tool for the cultural prehistorian. Not only can individual items be reconstructed, as in this case, but often a whole cultural complex is revealed. Farming, and specifically the use of corn, by Uto-Aztecan-speaking peoples presents an example. The economies of those belonging to the southern branch (the Aztecan languages and the Sonoran languages in northwest Mexico) are all based on corn. In the north, only the Hopi are farmers and corn cultivators, while the rest, Takic, Tubatulabal and Numic, were hunters and gatherers.

How far back can we reconstruct the use of corn? For Southern Uto-Aztecan, but not for Uto-Aztecan as a whole, we can reconstruct the word for corn, which is *sunu, along with words that reflect its preparation, such as the tamale, and the roasting of grains of corn, to make it into a type of popcorn; thus we can reconstruct this cultural complex for the speakers of Proto-Southern-Uto-Aztecan. We will see in section 13.4 that there is linguistic evidence for the later introduction of the technology used in the preparation of corn into tortillas.

Whereas corn is very important to the economy of the Hopi, it is noteworthy that none of the words for corn or for its preparation are cognate with the words used farther south. This is a good indication that the introduction of corn, along with methods for its preparation, represent separate historical events in the southern Uto-Aztecan groups and Hopi.

The reconstructed vocabulary for the whole of the language family tells us that the Proto-Uto-Aztecan speakers were hunters and gatherers. The word for grinding stone or metate can be reconstructed as *ma·ta, an implement first used for grinding wild seeds and then later, in the south, for grinding corn. The reconstructed vocabulary is richer in plant foods than animal, presenting us a picture in which gathering was more important to the economy than hunting, and a picture in which the greatest share of the plants came from semiarid mountains.

Reconstructed vocabulary can also help in locating areas of dispersal, as the next two sections illustrate.

13.2 THE ALGONQUIAN HOMELAND

A family of languages, descended from a single protolanguage, may occupy an extended territory. It is not unreasonable to assume that, at an earlier time, the protolanguage occupied a more restricted range. How can we discover that location? One technique used is to reconstruct floral and faunal terms and then search for the region that contains the entire set of terms. One of the earliest and best applications of this technique was carried out for the Algonquian family.

Over fifty terms for various birds, mammals, fish, and trees for Proto-Algonquian were reconstructed. Since American Indian groups normally have far more than this number for the local flora and fauna, we can be fairly certain that the Algonquians had well over fifty, but this is the number that could be reconstructed. With fuller data, perhaps the number could be increased, but it is still large enough to be more than adequate for the task.

Some of the species, certain common birds, for example, have a very wide range, covering most or all of the area occupied by modern Algonquian groups. Such terms are of no help. Diagnostic are those species that occupy a restricted range. An example would be the term for "moose," because it is found in only the northern range of present-day Algonquian languages. If we can reconstruct a word for moose, then we know that the Proto-Algonquians lived somewhere in the northern area. Notice that it is not simply having a term for moose that is important. All of the more northern Algonquian-speaking peoples are familiar with the animal, so of course there will be a word for it in their languages. The question is: Are the various words cognate?

Care must be exercised in applying the technique. One must be sure that there is an accurate zoological or botanical identification in each of the languages, and keeping in mind that most recordings come from linguists who are not biologists, this is not an easy task. Some species, such as moose, are easy, but species identification of some smaller mammals (squirrels, for instance), smaller birds, fish, and many plants is sometimes problematical.

Care must also be taken in determining the range of individual species. There has been both extension and curtailment in the range of some species since the time of European contact, and climatic changes over the past few thousand years, dating back to the time Proto-Algonquian was spoken, may also have led to changes in distribution. Therefore one must enlist the aid of the paleobiologist.

The phonological reconstruction of the parent language must be done, with the sound changes in the daughter languages carefully isolated. If not, it would be difficult to differentiate between cognates and borrowings between closely related languages. Borrowing would, of course, be good evidence that the habitat occupied by the species in question was a new one for the speakers of the borrowing languages (section 11.1).

Finally, one must watch for changes in meaning. When a group moves into an area where the particular species is lacking, sometimes they will apply the old word to a similar species; for example, the word that reconstructs as *mo·swa means 'moose' in all the cognate forms except among the Miami, who moved into a more southern region that did not have moose; for the Miami, the cognate form means 'deer'. In this case, only one language disagrees in the meaning, so that it is fairly certain that a change from moose to deer took place in only one language, rather than a change from deer to moose in all the languages except Miami. But not all cases are this easy to resolve.

Because of these problems, we should expect that some of the conclusions on specific items may well be in error; however, if the determination of homeland is based on a large number of species and if a constellation of forms presents a consistent picture of the hypothesized habitat, a few erroneous forms should not be a problem. A consistent picture does in fact emerge from the Algonquian data, namely, of a habitat with a mixed forest of coniferous and deciduous trees, rich in a variety of fish, waterfowl, and game. The area for which the ranges of all the species overlap is in the Great Lakes area, specifically to the north of Lake Ontario, extending west to Georgian Bay on Lake Huron, with many lakes found in the region. (It is interesting to note that part of this area, the region immediately north of Lake Ontario, was occupied by non-Algonquian speakers, namely, Iroquoian-speaking tribes.) The evidence for the overlap in this region is based on over twenty forms; we give the evidence for six of them.

> *mo·swa 'moose' (*Alces americana*): Fox *mo·swa*, Menomini *mo·s*, Plains Cree *mo·swa*, Montagnais *mo·s*, Ojibwa *mo·ns*, Miami *moswa* (meaning 'deer'), Munsee *mo·s*, Penobscot *mos*. The original range of the moose extended from the Great Lakes northward.

> *pešehkiwa 'buffalo, bison': Menomini *pesɛhkiw*, Woodland Cree *pisihkiw*, Ojibwa *pišikki*, Abenaki *pəsihkó*, Penobscot *wə́sihko*. The Proto-Algonquian word probably did not refer to the Plains buffalo (*Bison bison bison*), but to the wood buffalo (*Bison bison pennsylvanicus*), which originally ranged from the Great Lakes southward. Notice that the moose and wood buffalo help bracket the homeland in the Great Lakes area.

> *a·skikwa 'seal', primarily 'the harbor seal (*Phoca vitulina concolor*)': Woodland Cree *a·hkik*, Montagnais *a·hčok*, Ojibwa *a·skik*, Penobscot *àhkik^w*. The harbor seal was found along the Atlantic Coast, Hudson Bay, and the St. Lawrence River up to Niagara Falls, where their upriver distribution was blocked. This third term, then, helps to further restrict the potential area of the Proto-Algonquians.

> *po·hpo·hkwa (?) 'bobwhite' (*Colinus virginianus*): Fox *po·hkwi·ha*, Miami *pohkosisia* (with the diminutive suffix), Delaware *po·hpó·hkəs*, Munsee *po·hpó·hkwi·s* (with the diminutive suffix), Natick *poohpoohqu-tteh* (in an early translation of the Bible, where it translated 'quails'). The bobwhite has a generally southern distribution, extending north of only two of the Great Lakes, Lake Ontario and Lake Erie.

> *a?šikanwa 'black bass' (*Micropterus dolomieu*): Fox *ašikanwa*, Menomini *a?sekam*, Ojibwa *aššikan*, Shawnee *a?šika*, Penobscot *ásikan*. Some Algonquian languages in the Mississippi River drainage use the word for the large mouth bass (*Micropterus salmoides*), but the Proto-Algonquian word probably was limited

to the black bass, which was not natively found in Maine or
other areas west of the Appalachian Mountains. The Penobscot
of Maine knew of this fish in Lake Champlain, located out of
Penobscot territory to the west.

*ka·wa·ntakwa 'white spruce' (*Picea glauca*): Fox *papa-ka·takwa*
(meaning 'evergreen tree'), Ojibwa *ka·wa·ntak*, Penobscot
káwatak^w; probably also, Menomini *ka·wa·htek* 'spruce', but
there are some phonological problems if this form is cognate.
The white spruce is a northern tree with its southern extension
extending to the Great Lakes.

These six species overlap only to the north of Lake Ontario. This pattern of overlap is repeated in more than fifteen additional forms.

13.3 THE NUMIC HOMELAND

The patterns of language and dialect diversity reflect population movements. Because linguistic differentiation is a function of time, the area of greatest differentiation is the area of longest occupation. This principle has been applied to Numic,
the northernmost branch of the Uto-Aztecan language family. The Numic languages are divided into three groups, each with two or three languages: Western
Numic, with Mono and Northern Paiute; Central Numic, with Panamint, Shoshoni,
and Comanche; and Southern Numic, with Kawaiisu and Ute-Southern Paiute (Ute
and Southern Paiute, distinct ethnic groups, speak the same language). The three
branches are spread out in a fan shape, with the apex of the fan in the southwestern part of the Great Basin, near Death Valley. We can divide each of the three
branches into inner and outer languages, with the inner languages, Mono, Panamint, and Kawaiisu, located in the apex of the fan. The inner languages occupy a
much more restricted area and display greater internal dialect diversity than do the
outer languages. Furthermore, the dialects of the outer languages that are closest
to the apex show greater internal diversity than the dialects located further away.

An example can be seen in the cognate density chart for Central Numic dialects
(table 13.1): A, B, and C are Panamint dialects; D, E, and F are Shoshoni dialects
closest to the apex, while G, H, I, J, K, and L are Shoshoni dialects farthest from
the apex (see section 12.5 for an explanation of cognate density charts). Although
this example is restricted to lexical diversity, phonological and grammatical diversity
show a similar pattern, not only in Central Numic, but in the other two branches
as well.

Table 13.1.   Cognate Density in Central Numic

(I)

	A	B	C	D	E	F	G	H	I	J	K	L
A												
B	89											
C	90	94										
D	88	85	86									
E	84	84	84	94								
F	83	82	82	89	90							
G	84	83	84	91	91	92						
H	83	85	82	89	90	89	95					
I	84	84	83	91	89	91	93	94				
J	85	83	84	92	88	89	95	94	96			
K	82	81	81	88	87	85	93	94	91	94		
L	84	83	83	90	88	86	94	94	94	97	95	

(II)

	A–C	D–F	G–L
A–C	90		
D–F	84	90	
G–L	84	89	94

Note:
(I) represents twelve speakers. Letters correspond to locations of the speakers on the Central Numic Map. A, B, and C are Panamint speakers; the rest are Shoshoni speakers, with D, E, and F closest to Panamint, and G through L farther away, to the northeast.
(II) gives the median figure of the cognate densities within and between these three groups.

Since, as we said, the area of greatest diversity is the area of longest occupation, the Numic homeland, then, is located in the southwest part of the Great Basin. The Proto-Numic speakers first divided into the three groups, which became the modern Western, Central, and Numic branches. The degree of diversity, along with the glottochronological figures, indicate that this division took place about two thousand years ago. Then about a thousand years ago, each group spread to the north, northeast, and east, occupying the whole of the Great Basin and the western fringes of the Plains.

The technique applied in determining the Algonquian homeland was also used to plot the distribution of the plants and animals that can be reconstructed for Numic.

Some of the items have a wide range, so that "piñon pine," is absent only in the far north of the Great Basin, while others, such as "turtle" have a more restricted range. But what they all have in common is that they occur in the southwestern area; thus there is additional evidence for the Proto-Numic speakers being from this area.

An examination of placenames also leads one to the same conclusion. When a people come into a new area, there are two common ways to provide for place-names: They may either be coined, using native techniques, or they may be bor-rowed from their neighbors. If occupation is recent, the analysis of the new coinages is transparent. Examples from Shoshoni, an outer language, are *isa-sonko* literally 'Coyote's lungs' (the Dolly Varden, a mountain in northeastern Nevada); *tono-pa·* literally 'greasewood-springs' (Tonopah); *pa·-wa·k-kati* literally 'water-juniper-sitting' (a river in Wyoming). One of the very few unanalyzable Shoshoni place-names is *wa·hkaima* (Pilot Peak, in northeastern Nevada). The inner languages show a different pattern. Panamint, for example, has many transparently analyz-able words, but it also has many that are only partially analyzable. In *si·-napiti* (Wild Rose Canyon) the first element is 'willow', but the second is meaningless in present-day Panamint. The partially meaningful placenames are of more interest than totally meaningless ones, because they tell us that such names were formed in Panamint, not borrowed from a neighboring language, but that the formations are of sufficient antiquity to allow the regular processes of language change to ob-scure their original composition.

The most northern Numic speakers live in the Snake River drainage of southern Idaho. Their aboriginal economy, along with that of their neighbors, the Nez Perce, who speak a Sahaptin language, depended a great deal upon fish. Northern Paiute and Shoshoni have only two root words for fish, and the various kinds of fish found in the Snake River area are derived by means of compounding, for example, Northern Paiute *pissáp-pakkʷi* 'trout', literally 'good-fish'; *pakkʷí papiʔi* 'sturgeon', literally 'fish's older-brother'. The Nez Perce, on the other hand, have single, unanalyzable roots for these words; thus we have a reflection of the Northern Paiute, basically dwellers of the desert where there were fewer kinds of fish and these were gener-ally less important as one moved into the Snake River area where the Nez Perce had lived for a longer period of time.

We have used three lines of argument for locating the Proto-Numic homeland, and it is gratifying that the three agree: the nature and distribution of language and dialect diversity, the distribution of reconstructible plants and animals (the same technique used for determining the Proto-Algonquian homeland), and the analysis of placenames.

The first study to make extensive use of linguistic data in tracing American Indian culture history appeared in 1916. In it, the principle of greatest linguistic differentia-tion was used to locate the Athapaskan homeland. The "linguistic center of gravity," that is, the greater diversity, found in the northern groups, points to longer occupation, so that the more uniform branches, the Apachean branch in the Southwest and the Pacific coast branch in Oregon and northern California, must have come from the north. The analysis of placenames was also used; for example, the Athapaskan-speaking Hupa in northern California use a descriptive term meaning "white mountain" for Mt. Shasta, while their neighbors the Yana use an unanalyzable term, providing evidence then for the priority of the Yana over the Hupa in this region.

We have noted that in Northern Paiute and Shoshoni (Snake River drainage area) there are only two unanalyzable words for fish in each language, whereas in Nez Perce there are several unanalyzable fish terms. This is evidence that the Nez Perce were the earlier occupants of the Snake River area. The use of this kind of evidence in tracing the antiquity of cultural practices was introduced in the 1916 study mentioned previously, in which there is an example from the Nootka potlatch ceremony. The Nootka language has a number of unanalyzable roots referring to the potlatch such as *-'o·'it* 'to ask for something as a gift in a girl's puberty potlatch'; *-t'o·ta* 'to give a potlatch for someone'; *-'int* 'to give a feast of some kind of food (in a potlatch)'. The fact that there are numerous unanalyzable terms for this cultural complex provides evidence that the potlatch is an old cultural institution.

13.4 EARLY SPANISH AND AZTEC LOANS IN NORTHWEST MEXICO

The use of linguistic data need not be limited to the prehistoric past. It can also shed light on post-Columbian events, particularly in studying contact with the European conquerors during the early period of colonization. Social and cultural events of considerable importance to aboriginal groups often went unrecorded or underrecorded. By studying the linguistic evidence in conjunction with the historical record, we can often obtain a much fuller picture than either body of evidence can supply by itself. The most important but not the only body of linguistic evidence is provided by loanwords from the European colonial languages.

As a case in point, we will examine the languages of northwest Mexico (table 13.2). The groups in question are the Uto-Aztecan-speaking tribes that belong to the Sonoran branch, along with Seri, a linguistic isolate spoken on the Sonoran coast. These languages have been in contact with Spanish for the past four centuries. The aboriginal inhabitants were introduced to new objects and ideas, all of which needed new names. These names were provided by external means, through the introduction of loanwords, or by internal means, through new coinages or semantic shift of old words (see section 11.3 for further discussion of the strategies used in

Table 13.2. **Distribution of Loanwords versus Native Creations in Northwest Mexico**

	River Guarijío	Mountain Guarijío	Western Tarahumara	Central Tarahumara	Eastern Tarahumara	
work	L	N	N	N	N	Nahuatl, *tekipanoa·*
money	L	N	N	N	N	Spanish, *tomín* (a colonial Spanish coin)
tortilla	L	N	N	N	–	Nahuatl, *taxcalli*
week	L	L	N	N	N	Spanish, *domingo* "Sunday"
knife	L	L	N	N	N	Spanish, *navaja*
Sunday	L	L	L	N	N	Spanish, *domingo*
Wednesday	L	L	L	L	N	Spanish, *miércoles*
Thursday	L	L	L	L	N	Spanish, *jueves*
church	L	L	L	L	L	Nahuatl, *teo·pantli*
chicken	L	L	L	L	L	Nahuatl, *to·tolin*

Note:
L = loanword (from either Spanish or Nahuatl); N = native creation; – = data missing; the languages run from west to east.
The model for the loanword is listed in the right column. Notice that in some cases the meaning of the loanword is not the same as in the donor language. (Based on Miller, 1990a.b.)

lexical acculturation). Loanwords were most often supplied by Spanish, but a few came from Nahuatl, supplied by the Aztec workers who accompanied the Spaniards during the early colonial period. The study of the cultural history can be enhanced if we can determine (1) if a borrowing was early or late, (2) if contact was direct or indirect, and (3) in the case of indirect contact, who the intermediaries were.

A borrowing from Nahuatl is necessarily evidence of early contact because the Nahuatl-speaking Aztec workers accompanied the Spaniards only in the early period. Spanish loanwords are identified as "early" if (1) the borrowings are of words that no longer have currency in local Spanish, (2) the borrowings are of words that reflect an earlier Spanish phonology, or (3) the borrowings show phonetic distortions from the Spanish models. We will examine each of these types, with examples. Evidence comes from seventeen communities, though the data are not complete for each of the words in question. The number of communities is so large that our examples will provide only a representative sample of the evidence.

There are four widespread borrowings from Nahuatl: *taxcal-li* 'tortilla' (pronounced [taškal-li]), *teo·-pan* 'church' (lit. 'God-place'), *tōtol-in* 'chicken' (the original meaning was 'turkey', but after the arrival of Spaniards, it shifted in meaning to include both animals), and *tekipanoā* 'work'. In a few of the languages, 'lime(stone)', used in making tortillas, is also a Nahuatl borrowing. (The elements *-li* and *-in* are absolute suffixes, elements added to Nahuatl nouns when they are neither possessed nor pluralized.) Some examples for 'tortilla':

Onevas:	*taskal*
Eudeve:	*táskari*
River Guarijío:	*takarí*
Yaqui:	*tása?im, táhka?i*
Mayo:	*táskari, táhkari*
Tubar:	*tasekałí-t*
Northern Tepehuan:	*taskali*
Seri:	*?atáskar*

The absolute suffix *-li*, which shows up variously as [-l(i)], [-r(i)], [-?i], [-ł i], is meaningful only in Nahuatl; it is simply part of the stem in the various borrowing languages. There are two Aztec forms for tortilla: *texcal-li* in the Classical Aztec of the Valley of Mexico, *taxcal-li* in most other dialects. Borrowings with the vowel [a] show that the Aztecs who came with the Spaniards were not speakers of Classical Aztec; probably they were Tlaxcalans.

The word for 'violin' and 'money' are borrowed from Spanish words that are no longer in use. 'Violin' is from *rabel* 'rebec', an instrument ancestral to the violin. Some examples:

Mountain Pima:	*la·wé·r*
Central and Western Tarahumara:	*rabéri*
Mountain Guarijío:	*yawéla*
River Guarijío:	*yawéra*
Yaqui:	*laában*
Southeastern Tepehuan:	*lavé·r*

'Money' is from *tomín*, a coin widely used in colonial Spanish America and widely borrowed throughout much of Spanish America, as well. In some languages, the native numerals 'two', 'four', and 'six' are used with this word, to express "twenty-five cents," "fifty cents," and "seventy-five cents"; for example, River Guarijío *woká tomí* 'twenty-five cents', or literally 'two money'. This way of counting money reflects the old "pieces of eight," still reflected in American English "two bits," "four bits," "six bits," but no longer used in Spanish. In one language, O'odham, the word for money is borrowed from Spanish *real*, also an old colonial coin.

Another example involves borrowings from *cabra* 'goat'. There are two words for goat still in use in the Spanish-speaking world, *chiva*, along with *cabra*, but only *chiva* is still in current use by Spanish speakers in northwest Mexico. Both have served as models for the indigenous languages of the area, for example:

O'odham:	*siwat*
Mountain Pima:	*ší·wkilʸ*
Mountain Guarijío:	*čiwá*
Yaqui: kabá·:	*číba*
Southeastern Tepehuan:	*kárvaš*
Cora: káu·ra:	*čí·vu*
Huichol:	*káa·pɨra·*

In some cases, the borrowing from *cabra* is used, but meaning 'sheep' instead of 'goat':

O'odham:	*ka·wal*
Mountain Pima:	*ká·wilʸ*
Mayo:	*kabara*
Seri:	*ka·r*

There are two differences between the phonetics of early colonial and present-day Spanish, involving sounds written with the letters "j" and "ll." Words written with the letter "j" were pronounced as a palatal sibilant [š], and borrowed usually as [š], [ṣ], or [s]; in current Spanish, "j" is pronounced as a velar fricative [x], so that later borrowings usually represent the sound with [h], the closest equivalent most of these languages have to [x]. In the second case, colonial Spanish pronounced "ll" as [lʸ], with borrowings representing the sound as [l] or [r]; in today's (Latin-American) Spanish, "ll" and "y" are pronounced identically, namely as [y]. An example of earlier [ṣ] for "j" is found in "orange," from Spanish *naranja*:

O'odham:	*nalaṣ*
Eastern Tarahumara:	*naláso, naʔlási*
Central Tarahumara:	*nalási*
Western Tarahumara:	*naráso*
Mountain and River Guarijío:	*naláso*
Yaqui:	*naáso, naʔso*

In a few cases, the word seems to represent a later borrowing, with [h], as for example, Mountain Pima *naráŋh*. Other words with "j" that were borrowed early are: *navaja* 'knife', *jarro* 'jar', *jabón* 'soap', and *jueves* 'Thursday'. Words with "ll" that were borrowed early are: *silla* 'saddle', *cuchillo* 'knife', and *castellano* 'Spaniard, White'.

The group characterized as containing phonetic distortions is a large one, and includes most of the words we have already discussed using other criteria. Some of the phonetic distortions are inexplicable, such as the appearance of [ʔ], the glottal stop, in these words in Mountain Guarijío:

toʔtorí	'chicken' (Nahuatl *tōtol-in*, 'turkey, chicken')
tuʔlasí	'peach' (Spanish *durazno*)
aʔrápa	'harp' (Spanish *arpa*)

In other cases, the changes are explicable in terms of the differences in the phonological systems of Spanish and the indigenous languages; thus consonant clusters not found in these languages are either simplified to a single consonant, or are broken by placing a vowel between them. An example is *cruz* 'cross', in which the /kr/ is either simplified to /k/, or is changed to /kur/, /kul/, or the like:

O'odham:	*kots*
Mountain Pima:	*kurš*
Yaqui:	*kús*
Northern Tepehuan:	*kurusi*

Later borrowings often maintain the cluster, presumably because of the increased number of fluent bilinguals. *Plátano* 'banana' provides an example:

Mountain Pima:	*plá·tan*
Central and Western Tarahumara:	*plátano*
Mayo:	*plá·tano*

Words in addition to "peach," "harp," and "cross" that have been borrowed with phonetic distortions of various kinds are: *vaca(s)* 'cow(s)', *buey(es)* 'ox(en)', *trigo* 'wheat', *manzana* 'apple', *Dios* 'God', *diablo* 'devil', *soldado* 'soldier', *martes* 'Tuesday', *miércoles* 'Wednesday', *viernes* 'Friday', and *domingo* 'Sunday' (borrowed with the meanings of both 'Sunday' and 'week').

A word of caution regarding evidence from phonetic distortions: it can be useful for identifying old borrowings, but lack of distortion does not guarantee late borrowings. The phonological sequence of some Spanish words is such that it is hard to imagine how early versus late borrowings might differ. An example given earlier is *chiva* 'goat': It contains no consonant clusters and no phonetic sequences or sounds that would be exotic for the aboriginal languages. Another complication is the fact that later generations of more fluent bilinguals can touch up an early borrowing if the model word is still to be found in current Spanish. A case in point, *trigo* 'wheat' in Mountain Guarijío shows considerable distortion: The cluster is divided by a vowel, the initial /t/ is replaced by /p/, and the accent is on the final syllable, rather than the second; in the River dialect of Guarijío, the consonant cluster is split, but otherwise the word is identical to Spanish:

> Mountain Guarijío: *pirikó*
> River Guarijío: *tirígo*

Nonlinguistic Information Gleaned from the Linguistic Evidence

A coherent picture emerges from a study of the early Nahuatl and Spanish loanwords, especially when coupled with the direct historical record. There are a number of domesticated plants and animals that are well integrated into the native economy, and which the linguistic evidence indicates were early introductions: peaches, oranges, apples, wheat, cows, oxen, goats, sheep, and chickens. Other plants and animals may well have been introduced early, such as the pig, but the linguistic evidence is silent. The early borrowing of "saddle" is indirect evidence of the early introduction of the horse (although most of the languages have borrowed the Spanish word *caballo* 'horse', it is in a form that gives no evidence of early introduction).

Except for the hunting and gathering Seri, all of the original inhabitants were farmers whose most important crop was corn. It is most frequently prepared in the form of the tortilla, which is made by boiling the corn in lime water, grinding it, and then shaping the resulting dough into balls, which are flattened out and baked on a comal or griddle. This method of preparation is so pervasive in Indian communities today that one would think it must be a pre-Columbian practice. The linguistic evidence clearly shows otherwise, however, with the word for "tortilla" being borrowed from the Aztec workers. Furthermore, in most languages, the word for "lime" is borrowed from Spanish, whereas in the remaining languages it is either clearly a new derivation or a borrowing from Nahuatl. While the cultivation of corn is pre-Columbian, the linguistic evidence shows that the tortilla, the most common means of preparing corn today, is new. The tortilla complex was, in fact, borrowed from the Nahuatl-speaking workers who accompanied the first Spanish colonists into the area.

The linguistic evidence indicates that the native populations were introduced early to a wider, nonsubsistence economy. That the word for "work" was borrowed from Nahuatl, not Spanish, is an indication that there was closer contact between the Aztec workers and the indigenous population than with the Spanish overlords, at least as far as this activity was concerned. The notion of work was, of course, not something novel for these people. Working for someone else, however, was new, whether working for wages, being drafted for working a certain number of days per week on mission farms, or working as virtual slaves in the mines. Other work-related words, namely, money and the days of the week, are from Spanish.

It is hardly surprising to find linguistic evidence for the early introduction of Christianity, with early Spanish borrowings of "God," "devil," and "cross." The use of the Nahuatl word for "church" is evidence that the Aztecs also played a role in this aspect of colonial acculturation.

The linguistic evidence shows that the violin and harp were early introductions. These two instruments are now well integrated into the native ceremonial life, so much so that without historical evidence to the contrary, one might think they were aboriginal inventions.

In later borrowings, the forms in each of the languages are sometimes different enough from each other to indicate that they were introduced separately into each of the communities. An example is *plato* 'plate':

Mountain Pima:	*pla·t*
Western Tarahumara:	*biráto*
Mountain Guarijío:	*ihpeláto*
Mayo:	*purá·to*

Many of the early loans, on the other hand, show evidence of having spread through intertribal borrowing. A striking example is the borrowing of *trigo* 'wheat' in these three languages:

O'odham:	*pilkani*
Opata:	*piliko*
Mountain Guarijío:	*pirikó*

The replacement of Spanish initial /t/ with /p/ is an unlikely substitution, one that probably took place only once; that is, the word was probably borrowed into one

Indian language, and then later borrowed from that language into other Indian languages.

The area of greatest Spanish contact was along the coastal plains. Some of the early loans spread to the most eastern communities in the mountainous interior, while others spread only a limited distance. As a result, the western communities have a larger number of borrowings for these early acculturative items, while those to the east have a larger proportion of native creations, through new coinages or semantic shift. Table 13.2, in which the distribution is plotted for selected loanwords, illustrates this pattern.

Establishing the Direction of Borrowing

Almost all the languages of the Americas have loanwords from colonial languages, notably from Danish, French, Russian, English, Spanish, and Portuguese. As in the case we have been looking at, the borrowing is often chronologically layered, and examples are found in the Spanish borrowing into the Pueblo languages. The intertribal spread of loanwords is also found elsewhere; for example, the spread of Spanish loanwords well beyond the area of direct Spanish contact, and it is possible to trace the routes these words traveled. Sometimes loanwords are found from colonial languages that are no longer the primary contact language; for example, Spanish in California and the southwestern United States, French in the southeastern United States, and Russian in Alaska.

The isolation of loanwords between the aboriginal languages provides evidence for prehistoric contact. In this case, one does not have available historical records to indicate who has borrowed from whom, but frequently there is linguistic evidence to determine the direction of borrowing. Sometimes phonetic evidence provides the clue. The word for 'mountain goat' in Haida, spoken on the Queen Charlotte Islands, is *mat*, while in Tsimshian, the neighboring language spoken along the British Columbia coast, the word is *mati*. The Haida must have borrowed from the Tsimshian, not the reverse, since the consonant /m/ is rare in Haida, being limited primarily to loanwords.

Another example is found in the Pueblo area, where the Keres-speaking Acoma use *k'azi·ná*, and the Uto-Aztecan-speaking Hopi use *kačina* as the name for a culturally very important set of rain gods (borrowed into Southwestern English as kachina). In this case, both phonetic and morphological evidence can be used to show that the direction of borrowing is from Acoma to Hopi. The Acoma word begins with a glottalized consonant, /k'/, a class of sounds absent in Hopi. Acoma would not change an unglottalized /k/ in Hopi to its glottalized counterpart in Acoma, but we would expect a Hopi borrowing to change a glottalized sound to its unglottalized counterpart. In word initial position, Hopi normally has [qa] rather than [ka], except in loanwords. Furthermore, the word is analyzable, or at least partly so, in Acoma. There is a technique for deriving nouns from verbs, by using the third person pronominal prefix *k'-*, and the noun forming suffix *–ná*, a suffix that lengthens and attaches the high tonal accent to the preceding vowel. In this particular case, the root, *–azi*, occurs only in this combination.

The comparative method can sometimes be enlisted for establishing the source of borrowing. Acoma and Hopi share another word, Acoma *húnani*, Hopi *honani*. (The difference in vowel is no clue, since Acoma lacks /o/ and Hopi lacks /u/.) In Acoma the word refers to a particular fetish used in the Badger cult. In Hopi, it has the same meaning, as well as meaning simply 'badger'. The occurrence of only the more specialized meaning is a clue that it is a borrowing into Acoma, but the more conclusive evidence is provided by the fact that the Hopi word for 'badger' finds cognates in other languages, and *huna must be reconstructed for Uto-Aztecan.

Borrowings between related languages provide special problems because one must determine if similarities between words are due to common retention (i.e., cognate) or borrowing. We noted an example in which there is evidence that the Guarijío word for 'tobacco' *wipá* was borrowed from a Tepiman language (section 12.2). The argument was that the word obeyed the Uto-Aztecan sound correspondences for the Tepiman languages, whereas it did not in Guarijío.

13.5 CALIFORNIA REVISITED

We have illustrated several methods that use linguistic clues for reconstructing linguistic prehistory. We apply them now to California, a particularly difficult and challenging case. We have seen that not only is California an area of great genetic diversity, but it is one in which a great deal of diffusion has taken place. California Indians have been in contact with each other for millennia, with much exchange of both linguistic and nonlinguistic material. First we give an overview in which the interpretation of the genetic units is the focal point. Then we take a close look at a situation that involves diffusion in relatively recent times. From earlier discussion (sections 9.2, 11.2, 12.5, and 12.6), it should be clear that we are touching upon only a small part of California linguistic prehistory.

Distribution and Diversity

Archaeological evidence shows in situ development in California for at least ten thousand years. There is also archaeological evidence that new groups entered California at various prehistoric periods. An archaeologist studying preliterate cultures has no way of tying a specific language to a specific culture, so that there is no certain way of tying archaeological evidence to language. Nevertheless, it is likely (in fact, almost certain) that some early archaeological cultures are ancestral to some of the modern Californian groups, and it is not unthinkable that members of these cultural groups spoke languages ancestral to some of the present-day languages. The most inclusive genetic classifications place the California languages into six genetic units. As we have seen, the two most inclusive stocks, Hokan and Penutian, have yet to be validated, while the genetic unity of the other four, Uto-Aztecan, Algic, Athapaskan, and Yukian, is unquestioned.

Hokan and Penutian incorporate approximately two-thirds of the languages of California. They display great internal diversity, which, in turn (assuming they are valid genetic constructs), would indicate great age within California. The Hokan languages surround the more geographically compact Penutian stock, which would suggest that perhaps the Penutians were later arrivals who pushed the Hokan peoples into peripheral positions.

The diversity within Uto-Aztecan is not as great as that for Hokan or Penutian, but it is nevertheless considerable. The bulk of these languages is found outside of California. It has been suggested that the homeland was not too far away, perhaps near the border of Arizona and Sonora. This argument is based on an examination of the center of greatest linguistic diversity and an examination of botanical terms. The nature of the evidence, however, is not as clear cut as in the case of the Numic speakers we discussed in section 13.3. There is evidence that Uto-Aztecan and Kiowa-Tanoan form a more inclusive stock called Aztec-Tanoan. Although the evidence for this remote relationship is not as good as it is for Algic and cannot be considered validated, it is nevertheless fairly convincing, more convincing than that considered for Iroquoian, Siouan, and Caddoan in section 12.7. The Tanoan languages are spoken in some of the Pueblos of New Mexico, and Kiowa is found nearby on the southern Plains, so that it is not unlikely that a homeland for the Proto-Uto-Aztecan lies somewhere in that general direction, not far from southeastern California.

Algic is equally diverse, and the majority of these languages are also found far afield. Of the three genetic units that comprise Algic, two are found in northern California (Wiyot and Yurok), while the third (Algonquian) is found much farther east. Despite the eastern location of the majority of Algic languages, the center of linguistic diversity is in northern California, the location of two of the three genetic units, so the most parsimonious hypothesis would place the homeland of Proto-Algic in northern California or environs, with a single group moving east and later diversifying into the Algonquian languages, rather than assuming a more eastern homeland, with two groups later moving to California.

The Pacific Coast Athapaskan languages are quite closely related and are recent arrivals from the north; the archaeological evidence suggests that they arrived less than a thousand years ago and this matches the linguistic evidence.

The Yukian family represents the California enigma. It is the only genetic unit that is not a part of a larger (real or putative) family and does not have (real or putative) relatives outside the California area. Various linguists have found (or claimed to have found) similarities between it and various other language families, including Athapaskan, Hokan, Penutian, and Siouan. Although some of the similarities are striking, no one has been able to demonstrate that they must reflect a genetic relationship, rather than chance or borrowing. With no certain linguistic relatives outside of northern California, one can speculate that they might represent the vestiges of a language group that is older in California than the Hokan stock; but one should bear in mind that this is mere speculation. A word of caution: The fact that the time depth within the Yukian family is shallow does not mean these languages are "younger," only that Proto-Yukian was spoken more recently than, for example, Proto-Uto-Aztecan or Proto-Hokan. Every protolanguage is derived from a still more ancient ancestral language, whether or not we have the evidence for the ancestral form.

Ethnic territories shifted frequently in precontact California, with some communities disappearing, others fusing together, and still others increasing in population and splitting into new communities. Over the centuries, particular groups may have moved repeatedly. Also, at various times, language boundaries would be more or less arbitrary or indefinite, tending to merge gradually, especially between peoples with strong social ties. The northern Hill Yokuts and Southern Sierra Miwok, for example, often intermarried and lived in mixed villages near their common border, and at least one Clear Lake Pomo village was occupied by speakers of Hill Patwin and five Pomo languages. We present this cautionary note, because situations of this sort preclude our knowing the details of the linguistic prehistory and can cloud our understanding of the larger picture. We can even be misled in seemingly simple situations with a shallow time depth, as the following example illustrates.

"The Case of the Broken Bottle"

The seven Pomoan languages are located in the area north of San Francisco Bay between the Pacific coast and the Sacramento Valley. Three of the languages, Kashaya Pomo, Southern Pomo, and Central Pomo, located along and close to the coast, form an especially closely related group within the Pomoan family. These languages share the following word for 'broken glass fragments':

Kashaya Pomo:	*putílka*
Southern Pomo:	*pʰot·ílka*
Central Pomo:	*pʰtílka*

The form in Central Pomo is restricted to the Coast Central dialect, where it means "glass in any form" but especially "broken fragments." Based on the sound correspondences in these three languages, one could reconstruct the protoword as *pʰutilka. In Kashaya Pomo, an initial aspirated stop loses aspiration when the following syllable begins with a plain stop (in this case /t/) or an aspirated stop; in Southern Pomo *u in initial syllables becomes /o/ if the following vowel is /o/ or (as in this case) /i/, and a single consonant is geminated if the following syllable ends with a heavy syllable (thus /t/ becomes /t·/, since the syllable /til/ ends with a consonant). In Central Pomo, all vowels except *a are lost in initial syllables.

If we were to reconstruct *pʰutilka in the protolanguage, it would be an error, in spite of the fact that the phonetic correspondences are perfect. This is because the word has been borrowed from Russian butílka (бутылка) 'bottle'. From 1811 to 1842 Russia maintained a military presence at Fort Ross, which is located in the middle of Kashaya Pomo country. The form was probably borrowed first into Kashaya Pomo, from whence it spread to the other two languages.

There are two problems to reconcile, one dealing with meaning, the other with form. The meaning in Russian is 'bottle' not 'broken glass'. We can speculate that the Pomos saw bottles more often in their broken rather than whole form, particularly after the end of the Russians' occupation, with broken bottles and other debris being left around the abandoned fort.

The problem in form is a bit more difficult. Since related languages are very frequently in the same area, and in contact with one another, it is not uncommon for them to borrow words from each other. One can normally distinguish cognates, that is, words inherited from the protolanguage (section 12.2), from borrowings, because cognates will obey the sound changes, and fit into the pattern of regular phonetic correspondences, while borrowings will not. Thus if Kashaya Pomo putílka were borrowed into Southern Pomo, one would expect the form to be *putílka since it would not undergo the sound changes discussed previously. One possible explanation would be that the word was borrowed before the sound changes took place, but that event would be extremely unlikely, because one would not expect all four sound changes to have taken place in the short span of a century and a half.

A much more likely explanation is that the speakers of these three languages, who were in close contact with one another, had come to know the sound changes. This would be intuitive not conscious knowledge; that is, Southern Pomo speakers would know that if a Kashaya Pomo word began with /pu/, a cognate word would likely begin with /pʰu/ or /pʰo/, and in this case it should be /pʰo/ since the vowel of the following syllable is /i/. Such an interpretation is all the more likely because the word is seemingly analyzable in Pomoan. There is a Proto-Pomoan prefix *pʰu- 'by blowing, by wind', which (following the regular correspondences) is Kashaya Pomo pu- (before a plain or aspirated stop), pʰu- (before other consonants), Southern

Pomo p^hu- or p^ho- (depending on the vowel of the next syllable), and Central Pomo p^h-. Further, Southern and Central Pomo have a suffix –*ka*, indicating that the speaker did not see the action, but rather infers it; it is best translated as "must have." Thus the forms could be interpreted as meaning "the wind must have broken the glass" or "it must have blown over and broken" (such an interpretation is not available for Kashaya Pomo, as the corresponding suffix is –*q*). The prefix "by blowing, by wind" is especially common with a group of imitative roots (section 12.5), so that the word could be analyzed by native speakers as containing an imitative root –*til*– meaning "the sound of glass breaking." Such an analysis is strengthened in Central Pomo because of the similarity of the root –*zil*– 'tinkle, the sound of small bells ringing or of shell pendants hitting each other', which occurs in derivations like *zi·li·liy* 'to tinkle once', *zi·lizliw* 'to be tinkling'. Southern Pomo speakers have treated –*til*– as an imitative root and have made new formations such as: *ti·li·liy* 'glass to tinkle from breaking all at once', and *ti·litliw* 'glass to be tinkling from breaking'.

There is a moral in all this. We are able to arrive at the correct historical conclusion, namely, that this word was borrowed into the three Pomoan languages, and that the three words were not cognates derived from a common protoword. We are able to do this because the nonlinguistic historical facts are clear. There were Russians in the Kashaya Pomo area early in the last century, and the Russian use of the word *butílka* (буты́лка) 'bottle', as well as their knowledge of bottles, predates their contact with Pomo speakers, so that it must be a borrowing from Russian into Pomo, not the reverse. Pre-Columbian California was an area of considerable linguistic diversity; bilingualism was rampant, as was linguistic borrowing. Thus we must take great care in trying to distinguish resemblances due to cognation from resemblances due to borrowing. Doubtless there will be cases in which we cannot distinguish between the two, or in which we will be fooled.

As a final note, it is interesting that the word for 'bottle' is *woté·ya* in these three Pomoan languages. It is derived from Spanish *botella* [botéya] and is probably an indirect borrowing, that is, with other Californian languages as intermediaries, since there was no direct contact with Spanish speakers. Both Spanish *botella* and Russian *butílka* are ultimately related to Latin *buticula*, with the Spanish word descended from the Latin, but the Russian word a borrowing.

SOURCES

In section 13.1 the discussion of the northern origin of the Navajo is based on Sapir 1936; in the commentary on reconstructed vocabulary and the Uto-Aztecan family, the remarks concerning plants and the significance of gathering in Proto-

Uto-Aztecan society draw from Fowler 1983. Section 13.2 draws from Siebert 1967. In section 13.3 the Numic discussion draws on Lamb 1958 and Miller 1986; in addition see Fowler 1972 (distribution of plants and animals) and Miller 1986:103 (Shoshoni examples); Liljeblad 1971 (cited in Miller 1986:103) (Northern Paiute, Shoshoni and Nez Perce terms for "fish"). On Linguistic data and culture history, see Sapir 1916. Section 13.4 is based on Miller 1990a,b.; on establishing the direction of borrowing, see Trager 1944 and Miller 1959–1960 (borrowing of Spanish terms by Pueblo languages); see also Shipley 1962, Kroskrity and Reinhardt 1984 (spread of loans beyond area of direct contact), and Sapir 1916 (Haida borrowing from Tsmishian). In section 13.5, on distribution and diversity, see Fowler 1983 (Uto-Aztecan homeland); see also Whorf and Trager 1937, Miller 1983:122 (evidence for Aztec-Tanoan), Moratto 1984:529–74, Whistler 1977 (California prehistory)*, and Moratto 1984:570–71 (Pacific coast Athapaskan entry into California). "The case of the broken bottle" discussion is based on Oswalt 1971b.

SUGGESTED READINGS

See Mithun 1984 for aspects of Iroquoian culture history. Sapir 1916 is a classic in the use of linguistic evidence as a tool for prehistory. See also Lathrop and Troike 1988 for discussion of relationship between archaeological and linguistic data in the Americas.

* Moratto's and Whistler's conclusions do not always match the view we present here.

CHAPTER 14

SPREAD AND DISTRIBUTION
OF LANGUAGE FAMILIES

Languages and language families are distributed unevenly throughout the Americas. In some cases, wide areas are covered by a single language family, while in other cases families are found in restricted areas. Some places in the Americas have a considerable number of language isolates, single languages with no proven or close relatives.

For discussion purposes, we divide North and South America each into three geographic areas. The divisions in North America correspond reasonably well to cultural and linguistic provinces. What we call eastern and western North America includes Canada, the United States, and the northern part of Mexico, divided, roughly, by the Rocky Mountains. Middle America includes the rest of North America, that is, Mesoamerica (as defined in section 12.4) plus the area to the south and east as far as the Panama-Colombia border. It should be noted that many of the languages of northern Mexico, especially in the east, became extinct rather early, so that in some cases the only record is a name, and, when we are lucky, a short word list.

The aim of the discussion in sections 14.1 through 14.4 is to present a general picture of the distribution of the languages of the Americas. In appendix 2 there is a complete listing of the families and languages of North America. Knowledge is too limited to allow an attempt at listing the languages for South America. The discussion in sections 14.1 through 14.3 includes only the briefest mention of remote relationships and excludes the more controversial linkages that would unite all or almost all of the languages of the Americas (section 12.7).

14.1 EASTERN NORTH AMERICA

There are four large language families in this region: Algonquian, Iroquoian, Muskogean, and Siouan. About half of the Algonquian languages belonged to the Eastern Algonquian branch and were spoken along the Atlantic coast; the remaining languages were spoken primarily in the eastern woodlands and northern Plains. Cree, with about eighty thousand speakers, is today one of the most widely spoken North American Indian languages (section 12.1). It is followed closely by Ojibwa with about fifty thousand speakers, found mostly in Canada (Quebec, Ontario, Manitoba, Saskatchewan). A few of the remaining languages have speakers that number between one thousand and five thousand: Micmac, Potawatomi, Blackfoot, Cheyenne, and Arapaho. Of the remaining languages, perhaps a third or more are now extinct, while those that are not extinct are spoken mostly by older people, with numbers ranging from a handful to a few hundred. Some of the Algonquian languages are now spoken in Oklahoma, sometimes exclusively so, while at other times in addition to places in or near their original homeland.

Yurok, Wiyot (northern coast of California), and Algonquian are members of the Algic stock. Yurok and Wiyot were first united under the name of Ritwan, but because it is generally accepted that Algic does not consist of two members, Ritwan and Algonquian, but rather of three coequal members, the term Ritwan is no longer needed (see sections 12.6 and 12.7).

Some have tried to link Beothuk, an extinct language of Newfoundland, to Algonquian. The language became extinct in the nineteenth century. Our knowledge of it is limited to short word lists recorded by untrained observers. Although the data are not of good quality, they are adequate to be sure that Beothuk is not an Algonquian language, but not adequate to determine if a more remote relationship exists. The major motivation for trying to link Beothuk and Algonquian is probably based on their geographic proximity.

The Iroquoian language family consists of two linguistic branches: Southern Iroquoian, a single language (Cherokee) and Northern Iroquoian, found in two geographic areas: one in the South, in Virginia, the Carolinas, Tennessee, Georgia, and Alabama; the other in the North, around or near the Great Lakes. Some of the languages classified linguistically as Northern Iroquoian were located in the south. There was considerable postcontact movement, with some of the southern Iroquoian peoples moving north, and others moving to Canada and Oklahoma. The largest Iroquoian language today is Cherokee, with about ten thousand speakers, most of whom reside in Oklahoma, but with a few in their aboriginal home in the Carolinas. There are about three thousand Mohawk speakers who straddle the border between New York and Quebec. The remaining extant linguistic groups have much smaller numbers of speakers.

The Muskogean languages were originally spoken in what is now the southeastern United States. There are four extant languages; possibly there were more in pre-Columbian times. The majority of the Muskogeans have either moved or been removed from their original homeland to Texas, Florida, and, especially, Oklahoma. Most of the language communities in Oklahoma are in decline, while those in Florida (especially Seminole Creek) and those in their original homeland are still very much alive. Choctaw and Creek have the largest numbers of speakers, with about ten thousand each.

Natchez, a language isolate, and Muskogean are probably related. The Natchez were a powerful tribe who lived near modern Natchez, Mississippi. They were defeated by the French in a war in 1731 and were scattered among a variety of other tribal groups in the Southeast, principally the Creek and Cherokee. The language survived into the middle of the twentieth century in Oklahoma.

The Siouan languages were found in scattered areas in the South in what are now Mississippi, the Carolinas, and Virginia; and in the Great Plains and bordering areas, particularly the eastern Plains. All of the languages formerly spoken in the South (Biloxi, Ofo, Quapaw, Tutelo, and Catawba, along with some languages in Virginia) are now extinct. There is also some evidence that there were additional Siouan languages in the east and south that became extinct before any record was made of them. The several quite different dialects of Dakota have perhaps fifteen thousand speakers or more, and are located in several places in the northern Plains, in both the United States and Canada. Several other Siouan languages have speakers whose numbers range into the high hundreds or low thousands: Crow, Hidatsa, Winnebago, Chiwere (Iowa and Oto), and Dhegiha (Omaha, Osage, and Ponca).

The Caddoan family consists of five languages, spoken in three small and widely scattered locations, from the northern Plains to Louisiana.

A number of language isolates were spoken along the Gulf coast and immediate interior. In addition to the Natchez, there were Timucua in Florida, Tunica in Mississippi, Chitimacha and Atakapa in Louisiana, and, extending along the Texas coast into northern Mexico, Tonkawa, Coahuilteco, Karankawa, and others. All are now extinct, with some, especially those in south Texas and northern Mexico, becoming extinct rather early, while others continued to be spoken by small numbers of speakers well into the twentieth century. Our knowledge of these languages is variable. For Tunica, Natchez, Chitimacha, and Tonkawa, we have fairly extensive twentieth-century recordings. Our knowledge of the rest comes from nineteenth-century records, with the data ranging from fairly extensive material to short word lists, and in some cases, little more than a tribal name with the comment from an early observer as to the linguistic or ethnic affiliation of the group. Therefore, there are a number of coastal tribes in southern Texas and northern Mexico that are linguistically unclassified and unclassifiable. There have been various suggestions linking some of these isolates to other families or to each other. Except for the genetic relationship between Natchez and the Muskogean family, none of the suggested linkages has received much support from experts on these languages. Our survey is completed with Yuchi, a language isolate. It was originally spoken in Georgia; today it is restricted to a few hundred speakers in Oklahoma.

As noted in section 1.2, the United States government began a policy in the 1830s of encouraging or forcing the removal of Indian tribes to territories that were to be incorporated into the state of Oklahoma. The policy was first applied to a number of tribes in the South, and later to Indians found in the northern and Plains states. As a result, many languages once spoken elsewhere are now spoken in Oklahoma, in some cases exclusively so, or in addition to places in or near their original location. Oklahoma now enjoys considerably more linguistic diversity than it did in earlier times.

14.2 WESTERN NORTH AMERICA

In contrast to eastern North America, western North America has many more language families and isolates with a restricted range. Even in areas of considerable population density, such as California, the number of speakers of a single language has seldom ranged above a few thousand. The families covering a wider range can be easily listed: Eskimo-Aleut, Athapaskan, Salish, and Uto-Aztecan.

Eskimo-Aleut languages stretch across the northern edge of North America from the Aleutian Islands to Greenland. The major division is between Aleut, a single language, and Eskimo, six closely related languages. Three of the Eskimo languages are spoken on the Chukchi Peninsula in Siberia. The largest language, both in terms of number of speakers and geographic extent, is Inuit-Inupiaq (also known as Eastern Eskimo), spoken in a dialect continuum from the Seward Peninsula in Alaska, across the Canadian Arctic, and along the coasts of Quebec, Labrador, and Greenland. In 1980, there were sixty-eight thousand speakers, with forty-three thousand in Greenland. The West Greenlandic dialect is very much alive with forty thousand speakers and, because of thriving literacy and its use in the school system and in local government, it is likely to remain so well into the future.

The languages in the Athapaskan family are closely related and are spoken in three areas: interior Alaska and northwest Canada, along the coast of southern Oregon and northern California, and in the Southwest. It is difficult to give an accurate count of the northern languages, since they form a dialect or language complex with few sharp boundaries; the most authoritative source lists twenty-three. Even though the area is huge, the population in this harsh environment is low. The largest language is Chipewyan, with five thousand speakers, spoken in the far northern part of Alberta, Saskatchewan, and Manitoba, and into the Northwest Territories. There are almost as many speakers for the Slavey-Hare dialect and language complex, spoken over a very wide area in the Northwest Territories to the north and west of Chipewyan. But some other languages have (and presumably had, in precontact times) only a few hundred speakers.

There are five Pacific coast Athapaskan languages. As was typical of much of California (section 12.6), these languages were spoken in limited areas, with a limited number of speakers, around a thousand in most cases. All the languages except Hupa are extinct or nearly so.

There are seven Apachean languages, spoken today mostly in Arizona and New Mexico, but in earlier times they ranged east and south into adjacent areas of Oklahoma, Texas, and Mexico. The Navajo constitute the largest Indian group north of central Mexico, numbering 166,519 in 1981, and they are still growing; of these, about two thirds still spoke the language at the time of that count. The Western Apache numbered almost sixteen thousand, with three-quarters being speakers. The numbers for the other five Apachean languages are considerably fewer, with three of the languages nearing extinction.

Athapaskan languages were also spoken in two isolated enclaves: Nicola in British Columbia, and Kwalhioqua-Tlatskanai, spoken near the mouth of the Columbia River. Both are extinct. Nicola was surrounded by Salish languages, and our knowledge of it is too fragmentary to be sure if it was a distinct language or merely a southern outlier of Carrier. Records of Kwalhioqua-Tlatskanai are complete enough to determine that it was a distinct language and, moreover, that it was not a member of the Pacific branch of languages found in southern Oregon and northern California.

The Athapaskan language family fits into a larger grouping called Athapaskan-Eyak, which consists of two branches, with Eyak as one branch and all the Athapaskan languages as the other. Eyak is a recently extinct language that was spoken on the southern coast of Alaska. The time depth of this larger grouping is relatively modest, perhaps about thirty-five hundred years. A still more inclusive grouping, called Na-dene, includes two additional languages, Tlingit and Haida. Tlingit is found on the Alaskan panhandle, while Haida is spoken on the Queen Charlotte Islands in British Columbia. Although there is a consensus that Tlingit and Athapaskan-Eyak are related, there is considerable doubt about the inclusion of Haida.

The Salish family consists of some twenty-three languages, which occupy the better part of Washington, southern British Columbia, and parts of Oregon, Idaho, and Montana. Two of the languages are separated from the main body: Bella Coola on the British Columbian coast to the north and Tillamook, on the Oregon coast to the south. The remaining languages form a continuous block. The genetic unity is clear, but not close. There has been considerable communication between neighboring groups, so that untangling the interinfluences between dialects and languages provides a challenge for the historical investigator. Few of the languages today have more than one or two thousand speakers.

The Uto-Aztecan languages are found over a wide area in western North America and northwest Mexico, and extend into Mesoamerica. Excluding the Aztecan languages of Mesoamerica, the largest language is Tarahumara, spoken in the mountains of Chihuahua, with an estimated population of over fifty thousand and still expanding. The Uto-Aztecan family was discussed in section 12.2. The Kiowa-Tanoan family of New Mexico and Oklahoma and Uto-Aztecan form the Aztec-Tanoan stock. Each of the three Tanoan languages is spoken by a few thousand speakers in a number of Pueblos of New Mexico and Arizona.

There are other language families that cover a more modest range. Those in California, such as Shastan, Pomoan, Utian, and Chumash, were discussed in section 12.6 There are a few others, such as Wakashan, consisting of six languages centering upon Vancouver Island and the coastal areas of the adjacent mainland; Yuman-Cochimí, consisting of eight Yuman languages in southern California, western Arizona, and northern Baja California; and two Cochimí languages in southern Baja California. Beyond these families, one begins to list language isolates or families of two or three languages with no clearly proven affiliations; for example Chemakuan, a family of two languages, both probably now extinct, spoken on the northern Washington coast; Kutenai, a language isolate spoken near the junction of Idaho, Montana, and British Columbia; Coos, an isolate, probably now extinct, found along the Oregon coast; the extinct Takelma, a language isolate of southern Oregon; Sahaptian, two languages of Idaho and eastern Oregon and Washington; Chimariko, an extinct isolate spoken in a single valley in northwestern California; Wintuan, a family of three languages in the Sacramento valley of California; Zuni, an isolate in the Pueblo Southwest; Keres, an isolate spoken at seven Pueblos in the Southwest; Seri, an isolate on the Sonoran coast; and many others.

As with the isolates in the eastern part of North America, there have been many attempts to link these single languages or small language families to other groups or to each other. The most ambitious schemes involve the proposed Penutian family (numbers 26–41 on the list in appendix 2) and the Hokan family (42–53 in appendix 2), which have been discussed in section 12.6. Undoubtedly some of the suggested but unproven affiliations will be validated as work on these languages continues.

There are three noteworthy facts about the distribution of these language families and isolates; first, there is a great deal more diversity among the languages west of the Rockies than those east of the Rockies; second, within this western zone, there is more diversity along the coast than in the interior; and last, it is striking that there is a rather strict division into east and west, defined generally by the Rocky Mountains. The exceptions to this division are easily listed. In the north, the Eskimo-Aleut family extends from the far west to the far east. The Athapaskan languages are generally in the west, with two exceptions: one is Sarcee, a northern Athapaskan group that has moved into the Plains; the other involves the Apachean group to the south, in which two languages, Kiowa-Apache (not to be confused with Kiowa) and Lipan Apache moved out into the southern Plains. (Evidence from a variety of sources suggests that the Apachean group split off from their northern cousins and traveled along the east side of the Rockies before moving into the

Southwest; see section 13.1.) The Kiowa-Tanoan family consists of four languages, with three of them in the Pueblo Southwest, but with Kiowa in the southern Plains. Some Numic-speaking peoples (Uto-Aztecan) are also found in the Plains: some Shoshonis, some Utes, and the Comanche (section 13.3). Finally, the distantly related Algic family is found in both areas: Two of the branches consist of single languages, Wiyot and Yurok found in northwestern California, while the third branch, the closely related but well diversified Algonquian languages, are found to the east (sections 12.6 and 12.7).

Any discussion of linguistic diversity must be concerned with uniform units. One study that carefully controlled this factor grouped North American languages north of Mexico into ninety-two "conservative" families, those families that had about the same or less diversity than Germanic. This would give each family a time depth of no more than about twenty-five hundred years. The study was then able to show much more accurately the range of linguistic diversity than studies that have not controlled for degree of time depth: Of these ninety-two families, forty-five were represented along the Pacific strip, and sixty-six were represented west of the Rockies.

14.3 MIDDLE AMERICA

The diversity found in western America continues on into Middle America, though not to the same degree. In Mesoamerica proper, which covers all but the southeastern range of Middle America, there were, and in some cases still are, large populations, because of the pre-Columbian urban populations in this area (section 4.4). The area of greatest diversity was and still is in Oaxaca, on the Pacific side of the Isthmus of Mexico, where scores of distinct languages are spoken. There are some languages, sometimes restricted in geographic area, sometimes not, that were important because of their political and cultural position, and were (and often still are) important because of their numbers. Some of the languages, such as Yucatec Mayan, are spoken in a contiguous or connected geographic area, while others such as Nahuatl and Otomí, are found in a number of enclaves, reflecting the kind of movement brought about by the political upheavals of empire building.

The Uto-Aztecan languages in this area represent a southern extension. The two Corachol languages, Cora and Huichol, are spoken in the northwest, in the state of Nayarit. There are three Aztecan languages: Nahuatl, still spoken by a half million or more people, Pipil, nearly extinct, and Pochutla, now extinct. Nahuatl displays considerable dialect diversity, with the dialects being different enough that they should probably be considered a cluster of closely related languages; they were (and still are) spoken over a wide area centering around Mexico City, along with a number of enclaves to the south and east (section 4.4). The main body of Pipil was spoken in Nicaragua, but with a number of enclaves elsewhere. Pochutla was spoken on the Pacific coast in Oaxaca.

The Otopamean family is represented by about a dozen languages. Most of the languages occupied a solid block of territory to the north and west of present day Mexico City, along with numerous enclaves elsewhere in central Mexico. Mazahua and the Otomí languages number their speakers in the tens of thousands, while most of the remaining languages are represented by much more modest figures.

Popolocan contains about half a dozen languages, spoken in scattered enclaves in Oaxaca and Puebla. The largest is Mazatec, spoken by about eighty-five thousand people.

The Mixtecan family, found in Oaxaca and adjacent states, consists of three groups: the Mixtec languages, Cuicatec, and the Trique languages. The closely related Mixtec languages have about one hundred and seventy thousand speakers.

The Zapotecan family, also in Oaxaca, includes the Zapotec and Chatino languages. Speakers of the Zapotec languages were the carriers of the civilization represented at Monte Alban, an important city for well over a thousand years, with a population reaching into the tens of thousands, and with an even larger population in the surrounding areas. The languages are still spoken by about two hundred thousand people. The Chatino languages are spoken by smaller numbers, about twenty-five thousand.

Totonacan consists of two languages, Totonac and Tepehua, spoken on and near the Gulf Coast, to the north of the Nahuatl. There is some evidence that the important cultural center of Teotihuacan was founded by Totonac speakers, which, if correct, would make it a culturally important language during the prehistoric period when this city was the cultural and political center of western Mesoamerica and boasted a population of tens or hundreds of thousands. There are almost a hundred thousand speakers of Totonac today.

The Mixe-Zoquean family is spoken primarily in Oaxaca, bounded by Nahuatl to the west, the Zapotecan languages to the south, and the Mayan languages to the east. These languages were probably spoken by people known in the archaeological literature as the Olmecs, people who are seen as the fountainhead of Mesoamerican civilization. The numbers of speakers today are more modest (by Mesoamerican standards), never reaching above the low tens of thousands for the individual languages.

There are about thirty Mayan languages, located mostly in the Yucatán Peninsula, Chiapas, Guatemala, and Belize. One Mayan language, Huastec, is found in Veracruz, on the Gulf coast well to the northwest of the main body of Mayan languages. Many of the languages are still thriving, with speakers numbering in the tens and hundreds of thousands. Among the largest is Yucatec (also sometimes, but ambiguously, known as Mayan); it is spoken on the Yucatán Peninsula. Yucatec and the language to the south, Chol, are the Mayan languages represented in the hieroglyphic writing system (section 8.2).

Languages belonging to the Chibchan family are found in Costa Rica and Panama, along with a few outliers farther north. The number of languages is uncounted, but clearly there are many, some extinct or moribund, whereas others are very much alive, such as Rama in southern Nicaragua, and Kuna (or Cuna) in Panama (discussed in section 5.6). The four languages belonging to the Misumalpan family, originally spoken throughout the better part of Nicaragua, and parts of Honduras and El Salvador, are thought by many to be related to Chibchan, but as yet little evidence has been presented to support this relationship. Two of the four languages are extinct, but Mískito is very much alive, with about thirty-five thousand speakers along the Caribbean coast of Nicaragua and Honduras. It has also been suggested that Paya, a language isolate of Honduras, is also related to Chibchan. In this case, we are on firmer ground: there is evidence that Paya is not merely related to, but is, a Chibchan language.

This does not complete the roster of Middle American language families. There are about a half-dozen or more language isolates or families consisting of just a few closely related languages. Some like Huave, found along the Pacific coast in Oaxaca, have a few thousand speakers and were unimportant in the pre-Columbian civilizations. Other unaffiliated languages were and are spoken by larger populations, such as Purpecha (Tarascan), still with about fifty thousand speakers in the state of Michoacan; speakers of this language founded a powerful state which challenged the Nahuatl-speaking Aztec empire to the east.

An Arawakan language, spoken aboriginally in the islands of the Caribbean and the northern coast of South America, is now spoken by about a hundred thousand speakers along the coast from Belize to Nicaragua. It is known as Black Carib and is spoken by the descendants of runaway slaves and their Indian hosts, who were brought to the mainland in the late eighteenth century.

There have been numerous proposals to link some of the Middle American families into larger linguistic stocks, including the proposed Penutian and Hokan stocks we discussed for western North America. The inclusion of Middle American languages into these two stocks is often based on very flimsy evidence, so that such remote genetic groupings are even more tenuous than the more northern groupings.

An Otomanguean stock has been proposed, a stock composed only of Middle American languages. Its suggested membership is made up of Otopamean, Popolocan, Mixtecan, Amuzgo, Zapotecan, Chinatecan, and Manguean; some would also include Subtiaba-Tlapanec (numbers 60–67 on the list in appendix 2). Although the relationships are quite remote, and the nature of the interconnections within the stock are yet to be worked out and validated, fairly good evidence has been given in its support. There is general if not universal agreement that it is a valid grouping.

14.4 SOUTH AMERICA

With some important exceptions, the linguistic research on the languages of South America before the middle of the twentieth century has been limited. In the past few decades, however, there has been a flurry of work. Unfortunately, by now, many languages are extinct and many others, especially in the Lowlands, are in fragile condition. The earliest linguistic classifications were made over a century ago, but researchers were hampered by the paucity of data. While considerable data are now available, the most recent and comprehensive classification was able to reduce the number of clearly related genetic units to only 117; 8 of the units were families consisting of ten or more languages, 49 were families with two to eight languages, while the rest (60) were single languages. As more data become available and as more comparative work is done, the number will doubtlessly be reduced and, in fact, there is good (though not yet conclusive) evidence for incorporating a number of them into more inclusive groupings. The total number of languages in the classification is 464: 274 still spoken, 190 extinct. It is likely that a few additional languages will be discovered, and it is certain that the number of languages that have become extinct is much greater than 190, since the classification only included languages for which there were some data.

For discussion purposes, we divide South America into three regions, the Highlands, Lowlands, and Southern Cone. Of the 464 languages in the classification, 22 are in the Highlands, 30 in the Southern Cone, and 412 in the Lowlands.

The Highlands

The Andean highlands are located in parts of Colombia, Ecuador, Peru, Bolivia, and Argentina. The Quechuan languages and Aymara are the dominant languages. Estimates range between ten and twenty million speakers for the more than half a dozen closely related Quechuan languages. They are found over a wide area in Colombia, Ecuador, Peru, and Argentina. In Ecuador, their speakers comprise over 50 percent of the total population, in Bolivia 40 percent, and in Peru 25 percent.

There are between two and three million speakers of Aymara. Most of them are in Peru, Bolivia, and Argentina, with a relatively modest number (twenty thousand) in Chile. They make up almost 25 percent of the population of Bolivia. Aymara belongs to the Jaqi language family, which contains, in addition to Aymara, Jaqaru and Kawki, two languages spoken by a small number of people in the Peruvian Highlands. The Quechuan languages have not been clearly demonstrated to be related to any other languages. There is some evidence that they may be related to the Jaqi family. It has so far proved impossible, however, to validate this larger linguistic grouping, because Aymara, Jaqaru, Kawki, and Quechua have been in contact for centuries, and at least some of the similarities between these languages are due to mutual borrowing. While Quechuan and Aymara were and still are the dominant languages of the area, there were a number of other languages spoken by smaller populations. Almost all of them are extinct.

The Lowlands

The South American Lowlands comprise the river drainages of the Amazon, Orinoco, and other nearby areas of the South American tropical rain forest. Included are all of Venezuela, the Guianas, and Brazil, and parts of Colombia, Ecuador, Peru, Bolivia, Paraguay, and Argentina. The area is one of extreme linguistic complexity. At time of contact, it is doubtful that many languages had more than a few thousand speakers. Most of those that have not become extinct are found in the hinterlands, areas that had little contact with Spanish or Portuguese speakers until this century. Modern technology has made these remote areas more accessible, an accessibility that is threatening the survival of the tropical forests, and genocide is an accepted practice in some areas, threatening the survival of their people, languages, and cultures. Speakers of many of the languages number in the tens or hundreds. The outstanding exception is Guaraní, one of the two national languages of Paraguay (section 9.4). In addition to the almost three million speakers in Paraguay, there are about one million more who have relocated in recent years in Brazil and Argentina.

Because classificatory work is still in its infancy in this part of the world, there are only a few well-delineated language families that include large numbers of languages: Chibchan, Arawakan, Cariban, Tupí (or Tupí-Guaraní), Je , Tucanoan, and Panoan. While each of these families has certain areas where it predominates, there are almost no areas in which a given family forms a solid geographic block: unclassified languages and languages from other families intermesh. Frequently, in fact, the languages themselves intermesh (see section 9.1 for an example in the Vaupés).

The Chibchan languages are found in Central America (section 14.3), Colombia, and Venezuela. The family includes about twenty-five languages, three quarters of which are still spoken.

Most of the languages that belong to the Arawakan family are found to the north of the Amazon River, and, formerly, on the Caribbean Islands. Some members of the family, however, are located much farther afield, in every country in South America

except Uruguay (which has no Indian population today) and Chile. There were over
sixty known languages, about half of which are still spoken. The total number at
the time of contact was probably much greater than we can ever know, because
they were the predominant languages in the Caribbean where many languages and
cultures became extinct before their identity was recorded.

The Cariban family consists of more than forty languages, with more than half of
them still spoken. They center in the Guianas, with outliers in Colombia, Venezuela,
and Brazil. Most languages have a few thousand or fewer speakers; the exception
is Carib, with fifteen thousand speakers scattered in several communities in the
Guianas, Colombia, Venezuela, and Brazil. Even though the Caribbean Sea takes its
name from Carib, it was not a major language of the people in this region. Caribs
did, however, form raiding parties and sent invasions at least as far north as Cuba.

The majority of the Tupí, or Tupí-Guaraní, languages are found in the central
Amazon Basin, but there are numerous outliers so that this far-flung family is
represented in Brazil, Colombia, Venezuela, Bolivia, Paraguay, and Argentina. Tupí
languages are represented in the Vaupés area, discussed in section 9.1. Guaraní (section 9.4) belongs to this family. About twenty-five of the languages are still spoken.

Je consists of about a dozen languages in eastern Brazil. A more inclusive family,
Macro-Je, has been proposed, which includes about three dozen languages. About
half the languages are extinct; the extant languages normally have speakers numbering in the hundreds or less.

There are slightly over a dozen Tukanoan languages, scattered through a wide
area in Colombia, Brazil, Ecuador, and Peru. The speakers of the languages are not
numerous, a few thousand at most. The extensive bilingualism in the Eastern Tukanoan languages was discussed in section 9.1.

The Panoan languages are found in the western Amazon Basin in Brazil, Peru,
and Bolivia. There were almost thirty languages, about half of which are still spoken. The speakers number in the low thousands or less.

The Southern Cone

This area includes the better part of Chile, Argentina, and part of Paraguay. The only
extant language with large numbers of speakers is Mapuche. Most speakers live in
Chile, with population estimates at around four hundred thousand. A smaller number live in adjacent areas of Argentina. The language is not known to be related to
any others.

Members of the Guacurú language family are located principally on the Chaco
plains in northern Argentina, with some outliers in Paraguay, Brazil, and Bolivia.
Four of the languages still survive; the largest is Toba, with about twenty thousand
speakers. Except for small families that consist of two or three languages, and out-

liers of the Tupí-Guaraní family, the remaining fifteen or twenty languages of the Argentinean and Paraguayan Chaco have not been shown to be members of any language family.

Tierra del Fuego was the homeland of people who spoke a number of languages, but just how many is not clear. There were twelve speakers of Yagan (or Yahgan) in 1968, twelve of Ona in 1968, between fifty and a hundred of Tehuelche in the late 1970s, and forty-seven of Kawaskar in 1972. The remaining Tierra del Fuego languages are extinct.

SOURCES

Section 14.1 is based on Campbell and Mithun 1979, Chafe 1979, Crawford 1975, Goddard 1978a, 1978b, 1979, Haas 1979, Hoijer 1946, and Rood 1979. Section 14.2 is based on Campbell and Mithun 1979, Jacobsen 1979a, 1979d, Krauss 1979, Krauss and Golla 1981 (authoritative source for Athapaskan), Mixco 1978, Shipley 1978, Silverstein 1979, Thompson 1979, Woodbury 1984, and Young 1983; see also Krauss 1979 and Levine 1979 (inclusion of Haida in Na-dene). On language distribution, see Jacobsen 1979c for a study of linguistic diversity, controlled for uniform units. Section 14.3 is based on Campbell 1979, Kaufman 1991, Mason 1940, Suárez 1983, and Voegelin and Voegelin 1964, 1965. See Campbell 1979:942–43 for evidence that Paya is a Chibchan language. Section 14.4 is based on Grimes 1988, Kaufman 1990 (most recent and comprehensive classification), Klein and Stark 1985a, most of the chapters in Klein and Stark 1985b and Hardman de Bautista 1985b. Unless a specific date is mentioned, estimates for the number of speakers in sections 14.1 and 14.2 are based on figures found in Chafe 1962 and 1965. The demographic situation for a number of the languages has changed since that time.

SUGGESTED READINGS

For section 14.4, Derbyshire and Pullum 1986 contains an introductory chapter on the general linguistic and cultural background of Amazonia and two survey chapters on comparative morphology and syntax within Arawakan; one chapter is concerned with eight Brazilian, the other with eight Peruvian languages. See also Durbin 1977 for a survey of the Carib language family and Payne 1985 for discussion of the genetic classification of Resigaro, a moribund language of lowland Colombia and Peru.

PHONETIC SYMBOLS AND THEIR MEANING

Positions of articulation not in table AI.I:

labiovelar: kʷ, xʷ, gʷ, and so on (symbols from velar row with raised "w")

retroflex: ṭ, ṣ, c̣, ṇ, and so on (symbols from alveolar row with subscript dot)

uvular: ḳ (or q), x̣, ŋ̣, and so on (symbols from velar row with subscript dot)

palatalized: kʸ, lʸ, and so on (symbols from velar or alveolar row with raised "y")

Since many phonetic symbols are identical to the letters of the Roman alphabet, it is customary to enclose them in square brackets, for example, [q], [c] to distinguish them from the written letter. Slashes, e.g., /q/, /c/, are used when writing phonemically, which is akin to phonetic writing, except leaving out the phonetic detail that is not important or contrastive for the particular language in question. If the context is clear as to the type of notation, the square brackets or slashes are sometimes omitted. The reader is also referred to the discussion in 3.8 for more on the nature of phonological systems.

CONSONANTS

These sounds have greater blockage in the vocal tract than do vowels. They are found on the margins (beginning or end) of the syllable. Three primary dimensions are used for describing consonant sounds: voicing, place of articulation, and manner of articulation. Additional features, such as glottalization, aspiration, and length are important in some languages.

Voicing

There are two degrees, voiceless (vl.) and voiced (vd.). Voiced sounds are produced by stretching the vocal cords just enough so that when air passes between them

Table AI.I. Consonant Symbols

	Bilabial	Labio-dental	Dental	Alveolar	Palatal	Velar	Glottal
Stops							
Plain vl.	p		ṭ	t	t^y	k	ʔ
Plain vd.	b		ḍ	d	d^y	g	
Vl.glottalized	p'		ṭ'	t'	t$^{y'}$	k'	
Vl.aspirated	p^h		ṭ^h	t^h	t^{yh}	k^h	
Fricatives							
Plain vl.	ɸ	f	θ	s	š	x	h
Plain vd.	β	v	ð	z	ž	ɣ	
Vl.glottalized				s'	š'	x'	
Affricates							
Plain vl.				c	č		
Plain vd.				ʒ	ǯ		
Vl.glottalized				c'	č'		
Laterals							
Plain vl.				ɬ			
Plain vd.				λ			
Vl.glottalized				ƛ'			
Flap or trill				r			
Sonorant (voiced)							
Nasal	m		ṇ	n	ñ	ŋ	
Liquid				r			
Lateral				l			
Glide							
(semivowel)	w [high back rounded]				y [high front unrounded]		

Key: vd. = voiced
    vl. = voiceless

they vibrate to produce a buzzing sound. The vocal cords are relaxed with voiceless sounds, so that the air passes through with no obstruction. The difference between voiced and voiceless sounds can most easily be perceived with fricatives: place your fingers on your throat and notice the vibration in the voiced sounds [v, z, ð] in "vat, zoo, thy"; contrast this with the lack of vibration in the voiceless [f, s, θ] in "fat, Sue, thigh."

Table A1.2. Vowel Symbols

Tongue Position	Front		Central	Back	
	Rounded	Unrounded	Unrounded	Rounded	Unrounded
High	u	i	ɨ	ʊ	ï
Lower-high		ɪ			
Mid	ö	e	ə	o	
Lower mid		ɛ			
Low		æ	a	ɔ	

Place of Articulation

This refers to the place in the vocal tract in which the blockage or partial occlusion occurs. We define the positions shown on the chart, starting from the front of the mouth and moving back. First are labial, which involve the lips. With bilabial, both lips are used, as the initial consonants in the English words "pan, ban, man, won." Labiodental sounds are produced when there is contact between the upper teeth and the lower lip, as in the initial segment in "fan, van."

The tip of the tongue is used in making dental, alveolar, and retroflex sounds. For alveolars, the tip is placed on the alveolar ridge, or gum ridge, as in the initial consonants of English "two, do, no," [t, d, n]. Dentals have the tongue placed on the back of the upper teeth, with the tongue making contact with the upper teeth. The fricatives [θ] and [ð] are, strictly speaking, interdental rather than dental, which is to say that the tongue is placed between the upper and lower teeth, as in "thigh, thy" ([θay], [ðay]). Dental sounds (excluding interdentals) are rare in English and normally come from alveolars that are next to an interdental, as in "month" [manθ]. The Spanish sounds that are spelled "t, d, n" are dental, unlike English, which are alveolar. Some languages have alveolar consonants, others have dental consonants, while some have both. If a language has dental but no alveolar consonants, it is customary to simply use the alveolar symbols for the dentals. Retroflex consonants (not on chart and represented by placing a subscript dot under the corresponding alveolar symbol) are made by curling the tongue so that the tip touches the roof of the mouth rather than the alveolar ridge. In some languages these are common and fundamental sounds; in English they are found only when an "r" follows, as in "dry, try" [ḍray], [ṭray], and come from alveolars.

To produce the palatals, the fat part of the tongue touches the hard roof of the mouth, or palate: [š] as in English "shoe"; [ž] as in the medial consonants of English "pleasure, azure, division"; [č] as in English "chew"; [ž] as in both the first and final consonant of English "judge."

Velar sounds have the back of the tongue against the velum, which is the soft roof of the mouth behind the bony palate. Examples in English are "key, go" and the final sound in "sing" (phonetically [siŋ]). Uvular consonants (not on chart), also called postvelar, are made in the same general way, but the tongue is placed further back. Notice the position of the tongue in English "key," which is close to the true velar position, as opposed to its position in "coo" in which it approaches the post-velar or uvular position. Uvular sounds are written with a subscript dot under the corresponding velar sound. While the voiceless uvular stop can be written [ḳ], the unitary symbol [q] is more commonly used, a symbol that is reserved for this sound. Labiovelar sounds (not on chart) are velars with a labial after release. They are similar to the initial sounds of English "queen" [kwin] and "Gwendolyn" [gwendəlɪn], where they are best treated as a velar stop plus [w]: [kw] and [gw]. In some languages they act as a unitary sound and are written with the corresponding velar symbol plus a raised [ʷ]: [kʷ, gʷ, xʷ, ŋʷ], and so on. In some languages there are labialized uvular sounds. They are written with a raised [ʷ] after the corresponding uvular symbol, e.g., [qʷ, ġʷ, x̣ʷ], and so on.

The glottal sounds are produced in the glottis, where the vocal cords are housed. The glottal stop [ʔ] is not a familiar sound in English; it can be found in the exclamation of warning "oh-oh" [oʔo] and in the American English pronunciation of "t" in words like "cotton" [kaʔn̩] and "mountain" [mawʔn̩]. The glottal fricative [h] is as in English "he."

Manner of articulation refers to the manner of obstruction used in making the consonant. Stops have the greatest, sonorants the least obstruction. For stops, there is total obstruction of the air flow. Fricatives, such as [f, v, s], and so on have partial obstruction, but the airflow is continuous. Affricates start with total stoppage, and then are released to partial obstruction. Thus affricates are very much like a stop followed by a fricative. For example, the initial segment in "cheese" [čiz] could just as well be represented as [tšiz]. Dental and alveolar affricates are very common, especially in American Indian languages. They are difficult to illustrate on the printed page, however, since they are lacking in English. The closest English equivalent to the alveolar affricate [c] [ʒ] (voiceless and voiced) are the "ts" in "hats" and the "dz" in "adze." The voiced palatal affricate is normally represented by [ǰ], as in English "judge" [ǰəǰ]; some languages, like Navajo, represent this sound with [j].

The most common laterals are dental or alveolar sounds in which the air flows over the side of the tongue. English has no lateral fricatives or affricates, although the affricates [ƛ] and [λ] would be something like English "tl" and "dl," if such combinations were to be found in English. In fact, the sequences [tl] and [dl] are sometimes used to represent these sounds. Laterals are sometimes also found in the retroflex and palatal positions.

Sonorants can be voiceless but typically are voiced. The nasals are, strictly speaking, stops in which there is total stoppage in the mouth (the oral cavity), but with escape of the air flow through the nose before the stop is released.

There are a variety of different [r] sounds in the languages of the world, but the most common are flapped and trilled. Some languages have more than one [r] sound, as in Spanish, in which the flapped [r] is written (in the orthography, or regular spelling) as a single "r," the trilled [r] as double "rr." The English "r" is, for most speakers, retroflex, with the tongue curled up; this type of "r" is a rare sound, found in only a few languages, including Mandarin Chinese and Yurok (spoken in northwest California). American English "t" and "d" between vowels is often a flapped [r], as in "water" and "ready."

In the chart we have placed the voiced lateral [l] among the sonorants, but the voiceless lateral [ɬ] among the fricatives. The classification of [ɬ] depends on how much friction or occlusion there is; in some languages it might best be placed with the sonorants.

Semivowels are akin to vowels, so that [w] is the consonantal counterpart of [u] and [y] is the consonantal counterpart of [i]. Semivowels are sometimes considered apart from consonants, so that there would be three classes of sounds: consonants, semivowels and vowels.

Other Consonantal Distinctions:
Glottalization, Aspiration, and Length

We have noted (in section 2.8) that glottalized consonants are found in a number of American Indian languages. These consonants are produced by releasing the flow of air from the glottis or vocal cords at the same time that the consonant is released from another position of articulation, so that, for example, an unglottalized [p] is released only from the bilabial position, while a glottalized [p'] is released from both the bilabial and the glottal position.

Aspirated consonants are marked by a following raised [h], while unaspirated consonants are unmarked. Aspiration is a short puff of air that follows the release of a consonant. In English, a stop at the beginning of a word is aspirated, for example, "peak" [pʰik] which begins with an aspirated bilabial stop; if an [s] comes before the stop, the stop is unaspirated, for example, "speak" [spik], which has an unaspirated bilabial stop after the [s]. You can feel the puff of air or its absence if you hold your hand in front of your mouth as you say "peak" and "speak." In English, aspirated and unaspirated consonants can be predicted by such things as the presence or absence of a preceding [s]; however, in some other languages, such as Lake Miwok, these sounds are fundamentally distinct and are used for distinguishing words with different meanings.

Long or geminated consonants are either written double—[kk, mm], and so on—or with a raised dot [k·, m·], and so on.

The chart does not include symbols for all the possible sounds of the world's languages, or even for those found in the Americas. Many of the missing consonants, however, can be filled into the chart once the underlying system of notation is observed. Thus [m'] would be a glottalized labial nasal; [ɬʸ] a palatalized voiceless lateral fricative.

VOWELS

Vowels are classified according to three primary dimensions: tongue height (high to low), position (front, central, back), and type of lip rounding (rounded, unrounded). Some languages, like English, have only front unrounded vowels, while others, like German, have both front unrounded and front rounded vowels; a language never has only front rounded vowels. In a similar fashion, some languages, like English, have only back rounded vowels, while others like Turkish have both back rounded and back unrounded vowels; a language never has only back unrounded vowels. Thus front vowels are typically unrounded while back vowels are typically rounded.

Tongue height is a continuous dimension, and some languages utilize more than the four places we have provided for on the chart; for such cases, there are additional vowel symbols that we have not listed. For tongue height, notice the placement of your tongue in the English words "seat, suit" (high vowels, [i], [u]), "bait, but, boat" (mid vowels, [e], [ə], [o]), and "cat, cot, caught" (low vowels [æ], [a], [ɔ]). For some speakers, "cot" and "caught" are pronounced the same, [kat], while for others "caught" is pronounced differently, [kɔt].

For position of the tongue, notice the placement of your tongue in "beat, bait, bat" (front unrounded vowels [i], [e], [æ]), "cut, cot" (central unrounded [ə], [a]), and "boot, boat, bought" (back rounded [u], [o], [ɔ]). Some people pronounce "bought" as [bat] rather than [bɔt]. The front rounded and back unrounded vowels are not found in English and are found in only a few American Indian languages, such as Hopi. Those familiar with German are familiar with front rounded vowels, the so-called umlauted vowels. The high central unrounded [ɨ] is unfamiliar to speakers of English, but it is found in a number of American Indian languages. It is somewhat like the unstressed vowel in the second syllable of "roses" [rózəz], except that the tongue is in a still higher position.

Nasalized vowels are indicated by a tilde, for example, [ã, õ], or a subscript hook, for example, [ą, ǫ]. These are vowels produced with airflow through the nose. They are familiar to speakers of French and Portuguese. Vowel length, which refers to the absolute temporal length, is marked by doubling the vowel, for example, [aa, oo], or by a raised dot, for example, [a·, o·].

ADDITIONAL COMMENTS

In some languages, tone or musical pitch is part of the phonological system and is used to differentiate words in the same way as consonants and vowels. In Navajo, high tone is usually marked by an acute accent, for example, [á], low tone is either marked by a grave accent or it is unmarked, for example, [à] or [a]. Other languages, for example, Acoma, have a falling tone, marked [â], and a falling glottal tone, marked [ą]. Some languages have distinctive stress or accent, which is marked in similar ways, for example, [á] indicates a stressed vowel. Notice that the same set of symbols is used for tone and for accent, so that one must know how the symbols are used for the language in question.

Special writing conventions have developed for some languages. Of the languages used in this book, the most notable case is Classical Aztec or Nahuatl. It was first recorded in the sixteenth century by Spanish-speaking missionaries, and it has become traditional to write the language with a modified Hispanicized alphabet:

"qui, que, ca, co" = [ki, ke, ka, ko]
"ci, ce, za, zo" = [si, se, sa, so]
"cu" (syllable initial) and "uc" (syllable final) = [kʷ]
"x" = [š]
"tz, ch, tl" = [c, č, ƛ] (alveolar, palatal, and lateral affricates)
"hu" = [w]
"ī, ē, ā, ō" = [i·, e·, a·, o·]

In chapter 12, where Aztec is compared to other languages, a phonetic writing is used in place of the hispanicized orthography. But in other places (e.g., sections 4.4 and 6.1) the traditional writing system is used.

In some languages (e.g., Navajo, Acoma), it has become traditional to use voiceless stop symbols for the aspirated stops ("p, t, k" for [pʰ, tʰ, kʰ]) and voiced stop symbols for the unaspirated ("b, d, g" for [p, t, k]). This convention is a useful one for a language that has voiceless unaspirated and voiceless aspirated stops, but no voiced stops. Further conventions apply to Navajo: the voiceless unaspirated lateral affricate [λ] is written "dl," and the voiceless aspirated lateral affricate [λʰ] is written "tl"; the voiceless unaspirated affricate [č] is written "j"; and a number of other consonants are written with two letters so that [š, ž, ɣ, c, cʰ, c', čʰ, č'] are written "sh, zh, gh, dz, ts, ts', ch, ch'."

A LIST OF LANGUAGE FAMILIES
OF NORTH AMERICA

Extinct languages are marked with a dagger (†). Doubtlessly some of the languages that are unmarked are now extinct, because we have had to base our report on information that is sometimes one, two, or more decades old. Geographic locations are approximate. There is almost always some difference between the present-day and contact locations. Such differences are indicated only when they are considerable, particularly for those cases in which the group or part of the group was moved to Oklahoma (see end of section 14.1).

Because of language extinction, the total number of languages at time of contact was undoubtedly much greater than the following list would indicate. This is for two reasons. A number of groups became extinct before information on their languages was recorded. In some cases, only a name was recorded along with a few poorly transcribed words, in other cases only a name for the group survives, and in still other cases we lack even that. It is clear that some groups that spoke the same language were recorded under different names, while in other instances a named group included more than one language. We have tended to be conservative in regard to extinct languages, listing only those for which there is sufficient information to be sure we are really dealing with a distinct language. A second cause for undercounting relates to the reporting of so-called dialects. We know from examples of languages that survived into the modern period that there was a tendency for early travellers to speak of a single language, sometimes with "dialects," but when studied by modern investigators they proved to be a cluster of related languages. Even if we were to have complete information on the language situation, it would be impossible to specify the exact number of languages, because of the many instances in which it is impossible to distinguish between divergent dialect versus closely related language.

There are few language families for which there is universal agreement concerning the classification into branches and sub-branches, the result in some cases stemming from honest disagreement, while in others from ignorance or lack of information. We list only the branches (never subbranches) and then only when there seems to be a consensus.

Each language family is provided a number, and each language within the family (excepting language isolates) is also given a number, which is used in the alphabetized guide that precedes the list. For example, Oneida is referred to as 5.2, with 5 referring to the Iroquoian family, and 2 referring to the language within that family; Yurok is 2, with the number referring to family and, since it is an isolate, there is no further number.

A number of languages are known by more than one name. We list the more common alternates with no attempt to provide a complete tribal synonymy. In some cases, the alternate names are subdivisions (within the group) that name dialects or ethnic groups that speak the same language. Needless to say, we have had to make decisions about closely related varieties; whether to group them as divergent dialects of a single language or as closely related but distinct languages. Since we cannot know the linguistic situation in detail for all the Americas, we have doubtlessly not made the right decision in all cases.

ALPHABETICAL GUIDE TO THE LIST

Abenaki: 1.4–5
Acatec: 74.16
Achumawi: 45.1
Acoma: 59
Aguacatec: 74.21
Ahtna: 19.5
Alabama: 6.2
Alaskan Yupic: 18.5
Aleut: 18.1
Algonquian: 1
Algonquin: 1.19
Alsea: 32
Amuzgo: 63
Apache: 19.31–37
Aranama: 16
Arapaho: 1.25
Arikara: 9.1
Arizona Tewa: 25.1
Arkansa: 8.5
Assiniboine: 8.7
Atakapa: 13
Athapaskan: 19
Atsina: 1.25
Atsugewi: 45.2

Awaswas: 39.12
Ayautla: 61.2
Aztec: 24.28
Babine: 19.20
Bannock: 24.2
Barbareño: 50.2
Bear River: 19.29
Beaver: 19.16
Bella Bella: 56.2
Bella Coola: 23.1
Beothuk: 4
Biloxi: 8.4
Blackfoot: 1.27
Cacaopera: 79.3
Caddo: 9.5
Caddoan: 9
Cahita: 24.24
Cahto: 19.30
Cahuilla: 24.13
Cakchiquel: 74.27
Carolina Algonquian: 1.17
Carrier: 19.20–21
Catawba: 8.1

Cayuga: 5.5
Cayuse: 29
Central Pomo: 47.5
Central Sierra Miwok: 39.6
Chalon: 39.15
Chaplinski: 18.3
Chasta Costa: 19.26
Chatino: 64.6–8
Chehalis: 23.7, 23.12, 23.15
Chemehuevi: 24.7
Cherokee: 5.10
Cheyenne: 1.26
Chiapanec: 67.1
Chiapas Zoque: 73.6
Chibchan: 80
Chicahuaxtla Trique: 62.5
Chichimec-Jonaz: 60.4
Chickasaw: 6.1
Chicomuceltec: 74.2
Chilanga: 77.2

Chilcotin: 19.22
Chimakuan: 57
Chimakum: 57.2
Chimariko: 44
Chinantecan: 65
Chinook: 27
Chipewyan: 19.17
Chippewa: 1.19
Chiquihuiltan: 61.4
Chiquimulilla: 76.2
Chiricahua Apache:
  19.33
Chitimacha: 12
Chiwere: 8.6
Chochenyo: 39.9
Chocho: 61.6
Choctaw: 6.1
Chol: 74.7
Choltí: 74.9
Chontal: 74.8
Chorotegan: 67
Chortí: 74.10
Chuj: 74.14
Chumashan: 50
Clallam: 23.8
Coahilteco: 16
Coast Miwok: 39.2
Coast Yuki: 58.1
Cochimí: 51.9-10
Cochiti: 59
Cocopa: 51.7
Coeur d'Alene: 23.23
Columbian: 23.20
Colville: 23.21
Comanche: 24.5
Comecrude: 16
Comox: 23.2
Concow: 38.2
Coos: 34
Copala Trique: 62.6

Cora: 24.26
Costanoan: 39.8-15
Cotoname: 16
Cowichan: 23.7
Cowlitz: 23.13
Cree: 1.18
Creek: 6.4
Crow: 8.11
Cuicatec: 62.4
Cuitlatec: 70
Cupeño: 24.12
Dakota: 8.7
Delaware: 1.14
Dhegiha: 8.5
Diegueño: 51.6
Dogrib: 19.19
Eastern Pomo: 47.2
Emigdiano: 50.1
Eskimo-Aleut: 18
Esselen: 48
Etchemin: 1.3
Eudeve: 24.21
Eyak: 20
Flathead: 23.22
Foothill Yokuts: 40.1
Fox: 1.22
Gabrielino: 24.11
Galice: 19.26
Garza: 16
Guaikura: 54
Guarijío: 24.23
Guazacapán: 76.1
Haida: 22
Haisla: 56.3
Halkomelem: 23.7
Han: 19.10
Hanis: 34.1
Hare: 19.18
Hat Creek: 45.2
Havasupai: 51.1

Heiltsuk: 56.2
Hidatsa: 8.10
Hitchiti: 6.3
Holikachuk: 19.2
Hopi: 24.15
Huamelultec: 71.1
Huastec: 74.1
Huautal: 61.1
Huave: 72
Huchiti: 54
Huchnom: 58.1
Huichol: 24.27
Hupa: 19.28
Huron: 5.7
Illinois: 1.23
Ingalik: 19.3
Inuit: 18.7
Inupiaq: 18.7
Iowa: 8.6
Ipai: 51.6
Iroquoian: 5
Island Chumash:
  50.5
Isleta: 25.2
Itzá: 74.6
Ixcatec: 61.5
Ixil: 74.22
Ixtenco: 60.6
Jacaltec: 74.17
Jalapa: 61.3
Jemez: 25.3
Jicaque: 75
Jicarilla Apache:
  19.35
Jumaytepeque: 76.3
Kalapuya (proper):
  30.2
Kalapuyan: 30
Kalispel: 23.22
Kamia: 51.6

Kanjobal: 74.15
Kansa: 8.5
Kansas: 8.6
Karankawa: 15
Karkin: 39.8
Karuk: 42
Kashaya: 47.7
Kaska: 19.14
Kato: 19.30
Kawaiisu: 24.6
Kekchí: 74.30
Keres: 59
Kickapoo: 1.22
Kiliwa: 51.8
Kiowa: 25.4
Kiowa-Apache: 19.37
Kiowa-Tanoan: 25
Kitamat: 56.3
Kitanemuk: 24.10
Kitsai: 9.4
Klallam: 23.8
Klamath: 36
Klikitat: 28.1
Koasati: 6.2
Kolchan: 19.6
Konkow: 38.2
Konomihu: 43.4
Koyokon: 19.1
Kutchin: 19.11
Kutenai: 55
Kwakiutl: 56.1
Kwalhioqua: 19.25
Lacandón: 74.4
Laguna: 59
Lake Miwok: 39.1
Lakota: 8.7
Lalana: 65.5
Lassik: 19.30
Laurentian: 5.9
Lenca: 77

Lillooet: 23.17
Lipan Apache: 19.36
Loucheux: 19.11
Loup A: 1.6
Loup B: 1.7
Lower Chehalis: 23.15
Lower Chinook: 27.2
Lower Tanana: 19.7
Lower Umpqua: 33
Luiseño: 24.14
Lushootseed: 23.10
Lutuamian: 36
Mahican: 1.12
Maidu: 38.1
Maiduan: 38
Makah: 56.6
Maliseet: 1.2
Mam: 74.20
Mandan: 8.8
Mangue: 67.2
Manguean: 67
Maricopa: 51.5
Massachusetts: 1.8
Matagalpa: 79.4
Matlatzinca: 60.10
Mattole: 19.29
Mayan: 74
Mayo: 24.24
Mazahua: 60.9
Mazatec: 61.1–4
Mazatlan: 61.1
Menominee: 1.21
Mescalero Apache: 19.34
Miami: 1.23
Micmac: 1.1
Mikasuki: 6.3
Miluk: 34.2
Mískito: 79.1

Mississauga: 1.19
Missouri: 8.6
Misumalpan: 79
Miwok: 39.1–7
Mixe-Zoque: 73
Mixe: 73.1–2
Mixtec: 62.1–3
Mixtecan: 62
Mochó: 74.18
Modoc: 36
Mohave: 51.3
Mohawk: 5.1
Mohegan: 1.10
Molale: 31
Mono: 24.1
Montagnais: 1.18
Montauk: 1.11
Mopán: 74.5
Mototzintlec: 74.18
Mountain Pima: 24.17
Munsee: 1.13
Muskogean: 6
Muskogee: 6.4
Mutsun: 39.13
Nahuatl: 24.28
Nakota: 8.7
Nambe: 25.1
Nanaimo: 23.7
Nanticoke: 1.15
Narraganset: 1.9
Naskapi: 1.18
Natchez: 7
Naukanski: 18.4
Navajo: 19.31
Nawathinehena: 1.25
Nebraska: 8.6
Neutral: 5.7
Névome: 24.16
New River Shasta: 43.2

Sauk: 1.22
Saulteaux: 1.19
Sayula Popoluca: 73.3
Sekani: 19.15
Seminole: 6.4
Seneca: 5.6
Seri: 53
Serrano: 24.9
Seshelt: 23.4
Shasta (proper): 43.1
Shastan: 43
Shawnee: 1.24
Shinnecock: 1.11
Shoshoni: 24.4
Shuswap: 23.19
Siammon: 23.2
Siberian Yupic: 18.3
Sierra Popoluca: 73.7
Sinkyone: 19.30
Siouan: 8
Sipacapa: 74.24
Sipacepeño: 74.24
Sirenikski Yupic: 18.2
Siuslaw: 33
Skiri: 9.2
Slavey: 19.18
Solano: 16
Southeastern Pomo: 47.3
Southern Cochimí: 51.10
Southern Maidu: 38.3
Southern Paiute: 24.7
Southern Pomo: 47.6
Southern Sierra Miwok: 39.7
Southern Tepehuan: 24.19

Soyaltepec: 61.2
Spokan: 23.21
Squamish: 23.5
St. Lawrence Iroquois: 5.9
Stoney: 8.7
Straits: 23.8-9
Subtiaba: 66.2
Sumu: 79.2
Susquehannock: 5.4
Tagish: 19.14
Tahltan: 19.14
Takelma: 35
Tamyen: 39.10
Tanacross: 19.8
Tanaina: 19.4
Tanana: 19.7, 19.9
Tanoan: 25
Taos: 25.2
Tapachultec: 73.9
Tarahumara: 24.22
Tarascan: see Purepecha
Tatalpepec: 64.7
Tectiteco: 74.19
Tepecano: 24.19
Tepehua: 68.2
Tepehuan: 24.18-19
Tequistlatec: 71.2
Tequistlatecan: 71
Tesuque: 25.1
Teton: 8.7
Tewa: 25.1
Texistepec: 73.8
Thompson: 23.18
Tillamook: 23.16
Timucua: 10
Tipai: 51.6
Tiwa: 25.2
Tlapanec: 66.1

Tlatskanai: 19.25
Tlingit: 21
Tojolabal: 74.13
Tolowa: 19.27
Tonkawa: 14
Totonac: 68.1
Totonacan: 68
Towa: 25.3
Trique: 62.5-6
Tsetsaut: 19.13
Tsimshian: 26
Tualatin: 30.1
Tubar: 24.25
Tubatulabal: 24.8
Tuchone: 19.12
Tunica: 11
Tuscarora: 5.8
Tutelo: 8.2
Tututni: 19.26
Twana: 23.11
Tzeltal: 74.12
Tzotzil: 74.11
Tzutujil: 74.26
Umatilla: 28.1
Umpqua, Lower: 33
Unami: 1.14
Unquachog: 1.11
Upland Yuman: 51.1
Upper Chehalis: 23.12
Upper Chinook: 27.1
Upper Tanana: 19.9
Usila: 65.1
Uspantec: 74.31
Ute: 24.7
Utian: 39
Uto-Aztecan: 24
Valley Yokuts: 40.2
Ventureño: 50.1
Waikuri: 54

Wailaki: 19.30
Wakashan: 56
Walapai: 51.1
Wappo: 58.2
Wasco: 27.1
Washo: 52
Wenatchi: 23.20
Wenro: 5.7
Western Apache:
   19.32
Wichita: 9.3
Winnebago: 8.9
Wintu: 37.1
Wintuan: 37
Wishram: 27.1

Wiyot: 3
Wyandot: 5.7
Xinca: 76
Yahi: 46.2
Yaitepec: 64.6
Yakima: 28.1
Yamhill: 30.1
Yana: 46.1
Yanan: 46
Yankton: 8.7
Yaqui: 24.24
Yavapai: 51.1
Yneseño: 50.3
Yokutsan: 40
Yonkalla: 30.3

Yopi: 66.1
Yucatec: 74.3
Yuchi: 17
Yuki: 58.1
Yukian: 58
Yuman: 51
Yupic: 18.2-6
Yupiltepeque: 76.4
Yurok: 2
Zapotec: 64.1-5
Zapotecan: 64
Zenzontepec: 64.8
Zia: 59
Zoque: 73.5-6
Zuni: 41

LANGUAGE FAMILIES OF NORTH AMERICA

I. Algonquian
Eastern Algonquian branch
1. Micmac (Maritime Provinces)
2. Maliseet-Passamaquoddy (New Brunswick and Maine)
3. †Etchemin (Maine)
4. Eastern Abenaki, including Penobscot (Maine)
5. Western Abenaki (Vermont, New Hampshire)
6. †Loup A (central New England)
7. †Loup B (central New England)
8. †Massachusetts (southeastern coastal New England)
9. †Narraganset (Rhode Island)
10. †Mohegan-Pequot (Connecticut)
11. †Montauk, †Quiripi, †Unquachog, †Shinnecock (language[s] of Connecticut and Long Island)
12. †Mahican (New York)
13. Munsee (originally New York; later scattered in various locations in Canada, Kansas, Wisconsin, Oklahoma)
14. Unami, or Delaware (New Jersey, Pennsylvania; today, Oklahoma)

15. †Nanticoke (Maryland)
16. †Powhatan (Virginia)
17. †Carolina Algonquian (North Carolina)
18. Cree, including Montagnais-Naskapi (Labrador, Quebec, Ontario, Manitoba, Saskatchewan, Alberta, Montana; see section 12.1)
19. Ojibwa, including Chippewa, Saulteaux, Ottawa, Mississauga, Nipissing, and Algonquin (northern Great Lakes region)
20. Potawatomi (originally Michigan, now also Wisconsin, Kansas, Oklahoma)
21. Menominee (Michigan, Wisconsin)
22. Fox, including Sauk and Kickapoo (originally Michigan, but now in Iowa, Oklahoma, and Coahuila, Mexico; see section 7.2)
23. †Miami-Illinois (Indiana, Illinois)
24. Shawnee (probably originally Ohio, but now in Oklahoma)
25. Arapaho, including Atsina and Nawathinehena (northern Plains states now, also Oklahoma)
26. Cheyenne (northern Plains states, now also Oklahoma)
27. Blackfoot (northern Plains states, Alberta)

2. Yurok (northwestern California)
3. Wiyot (northwestern California)
4. †Beothuk (Newfoundland)
5. Iroquoian

Northern Iroquoian branch

1. Mohawk (New York, now also Quebec and Ontario)
2. Oneida (New York, now also Ontario and Wisconsin)
3. Onandaga (New York)
4. †Susquehannock (Pennsylvania)
5. Cayuga (New York, now also Ontario and Oklahoma)
6. Seneca (New York, now also Ontario)
7. †Huron-Wyandot, and probably including Neutral, Petun, Wenro (Ontario and New York)
8. Tuscarora-Nottaway (originally the Carolinas, now New York and Ontario)
9. †Laurentian, or St. Lawrence Iroquois (Quebec)

Cherokee
  10. Cherokee (originally Tennessee, North and South
       Carolina, but today Oklahoma and North Carolina)

6. Muskogean
  1. Choctaw-Chickasaw (originally Mississippi, Louisiana,
      Kentucky, and Tennessee, now also Oklahoma and
      Mississippi)
  2. Alabama-Koasati (originally Alabama, now Texas and
      Louisiana)
  3. Hitchiti-Mikasuki (originally Georgia and Florida, now
      only Florida)
  4. Creek or Muskogee, including Seminole (originally
      Alabama, Georgia, and Florida, now Alabama, Florida,
      and Oklahoma)

7. †Natchez (Mississippi, later Oklahoma)

8. Siouan
  1. †Catawba (the Carolinas)
Southeastern branch
  2. †Tutelo (Virginia)
  3. †Ofo (Mississippi)
  4. †Biloxi (Mississippi)
Mississippi Valley branch
  5. Dhegiha, including Quapaw or Arkansa, Kansa,
      Osage, Omaha, and Ponca (Arkansas, Kansas, now
      Oklahoma and Nebraska)
  6. Chiwere, including Iowa, Oto, Missouri (Kansas,
      Nebraska, and now Oklahoma)
  7. Dakota, including Lakota, Nakota, Santee, Yankton,
      Teton, Assiniboine, Stoney (Minnesota, the Dakotas,
      Nebraska, Montana, Manitoba, Saskatchewan, and
      Alberta)
  8. Mandan (the Dakotas)
  9. Winnebago (Wisconsin)
Missouri River branch
  10. Hidatsa (the Dakotas)
  11. Crow (Montana)

9. Caddoan
  1. Arikara (the Dakotas)
  2. Pawnee, including Skiri (originally Nebraska, now
      Oklahoma)

      3.   Wichita (Kansas and Oklahoma)

      4.   †Kitsai (Oklahoma)

      5.   Caddo (originally Louisiana, Arkansas, and Texas, now Oklahoma)

10. †Timucua (Florida)

11. †Tunica (Mississippi)

12. †Chitimacha (Louisiana)

13. †Atakapa (Louisiana and Texas)

14. †Tonkawa (originally central Texas, later Oklahoma)

15. †Karankawa (south Texas coast)

16. †Coahilteco and other unclassified and unclassifiable languages of Texas and northern Mexico: Coahilteco, Comecrude, Cotoname, Garza, Solano, Aranama, and others. While some of these languages may be related, evidence is too skimpy to propose any meaningful genetic grouping.

17. Yuchi (originally Georgia, now Oklahoma)

18. Eskimo-Aleut

      1.   Aleut (Aleutian Islands)

Eskimo

      2.   Sirenikski Yupic (Chukchi Peninsula, Siberia)

      3.   Central Siberian Yupic, or Chaplinski (Chukchi Peninsula, Siberia, and Alaska)

      4.   Naukanski (Chukchi Peninsula, Siberia)

      5.   Central Alaskan Yupic (Norton Sound to Nushagak River, Alaska)

      6.   Pacific Yupic (southern coast of the Alaska Peninsula)

      7.   Inuit-Inupiaq (Arctic Coast of northern Alaska, Canada, and Greenland)

19. Athapaskan

      1.   Koyokon (interior Alaska)

      2.   Holikachuk (interior Alaska)

      3.   Ingalik (interior Alaska)

      4.   Tanaina (interior Alaska)

      5.   Ahtna (interior Alaska)

      6.   Kolchan (interior Alaska)

      7.   Lower Tanana (interior Alaska)

      8.   Tanacross (interior Alaska)

      9.   Upper Tanana (interior Alaska)

   10.   Han (interior Alaska and Yukon Territory)

11. Kutchin or Loucheux (interior Alaska and Yukon Territory)
12. Tuchone (Yukon Territory)
13. †Tsetsaut (British Columbia and Alaskan panhandle)
14. Tahltan-Kaska-Tagish (British Columbia and Yukon Territory)
15. Sekani (British Columbia)
16. Beaver (British Columbia and Alberta)
17. Chipewyan (Northwest Territories)
18. Slavey-Hare (Northwest Territories)
19. Dogrib (Northwest Territories)
20. Babine, or Northern Carrier (British Columbia)
21. Carrier (British Columbia)
22. Chilcotin (British Columbia)
23. Sarcee (Alberta)
24. †Nicola (British Columbia)
25. †Kwalhioqua-Tlatskanai (Washington and Oregon)

Pacific Coast branch

26. †Chasta Costa, including Tututni and †Galice (southwestern Oregon)
27. Tolowa (Oregon and California border)
28. Hupa (northwestern California)
29. †Mattole, including Bear River (northwestern California)
30. †Wailaki, including Kato (or Cahto), †Nongatl, †Lassik, and †Sinkyone (northwestern California)

Apachean branch

31. Navajo, or Navajo Apache (New Mexico, Arizona, Utah)
32. Western Apache (Arizona)
33. Chiricahua Apache (Arizona and New Mexico, now also Oklahoma)
34. Mescalero Apache (New Mexico)
35. Jicarilla Apache (New Mexico)
36. †Lipan Apache (Texas)
37. Kiowa-Apache (Oklahoma)

20. **†Eyak** (Alaskan panhandle)

21. **Tlingit** (Alaskan panhandle and British Columbia)

22. **Haida** (British Columbia)

23.   Salish

      1.   Bella Coola (British Columbia)

Coast Salish branch

      2.   Comox, including Siammon (British Columbia)

      3.   †Pentlatch (Vancouver Island, British Columbia)

      4.   Seshelt (British Columbia)

      5.   Squamish (British Columbia)

      6.   Nooksack (Washington)

      7.   Halkomelem, including Chehalis, Cowichan and Nanaimo (Vancouver Island and mainland of British Columbia)

      8.   Clallam, or Klallam, or Straits (British Columbia and Washington)

      9.   Northern Straits (British Columbia and Washington)

   10.   †Lushootseed (Washington)

   11.   Twana (Washington)

   12.   Upper Chehalis (Washington)

   13.   Cowlitz (Washington)

   14.   Quinault (Washington)

   15.   Lower Chehalis (Washington)

   16.   Tillamook (Oregon)

Interior Salish branch

   17.   Lillooet (British Columbia)

   18.   Thompson (British Columbia)

   19.   Shuswap (British Columbia)

   20.   Columbian, including Wenatchi (Washington)

   21.   Okanagan, including Sanpoil, Colville, and Spokan (British Columbia and Washington)

   22.   Kalispel, including Flathead and Pend d'Oreille (Washington and Montana)

   23.   Coeur d'Alene (Idaho)

24.   Uto-Aztecan (see section 12.2)

Numic branch

      1.   Mono (California and Nevada)

      2.   Northern Paiute, including Bannock (Nevada, Oregon, and Idaho)

      3.   Panamint (California and Nevada)

      4.   Shoshoni (Nevada, Utah, Idaho, and Wyoming)

      5.   Comanche (originally the southern Plains, today Oklahoma)

    6.   Kawaiisu (California)

    7.   Ute-Southern Paiute, including Chemehuevi (California, Nevada, Utah, and Colorado)

    8.   Tubatulabal (California)

Takic branch

    9.   †Serrano (California)

  10. †Kitanemuk (California)

  11. †Gabrielino (California)

  12. Cupeño (California)

  13. Cahuilla (California)

  14. Luiseño (California)

  15. Hopi (Arizona)

Sonoran branch

  16. O'odham [Papago], including Pima, Névome, and Onavas (Arizona and Sonora)

  17. Mountain Pima (Sonora and Chihuahua)

  18. Northern Tepehuan (Chihuahua and Durango)

  19. Southern Tepehuan, including Tepecano (Durango)

  20. †Opata (Sonora)

  21. †Eudeve (Sonora)

  22. Tarahumara (Chihuahua)

  23. Guarijío (Chihuahua, Sonora)

  24. Cahita, including Mayo and Yaqui (Sonora and Sinaloa)

  25. †Tubar (Chihuahua)

  26. Cora (Nayarit)

  27. Huichol (Nayarit)

Aztecan branch

  28. Nahuatl, including Aztec (Valley of Mexico, and a wide area to the south and east; probably more than a single language)

  29. Pipil (Nicaragua, but with enclaves elsewhere)

  30. †Pochutec (Oaxaca)

25. Kiowa-Tanoan

    1.   Tewa (Santa Clara, San Juan, San Ildefonso, Nambe, Tesuque, and Pojoaque Pueblos of the Rio Grande Valley of New Mexico and the Arizona Tewa Pueblo)

    2.   Tiwa (Taos, Picuris, Sandia, and Isleta Pueblos of New Mexico)

    3.   Towa (Jemez Pueblos of New Mexico)

        4.   Kiowa (Oklahoma)

26. **Tsimshian** (British Columbia)

27. **Chinook** (along the Columbia River in Oregon and
Washington)
   1.   Upper Chinook, including Wishram and Wasco
   2.   †Lower Chinook

28. **Sahaptian**
   1.   Sahaptin, including Yakima, Klikitat, and Umatilla
   (eastern Oregon and eastern Washington)
   2.   Nez Perce (Idaho)

29. **†Cayuse** (northeastern Oregon and southwestern
Washington)

30. **Kalapuyan** (Willamette Valley, Oregon)
   1.   †Northern Kalapuya, or Yamhill and Tualatin
   2.   †Central Kalapuya, Santiam, or Kalapuya (proper)
   3.   †Southern Kalapuya, or Yonkalla

31. **†Molale** (central Oregon)

32. **†Alsea** (Oregon coast)

33. **†Siuslaw-Lower Umpqua** (Oregon coast)

34. **Coos** (Oregon coast)
   1.   †Hanis
   2.   †Miluk

35. **†Takelma** (southern Oregon)

36. **Klamath,** or Modoc, or Lutuamian (southern Oregon and
northern California)

37. **Wintuan** (northern California; see section 12.6)
   1.   Wintu
   2.   Nomlaki
   3.   Patwin

38. **Maiduan** (northeastern California; see section 12.6)
   1.   Maidu, or Northeastern Maidu
   2.   Konkow, Concow, or Northwestern Maidu
   3.   Nisenan, or Southern Maidu

39. **Utian** (central California; see section 12.6)
   Miwokan branch
   1.   Lake Miwok
   2.   †Coast Miwok
   3.   †Saclan
   4.   †Plains Miwok
   5.   Northern Sierra Miwok

      6.   Central Sierra Miwok

      7.   Southern Sierra Miwok

Costanoan branch

      8.   †Karkin

      9.   †Chochenyo

     10.   †Tamyen

     11.   †Ramaytush

     12.   †Awaswas

     13.   †Mutsun

     14.   †Rumsen

     15.   †Chalon

40. **Yokutsan** (central California; see section 12.6)

      1.   Foothill Yokuts (a group of six interlinking dialects or languages)

      2.   Valley Yokuts (a group of six interlinking dialects or languages)

41. **Zuni** (a Pueblo of New Mexico)

42. **Karuk** (northern California; see section 12.6)

43. **Shastan** (northern California and southern Oregon; see section 12.6)

      1.   †Shasta (proper)

      2.   †New River Shasta

      3.   †Okwanuchu

      4.   †Konomihu

44. **†Chimariko** (northern California; see section 12.6)

45. **Palaihnihan** (northern California; see section 12.6)

      1.   Achumawi, or Pit River

      2.   Atsugewi, or Hat Creek

46. **Yanan** (northern California; see section 12.6)

      1.   †Yana

      2.   †Yahi

47. **Pomoan** (Central California; see section 12.6)

      1.   †Northeastern Pomo

      2.   Eastern Pomo

      3.   Southeastern Pomo

Western Pomo Branch

      4.   Northern Pomo

      5.   Central Pomo

      6.   Southern Pomo

      7.   Kashaya

48. **†Esselen** (southern California coast; see section 12.6)
49. **†Salinan** (southern California coast; see section 12.6)
50. **Chumashan** (southern California coast; see section 12.6)
    1. †Ventureño-Emigdiano
    2. †Barbareño
    3. †Ineseño
    4. †Purisimeño
    5. †Island Chumash
    6. †Obispeño
51. **Yuman-Cochimí** (see section 12.6)
    Yuman branch
    1. Upland Yuman or Northern Pai, including Havasupai, Yavapai, and Walapai (western Arizona)
    2. Paipai (northern Baja California)
    3. Mohave (along the Colorado River in California and Arizona)
    4. Quechan (along the Colorado River in California and Arizona)
    5. Maricopa (southern Arizona)
    6. Diegueño, including Tipai, Ipai, and Kamia (southern California and northern Baja California)
    7. Cocopa (mouth of the Colorado River in Mexico and the United States)
    8. Kiliwa (northern Baja California)
    Cochimí branch (southern Baja California)
    9. †Northern Cochimí
    10. †Southern Cochimí
52. **Washo** (Lake Tahoe area of Nevada and California; see section 12.6)
53. **Seri** (Sonora)
54. **†Guaikura** (Waikuri) and two other unclassified and unclassifiable languages of southern Baja California: Huchiti and Pericú. They are probably three isolates.
55. **Kutenai** (British Columbia, Montana, and Idaho)
56. **Wakashan** (Vancouver Island, and adjacent mainland in British Columbia and Washington)
    Kwakiutlan, or Northern Wakashan
    1. Kwakiutl
    2. Heiltsuk, or Bella Bella
    3. Kitamat, or Haisla

Nootkan, or Southern Wakashan

    4.   Nootka

    5.   Nitinat

    6.   Makah

57. **Chimakuan** (western Washington)

    1.   Quileute

    2.   †Chimakum

58. **Yukian** (northern California)

    1.   Yuki, including Yuki (proper), Coast Yuki, and Huchnom

    2.   Wappo

59. **Keres** (Cochiti, Santo Domingo, San Felipe, Santa Ana, Zia, Laguna, and Acoma Pueblos of New Mexico)

60. **Otopamean**

Pamean branch (San Luís Potosí, Hidalgo, and Guanajuato)

    1.   Northern Pame

    2.   Central Pame

    3.   †Southern Pame

    4.   Chichimec-Jonaz

Otomí branch

    5.   Mezquital Otomí (Hidalgo, México, and Querétaro)

    6.   Ixtenco (Tlaxcala)

    7.   Puebla Otomí (Puebla, Veracruz, and Hidalgo)

    8.   México Otomí (state of México)

    9.   Mazahua (states of México and Michoacán)

    10. Matlatzinca (state of México)

    11. Ocuiltec (state of México)

61. **Popolocan**

Mazatec branch (Oaxaca and Puebla)

    1.   Huautal-Mazatlan

    2.   Ayautla-Soyaltepec

    3.   Jalapa

    4.   Chiquihuiltan

    5.   Ixcatec (Oaxaca)

Chocho-Popoloca branch (Oaxaca)

    6.   Chocho

    7.   Northern Popoloca

    8.   Western Popoloca

    9.   Eastern Popoloca

62. **Mixtecan**
    Mixtec branch (Oaxaca)
    1. Northern Mixtec
    2. Central Mixtec
    3. Southern Mixtec
    4. Cuicatec (Oaxaca)
    Trique branch (Oaxaca)
    5. Chicahuaxtla Trique
    6. Copala Trique
63. **Amuzgo** (Guerrero)
64. **Zapotecan** (Oaxaca and Gerrero)
    Zapotec branch
    1. Northern Zapotec
    2. Eastern Zapotec
    3. Central Zapotec
    4. Western Zapotec
    5. Southern Zapotec
    Chatino branch
    6. Yaitepec
    7. Tatalpepec
    8. Zenzontepec
65. **Chinantecan** (Oaxaca)
    1. Usila
    2. Palantla
    3. Ojitlán
    4. Quiotepec
    5. Lalana
66. **Subtiaba-Tlapanec**
    1. Tlapanec (once known as Yopi, found in Guerrero)
    2. †Subtiaba (Nicaragua)
67. **Manguean** (also Chiapanec-Mangue, or Chorotegan)
    1. †Chiapanec (Chiapas)
    2. †Mangue (Nicaragua, Costa Rica, and Honduras)
68. **Totonacan**
    1. Totonac (probably more than one language, in Veracruz and Puebla)
    2. Tepehua (Veracruz and Hidaldo)
69. **Purepecha** [Tarascan] (Michoacán)
70. **†Cuitlatec** (Guerrero)

71. **Tequistlatecan** (Chontal of Oaxaca)
    1. Huamelultec (Lowland Chontal)
    2. Tequistlatec (Highland Chontal)
72. **Huave** (Oaxaca) .
73. **Mixe-Zoque**
    Mixean branch (Oaxaca)
    1. Northern Mixe
    2. Southern Mixe
    3. Sayula Popoluca
    4. Oluta Popoluca
    Zoquean branch
    5. Oaxaca Zoque (Oaxaca)
    6. Chiapas Zoque (Chiapas)
    7. Sierra Popoluca (Veracruz)
    8. Texistepec (Oaxaca)
    9. †Tapachultec (Oaxaca)
74. **Mayan**
    1. Huastec (Veracruz)
    2. †Chicomuceltec (Chiapas)
    3. Yucatec (Yucatán Peninsula)
    4. Lacandón (Guatemala and Chiapas)
    5. Mopán (Guatemala and Belize)
    6. Itzá (Yucatec)
    7. Chol (Tabasco and Chiapas)
    8. Chontal (Tabasco)
    9. †Choltí (Guatemala)
    10. Chortí (Honduras and Guatemala)
    11. Tzotzil (Chiapas)
    12. Tzeltal (Chiapas)
    13. Tojolabal (Chiapas)
    14. Chuj (Guatemala)
    15. Kanjobal (Guatemala)
    16. Acatec (Guatemala)
    17. Jacaltec (Guatemala)
    18. Mochó, or Mototzintlec (Chiapas)
    19. Tectiteco (Chiapas)
    20. Mam (Chiapas and Guatemala)
    21. Aguacatec (Guatemala)
    22. Ixil (Guatemala)

23.   Quiché (Guatemala)
24.   Sipacapa, or Sipacepeño (Guatemala)
25.   Sacapultec (Guatemala)
26.   Tzutujil (Guatemala)
27.   Cakchiquel (Guatemala)
28.   Pocomam (Guatemala)
29.   Pocomchí (Guatemala)
30.   Kekchí (Guatemala)
31.   Uspantec (Guatemala)

75. Jicaque (Honduras)
1.   †Jicaque of El Palmar
2.   Jicaque of La Flor

76. Xinca (Guatemala)
1.   Guazacapán
2.   Chiquimulilla
3.   Jumaytepeque
4.   †Yupiltepeque

77. Lenca
1.   †Honduran Lenca
2.   Salvadorian Lenca, or Chilanga

78. Paya (Honduras)

79. Misumalpan
1.   Mískito (Honduras and Nicaragua)
2.   Sumu (Honduras and Nicaragua)
3.   †Cacaopera (El Salvador)
4.   †Matagalpa (Honduras)

80. Chibchan (a number of languages, in Costa Rica, Panama,
Colombia, and Venezuela)

BIBLIOGRAPHY

ABBOTT, CLIFFORD

1984   Two Feminine Genders in Oneida. *Anthropological Linguistics* 261:25–137.

ABBOTT, MIRIAM

1991   Macushi. In *Handbook of Amazonian Languages*, ed. Desmond C. Derbyshire and Geoffrey K. Pullum, vol. 3, 23–160. Berlin: Mouton de Gruyter.

ALLEN, PAULA GUNN

1991   *Grandmothers of the Light: A Medicine Woman's Sourcebook*. Boston: Beacon Press.

ANDREWS, J. RICHARD

1974   *Introduction to Classical Nahuatl*. Austin: University of Texas Press.

AOKI, HARUO

1970   *Nez Perce Grammar*. University of California Publications in Linguistics 62. Berkeley and Los Angeles: University of California Press.

APPLEGATE, RICHARD B.

1974   Chumash Placenames. *Journal of California Anthropology* 1:187–205.

ARMSTRONG, JEANETTE

1985   *Slash*. Penticton, British Columbia: Theytus.

ASCHER, MARCIA

1986   Mathematical Ideas of the Incas. In *Native American Mathematics*, ed. Michael P. Closs, 261–89. Austin: University of Texas Press.

ASCHER, MARCIA, AND ROBERT ASCHER

1981   *Code of the Quipu: A Study in Media, Mathematics, and Culture*. Ann Arbor: University of Michigan Press.

ATWOOD, MARGARET

1990   Scrooge McDuck vs. the Trickster. *Times Literary Supplement*, March 16–22.

BABCOCK, BARBARA, AND JAY COX

1994   The Native American Trickster. In *Dictionary of Native American Literature*, ed. Andrew Wiget, 99–105. Garland Reference Library of the Humanities, vol. 1815. New York: Garland Publishing.

BAETENS BEARDSMORE, HUGO

1986   *Bilingualism: Basic Principles*. 2d ed. San Diego: College Hill Press.

BAKKER, PETER

1991   Trade Languages in the Strait of Belle Isle. *Journal of the Atlantic Provinces Linguistic Association* 13:1–19.

BASSO, KEITH H.

1967   Semantic Aspects of Linguistic Acculturation. *American Anthropologist* 69:471–77. (Reprinted, 1990, in Keith H. Basso, *Western Apache Language and Culture: Essays in Linguistic Anthropology*, 15–24. Tucson: University of Arizona Press.)

1970   "To Give Up on Words": Silence in Western Apache Culture. *Southwestern Journal of Anthropology* 26:213–30. (Reprinted, 1990, in Keith H. Basso, *Western Apache Language and Culture: Essays in Linguistic Anthropology*, 80–98. Tucson: University of Arizona Press.)

1972   Ice and Travel among the Fort Norman Slave: Folk Taxonomies and Cultural Rules. *Language in Society* 1:31–49.

1984   Stalking with Stories. In *Text, Play, and Story: The Reconstruction of Self and Society*, ed. Eduard Bruner, 19–55. (Proceedings of the American Anthropological Association). Washington, D.C.: American Ethnological Society. (Reprinted, 1990, in Keith H. Basso, *Western Apache Language and Culture: Essays in Linguistic Anthropology*, 99–137. Tucson: University of Arizona Press.)

1988   'Speaking with Names': Language and Landscape among the Western Apache. *Cultural Anthropology* 3:99–130. (Reprinted, 1990, in Keith H. Basso, *Western Apache Language and Culture: Essays in Linguistic Anthropology*, 138–73. Tucson: University of Arizona Press.)

1990   *Western Apache Language and Culture: Essays in Linguistic Anthropology*. Tucson: University of Arizona Press.

BEAN, LOWELL JOHN

1976   Social Organization in Native California. In *Native Californians: A Theoretical Retrospective*, ed. Lowell J. Bean and Thomas C. Blackburn, 99–123. Socorro, New Mexico: Ballena Press.

1978   Social Organization. In *California*, ed. Robert Heizer, 673–82. *Handbook of North American Indians*, vol. 8, William C. Sturtevant, gen. ed. Washington, D.C.: Smithsonian Institution.

BEAN, LOWELL JOHN, AND CHARLES R. SMITH

1978   Gabrielino. In *California*, ed. Robert Heizer, 538–49. *Handbook of North American Indians*, vol. 8, William C. Sturtevant, gen. ed. Washington, D.C.: Smithsonian Institution.

BEAN, LOWELL JOHN, AND DOROTHY THEODORATUS

1978   Western Pomo and Northeastern Pomo. In *California*, ed. Robert Heizer, 289–305. *Handbook of North American Indians*, vol. 8, William C. Sturtevant, gen. ed. Washington, D.C.: Smithsonian Institution.

BEAN, LOWELL JOHN, AND SYLVIA BRAKKE VANE

1978   Cults and Their Transformations. In *California*, ed. Robert Heizer, 662–72. *Handbook of North American Indians,* vol. 8, William C. Sturtevant, gen. ed. Washington, D.C.: Smithsonian Institution.

BEELER, MADISON S.

1964 Ventureño Numerals. In *Studies in California Linguistics,* ed. William Bright, 13–18. University of California Publications in Linguistics 34. Berkeley: University of California Press.

1986 Chumash Numerals. In *Native American Mathematics,* ed. Michael P. Closs, 109–28. Austin: University of Texas Press.

BERDAN, FRANCES F.

1982 *The Aztecs of Central Mexico: An Imperial Society.* New York: Holt, Rinehart and Winston.

BERLIN, BRENT

1972 Speculations on the Growth of Ethnobotanical Nomenclature. *Language in Society* 1:51–86.

1976 The Concept of Rank in Ethnobiological Classification: Some Evidence from Aguarana Folk Botany. *American Ethnologist* 3:381–99.

BERLIN, BRENT, AND A. KIMBALL ROMNEY

1964 Descriptive Semantics of Tzeltal Numeral Classifiers. *American Anthropologist* 66: 79–98.

BERLIN, BRENT, DENNIS E. BREEDLOVE, AND PETER H. RAVEN

1966 Folk Taxonomies and Biological Classification. *Science* 154:273–75. (Reprinted, 1969, in *Cognitive Anthropology,* ed. Stephen A. Tyler, 60–66. New York: Holt, Rinehart and Winston.)

1973 General Principles of Classification and Nomenclature in Folk Biology. *American Anthropologist* 75:214–42.

1974 *Principles of Tzeltal Plant Classification: An Introduction to the Botanical Ethnography of a Mayan Speaking Community in Highland Chiapas.* New York: Academic Press.

BICKERTON, DEREK

1981 *Roots of Language.* Ann Arbor: Karoma.

BLACK, ROBERT A.

1967 Hopi Grievance Chants: A Mechanism of Social Control. In *Studies in Southwestern Ethnolinguistics,* ed. Dell H. Hymes and William E. Bittle, 54–67. The Hague: Mouton.

BLACKBURN, THOMAS

1976 Ceremonial Integration and Social Interaction in Aboriginal California. In *Native Californians: A Theoretical Perspective,* ed. Lowell J. Bean and Thomas C. Blackburn, 225–43. Socorro, New Mexico: Ballena Press.

1989 California and the Intermountain Region. In *Native American Religions: North America,* ed. Lawrence E. Sullivan, 75–88. New York: Macmillan.

BLACK-ROGERS, M. B.

1982   Algonquian Gender Revisited: Animate Nouns and Ojibwa "Power"-An Impasse?
       Papers in Linguistics 15(1):59-76.

BLOOMFIELD, LEONARD

1927   Literate and Illiterate Speech. *American Speech* 10:432-49. (Reprinted, 1964, in *Lan-
       guage in Culture and Society: A Reader in Linguistics and Anthropology*, ed. Dell H.
       Hymes, 391-96. New York: Harper and Row.)

1946   Algonquian. In *Linguistic Structures of Native America*, ed. Harry Hoijer, 85-129. Pub-
       lications in Anthropology 6. New York: Viking Fund.

BOAS, FRANZ

1911   Introduction. In *Handbook of American Indian Languages*, ed. Franz Boas, 1-83.
       Bureau of American Ethnology, Bulletin 40, pt. 1. Washington, D.C.: Smithsonian
       Institution.

1934   *Geographical Names of the Kwakiutl Indians*. Columbia University Contributions
       to Anthropology, vol. 20. New York. (Reprinted, 1964, in *Language in Culture and
       Society: A Reader in Linguistics and Anthropology*, ed. Dell H. Hymes, 171-76. New
       York: Harper and Row.)

BONVILLAIN, NANCY

1989   Noun Incorporation and Metaphor Semantic Process in Akwesasne Mohawk. *Anthro-
       pological Linguistics* 31(3-4):173-94.

BRANDT, ELIZABETH

1970   On the Origins of Linguistic Stratification: The Sandia Case. *Anthropological Linguis-
       tics* 12:46-50.

BRIGGS, CHARLES L.

1992   Since I Am a Woman, I Will Chastise My Relatives: Gender, Reported Speech, and Re-
       production of Social Relations in Warao Ritual Wailing. *American Ethnologist* 19(2):
       337-61.

BRIGGS, LUCY T.

1981   Politeness in Aymara Language and Culture. In *The Aymara Language in Its Social
       and Cultural Context*, ed. Martha J. Hardman, 90-113. University of Florida Mono-
       graphs in the Social Sciences No. 67. Gainesville: University Presses of Florida.

1983   Bilingual Education in Bolivia. In *Bilingualism: Social Issues and Policy Implications*,
       ed. Andrew W. Miracle, Jr., 84-95. Southern Anthropological Society Proceedings
       No. 16. Athens: University of Georgia Press.

BRIGHT, WILLIAM

1952   Linguistic Innovations in Karok. *International Journal of American Linguistics* 18:53-
       62.

1957   *The Karok Language*. University of California Publications in Linguistics 13. Berkeley:
       University of California Press.

1960   *Animals of Acculturation in California Indian Languages*. University of California
       Publications in Linguistics 4(4). Berkeley: University of California Press.

1973   North American Indian Languages Contact. In *Current Trends in Linguistics*, vol. 10, ed. Thomas A. Sebeok, 713–26. The Hague: Mouton.

1979   Toward a Typology of Verbal Abuse; Naming Dead Kin in Northwestern California. *Maledicta* 3:177–80.

1984   A Karok Myth in "Measured Verse": The Translation of a Performance. In *American Indian Linguistics and Literature*, by William Bright, 91–100. Berlin: Mouton. (First published, 1979, in *Journal of California and Great Basin Anthropology* 1:117–23.)

1990   "With One Lip, With Two Lips": Parallelism in Nahuatl. *Language* 66:437–52.

BRIGHT, WILLIAM, AND JANE O. BRIGHT

1965   Semantic Structures in Northwestern California and the Sapir-Whorf Hypothesis. *American Anthropologist* (Special Publication) 67(5,pt.2):249–58. (Reprinted, 1969, in *Cognitive Anthropology*, ed. Stephen A. Tyler, 66–78. New York: Holt, Rinehart and Winston.)

BROWN, ALANNA K.

1994   Mourning Dove. In *Dictionary of Native American Literature*, ed. Andrew Wiget, 259–64. Garland Reference Library of the Humanities, vol. 1815. New York: Garland Publishing.

BROWN, C. H.

1983   Where Do Cardinal Direction Terms Come From? *Anthropological Linguistics* 25(2): 121–26.

BRUGMAN, CLAUDIA

1983   The Use of Body-Part Terms as Locatives in Chalcatongo Mixtec. In *Survey of California and Other Indian Languages Report #4*, ed. Alice Schlicter, Wallace L. Chafe, and Leanne Hinton, 235–90. Report No. 4. Berkeley: Department of Linguistics, University of California.

BUCKLEY, THOMAS

1984   Yurok Speech Registers and Ontology. *Language and Society* 13:467–88.

1989   California and the Intermountain Region. In *Native American Religions: North America*, ed. Lawrence E. Sullivan, 75–88. New York: Macmillan.

BUNTE, PAMELA A., AND ROBERT J. FRANKLIN

1988   San Juan Southern Paiute Numerals and Mathematics. In *In Honor of Mary Haas: From the Haas Festival Conference on Native American Linguistics*, ed. William Shipley, 15–36. New York: Mouton de Gruyter.

BURWASH, NATHANIEL

1911   The Gift to a Nation of Written Language. *Proceedings and Transactions of the Royal Society of Canada*, 3rd series, section 2, 5:3–21.

CALLAGHAN, CATHERINE A.

1964   Phonemic Borrowing in Lake Miwok. In *Studies in Californian Linguistics*, ed. William Bright, 46–53. University of California Publications in Linguistics 34. Berkeley: University of California Press.

CALNEK, EDWARD E.

1976   The Internal Structure of Tenochtitlan. In *The Valley of Mexico*, ed. Eric R. Wolf, 287–302. Albuquerque: University of New Mexico Press.

CAMPBELL, LYLE

1979   Middle American Languages. In *The Languages of Native America: Historical and Comparative Assessment*, ed. Lyle Campbell and Marianne Mithun, 902–1000. Austin: University of Texas Press.

1988   Review of *Language in the Americas*, by J. H. Greenberg. *Language* 64:591–615.

CAMPBELL, LYLE, TERENCE KAUFMAN, AND THOMAS C. SMITH-STARK

1986   Meso-America as a Linguistic Area. *Language* 62:530–70.

CAMPBELL, LYLE, AND MARIANNE MITHUN

1979   Introduction: North American Indian Historical Linguistics in Current Perspective. In *The Languages of Native America: Historical and Comparative Assessment*, ed. Lyle Campbell and Marianne Mithun, 3–69. Austin: University of Texas Press.

CAMPBELL, LYLE, AND MARTHA C. MUNTZEL

1989   The Structural Consequences of Language Death. In *Investigating Obsolescence Studies in Language Contraction and Death*, ed. Nancy D. Dorian, 181–96. New York: Cambridge University Press.

CANGER, UNA

1978   Nahuatl Dialect Subgroupings. Paper given at the 6th annual Friends of Uto-Aztecan Working Conference, Reno.

1980   Five Studies Inspired by Nahuatl Verbs in *-oa*. *Travaux du cercle linguistique de Copenhague*, vol. 14.

CAPITAINE, FERNANDO WINFIELD

1988   La Estela 1 de la Mojarra, Veracruz, México. *Research Reports on Ancient Maya Writing* No. 16. Washington, D.C.: Center for Maya Research.

CARRANZA, ROMERO F.

1983   Los insultos en el quechua de Ancash. *Revista latinoamericana de estudios ethnolingüísticos* 3.

CARRASCO, PEDRO

1971   Social Organization in Ancient Mexico. In *Archaeology of Northern Mesoamerica*, vol. 10, part 1, *Handbook of Middle American Indians*, ed. Gordon F. Ekholm and Ignacio Bernal, 349–75. Austin: University of Texas Press.

CARROLL, JOHN B.

1956   *Language, Thought, and Reality: Selected Writings of Benjamin Lee Whorf*. New York: John Wiley; Cambridge, Mass.: Technology Press.

CASAGRANDE, JOSEPH B.

1948   Comanche Baby Language. *International Journal of American Linguistics* 14:11–14. (Reprinted, 1964, in *Language in Culture and Society: A Reader in Linguistics and Anthropology*, ed. Dell H. Hymes, 245–349. New York: Harper and Row.)

1954 Comanche Linguistic Acculturation: I, II. *International Journal of American Linguistics* 20:140-52, 217-37.

1955 Comanche Linguistic Acculturation: III. *International Journal of American Linguistics* 21:8-25.

CHAFE, WALLACE L.

1962 Estimates Regarding the Present Speakers of North American Indian Languages. *International Journal of American Indian Languages* 28:162-71.

1965 Corrected Estimates Regarding Speakers of Indian Languages. *International Journal of American Indian Languages* 31:345-46.

1973 Siouan, Iroquoian, and Caddoan. In *Trends in Linguistics*, vol. 10, ed. Thomas Sebeok, 1164-1209. The Hague: Mouton. (Reprinted, 1976, in *Native Languages of the Americas*, vol. 1, 527-72. New York: Plenum Press.)

1979 Caddoan. In *The Languages of Native America: Historical and Comparative Assessment*, ed. Lyle Campbell and Marianne Mithun, 213-35. Austin: University of Texas Press.

1981 Differences between Colloquial and Ritual Seneca, or How Oral Literature Is Literary. In *Survey of California and Other Indian Languages*, ed. Alice Schlicter, Wallace L. Chafe, and Leanne Hinton, 131-45. Report No. 1. Berkeley: Department of Linguistics, University of California.

1993 Seneca Speaking Styles and the Location of Authority. In *Responsibility and Evidence in Oral Discourse*, ed. Jane H. Hill and Judith T. Irvine, 72-87. Cambridge: Cambridge University Press.

CHAFE, WALLACE L., AND JOHANNA NICHOLS, EDITORS

1986 *Evidentiality: The Linguistic Coding of Epistemology*. Norwood, N. J.: Ablex.

CHAMBERLAIN, ALEXANDER F.

1910 Nith-Songs. *Handbook of American Indians North of Mexico*, ed. Frederick Webb Hodge. Bureau of American Ethnology Bulletin, 30(2):77.

CHAMPAGNE, DUANE, EDITOR

1993 *Native America: Portrait of the Peoples*. Detroit: Visible Ink Press.

CHAPMAN, SHIRLEY, AND DESMOND C. DERBYSHIRE

1991 Paumarí. In *Handbook of Amazonian Languages*, vol. 3, 161-352. Berlin: Mouton de Gruyter.

CHILDE, V. GORDON

1936 *Man Makes Himself*. London: London, Watts.

CLAIRIS, CHRISTOS

1985 Indigenous Languages of Tierra del Fuego. In *South American Indian Languages: Retrospect and Prospect*, ed. Harriet E. Manelis Klein and Louisa R. Stark, 753-83. Austin: University of Texas Press.

CLARK, WILLIAM PHILO

1885 *Indian Sign Language*. Philadelphia: L. R. Hamersly.

CLAVAUD, DONNA

1977 Playing Leaves: A Study of a Traditional Kashaya Pomo Play Behavior. *Journal of California Anthropology* 4(2):191–205.

CLEWLOW, C. WILLIAM, JR.

1978 Prehistoric Rock Art. In *California,* ed. Robert H. Heizer, 619–25. *Handbook of North American Indians,* vol. 8, William C. Sturtevant, gen. ed. Washington, D.C.: Smithsonian Institution.

CLOSS, MICHAEL P.

1986a Native American Number Systems. In *Native American Mathematics,* ed. Michael P. Closs, 3–43. Austin: University of Texas Press.

CLOSS, MICHAEL P., EDITOR

1986b *Native American Mathematics.* Austin: University of Texas Press.

COE, MICHAEL D.

1962 *Mexico.* New York: Praeger.

1973 *The Maya Scribe and His World.* New York: Grolier Club.

1976 Early Steps in the Evolution of Maya Writings. In *Origins of Religious Art and Iconography in Preclassic Mesoamerica,* ed. H. B. Nicholson, 109–22. Los Angeles: University of California, Los Angeles, Latin American Center.

COLTELLI, LAURA

1990 *Winged Words: American Indian Writers Speak.* Lincoln: University of Nebraska Press.

COOK, SHERBURNE F.

1978 Historical Demography. In *California,* ed. Robert Heizer, 91–99. *Handbook of North American Indians,* vol. 8, William C. Sturtevant, gen. ed. Washington, D.C.: Smithsonian Institution.

CORBETT, GRENVILLE

1991 *Gender.* Cambridge: Cambridge Unversity Press.

CORNYN, JOHN HUBERT

1938 Aztec Literature. *International Congress of Americanists, Mexico,* 322–36.

COTTON, ELIZABETH G., AND JOHN M. SHARP

1988 *Spanish in the Americas.* Washington, D.C.: Georgetown University Press.

COWAN, GEORGE M.

1948 Mazateco Whistle Speech. *Language* 24:280–86. (Reprinted, 1964, in *Language in Culture and Society: A Reader in Linguistics and Anthropology,* ed. Dell H. Hymes, 305–10. New York: Harper and Row.)

CRAIG, COLETTE GRINEVALD

1979 Jacaltec: Field Work in Guatemala. In *Languages and Their Speakers,* ed. Timothy Shopen, 3–57. Cambridge, Mass: Winthrop.

1986 Jacaltec Noun Classifiers: A Study in Grammaticalization. *Lingua* 70:241–84.

CRAIK, BRIAN

1982   The Animate in Cree Language and Ideology. In *Papers of the Thirteenth Algonquian Conference*, ed. William Cowan, 29–35. Ottawa: Carleton University.

CRAWFORD, JAMES M.

1970   Cocopa Baby Talk. *International Journal of American Linguistics* 36:9–13.

1975   Southeastern Indian Languages. In *Studies in Southeastern Indian Languages*, ed. James M. Crawford, 1–120. Athens: University of Georgia Press.

1978a   More on Cocopa Baby Talk. *International Journal of American Linguistics* 44:17–23.

1978b   *The Mobilian Trade Language*. Knoxville: University of Tennessee Press.

CRUM, BEVERLY

1980   Newe Hupia-Shoshoni Poetry Songs. *Journal of California and Great Basin Anthropology–Papers in Linguistics* 2:3–23.

DAKIN, KAREN

1981   The Characteristics of a Nahuatl Lingua Franca. In *Nahuatl Studies in Memory of Fernando Horcasitas*, ed. Frances Karttunen, 55–67. Texas Linguistic Forum 18. Austin: Department of Linguistics, University of Texas.

DARNELL, REGNA

1985   The Language of Power in Cree Interethnic Communication. In *Languages of Inequality*, ed. Nessa Wolfson and Joan Manes, 61–72. Contributions to the Sociology of Language No. 36. Berlin: Mouton.

DARNELL, REGNA, AND A. L. VANECK

1976   The Semantic Basis of the Animate/Inanimate Distinction in Cree. *Papers in Linguistics* 9(3–4):59–180.

DARNELL, REGNA, AND DELL HYMES

1986   Edward Sapir's Six-Unit Classification of American Indian Languages: The Search for Time Perspective. In *Studies in the History of Western Linguistics in Honour of R. H. Robins*. Cambridge: Cambridge University Press.

DAUENHAUER, NORA MARKS, AND RICHARD DAUENHAUER

1987   *Haa Shuka, Our Ancestors: Tlingit Oral Narratives*. Seattle: University of Washington Press; and Juneau: Sealaska Heritage Foundation.

DAVIES, NIGEL

1987   *The Aztec Empire*. Norman: University of Oklahoma Press.

DAY, CYRUS LAWRENCE

1967   *Quipus and Witches' Knots: The Role of the Knot in Primitive and Ancient Cultures*. Lawrence: University of Kansas Press.

D'AZEVEDO, WARREN L.

1963   *The Washo Indians of California and Nevada*. Anthropological Papers 67. Salt Lake City: University of Utah Press.

1986a   Washo. In *Great Basin*, ed. Warren L. d'Azevedo, 466–98. *Handbook of North Ameri-*

can Indians, vol. ii, William C. Sturtevant, gen. ed. Washington, D.C.: Smithsonian Institution.

D'AZEVEDO, WARREN L., EDITOR

1986b *Great Basin. Handbook of North American Indians*, vol. ii, William C. Sturtevant, gen. ed. Washington, D.C.: Smithsonian Institution.

DEDRICK, JOHN M.

1977   Spanish Influences on Yaqui Grammar? *International Journal of American Linguistics* 43:144-9.

DELORIA, ELLA

1988   *Waterlily*. Lincoln: University of Nebraska Press.

DELORIA, VINE, JR.

1970   *We Talk, You Listen*. New York: Macmillan.

DENNIS, WAYNE

1940   *The Hopi Child*. University of Virginia Institute for Research in the Social Sciences Institute Monograph 26. New York: D. Appleton-Century.

DENNY, J. PETER

1989   The Nature of Polysynthesis in Algonquian and Eskimo. In *Theoretical Perspectives on Native American Languages*, ed. Donna B. Gerdts and Karin Michelson, 230-58. Albany: State of New York University Press.

DERBYSHIRE, DESMOND C., AND GEOFFREY K. PULLUM, EDITORS

1986   *Handbook of Amazonian Languages*, vols. i, 2. Berlin: Mouton de Gruyter.

DE REUSE, WILLEM J.

1989   'Magic Words' and Formulaic Speech in Siberian Yupik Eskimo Folklore. Paper delivered to the Society for the Study of the Indigenous Languages of America, Tucson.

DEVEREUX, GEORGE

1951   Mohave Indian Verbal and Motor Profanity. *Psychoanalysis and Social Sciences* 3:99-127.

DE WOLF, PAUL P.

n.d.   *Aculturación lingüística y expansión léxica en el Pima Bajo de Yecora* (Sonora, Mexico). Ms. available from author.

DIBBLE, CHARLES E.

1963   Glifos fonéticos del Codece Florentino. *Estudios de cultura Nahuatl* 4:55-60.

1971   Writing in Central Mexico. In *Handbook of Middle American Indians*, vol. 10, ed. Gordon F. Ekholm and Ignacio Bernal, 322-31. Austin: University of Texas Press.

1972   The Syllabic-Alphabetic Trend in Mexican Codices. *Atti del XL Congresso Internazionale degli Americanisti*.

DIEBOLD, A. RICHARD, JR.

1960   Incipient Bilingualism. *Language* 37:97-112. (Reprinted, 1964, in *Language in Culture and Society: A Reader in Linguistics and Anthropology,* ed. Dell H. Hymes, 495–508. New York: Harper and Row.)

DIXON, ROLAND B., AND A. L. KROEBER

1907   Numerical Systems of the Languages of California. *American Anthropologist* 9:663–90.

1913   New Linguistic Families in California. *American Anthropologist* 15:647–55.

1919   Linguistic Families of California. *University of California Publications in American Archaeology and Ethnology* 16(3):47–118.

DORRIS, MICHAEL

1988   *A Yellow Raft on Blue Water.* New York: Warner.

DOWNS, JAMES F.

1966   *The Two Worlds of the Washo, an Indian Tribe of California and Nevada.* New York: Holt, Rinehart and Winston.

DOZIER, EDWARD P.

1954   The Hopi-Tewa of Arizona. *University of California Publications in American Archaeology and Ethnology,* 44(3):259–376. Berkeley: University of California Press.

1956   Two Examples of Linguistic Acculturation: The Yaqui of Sonora and Arizona and the Tewa of New Mexico. *Language* 32:46–57. (Reprinted, 1964, in *Language in Culture and Society: A Reader in Linguistics and Anthropology,* ed. Dell H. Hymes, 509–16. New York: Harper and Row.)

1970   *The Pueblo Indians of North America.* New York: Holt, Rinehart and Winston.

DRIVER, HAROLD E.

1961   *Indians of North America.* Chicago: University of Chicago Press.

DURBIN, M.

1977   A Survey of the Carib Language Family. In *Carib-speaking Indians: Culture, Society and Language,* ed. Ellen B. Basso, 23–38. Tucson: University of Arizona Press.

EGESDAL, STEVEN M.

1992   *Stylized Characters' Speech in Thompson Salish Narrative.* University of Montana Occasional Papers in Linguistics 9. Missoula: University of Montana Linguistics Laboratory.

EGGAN, FRED R.

1950   *Social Organization of the Western Pueblos.* Chicago: University of Chicago Press.

1979   Pueblos: Introduction. In *Southwest,* ed. Alfonso Ortiz, 224–35. *Handbook of North American Indians,* vol. 9, William C. Sturtevant, gen. ed. Washington, D.C.: Smithsonian Institution.

ELMENDORF, WILLIAM W.

1951   Word Taboo and Lexical Change in Coast Salish. *International Journal of American Linguistics* 17:205–8.

EVERS, LARRY, AND FELIPE S. MOLINA

1987   *Yaqui Deer Dance: Maso Bwikam, a Native American Poetry.* Tucson: University of Arizona Press.

FAGAN, BRIAN M.

1984   *The Aztecs.* New York: W. H. Freeman.

FARRELL, PATRICK, STEPHEN A. MARLETT, AND DAVID M. PERLMUTTER

1991   Notions of Subjecthood and Switch Reference Evidence from Seri. *Linguistic Inquiry* 22(3):431–56.

FLANNERY, REGINA

1953   *The Gros Ventres of Montana:* Part I, Social Life. Anthropological Series No. 15. Washington, D.C.: Catholic University of America.

FOREMAN, GRANT, EDITOR

1930   *A Traveler in Indian Territory: The Journal of Ethan Allen Hitchock, Late Major-General in the United States Army.* Cedar Rapids, Iowa: Torch Press.

FOSTER, MICHAEL K.

1974a   From the Earth to Beyond the Sky: An Ethnographic Approach to Four Longhouse Iroquois Speech Events. Unpublished Ph.D. dissertation, University of Pennsylvania, Philadelphia.

1974b   When Words Become Deeds: An Analysis of Three Iroquois Longhouse Speech Events. In *Explorations in the Ethnography of Speaking,* ed. Richard Bauman and Joel Sherzer, 354–67. London: Cambridge University Press.

FOWLER, CATHERINE S.

1972   Some Ecological Clues to Proto-Numic Homelands. In *Great Basin Cultural Ecology: A Symposium,* ed. Don D. Fowler, 105–21. Desert Research Institute Publications in the Social Sciences 8. Reno: University of Nevada.

1982a   Food-Named Groups among the Northern Paiute in North America's Great Basin: An Ecological Interpretation. In *Resources Managers: North American and Australian Hunter-gatherers,* ed. N. M. Williams and E. S. Hunn, 113–29. American Association for the Advancement of Science Selected Symposium 67, Boulder, Colorado.

1982b   Settlement Patterns and Subsistence Systems in the Great Basin: The Ethnographic Record. In *Man and Environment in the Great Basin,* ed. David B. Madsen and James F. O'Connell, 121–38. Society of American Archaeology Papers 2. Washington, D.C.

1983   Some Lexical Clues to Uto-Aztecan Prehistory. *International Journal of American Linguistics* 49:224–57.

FOWLER, CATHERINE S., AND SVEN LILJEBLAD

1986   Northern Paiute. In *Great Basin,* ed. Warren L. d'Azevedo, 435–65. *Handbook of North American Indians,* vol. 11, William C. Sturtevant, gen. ed. Washington, D.C.: Smithsonian Institution.

FOWLER, DON D.

1966   Great Basin Social Organization. In *The Great Basin: 1964*, ed. Warren L. d'Azevedo, 57–73. Reno: Desert Research Institute.

FOX, ROBIN

1959   A Note on Cochiti Linguistics. In *Cochiti, a New Mexico Pueblo, Past and Present*, ed. Charles H. Lange, 557–72. Austin: University of Texas Press.

FRIED, MORTON

1967   *The Evolution of Political Society: An Essay in Political Anthropology*. New York: Random House.

FRISCH, J. A.

1968   Maricopa Foods: A Native Taxonomic System. *International Journal of American Linguistics* 34:16–20.

GAMBLE, GEOFFREY

1975   Consonant Symbolism in Yokuts. *International Journal of American Linguistics* 41: 306–9.

GARDNER, HOWARD

1985   *The Mind's New Science: A History of the Cognitive Revolution*. New York: Basic Books.

GARIBAY K., ANGEL M.

1954–55   *Historia de la literatura nahuatl*. 2 vols. Mexico City: Editorial Porrua.

1964   *La literatura de los aztecas*. Mexico City: Editorial Joaquin Mortiz.

GARTH, T. R.

1978   Atsugewi. In *California*, ed. Robert F. Heizer, 236–43. *Handbook of North American Indians*, vol. 8, William C. Sturtevant, gen. ed. Washington, D.C.: Smithsonian Institution.

GARVIN, PAUL L., AND MADELEIN MATHIOT

1960   The Urbanization of the Guaraní Language–A Problem in Language and Culture. In *Men and Cultures*, ed. F. C. Wallace, 783–90. Philadelphia: University of Pennsylvania Press. (Reprinted, 1968, in *Readings in the Sociology of Language*, ed. Joshua A. Fishman, 365–74. The Hague: Mouton.)

GATSCHET, ALBERT S.

1884   *A Migration Legend of the Creek Indians, with a Linguistic, Historic and Ethnographic Introduction*. Reprinted, 1969, New York: AMS Press.

GAYTON, ANNA H.

1976   Culture-environment Integration: External References in Yokuts Life. In *Native Californians: A Theoretical Perspective*, ed. Lowell J. Bean and Thomas C. Blackburn, 79–97. Socorro, N.M.: Ballena Press.

GAYTON, ANNA H., AND STANLEY S. NEWMAN

1940   Yokuts and Western Mono Myths. *University of California Anthropological Records*

5(1):1-110. (Reprinted in part, 1964, in *Language in Culture and Society: A Reader in Linguistics and Anthropology*, ed. Dell H. Hymes, 372-81. New York: Harper and Row.)

GEIOGAMAH, HANAY

1980   *New Native American Drama.* Norman: University of Oklahoma Press.

GENSLER, O. D.

1983   θ and *ha* in Walapai Foregrounding and Sound Symbolism. *Journal of California and Great Basin Anthropology Papers in Linguistics* 3:17-63.

GERDTS, DONNA B., AND KARIN MICHELSON

1989   *Theoretical Perspectives on Native American Languages.* Albany: State University of New York Press.

GODDARD, IVES

1975   Algonquian, Wiyot, and Yurok: Proving Distant Linguistic Relationships. In *Linguistics and Anthropology: In Honor of C.F. Voegelin*, ed. M. Dale Kinkade, Kenneth L. Hale, and Oswald Werner, 249-62. Lisse: Peter de Ridder Press.

1978a Central Algonquian Languages. In *Northeast*, ed. Bruce Trigger, 583-87. *Handbook of North American Indians*, vol. 15, William C. Sturtevant, gen. ed. Washington, D.C.: Smithsonian Institution.

1978b Eastern Algonquian Languages. In *Northeast*, ed. Bruce Trigger, 70-77. *Handbook of North American Indians*, vol. 15, William C. Sturtevant, gen. ed. Washington, D.C.: Smithsonian Institution.

1978c Synonymy. In "Northern Iroquoian Culture Patterns" by William N. Fenton, 296-321, *Northeast*, ed. Bruce G. Trigger, 319-21. *Handbook of North American Indians*, vol. 15, William C. Sturtevant, gen. ed. Washington, D.C.: Smithsonian Institution.

1979   The Languages of South Texas and the Lower Rio Grande. In *The Languages of Native America: Historical and Comparative Assessment*, ed. Lyle Campbell and Marianne Mithun, 355-89. Austin: University of Texas Press.

1986   Sapir's Comparative Method. In *New Perspectives in Language, Culture, and Personality: Proceedings of the Edward Sapir Centenary Conference*, ed. William Cowan, Michael K. Foster, and Konrad Koerner, 191-210. Amsterdam: John Benjamins.

GODDARD, IVES, AND KATHLEEN J. BRAGDON

1988   *Native Writings in Massachusetts.* Philadelphia: American Philosophical Society.

GOLDSCHMIDT, WALTER

1978   Nomlaki. In *California*, ed. Robert F. Heizer, 341-49. *Handbook of North American Indians*, vol. 8, William C. Sturtevant, gen. ed. Washington, D.C.: Smithsonian Institution.

GOODRICH, JENNIE, CLAUDIA LAWSON, AND VANA PARRISH LAWSON

1980   *Kashaya Pomo Plants.* American Indian Monograph Series, No. 2. Los Angeles: University of California, Los Angeles, American Indian Studies Center.

GOODY, JACK

1977   *The Domestication of the Savage Mind.* Cambridge: Cambridge University Press.

GOSS, JAMES A.

n.d.   Gumming to Glory. Ms. available from author.

GREENBERG, JOSEPH H.

1987   *Languages in the Americas.* Stanford: Stanford University Press.

GRIMES, BARBARA F.

1985   Language Attitudes: Identity, Distinctiveness, Survival in the Vaupes. *Journal of Multilingual and Multicultural Development* 6(5):389-401.

GRIMES, BARBARA F., EDITOR

1988   *Ethnologue: Languages of the World.* 11th ed. Dallas: Summer Institute of Linguistics.

GUMPERZ, JOHN J.

1962   Types of Linguistic Communities. *Anthropological Linguistics* 4:28-40. (Reprinted, 1968, in *Readings in the Sociology of Language,* ed. Joshua A. Fishman, 460-72. The Hague: Mouton.)

1969   Communication in Multilingual Societies. In *Cognitive Anthropology,* ed. Stephen A. Tyler, 435-49. New York: Holt, Rinehart and Winston.

GUMPERZ, JOHN J., AND ROBERT WILSON

1971   Convergence and Creolization: A Case from the Indo-Aryan/Dravidian Border in India. In *Pidginization and Creolization of Languages,* ed. Dell H. Hymes, 151-67. Cambridge: Cambridge University Press.

HAAS, MARY R.

1944   Men's and Women's Speech in Koasati. *Language* 20:142-49. (Reprinted, 1964, in *Language in Culture and Society: A Reader in Linguistics and Anthropology,* ed. Dell H. Hymes, 228-32. New York: Harper and Row.)

1945   Dialects of the Muskogee Language. *International Journal of American Linguistics* 11: 69-47.

1946   A Grammatical sketch of Tunica. In *Linguistic Structures of Native America,* ed. Harry Hoijer, 337-66. Publications in Anthropology No. 6. New York: Viking Fund.

1958   Algonkian-Ritwan: The End of Controversy. *International Journal of American Linguistics* 24:159-73.

1967   Language and Taxonomy in Northwestern California. *American Anthropologist* 69: 358-61.

1969   Grammar or Lexicon? The American Indian Side of the Question from Duponceau to Powell. *International Journal of American Linguistics* 35:239-55. (Reprinted, 1978, in *Language, Culture and History: Essays by Mary R. Haas,* selected and introduced by Anwar S. Dil, 130-63. Stanford: Stanford University Press.)

1970   Diminutive Symbolism in Northern California: A Study in Diffusion. In *Languages and Cultures of Western North America,* ed. Earl H. Swanson, Jr., 86-96. Pocatello: Idaho State University Press.

1973a   The Expression of the Diminutive. In *Studies in Linguistics in Honor of George L. Trager,* ed. M. Estelle Smith, 148-52. The Hague: Mouton.

1973b   The Southeast. In *Current Trends in Linguistics*, vol. 10, *Linguistics in North America*, ed. Thomas A. Sebeok, 1210–49. The Hague: Mouton.

1975   What Is Mobilian? In *Studies in Southeastern Indian languages*, ed. James M. Crawford, 257–63. Athens: University of Georgia Press.

1976   Boas, Sapir and Bloomfield. In *American Indian Languages and American Linguistics*, ed. Wallace L. Chafe, 59–69. Lisse: Peter de Ridder Press. (Reprinted, 1978, in *Language, Culture and History: Essays by Mary R. Haas*, selected and introduced by Anwar S. Dil, 194–206. Stanford: Stanford University Press.)

1978a   *Language, Culture and History: Essays by Mary R. Haas*, selected and introduced by Anwar S. Dil. Stanford: Stanford University Press.

1978b   The Study of American Indian Languages: A Brief Historical Sketch. In *Language, Culture and History: Essays by Mary R. Haas*, selected and introduced by Anwar S. Dil, 110–29. Stanford: Stanford University Press. (Revised version, Anthropological Linguistics: History, in *Perspectives in Anthropology* [1976], ed. Anthony F. C. Wallace et al., 33–47. Special publication of the American Anthropological Association No. 10.)

1979   Southeastern Languages. In *The Languages of Native America: Historical and Comparative Assessment*, ed. Lyle Campbell and Marianne Mithun, 299–326. Austin: University of Texas Press.

HAGE, PER, AND WICK R. MILLER

1976   "Eagle" = "Bird": A Note on the Structure and Evolution of Shoshoni Ethnoornithological Nomenclature. *American Ethnologist* 3:481–88.

HAIMAN, JOHN, AND PAMELA MUNRO

1993   *Switch Reference and Universal Grammar.* Amsterdam: John Benjamins.

HAJDA, YVONNE, HENRY ZENK, AND ROBERT BOYD

1988   The Early Historiography of Chinook Jargon. Paper presented at the 87th Annual Meeting of the American Anthropological Association.

HALE, JANET CAMPBELL

1985   *The Jailing of Cecilia Capture.* New York: Random House

HALE, KENNETH

1992   Endangered Languages. *Language* 68(1):1–42.

HALLIDAY, M.A.K, ANGUS MCÍNTOSH, AND PETER STREVENS

1965   *The Linguistic Sciences and Language Teaching.* London: Longmans, Green.

HALPERN, A.

1980   Sex Differences in Quechuan Narration. *Journal of California and Great Basin Anthropology, Papers in Linguistics* 2. Banning, CA: Malki Museum.

HANKS, WILLIAM F.

1989   Word and Image in a Semiotic Perspective. In *Word and Image in Maya Culture: Explorations in Language, Writing, and Representation*, ed. William F. Hanks and Don S. Rice, 8–21. Salt Lake City: University of Utah Press.

1990   *Referential Practice: Language and Lived Space Among the Maya.* Chicago: University
        of Chicago Press.

HARDMAN, MARTHA JAMES

1986   Data-Source Marking in the Jaqi Languages. In *Evidentiality: The Linguistic Coding of
        Epistemology,* ed. Wallace Chafe and Johanna Nichols, 113–36. Norwood, N. J.: Ablex.

HARDMAN DE BAUTISTA, MARTHA JAMES

1985a   Aymara and Quechua: Languages in Contact. In *South American Indian Languages:
        Retrospect and Prospect,* ed. Harriet Manelis Klein and Louisa R. Stark, 617–43. Austin:
        University of Texas Press.

1985b   The Imperial Languages of the Andes. In *Languages of Inequality,* ed. Nessa Wolf-
        son and Joan Manes, 182–93. (Contributions to the Sociology of Language, No. 36.)
        Berlin: Mouton.

HARDY, HEATHER K., AND TIMOTHY R. MONTLER

1988   Alabama Radical Morphology: H-infix and Disfixation. In *In Honor of Mary Haas:
        From the Haas Festival Conference on Native American Linguistics,* ed. William Shipley,
        377–409. New York: Mouton de Gruyter.

HARJO, JOY

1990   *In Mad Love and War.* Middleton, Conn: Wesleyan University Press.

HARRINGTON, J. P.

1916   *The Ethnogeography of the Tewa Indians.* Bureau of American Ethnology, Annual Re-
        port, 1907–1908, vol. 29. Washington, D.C.: Smithsonian Institution.

HARVEY, GINA

1974   Dormitory English. In *Southwestern Areal Linguistics,* ed. Garland Bills, 283–93. San
        Diego: Center for Cultural Pluralism.

HAUGEN, EINAR

1950   The Analysis of Linguistic Borrowing. *Language* 16:210–31. (Reprinted, 1972, in *The
        Ecology of Language,* by Elinor Haugen, 79–109; Stanford: Stanford University Press.)

1966   *Language Conflict and Language Planning: The Case of Modern Norwegian.* Cam-
        bridge, MA: Harvard University Press.

HEATH, SHIRLEY BRICE, AND RICHARD LAPRADE

1982   Castilian Colonization and Indigenous Languages: The Case of Quechua and Aymara.
        In *Language Spread: Studies in Diffusion and Social Change,* ed. Robert L. Cooper,
        118–47. Bloomington: Indiana University Press.

HEIZER, ROBERT

1978   Trade and Trails. In *California,* vol. 8, William C. Sturtevant, gen. ed. *Handbook of
        North American Indians,* ed. Robert Heizer, vol. 8, 690–3. Washington, D.C.: Smith-
        sonian Institution.

HIGHWAY, TOMSON

1988   *The Rez Sisters.* Saskatoon: Fifth House.

HILL, ARCHIBALD

1952   A Note on Primitive Languages. *International Journal of American Linguistics* 18:172–
        77. (Reprinted, 1964, in *Language in Culture and Society: A Reader in Linguistics and
        Anthropology*, ed. Dell H. Hymes, 86–89. New York: Harper and Row.)

HILL, JANE H.

1978   Language Contact Systems and Human Adaptations. *Journal of Anthropological Re-
        search* 34:1–26.

HILL, JANE H., AND KENNETH C. HILL

1978   Honorific Usage in Modern Nahuatl: The Expression of Social Distance and Respect
        in the Nahuatl of the Malinche Volcano Area. *Language* 54:123–55.

1986   *Speaking Mexicano: Dynamics of Syncretic Language in Central Mexico.* Tucson: Uni-
        versity of Arizona Press.

HILL, JONATHAN

1993   *Keepers of the Sacred Chants: The Poetics of Ritual Power in an Amazonian Society.*
        Tucson: University of Arizona Press.

HINTON, LEANNE

1984   *Havasupai Songs: A Linguistic Perspective.* Ars Linguistica 6. Tübingen: Gunter Narr.
1989a   California Counting. *News from Native California* 3(1):25–27.
1989b   Coyote Talk. *News from Native California* 4(1):29–30.
1994   *Flutes of Fire: Essays on California Indian Languages.* Berkeley: Heyday Books.

HINTON, LEANNE, AND LUCILLE J. WATAHOMIGIE, EDITORS

1984   *Spirit Mountain: An Anthology of Yuman Story and Song.* Sun Tracks, vol. 10. Tucson:
        University of Arizona Press.

HODGE, FREDERICK W., EDITOR

1959   *Handbook of American Indians North of Mexico*, Part 1. New York: Pageant Books.
        (First published, 1907, Bureau of American Ethnology Bulletin 30. Washington, D.C.:
        Smithsonian Institution.

HOIJER, HARRY

1945   Classificatory Verb Stems in the Apachean Languages. *International Journal of Ameri-
        can Linguistics* 11:13–23.
1946   Introduction. In *Linguistic Structures of Native America*, ed. Harry Hoijer, 9–29. Pub-
        lications in Anthropology No. 6. New York: Viking Fund.
1951   Cultural Implications of Some Navaho Linguistic Categories. *Language* 27:111–20.
        (Reprinted, 1964, in *Language in Culture and Society: A Reader in Linguistics and
        Anthropology*, ed. Dell H. Hymes, 142–9. New York: Harper and Row.)
1954   Some Problems of American Indian Linguistic Research. In *Papers from the Symposium
        on American Indian Linguistics, held at Berkeley, July 7, 1951*, ed. C. Douglas Chrétien
        et al., 3–12. Publications in Linguistics 10. Berkeley: University of California Press.

HOIJER, HARRY, EDITOR

1964   *Language in Culture.* Comparative Studies of Cultures and Civilizations, No. 3; Memoirs of the American Anthropological Association, No. 79. Chicago: University of Chicago Press.

HOLM, BILL

1990   Art. In *Northwest Coast,* ed. Wayne Suttles, 602-32. *Handbook of North American Indians,* vol. 7, William C. Sturtevant, gen. ed. Washington, D.C.: Smithsonian Institution.

HOPKINS, JILL D.

1992   On the Significance of Names: An Analysis of Terms for God in the Native American Church Songs of the Otoe-Missioura and Ioway. Paper presented at the 31st CAIL Session, American Anthropological Association annual meeting.

HOPKINS, SARAH WINNEMUCCA

1883   *Life among the Piutes, Their Wrongs and Claims,* ed. Mrs. Horace Mann. Boston: Cupples, Uppham. (Reprinted, 1964, Bishop, CA: Chalfant Press.)

HOUSTON, S. D.

1989   *Maya Glyphs.* Berkeley: University of California Press.

HOWARD, GREGG, AND RICHARD EBY

1993   *Introduction to Choctaw,* rev. ed. Fayetteville, Ark.: VIP Publishing.

HOWARD, NORMAN

1987   Wesucechak Becomes a Deer and Steals Language: An Anecdotal Linguistics Concerning the Swampy Cree Trickster. In *Recovering the Word: Essays on Native American Literature,* ed. Brian Swann and Arnold Krupat, 402-21. Berkeley: University of California Press.

HUDSON, TRAVIS, AND GEORGIA LEE

1981   Function and Purpose of Chumash Rock Art. *The Masterkey* 55(3):92-99.

HYMES, DELL H.

1960   Lexicostatistics So Far. *Current Anthropology* 1:3-44.

1966   Two Types of Linguistic Relativity (with Examples from Amerindian Ethnography). In *Sociolinguistics: Proceedings of the UCLA Sociolinguistics Conference, 1964,* ed. William Bright, 114-67. The Hague: Mouton.

1974a *Foundations in Sociolinguistics: An Ethnographic Approach.* Philadelphia: University of Pennsylvania Press.

1974b Speech and Language: On the Origins and Foundations of Inequality among Speakers. In *Language as a Human Problem,* ed. Morton Bloomfield and Einar Haugen, 45-71. New York: W. W. Norton Company. (Originally published in *Daedalus,* summer 1973.)

1975   Breakthrough into Performances. In *Folklore: Performance and Communication,* ed. Dan Ben-Amos and Kenneth S. Goldstein, 11-74. The Hague: Mouton. (Reprinted, 1981, in *"In Vain I Tried to Tell You": Essays in Native American Ethnopoetics,* by Dell H. Hymes, 79-141. Philadelphia: University of Pennsylvania Press.)

1980 Commentary. In *Theoretical Orientations in Creole Studies*, ed. Albert Valdman and Arnold Highfield, 389–423. New York: Academic Press.

1981 *"In Vain I Tried to Tell You": Essays in Native American Ethnopoetics*. Philadelphia: University of Pennsylvania Press.

1983 *Essays in the History of Linguistic Anthropology*. Amsterdam Studies in the Theory and History of Linguistic Science, vol. 25. Amsterdam: John Benjamins.

1984 Bungling Host, Benevolent Host: Louis Simpson's "Deer and Coyote." *The American Quarterly* 8:171–98.

1990 Mythology. In *Northwest Coast*, ed. Wayne Suttles, 593–601. *Handbook of North American Indians*, vol. 7, William C. Sturtevant, gen. ed. Washington, D.C.: Smithsonian Institution.

HYMES, DELL H., EDITOR

1964 *Language in Culture and Society: A Reader in Linguistics and Anthropology*. New York, Evanston, and London: Harper and Row.

JACKSON, JEAN

1974 Language Identity of the Colombian Vaupés Indians. In *Explorations in the Ethnography of Speaking*, ed. Richard Bauman and Joel Sherzer, 50–64. New York: Cambridge University Press.

1983 *The Fish People: Linguistic Exogamy and Tukanoan Identity in Northwest Amazonia*. Cambridge: Cambridge University Press.

JACOBS, MELVILLE

1937 Historical Perspectives in Indian Languages of Oregon and Washington. *Pacific Northwest Quarterly* 28:55–74.

JACOBSEN, WILLIAM H., JR.

1966 Washo Linguistic Studies. In *The Current Status of Anthropological Research in the Great Basin: 1964*, ed. Warren L. d'Azevedo, 113–36. Reno: Desert Research Institute.

1967 Switch-reference in Hokan-Coahuiltecan. In *Studies in Southwestern Ethnolinguistics: Meaning and History in the Languages of the American Southwest*, ed. Dell Hymes, 238–63. The Hague: Mouton.

1979a Chimakuan Comparative Studies. In *The Languages of Native America: Historical and Comparative Assessment*, ed. Lyle Campbell and Marianne Mithun, 792–803. Austin: University of Texas Press.

1979b Gender and Personification in Washo. *Journal of California and Great Basin Anthropology Papers in Linguistics* 1:75–84.

1979c Hokan Inter-Branch Comparisons. In *The Languages of Native America: Historical and Comparative Assessment*, ed. Lyle Campbell and Marianne Mithun, 545–91. Austin: University of Texas Press.

1979d Wakashan Comparative Studies. In *The Languages of Native America: Historical and Comparative Assessment*, ed. Lyle Campbell and Marianne Mithun, 766–91. Austin: University of Texas Press.

1980 Inclusive/Exclusive: A Diffused Grammatical Category in Native Western North

America. In *Parasession on Pronouns and Anaphora*, 204–27. Chicago: Chicago Linguistic Society.

1986   Washo Language. In *Great Basin*, ed. Warren L. d'Azevedo, 107–12. *Handbook of North American Indians*, vol. 11, William C. Sturtevant, gen. ed. Washington, D.C.: Smithsonian Institution.

JELINEK, ELOISE, AND FERNANDO ESCALANTE

1988   "Verbless" Possessive Sentences in Yaqui. In *In Honor of Mary Haas: From the Haas Festival Conference on Native American Linguistics*, ed. William Shipley, 411–29. New York: Mouton de Gruyter.

JOE, RITA

1988   *Song of Eskasoni*. Charlottetown, Prince Edward Island: Ragweed.

JOHNSON, ALLEN W., AND TIMOTHY EARLE

1987   *The Evolution of Human Societies from Foraging Groups to Agrarian State*. Stanford: Stanford University Press.

JUSTESON, JOHN S., AND TERRENCE KAUFMAN

1993   A Decipherment of Epi-Olmec Hieroglyphic Writings. *Science* 259:1703–11.

JUSTESON, JOHN S., WILLIAM M. NORMAN, LYLE CAMPBELL, AND TERRENCE KAUFMAN

1985   *The Foreign Impact on Lowland Mayan Language and Script*. Middle American Research Institute Publication 53. New Orleans: Tulane University Press.

KALMÁR, IVAN

1979   *Case and Context in Inuktitut (Eskimo)*. Mercury Series, Canadian Ethnology Service Papers, 49. Ottawa: National Museum of Man.

KARTTUNEN, FRANCES

1983   *An Analytical Dictionary of Nahuatl*. Austin: University of Texas Press.

KARTTUNEN, FRANCES, AND WILLIAM LOCKHART, EDITORS

1991   *The Art of Nahuatl Speech: The Bancroft Dialogues*.

KAUFMAN, TERRENCE S.

1971   A Report on Chinook Jargon. In *Pidginization and Creolization of Languages*, ed. Dell Hymes, 275–78. Cambridge: Cambridge University Press.

1990   Language History in South America: What We Know and How to Know More. In *Amazonian Linguistics: Studies in Lowland South American Languages*, ed. Doris L. Payne, 12–73. Austin: University of Texas Press.

1991   The Languages of Mesoamerica and Northern Mexico and Their Classification. Manuscript.

KELLEY, DAVID HUMISTON

1976   *Deciphering the Maya Script*. Austin: University of Texas.

KELLY, ISABEL T., AND CATHERINE S. FOWLER

1986   Southern Paiute. In *Great Basin*, ed. Warren L. d'Azevedo, 368–97. *Handbook of*

North American Indians, vol. 11, William C. Sturtevant, gen. ed. Washington, D.C.: Smithsonian Institution.

KENNY, GEORGE

1977   *Indians Don't Cry.* Toronto: Chimo.

KENNY, MAURICE

1985   *In Summer This Bear.* Saranac Lake, N.Y.: Chauncy Press.

KESS, J. F., AND A. C. KESS

1986   On Nootka Baby Talk. *International Journal of American Linguistics* 53:201-11.

KIMBALL, GEOFFREY

1987   Men's and Women's Speech in Koasati: A Reappraisal. *International Journal of American Linguistics* 53:30-38.

1988   Koasati Reduplication. In *In Honor of Mary Haas: From the Haas Festival Conference on Native American Linguistics,* ed. William Shipley, 431-42. New York: Mouton de Gruyter.

1989   Huastec and Totonac Loanwords in Huastec Nahuatl. Paper presented to the Friends of Uto-Aztecan, Tucson.

KING, THOMAS

1994   Native Literature of Canada. In *Dictionary of Native American Literature,* ed. Andrew Wiget, 353-69. Garland Reference Library of the Humanities, vol. 1815. New York: Garland Publishing.

KLEIN, HARRIET E. MANELIS, AND LOUISA R. STARK

1985a   Introduction. In *South American Indian Languages: Retrospect and Prospect,* ed. Harriet E. Manelis Klein and Louisa R. Stark, 3-14. Austin: University of Texas Press.

KLEIN, HARRIET E. MANELIS, AND LOUISA R. STARK, EDITORS

1985b   South American Indian Languages: Retrospect and Prospect. Austin: University of Texas Press.

KOLLER, JAMES, 'GOGISGI,' CARROLL ARNETT, STEVE NEMIROW, AND PETER BLUE CLOUD

1982   *Coyote's Journal.* Berkeley: Wingbow Press.

KRAUSS, MICHAEL E.

1979   Na-Dene and Eskimo-Aleut. In *The Languages of Native America: Historical and Comparative Assessment,* ed. Lyle Campbell and Marianne Mithun, 803-901. Austin: University of Texas Press.

KRAUSS, MICHAEL E., AND VICTOR K. GOLLA

1981   Northern Athapaskan Languages. In *Subarctic,* ed. June Helm, 67-85. *Handbook of North American Indians,* vol. 6, William C. Sturtevant, gen. ed. Washington, D.C.: Smithsonian Institution.

KROEBER, ALFRED L.

1906   The Dialectic Divisions of the Moquelumnan Family in Relation to the Internal Differentiation of the Other Linguistic Families of California. *American Anthropologist* 8:652–63.

1911   *The Languages of the Coast of California North of San Francisco.* University of California Publications in American Archaeology and Ethnology, 9(3):373–438. Berkeley: University of California Press.

1925–26 *Handbook of the Indians of California.* Bureau of American Ethnology, Bulletin 78. Washington, D.C.: Smithsonian Institution. (Reprinted, 1953, Berkeley: California Book Co.; 1976, New York: Dover.)

1962   The Nature of Landholding Groups in Aboriginal California. In *Two Papers in the Aboriginal Ethnography of California,* ed. Dell Hymes and Robert F. Heizer, 19–58. Archaeological Survey Reports No. 56. Berkeley: University of California.

1971   Principal Local Types of the Kuksu Cult. In *The California Indians: A Source Book,* 2d. ed., ed. R. F. Heizer and M. A. Whipple, 485–95. Berkeley: University of California Press.

KROEBER, ALFRED L., AND GEORGE WILLIAM GRACE

1960   *The Sparkman Grammar of Luiseño.* Publications in Linguistics No. 16. Berkeley: University of California Press.

KROEBER, KARL, ET AL.

1981   *Traditional American Indian Literatures: Texts and Interpretations.* Lincoln: University of Nebraska Press.

KROSKRITY, PAUL V.

1981   Toward a Sociolinguistic History of the Tewa. Paper presented at the School of American Research Advanced Seminar on the Tewa, Santa Fe.

1983   On Male and Female Speech in the Pueblo Southwest. *International Journal of American Linguistics* 49:88–91.

1985   Growing with Stories: Line, Verse, and Genre in an Arizona Tewa Text. *Journal of Anthropological Research* 41:183–99.

1993a   How to "Speak the Past": An Evidential Particle and the Text-Building of Traditional Stories. In *Language, History and Identity: Ethnolinguistic Studies of the Arizona Tewa,* 143–75. Tucson: University of Arizona Press.

1993b   *Language, History, and Identity: Ethnolinguistic Studies of the Arizona Tewa.* Tucson: University of Arizona Press.

KROSKRITY, PAUL V., AND GREGORY A. REINHARDT

1984   Spanish and English Loanwords in Western Mono. *Journal of California and Great Basin Anthropology* 4:107–39.

LAMB, SYDNEY M.

1958   Linguistic Prehistory in the Great Basin. *International Journal of American Linguistics* 24:95–100.

LANG, JULIAN

1994   *Ararapikva: Traditional Karuk Indian Literature from Northwestern California.* Berkeley: Heyday Books.

LANGDON, MARGARET

1970   *A Grammar of Diegueño: The Mesa Grande Dialect.* Publications in Linguistics No. 66. Berkeley: University of California Press.

1971   Sound Symbolism in Yuman Languages. In *Studies In American Indian Languages,* ed. Jesse O. Sawyer, 149–74. Publications in Linguistics No. 65. Berkeley: University of California Press.

1978   Animal Talk in Cocopa. *International Journal of American Linguistics* 44:10–16.

1988   Number Suppletion in Yuman. In *In Honor of Mary Haas: From the Haas Festival Conference on Native American Linguistics,* ed. William Shipley, 483–96. New York: Mouton de Gruyter.

LANGDON, MARGARET, AND SHIRLEY SILVER

1984   California t/ṭ. *Journal of California and Great Basin Anthropology Papers in Linguistics* 4:139–65.

LANGE, CHARLES H.

1959   *Cochiti: A New Mexico Pueblo, Past and Present.* Austin: University of Texas Press.

LASKI, VERA

1958   *Seeking Life.* Memoirs of the American Folklore Society, vol. 50.

LASTRA DE SUÁREZ, YOLANDA

1986   *Las áreas dialectales del náhuatl moderno.* Mexico City: Universidad Nacional de México.

LATHROP, D. W., AND R. C. TROIKE

1988   Relationships between Linguistic and Archaeological Data in the New World. In *Archaeology and Linguistics* (Journal of Steward Anthropological Society for 1983–1984) 15(1,2):99–157.

LEAP, WILLIAM L.

1973   Language Pluralism in a Southwestern Pueblo: Some Comments on Isletan English. In *Bilingualism in the Southwest,* ed. Paul R. Turner, 275–93. Tucson: University of Arizona Press.

1974   Ethnics, Emics, and the New Ideology: The Identity Potential of Indian English. In *Social and Cultural Identity,* ed. Thomas K. Fitzgerald, 51–62. Athens: University of Georgia Press.

1981a American Indian Language Maintenance. *Annual Review of Anthropology* 10:209–36.

1981b American Indian Languages. In *Language in the USA,* ed. Charles Ferguson and Shirley B. Heath, 116–44. New York: Cambridge University Press.

1993   *American Indian English.* Salt Lake City: University of Utah Press.

LEE, DOROTHY

1938   Conceptual Implications of an Indian Language. *Philosophy of Science* 5:89–102.

1943   The Linguistic Aspect of Wintu Acculturation. *American Anthropologist* 45:435–40.

1944a Categories of the Generic and Particular in Wintu. *American Anthropologist,* new ser., 46:362–69.

1944b Linguistic Reflections of Wintu Thought. *International Journal of American Linguistics* 10:181–87.

1946 Stylistic Use of the Negative in Wintu. *International Journal of American Linguistics* 12:79–81.

LEEDS-HURWITZ, WENDY

1989 *Communication in Everyday Life: A Social Interpretation.* Norwood, N.J.: Ablex.

LELAND, JOY

1986 Population. In *Great Basin,* ed. Warren L. d'Azevedo, 608–19. *Handbook of North American Indians,* vol. 11, William C. Sturtevant, gen. ed. Washington, D.C.: Smithsonian Institution.

LEÓN-PORTILLA, MIGUEL

1969 *Pre-Columbian Literatures of Mexico.* Norman: University of Oklahoma Press.

1971a Philosophy in Ancient Mexico. In *Archaeology of Northern Mesoamerica,* vol. 10, part 1. *Handbook of Middle American Indians,* ed. Gordon F. Ekholm and Ignacio Bernal, 447–51. Austin: University of Texas Press.

1971b Pre-Hispanic Literature. In *Archaeology of Northern Mesoamerica,* vol. 10, pt. 1. *Handbook of Middle American Indians,* ed. Gordon F. Ekholm and Ignacio Bernal, 452–85. Austin: University of Texas Press.

1993 Poems and Songs of the Cuicapicque, Contemporary Nahuatl Poets. In *New Voices in Native American Literary Criticism,* ed. Arnold Krupat, 186–201. Washington, D.C.: Smithsonian Institution Press.

LERNER, ANDREA, EDITOR

1990 *Dancing on the Rim of the World: An Anthology of Contemporary Northwest Native American Writing.* Sun Tracks, vol. 19. Tucson: University of Arizona Press.

LEVINE, ROBERT D.

1979 Haida and Na-Dene: A New Look at the Evidence. *International Journal of American Linguistics* 45:157–70.

LEVITAS, GLORIA, FRANK R. VIVELO, AND JACQUELINE J. VIVELO, EDITORS

1974 *American Indian Prose and Poetry: We Wait in Darkness.* New York: Capricorn Books.

LI, FANG-KUEI

1946 Chipewyan. In *Linguistic Structures of Native America,* ed. Harry Hoijer, 398–423. Publications in Anthropology No. 6. New York: Viking Fund.

LILJEBLAD, SVEN

1971 The History of Indian Tribes in Idaho: Languages. Ms. in Liljeblad's possession (cited in Miller 1986).

1986 Oral Traditions: Content and Style of Verbal Arts. In *Great Basin,* ed. Warren L. d'Azevedo, 641–59. *Handbook of North American Indians,* vol. 11, William C. Sturtevant, gen. ed. Washington, D.C.: Smithsonian Institution.

LOUNSBURY, FLOYD

   1953   *Oneida Verb Morphology.* Publications in Anthropology 48. New Haven: Yale University Press.

LOWIE, ROBERT H.

   1935   *The Crow Indian.* New York: Farrar and Rinehart.

   1959   Crow Curses. *Journal of American Folklore* 72:105.

LUOMALA, KATHARINE

   1978   Tipai and Ipai. In *California,* ed. Robert F. Heizer, 592–609. *Handbook of North American Indians,* vol. 8, William C. Sturtevant, gen. ed. Washington, D.C.: Smithsonian Institution.

MACLAY, HOWARD

   1958   An Experimental Study of Language and Non-linguistic Behavior. *Southwestern Journal of Anthropology* 14:220–29.

MALLERY, GARRICK

   1880   *A Collection of Gesture-Sign and Signals of the North American Indians, with Some Comparisons.* Bureau of American Ethnology. Washington, D.C.: Smithsonian Institution. (Reprinted, 1978, *Aboriginal Sign Languages of the Americas and Australia,* vol. 1, ed. D. Jean Umiker-Sebeok and Thomas A. Sebeok. New York: Plenum Press.)

   1881   Sign Language among North American Indians Compared with That among Other Peoples and Deaf Mutes. *Annual Report of the Bureau of Ethnology* 1:263–552. Washington, D.C.: Smithsonian Institution. (Reprinted, 1972, *Approaches to Semiotics* 14. The Hague: Mouton.)

MALOTKI, EKKEHART

   1983   *Hopi Time: A Linguistic Analysis of the Temporal Concepts in the Hopi Languages.* Berlin: Mouton.

MANNHEIM, BRUCE

   1991   *The Language of the Inka since the European Invasion.* Austin: University of Texas Press.

MARCUS, JOYCE

   1976   The Origins of Mesoamerican Writing. *Annual Review of Anthropology* 5:35–67.

   1980   Zapotec Writing. *Scientific American* 242(2):50–64. (Reprinted, 1982, in *Human Communication: Language and Its Psychobiological Bases,* ed. William S-Y. Wang, 90–104. San Francisco: W. H. Freeman.

   1992   *Mesoamerican Writing Systems: Propaganda, Myth, and History in Four Ancient Civilizations.* Princeton, N.J.: Princeton University Press.

MARKOOSIE

   1970   *Harpoon of the Hunter.* Kingston: McGill-Queen's University Press.

MARTIN, LAURA

   1986   "Eskimo Words for Snow": A Case Study in the Genesis and Decay of an Anthropological Example. *American Anthropologist* 88:418–23.

MASON, J. ALDEN

1940   The Native Languages of Middle America. In *The Maya and Their Neighbors*, ed.
       Clarence L. Hay et al., 52–87. New York: D. Appleton-Century. (Reprinted, 1962, Salt
       Lake City: University of Utah Press.)

MATHIOT, MADELEINE

1991   The Reminiscences of Juan Delores, an Early O'odham Linguist. *Anthropological Lin-
       guistics* 33:233–315.

McCORMACK, WILLIAM C., AND STEPHEN A. WURM, EDITORS

1977   *Language and Thought*. The Hague: Mouton.

McLAUGHLIN, DANIEL

1992   *When Literacy Empowers: Navajo Language in Print*. Albuquerque: University of New
       Mexico Press.

McLENDON, SALLY

1969   Spanish Words in Eastern Pomo. *Romance Philology* 23:39–53.

McLENDON, SALLY, AND MICHAEL J. LOWY

1978   Eastern Pomo and Southeastern Pomo. In *California*, ed. Robert F. Heizer, 306–23.
       Handbook of North American Indians, vol. 8, William C. Sturtevant, gen. ed. Wash-
       ington, D.C.: Smithsonian Institution.

McNICKLE, D'ARCY

1978   *Wind from an Enemy Sky*. San Francisco: Harper and Row.

McQUOWN, NORMAN

1955   The Indigenous Languages of Latin America. *American Anthropologist* 57:501–70.

METZGER, DUANE, AND G. WILLIAMS

1966   Some Procedures and Results in the Study of Native Categories: Tzeltal "Firewood."
       American Anthropologist 68:389–407.

MILLER, WICK R.

1959–60   Spanish Loanwords in Acoma. *International Journal of American Linguistics* 25:
          147–53, 26:41–49.

1965   *Acoma Grammar and Texts*. Publications in Linguistics No. 40. Berkeley: University
       of California Press.

1966   Anthropological Linguistics in the Great Basin. In *The Current Status of Anthropologi-
       cal Research in the Great Basin: 1964*, ed. Warren L. d'Azevedo, 75–112. Reno: Desert
       Research Institute.

1970   Western Shoshoni Dialects. In *Languages and Cultures of Western North America:
       Essays in Honor of Sven S. Liljeblad*, ed Earl H. Swanson, Jr., 17–36. Pocatello: Idaho
       State University Press.

1972   Obsolescing Languages: The Case of the Shoshoni. *Language in American Indian
       Education: A Newsletter of the Office of Education Program, Bureau of Indian Affairs,
       Winter*:1–12. Salt Lake City: University of Utah.

1978   Multilingualism in Its Social Context in Aboriginal North America. *Berkeley Linguistics Society* 4:610–36.

1980   Speaking for Two: Respect Speech in the Guarijío of Northwest Mexico. *Berkeley Linguistics Society* 6:196–206.

1983   Uto-Aztecan Languages. In *Southwest*, ed. Alfonso Ortiz, 113–24. *Handbook of North American Indians*, vol. 10, William C. Sturtevant, gen. ed. Washington, D.C.: Smithsonian Institution.

1984   The Classification of the Uto-Aztecan Languages Based on Lexical Evidence. *International Journal of American Linguistics* 50:1–24.

1986   The Numic Languages. In *Great Basin*, ed. Warren L. d'Azevedo, 98–106. *Handbook of North American Indians*, vol. 11, William C. Sturtevant, gen. ed. Washington, D.C.: Smithsonian Institution.

1987   The Possession of Pets in the Great Southwest. Paper presented to the Friends of Uto-Aztecan and Hokan-Penutian joint meeting, Salt Lake City.

1988   Componential Analysis of the Guarijío Orientational System. In *In Honor of Mary Haas: From the Haas Festival Conference on Native American Linguistics*, ed. William F. Shipley, 497–515. Berlin: Mouton de Gruyter.

1990a   Early Lexical Acculturation in Northwest Mexico. In *Languages in Contact: Proceedings of Symposium 16.1 of the 12th International Congress of Anthropological and Ethnological Sciences, Zagreb, Yugoslavia, July 1988*, ed. Rudolf Filipović and Maja Bratanić, 237–47. Zagreb: Institute of Linguistics, Faculty of Philosophy, University of Zagreb.

1990b   Early Spanish and Aztec Loan Words in the Indigenous Languages of Northwest Mexico. In *Homenaje a Jorge A. Suárez: Lingüística indoamericana e hispánica*, ed. Beatriz Garza Cuarón and Paulette Levy, 351–65. Mexico City: El Colegio de México.

n.d.a. Shoshoni (Gosiute Dialect). To appear in *Handbook of North American Indians*, Languages, vol. 17.

n.d.   The Ethnography of Speaking. To appear in *Handbook of North American Indians*, Languages, vol. 17.

MITHUN, MARIANNE

1983   The Genius of Polysynthesis. In *North American Indians: Humanistic Perspectives*, ed. James J. Thayer, 222–42. Papers in Anthropology 24(2). Norman: Department of Anthropology, University of Oklahoma.

1984   The Proto-Iroquoian Cultural Reconstruction from Lexical Materials. In *Extending Rafters: Inter-disciplinary Approaches to Iroquoian Studies*, ed. Mary Foster et al. Albany: State University of New York Press.

1988   Lexical Categories and Number in Central Pomo. In *In Honor of Mary Haas: From the Haas Festival Conference on Native American Linguistics*, ed. William Shipley, 517–37. New York: Mouton de Gruyter.

1989   The Incipient Obsolescence of Polysynthesis: Cayuga in Ontario and Oklahoma. In *Investigating Obsolescence Studies in Language Contraction and Death*, ed. Nancy C. Dorian, 243–57. New York: Cambridge University Press.

MIXCO, MAURICIO J.

1978   Cochimí and Proto-Yuman: Lexical and Syntactic Evidence for a New Language Family in Lower California. Anthropological Papers No. 101. Salt Lake City: University of Utah Press.

MOLINA, FRAY ALONSO DE

1977   Vocabulario en lengua castellana y mexicana y mexicana y castellana. Estudio preliminar de Miguel Léon-Portilla. 2d. ed. Mexico City: Editorial Porrua. (First ed., Mexico City, 1555–71.)

MOMADAY, N. SCOTT

1976   The Names: A Memoir. Tucson: University of Arizona Press. (Originally published New York: Harper and Row.)

MONTEITH, CARMELETA L.

1984   Literacy among the Cherokee in the Early Nineteenth Century. Journal of Cherokee Studies 9(2):56–75. Chattanooga: Museum of the Cherokee Indian; Chattanooga Printing and Engraving.

MOORE, DENNY, SIDNEY FACUNDES, AND NÁDIA PIRES

1994   Nheengatú (Língua Geral Amazonia), Its History, and the Effects of Language Contact. In Survey of California and Other Indian Languages, ed. Margaret Langdon, 93–137. Report No. 8. Berkeley: Department of Linguistics, University of California.

MORATTO, MICHAEL J.

1984   California Archaeology. New York: Academic Press.

MORLEY, SYLVANUS GRIWOLD

1975   An Introduction to the Study of the Maya Hieroglyphics. New York: Dover. (Originally published, 1915, as Bureau of American Ethnology Bulletin 56. Washington, D.C.: Smithsonian Institution.)

MOURNING DOVE

1981   Cogewea, the Half-Blood. Lincoln: University of Nebraska Press. (Originally printed, 1927, n.p.)

MUNRO, PAMELA

1988   Diminutive Syntax. In In Honor of Mary Haas: From the Haas Festival Conference on Native American Linguistics, ed. William Shipley, 539–55. New York: Mouton de Gruyter.

MURPHY, ROBERT F., AND YOLANDA MURPHY

1986   Northern Shoshone and Bannock. In Great Basin, ed. Warren L. d'Azevedo, 284–307. Handbook of North American Indians, vol. 11, William C. Sturtevant, gen. ed. Washington, D.C.: Smithsonian Institution.

MYERS, JAMES E.

1978   Cahto. In California, ed. Robert F. Heizer, 244–48. Handbook of North American Indians, vol. 8, William C. Sturtevant, gen. ed. Washington, D.C.: Smithsonian Institution.

NARANJO-MORSE, NORA

1992   *Mud Woman: Poems from the Clay.* Sun Tracks, vol. 20. Tucson: University of Arizona Press.

NEWMAN, STANLEY

1955   Vocabulary Levels: Zuñi Sacred and Slang Usage. *Southwestern Journal of Anthropology* 11:345-55.

NIATUM, DUANE

1981   *Songs for the Harvester of Dreams.* Seattle: University of Washington Press.

NICHOLS, JOHANNA

1971   Diminutive Consonant Symbolism in Western North America. *Language* 47:826-48.

1988   On Alienable and Inalienable Possession. In *In Honor of Mary Haas: From the Haas Festival Conference on Native American Linguistics*, ed. William Shipley, 557-609. New York: Mouton de Gruyter.

1992   *Linguistic Diversity in Space and Time.* Chicago: University of Chicago Press.

NICOLAU D'OLWER

1987   *Fray Bernardino de Sahagún, 1499-1590.* Trans. Mauricio J. Mixco. Salt Lake City: University of Utah Press.

NOGUERA, EDUARDO

1971   Minor Arts in the Central Valleys. In *Archaeology of Northern Mesoamerica*, vol. 10, pt. 1, *Handbook of Middle American Indians*, ed. Gordon F. Ekholm and Ignacio Bernal, 258-69. Austin: University of Texas Press.

NORCROSS, AMOENA B.

1993   Noun Incorporation in Shawnee. Unpublished Ph.D. dissertation, University of South Carolina, Columbia.

NORMAN, HOWARD, EDITOR

1976   *The Wishing Bone Cycle: Narrative Poems from the Swampy Cree Indians.* New York: Stonehill.

OANDASAN, WILLIAM

1984   *Round Valley Songs.* Minneapolis: West End.

OLMSTED, DAVID L., AND OMER C. STEWART

1978   Achumawi. In *California*, ed. Robert F. Heizer, 225-35. *Handbook of North American Indians*, vol. 8, William C. Sturtevant, gen. ed. Washington, D.C.: Smithsonian Institution.

OLSON, JAMES S.

1991   *The Indians of Central and South America: An Ethnohistorical Dictionary.* New York: Greenwood Press.

OPLER, MORRIS EDWARD

1941   *An Apache Life-Way: The Economic, Social, and Religious Institutions of the Chiricahua Indians.* Chicago: University of Chicago Press.

1952   The Creek "Town" and the Problem of Creek Indian Political Reorganization. In
        Human Problems in Technological Change: A Casebook, ed. Edward H. Spicer, 165–
        80. New York: Russell Sage Foundation.

ORTIZ, ALFONSO, EDITOR

1979   *Southwest. Handbook of North American Indians,* vol. 9, William C. Sturtevant, gen.
        ed. Washington, D.C.: Smithsonian Institution.

ORTIZ, SIMON J.

1992   *Woven Stone.* Sun Tracks, vol. 21. Tucson: University of Arizona Press.

ORTIZ, SIMON J., EDITOR

1983   *Earth Power Coming: Short Fiction in Native American Literature.* Tsaile, Ariz.: Navajo
        Community College Press.

OSWALT, ROBERT L.

1961   A Kashaya Grammar (Southern Pomo). Unpublished Ph.D. dissertation, University
        of California, Berkeley.

1971a   Inanimate Imitatives in Pomo. In *Studies in American Indian Languages,* ed. Jesse O.
        Sawyer, 175–90. Publications in Linguistics No. 65. Berkeley: University of California
        Press.

1971b   The Case of the Broken Bottle. *International Journal of American Linguistics* 36:48–49.

OWEN, ROGER C.

1965   The Patrilocal Band: A Linguistically and Culturally Hybrid Social Unit. *American
        Anthropologist* 67:675–90.

PARSONS, ELSIE CLEWS

1923   Laguna Genealogies. *Anthropological Papers of the American Museum of Natural His-
        tory* 19:133–292. New York.

PAYNE, DORIS L.

1985   The Genetic Classification of Resigaro. *International Journal of American Linguistics*
        51(2):222–31.

1990   *Amazonian Linguistics: Studies in Lowland South American Languages.* Austin: Uni-
        versity of Texas Press.

PAYNE, JUDITH

1982   Directionals as Time Referentials in Asheninca. *Anthropological Linguistics* 23(3):
        325–37.

PAYNE, STANLEY, AND MICHAEL P. CLOSS

1986   A Survey of Aztec Numbers and Their Uses. In *Native American Mathematics,* ed.
        Michael P. Closs, 213–35. Austin: University of Texas Press.

PERCHONOCK, N., AND OSWALD WERNER

1968   Navajo Systems of Classification: The Domains of Foods. *Ethnology* 8:229–42.

PEYER, BERND C.

1994   William Apes. In *Dictionary of Native American Literature,* ed. Andrew Wiget, 207–

10. Garland Reference Library of the Humanities, vol. 1815. New York: Garland Publishing.

PEYER, BERND C., EDITOR

1990   *The Singing Spirit: Early Short Stories by North American Indians.* Tucson: University of Arizona Press.

PHILIPS, SUSAN U.

1970   Rules for Appropriate Speech Usage. In the *Twenty-first Annual Round Table, Bilingualism and Language Contact,* ed. James E. Alatis, 77–101. Washington, D.C.: Georgetown University Press.

1983   *The Invisible Culture: Communication in Classroom and Community on the Warm Springs Indian Reservation.* New York: Longman.

PILLING, ARNOLD R.

1978   Yurok. In *California,* ed. Robert F. Heizer, 137–44. *Handbook of North American Indians,* vol. 8, William C. Sturtevant, gen. ed. Washington, D.C.: Smithsonian Institution.

POSEY, ALEXANDER

1993   *The Fus Fixico Letters,* ed. Daniel F. Littlefield, Jr., and Carol A. Petty Hunter. Lincoln: University of Nebraska Press.

POWELL, JOHN WESLEY

1891   Indian Linguistic Families of America North of Mexico. In the *Seventh Annual Report of the Bureau of American Ethnology for the Years 1885–1886,* 1–142. Washington, D.C. (Reprinted, 1966, Lincoln: University of Nebraska Press.)

POWERS, STEPHEN

1877   Tribes of California. *Contributions to North American Ethnology,* vol. 3. Washington, D.C.: U.S. Geographical and Geological Survey of the Rocky Mountain Region.

PULLUM, GEOFFREY K.

1991   *The Great Eskimo Vocabulary Hoax, and Other Irreverent Essays on the Study of Language.* Chicago: University of Chicago Press.

PURDY, J. L.

1989   *Word Ways: The Novels of D'Arcy McNickle.* Tucson: University of Arizona Press.

PYE, CLIFTON

1986   Quiché Mayan Speech to Children. *Journal of Child Language* 13:85–100.

RADIN, PAUL

1919   The Genetic Relationship of the North American Indian Languages. *University of California Publications in American Archaeology and Ethnology* 14(5):489–502.

RANKIN, ROBERT L.

1992   Review of *Language in the Americas,* by Joseph H. Greenberg. *International Journal of American Linguistics* 58:324–51.

RANSOM, JOY ELLIS

1946   Aleut Linguistic Perspectives. *Southwestern Journal of Anthropology* 2:48-55.

REICHARD, GLADYS A.

1944   *Prayer: The Compulsive Word.* Monographs of the American Ethnological Society.
        New York: J. J. Augustin.

REID, BILL

1984   *Raven Steals the Light.* Vancouver: Douglas and McIntyre.

REVARD, CARTER

1993   *An Eagle Nation.* Sun Tracks, vol. 24. Tucson: University of Arizona Press.

REX, JIM

1989   *Mazii Diné-tsoi. Ahí Ní Nikisheegish. Lenape Yaa Deez'á T-oh Nii-ne'éh.* (The Prince-
        ton Collection of Americana.)

RHODES, RICHARD

1977   French Cree — A Case of Borrowing. In *Actes du Huitième Congrès des Algonquinistes,*
        ed. William Cowan, 6-26. Ottawa: Carleton University.

RHODES, RICHARD, AND EVELYN M. TODD

1981   Subarctic Algonquian Languages. In *Subarctic,* ed. June Helm, 52-66. *Handbook of
        North American Indians,* vol. 6, William C. Sturtevant, gen. ed. Washington, D.C.:
        Smithsonian Institution.

RICE, JULIAN

1987   How the Bird that Speaks Lakota Earned a Name. In *Recovering the Word: Essays on
        Native American Literature,* ed. Brian Swann and Arnold Krupat, 422-45. Berkeley:
        University of California Press.

RIGGS, LYNN

1936   *Green Grow the Lilacs.* New York: Samuel French.

RITZENTHALER, ROBERT E., AND F. FREDERICK A. PETERSON

1954   Courtship Whistling of the Mexican Kickapoo Indians. *American Anthropologist* 56:
        1088-89.

ROBINS, R. H.

1958   *The Yurok Language: Grammar, Texts, Lexicon.* Publications in Linguistics No. 15.
        Berkeley: University of California Press.

RODRIGUES, ARYON D.

1985   Evidence for Tupi-Carib Relationships. In *South American Indian Languages,* ed.
        Harriet E. Manelis Klein and Louisa R. Stark, 371-404. Austin: University of Texas
        Press.

ROOD, DAVID S.

1979   Siouan. In *The Languages of Native America: Historical and Comparative Assessment,*
        ed. Lyle Campbell and Marianne Mithun, 236-98. Austin: University of Texas Press.

ROSE, WENDY

1982   *What Happened When the Hopi Hit New York*. New York: Contact II.

RUBIN, JOAN

1968   *National Bilingualism in Paraguay*. The Hague: Mouton.

1985   The Special Relation of Guaraní and Spanish in Paraguay. In *Language of Inequality*,
       ed. N. Wolfson and J. Manes, 111–20. Berlin: Mouton.

RUOFF, A. LAVONNE BROWN

1994   George Copway. In *Dictionary of Native American Literature*, ed. Andrew Wiget,
       225–30. Garland Reference Library of the Humanities, vol. 1815. New York: Garland
       Publishing.

SAHAGÚN, FRAY BERNARDINO

1950–70   *Florentine Codex: History of the Things of New Spain*, 12 vols. ("books"), trans.
          Charles E. Dibble and Arthur J. O. Anderson. Santa Fe and Salt Lake City: School of
          American Research and the University of Utah Press.

SALZMANN, ZDENĚK

1951   Contrastive Field Experience with Language and Values of the Arapaho. *International
       Journal of American Linguistics* 17:98–101.

1969   Salvage Phonology of the Gros Ventre (Atsina). *International Journal of American
       Linguistics* 35:307–14.

SANDERS, WILLIAM T.

1971   Settlement Patterns in Central Mexico. In *Archaeology of Northern Mesoamerica*,
       vol. 10, pt. 1, *Handbook of Middle American Indians*, ed. Gordon F. Ekholm and Ignacio
       Bernal, 3–44. Austin: University of Texas Press.

SANTAMARÍA, FRANCISCO J.

1974   *Dicionario de Mejicanismos*, 2d. ed., corregida y aumentada. Mexico City: Editorial
       Porrua.

SAPIR, EDWARD

1910   Song Recitative in Paiute Mythology. *Journal of American Folk-Lore* 23:455–72.

1911   The Problem of Noun Incorporation in American Languages. *American Anthropolo-
       gist* 13:250–82.

1913   Wiyot and Yurok, Algonkin Languages of California. *American Anthropologist* 15:617–
       46.

1915   *Abnormal Types of Speech in Nootka*. Memoirs of the Canadian Geological Survey, 62,
       Anthropological Series No. 5. Ottawa. (Reprinted, 1951, in *Selected Writings of Edward
       Sapir*, ed. David G. Mandelbaum, 179–96. Berkeley: University of California Press.)

1916   *Time Perspective in Aboriginal American Culture: A Study in Method*. Memoirs of the
       Canadian Geological Survey 90, Anthropological Series 13. Ottawa. (Reprinted, 1951,
       in *Selected Writings of Edward Sapir*, ed. David G. Mandelbaum, 389–462. Berkeley:
       University of California Press.)

1917   *The Position of Yana in the Hokan Stock*. Publications in American Archaeology and
       Ethnology 13–34. Berkeley: University of California.

1921a A Bird's-eye View of American Languages North of Mexico. *Science* 54:408.

1921b *Language.* New York: Harcourt, Brace.

1923 A Characteristic Penutian Form of Stem. *International Journal of American Linguistics* 2(1–2):58–67.

1925 The Hokan Affinity of Subtiaba in Nicaragua. *American Anthropologist* 27:402–35; 491–527.

1929a Central and North American Languages. *Encyclopaedia Britannica,* 14th ed. 5:138–41. (Reprinted, 1951, in *Selected Writings of Edward Sapir,* ed. David G. Mandelbaum, 169–78. Berkeley: University of California Press.)

1929b Male and Female Forms of Speech in Yana. In *Donum Natalicium Schrijnen,* ed. St. W. J. Teeuwen, 79–85. Nijmegen-Utrecht: Dekker and Van de Vegt. (Reprinted, 1951, in *Selected Writings of Edward Sapir,* ed. David G. Mandelbaum, 206–12. Berkeley: University of California Press.)

1931 The Concept of Phonetic Law as Tested in Primitive Languages by Leonard Bloomfield. In *Methods in Social Science: A Case Book,* ed. Stuart A. Rice, 297–306. Chicago: University of Chicago Press. (Reprinted, 1951, in *Selected Writings of Edward Sapir,* ed. David G. Mandelbaum, 73–82. Berkeley: University of California Press.)

1936 Internal Linguistic Evidence Suggestive of the Northern Origin of the Navaho. *American Anthropologist* 38:224–35. (Reprinted, 1951, in *Selected Writings of Edward Sapir,* ed. David G. Mandelbaum, 213–24. Berkeley: University of California Press.)

1951 *Selected Writings of Edward Sapir,* ed. David G. Mandelbaum. Berkeley: University of California Press.

SAPIR, EDWARD, AND MORRIS SWADESH

1946 American Indian Grammatical Categories. *Word* 2:103–12. (Reprinted, 1964, in *Language in Culture and Society: A Reader in Linguistics and Anthropology,* ed. Dell H. Hymes, 101–7. New York: Harper and Row.)

SARRIS, GREG

1993 *Keeping Slug Woman Alive.* Berkeley: University of California Press.

SAVILLE-TROIKE, MURIEL

1985 The Place of Silence in an Integrated Theory of Communication. In *Perspectives on Silence,* ed. Deborah Tannen and Muriel Saville-Troike, 3–18. Norwood, N.J.: Ablex.

1988 A Note on Men's and Women's Speech in Koasati. *International Journal of American Linguistics* 54(2):241–42.

SAXTON, DEAN F., AND LUCILLE SAXTON, COMPILERS

1969 *Dictionary: Papago and Pima to English, English to Papago and Pima: O'odham-Mil-O'odham.* Tucson: University of Arizona Press.

SCHELE, LINDA

1982 *Maya Glyphs: The Verbs.* Austin: University of Texas Press.

1984 *Notebook for the Maya Hieroglyphic Writing Workshop at Texas.* Austin: University of Texas, Institute of Latin American Studies.

SCHELE, LINDA, AND DAVID FREIDEL

1990   A Forest of Kings: The Untold Story of the Ancient Maya. New York: William Morrow.

SCHLICTER, ALICE

1981   Notes on the Wintu Shamanistic Jargon. In Survey of California and Other Indian
       Languages, ed. Alice Schlicter, Wallace L. Chafe, and Leanne Hinton, 95–130. Report
       No. 1. Berkeley: Department of Linguistics, University of California.

SCHMANDT-BESSERAT, DENISE

1978   The Earliest Precursor of Writing. Scientific American 238(6):50–59. (Reprinted, 1991,
       in The Emergence of Language Development and Evolution, ed. William S-Y. Wang,
       31–45. San Francisco: W. H. Freeman.)

SCOLLON, RON

1985   The Machine Stops: Silence in the Metaphor of Malfunction. In Perspectives on Silence,
       ed. Deborah Tannen and Muriel Saville-Troike, 21–30. Norwood, N.J.: Ablex.

SERVICE, ELMAN

1954   Spanish-Guaraní Relations in Early Colonial Paraguay. Anthropological Papers of the
       Museum of Anthropology No. 9. Ann Arbor: University of Michigan Press. (Re-
       printed, 1971, Westport Conn.: Greenwood Press.)

1962   Primitive Social Organization. New York: Random House.

SHAFFER, P.

1990   A Tree Grows in Montana: Indians Turn to Old Ways to Meet New Challenges, Utne
       Reader, Jan/Feb.:54–60. (Originally in Areté, April/May 1988.)

SHERZER, JOEL

1970   Talking Backwards in Cuna: The Sociological Reality of Phonological Descriptions.
       Southwestern Journal of Anthropology 26:343–53.

1976   Play Languages: Implications for (Socio) Linguistics. In Speech Play, ed. Barbara
       Kirshenblatt-Gimblett, 19–36. Philadelphia: University of Pennsylvania Press.

1983   Kuna Ways of Speaking: An Ethnographic Perspective. Austin: University of Texas
       Press.

1986   The Report of a Kuna Curing Specialist: The Poetics and Rhetoric of an Oral Per-
       formance. In Native South American Discourse, ed. Joel Sherzer and Greg Urban,
       169–212. Berlin: Mouton de Gruyter.

1990   Verbal Art in San Blas: Kuna Culture through Its Discourse. Cambridge: Cambridge
       University Press.

1992   A Richness of Voices. In America in 1492: The World of the Indian Peoples before the
       Arrival of Columbus, ed. Alvin M. Josephy, 251–75. New York: Alfred A. Knopf.

SHERZER, JOEL, AND GREG URBAN, EDITORS

1986   Native South American Discourse. Berlin: Mouton.

SHERZER, JOEL, AND ANTHONY C. WOODBURY, EDITORS

1987   Native American Discourse: Poetics and Rhetoric. Cambridge: Cambridge University
       Press.

SHIPLEY, WILLIAM

1962   Spanish Elements in the Indigenous Languages of Central California. *Romance Philology* 16:1–21.

1978   Native Languages of California. In *California*, ed. Robert F. Heizer, 80–91. *Handbook of North American Indians*, vol. 8, William C. Sturtevant, gen. ed. Washington, D.C.: Smithsonian Institution.

1991   *The Maidu Indian Myths and Stories of Hanc'ibyjim*. Berkeley: Heyday Books.

SHUTIVA, CHARMAINE

1994   Native American Culture and Communication through Humor. In *Our Voices: Essays in Culture, Ethnicity, and Communication, an Intercultural Anthology*, ed. Alberto González, Marsha Houston, and Victoria Chen, 117–21. Los Angeles: Roxbury.

SIEBERT, FRANK C.

1967   The Original Home of the Proto-Algonquian People. In *Contributions to Anthropology Linguistics I (Algonquian)*. Anthropological Series 78, National Museum of Canada Bulletin 214, 12–47. Ottawa: National Museum of Canada.

SILKO, LESLIE

1991   *Almanac of the Dead: A Novel*. New York: Simon and Schuster.

SILVER, SHIRLEY

1966   The Shasta Language. Unpublished Ph.D. dissertation, University of California, Berkeley.

SILVERSTEIN, MICHAEL

1979   Penutian: An Assessment. In *The Languages of Native America: Historical and Comparative Assessment*, ed. Lyle Campbell and Marianne Mithun, 650–91. Austin: University of Texas Press.

SIMS, CHRISTINE P., AND HILAIRE VALIQUETTE

1990   More on Male and Female Speech in (Acoma and Laguna) Keresan. *International Journal of American Linguistics* 56:162–66.

SLOBODIN, RICHARD

1981   Subarctic Métis. In *Subarctic*, ed. June Helm, 361–71. *Handbook of North American Indians*, vol. 6, William C. Sturtevant, gen. ed. Washington, D.C.: Smithsonian Institution.

SMITH, MARTIN CRUZ

1986   *Stallion Gate*. New York: Random House.

SMITH, WATSON, AND JOHN M. ROBERTS

1954   *Zuni Law: A Field of Values*. Papers of the Peabody Museum of American Archaeology and Ethnology, Harvard University, 43(1). Cambridge, MA: Harvard University.

SMITH-STARK, THOMAS

1982   *Mesoamerican Calques*. 44th International Congress of Americanists. Manchester, England.

SNYDER, WARREN A.

1968   *Southern Puget Sound Salish Phonology and Morphology.* Paper 8. Sacramento, Calif.: Sacramento Anthropology Society, Sacramento State College.

SORENSEN, ARTHUR P.

1967   Multilingualism in the Northwest Amazon. *American Anthropologist* 69:670–83.

1973   South American Indian Linguistics at the Turn of the Seventies: An Anthropological Reader. In *Peoples and Cultures of Native South America,* ed. Daniel R. Gross, 312–41. Garden City, N.Y.: Doubleday (The Natural History Press).

1985   An Emerging Tukanoan Linguistic Regionality: Policy Pressures. In *South American Indian Languages: Retrospect and Prospect,* ed. Harriet Manelis Klein and Louisa R. Stark, 140–56. Austin: University of Texas Press.

SOUSTELLE, JACQUES

1962   *Daily Life of the Aztecs: On the Eve of the Spanish Conquest.* Stanford: Stanford University Press.

SPECK, FRANK G.

1909   *Ethnology of the Yuchi Indians.* Anthropological Publications of the University Museum, University of Pennsylvania, vol. 1, no. 1. Philadelphia: University of Pennsylvania.

1911   *Ceremonial Songs of the Creek and Yuchi Indians.* Anthropological Publications of the University Museum, vol. 1, no. 2. Philadelphia: University of Pennsylvania.

1945   *The Iroquois: A Study in Cultural Evolution.* Bulletin 23. Detroit: Cranbrook Institute of Science.

SPENCER, ROBERT F., JESSE D. JENNINGS, ET AL.

1965   *The Native Americans: Prehistory and Ethnology of the North American Indians.* New York: Harper and Row.

SPICER, EDWARD H.

1962   *Cycles of Conquest.* Tucson: University of Arizona Press.

SPIER, ROBERT F. G.

1978   Monache. In *California,* ed. Robert. F. Heizer, 426–36. *Handbook of North American Indians,* vol. 8, William C. Sturtevant, gen. ed. Washington, D.C.: Smithsonian Institution.

SPOLSKY, BERNARD

1978   American Indian Bilingual Education. In *Case Studies in Bilingual Education,* ed. Bernard Spolsky and R. Cooper, 332–61. Rowley, Mass: Newbury House.

STARK, LOUISA R.

1983   Alphabets and National Policy: The Case of Guaraní. In *Bilingualism: Social Issues and Policy Implications,* ed. Andrew W. Miracle, Jr., 70–83. Southern Anthropological Society Proceedings No. 16. Athens: University of Georgia Press.

ST. CLAIR, ROBERT, AND WILLIAM L. LEAP

1982   *Language Renewal among American Indian Tribes: Issues, Problems and Prospects.*
        Arlington: Virginia National Clearing House for Bilingual Education.

STEPHEN, ALEXANDER M.

1936   *Hopi Journal of Alexander M. Stephen.* 2 vols., ed. Elsie C. Parson. Contributions to
        Anthropology No. 23. New York: Columbia University.

STEVENSON, MATILDA COX

1904   *The Zuni Indians; Their Mythology, Esoteric Fraternities, and Ceremonies.* Twenty-third
        Annual Report of the Bureau of American Ethnology. Washington, D.C.: Smith-
        sonian Institution.

STEWARD, JULIAN

1938   *Basin-Plateau Aboriginal Sociopolitical Groups.* Bureau of American Ethnology Bul-
        letin 120. Washington, D.C.: Smithsonian Institution.

1965   Some Problems Raised by Roger C. Owen's "The Patrilocal Band . . ." *American
        Anthropologist* 67:732–34.

1970   The Foundations of Basin-Plateau Shoshonean Society. In *Languages and Cultures of
        Western North America: Essays in Honor of Sven S. Liljeblad,* ed. Earl H. Swanson, Jr.,
        113–51. Pocatello: Idaho State University Press.

STEWARD, JULIAN, AND LOUIS C. FARON

1959   *Native Peoples of South America.* New York: McGraw-Hill.

STEWART, JOSEPH L.

1960   *The Problem of Stuttering in Certain North American Indian Societies.* Journal of Speech
        and Hearing Disorders, Monograph Supplement 6.

STRAUSS, A. T., AND R. BRIGHTMAN

1982   The Implacable Strawberry. *Papers in Linguistics* 15:97–137.

STREHLOW, T.G.H.

1947   *Aranda Traditions.* Melbourne: Melbourne University Press. (Reprinted, 1964, in *Lan-
        guage in Culture and Society: A Reader in Linguistics and Anthropology,* ed. Dell H.
        Hymes, 79–82. New York: Harper and Row.)

STUART, DAVID

1987   *Ten Phonetic Syllables.* Research Reports on Ancient Maya Writing 14. Washington,
        D.C.: Center for Maya Research.

STUART, DAVID, AND STEPHEN D. HOUSTON

1989   Maya Writing. *Scientific American* 261(2):82–89.

STUART, GEORGE E.

1993   New Light on the Olmec. *National Geographic* 184(5):88–114.

STURTEVANT, WILLIAM C.

1971   Creek into Seminole. In *North American Indians in Historical Perspective,* ed. Elonor
        Burke Leacock and Nancy Oestreich Lure, 92–128. New York: Random House.

SUÁREZ, JORGE A.

1983   *The Mesoamerican Indian Languages.* Cambridge: Cambridge University Press.

SULLIVAN, THELMA D.

1976   *Compendio de la gramática náhuatl.* Mexico City: Universidad Nacional Autónoma de México.

1988   *Compendium of Nahuatl Grammar,* trans. Thelma D. Sullivan and Neville Stiles, ed. Wick R. Miller and Karen Dakin. Salt Lake City: University of Utah Press.

SWANTON, JOHN R.

1911   Haida. In *Handbook of American Indian Languages,* ed. Franz Boas, 205–82. Bureau of American Ethnology Bulletin 40, pt. 1. Washington, D.C.: Smithsonian Institution.

1922   *Early History of the Creek Indians and Their Neighbors.* Bureau of American Ethnology Bulletin 73. Washington, D.C.: Smithsonian Institution.

1928a   Aboriginal Culture of the Southeast. *Bureau of American Ethnology, Annual Report* 42:673–726. Washington, D.C.: Smithsonian Institution.

1928b   Religious Beliefs and Medicinal Practices of the Creek Indians. *Bureau of American Ethnology, Annual Report* 42:473–673. Washington, D.C.: Smithsonian Insitution.

1928c   Social Organization and Social Usages of the Indians of the Creek Confederacy. *Bureau of American Ethnology, Annual Report* 42:23–472. Washington, D.C.: Smithsonian Institution.

1931   *Source Material for the Social and Ceremonial Life of the Choctaw Indians.* Bureau of American Ethnology, Bulletin 103. Washington, D.C.: Smithsonian Institution.

1946   *The Indians of the Southeastern United States.* Bureau of American Ethnology, Bulletin 137. Washington, D.C.: Smithsonian Institution.

SZASZ, MARGARET CONNELL, AND CARMELITA S. RYA

1988   American Indian Education. In *History of Indian-White Relations,* ed. Wilcomb W. Washburn, 284–300. *Handbook of North American Indians,* vol. 4, William C. Sturtevant, gen. ed., Washington, D.C.: Smithsonian Institution.

TAPAHONSO, LUCI

1987   *A Breeze Swept Through.* Albuquerque: West End Press.

1993   *Sáanii Dahataał, the Women Are Singing: Poems and Stories.* Sun Tracks, vol. 23. Tucson: University of Arizona Press.

TAYLOR, ALLAN R.

1975   Nonverbal Communication Systems in Native North America. *Semiotica* 13:329–74.

1978   Nonverbal Communication in Aboriginal North America: The Plains Sign Language. In *Aboriginal Sign Languages of the Americas and Australia,* vol. 2, ed. D. Jean Umiker-Sebeok and Thomas A. Sebeok, 223–44. New York: Plenum Press.

1981   Indian Lingua Francas. In *Language in the USA,* ed. Charles Ferguson and Shirley Brice Heath, 179–95. Cambridge: Cambridge University Press.

1982   "Male" and "Female" Speech in Gros Ventre. *Anthropological Linguistics* 24:301–7.

TEETER, KARL V.

1959   Consonant Harmony in Wiyot, With a Note on Cree. *International Journal of American Linguistics* 25:41-43.

THOMAS, DAVID H., LORANN S. A. PENDELTON, AND STEPHEN C. CAPPANNARI

1986   Western Shoshone. In *Great Basin*, ed. Warren L. d'Azevedo, 262-83. *Handbook of North American Indians*, vol. 11, William C. Sturtevant, gen. ed. Washington, D.C.: Smithsonian Institution.

THOMASON, SARAH GRAY

1983   Chinook Jargon in Areal and Historic Context. *Language* 59:820-70.

THOMASON, SARAH GRAY, AND TERRENCE KAUFMAN

1988   *Language Contact, Creolization, and Genetic Linguistics.* Berkeley: University of California Press.

THOMPSON, J. ERIC S.

1972   *Maya Hieroglyphs without Tears.* London: British Museum.

THOMPSON, LAURENCE C.

1979   Salishan and the Northwest. In *The Languages of Native America: Historical and Comparative Assessment*, ed. Lyle Campbell and Marianne Mithun, 692-765. Austin: University of Texas Press.

THWAITES, REUBEN GOLD, EDITOR

1896-1901   *The Jesuit Relations and Allied Documents: Travel and Explorations of the Jesuit Missionaries in New France, 1610–1791* (Original French, Latin, and Italian Texts, with English translation and notes). Cleveland: Burroughs Bros.

TITIEV, MISCHA

1946   Suggestions for the Further Study of Hopi. *International Journal of American Linguistics* 12:89-91.

TOMKINS, WILLIAM

1929   *Universal Indian Sign Language of the Plains Indians of North America.* San Diego: William Tomkins. (Reprinted, 1969, New York: Dover Press.)

TOOKER, ELISABETH

1978   The League of the Iroquois: Its History, Politics, and Ritual. In *Northeast*, ed. Bruce Trigger, 418-41. *Handbook of North American Indians*, vol. 15, William C. Sturtevant, gen. ed. Washington, D.C.: Smithsonian Institution.

TRAGER, GEORGE L.

1939   "Cottonwood" = "Tree": A Southwestern Linguistic Trait. *International Journal of American Linguistics* 9:117-18. (Reprinted, 1964, in *Language in Culture and Society: A Reader in Linguistics and Anthropology*, ed. Dell H. Hymes, 467-68. New York: Harper and Row.)

1944   Spanish and English Loanwords in Taos. *International Journal of American Linguistics* 10:14-18.

ULTAN, RUSSELL

1970   Size-Sound Symbolism. Working paper on Language Universals, Stanford University,
        3:1-31.

1971   A Case of Sound Symbolism in Konkow. In *Studies in American Indian Languages*,
        ed. Jesse O. Sawyer, 295-301. Publications in Linguistics, vol. 65. Berkeley: Univer-
        sity of California.

UMIKER-SEBEOK, D. JEAN, AND THOMAS A. SEBEOK, EDITORS

1978   *Aboriginal Sign Languages of the Americas and Australia.* New York: Plenum Press.

URBAN, GREG

1991   The Semiotics of State-Indian Linguistic Relationships: Peru, Paraguay, and Brazil. In
        Nation-States and Indians in Latin America, ed. Greg Urban and Joel Sherzer, 307-30.
        Symposia on Latin America Series, Institute of Latin American Studies, University
        of Texas at Austin. Austin: University of Texas Press.

VALDMAN, ALBERT, AND ARNOLD HIGHFIELD, EDITORS

1980   *Theoretical Orientations in Creole Studies.* New York: Academic Press.

VANDER, JUDITH

1988   *Song Prints: The Musical Experience of Five Shoshoni Women.* Urbana: University of
        Illinois Press.

VÁSQUEZ, JUANA

1992   Chuyma Manquit Yurir Arunaka: Suxtalla. *Latin American Literatures Journal*, 8(1):
        92-94.

VELÁSQUEZ-CASTILLO, MAURA M.

1993   The Grammar of Inalienability Possession and Noun Incorporation in Paraguayan
        Guaraní. Unpublished Ph.D. dissertation, University of California, San Diego.

VIZENOR, GERALD

1991   *The Heirs of Columbus.* Hanover, NH: University Press of New England.

VOEGELIN, CHARLES F.

1960   Casual and Noncasual Utterances Within Unified Structure. In *Styles in Language*,
        ed. Thomas A. Sebeock, 57-68. New York: Wiley; Cambridge, MA: Technology Press.

VOEGELIN, CHARLES F., AND ROBERT C. EULER

1957   Introduction to Hopi Chants. *Journal of American Folklore* 70:115-36.

VOEGELIN, CHARLES F., FLORENCE M. VOEGELIN, AND NOEL W. SCHUTZ, JR.

1967   The Language Situation in Arizona as Part of the Southwestern Culture Area. In
        Studies in Southwestern Ethnolinguistics, ed. Dell H. Hymes and William E. Bittle,
        403-51. The Hague: Mouton.

VOEGELIN, CHARLES F., AND FLORENCE M. VOEGELIN

1957   *Hopi Domains: A Lexical Approach to the Problem of Selection.* Publications in Anthro-
        pology and Linguistics, Memoir 14. Bloomington: Indiana University.

1964   Languages of the World: Native America Fascicle One. *Anthropological Linguistics*
        6(6):1–149.

1965   Languages of the World: Native America Fascicle Two. *Anthropological Linguistics*
        7(7):1–150.

VOORHIES, BARBARA

1989   An Introduction to the Soconusco. In *Ancient Trade and Tribute: Economies of the
        Soconusco Region of Mesoamerica*, ed. Barbara Voorhies, 1–18. Salt Lake City: University of Utah Press.

VOORHIS, PAUL

1971   Notes on Kickapoo Whistle Speech. *International Journal of American Linguistics* 37:
        238–43.

WALKER, WILLARD

1969   Notes on Native Writing Systems and the Design of Native Literacy Programs.
        Anthropological Linguistics 11:148–66.

1975   Cherokee. In *Studies in Southeastern Indian Languages*, ed. James M. Crawford, 189–
        236. Athens: University of Georgia Press.

1980   Incidental Intelligence on the Cryptographic Use of Muskogee Creek in World War II
        Tactical Operations by the United States Army. *International Journal of American
        Linguistics* 46:144–45.

1981   Native American Writing Systems. In *Language in the USA*, ed. Charles A. Ferguson
        and Shirley Brice Heath, 145–74. Cambridge: Cambridge University Press.

1983   More on the Cryptographic Use of Native American Languages in Tactical Operations by United States Armed Forces. *International Journal of American Linguistics*
        49:93–97.

n.d.   Native Writing Systems. To appear in *Handbook of North American Indians*, Languages vol. 17. Washington, D.C.: Smithsonian Institution. (Written 1974.)

WALKER, WILLARD, AND JAMES SARBAUGH

1993   The Early History of the Cherokee Syllabary. *Ethnohistory* 40(1):70–94.

WALLACE, WILLIAM J.

1978   Comparative Literature. In *California*, ed. Robert F. Heizer, 658–61. *Handbook of
        North American Indians*, vol. 8, William C. Sturtevant, gen. ed. Washington, D.C.:
        Smithsonian Institution.

WATAHOMIGIE, LUCILLE J. ET AL.

1982   *Hualapai Reference Grammar*. Los Angeles: University of California American Indian
        Studies Center.

WEINREICH, URIEL

1953   *Languages in Contact*. New York: Linguistic Circle of New York.

WELCH, JAMES

1990   *The Indian Lawyer*. New York: W.W. Norton & Co., Inc.

WEST, LA MONT, JR.

1960   The Sign Language, An Analysis. Unpublished Ph.D. dissertation, Indiana University, Bloomington.

WHISTLER, KENNETH

1977   Wintun Prehistory: An Interpretation Based on Linguistic Reconstruction of Plant and Animal Nomenclature. *Proceedings of the Third Berkeley Linguistic Society Meeting, BLS* 3:157-74.

WHITE, JOHN K.

1962   On the Revival of Printing in the Cherokee Language. *Current Anthropology* 3:511-14.

WHITE, LESLIE A.

1935   *The Pueblo of Santo Domingo, New Mexico.* Memoirs 43. Menasha, Wis.: American Anthropological Association.

1944   A Ceremonial Vocabulary Among the Pueblos. *International Journal of American Linguistics* 10:161-67.

WHITEMAN, ROBERTA

1984   *Star Quilt.* Minneapolis: Holy Cow! Press.

WHORF, BENJAMIN LEE

1938   Some Verbal Categories of Hopi. *Language* 14:275-86. (Reprinted, 1956, in *Language, Thought, and Reality: Selected Writings of Benjamin Lee Whorf*, ed. John B. Carroll, 112-24. New York: John Wiley; Cambridge, Mass.: Technology Press.)

1940   Science and Linguistics. *Technological Review* 42:229-31, 247-48. (Reprinted, 1956, in *Language, Thought, and Reality: Selected Writings of Benjamin Lee Whorf*, ed. John B. Carroll, 207-19. New York: John Wiley; Cambridge, Mass.: Technology Press.)

1941a Language and Logic. *Technological Review* 43:250-52, 266, 268, 272. (Reprinted, 1956, in *Language, Thought, and Reality: Selected Writings of Benjamin Lee Whorf*, ed. John B. Carroll, 233-45. New York: John Wiley; Cambridge, Mass.: Technology Press.)

1941b The Relation of Habitual Thought and Behavior to Language. In *Language, Culture, and Personality, Essays in Memory of Edward Sapir*, ed. Leslie Spier, 75-93. Menasha, Wis.: Sapir Memorial Publication Fund. (Reprinted, 1956, in *Language, Thought, and Reality: Selected Writings of Benjamin Lee Whorf*, ed. John B. Carroll, 134-59. New York: John Wiley; Cambridge, MA: Technology Press.)

1942   Language, Mind, and Reality. *The Theosophist* (Madras, India), 63(1):281-90, 63(2):25-37. (Reprinted, 1956, in *Language, Thought, and Reality: Selected Writings of Benjamin Lee Whorf*, ed. John B. Carroll, 246-70. New York: John Wiley; Cambridge, Mass.: Technology Press.)

1945   Grammatical Categories. *Language* 21:1-11. (Reprinted, 1956, in *Language, Thought, and Reality: Selected Writings of Benjamin Lee Whorf*, ed. John B. Carroll, 87-101. New York: John Wiley; Cambridge, Mass.: Technology Press.) (Written about 1937.)

1956   A Linguistic Consideration of Thinking in Primitive Communities. In *Language, Thought, and Reality: Selected Writings of Benjamin Lee Whorf*, ed. John B. Carroll, 65-86. New York: John Wiley; Cambridge, Mass.: Technology Press. (Reprinted, 1964, in

Language in Culture and Society: A Reader in Linguistics and Anthropology, ed. Dell H. Hymes, 129–41. New York: Harper and Row.) (Written about 1936.)

WHORF, BENJAMIN LEE, AND GEORGE L. TRAGER

1937   The Relationship of Uto-Aztecan and Tanoan. *American Anthropologist* 39:609–24.

WICHMANN, SØREN

1993   Grammaticalization in Mixe-Zoquean Languages. *Sprachtypologie und Universalien-forschung* 46(1):45–60.

WIERZBICKA, ANNA

1984   Apples Are Not a "Kind of Fruit": The Semantics of Human Categorization. *American Ethnologist* 11:313–28.

WIGET, ANDREW, EDITOR

1994   *Dictionary of Native American Literature.* Garland Reference Library of the Humanities, vol. 1815. New York: Garland Publishing.

WILLIAMS, SAMUEL COLE

1930   *Adair's History of the American Indians.* Johnson City, Tenn.: Watauga Press.

WISSLER, CLARK

1942   The American Indian and the American Philosophical Society. *Proceedings of the American Philosophical Society* 86:189–204.

WITHERSPOON, GARY

1977   *Language and Art in the Navajo Universe.* Ann Arbor: University of Michigan Press.

1980   Language in Culture and Culture in Language. *International Journal of American Linguistics* 46:1–13.

WOLFART, H. CHRISTOPH

1973a   Boundary Maintenance in Algonquian: A Linguistic Study of Island Lake, Manitoba. *American Anthropologist* 75:1305–23.

1973b   *Plains Cree: A Grammatical Study.* American Philosophical Society. Philadelphia, Transactions, n.s., vol. 63, part 5.

1978   How Many Obviatives: Sense and Reference in a Cree Verb Paradigm. In *Linguistic Studies of Native Canada,* ed. Eung-Do Cook and Jonathan Kaye, 255–72. Vancouver: University of British Columbia Press.

WOLFART, H. CHRISTOPH, AND JANET F. CARROLL

1981   *Meet Cree: A Guide to the Language,* 2d. ed. Lincoln: University of Nebraska Press.

WOLFF, HANS

1951   Yuchi Text with Analysis. *International Journal of American Linguistics* 17:48–53.

WOODBURY, ANTHONY C.

1984   Eskimo and Aleut Languages. In *Arctic,* ed. David Damas, 49–63. *Handbook of North American Indians,* vol. 5, William C. Sturtevant, gen. ed. Washington, D.C.: Smithsonian Institution.

YOUNG, ROBERT W.

   1983   Apachean Languages. In *Southwest*, ed. Alfonso Ortiz, 393–400. *Handbook of North American Indians*, vol. 10, William C. Sturtevant, gen. ed. Washington, D.C.: Smithsonian Institution.

YOUNG, ROBERT W., AND WILLIAM MORGAN

   1980   *The Navajo Language: A Grammar and Colloquial Dictionary.* Albuquerque: University of New Mexico Press.

ZEPEDA, OFELIA, EDITOR

   1982   *When It Rains, Papago and Pima Poetry* = *Mat hekid o ju, 'O'odham Na-cegitodag.* Tucson: University of Arizona Press.

   1991   The Condition of Native American Languages in the United States. *Diogenes* 15:545–47.

INDEX

ABOUT THE AUTHORS

Shirley Silver has taught cultural/linguistic anthropology and linguistics at Sonoma State University since 1970. With California as an areal specialty, her linguistic/ethnographic fieldwork experience is focused in northern California. She also has been the principal investigator of a project on the Kashaya Pomo language in culture sponsored by the National Endowment for the Humanities (Education Division), a consultant for a cultural heritage training program conducted under the auspices of Ya-Ka-Ama Indian Education and Development, Inc., and a consultant for various language and culture curriculum development projects. Her publications concerning American Indian languages include a co-edited bilingual collection of northern California Indian texts and two co-edited collections of articles on American Indian languages. In addition, she wrote ethnographic sketches of the Chimariko and Shastan peoples for volume 8 (*California*) of the *Handbook of North American Indians*.

Wick R. Miller taught anthropology and linguistics at the University of Utah from the early 1960s until his untimely death in May 1994. His primary fieldwork was with three languages: Acoma, Shoshoni, and Guarijío. He served as an advisor to a bilingual education project (Acoma) and worked in a variety of language and literacy programs among the Shoshoni of Utah, Nevada, and Idaho. His publications involving American Indian languages range from topics on descriptive linguistics to sociolinguistics, linguistic acculturation, and historical linguistics. His most recent publications include an article on the ethnography of speaking and a grammatical sketch of Shoshone, which appear in volume 17 (*Languages*) of the *Handbook of North American Indians*.